The Social World of Galleries

Contextualizing Art Markets

This series presents new, original research that reconceives the scope and function of art markets throughout history by examining them in the context of broader institutional practices, knowledge networks, social structures, collecting activities, and creative strategies. In many cases, art market activities have been studied in isolation from broader themes within art history, a trend that has tended to stifle exchange across disciplinary boundaries. Contextualizing Art Markets seeks to foster increased dialogue between art historians, artists, curators, economists, gallerists, and other market professionals by placing art markets around the world within wider art historical discourses and institutional practices.

The series has been developed in the belief that the reciprocal relation between art and finance is undergoing a period of change: artists are adopting innovative strategies for the commercial promotion of their work, auction houses are expanding their educational programmes, art fairs are attracting unprecedented audience numbers, museums are becoming global brands, private galleries are showing increasingly 'curated' exhibitions, and collectors are establishing new exhibition spaces.

As the divide between public and private practices narrows, questions about the social and ethical impact of market activities on the production, collection, and reception of art have become newly pertinent. By combining trends within the broader discipline of art history with investigations of marketplace dynamics, Contextualizing Art Markets explores the imbrication of art and economics as a driving force behind the aesthetic and social development of the art world. We welcome proposals that debate these issues across a range of historical periods and geographies.

Published Books in the Series:

Women Art Dealers, Creating Markets for Modern Art, 1940–1990, edited by Véronique Chagnon-Burke and Caterina Toschi

The New York Market for French Art in the Gilded Age, 1867–1893, Leanne M. Zalewski

Art Markets, Agents and Collectors: Collecting Strategies in Europe and the United States, 1550–1950, edited by Adriana Turpin and Susan Bracken

Collecting Prints, Posters, and Ephemera: Perspectives in a Global World, edited by Ruth E. Iskin and Britany Salsbury

Corporate Patronage of Art and Architecture in the United States, Late Nineteenth Century to the Present, edited by Monica E. Jovanovich and Melissa Renn

Ellen Emmet Rand: Gender, Art, and Business, edited by Alexis L. Boylan

Ethnographic Collecting and African Agency in Early Colonial West Africa: A Study of Trans-Imperial Cultural Flows, by Zachary Kingdon

Old Masters Worldwide: Markets, Movements and Museums, 1789–1939, edited by Susanna Avery-Quash and Barbara Pezzini

Pioneers of the Global Art Market: Paris-Based Dealer Networks, 1850–1950, edited by Christel H. Force

Reframing Japonisme: Women and the Asian Art Market in Nineteenth-Century France, 1853–1914, by Elizabeth Emery

Théodore Rousseau and the Rise of the Modern Art Market: An Avant-Garde Landscape Painter in Nineteenth-Century France, by Simon Kelly

Women, Art and Money in Late Victorian and Edwardian England, 1880–1914: The Hustle and the Scramble, by Maria Quirk

The Social World of Galleries

Contemporary Art, the Market and Internationalization

Alain Quemin

Translated by Keara Engelhardt

BLOOMSBURY VISUAL ARTS

LONDON • NEW YORK • OXFORD • NEW DELHI • SYDNEY

BLOOMSBURY VISUAL ARTS
Bloomsbury Publishing Plc
50 Bedford Square, London, WC1B 3DP, UK
1385 Broadway, New York, NY 10018, USA
29 Earlsfort Terrace, Dublin 2, Ireland

BLOOMSBURY, BLOOMSBURY VISUAL ARTS and the Diana logo are trademarks of Bloomsbury Publishing Plc

Originally published in French as *Le monde des galeries: Art contemporain, structure du marché et internationalisation*, 2021

This edition published in Great Britain 2024

For legal purposes the Acknowledgements on p. xi constitute an extension of this copyright page.

Cover Image: 'Dimensions of Reality: Female Minimal', exhibition view. Curated by Anke Kempkes and Pierre-Henri Foulon at Thaddaeus Ropac Paris Pantin in February-June 2020 with works by Rosemarie Castoro in the foreground and Lydia Okumura in the background. Photo: Charles Duprat. Courtesy Thaddaeus Ropac gallery, London · Paris · Salzburg · Seoul

A catalogue record for this book is available from the British Library.

ISBN: HB: 978-1-3503-7092-0
ePDF: 978-1-3503-7093-7
eBook: 978-1-3503-7094-4

Series: Contextualizing Art Markets

Typeset by RefineCatch Limited, Bungay, Suffolk
Printed and bound in Great Britain

To find out more about our authors and books visit www.bloomsbury.com and sign up for our newsletters.

In memory of Raymonde Moulin (1924–2019),
a pioneer in the sociology of the art market.

CONTENTS

ACKNOWLEDGEMENTS

This book would not have been possible without the help of numerous people, and it would be impossible to thank them all by name here. However, I must express my immense gratitude toward various actors in the art market—especially gallerists and their staff—who always welcomed me into their spaces over a period of 10 years. My thanks also go out to several periodicals in the French art media—*Le Journal des Arts, La Gazette Drouot, Artpress*, and *Artension*—who regularly published my articles on the art market in their columns, and who gave me easier access to the art world.

Being elected as a senior member of the Institut Universitaire de France in 2020 proved enormously helpful in writing this book after all my research. I therefore want to thank the selection jury, as well as the Sorbonne Research Group of Analysis of Sociological Methods (GEMASS – Sorbonne Université), which has supported me since the very beginning of my time at the Institut.

Several sections of this book were written over many months spent as a researcher or a visiting professor at foreign universities, where conversations with my colleagues led to deeper conceptualization. I would therefore particularly like to thank Arturo Rodríguez Morató, professor at the University of Barcelona and director of CECUPS (Center for the Study of Culture, Politics and Society), an institution that warmly hosted me for many months over the last few years. I must also extend my gratitude to my other colleagues, professors David Halle, Luca Zan, and Nicolas Galley at UCLA, at the University of Bologna (GIOCA masters program), and the University of Zurich (EMAMS masters program) respectively, who allowed me to teach regularly and nearly continuously in their institutions over all these years. My discussions with these colleagues, as well as with their students, gave valuable insight into my analyses.

The book that resulted from all this research benefited from the financial contribution of the European Horizon 2020 project "Uncharted" (Understanding, Capturing and Fostering the Societal Value of Culture) (H2020-EU.3.6.3.2), which I would like to thank here. The translation was partly funded by Institut d'Etudes Européennes / Université Paris 8.

I also want to express my gratitude to Clara Lévy, professor of sociology at the University of Paris-8, as well as Gisèle Sapiro, director of research at the French National Center for Scientific Research (CNRS) and manager of the CNRS Editions collection where the French version of this book was published, for three decades of unceasing friendship and discourse.

Finally, my thanks go to Isotta Bosi and Gloria Romanello, whose quintessential contributions as research assistants provided the core statistical data for this book, and to Keara Engelhardt who translated from French into English the adapted and updated version of *Le monde des galeries* that was initially published by CNRS Editions in France.

SERIES EDITOR PREFACE

Gallerists are crucial players in global art commerce. They constitute a vital conduit between artists and collectors, generate public discourses about art, contribute to celebrity culture, and mediate ideas between a wide range of cultural institutions. Yet for most people, the social world of galleries is perceived as elitist and closed to outsiders. Despite the fact that many of these businesses are multi-national and highly visible in the art press, their ways of operating remain opaque.

Alain Quemin's meticulous study unveils the socio-cultural dynamics of contemporary art galleries. This book takes readers on a journey that begins with the historical underpinnings of commercial galleries in Europe and ends with an examination of their recent evolution in an increasingly globalized art world. Throughout the discussion, Quemin peels back the multi-layered personal and professional relationships that propel this part of the art market. He reveals the importance of friendships, client management, and social events as well as the tensions that arise behind the scenes of commercial operations. Gallerists may be gatekeepers who control artists' access to opportunities and commercial success, but the ways in which they wield that power can be barely visible to those outside their milieu.

One of the strengths of this book is its methodology. Rather than relying solely on quantitative or qualitative sociological approaches to the analysis, Quemin opts for their combination and places special focus on ethnographic observation. This immersive method reduces the temptation to write from a pre-determined perspective and allows Quemin to give voice to the gallerists themselves. In consequence, the reader is exposed to a range of refreshingly candid views as gallerists share information about their experiences and ways of working.

Yet Quemin's journey also extends beyond such personal testimony and takes into account the wider physical and conceptual networks in which art galleries are embedded. Chapters reveal the importance of geographical location, the tensions between community and competition at art fairs, and the significance of relationships to museums and other art world institutions. Complementing his ethnographic analysis, Quemin turns his attention to the role of data in the study of contemporary art markets. Strategies for ranking galleries and fashioning hierarchies of prestige from complex information flows are shown to be vital factors in the structuring of this unique art economy. *The Social World of Galleries* makes an important contribution to a book series that seeks to contextualize art markets. Quemin invites readers to listen closely to the voices of contemporary gallerists and to understand their multi-faceted activities, ambitions, and vulnerabilities from a position within a hitherto closed part of the art world.

Kathryn Brown
Loughborough, Spring 2024

Introduction

It seems virtually impossible to introduce this book, after conducting so much research on the art market, without immediately referencing the works produced by pioneers in the field; foremost in France is sociologist Raymonde Moulin who, in the 1960s, wrote *Le marché de la peinture en France* (*The French Art Market*) (Moulin, 1987).[1] Over half a century ago, gallerists had already come to occupy a prime position in the art market, among the other major players that Moulin met and analyzed.[2] Moulin's second major work—*L'artiste, l'institution et le marché* (*Artists, Institutions, and the Market*), which focuses on the art market and the question and undoubtedly constitutes her masterpiece (Moulin, 1992)—was written after further encounters with these professionals. In the shadow of these two sweeping studies, any quality work dedicated to contemporary art galleries and gallerists falls short.

The changes within this professional and social group, not unlike the evolution of the occupation and the market, made it all the more important to take another look at gallerists. The context of the art market, and specifically that of the contemporary art market, has evolved drastically since the 1960s and even since the beginning of the 1980s and the very beginning of the 1990s; the two main time periods that Raymonde Moulin studied. Although, as we will see throughout this book, it is hardly realistic to cite statistics that accurately represent the breadth of the art market, including private transactions that are by their very nature discreet, recent decades have seen significant growth in the art auction market. This growth is visible, not only in terms of number of auctions being held globally, but also in the number of record-breaking sales. Both factors underline the notion of a considerable advancement in artistic transactions.

According to the Artprice Annual Report, which indexes the total number of artworks auctioned throughout the world—possibly the only reliable data on the art market— the total amount of auction sales for art reached $17 billion in 2019 (Artprice, 2021a), and the amount for contemporary art reached $2.7 billion in the same year (Artprice, 2021b). In 2019, a previous Artprice report on contemporary art explained: "Driven by growing demand, revenue from contemporary art sales doubled in this century. Sales momentum is higher than ever, in affordable and high-end markets alike." (Artprice, 2019). Growth has continued even more since then, with auction sales of contemporary art going from $1.89 billion to $2.7 billion between 2019 and 2021 (a 40 percent growth), even during the COVID-19 pandemic. In 2021, contemporary art made up 20 percent of auction art sales (as opposed to 15 percent in 2019 and only 3 percent in 2000). This is behind modern art (38 percent) and post-war art (23 percent), but ahead of nineteenth-century art (10 percent) and the Old Masters (9 percent) (Artprice, 2021b).[3]

The art market recently saw record sales prices, which also illustrates the growing power of contemporary creations. To boost the value of the most popular artworks of the past, auction houses are now incentivized to include them in auction sales that also feature the most recently produced works of art. Christie's in New York did so when they sold Pablo Picasso's *Les Femmes d'Alger (version O)* in May 2015, during an auction that also featured contemporary art; the painting ultimately reached a price of nearly $180 million. The same auction house repeated this feat by selling *Salvator Mundi*, attributed to Leonardo da Vinci, for over $450 million in November 2017, also in New York. There as well, the act of selling art at an astronomical price[4] was not relegated to a specialized auction in classical art, as it traditionally would have been, but rather accompanied by other prestigious works of art, notably contemporary ones. Today, contemporary art can even enhance the value of the classical art sector, and it is thanks to auction sales wherein the common denominator appears essentially to be a wealthy target audience that artworks from different eras can change owners.

Contemporary art itself is not an exception. In May 2019, also at Christie's auction house in New York, the Jeff Koons sculpture *Rabbit* sold for $91 million, thereby making it the most expensive piece by a living artist ever sold. It broke the record held by David Hockney's *Portrait of an Artist (Pool with Two Figures)*—which sold for $90 million in November 2018—which itself broke the record for most expensive piece by a living artist—Jeff Koons's sculpture, *Balloon Dog (Orange)*—which sold for "only" $58 million in 2013. The three years above—2013, 2018, and 2019—as well as the record sales for these pieces by living artists—$58 million, $90 million, and $91 million, respectively—paint a portrait of a real acceleration of the contemporary art market, especially for newer pieces, whose creators are still alive.

These highly publicized sales, which are nonetheless rare, have drawn a great deal of attention to art markets, especially the contemporary one, over recent years. Coupled with these events are other, more common occurrences: art fairs (Quemin, 2013a). Now recognized outside of the art world alone, these gatherings have become essential for the media, and even mainstream sources that do not specialize in the art market.

In spite of the market's constantly growing visibility in mainstream media, and the awareness among the social sciences of the art market's increasing ability to generate art value (more so than institutions such as museums and contemporary art centers), galleries (especially contemporary art galleries) remain even to this day a little-known universe. How, then, can we come to terms with this shortcoming? In the introduction to *The French Art Market*, Raymonde Moulin focuses on the rule of secrecy that prevails over art dealers more than the other players that she studied, and indicates that they are the ones who transgressed this rule the least (Moulin, 1987). This characteristic, which is common among gallerists, most likely explains why so few quality studies on galleries and their owners have been produced. Too often, the galleries are examined more than the gallerists, and most frequently through the lens of transactions; or, more precisely, revenue (Velthuis, 2002, 2003, and 2005). This approach, in reality, translates into a considerable misrepresentation of the field. We will further see that it appears to be a *de facto* impossibility to analyze accurate sales totals made by galleries with any kind of relevance. Unlike the economic approach, which too often winnows itself down to the theme of transactional amounts, or at least pays substantial attention to them, the perspective on contemporary art galleries in this book will consist of that of their owners (and staff). The term "gallerist" has been established broadly within the contemporary art field for these individuals, and more generally in the English language. Leo Castelli, who was the most important international contemporary gallerist from the 1960s to the 1980s, did not appreciate being identified as a "dealer," preferring to be known as an entrepreneur who promoted artists (Hindry, 1990). He was also known for saying, on many occasions, "I am not an art dealer, I am a gallerist" (Cohen-Solal, 2009). The term "gallerist" essentially refers to a profusion of tasks,[5] including sales, but more broadly the promotion of the artists' works represented by the gallery. This is illustrated in the following excerpt of an interview with two such art professionals:

> Daniel Templon, you say that you don't like the term 'gallerist,' and even less the term 'dealer.' What, therefore, is your job title?"
>
> Daniel Templon: Did I say that? (laughs) In reality, both of those terms suit me perfectly. When I began, we only talked about dealers. Then, as the term 'gallerist' has become more common, it sounds more contemporary and accentuates the activity of presenting artworks rather than commercial dimension. However, we are art dealers above all else. A gallery isn't a museum. Our occupation consists of displaying art with the goal of selling it. That's what the artists want.
>
> Mathieu Templon: I'm going to build on that a bit. . . A dealer's activity is only a piece of our work. Of course, it's important, but the term 'gallerist' seems to me more representative of what the job is today. It involves organizing exhibitions, logistics, and relationships with institutions. We also do a lot of promotion, which is key for up-and-coming artists. [. . .]
>
> "The Templons, father-and-son gallerists", *La Gazette Drouot*, issue no. 2, January 17, 2020, pp. 158–161

As we will see in this book, sales even to this day represent the core of a gallery's business, which is logically oriented toward the commercial aspect. Yet, as we have just seen, sales far from represent all of the tasks performed by gallerists, contemporary art being distinct from other sectors of the art market due to additional, specific productive activities. Incidentally, as with several occupations, a gallerist's trade is often vocational,[6] and typically "takes over one's life", as we will see particularly in the chapter of this book devoted to sociability. This is perfectly illustrated in the words of this gallerist: "for me, being a gallerist isn't a job, it's my life. It's a real vocation, or else it isn't viable. A gallerist has to fulfill their role with passion and perseverance, that's how they gain the trust and fidelity of artists and collectors." ("Marie-Hélène de la Forest Divonne, a Breath of Fresh Air," *La Gazette Drouot*, issue no. 32, September 21, 2018, p. 23).

It would be pertinent in this introduction, in addition to explaining what a gallerist does, to also establish what contemporary art is. Throughout all of my research on this subject, it always seemed crucial to define what falls under the umbrella of contemporary art, as conducive to misunderstandings as it is (Quemin, 2001, 2002).

First of all, in the context of customs law in a country like France, artworks produced by living artists (or if the creators have passed away, produced within the past 20 years), are considered contemporary. There is no aesthetic consideration in this approach. A focus that is more central to my viewpoint is that, even in the art world, there is a dual definition of contemporary art that refers to the positions occupied in this universe. Art historians generally define contemporary art as anything produced after 1945, following modern art, which spanned the decades from the 1860s—along with the advent of impressionism—up to the end of the World War II (Quemin, 2013b). From this perspective, the beginning of the contemporary period is therefore linked with a major historical moment—a global conflict—outside of the art world, resulting in a clear watershed moment: art historians here find themselves in agreement with other historians. However, it must be noted that art historians do not refer to the categories of "modern" and "contemporary" in the same chronological senses as their historian colleagues studying other domains. This exemplifies the importance of conventions, even between individuals from the same institution (here, universities), as well as those from different sectors within the same discipline (here, history).

For a very long time, the preeminent auction houses—with the two market powerhouses Christie's and Sotheby's foremost among them—shared their definition of contemporary art with art historians. Their auction sales dedicated to this category included artworks made in 1945 or after. Nevertheless, at the very end of the 1990s, due to the public's appetite for contemporary art, auction houses sought on occasion to promote contemporaneity even more pronouncedly in some of their sales. They therefore separated the period from 1945 to the present day into two subcategories: "post-war," for the period between 1945 and 1970, and "contemporary," for the period between 1970 and the present day. As the more recent contemporary art sector in particular grew in visibility, auction houses also adopted initiatives to market recently produced collections under a new distinct category of contemporary art, giving it such labels as "contemporary now" or "new now."[7] The distinction imposed on post-war and contemporary art is now so entrenched that, when organizing auction sales that feature pieces made between 1945 and the present day, auction houses must now clarify that the sales blend "post-war *and* contemporary," where before they would have been labeled solely as "contemporary" art.

If auction houses have decided to move on from their former classification system (which held that contemporary art had to be made between 1945 and the present day) by truncating the period at the year 1970, it is because they took their inspiration from the prevailing tendency among museum management and exhibition curators. For these professionals, contemporary art as we conceptualize it today originated from the seminal exhibition, *When Attitudes Become Form*, organized in 1969 by Harald Szeemann, then director of the Kunsthalle in Bern, Switzerland. This sweeping exhibition, which predominantly presented conceptual and minimalist artists, largely contributed to the redefinition of what art from our era is, thereby sketching the main outlines of a new model. It is therefore widely held that this exhibition marked a turning point in the conception of what art should be, which justifies considering it as pivotal in the emergence of contemporary art as a category in its own right.

These examples make clear that establishing chronologies and time periods constitutes an important criterion when determining what is or is not contemporary art, and also that sector players subscribe to conventions that are absolutely not immutable; on the contrary, these conventions are directly linked to the sector to which these actors belong. It is important to note, incidentally, that while the criterion of periodization plays an overt role in characterizing contemporary art, it is nonetheless neither necessary nor sufficient. Although it may seem logical for contemporary art to be produced today (or at least very recently), it would not be improper to include Marcel Duchamp—who created his most emblematic artworks during the 1910s, before the 1945 benchmark and even earlier than that of 1969—in the category of contemporary art. Here, it is the nature of the categorization process, which is conceptual rather than chronological, that ascribes the creator to an artistic category that did not technically exist in its own right until much later. We may therefore conclude that, in order to define contemporary art, the criterion of the timeline, though generally necessary, is not always systematically so.

Marcel Duchamp's work is a perfect example of pieces that were produced well before the period generally being accepted as the chronological delineation of the contemporary classification. Likewise, as it is not strictly necessary, the timeline criterion is in no way solely adequate to determine what contemporary art is. Thus, the vast majority of artworks produced today are not *contemporary* in the sense that they do not fit into this specific category; to be considered definitively as contemporary, a piece must be *labeled* (Becker, 1985) as such by the art world. This procedure is carried out by a community immersed in contemporary art, which constitutes a sort of "informal academy" (Moulin, 1992). It certifies some works and artists as contemporary, and keeps other pieces and creators—whose status as "contemporary" has been called into question—at a distance, with their very artistic qualities being contested. Norms emerge via a regular exchange of information, be it verbal, in the form of conversations; textual, in the publication of magazines and catalogues, as well as private correspondence (especially email); or even in visual decisions, especially aesthetic ones, taking place during exhibitions. The contours of what is contemporary or not are therefore collectively drawn. Informal academies thus operate as gatekeepers and control access to the social world of contemporary art (Becker, 1988). Anything not validated by the members of this social world will be relegated to the category of "chromos" (Couture, 1981; Moulin, 1992); that is, works created without real aesthetic qualities recognized by the legitimate art world and produced with the intention of appealing to the masses. We must bear in mind the fact that, today, the contemporary category is very much linked to the international dimension, but the simple notion of having recognition in other countries does not guarantee the bestowal of the contemporary label. Some countries are more leaders and influencers than others (Quemin, 2001), and within those, some institutions and players possess a clearly superior qualifying power.

The quality of "contemporary" that fundamentally constitutes a social construct is based on an accumulation of signals, and acquired by confronting points of view (Becker, 1988; Quemin, 2002). If, even today, some external commentators cast a suspicious or ironic eye on the actions that allow certain artists and their works to be accepted into the contemporary category, we must then underscore the intense individual and collective activity that this implies. Where outside observers sometimes naively believe that "anything and everything" could be contemporary art, there is in reality a veritable effort of prospection, selection, and construction that, though it is partially invisible (Strauss, 1992), nonetheless objectively exists. If it were so simple as to arbitrarily designate certain artworks as contemporary and to have everyone accept them as such, the most central professionals in the domain would not be obligated to constantly gather information, to endlessly visit exhibition spaces and to travel as diligently as they do. For any person belonging to this social world in a professional capacity (Becker, 1988), it is obvious that the exchange and accumulation of information makes not only for more or less unanimous consensuses, but also helps to concretely establish the social world that is oriented around contemporary art.[8] It is a question of drawing the contours of contemporary art and allowing the functioning of the social world built around it based on the norms and agreements produced therein. To summarize, contemporary art is fundamentally a socially defined category, obeying certain norms which are themselves founded and nourished in the social world that has developed around art.

In my work, I had to return to the definition of contemporary art, for it has a direct impact on how to delineate the contemporary art galleries that I study in this book. Even here, this task is not elementary, precisely because, based on the definition that is generally applied to contemporary art, the demarcations of gallery populations can vary significantly. It follows logically that it is totally impossible to define the population of contemporary art galleries without delving deeply into the notion of contemporary art itself. Yet, the public statistics of a country such as France completely neglect this point. A light must therefore be shed on the highly dissatisfactory public data currently available in France on "contemporary" art galleries (the quotation marks being particularly necessary here). As François Rouet, former researcher at the French Ministry of Culture and Communication, explained:

> all the studies conducted on art galleries contend with a dual question: first, that of the gallery's domain, in the absence of a characterizing activity in the nomenclature of French businesses (NAF rév. 2), especially for contemporary art galleries, which requires us to cross-reference files and sources that are both accessible and relevant; second, that of being able to distinguish 'promotion-driven' galleries, which are particularly dedicated to the search for new artists.
>
> Rouet, 2013, p. 1

As it happens, the author of the previously cited study included all the galleries selling pieces by living artists and benefiting from a minimal amount of promotion; for instance, by organizing introductory exhibitions without leaning on the label of the "contemporary" category. However, in reality, entities that are defined and maintained as such contribute more to the "chromo" market than to the strictly contemporary art market. Such it was that no fewer than 2,191 galleries were identified in 2012 in France, and ultimately qualified by the abovementioned author as contemporary art galleries! Certain characteristics should, however, have alerted him. Taking into account the sole factor of space, the study stated that Paris was home to only 48 percent of these establishments. The third and the sixth districts[9] of the city boasted a nearly identical number of contemporary art galleries—around 200 each—with the eighth district coming in third, with 152 galleries (Rouet, 2013).[10] In reality, little of the data produced and interpreted in the study made any sense, as it theoretically analyzed contemporary art galleries, but in actuality referred to an extremely heterogeneous assortment of structures, of which proper *contemporary* art galleries were very few.

The 2019 report, *Key Figures*—another source taken from French public authorities (the Ministry of Culture)—cited statistics taken from the Maison des Artistes, an institution whose last dataset had been gathered in 2012. In that year, 1,545 galleries contributed to the social insurance of artists and authors in France (as opposed to 1,157 in 2010 and 1,244 in 2011) (*Chiffres clés*, 2019).[11]

Even among gallerists, public data, when it is available, is a serious cause for concern. In an informal interview that I conducted with a French gallerist, he deplored the vague surveys that are occasionally performed on art galleries and produce absurd results:

> I have to say that stupid things are sometimes published about French art galleries that don't pay any attention to what the companies are selling! If shops are selling souvenirs, like postcards, and if they have a little painting, some of them may say that they are contemporary art galleries, it's total nonsense. Once, I even saw a survey where they had mixed us up with all the businesses that sell postcards or I don't know what kind of stuff, because they were basing their research off the same SIRET number,[12] and apparently a gallery SIRET number can cause a certain amount of confusion. But come on, these people, later on, don't they see that the results they get don't make any sense?

Like this gallerist, the overly disproportionate figures previously mentioned in this introduction seem to me, on the whole, to be artificially inflated by the fact that they include a high number of galleries that do not truly sell *contemporary* art, and that therefore belong to a professional and social world that is very different from that which I will review and analyze here. It is especially the galleries that sell "chromo" pieces (Couture, 1981; Moulin, 1992) for which the rationale of demand takes precedence over that of supply. To be clear, contrary to what many people may sometimes think, it is not the price of the piece that helps us differentiate between the market for contemporary art and other kinds of art produced today that do not fall under the same category. Of these galleries that fall outside of the world of contemporary art, some even sell "luxury" chromos, produced by expensive artists who have no recognition in the contemporary art world. Such was the case in 2021 for one French gallery—where the most expensive paintings were sold for €50,000 and the most expensive sculptures went as high as €120,000—but where staff members acknowledged (in private) that they were not really a contemporary art gallery, even though the qualifier "contemporary" had been broadcast to their clients in order to promote the gallery, as well as the artists and their works. As the staff member of such a space explained during an interview:

> Well, it's true, the gallery isn't truly contemporary, it follows a different logic. The website doesn't work, there's even a gallery like ours that took

> out an ad in the subway (!), but our prices can be high. The other day (a very wealthy, famous foreign head of state) came to the gallery, and he bought €150,000 worth of art. More generally, at the gallery, the average price of a piece that we sell is around €20,000 . . . and we sell them! Right now, we even have a piece going for €120,000, our highest price ever. There are people who walk by the gallery, who come in and buy a piece because they like it.

Clearly, from that last extract, it is not the price of a piece that can distinguish contemporary art from current generic art productions; the prices being quoted can be very similar between incontestable contemporary art galleries, and the other kinds of galleries cited above. It is a question of distinct commercial circuits (Couture, 1981), as well as different social worlds (Becker, 1982).

In the absence of reliable data, particularly public data, that can give an accurate estimate of how many contemporary art galleries currently exist in France—and in the world—I sought to address this considerable shortcoming in my previous work (Quemin, 2013a). To do so, it was essential that I be able to make use of representations and definitions prevailing throughout the contemporary art world itself, notably by incorporating the fact that this social world operates by drawing symbolic lines to establish its dimensions. Upon reflection, I came to the conclusion that one of the best means of inventorying contemporary art galleries was to consider participation in art fairs. Thanks to a partnership with the company Artprice, I first made a tally of all the art fairs held throughout the world in a given year (in this case, 2008). As fairs are by their nature highly diverse, I only took into account those that are dedicated to contemporary art and fulfil two criteria: that they be international, meaning that they display works by foreign artists, not only works from the host country; and that they be sufficiently diverse in terms of the home countries of their displayed artists, so as to avoid being classed as a bi- or tri-national fair. To the extent that having an international dimension now constitutes a strong component of qualifying as contemporary (Quemin, 2002), no matter the impact of a particular work or event, this criterion tends to be exaggerated by lesser known fairs in their press releases, which I therefore had to investigate. In proceeding thus, I concluded that in the year 2008, 41 truly international contemporary art fairs were held throughout the world. It is important to note that, in this census, I chose to be very inclusive, with the goal of considering not only the most international—and often very prestigious—events, but also other fairs of less acclaim, in order to encompass as many galleries as possible (while ensuring all the same that they have a connection to the contemporary art world as demonstrated by the criterion of participating in one or more really international art fairs.)

For the year 2008 and the 41 fairs that I considered, I counted 4,113 contributions from 2,322 different galleries (which themselves participated in 1.8 art fairs that year, on average). The number that I then calculated for the total contemporary art galleries in the world,[13] while adhering as closely as possible[14] to the strict category of contemporary, seems overall fairly close to that provided by the French Ministry of Culture for contemporary art galleries in France alone! Among all the galleries that I identified throughout the world, 9.4 percent (Quemin, 2013a), or 150, were French. The number that I obtained via data that accounted for the "contemporary" category is over 10 times smaller than official French statistics, which make no effort to clarify their categories to allow for further study. In addition to the number of galleries present at art fairs with a more or less international scope, we should also include fledgling entities that are too new to participate in these events, and we must keep in mind that over the last decade the number of contemporary art galleries has markedly grown due to the rapid development of the market. Thus, it is possible to propose an estimated number of around 200 contemporary art galleries in France today, and around 3,000 in the world (keeping in mind that it is more important to estimate a realistic *order of magnitude* than claim to be able to calculate exact numbers to within a few digits, or even to the nearest 10). The unfathomable gap between the data provided by the French Ministry of Culture and my own estimation seems rooted in what Raymonde Moulin asserted in 1967: "There is not one, but several art markets," (Moulin, 1967, p. 69). If we set aside the categories of ancient, classical, and modern art, and only focus on the most recent time period, then we are left with two co-existing markets: a contemporary art market, in the strictest of terms, and another market where artworks are produced in a conventional and largely interchangeable manner (designated by Francine Couture and Raymonde Moulin as "chromos") (Couture, 1981; Moulin, 1992).

It seems necessary here to compare my estimate for France with other sources that are likely to either corroborate my results or challenge them. To do so, we may consider the inside sources—within the contemporary art world—that are available. The most relevant of these sources appears to be the number of members of the Professional Committee of Art Galleries (Comité Professionnel des Galeries d'Art, CPGA). The committee was formed in 1947, and today represents 280 member galleries in France;[15] many, but not all of which, are contemporary galleries. Though it also aims to respond to ethical concerns, its main role is that it ensures representation in public institutions for the professional group, which is key for galleries.

It could be asserted that, unlike a decent number of other professional associations, the CPGA represents most of the professionals within the field, and even more so the galleries that specialize in contemporary art. To the extent that the association operates through cooptation—a prospective member must be sponsored by two existing members of the organization in order to apply—and because, as previously stated, as contemporary art consists of a label, being a member of the CPGA is essential for French galleries that are eligible. Membership constitutes not only a guarantee of professionalism, but it also bestows a kind of certification of being a "real" gallery. In the particular case of contemporary art, this can only be granted if the gallery sells "real" contemporary art. This certification is therefore determined by the informal academies that govern the art world (Moulin and Quemin, 1993).

As this gallerist and chair of the CPGA stated:

> As a union, we defend the interests of the profession. The growing number of members also demonstrates that the committee has proved its legitimacy. When Georges-Philippe Vallois arrived in 2011, we had 170 member galleries. Since then, 70 of them have closed their doors, but nearly 200 have joined our organization. We currently have 284 member galleries, 90 percent of which are in Paris, including antiques dealers, modern art dealers, and half of which are contemporary art galleries, which have joined our ranks abundantly these last few years.
>
> Marion Papillon in "Une Combattante pour le CPGA," *La Gazette Drouot*, issue no. 1 from January 10th, 2020, p. 123

According to this source, 170 contemporary art galleries were members of the CPGA at the time; however, when I reached out to them directly to find out the number of members in March 2020, I was informed that they had a total of 287 members, 230 of which were contemporary galleries. If we factor in galleries that have not yet joined the CPGA because they are too new, we found ourselves somewhere between 200 and 250 contemporary art galleries in France at the beginning of 2020. This seems to align perfectly with the order of magnitude that we calculated by including art fair participation as a means of identifying these entities within France and other countries. Conversely, this result once again completely contradicts the number of contemporary art galleries cited by the Ministry of Culture and Communication in its 2012 study (Rouet, 2013). Let us reestablish, incidentally, that of the total number of CPGA members specializing in contemporary art (as indicated to me in February 2019), only 5 percent were located outside of the Paris area. Once again, we are far from the statistics provided by the Ministry of Culture, which estimated that of the 2,191 contemporary art galleries that it recognized in France, nearly half of them (47 percent) were located outside of the French capital (Rouet, 2013). In 2016, this statistic was repeated (*Chiffres clefs 2016. Statistiques de la culture et de la communication*, Paris, Ministère de la culture et de la communication, DEPS, la documentation Française, 2016).

Another source that could be helpful in the attempt to take a census of the population that will be studied in this book could be the MAP (Metropolitan Art Paris) register of contemporary art galleries: the foremost index available to the Parisian public. This booklet of member Paris galleries, formerly called the Gallery Guide, until March 2017 and curated by the

MAP association (of the same name), has been freely available for the last 30 years. It indexed 72 Parisian galleries in 2017 (*Le Journal des Arts*, issue no. 475, March 17–30, 2017, p. 25), (http://www.cnap.fr/map-metropolitain-art-paris), and 89 galleries in February 2020 (parisgallerymap.com). Like becoming a member of the CPGA, in order to join the ranks, a gallery has to be sponsored by two existing MAP members, and subsequently be voted in by the remaining members. Here as well, appearing on this list amounts to a sign of inclusion and professional recognition for the galleries that subsequently greatly benefit from being included. If these numbers seem much lower than my own estimate of French galleries, which is generally corroborated by CPGA date, they are even much further from those provided by public authorities on contemporary art galleries.

The case above refers solely to the situation in France, but that is just one example. All countries, particularly those that are home to the most internationally impactful galleries (the United States foremost among them, as well as Germany and the United Kingdom), experience highly comparable issues.

To conclude these questions of definitions and indexing, which are important preliminary steps in this research, it is important to stress that I am interested in galleries that sell artworks that have not been previously owned, or whose central business is in primary sales. Some galleries, especially the most established ones, also operate in the secondary sales market by reselling artworks. As Juan Pablo Pardo-Guerra states, the organization of the contemporary art market is historically oriented around a division of labor that unites two different sectors: the primary market, where gallerists introduce and promote new and established artists in the sector, and the secondary market, where art dealers and auction houses sell pieces that have already appeared on the market (Pardo-Guerra, 2013). The primary market corresponds to professionals whom Raymonde Moulin named as entrepreneur dealers (Moulin, 1967). As she later wrote: "Since the end of the 19th century, the cornerstone of the system is the entrepreneur dealer [. . .], someone who acts as a risk taker, a backer, an organizer, and an innovator" (Moulin, 2009, p. 32). Even if the distinction between the primary market—over which these entrepreneurs essentially preside—and the secondary market seems more blurred now than it did in the past, it is still possible to identify which of these two markets is more important for galleries, especially in terms of the image that they want to project.

Before presenting the primary results of my research in the chapters of this book, I must begin with a quick introductory foreword. First of all, I will explain the methodology that I used in my research; then, I will lay out the broad strokes of the emergence of contemporary art galleries by attempting to illustrate how they are the product of a historical process.

I will then turn my attention to spatial aspects in the first part of the book, which will be addressed over three chapters. The first will analyze the physical space of the gallery itself; even though all galleries today have websites—the social codes of which replicate those of the brick-and-mortar gallery, particularly the characteristics of the "white cube" (O'Doherty, 2008)—their physical space remains a highly significant factor. It is also the physical space that gives its name to the economic activity that takes place within the structure: that of gallery, according to the principle of metonymy. The second chapter will continue this spatial analysis by reviewing districts or clusters of galleries by neighborhood, which reveals the importance of location in developing an art gallery's business. Finally, the third chapter will conclude this first part with a focus on art fairs, which are today essential for contemporary art galleries, and will raise the question of regional anchoring (regional designating here a group of neighboring countries, and not a territorial unit inside a given country). Although they seem to extend a gallery's activity beyond their primary space, and as they also seem not to be subject to geographical determinism due to their international nature, we will see that art fairs are in reality contingent upon extremely impactful spatial rationales. Though they were largely suspended during the COVID-19 pandemic in 2020, they remain nevertheless fundamental for the operation of the contemporary art market, and their absence was very deeply felt.

The second part of this book will review what takes place inside the gallery: the operations performed, and particularly the sales that will be the main focus of the fourth chapter. The fifth chapter will highlight sociability and friendship as specific resources for selling artworks. The sixth chapter will expand the analysis to other activities that contribute to the promotion of artists being displayed in the gallery. Finally, the seventh chapter—which will conclude the second part of the book—will look at recent trends and transformations in the occupation of gallerist.

The third and final part of the book will consist of presenting a ranked list of international contemporary art galleries that I have put together based on those participating in the biggest art fair in the world, Art Basel. Chapter eight will give a detailed explanation of the methodology I used, and chapter nine will present, review, and explain the ranking of the main galleries around the world that I included on the list. I will analyze it in depth to reflect both the professional universe studied in this book and the prevailing hierarchy in this social world. Since this ranking presents an inherently heuristic quality, it will be possible to test and reconsider some points in the essentially spatial analysis presented in the first part of the book, and the functioning of galleries as developed in the second part.

Foreword 1:

A few methodological notes—researching the art market and its social world

In the introduction to *The French Art Market* (as previously stated in the introduction of this book), Raymonde Moulin emphasized the rule of secrecy that prevails over art dealers more than other players in the art market. In the book, she asserted that it was dealers who transgressed this rule the least (Moulin, 1987). The difficulty of gaining admittance to the field explains why her research was so rarely expanded on after publication. Her works are therefore still broadly cited to this day.[1]

However, in the 1950s and 1960s—and even after her second major book on the art market, *L'artiste, l'institution et le marché* (The Artist, the Institution, and the Market) (Moulin, 1992) was published a quarter of a century later (and never in English)—Moulin remained an external observer, even though she had developed a wealth of knowledge pertaining to her field of study. Though she conducted numerous interviews, nearly all were of a formal nature, which she supplemented with document analysis. Conversely, she never truly practiced the method of ethnographic field observations (Arborio & Fournier, 2015; Beaud & Weber, 1997; Peneff, 2009; Peretz, 1998), despite the rich insights afforded by this method. This fact brings to light an interesting trait of the sociology of art: the use of participatory observation is, it would seem, highly variable depending on the artistic domain being studied. It is commonplace, and even conventional, for the sociology of music, starting from the work produced by Howard S. Becker, sociologist and jazz pianist (Becker, 1982); and is also present in more recent research like that produced by Marie Buscatto, sociologist and jazz singer (Buscatto, 2007), Hyacinthe Ravet, sociologist, musicologist, and musician (Ravet, 2011 and 2015), and Marc Perrenoud, sociologist and musician (Perrenoud, 2007). Incidentally, the list of sociologist-musicians may be even longer, as the artistic domain of music traditionally seems to call for those who write about it from a sociological perspective to also perform in some capacity, thus directly linking them to their field of study.

The same remark could be made in the world of dance for Sylvia Faure, a former professional dancer turned sociologist (Faure, 2000); or Pierre-Emmanuel Sorignet, in his dual careers as dancer, and as a sociology professor and researcher (Sorignet, 2010). Admittedly, not all sociologists studying these fields conduct systematic ethnographic-style research, but it is clear that, when they do employ this method, it is often paired with a personal practice of the discipline, which affords them a highly integrated status within the social world that they are studying.

It would nevertheless be incorrect to use the examples above to make generalizations of all artistic disciplines, as they are taken from very specific domains. The matter is, in fact, very different for the sociology of visual arts: in this case, it is much rarer, or even exceptional, for those writing in this discipline as sociologists to also participate actively in the world of visual arts. As such, Raymonde Moulin, even though she studied the art market extensively, did so nearly exclusively with a professionalism borne of her profession as a sociologist. She herself even remarked that she had only directly engaged with the social world of the art market a single time, by writing a piece for a catalogue; however, this was written under a pseudonym, as she felt it would be improper for an art sociologist to be directly involved with the social world that they intended to study. From this perspective, and in the tradition that she initiated, in the sector of the sociology of visual arts, sociologists do not generally engage in this social world themselves; rather, they generally study it from an external perspective. The comparison with the other artistic domains previously cited demonstrates that it is sometimes misleading to generalize, as there are different, specific rationales within various artistic disciplines.

Having been advised by Raymonde Moulin during my doctoral thesis (Quemin, 1994 and 1997), I myself had never thought of permeating the art market by performing an internal role that traditionally exists within this social world. However, in 2011, the bi-monthly publication *Le Journal des Arts* interviewed me for an article that marked the 10th anniversary of a report that I had submitted to the French Ministry of Foreign Affairs in 2001 entitled *Le rôle des pays prescripteurs sur le marché et dans le monde de l'art contemporain* (The Role of Influential Countries on the Contemporary Art Market and World) (Quemin, 2001). The newspaper's owner, Jean-Christophe Castelain, interviewed me on this subject. At the end of the conversation, after we had discussed many topics related to the art world, he offered to regularly publish my contributions to his paper, while I would simultaneously continue my university work. Thus, I became a journalist specializing in the contemporary art market and, soon after, an art critic as well.

Being a journalist specializing in the art market led me to assume the hectic pace of international art galleries by participating in a dozen fairs around the world over the course of a year, some of which I covered for the art press. This allowed me to operate under the same conditions (particularly physical ones, as well as the notion of reconciling my private life with a partially itinerant occupation) as professionals from prominent galleries that participate in numerous international events in quick succession. In short, I was able to go beyond the usual simple collection of empirical data from an exterior position, as I was no longer an outsider.

My new position as a professional in the art market also completely changed my relationship with the field, and it is evident that the quality of information that I gathered over the 10 years that followed was considerably impacted for the better.

The most notable improvement that I made is probably the radical evolution in conducting interviews. Up to that point, I had upheld the formal, semi-structured style of interviews common in sociology (Blanchet & Gotman, 2007; Kaufmann, 2016). For these interviews, I first had to make an appointment, which often required several attempts. Players within the art world and the art market nearly always agreed to meet with me, as I was already a known entity within this social world, but I often had to send one, or several, reminders to schedule these interviews. When I became a regular contributor to various French press publications—*Le Journal des Arts*, initially, then *La Gazette Drouot*, to name the two main publications, as well as *Artpress* and *Artension* more intermittently, and even *Beaux-Arts Magazine* once in a while—I performed a clearly identified function within the social world that I was studying, which made my presence therein self-evident. Moreover, although sociologists hardly ever compensate their interviewees for their time, other than the opportunity to perform a reflective analysis and to see their ideas and points of view represented, a journalist and art critic can provide a certain amount of access to the press that can boost the visibility of a gallery or an artist. They therefore participate in artistic promotion (Moulin, 1987), which constitutes one of a contemporary art gallery's objectives, and a very important one at that. As such, after becoming a journalist and art critic, the process of requesting and completing interviews became very simple. This could be explained, in utilitarian terms, by the publicity that the galleries and their artists were likely to receive, but also more broadly by the notion of belonging to the same social world, which creates a sense of familiarity and community (Tönnies, 1988). Indeed, over the 10 years spent researching this book, I have been able to maintain a strong presence among art galleries, which has allowed me to develop relationships that are often cordial, or even friendly. In point of fact, as we will see later in this book, friendship (Bidart, 1997) constitutes a very important value in the social world of galleries, as it is a social construct that helps this universe to operate at its best.

Insofar as I was so frequently present in galleries, I had access to more accurate information, as it was not adulterated by the perception of my being an outside observer of the social world of contemporary art. This is how I was often able, via informal interviews (either simple discussions that were nevertheless steered by my research objectives, or by being present to hear remarks) to accumulate comments that completely contradicted information that I had previously obtained during formal interviews. Upon realizing this, it became highly important for me to allow my interlocutors to speak freely, which is much easier to do as an individual integrated into the art world, rather than as an "outsider" sociologist.

In one of my previous books, *Les stars de l'art contemporain* (The Stars of Contemporary Art) (Quemin, 2013b), I was particularly interested in the factor of the artists' ages. A few years before the book was published, when I was still conducting formal interviews and not being perceived as integrated into the social world I was studying, if I asked my interlocutors whether they thought that the age of an artist impacted their reputation, they answered by and large in the negative. Since they perceived these formal interviews as a kind of test (Blanchet & Gotman, 2007), they generally (though sometimes subconsciously) gave normative answers[2] that they considered to be "accurate," fearing that they would be poorly judged if they veered too far from the norm. Given the results that derived from these formal interviews, various players in the art world seemed to consider that age had little, or even no influence on how artists were recognized. Once I became an art journalist and critic, I was invited to travel to Brazil in 2012 to participate in an event—organized by the Brazilian Association of Contemporary Art Galleries (Associação Brasileira de Arte Contemporânea, ABACT)—for international art critics and exhibition curators. I was struck by the fact that every time an attendee mentioned the name of an artist that their interlocutor did not know, the interlocutor would ask how old the artist was! The discussions that followed often showed that, in this informal and spontaneous context, an artist's age was a factor that played a major role in how satisfactory (or not) the degree of visibility or recognition of a given artist was in their eyes. This stands as a clear example of how formal and informal interviews can produce radically different information. The former tend to reinforce norms, while the latter seem to produce a more realistic overview of the practices and even representations of this social world, since in this case these results are less susceptible to the (often significant) pressure of producing discourse that is socially acceptable.

Informal interviews therefore provide a means of gathering information that is highly unlikely to be conferred during formalized interviews. This is particularly evident in the following quote, when a gallerist told me in jest, "Oh, you know, being a gallerist, it's a job where you lie a lot!" It is improbable that an interviewee would make such a remark in a formal setting; it is much more plausible to imagine it during a more light-hearted exchange, as was precisely the case in this instance.

If it does indeed seem incontestable that informal interviews are ultimately more relevant when attempting to comprehend a social reality (in this case, that of the art world) and not only the representations intended for outsiders, how have formalized, semi-structured, or in-depth interviews (Blanchet & Gotman, 2007; Kaufmann, 2016) had such broad success in the social sciences, and in sociology in particular? This can be explained, at least in part, by the notion that conducting informal interviews is very time-consuming, and requires a considerable amount of commitment to become truly immersed in the domain.[3] The first phase is a long process of penetrating or infiltrating the terrain or community (Peretz, 1998), the second phase is waiting for the best moment to either begin a conversation (when conditions are conducive to ensuring that one's interlocutor feels at ease), or being in "the right place at the right time" to hear spontaneous remarks that are extremely relevant to one's research.

Other than gathering information from informal interviews, a lasting presence in the social world being studied also makes it possible to carry out ethnographic observations, which can evince revealing depths of knowledge (Arborio & Fournier, 2015; Beaud & Weber; Peneff, 2009; Peretz, 1998). Here as well, the conclusions resulting from this kind of data can contradict statements made during formal interviews. This point can also be illustrated with an example taken from the fieldwork carried out for my previous book, *The Stars of Contemporary Art* (Quemin, 2013b). I was interviewing a gallerist who was working in Dubai about lists of ranked artists. On several occasions during our long conversation, my interviewee made the same statement: ranked lists made no sense, and he did not use them. Once the formal interview had finished, and the recording device had been turned off (even though I had previously guaranteed that he would remain anonymous), he wanted to carry on the discussion. As he had discerned that I was very familiar with the French and European visual arts scenes, he asked if I could give him the names of some artists that I thought a gallery like his could represent, after which he immediately asked me how old they were. Then, although he had previously repeatedly and vehemently claimed during the formal interview that he did not believe in artist rankings, he immediately consulted a website — Artfacts–in my presence, to verify their ranking! Just as confusingly, when the ranking on this website appeared to be at odds with what he had expected based on the information I gave him on these artists, the gallerist wanted to understand why (as though he then believed that the information from the website was truly reliable). This example perfectly illustrates how the chosen methods can directly impact the result obtained, and even produce completely contradictory conclusions. In the first context of a qualitative study, albeit thorough, the interviewee seemed profoundly skeptical about the fairness of artist rankings. However, after shifting to the ethnographic observation method it seemed that, in reality, the same interviewee himself used these rankings, despite his repudiation thereof, and even patently subscribed to their credibility. Of course, utilizing both methods can ultimately result in two kinds of information; moreover, analyzing the discrepancies between them constitutes another kind of information in and of itself. Incidentally, I have identified this tendency under different circumstances, but about the same situation: it is the social norm for contemporary art galleries to insist on their disdain for ranking lists of artists, even if in reality these lists are employed by some gallerists. However, it is important to keep in mind that, when conducting formal interviews, the only information gathered is that of representations, which are more or less inevitably stamped with the norms that prevail in the social world being studied. To comprehend these practices, ethnographic observation of the milieu constitutes a method that is much more relevant, but as I previously mentioned, and as should be emphasized, it requires long-term immersion in order for the researcher to be present "at the right time." In essence, the observer must ensure that they are not perceived as an outsider (Peretz, 1998), which is a position that tends to influence and introduce bias into a given situation in order to adhere to social norms.

Belonging to the same social world can bring to light shared values, and sometimes even shared skills, which can contribute to recognition in the community. This can be illustrated via a successful interaction that I had during my first real encounter with an important German gallerist who had a reputation of being "rough around the edges." Up to that point, during each of my visits to his gallery, even when I had been invited to an opening dinner, our interactions were limited to a handshake, and not a word of conversation. One day, when this gallerist had just added a Brazilian artist to his roster (an artist who up to that point had been totally unknown in Europe, and whom he was going to exhibit as a solo show for the first time on the European continent), I was visiting his gallery, and we struck up a conversation. I told him that, nearly 10 years prior, I myself had noticed the work of this artist when I was visiting Brazil, and when back in Europe another gallerist friend of mine asked me if I could recommend any Brazilian artists. I enthusiastically recommended the artist in question, but this other gallerist did not seem remotely interested. Two years later, after seeing pieces from this same artist in another exhibition in Brazil, I once again expressed my admiration to this other European gallerist . . . who remained uninterested. Though it was simply an anecdote, I had the impression that this story not only amused the German gallerist, but also established me in his eyes as an equal in being able to identify the best artists, even over his fellow gallerists. From that point on, he was much more inclined to speak to me openly, and I was able to have conversations that would have been impossible during a formal interview with an interviewer who was perceived as a mere sociologist, and not an almost-peer.

The possibility of regularly obtaining unfiltered information is also due to the fact that familiarity and in-depth insertion into a social world can allow interviewees to take the lead in conversations with a friendly tone. Such was the case with a private email (below) that I received in December 2018 from a Swiss gallerist friend. The comments made would have been practically impossible to obtain during a formal interview, even if the interviewer and interviewee knew each other very well, since maintaining confidence in the health of the market generally takes precedence over any other consideration:

> I think 2019 is going to be a huge wake-up call for so many people. The massive injection of fresh money into this fall's auction sales is a strategic purchasing error made by people who buy with their ears and are fed nonsense by art advisers and major galleries with no scruples . . . Pieces that are really bad, or mediocre at best, are selling for huge prices . . . These new buyers don't know the rules, and they're going to end up with pieces on their hands that they're going to want to sell 18 months later.

We will see further on in this book that this kind of statement would almost assuredly never have come from a formal interview.

Other than the fact that informal interviews can go beyond the limits of formal interviews when analyzing practices, interviews with an ethnographic observation component can also help to avoid biases that are inherent in other methods, especially those that utilize questionnaires, which are often too removed. The domain of the art market offers some striking examples that accentuate the substantial limits that come with this method, like when researchers ask gallerists questions about sales and their turnover. It is highly surprising that sociologists (and more often, economists), who are meant to analyze a social world, can be so naïve as to believe that promising anonymity for their subjects will ensure that they provide accurate figures.[4] Therefore, as some research may cite a gallery's sales amounts or turnover declarations, and believe—with an extremely strong assumption that is generally rarely, if ever addressed—that the amounts are correct, several of my contacts, even those whom I speak with regularly and with whom I have maintained trusting relationships for many years, informed me that they were profoundly reluctant to communicate data (and accurate data even more so). This can be explained both in terms of competition and of fear of tax implications. Spending so much time in galleries has, incidentally, allowed me to notice that many of them circulate large sums of cash that often come from undeclared transactions.[5] They may even give their staff cash bonuses, particularly at the end of the year. Again, participatory observation and informal conversations have made me realize that claiming to provide data on a gallery's economic situation is impossible, even though this is often taken for granted. Thus, during a conversation with an accountant for a well-known gallery, I was able to obtain some very illuminating information when she spoke about her workload for the following day:

– I can't have another drink. Tomorrow I have to work on our tax return.
– *Oh yes, if you don't manage to bring the actual sales figures down by 10 or 20%, you're going to be in trouble with your boss! (we laugh)*
– You know, if I hadn't brought the figures down by even more than that, I would already be in trouble with him!

- *Please tell me that if I were to ask what your sales numbers or turnover were in an anonymous survey, you would tell me the truth . . .*
- Of course not, I'd lie!
- *Really? Even if it's anonymous? And keeping in mind that we know each other very well?*
- (She smiles) Yes of course, that's professionalism.

The conversation above illustrates the indispensable nature of fieldwork, not only to gather empirical data of the highest quality, but also to know what it is possible (or not) to study. There are topics where biases are extremely strong and practically impossible to monitor. In the previous case, it seemed that the results would be underreported, but to an extent that would be difficult, or even impossible to quantify. Conversely, a gallery that wanted to artificially inflate its image could exaggerate its results, even if they were later made anonymous, in order to boost their image. In such an event, the knowledge obtained from fieldwork must be compelling enough to give up studying a gallery's economic performance or financial results, so as not to produce completely unreliable results.

Although ethnographic research can produce extremely valuable information and the observer is deeply integrated into the social world that they are studying, this familiarity can, paradoxically, overlook certain qualities that are much more obvious to external observers (Peretz, 1998). An example of this is the cocktail reception hosted by the auction house Sotheby's in Paris to present an upcoming contemporary art sale, to which I was accompanied by a friend outside of the contemporary art world. During the reception, she made two comments to me: that the women were strikingly thinner at this event, presenting an average body mass index much lower than most social groups; and that people spoke very freely about money,[6] even though discussions about money in France are much more taboo.[7] The simple fact of hearing these two observations brought them fully to my attention. They were extremely fair but since, as far as I was concerned, I was so integrated into the art market world, they had become nearly invisible to me. It should be noted that the friend in question was herself a sociologist in training, and was undoubtedly more sensitive to the social dimension, and likely equipped with a more developed sense of observation than other people who do not possess this characteristic.

This last exception notwithstanding, I have on the whole emphasized the advantages of integrating into the social world in question in order to benefit from all the resources that the participatory observation method affords (Arborio & Fournier, 2015; Peretz, 1998). It is nonetheless useful to clarify the following: in my case, my strictly professional encounters were superimposed with a sort of convivial, and even friendly sociability insofar as, in the world of galleries, they are intimately linked, or tightly interwoven, which I will develop in the second part of this book. These occasions make it all the more possible to speak openly with the art community, for various reasons.

This research would certainly not have been the same if over the last ten years I had not been invited to hundreds of dinners or cocktail receptions for museum and gallery openings, sometimes three or four per week, in galleries of various sizes (some fairly small, others among the biggest in France or the world). Before they retired and set aside their academic research, French sociologists Michel Pinçon and Monique Pinçon-Charlot produced remarkable work that provided a spectacular analysis of the sociability of the upper class (Pinçon & Pinçon-Charlot, 1996, 1997, and 2016). Where it is routine to see social practices that are superficial, as well as artificial, in the form of "niceties," these authors demonstrated that the sociability common in this group gives them a kind of structure and draws a boundary with the outside world. They also emphasized that, unlike other social milieus, there is no hard wall between the private and the professional spheres. This point had previously been analyzed by anthropologist Béatrix Le Wita in her analysis of bourgeois culture. For my part, I have always made sure to respect basic research ethics by showing loyalty to the individuals who welcomed me. To do so, I kept my observation sessions and interview extracts as anonymous as possible, which was at times fairly difficult in a professional and social context where many communities are tight-knit. Likewise, it was important to understand the social world but not to pass moral judgment on it. I sought never to denounce or ridicule the people who opened their doors to me and gave me their trust.

I myself was subject to a naive external perspective on how sociability in the art market manifests. One day, a university colleague that had looked me up online and found several photos of museum and gallery openings with me in them told me he was surprised to discover that I was "a socialite." In the moment, I was quite shocked by the use of this description taken from an outside perspective. Conversely, for me, on a subjective level, participating in objectively worldly activities amounted to a consequence of my strong interest in art, and directly linked to my professional research on the art gallery world.

Incidentally, it is interesting that this theme of the worldly (or not) nature of the professional activity of the most integrated players in the art world was spontaneously brought up during a dinner conversation with friends who worked at a major French gallery (while we were at an art fair in Cologne, Germany). The fact of being gathered around a table after a hard day of work, both for them and for myself working as a journalist all day (while at the same time playing the dual role of sociologist and participatory observer), allowed us to launch into a very interesting debate on the question, "when you work in the art world as a gallery director (or associate/assistant director), or even as a highly-integrated journalist (and sociologist), are you 'worldly?'" The conversation among the participants had a very open tone, as no one felt they were in an interview environment, strictly speaking. The remarks were very unrestrained, since the speakers did not feel judged. Ultimately, we came to something of an agreement: in a professional situation like that of a gallerist, where conversations provide an opportunity to develop one's business, particularly the commercial aspect, it is admittedly possible to speak about worldliness, but this is instrumental and aimed at developing both professional connections and sales. I will address this point again later in this book when discussing the importance of friendship in this social world.

The fact of so much information being gathered in the form of informal interviews and observation sessions that took place during festive events, cocktail receptions and dinners, underlines the enabling role often played by alcohol in loosening proverbial lips. This may be a funny consideration, but an interviewer cannot generally offer an alcoholic beverage to their interviewee during a formal interview in order to lower their guard. Yet, in the art world, although the excessive consumption of alcoholic beverages is very poorly perceived, partaking in a festive and controlled drinking environment has social value, particularly when there is champagne involved. In France, champagne (or some reasonable facsimiles in other countries) symbolizes the sociability that has grown around art and its market.

To conclude this methodological foreword, it is important to clarify for which readerships we in the social sciences write. When social science research is intended exclusively for peers, especially in sociology, it seems to me that we often run the risk of developing a supposedly scholarly approach by using a specialized language, while in reality the heuristic contribution to the social reality being studied can prove to be extremely limited. Conversely, having a readership composed of members of the social world under analysis calls for the use of a language that is relatively accessible. This also implies accepting that one's work will be subject to the criterion of its purpose and contribution in terms of knowledge, even by those who are most familiar with the field being studied. To be perfectly clear, sociological theories that lead to real perspectives on the intellection of the social world are extremely rare. Too often, sociology evolves in large part in a world that is almost parallel to that in which the social reality it claims to study operates. If scholarly language does not afford a better understanding of the social world, it amounts merely to a language exchanged between a handful of specialists whose contribution is extremely limited. While I will continue to build on the work of my predecessors in the social sciences, I will also ensure that I remain accessible to players within the art market, as their familiarity with the market constitutes another source of knowledge that is also perfectly respectable and that can challenge the contribution of my own analyses as a sociologist.

Foreword 2:

The invention of the gallerist profession and its development up to the contemporary period

Like all social structures, art galleries are the result of a historical evolution. Such is the case for all social groups; particularly in a professional context, including those with a connection to the art market (Freidson, 1984; Heinich, 1993; Moulin, 1995; Paicheler, 1992; Quemin, 1997), especially gallerists. Before presenting the results of my 10-year-long field study and the analyses that I derived from it, I will provide an overview of the evolution that allowed contemporary art galleries and gallerists to emerge and grow into their different iterations, as they exist today.[1]

To establish the main through lines of this history, we may once again turn to Raymonde Moulin's pioneering book *Le marché de la peinture en France* (The French Art Market) (Moulin, 1987). In her book, Moulin asserts that the mere existence of professionals who specialize in the commerce of contemporary artworks is not self-evident; it is the clear result of a social construction. As such, Moulin stipulates the following: when the guild of painters and sculptors was created in Paris in 1391, each artist was his own art dealer, and sold his own works himself. Belonging to the guild of painters and sculptors also conferred the right to open a workshop (Moulin, 1987). The first progressive phase of evolution began in Renaissance Italy at the end of the fifteenth century, where painters, sculptors, and architects were gradually recognized as men of knowledge as well of craft (Moulin, 1995).

The first art dealers developed independently of one another in the seventeenth and eighteenth centuries, playing the role of intermediary between penniless noble families who had to sell their art collections, and newly wealthy families who had the financial means to buy them. These intermediaries then benefited from the weakening of professional guilds, as well as the rise in power of the Royal Academy, which upon its creation included regulations that opened the "contemporary art" market of the time to these art dealers (Heinich, 1993; White & White, 1965). With the establishment of the Royal Academy of Painting and Sculpture, inaugurated in France in 1648 at the beginning of Louis XIV's reign, the founding statutes of the Academy declared that, "all members of the Academy body, on penalty of expulsion, will refrain from opening a storefront to hang their works, to display them in the windows of their abode [. . .] or finally to engage in any other activity that may conflate the two highly distinct notions of performing a self-serving profession and upholding the Academy's integrity" (Vitet, 2012 (1861, p. 72); Verley, 2020). A major innovation was therefore introduced, resulting from the slow transformation of the professional group's status: the Academy's original statutes forbade its members from hanging their proverbial shingle. The function of art dealers, as intermediaries between artists and their clients, therefore, became essential for members of the Academy (incidentally, the importance of this function was compounded by its ability to put these dealers in contact with the most famous artists). It was necessary to wrest all commercial activities away from painters and sculptors, and these tasks that were considered trivial were left to the mundane world. Indeed, for two centuries, artists had strived to remove themselves from the artisanal universe to which they were traditionally linked, and aspired to move toward a creative, more intellectual occupation (Moulin, 1987). To do so, however, they were obligated to break from the more trivial aspects of their professions—especially the commercial elements heretofore performed by the artists themselves—by leaving them to other specialized tradesmen. The political and social upheavals that wreaked havoc on eighteenth-century France—the French Revolution being particularly impactful—led to an amplification and acceleration of the art market.

As art was—due in particular to the creation of the Academy—socially recognized as an intellectual activity in its own right, and broadly liberated from its connotation with traditional artisanship, art criticism was then also able to emerge in turn during the eighteenth century as a specialized occupation. Printed reviews of art salons appeared for the first time in the art revue, *Le Mercure,* in 1738. The movement then endured and expanded into the nineteenth century, with art criticism growing significantly in importance in the press (Moulin, 1987).

Paul Durand-Ruel: inventor of the figure of gallerist in nineteenth-century France

In the context of a fine arts world that was becoming increasingly institutionalized, and newly endowed with a real market that had been entrusted to specialized professionals, a new major phase was initiated by Paul Durand-Ruel (1831–1922), the *de facto* ancestor of all gallerists who specialize in contemporary art. Sylvie Patry, curator and art historian, dedicated a remarkable exhibition to him at the Musée du Luxembourg in Paris,[2] presenting him as: "the greatest art dealer of the 19th century, discoverer of impressionists, and inventor of the modern art market" (Patry, 2014). In the leaflet, *Galleries of the 20th Century: France 1905–1970*, produced for another exhibition of the same name organized by the Centre Pompidou in Paris,[3] the pioneering role played by Durand-Ruel in the domain of art galleries is situated thus:

> First appearing in the late 19th century, gallery owners nevertheless quickly became indispensable intermediaries between artists and the public, like Durand-Ruel, a pioneer and dealer in Impressionist art. From the beginning of the 20th century the role of the galleries was thus closely linked to the development of 'living art'. By promoting the reputation of artists in France, and abroad in the case of the more enterprising galleries, they quickly became the main instruments of artistic legitimization. In the history of 20th century art, they played an essential role in the development of the Fauvist and Cubist movements, the first abstract trends and Surrealism. After 1945 they also played a role in the development of gestural or geometric abstraction, as well as Nouveau Réalisme.

Durand-Ruel had essentially set in motion a veritable revolution in the occupation of art dealers. The 2014–2015 exhibition at the Musée du Luxembourg, accompanied by a catalogue (Patry, 2014), has rounded out the public's knowledge of this great French art dealer, whose work is inextricably linked to the economic success of impressionist artists. Although he succeeded his father, Jean-Marie, in the art dealing business upon the latter's death in 1865, Paul Durand-Ruel went on to completely redefine the occupation of art dealer. While traditionally, this line of work operated by responding to a clearly identified client demand, Durand-Ruel shifted the profession to focus on the supply, and presented and supported artists for whom there was no demand, wagering that the demand simply did not exist . . . yet. By banking on a group of new artists who would not grow popular until later, and going against the taste of the public, Durand-Ruel soon lost his first client base, which he had inherited from his father's business.

Based in the 9th arrondissement[4] in Paris—the neighborhood at the heart of the art market at that time—Durand-Ruel bought artworks by Claude Monet, Camille Pissarro, Auguste Renoir, Edgar Degas, and Alfred Sisley at the beginning of the 1870s, when these artists were not yet known as "impressionists," and when they had no public recognition (Nahon, 1998; Assouline, 2002; Verley, 2020).

By choosing to support these impressionist artists, who initially garnered no public interest, Durand-Ruel was forced to attempt to generate demand for these artists by engaging in a monumental amount of promotional work (Moulin, 1967), which drove him to take on new initiatives. In 1869, four years after taking over the family business, he created an art magazine, and later a weekly newspaper that lasted a few months, with the goal of educating the public and coaxing them into appreciating the artists that he championed. Starting in 1883, Durand-Ruel organized exhibitions for his artists: a method that was still fairly rare. It is interesting to note that, at a time when access to exhibitions generally required an entrance fee, Durant-Ruel held these showings in galleries or in his apartment, at no cost to visitors. Where artists of the era were typically presented in groups, with the salon serving as an archetype of this kind of presentation, Durand-Ruel often opted for solo exhibitions, so as to accentuate the singularity of the artists under his aegis. In 1870, Durand-Ruel opened a gallery in London, and another in Brussels in 1871 (Durand-Ruel, 2014). In 1888, he even founded a gallery in the New World, in New York. Durand-Ruel was not the first to break ground in the United States, as his fellow Parisian art dealer Adolphe Goupil had already opened an office in New York in 1848 (this organization soon came under the direction of Michel Knoedler); however, the Maison Goupil occupied a different position in the market due to its specialization in reproductions (Nahon, 1998). When it came to migrating his operations to the United States, Durand-Ruel was a pioneer as well. For each new gallery, he selected a prestigious address. As French collectors could not recognize and enjoy what was right in front of them, he had to go abroad to both conquer and create new markets (Joyeux-Prunel, 2009). Beyond opening satellite galleries in other countries, Durand-Ruel organized exhibitions in large cities such as Vienna, Manchester, Rotterdam, Boston, Berlin, and Munich (Durand-Ruel, 2014). He implemented another *modus operandi* that went on to find tremendous success in the long run: he frequently bought artworks *en masse*, which was all the easier given that the artists he bought from were initially unknown, and their pieces were inexpensive. This allowed him to create a stockpile of art, while he waited for his artists to grow in popularity. For instance, in 1866 he bought 70 paintings by Théodore Rousseau, and in 1872 he acquired all of the works available for sale—no fewer than 23 paintings—by Edouard Manet (Moulin, 1987). Even when he did not manage to sell the art produced by his artists, Durand-Ruel continued to buy from them and pay them a stipend to maintain their professional relationship. In doing so, he made a clear display of confidence in their work and in the accolades that they would soon receive (White & White, 1965). As the model established by Durand-Ruel required significant amounts of capital, he was quick to merge the art world with the finance world, finding supporters among bankers or major investors (Durand-Ruel, 2014), which today would be called "backers." The 2014–2015 exhibition at the Palais du Luxembourg in Paris laid out Durand-Ruel's in-depth knowledge of networks, especially geographical ones. It also highlighted the mastery of speculation that he possessed, as he readily sold and bought back the same pieces over and over again, each time making a tidy profit (Patry, 2014; Verley, 2020). He also sought to secure his monopoly over his artists' productions even if, once impressionists found fame and were rewarded for their success, Durand-Ruel did not manage to maintain his monopoly over their distribution. Nevertheless, both because he was able to boost the popularity of his artists, and because he had set aside large stockpiles of art (or perhaps because he was replenishing them), Durand-Ruel finally met with resounding success.

While Durand-Ruel is undoubtedly a trailblazer for gallerists in the sense of creating a new model of distribution for the field of painting that gave precedence to supply rather than demand, thereby reversing the traditional pattern of the time, it would be appropriate to situate this revolution in a broader context. As a matter of fact, Durand-Ruel introduced the same reversal to the world of fine arts that the British-born French couturier Charles Frederick Worth (1825–1895) had just accomplished in the fashion sector. The founder of the eponymous fashion house, but also more broadly of Parisian *haute couture* (of which he created the very concept and essential rules) (Godart, 2012), Worth moved to Paris in 1845, where he first worked for Maison Gagelin, a large company that sold textiles, shawls, and ready-to-wear clothing. After becoming the lead salesman, he launched a couture division, which was his first foray into professional fashion design. Beyond the company where he presided, his recognition grew thanks to his prize-winning designs at the World's Fairs in London (in 1851) and Paris (in 1855). These designs contributed to the reputation of Maison Gagelin, and they also shone a spotlight on Worth himself. In 1858, along with an associate, Otto Bobergh, he founded his own company at 7, rue de la Paix, the famous epicenter of fashion in Paris.

Breaking completely from the conventions of fashion design at that time, Worth managed to implant his own vision. Up to that point, the designer had only fulfilled orders placed by his clientele; the client requested an item of clothing, and the designer had only to sew it. This procedure was therefore, on the whole, artisanal. However, Worth decided to create designs that had never been seen before, clearly demonstrating aesthetic inspiration and an artist's status. He chose to launch his own collections, constructed based on one-of-a-kind designs that he had pre-made, and presented at luxury salons, so that they would be better publicized. He also introduced a commerce of rarity,[5] as he regularly changed his collections (spring–summer and autumn–winter), and his clothing designs were only available for a limited time. Designing clothing became his main endeavor, and the client was limited to simply choosing the color and type of fabric they wanted. Worth serves as an excellent illustration of how fashion design went from a simple artisanal activity to a real creative process that stands on its own merit. To establish his influence, he fundamentally reversed the traditional relationship between supply and demand, giving primacy to the former over the latter, and having charge of the now-essential supply.

This is more or less what Durand-Ruel managed to do in the painting world a few years after Worth's transformation of the fashion world. There is, however, an important distinction between them: the latter elicited a reversal in the business of fashion creation itself, where sales were part-and-parcel of the process, and not outsourced to an intermediary. Durand-Ruel, for his part, enacted his own reversal between supply and demand at the level that he could influence: that of commercialization, which was a true innovation. These radical transformations that touched different creative domains must be resituated more broadly in the context of Paris in the second half of the nineteenth century. They are but two of the profound transformations of the artistic field that Pierre Bourdieu analyzed in his book, *The Rules of Art* (Bourdieu, 1996).

Paul Durand-Ruel's followers: Ambroise Vollard and Daniel-Henry Kahnweiler, and the impact of the great French gallerists up to the 1960s

Among the other eminent art dealers who clearly followed in the footsteps of Paul Durand-Ruel, and who helped to consolidate the role of 'gallerist' as we know it today, are the great entrepreneurs Ambroise Vollard (1865–1939) and Daniel-Henry Kahnweiler (1884–1979). In the brochure *Galleries of the 20th Century: France 1905–1970* for the exhibition of the same name at the Centre Pompidou,[6] Ambroise Vollard was presented as such: born on Reunion Island,[7] he

> moved to Paris in 1887, where he opened a small gallery in 1893, then another in 1895, where he organized the first exhibition for Cézanne, who was still at that point relatively unknown. In 1896, he moved into a bigger space, where he held the first Parisian exhibition for Picasso in 1901. After mounting a show for Matisse in 1904, Vollard became the preeminent dealer for Fauvists. Forced to close his gallery in 1914, Vollard then dedicated himself to publishing artists' books, notably that of Rouault.

In these four sentences, Vollard's commitment to *avant-garde* artists is apparent (Nahon, 1998; Morel, 2007), as is his penchant for supporting artistic movements (here, Fauvists). These two qualities link him to the model set by his predecessor, Paul Durand-Ruel.

The second, Daniel-Henry Kahnweiler, was the son of prosperous German parents, who planned for him to have a career in finance. Once he had convinced his family to allow him to become an art dealer (and to finance this decision), he chose to present the artists belonging to his generation, desiring to pave their way to success. He is presented in the same synoptic brochure cited above, as

> Having discovered great artists like Picasso, Braque, Derain, Gris, and Léger, Daniel-Henry Kahnweiler (1884-1979) was also a daring publisher and one of the first Cubist historians. From the beginning of his career, the young German dealer organized several exhibitions of international scope and relied on a small network of collectors. In 1914, forced into exile, he saw his stock of art sequestered by the French state as 'enemy assets'. After the First World War, his gallery reopened with a new generation of artists, revolving around André Masson and the surrealist artists of rue Blomet.[8]

Here as well, this brief biography shows that Kahnweiler adopted the business model invented by Paul Durand-Ruel. Interestingly, Kahnweiler developed the notion of a contract of exclusivity, allowing him to swim against the proverbial tide of public taste, and to operate in the long term. He therefore embraced one of the principles that had led Durand-Ruel to success, by establishing a legal framework for a longstanding contractual relationship. Kahnweiler has gone down in art history as the preeminent dealer for cubist paintings (Gee, 1981), as Durand-Ruel is for impressionists. Like his predecessor, he started his career by championing *avant-gardism* (a field with which he has remained associated), even at the beginning when it was not popular. Once again following Durand-Ruel's lead, he bought all of the works made by *avant-garde* artists in order to gain a monopoly and set his prices according to the piece's format. Also like his predecessor, he sold works by these young artists for little money, at prices for which he was prepared to buy the paintings back. Although he signed representation contracts with his artists at the beginning of his career, he later renounced this practice. In opening his first large gallery in 1907 on rue Vignon, a street located in the 8th and 9th arrondissements of Paris, he managed to follow the migration of the art gallery market from the area around rue Drouot (a neighborhood in the 9th arrondissement traditionally associated with art commerce) to the Madeleine neighborhood, toward the west of Paris.[9] Giving his establishment the new name of Galerie Simon in 1920,[10] just after the end of the First World War, then changing the name again to Louise Leiris in 1941 during the Second World War, the gallery eventually moved to 47 rue de Monceau (still in the 8th arrondissement) in 1957, to a neighborhood that had become a hub for art commerce after the French Liberation.

The occupation of art dealer was transformed by a societal evolution, particularly with respect to time. After the First World War, *avant-gardists* were quickly embraced by Parisian high society. As a sign of this radical transformation, Pablo Picasso moved to 23 rue de la Boétie in 1918—in the heart of the chic 8th arrondissement in Paris (which was heavily populated with galleries)—where he lived a very bourgeois lifestyle. The beginning of the 1920s therefore represented a prosperous period for the contemporary art market. After the First World War, between 1921 and 1923, the sales of paintings confiscated from collector (and art critic and dealer) Wilhelm

Uhde (1874–1947) and dealer Daniel-Henry Kahnweiler—both of whom were Germans and had therefore been stripped of their assets—caused a flood of artworks on the market: no fewer than 1,500 paintings and sketches were dispersed, sparking excitement about contemporary art (Moulin, 1987). Among the great artisans of this thriving market was Alphonse Bellier (1886–1980), who began to work as an auctioneer in 1920, but also took advantage of the surplus of art to create a modern painting market. At the time, the pieces being sold were too "fresh," lacking the patina of time and the cultural legitimacy that it traditionally affords (Moulin & Quemin, 1993), and were viciously critiqued. These sales nevertheless contributed to the growing visibility of newer paintings on the market, thus causing the market to expand. After the 1929 economic crisis and the beginning of the Great Depression, the market's momentum slowed down drastically; dealers could no longer sell, as prices had crashed. Some collectors, however, were able to acquire artworks at slashed prices at auction events (Moulin, 1987).

Due to the Second World War, the art market was profoundly transformed, as many of the art dealers who came to prominence during the interwar period were of the Jewish faith.[11] As we have already seen, Kahnweiler's gallery was renamed the Galerie Louise Leiris during the Second World War, when Georges Wildenstein and Paul Rosenberg were also forced to flee to the United States. All of these great dealers could draw a direct line back to Paul Durand-Ruel with their occupational *modus operandi*. As such, Georges Wildenstein (1892–1963), son of Nathan Wildenstein—after taking over the Paris, New York, London, and Buenos Aires branches of his family business upon the death of his father—operated under the fundamental principle of buying *en masse* and waiting until prices rose to sell his stock.

Many other institutions stand as examples of the continued emergence of gallerists who have marked the history of the French contemporary art market in the wake of Durand-Ruel's innovation up to the 1960s.[12] Summarizing the evolution of Durand-Ruel's sales of contemporary art up to the 1950s (mainly taking place in galleries), Raymonde Moulin posited the following: "along with the commercialization of art came the taming of the public" (Moulin, 1987). Just as impactful was the consolidation of the model implemented by Durand-Ruel, beginning essentially in the 1870s, allowing him to lay the foundation for a new professional occupation (i.e., gallerist), which rounded out the traditional métier of art dealer by introducing an original model whose elemental characteristics are still in effect to this day with the fundamental preeminence of supply over demand.

The revolutionary Leo Castelli: the triumph of the American gallerist

While it was Paul Durand-Ruel who created the model of the professional gallerist in France at the end of the nineteenth century and the beginning of the twentieth century, the primary figure who embodies the history of this occupation is undeniably Leo Castelli. He was born in Trieste in 1907 (a city in present-day Italy, but which at the time was located in the Austro-Hungarian Empire), and died in 1999 in New York City. Even to this day, Leo Castelli constitutes a major player in the collective memory and imaginary of gallerists (Halbwachs, 1992) due to his status as a great American gallerist in the second half of the twentieth century. He also established long-lasting trends and artists within the global market and on the international contemporary scene, and strove to bring success to galleries in the United States, and thus shift the creative epicenter away from France (Guilbaut, 1985; Cohen-Solal, 2009).

Leo Castelli was born Leo Krauss into a wealthy and very cosmopolitan Jewish family. His paternal family, from which he inherited his Hungarian name, chose to change their name to Castelli in an attempt to seem more Italian. After completing his studies in Milan, Castelli began working for an insurance company in Bucharest, where he met Ileana Schapira, a wealthy heiress who went on to become his wife. Years later, after she divorced Castelli in 1959 and married Michael Sonnabend in 1960 (and took his last name), she became a gallerist herself and was eventually one of her ex-husband's major business partners. In 1935, the couple moved to Paris, and in 1939 Castelli opened his first gallery (financed by his wife's fortune), teaming up with interior designer René Drouin. Located in the Place Vendôme, his gallery displayed surrealist artists more than anyone else. The Second World War forced the Castellis to leave France, and after a long journey they arrived in New York City in 1941. In 1942, the couple moved into the very wealthy Upper East Side, to a townhouse purchased by Castelli's father-in-law. Thus, he became established in the United States, but belonged to the European cosmopolitan class and was in possession of a long list of international contacts, as well as speaking perfect German. As a result, Castelli worked with (and eventually became a partner of) the CIA during the war. Having quickly assimilated into New York high society, Castelli developed an art trading business, as he had done in Paris before opening his gallery in the 1st arrondissement. In 1957, when he was 50 years old, he inaugurated his first New York gallery on East 77th Street, in the Upper East Side, in his own apartment. His people skills, combined with his visionary artistic choices (as well as financial support that we now know came from the CIA (Guilbaut, 1985) to promote American contemporary art and bring it to the international stage (Obadia, 2019)), constituted the primary factors on which Castelli built his success. In 1958, Castelli enthusiastically organized Jasper Johns' first solo show; Alfred Barr, then-director of the MoMA, came to see the exhibition, and stayed for three hours, buying four pieces for his museum, thereby immediately cementing the emergence of a young artist (Moulin & Quemin, 1993).

Throughout his career, Leo Castelli remained loyal to the Upper East Side and to East 77th Street, although he later invested in other spaces on the same street that were larger than his first apartment, moving from number 8 to number 18. He understood the importance of moving into more spacious galleries (see Part 1 of this book), later adding two galleries in SoHo to his main location in the Upper East Side. In 1971, he moved into a second-floor space in a SoHo building; his former wife, now going by Ileana Sonnabend (who had in 1970 moved onto Madison Avenue, also in the Upper East Side), had a space just above Castelli's. The top floor of the building was occupied by André Emmerich, another gallerist. During the 1980s, at the height of his glory, Castelli opened another, even larger space, also in SoHo, where he on occasion organized exhibitions along with other gallerists such as Mary Boone, who had moved into the same building as Castelli (420 West Broadway) in 1977. Like Castelli, she was one of the prominent figures of the contemporary art market in the 1980s.[13]

As Paul Durand-Ruel decided to play the long game in order to support his artists, banking on a long-term strategy of artistic validation, so Leo Castelli took inspiration from his illustrious predecessor. He was not satisfied with simply fulfilling the demand that already existed; instead, he staked his career on validation by geographical distance (Moulin & Quemin, 1993) paired with extensive knowledge of the international market. Castelli worked directly toward the success of the great American art movements of his time (pop art, minimalist art, and conceptual art) notably by guaranteeing them a fast ascent well outside of their domains. However, he also made sure to maintain long-term relationships with his artists,[14] providing them with regular stipends whether they sold their works or not. Such it was that pop artists Robert Rauschenberg and Jasper Johns, both discovered and supported by Castelli, received a monthly income of $500 from him to pay their rent and buy art supplies (Robson, 1995). Minimalist artists Richard Serra and Donald Judd also received monthly payments (during three years for the former, and 14 years for the latter). In exchange for these monthly payments, Castelli received any art that they produced; even if Castelli did not manage to sell any of these works, he continued to finance them (Velthuis, 2002, p. 113). Castelli's hard work quickly paid off, as in 1964 Robert Rauschenberg, one of the Castelli Gallery's emblematic artists, won the Golden Lion award at the Venice Biennale (Malbert, 2006). Up to that point, it had seemed nearly impossible for an American artist to win such an award, as the winners tended to be artists from "haute culture" countries (i.e., European), France being foremost among them. Castelli's gallery had another success in 1988, when Jasper Johns won the same prestigious award.

By capitalizing on both his society contacts and the political ones that he developed during the Second World War, Castelli was able to take full advantage of the post-war shift toward contemporary art that took place in American institutions. He wasted no time in forming relationships with directors of the greatest museums and the most influential art critics like Alfred Barr, Clement Greenberg, and Robert Rosenblum. As a result, his artists' works were soon being displayed in the best European and American museums (notably the MoMA in the US, as well as the Jewish Museum and regional arts councils). Additionally, as he was quite cosmopolitan and spoke many languages, Castelli was able to take advantage of the increasingly internationalized art market and the artistic scene, and he significantly helped to propel this movement forward. In doing so, he relied on a dense network of "friendly galleries" (i.e., business partners sharing the representation of some of his artists with him): French historian Annie Cohen-Solal cites no fewer than 12 of these partners in Europe and 18 in North America during the 1970s (Cohen-Solal, 2009). As a matter of fact, Castelli was one of the first people to work with a network of partner galleries in Europe, and was undisputedly the first to develop this model on such a scale. The share that was intended to reward the transaction and not the artist's production was split between the two galleries, Leo Castelli and the partner who had made the deal. In Europe, Castelli's gallery partners (from 1962 to 1968) included Konrad Fischer in Düsseldorf, Gian Enzo Sperone in Turin, and his former wife Ileana Sonnabend (with whom he remained very close, even after they separated) when she moved to the quai des Grands Augustins in Paris. Thus, Castelli was in a position to oversee the entire distribution network for his artists and to keep sole control over how their work was promoted (Moulin & Quemin, 1993). After the Second World War, Castelli became an archetype for a leading gallerist, relying on his international network and his commercial partners: "Promoting the artists that he supported required a cultural, worldly, media-friendly, and commercial network" (Moulin, 1992, p.50). Although no less than 70 percent of Castelli's sales took place in other galleries in the middle of the 1970s, this rate dropped over the 1980s, partly because new artistic trends began to appear in Europe, and also because Castelli's artists had become much too expensive (Moulin, 1992), and his gallery progressively lost its luster.

It is important to note that Castelli was a sort of mentor for some American gallerists like Mary Boone (cited above), as well as Jeffrey Deitch and Larry Gagosian; Gagosian went on to become a father figure of sorts for gallerists at the beginning of the twenty-first century, and stands unquestionably among the most powerful gallerists of our era. Demonstrating the model that he inherited directly from Castelli, Gagosian completely assimilated the necessity of controlling the international dimension of the market. However, unlike Castelli, who worked in cooperation with partner galleries, Gagosian took his occupation a step further into internationalization by implementing a policy of internalization and expansion: he instituted an unprecedented number of subsidiaries throughout the world, thereby affording himself even more control over his artists' supply than his predecessor.

Given this quick historical overview, it is clear that the role of "gallerist" corresponds to a professional model that differs from that of traditional art dealers, whose primary concern is fulfilling a preexisting demand. Paul Durand-Ruel was a veritable art entrepreneur (Schumpeter, 2008), who developed strategies to generate a demand that did not yet exist. The new model that he created persists to this day, albeit with some evolutions, the most notable being the shift of the art market from France toward the United States, particularly during the 1960s. Leo Castelli contributed to the transformation of the occupation, enhancing the value of art (Moulin, 1995), and heavily accentuating the international dimension of the market. Of course, Paul Durand-Ruel also took this dimension into account, but to a much lesser extent. This mastery over the supply of artworks at the international level was taken a step further with the inauguration of the next generation of gallerists as introduced by Larry Gagosian. Today, the international dimension is very closely associated with contemporary art, and is even a fundamental aspect of it (Quemin, 2002).

PART ONE

A spatial approach to contemporary art galleries

1

The gallery as a physical space

Traditionally, a gallery's space has been inextricably linked to the gallerist's business, as evidenced by the fact that the profession takes its name from the word "gallery." According to the metonymic principle previously mentioned in the introduction of this book, the gallery simultaneously designates a space and the commercial activity that takes place therein. In *Le marché de la peinture en France* (*The French Art Market*), Raymonde Moulin regularly made a point of differentiating gallerists from people who simply rented their spaces for a day to display their pieces, or art brokers who do not own professional premises outside of their residences (Moulin, 1987); essentially, the fact of possessing a professional space for permanent exhibitions sets gallerists apart from the other two groups. Even today, art fairs generally require any applicants hoping to participate in their main sector to have a physical space where they organize exhibitions and receive the general public, insofar as their aim is to feature *galleries*, not structures that sell artworks without having an exhibition space. Interestingly, certain professionals denounce this practice, as they are consequently not able to "stay in the race," as it were. In 2017, after closing her public space—even though she had been a gallerist in Paris since 1976, and for a time had a location in the SoHo neighborhood of New York (from 1985 to 1993)—Farideh Cadot made the following incendiary remark:

> When over half of the galleries in the Marais[1] are still empty, we have to wonder how they survive. Why do they have to maintain a physical space? Because of the tyranny imposed by art fairs, from Basel to Chicago, from Fiac [in Paris] to Arco [in Madrid], where I participated right from the start. I've been going to these kinds of events for the past 20 years. I stopped because the artists that I work with were like me: they didn't want to be displayed in those windows. What's more, today, the fair directors tell us what kind of art we can display because that's what the market wants.
>
> "Farideh Cadot, Parisian gallerist: 'Art is disappearing'", *Le Journal des Arts*, no. 483, July 7, 2017

However, despite this kind of criticism, the physical space of the gallery continues to be essential, even more so because it is tied to the gallery's identity. I will not go in depth into the question of a gallery's geographic location here, as it is such an important topic that I will discuss it in the next chapter; but, to put it briefly: territory is not neutral, be it related to a country or a metropolitan area (Grafmeyer & Authier, 2008). The choice of location is a commitment, a stance taken by the gallerist (Bourdieu & Delsaut, 1975).

The statement inherent in a gallery's street address is supported by the characteristics of the very space wherein the gallery welcomes its visitors. From the time that contemporary art emerged as a specific category and was integrated into the market, there has been a general, broadly imposed consensus regarding the code of the "white cube" (O'Doherty, 2000). It involves the notion of presenting works of art in an environment that is as pared down as possible, and is now practically unavoidable in contemporary art galleries,[2] although a gallery's design will occasionally break from this norm to be more memorable. In truly contemporary galleries, it is also essential not to display too many pieces at once, to space the pieces out, and even to leave some walls completely blank, based on the principle of conspicuous waste (Veblen, 1899); all of which aims to promote artists and their works, as well as to appeal to their potential buyers. Walls that are uniformly white, and preferably high, are enhanced by lighting. This lighting also tends to be standardized, which is why overhead light is so highly valued.[3] Skylights are very popular, especially in galleries located in Paris or in the New York neighborhood of Chelsea. Gallery floors are often made of polished concrete that is almost always grey, in varying shades. However, stone, though rather similar in appearance, is sometimes preferred to polished concrete, due to its more distinctive and higher-quality nature. This French gallerist shows what is symbolically at stake when it comes to a space's layout, particularly in terms of the choice of flooring: "for my new gallery, I'm going to have stone floors, like Gagosian and Dominique Lévy." Clearly, the interior design qualifies the gallery, and in this case it allows the gallery in question to emulate two very influential establishments, based on a strategy of distinction (Veblen, 1899; Bourdieu, 1987). However, some galleries—often those that have existed for a long time (as far as contemporary art is concerned)—still occasionally prefer to have parquet floors.

Symbolically, from a very Goffman-esque perspective, the gallery layout is split in two (Goffman, 1959) between the exhibition space—where any indicators of the commercial aspect must disappear—and the back office, where most of the transactions and administrative work take place. The first part, which is accessible to the public, employs visual codes that have stronger associations with museums than they do with stores: lighting, uncluttered spaces, the absence of furniture. The person stationed at the front desk does not generally approach visitors to ask if they need any assistance or to give explanations of the art on display. Not only is the art not listed with prices, but this public-facing space does not have a register at all; the machine used to process purchases is kept in a discreet place. When in this first gallery space, the gallerist practically plays the role of a curator, conversely, in the back office, the focus is completely oriented toward more commercial aspects. This space is much more cluttered, be it with furniture or equipment (desks, shelves, computers, printers, telephones, and various papers). It is also in this second space where large galleries frequently have one or two sales rooms (Velthuis, 2002 and 2005). The functional yet symbolic schism between these two spaces is therefore particularly evident.

The contemporary art gallery is symbolically presented as a closed universe that does not seek to be accessible to the whole city. In most countries, galleries avoid being highly visible from the street; instead, they may open onto a courtyard, in a layout that is very common in cities like Berlin and Paris. Even when they look onto the street, which is frequently the case in a neighborhood like Chelsea in New York, the design of the façade aims more often than not to cut the gallery off from the outside world. Even if the gallery has large windows, they are frequently opaque or obstructed by hanging fixtures that block them from view and isolate the interior from the exterior. This simple feature operates as a sign, and clearly differentiates galleries that sell true contemporary art from those that pretend to do the same, but that in reality operate more in the market of chromos (Couture, 1981; Moulin, 1992).[4]

Contemporary art galleries tend to favor a common model for their physical spaces that marks them as being truly "contemporary galleries" rather than making their space different from all the others of their kind. This goal of singularization does exist, but as a secondary consideration, such as competing for the most desirable addresses, moving into the largest spaces possible for the neighborhood, and meticulously planning every facet of their design plan. How a gallery's space is presented conveys a message about the quality (Misdrahi Flores, 2013) of the art that is displayed. In addition to the costs associated with the gallery's design and the maintenance of its permanent space, there is also the expense of mounting new exhibitions; however, according to an associate director of an international European gallery, there can be no question about reducing these expenses:

> We have a large space, so when we put on a new exhibition in the gallery, we have to repaint everything, we knock down the walls and put them back up in a new place. All that can cost €30,000, but it has to be done, otherwise it doesn't work. In New York, a fellow gallerist at Gallery [X] is so excited that Perrotin just set up shop next to him in the Lower East Side, he says that that will bring important collectors to the area and increase foot traffic in his space, but he doesn't realize that his gallery looks really slapdash, and any clients that come to his gallery because of his new neighbor will recoil when they see how poorly thought out his space is!

Hence, to present their premises in the most flattering manner possible, gallerists are eager to collaborate with well-known architects (when they have the budget for it); some of whom are even specialized in gallery or museum design. This latter attests to the gallerist's financial means as well as their level of taste (Bourdieu, 1987) and can better showcase their artists' work. As we will see at the end of this chapter, this trend has become stronger over the last few years.

The rivalry between galleries (especially those with similar positions on the market) leads them to reproduce the same codes, which in part explains why, even though they are competitors, they often hire the same architects with a signature style (Bourdieu & Delsaut, 1975). Even if this is not the case, they may deliberately copy a rival gallery's space. A former staff member of a famous Parisian gallery once confided to me: "[X] admires two people, Gagosian and Ropac. When he designed the space for his gallery in the Marais, he really wanted the same staircase as Ropac, his staircase is magnificent. He sent me to secretly photograph the place, I even had to measure the height of the steps, how thick the metal was! (he laughs) Well ultimately, his staircase is very beautiful, but it makes noise when you walk on it, Ropac's is better!"

From "mega-galleries"—the largest galleries of all, which have significant financial resources—to smaller-scale ones, the presentation of a professional space must be suitably tidy. A staff member of one of the biggest French galleries explained:

> Once, I had to use a colleague's desk when dealing with a collector, and it was an absolute mess, there were crumbs on his keyboard! When I turned on the computer to show the client some pieces, it was also in disarray, my colleague had left a music video by [French rapper] Booba open on his screen, I didn't know where to go.

He went on:

> We had a kitchen where our interns would heat up their food, and if collectors came in afterwards it smelled truly awful. Our boss gave them a telling off, and even though my office was one floor below, I could feel the walls vibrating, he was shouting so loudly!

An associate for an international gallery shared a similar point of view:

> In the gallery, at the beginning, I had to chase down my staff so that they would make sure everything would be neat and tidy before they left in the evening, because you never know, the next day you might have to open the gallery half an hour early for a collector, and if it's a pigsty, the effect is catastrophic.

Essentially, the care afforded to the gallery space generally appears to correlate with the level of prestige associated with it. What is acceptable for a small, emerging gallery is not so for a more established entity; this is even more true if it charges high prices for its art. While gallerists typically do not like their premises to be too similar to luxury businesses, the parallel can occasionally be drawn when talking about the spaces that accommodate the public, with particular regard to the clientele. An associate for an international European gallery explained it thus:

> Well, it's not something that we say very often, but it's true that, even though we don't like to use the word when talking about contemporary art, we are a luxury business. A luxury handbag costs €5,000; but we as a contemporary art gallery go way beyond that, so clearly the gallery has to be immaculate. If we have to change a light switch because it's broken or damaged, it has to be fixed right away, we can't wait. The presentation of the gallery is essential for us to stay credible, given our high prices.

The projected image influences collectors, as well as other players within the art world. A gallery's space can entice artists, but if the space is less than flattering—i.e. in an undesirable neighborhood, smaller, or less visually appealing—the artists will be unattainable, and the galleries will not be able to represent them.

One of today's most influential Parisian gallerists confirmed this notion:

> For me, it was totally impossible to represent [B] when I had my previous gallery, right down the street from this one, but much smaller. I had already met him, the introduction went well, I would have loved to represent him since he's an important artist, he's one of the most famous French artists on an international level. But there was no doubt, he couldn't have joined my gallery before I found this new space and had the means to work with him. Once it was sure, I got back in touch with him, and he accepted immediately. Before I had this space, I was still the same person, but he never would have been able to accept. It's normal, I understand completely.

The same phenomenon is perfectly illustrated by the French gallery RX, which was originally founded in Paris (but in a different neighborhood than the main contemporary art establishments), and later moved into a much larger space in Ivry-sur-Seine, a suburb of Paris. In 2016, the gallery returned to Paris, and invested in a large, beautiful space in the middle of the Marais neighborhood; right next to the most famous contemporary art galleries. The new premises boasted 7,200 square feet, of which about 5,000 square feet were dedicated to exhibition space.

A few weeks after inaugurating this new property, the gallery issued a press release announcing that it was representing three artists, two of whom were more famous by far than the artists the gallery had been representing up to that point. These artists would most likely have been inaccessible to the gallery if it had not been able to offer an exhibition space commensurate to their reputation (Quemin, 2013b). The press release was presented as thus:

> New collaborations 2016–2017 / Permanent artists:
>
> El Anatsui
> Born in 1944 in Anyako, Ghana. Lives and works between Ghana and Nigeria. Globally recognized and respected, even more so since winning the Golden Lion at the Venice Biennial in 2015 for his collected works, El Anatsui is known for his sculptures of wood and clay, and his complex constructions made of recycled materials.
>
> Elger Esser
> Born in 1967 – lives and works in Düsseldorf.
> In collaboration with the Thaddaeus Ropac gallery
>
> Joel Andrianimearisoa
> Born in 1977 – lives and works in Paris and Antananarivo.[5]

The prestigious Golden Lion at the Venice Biennale was inevitably mentioned in reference to El Anatsui, thus simultaneously qualifying the artist and the gallery (Moulin and Quemin, 1993). Incidentally, pertaining to Elger Esser, the then-collaboration with the Parisian gallery Thaddaeus Ropac (which also had locations in Salzburg, London, and later in Seoul)—one of the most prestigious galleries in Europe and in the world—also constituted a means of promoting the artist as well as his new gallery.

To accurately situate the gallery's leap in status—at least in terms of the reputation or recognition of the artists being represented—by moving to a new space, combining the benefits of a large surface area and an appealing interior design with a perfectly appropriate location, we may refer to the global ranking of the artists on the gallery's roster[6] at the time when the previously mentioned press release was issued, and compare it with the newcomers who also appeared on that list by considering the data provided by the Artfacts[7] website (Quemin, 2013b):

Artfacts ranking of artists represented by the RX gallery in 2016:	
Elger Esser	787
El Anatsui	953
Georges Rousse	1,596
Anna Malagrida	2,618
Samuel Rousseau	2,732
Fabien Verschaere	3,805

Bae Bien-U	4,626
Joël Andrianomearisoa	5,105
Denis Darzacq	6,123
Lee Bae	6,499
Philippe Pasqua	8,775
Ivan Plusch	13,981
Mrdjan Bajic	15, 547
Xiao Fan	28,761

These numbers clearly show that the fact of moving into a new, more prestigious space led to the representation of artists who are much more renowned than those who had been with the gallery up to that point, not least of which included Elger Esser and El Anatsui. This shows that a gallery's space conveys a message not only to collectors—who would be the obvious targets—and to artists—as we have just seen—but also to all the other players in the art world, particularly as regards art fair organizers, who visit galleries and judge their quality (Misdrahi Flores, 2013) regarding their lineup, as well as their space. A French gallerist, who ran a fairly small space in Paris' Haut Marais, admitted as much two years before opening at a second location in Romainville, a Paris suburb:

> – *Is the size of this new space a factor?*
>
> – Yes, this gallery on the Passage des Gravilliers is great, but I have this dream of a bigger space, so I can give artists a chance to mount new exhibitions, and, to be quite honest, because it's also a sign of power, a way of showing that things are going really well. I think it might be a beacon to draw the attention of major international fairs, and it would also be exciting and motivating for me and my team.
>
> Vincent Sator in "Vincent Sator, a Gallerist on the Move," in *La Gazette Drouot*, no. 41, November 24, 2017, p. 25

Just like its physical space, a gallery's virtual space (i.e. its website) is as much a conveyor as it is an extension of the gallery's image. Nowadays, it is difficult to find brands or companies that do not have their own website.[8] Just as much as their physical location, their website (which must certify that the gallery does indeed belong to the contemporary art world) is a conveyor of identity. As such, it adheres to a series of implicit, extremely precise codes like clean graphics and a white background that echoes the "white cube" of the physical space (O'Doherty, 2000). Starting with the homepage, the visitor must be reassured that they have well and truly entered the website of a *real* contemporary art gallery.

Among the items listed on the homepage's dropdown menu, there is systematically a reference to "artists," which must also attest to the gallery's "contemporaneity" and reflect its "line" (i.e. its positioning in the contemporary art world in terms of the tendencies that it promotes). The link leads to the gallery's roster, which grows based on how long the gallery has existed and how influential it has become. Although the smaller, truly contemporary galleries typically have a dozen or so artists, the most influential institutions (like Gagosian, whose flagship gallery is located in New York and boasts 18 points of sale throughout the world) once featured a record 130 artists on its roster.

Like a gallery's physical and virtual spaces, the design of the invitation cards for exhibition openings (*vernissages* in French) are also conveyors of identity and can be an extension of the gallery. The cardstock must be sufficiently thick (sometimes, as thick as possible) to demonstrate the gallery's importance and the social quality that it accords to the recipient to whom the card is addressed. However, this strategy of conspicuousness (Veblen, 1899) is only feasible up to a certain point. Essentially, galleries must show moderation, lest the invitation design go beyond the commonly accepted conventions of good taste and appear to be showing off. Any organization displaying such an overly assertive attempt at distinction (Bourdieu, 1987) would be broadly discredited. As this journalist explains: "[T] Gallery's invitation cards were a disaster, they were so thick that it became somewhat crude. When I reach into my mailbox and pick up my mail, I know that the card came from them without even reading the name on the envelope. Honestly, it's too much, it's like they have no class."

The gallery's space and everything that perpetuates it, especially in terms of visual communication, contribute directly to its branding. This is why the location is important, even when in the Internet age it would not be unreasonable to expect a certain amount of dematerialization; however, this is not the case. Physical space remains even to this day crucial for a gallery's business.

In 2019, the London art fair, Frieze, caused a controversy when it modified its rules to allow the participation of "galleries" that did not have a physical exhibition space. The subject has also been debated for several years by Art Basel, the leader in the art fair sector, which to date has nevertheless constantly resisted such an evolution. The influential player has always been of the belief that, in the long term, this would run the risk of making the contemporary art ecosystem more fragile, for which the fairs themselves would eventually pay the price. If the condition of requiring a physical space that hosted public exhibitions were to be removed in order for applicants to participate in the fair, many establishments could renounce the traditional gallery model that includes a permanent space, in order to cut costs and dedicate all their resources to short-term events such as pop-up shows. This would reduce the amount of contemporary art exhibitions in metropolitan areas and would cause the supply of contemporary art intended especially for collectors to dwindle, thus crippling the global artistic ecosystem.

This notion of questioning why physical exhibition spaces should be required is due to the pressure that galleries feel to determine in what ways a physical space is still necessary, and which means (particularly financial ones) must be utilized therein.

Many gallerists, including influential ones, argue in favor of having their own physical space, which to them is generally an indispensable resource for their work. As we will see in the following extract, art fairs can generate sales, as can gallery spaces, but for this gallerist who has locations in Paris and Brussels, the sales in her own spaces still clearly constitute the majority of her commercial activity:

> The Brussels gallery is its own business, but if you look at everything across the board, the French gallery earns three times as much as the Belgian one, and fairs only earn a third of what the galleries make. We make really good sales in the galleries. We have a great network of collectors and institutions in France, which allows us to make some really significant sales.

One of the most fervent statements in support of galleries having a physical space was given by the influential international gallerist Thaddaeus Ropac:[9]

> For my gallery, the fairs are important. But three-quarters of our business continues to be done in the galleries, and I'm happy to keep it this way. When we have a major gallery show on the horizon, we prefer not to offer one of the works at a fair. One of the reasons is that we want to incentivize collectors, and especially new collectors, to come to the gallery. There, they will see the work in the context that the artist envisioned, and become part of that artist's universe.
>
> "Thaddaeus Ropac on Why We Can't Give up on Galleries," *Artsy*, May 2, 2018

Ropac's attachment to the model of the gallery as a physical space is not surprising, as he has a very high-quality resource at his disposal (which very few competitors in the world are able to rival) in his various establishments in Salzburg, Paris, Pantin, London, and now Seoul. Therefore, for the few galleries that have comparable competitive advantages, the physical space plays a decisive role, as it allows them to maintain the exclusivity of this group of powerful organizations and keep all rivals at a distance.

More broadly, fairs—despite having become essential for galleries—now compete directly with them, as traditional gallery exhibition spaces tend to be neglected by art enthusiasts, to say nothing of collectors. As we will see in more detail in chapter 3, fairs today have become virtually indispensable for contemporary art galleries: it is often reported that galleries make about half of their profits at fairs. Incidentally, this statistic is confirmed in the following extract, which also underlines the fact that fairs offer the additional advantage of being less time-consuming, and therefore present a better return on investment from this point of view: "Our turnover comes down to 50% of profits from fairs and 50% in galleries, even though we spend most of our time taking care of the gallery and organizing exhibitions" (Alix Dionot-Morani and Axel Dibie, directors and founders of the French Galerie Crèvecœur in "We need alternative means of expression", *Le Journal des Arts*, no. 516, February 1, 2019).

More fundamentally, it is important to emphasize and preserve the current symbiosis between art fairs and gallery spaces. As this gallerist, who has locations in three countries, said: "Today, fairs are unavoidable, but we can't overestimate their role. While some collectors don't step foot in galleries anymore, others never come to art fairs, so you have to be everywhere!"

At less advanced levels of development, other gallerists also speak of the importance of having a physical space, which for them constitutes both a professional resource whose services are important in order to diversify their lineup, and a veritable showcase. However, for them, gaining access to a suitable physical space is more problematic.

While galleries seem, on the whole, to be required to have a physical space not only to receive the public—including collectors—but also to qualify for art fairs, some professionals—even those who are most assimilated into the art world—are beginning to take the plunge and give up their spaces. For instance, in June 2018, associates of the New York gallery Cheim & Reid–who had a beautiful space on the ground floor of a new building (built of concrete in the brutalist architectural style) located on West 25th Street in the middle of Chelsea—announced that they were closing their gallery and starting a brokerage business without having an exhibition space.

This example is the consequence of the following fact, described by this director of an American gallery in an unequivocal observation that is generally shared by many of his counterparts, albeit frequently in less stark terms: "Basically, fairs have become essential for galleries. Once an opening is over, many galleries don't have any visitors anymore. But we still need a place where we can receive the people who want to see our pieces. In fact, more and more, gallery spaces are for our image."

The same observation was made just as bluntly by art writer Kenny Schachter who, during his shocking speech at the 2020 professional symposium "Talking Galleries" in Barcelona, gave this bare-bones description of the "present model of the art world – art has become a hybrid offshoot of the luxury good business, the cesspool of the art market is rife with more crime than ever and attendance is dwindling at small and mid-level galleries that seem to be losing the battle to simply survive."

How can we address the "crisis of a gallery's physical space"?

Practically all of the art market players that I spoke with agree that it is becoming increasingly difficult to attract collectors or the public in general into galleries,[10] even during private exhibit openings.[11] This is due in part to the proliferation of venues for contemporary art (especially galleries) that have an extensive calendar of events, which thus compete with each other, not only when it comes to sales, but also to the time spent by art enthusiasts in a given space. However, one of the most formidable competitive activities is participating in art fairs, which have exploded in number since the beginning of the millennium (Quemin, 2013a), and which moreover occupy an increasingly important place on the contemporary art calendar. Collectors are traveling to fairs more and more, and it is very difficult for galleries to schedule events in their own spaces during the dates of the most important fairs. Even when a fair is not underway, it can be difficult to attract collectors into gallery exhibitions; their appetites having already been satisfied during a fair.

Today, the high (and still rising) cost of rent is all the more problematic as it is paired with a low number of visitors in the spaces in question, and therefore results in a particularly low return on investment.[12] Taking into consideration the additional fixed costs and the significant expense of participating in fairs, the gallery business model (Adam, 2018) appears to be increasingly unstable for many establishments, especially those that do not own their premises. As stated at the beginning of this chapter, galleries are traditionally faced with the problem of the cost of maintaining their physical space—rent constituting a significant budget item among their expenses—as this is necessary to qualify as a real gallery.

As renters, galleries are consistently confronted with the problem of rising rents, an issue of which David Halle and Elisabeth Tiso give a remarkable overview in their book, *New York's New Edge: Contemporary Art, the High Line, and Urban Megaprojects on the Far East Side* (Halle & Tiso, 2014). When galleries cluster together in an urban environment that had previously been undervalued, their presence alone prompts a reevaluation of the neighborhood in question, and the area's social image becomes much more desirable. Along with this, among other things, comes gentrification (Glass, 1964) in habitable areas, which pushes landlords to raise their rents to match the surging demand. This demand in turn is bolstered by fashion establishments that are particularly sensitive to the neighborhood's artistic aura, as is evident in New York's SoHo neighborhood or the Marais in Paris.

Two gallerists reported very different rents for the same space on a street in the Marais perpendicular to rue Beaubourg, which was fairly large and had spacious rooms, but was nevertheless not in the most reputed areas of Paris: "(the previous tenant) paid around €10,000 per month for the space, because she had rented it for a long time, and it was a friend's rate. But now, it's definitely closer to €25,000. Our colleague [X], just one street over, I know he pays €18,000 in rent per month, and it's much smaller." The same day, another gallerist informed me that he had heard that the gallery had been offered for a rent of €12,000 per month! A few streets away, but in a location further from the center, another Parisian gallerist told me that she paid €5,000 per month for her enormous space, but only because she was protected by her lease (the market price at that time would have been closer to €9,000). When the COVID-19 pandemic triggered an economic crisis in 2020, many galleries' ability to survive was tested, and some were forced to close their doors, while others had to downsize. In reaction to this development, this Swiss gallerist sent me an email that immediately mentioned the problem of fixed costs combined with the staggering rents of certain very well-known galleries: "[X] has to pay one million per month for rent in London . . . so it's absolute madness." Rent is a recurring concern for galleries and, as has just been shown, even though there is real uncertainty about the amounts to be paid, which vary considerably according to the person being interviewed, there seems to be a general consensus that the cost of rent (excluding for the most influential establishments) has gotten higher, some might even say to an excessive degree.

It is therefore particularly important for galleries to develop strategies to lower rent expenses. Among these strategies is the possibility of moving to a less expensive neighborhood (or, for brand new galleries, settling directly into such an environment), as we will see in the next chapter with the example on the rue Louise Weiss in the 13th arrondissement of Paris, or with the suburb of Romainville. In the United States, the manner in which the gallery districts of SoHo and Chelsea in New York were developed (Halle & Tiso, 2014) will also be enlightening.

Another option consists of divesting oneself of the gallery space model and focusing more on art fairs; even though, as we have seen, fairs take a candidate's physical space into consideration when selecting their participants.

The strategy of reducing fixed costs may involve relying on a gallery's website more than on its physical space. Investing more in the digital sphere might make it possible, at least in part, for a gallery to avoid the constraints of a physical space, especially the rising prices that almost inevitably accompany a high-performing space.

There is no shortage of initiatives, which makes it possible to view hundreds or even thousands of artworks, especially on a gallery's website – or nowadays on an art fair's website. Art Basel Hong Kong took on this initiative in 2020, and the ensuing website ultimately replaced the physical fair after it was canceled due to the COVID-19 pandemic, although it was initially intended to be only a complement. For a few years, online sales rooms have appeared on some galleries' websites; but in reality, they mainly present only the biggest galleries and the most famous artists. In general, the pieces are only on sale for a short time; in a space as wide-reaching as the Internet, it is necessary to reintroduce restriction and rarity (Moulin, 1995), here in terms of temporal availability. In March 2019, the mega-gallery Gagosian announced that it had sold a piece by Albert Oehlen for $6 million (thus breaking the artist's auction sale record) via an online sales room. However, as is always the case for private transactions, it is important to keep in mind that it is impossible to be sure that the transaction actually took place, or if it was merely a public relations tactic to appear avant-garde, technologically speaking. If art fairs, Art Basel Hong Kong foremost among them, decided to use virtual spaces to supplement the number of physical stands for participating galleries in their 2021 fair, it is most likely due to the fact that, at least today, these virtual spaces are not exact duplicates of the galleries' own websites; it is still rather premature to rely on this method in order for these establishments to significantly develop sales. It is also important to note that, while we often speak of developing "online" sales, unlike websites on the mass market, gallery websites do not constitute a sales tool that could function independently to process orders from the moment they are designed. Additionally, most of a gallery's work still consists of contacting and canvassing institutions such as museums and contemporary art centers, as well as collectors, by sending them files presenting artists (and their works), to promote them and possibly sell their productions.

Galleries can also attempt to reduce the costs of their current physical spaces via different means. Where they often used to organize exhibitions that lasted around six weeks (or sometimes even a month)—which typically resulted in around seven exhibitions per year—they are tending more and more to reduce this number by scheduling their exhibitions for longer periods of time, or by announcing prolongations of exhibitions that have already begun. Exhibitions lasting two months are no longer out of the ordinary. Hence, many galleries organize five exhibitions per year, and some are even scaling back to four per year, sometimes even three! This helps them to avoid accruing the installation expenses—which are sometimes quite costly—that come with new presentations. In April 2017, the American gallerist Jeffrey Deitch announced his upcoming installation in Los Angeles.[13] In an interview with *Artnet News*, he explained his decision to organize only three annual exhibitions in his new Angelino space (as he had already done in his New York gallery) by citing the museum-like caliber of his presentations and his desire that they be viewable for as many visitors as possible: "The idea in New York is to do three shows a year, and it will probably be the same here" he said. "When you do shows that are museum-level, you don't want to take them down after a month" (in "Jeffrey Deitch is Returning to LA to Open a New Gallery. The dealer has unfinished business on the West Coast," *Artnet News*, April 11, 2017). However, it is plausible that the desire to reduce costs was an additional factor behind this choice.

Another avenue that gallerists appear to be exploring with more interest is ensuring that the space generates income through activities that go beyond the sales of artworks, which nevertheless remain the gallery's primary purpose.

Over the last few years, galleries have sought out new revenue streams by diversifying the use of their spaces (this is particularly true for mid-size galleries, which were hit hardest by recent evolutions in the market). A gallery's space is therefore no longer used solely to display the works of its artists. This is clearly illustrated in this description of another Los Angeles gallery's services:

> James Gallery, for its part, cannot wait for an artist in its 35-strong stable to make it big, so it needs a variety of related sources of revenue. It will sell you art (a piece at a time or enough to fill an entire building), frame your art, commission artists to create specific works for you, evaluate your existing collection ('asset management'), and even let you throw a party right in the gallery. Such extras might already be rolled into the business of mega-galleries, which have been known to rent out their cavernous Chelsea spaces in New York for Fashion Week and some offer concierge-style services to collectors.
>
> But such endeavors are newer for smaller galleries, which are now pursuing them as separate profit-making endeavors rather than extras that a select few billionaire clients have come to expect.
>
> Providing such client services, or 'finding additional revenue streams,' as Andrew Schoelkopf, president of the New York-based Art Dealers Association of America, called it, might have been considered gauche in an earlier era. But it has become the new business model for smaller and regional galleries that are looking to compete with the growing quantity of online art sales, other galleries [. . .], and the hundreds of international art fairs where the elite galleries show their wares. It is a crowded field.
>
> "Galleries that Moonlight: How Smaller Dealers Are Making Money in Nontraditional Ways, From Helping Corporations to Hosting Weddings," *Artnet News*, July 29, 2019

The most common method for a gallery to turn a regular and considerable profit with an ancillary activity is renting out its space for Fashion Week. This practice is all the more beneficial because it does not damage the gallery's image, as associating fashion with art does not tarnish the latter's reputation (Bourdieu & Delsaut, 1975). The principle has now become widely accepted in the Marais in Paris, and in Chelsea in New York,[14] as the two cities are major fashion capitals (Godart, 2012) where the fashion industry supports the ecosystem and the particular economy of contemporary art galleries. In the Marais, only the most prestigious galleries do not take advantage of this possibility to turn a considerable profit. For the rest, this opportunity has become nearly unavoidable, and quite commonplace. As this Marais gallerist explained: "By renting their space out four times a year during Paris Fashion Week, galleries can pay between half and all of their annual rent, it's really an enormous source of income. Some galleries may even earn more than that." Unlike this gallerist, who was thrilled with the financial windfall that resulted from renting her space during Fashion Week, one of her Parisian colleagues expressed her disapproval:

> When over half of the galleries in the Marais are still empty, we have to wonder how they survive. Why do they have to maintain a physical space? Because of the tyranny imposed by art fairs [. . .] So these galleries, what are they doing to stay alive? They rent their spaces four times a year for the famous Paris 'Fashion Week,' which allows them to cover their own rent and even a bit more. If that's what you're living for, I don't want it. Also, there are no more real vernissages, it's just dinners organized the night before an opening for important buyers who don't want to bump into any other people.[15]
>
> "Farideh Cadot, Parisian gallerist: 'Art is disappearing'", *Le Journal des Arts*, no. 483, July 7, 2017[16]

Another reaction consists of trying to get the public—especially collectors—to find their way back to galleries. In order to do so, galleries may consider expanding their calendar to include other kinds of art exhibitions, or even attempting to make the galleries into "community spaces." In October 2018, the David Kordansky gallery in Los Angeles announced that they were launching an expansion intended to "enhance the experience" of their visitors, (collectors in particular). The overtly stated goal was to transform the gallery into a destination in and of itself.

Breaking down the boundaries between artistic disciplines thus has the aim of attracting new audiences, particularly by creating an event-based ambiance that can be added to potential art enthusiasts' social calendars (Bourdieu & Darbel, 1997). This tactic is no longer as effective for galleries if its sole focus is on contemporary art.

This range of activities is illustrated by Californian gallerist Peter Blake, who at the same time expressed his fondness of the traditional model, but acknowledged that it would be very outdated nowadays:

> Lately, my gallery no longer feels like the white box it was for 25 years. Now, it's become this kind of experimental space where we could have a pop-up dinner, music, tastings, poetry, show secondary market work, show design. I don't feel that compelled to be locked up in the white cube anymore. Mind you, I am a total white-cube enthusiast and if I could return to the old days, I would. But we've left that place.
>
> Peter Blake in "'You're Only as Good as Your Last Couple of Shows,' On the 25th Anniversary of His Gallery, Peter Blake Reflects on the Ups and Downs of Art Dealing," *Artnet News*, August 12, 2019

As previously stated, other initiatives involve explicit attempts to reintroduce the activity of visiting galleries to the social calendar to create more enthusiasm for contemporary art. Foremost among these initiatives[17] is unequivocally that of "gallery weekends". The first of these weekends was launched in Berlin in 2005, and its objective was to entice collectors from all over Germany, and even from other countries, to visit galleries. This is due to the fact that, while Berlin is a dynamic center for artists, it has a distinctive lack of art buyers. Moreover, Berlin's galleries are scattered over different neighborhoods, and even if they are in the same neighborhood, they are sometimes still too far from each other. This event has become closely associated with the city; in 2019, no fewer than 45 galleries participated. This model has expanded throughout the world in cities as varied as Brussels, Barcelona, Chicago, Seoul, Beijing, and Paris.

Gallery weekends attempt to compete with art fairs by concentrating the high-end art being showcased, as galleries may be inclined to display their best pieces on these occasions. The success of these events also derives from their short-term nature; while a gallery is permanently accessible (as opposed to fairs, which are temporary), the goal was to introduce a degree of exceptionality and an event atmosphere (Bourdieu & Darbel, 1997). Outside of gallery weekends, it is already the norm for galleries to be open on Saturdays, but extending to Sundays is uncommon. The weekend is supplemented with various events, such as cocktail receptions or private visits of institutions. Overall, it is fundamentally a question of establishing a social activity that will entice art lovers (and collectors in particular) to come to galleries.

Since 2014, Paris has organized a gallery weekend every year in May. In 2017, the coordinator of this event explained the project:

> Today, a city like Paris cannot afford not to have a gallery weekend, as it promotes the dynamism of the art scene and proves that there is more than fairs. The concept of the Gallery Weekend exists everywhere in the world, in Chicago, Seoul, Beijing . . . Berlin has a different status because it doesn't host a major fair. People have fewer excuses to go to Berlin than to Paris, where foreigners may want to come for several reasons, even if they come less since the [November 2015] terrorist attacks. That's another reason to use art and culture as an incentive to travel. For us, after four years, it's about becoming a key moment to promote the quality that Parisian contemporary art has to offer, on a weekend just after the Venice Biennial, for which many international collectors come to Europe (especially from across the Atlantic).
>
> Marion Papillon in "Choices Reveals the Program for the 4th Paris Gallery Weekend," *Lejournaldesarts.fr*, April 4, 2017

Since its launch, the Paris Gallery Weekend (PGW) has experimented with several formats—notably by discontinuing its initial collective exhibition, and by choosing a more emblematic name than the original

"Choices"—but it has maintained its primary goal of bringing collectors and the public back into the fold of galleries, which today are generally passed over in favor of fairs. To do so, it proposes a dinner for gallerists, collectors, artists, critics, and journalists, as well as a series of events such as talks at the Centre Pompidou, or exclusive visits of institutions or private collections. This weekend, which is far less expensive than a fair, amounts to about €3,000 in participation costs for Parisian galleries, while it costs at least €10,000 for a small fair. Everywhere in the world, the principle of these weekends is to resuscitate the practice of visiting galleries (and to promote their lineups) so that they will not have to concentrate all of their attention on fairs.

A final strategy related to gallery spaces that is frequently employed (and is essentially the most important among them) results in a sort of race for immensity. As collectors continue to give galleries a wide berth, it is crucial to ensure that when they do visit galleries, they be rewarded for their effort with a wide variety of high-quality artworks presented in the best condition. In addition to the intense competition that exists between galleries to offer the most beautiful exhibition spaces in the interest of attracting artists, having a large venue also means being able to bring in art enthusiasts with high expectations. The two pursuits of design and size are, ultimately, linked.

Across the board, the art market is moving toward an oligopoly-fringe economic model, wherein there are both juggernauts and a slew of smaller establishments (Benhamou, 1996). The biggest players tend to constantly absorb organizations that are smaller and more vulnerable than they are. This was illustrated in July 2019, when the Parisian gallery VnH was procured by the American mega-gallery David Zwirner.[18] Even more frequently, these large organizations turn smaller ones into non-viable galleries by "stealing" their most profitable artists from them. Once the promotional initiatives launched by smaller galleries begin to pay off (Moulin, 1987), the more prominent galleries often poach the artists for their own exhibitions and integrate them into their own rosters. This is a frequent occurrence that is typical of the structure of the market. It therefore motivates galleries to be constantly growing, especially as concerns moving into bigger spaces, in order to protect themselves from the voracity of the largest competitors. This is demonstrated by this international gallerist, whose exhibition space has undergone spectacular development over the years: "I was scared to lose my artists. I had to grow and offer them more and more services" (Emmanuel Perrotin at the "Talking Galleries" symposium in Barcelona on January 21, 2018).

Another prominent French gallerist expressed the same concern when opening a second space in Paris: "For the new gallery, we didn't really have a choice, we have to keep doing more if we don't want the biggest galleries to steal our best artists, we have to go with the tide."

This is particularly true for midsize or large galleries, but even the most prestigious establishments feel the pressure, as evidenced by the proliferation of points of sale around the world. In June 2019, in response to the heightened competition on the art market, three international galleries simultaneously announced that they were expanding their geographical scope by opening new physical spaces. The Goodman gallery, which has been the primary gallery on the South African art scene since 1966 and up to this point only had locations in Cape Town and Johannesburg, planned to expand into London in autumn of that year, so as to build better relationships with European museums and clients. At the same time, the giant Gagosian (originally founded in the United States) planned to buy a venue in Basel that, up to that point had only hosted temporary exhibitions. Finally, another major market player, Hauser & Wirth, launched an art center of 16,000 square feet on Isla del Rey—off the coast of Menorca (in the Spanish Balearic Islands)—where from April to October they would offer special events, exhibitions, and learning activities.

As we will see in the chapter dedicated to recent market trends regarding contemporary art galleries, it is important to situate the proliferation of exhibition spaces for leading galleries in the context of a broader competitive phenomenon, which plays a particular and very visible role in how these spaces are developed and how the public is received. The policy of "grow or go" has now become a mantra, as it is difficult for galleries not to expand if they do not want to lose their competitive edge, or even disappear from the market altogether.

The gallery space must now be even more expansive, and be able to mount exhibitions with a scrupulous attention to detail so that visitors will be more likely to attend. This trend is already prominent in France. A major event occurred in Paris when Thaddaeus Ropac, who already had a very beautiful space in the Marais on rue Debelleyme, acquired another mega-space (Halle & Tiso, 2014) in 2012 in Pantin (a Parisian suburb). In doing so, he gained an asset that surpassed all other galleries at that time in Paris, especially in terms of square footage. The new Pantin site offered an impressive array of benefits: 50,000 square feet (of which 21,000 were dedicated to exhibitions), with a magnificent central building composed of four naves with overhead lighting that allows the space to easily display even the most monumental pieces. Incidentally, the gallery showcased this very point during its inaugural exhibition—held in this massive building—which was dedicated to the illustrious German artist (Quemin 2013b) Anselm Kiefer, who had already been living in France for several years. At practically the same time, following in Ropac's footsteps, the incontestable market leader Larry Gagosian, who already had a space in the very bourgeois 8th arrondissement of Paris (right next to the great auction houses Christie's and Sotheby's), invested in a space in Le Bourget; another Parisian suburb, with similar characteristics to that of his counterpart. The space was formerly an immense air hangar that had been redesigned by the famous architect Jean Nouvel and transformed into a magnificent gallery.

In 2018, two great "historical" French contemporary galleries acquired a second space in Paris. Galerie Lelong, formerly Galerie Maeght, which was created in 1945 at its main location on rue de Téhéran in the elegant 8th arrondissement, inaugurated a second showcase space in the nearby upscale neighborhood of Matignon. Elsewhere in Paris, Galerie Templon, created in 1966 but situated in the Marais since 1972 on rue Beaubourg (Verlaine, 2016), opened another location a stone's throw away, on rue du Grenier-Saint-Lazare, thus doubling its exhibition capacity. The new space stretched over 7,000 square feet over three stories, with a large central skylight and a 130-foot façade that offered an additional 2,700 square feet of exhibition space. For the interior design of its second Paris space (which was inaugurated in 2018), Galerie Templon reached out to the famous architect Jean-Michel Wilmotte, who is known for his numerous interior design projects—for permanent or temporary exhibitions—in prestigious museums such as the Louvre.

Also in Paris, Kamel Mennour, whose first gallery is located on rue Saint-André-des-Arts in Saint-Germain-des-Près—a neighborhood that has long been important for galleries (Verlaine, 2013 and 2017) but has definitively become peripheral for contemporary art—endeavored to rectify this withdrawal by amplifying his presence in the neighborhood. He opened a second location on rue du Pont de Lodi, and in 2020 even inaugurated a third in the same neighborhood, just across the street from the second. While he has opened other spaces in London and in the 8th arrondissement of Paris, they are more modest in size, and his small London branch was closed in 2022. It is essentially in the 6th arrondissement of Paris where the gallery's main activity takes place—thus holding down the fort, so to speak—while at the same time expanding, not in other areas of Paris but in other countries (the international expansion being kept, nevertheless, to a very limited extent).[19]

However, this exacerbated competition for gallery space is no more pronounced than in Chelsea, New York, which is the uncontested nucleus of the international contemporary art market (Halle & Tiso, 2014). Today, the largest players in New York are no longer satisfied with having a single gallery space in the traditional sense; nowadays, they are literally investing in entire buildings.

In 2019, in Chelsea, three of the four main global players in the contemporary art market in terms of economic influence—David Zwirner, Hauser & Wirth, and Pace—had new buildings constructed simultaneously. This caused a decent amount of concern among other gallerists as to the massive financial resources disbursed by these few market players, as well as the considerable expansion of their professional square footage. A gallerist who manages an international, though much more modest enterprise, wrote to me in an email in December 2018:

> I'll be interested to see how the evolution of the 'big four' goes. As you know, the construction of the new sites for the three giga-galleries of

> Hauser & Wirth, Zwirner, and Pace have begun, and each one will be over 5,000 square meters, and they'll no doubt have restaurants, bookstores, etc. What's going to be left for us once they've sucked up 90% of the market?!

Larry Gagosian, who was for a long time the undisputed emperor of the market, now participates less actively (at least in New York) in the mad dash that recently took place between his three main competitors, which has notably resulted in the installation of new, immense spaces. However, it was Gagosian who, when he first became a gallerist in Los Angeles in 1980, and later opened a gallery in New York in 1985, introduced the model of the mega-gallery with the space that he created in 1999 on West 24th Street in Chelsea (Halle & Tiso, 2014). At the time, by entrusting the design of this massive 25,000 square foot space to the architect Richard Gluckman, Gagosian invented a kind of gallery that did not exist elsewhere in the world, and went unchallenged for a long time. As Gagosian grew older and had not designated a clear successor (and had no offspring, to put it bluntly),[20] a few prominent galleries started to become more ambitious. Their desire to rival the longtime uncontested market frontrunner often manifested in a significant development of their properties. This took place especially in competition in terms of development of their gallery spaces, which are the only assets they possess that are able both to represent their financial power and to appeal to the best artists (who are drawn to exceptional exhibition conditions), as well as art enthusiasts and collectors who want to find exhibitions that are more commonly on a par with contemporary art museums (Quemin, 2020b).

Two galleries currently play a decisive role at the top of the pack. Although the Pace gallery[21] may have seemed likely to succeed Gagosian as the market leader for a while, David Zwirner has since clearly positioned himself as a more serious challenger. His gallery, founded in 1993 in New York,[22] now has 150 staff members, represents around 80 artists, and generally participates in around 20 art fairs per year. The spectacular development of this gallery, which is considered one of the most prominent in the world, clearly demonstrates the importance of real estate, but also (at this level of excellence) the support of the most reputed architects to design spaces and even construct new buildings. These professionals are sometimes even specialists in structures of prestige, and may be counted among the ranks of "starchitects."[23]

The most emblematic example is that of the New York architect Annabelle Selldorf, who designed the spectacular five-story building for David Zwirner's gallery on West 20th Street, with nearly 30,000 square feet of space, a brutalist concrete façade, an impressive staircase, and multiple skylights and sources of natural light. In 2016, she was also called upon to design the new space for the prestigious Thaddaeus Ropac gallery in London's Ely House; a magnificent mansion in the Mayfair neighborhood.

Like Jean-Michel Wilmotte (a collaborator of the Louvre and other illustrious museums) who, as previously mentioned, designed Galerie Templon's second space in Paris, Annabelle Selldorf is associated with various museums for which her agency has completed extensions, notably the Frick Collection in New York and the contemporary art museum of San Diego in the United States, and the Fondation Luma in Arles, Southern France.

In the same vein of gallerists seeking to certify their talent (Moulin & Quemin, 1993) and that of their artists by collaborating with famous architects, the most recent building of David Zwirner's gallery in Chelsea was designed by the superstar architect Renzo Piano (before the project was eventually abandoned). Having never worked on a gallery project before, Piano was more familiar with museums and other immense buildings of prestige. Already a co-creator of the Centre Pompidou in Paris, Piano also designed the Beyeler Foundation near Basel in Switzerland, the Menil collection in Houston, United States and the Whitney Museum of American Art in New York, United States, among others.

Before the beginning of the COVID-19 pandemic, the opening of David Zwirner's fourth New York space, and seventh contemporary art gallery in the world, was initially announced for May 2020. The new building in New York (43,000 square feet over five floors) was estimated to cost $50 million. Aiming to reinvent the very concept of the art gallery, the architect explained that he wanted to establish a "psychological connection" between the building and the street, in a totally avant-garde and daring fashion, by moving away from the model of the white cube (O'Doherty, 2000), which as previously stated is the traditional presentation of commercial art galleries. By collaborating with a famous architect, it is clear that the mega-gallery intended to put itself on a par with even the most prominent museums. Alluding to the completely new concept designed by this superstar architect (who was more familiar with museums) into the world of galleries, David Zwirner explained that he had to remind his prestigious contractor that it would not be necessary to include a coatroom or booths for visitors to buy tickets, nor to build a grandiose lobby.

Another gallery in Chelsea, Hauser & Wirth—also a market juggernaut—rivals the Zwirner gallery in terms of space. It was founded in 1992 in Zurich, Switzerland by Ursula Hauser and married couple Iwan and Manuela Wirth. The gallery expanded internationally by opening several spaces around the world; but also, it should be noted, by investing in spectacular premises. In addition to its spaces in Zurich, the gallery first opened locations in six other cities: in London and Somerset in the United Kingdom, in Gstaad and St. Moritz in Switzerland, and in Los Angeles and two locations in New York (one in Chelsea and the other in the Upper East Side) in the United States. The gallery currently represents around 70 artists, including superstars Louise Bourgeois, Mike Kelley, Dan Graham, Isa Genzken, Paul McCarthy, and Cindy Sherman. On its website, the gallery introduces itself by citing projects that go far beyond those of traditional galleries, and that are comparable to non-profit organizations such as museums: "Hauser & Wirth has built a reputation for its dedication to artists and support of visionary artistic projects worldwide. In addition to presenting a dynamic schedule of exhibitions, the gallery collaborates with renowned curators to present museum quality surveys and invests considerable resources in new scholarship and research."

In February 2020, before the COVID-19 pandemic, the influential gallery issued a press release announcing that, in May of that year, they would be opening a new five-story, 38,000 square foot building in New York, on West 22nd Street (in the heart of Chelsea). The inaugural exhibition, entitled "The Bride of God," featured pieces by many of the gallery's celebrated artists, including Louise Bourgeois, Isa Genzken, Rodney Graham, Philip Guston, Jenny Holzer, Roni Horn, Mike Kelley, Maria Lassnig, Glenn Ligon, Paul McCarthy, Pipilotti Rist, and Lorna Simpson. This lineup was supplemented with pieces by famous artists not on the gallery's roster—such as Francis Bacon, Joseph Beuys, Robert Gober, Douglas Gordon, Robert Mapplethorpe, Agnes Martin, Piet Mondrian, Alice Neel, and Andy Warhol—which added a museum-quality touch.

The design of this building was also entrusted to Annabelle Selldorf, with whom the gallery has worked since it was founded. The ground floor and the fifth floor both have ceilings over 16 feet high. The top floor is able to accommodate monumental artworks, which can be installed from the street with the help of a crane. The second floor has a café and a reception hall for events such as conversations with artists or other kinds of interactive events. In many respects, both in terms of the volume of art on display and the amenities that were included in the conception of the building, the new gallery is not far from the museum model. Interestingly, when Hauser & Wirth came onto the Chelsea scene, the first phenomenal space that they occupied had previously (and for a long time) been a roller rink! The gallery then moved down the street into the former Dia building (Halle & Tiso, 2014), turning a space that had formerly been a contemporary art center into a commercial establishment.

In many ways, the Hauser & Wirth gallery broadly replicated the model that was introduced by its competitor, David Zwirner, with the construction of his building on West 20th Street, notably by hiring the same architect. However, it is essentially the immensity of the space—over 32,000 square feet—and the occupation of an entire building that were reproduced. Conversely, Hauser & Wirth follows a more specific model with its clear intention to rival museums in terms of a space that can accommodate many people, and amenities that make the gallery more of a real community space with a cultural purpose (Quemin, 2020b). This model was already in effect when Hauser & Wirth inaugurated its "mega-project" (Halle & Tiso, 2014) in Los Angeles in 2016. Stretching over 10,000 square feet, it could easily rival most of the city's major institutions. More than a commercial gallery in the traditional sense of the word, it is a veritable complex that boasts the obvious exhibition rooms with artworks available for sale. It also includes a renowned restaurant, educational programs, a bookstore, a gift shop, and an urban garden. To give another indicator of the influence of the museum model, the gallery had initially opened in Los Angeles under the name "Hauser, Wirth & Schimmel," thus incorporating the services of Paul Schimmel who, prior to this, had been the head curator for MOCA, the Museum of Contemporary Art, Los Angeles, which was not far away from the gallery (by Los Angeles standards). Even though this partnership came to an end not long after, it shows the museum-level ambition that steered the project from the outset (Quemin, 2020b). More recently, the gallery opened more traditional spaces in Monaco, Paris, Basel and in SoHo, in New York.

The competition for immense spaces between the largest worldwide galleries is particularly prominent in New York, especially in the emblematic Chelsea neighborhood, because the fiercest competition takes place in that district. Nevertheless, this kind of competition often occurs outside of Chelsea, and even outside of New York City. The race for enormous spaces has been a well-established trend among the biggest galleries for the past 10 years.

Even the Pace gallery, the third of Larry Gagosian's main New York rivals in terms of financial resources, was obliged to follow suit after having played the waiting game for a long time. The gallery, founded by Arne Glimcher at the very beginning of the 1960s, and now under the direction of his son Marc, currently has locations in eight cities and five countries throughout the world. Outside of New York, the gallery has outposts in Los Angeles, East Hampton, and Palm Beach in the United States; as well as in London, Geneva, Hong Kong, and Seoul.[24] In New York, the gallery already had several spaces in Manhattan when it commissioned the construction of a spectacular five-story, 21,000 square foot building that cost nearly $80 million. In its press release, Pace presented the newly inaugurated building in Chelsea as a response to the following question: what does it mean to be a contemporary art gallery in the twenty-first century? The introspection that was raised went beyond the building's prosaic commercial function in its attempt to respond to this more ontological question. As such, it is obvious that—as was previously illustrated by Hauser & Wirth—a gallery simultaneously constitutes a business and a space and now, as is more and more often the case with immense structures, like entire buildings, the gallery is being redefined.

Conclusion

Today, a gallery's physical space is a major point of consideration. Even in the Internet age, when the practicality of dematerialization seems to be indisputable, the physical space has not been put on the back burner. Essentially, it simultaneously constitutes a strong identity marker in its role as a conveyor of the gallery's image, and a sort of access pass to participate in fairs (which have become essential for a gallery's functioning), as well as to appeal to the most in-demand artists and the collectors with the highest expectations. While sales made during art fairs are meant to supplement those made in a gallery's physical space, in reality they often tend to compete with them. Small and midsize galleries, which are not permitted to participate in fairs (or at least, not first-rate ones, which are likely to be frequented by the most active collectors), tend to be particularly threatened, notably by the fact that maintaining their spaces takes a financial toll; a concern that is compounded by low foot traffic. These establishments must then find affordable spaces, or else transform their property in various ways into a veritable asset in order to turn a profit. They may also try to appeal to the public, which sometimes has a tendency to neglect their exhibitions, by diversifying their exhibition lineup and adding artworks that fall outside the category of contemporary art. On the other end of the spectrum, the largest galleries have endeavored to invest in ever-larger (and more spectacular) physical spaces. The New York neighborhood of Chelsea exemplifies this financial competition between the most influential galleries better than anywhere else in the world (Halle & Tiso, 2014). However, it must be noted that this competitiveness has brought about a shift in the traditional role of contemporary art galleries (Quemin, 2020b). At least for the largest galleries, beyond the abiding function of displaying art while at the same time maintaining the commercial aspect at the core of their existence, they are increasingly tending to take on the roles typically ascribed to contemporary art centers, museums, and institutions; thereby becoming more similar to them, not only by virtue of reproducing certain spatial elements (their dimensions being foremost among them), but also by the services that they offer.

2

The gallery in the urban space: Geography and neighborhoods

As we saw in the previous chapter, a gallery's true space—in terms of its physical size as well as other characteristics—remains decisive to this day, despite any associated tensions. The natural extension of this notion will be developed in this chapter: not only must the space be appropriate for the gallery's status, but it must also be located in the right place, as location still plays a key role. This may seem paradoxical, as fairs, which at first glance may seem to be beyond geographical affiliation—we will see in chapter 3 that the reality is much more complex—appear to allow the gallery to escape the boundaries of its physical space, either in terms of its capacity or location. Since many galleries make a large amount (if not the majority) of their sales at fairs,[1] the matter of their physical location can become less of a concern. Some establishments have come to be known in the contemporary art world as "fair galleries," which allows them to have one or several spaces in somewhat unconventional areas, as far as the geography of contemporary art is concerned (Quemin, 2001, 2002, and 2006). This is how the French gallery, Pietro Sparta, came to exist in Chagny, a small town in Burgundy with a population of only 6,000 people. Likewise the Italian gallery Continua got its start in the small tourist village of San Gimignano in Tuscany, later opening a successive series of spaces abroad. However, for a long time it avoided opening locations in major metropolitan hubs for contemporary art. It launched an outpost in Beijing, well before China became more influential in the contemporary art gallery scene, along with another location in Cuba, and Les Moulins, in the French countryside region of Seine-et-Marne. It recently launched additional locations in São Paulo, in the center of Rome, and in the heart of Paris. However, before doing so, the gallery had always preferred to take up residence in large spaces located in villages or cities with no pre-existing local contemporary art ecosystem, and with no regard as to the presence of collectors in its various locations. This attempt to break the trend of galleries clustering together in a given city that already has a strong concentration of galleries exists on a national scale as well as on a more local one; some individual galleries have begun to settle into neighborhoods that are more peripheral to the general market. In 2017, a French gallerist who had been operating in a working-class Parisian neighborhood for two years and was completely isolated from her contemporaries in other galleries stated:

> It's a little less expensive here for a space that's twice as big as what I used to have in the Marais. Obviously, that was a major factor when I was deciding whether to open this space. [. . .] in any case, contemporary art collectors live in the 16th, 7th, and 6th arrondissements, not in the Marais, so they already have to travel a bit to come to this neighborhood. [. . .] And today, in any case, people visit galleries less and less, we have to go to them at fairs, and people who come into the gallery randomly aren't very important visitors. The people who count for us will only make the trip to see what they already know and what they want to see, they're the motivated collectors, curators, and journalists. [. . .] Well anyway, I would love to find three or four other spaces like mine in the neighborhood so that my colleagues could come in droves, it would definitely be better than being all alone here.

It is clear in this extract that, even though she had given several justifications for her surprising and completely unconventional choice in location, the gallerist was aware of the limitations of being geographically isolated, and would have liked to have more of her fellow gallerists nearby (incidentally, two years later, she left this too-remote space to be closer to other galleries). Although there are some rare cases where geographical location does not have a real impact (in the short- or long-term) that are worth mentioning, they are in reality the exception that proves the rule.

Websites are another factor that could lessen the importance of a gallery's location in a particular place, as it affords a certain amount of visibility that is not directly impacted by geographical limitations. However, despite the dual impact of fairs and the Internet, galleries today remain (as they historically have been) extremely dependent on geographical patterns when choosing where to settle. Generally speaking, they must be sure to have a sufficient amount of foot traffic (including collectors in particular), and one of the best ways to do this is to assemble many galleries in the same neighborhood (Halle & Tiso, 2014). These groupings leave an imprint on a city in the form of urban development, which is influenced by these establishments, but also very often manifests in guidebooks or maps that are available in most big cities and identify the main galleries located in the area. This concentration in the same neighborhood or district has a dual benefit for galleries: moving into a space near one's competitors allows all parties involved to align with the market, and even influence it by encouraging collectors to frequent these locations by the simple fact of their collective presence. Traditionally, analysts have believed that commercial activities of a similar nature congregate spatially to better attract prospects and clients.

The principle also applies to the artistic and cultural sector (Markusen & Schrock, 2006; Lorenzen & Frederiksen, 2007; Lloyd Richard, 2010). Furthermore, this aggregation also makes it possible to establish and benefit from a collective qualifying function in terms of geographical location (Pinçon & Pinçon-Charlot, 1992 and 2016). In the domain of art galleries, a space carries an inherent statement that is absolutely identical to that analyzed by Pierre Bourdieu and Yvette Delsaut when studying spaces for fashion houses (Bourdieu & Delsaut, 1975). Only some spaces in a given city can be considered appropriate for a "real" contemporary art gallery. Moreover, based on the position that the gallery intends to assume and project to the world, the decision on whether to settle in a given gallery district depends on whether it identifies itself as avant-garde (especially for up-and-coming galleries) or more established (with more dedicated artists). Joaquim Rius-Ulldemolins describes the plurality of locations for the same line of business, or the existence of various artistic clusters (Mommaas, 2004) in the same city via the stances adopted by the galleries in the fields to which they belong (Rius-Ulldemolins, 2016). As such, over the course of a gallery's development, it often upgrades to a larger physical space that is more suitable for its new status, and it may also venture outside of the neighborhood where it was founded to integrate into an area that is more socially legitimate, and where there are more galleries that correspond to its new status. It would therefore be incorrect to assume that gallery districts are homogenous in relation to one another; in reality, urban environments can be interpreted based on existing norms, which themselves are subject to individual reinterpretations (Chombart de Lauwe, 1956). A gallery's space in a city is shaped by other establishments with a perceived affinity to the original gallery, as is perfectly illustrated by this gallerist:

> There was a lot of construction on avenue Matignon that was going to interfere with a gallery's business for years, so my friends asked me: why don't you leave Paris? On the contrary, I decided to double down with an even larger space. I wanted to send a positive message. [. . .] I also knew the places [in the Marais neighborhood], their flexibility, their dimensions, and their proximity to major galleries like Thaddaeus Ropac, Karsten Greve, and Almine Rech.
>
> Michele Casamonti, director of the Parisian gallery Tornabuoni Arte[2] in *La Gazette Drouot*, issue no. 14, April 7, 2017, p. 23

Despite the institutions named in this interview extract, there are other galleries that were much closer geographically to the new space that Tornabuoni Arte occupied when it was temporarily located in the Marais, most notable of which are gb agency, RX, and Chantal Crousel (this last gallery has a roster of very high-level artists and thus qualifies as a "major" gallery). However, these examples do not operate in the same segment of the art market as Tornabuoni Arte, particularly in terms of prices, sales of secondhand art, and networks of collectors. As is evident from the pioneering works of urban sociologist Paul-Henry Chombart de Lauwe, there is a subjective reality of a neighborhood's physical space that coexists with its objective reality, the latter of which is, in truth, determined by the experience that individuals have within these spaces (Chombart de Lauwe, 1956).

Galleries settle in districts on the basis of their social characteristics, as well as the gallery's own individual characteristics, according to the effect of structural homology, to borrow the terms from the theory developed by Pierre Bourdieu and his collaborators (Bourdieu & Delsaut, 1975). There is also the considerable task of qualifying the urban space. When the French gallery Perrotin announced that it was opening two new spaces in New York and Tokyo in its *Invitation Book* (the first edition, April–August 2017), it was clear how the social space is qualified by the presence of other galleries. Rather than glossing over the existence of other nearby establishments, even though they are also objective competitors, their presence in the same district was highlighted; in essence, they help to qualify the space by legitimizing it as a contemporary art gallery district. This also creates a dynamic of development, since the book also mentions establishments that were soon to come, demonstrating that it is a growing gallery district (i.e., not in decline), as the spatial and social qualities of a neighborhood (in art, as well as all other domains) evolve over time (Pinçon & Pinçon-Charlot, 1992, 1996, and 2016; Halle & Tiso, 2014). It is also clear how a building's characteristics in terms of size (which was reviewed in the previous chapter), are consistent with those of the street address and the environment wherein the building is situated. All of this contributes to the process of cultural legitimation, via the existence of galleries as well as artistic institutions as the following extract shows:

> **New space: Opening of Perrotin New York in the Lower East Side, April 27, 2017.**
>
> Since 2013, Perrotin New York has occupied a historic building on the Upper East Side's iconic Madison Avenue. After three successful years, Perrotin will expand to a 25,000-square-foot (2,300 sq.m.) space in New York City's most dynamic arts neighborhood, the Lower East Side [. . .]. The renovation remains faithful to Perrotin's signature design and also incorporates the existing character of the building. [. . .] The gallery space spans approximately 25,000 square feet (2,300 sq.m.) over five floors, with ceilings up to 20 feet (6 m.) high throughout" (p.16). "Perrotin is located at 130 Orchard Street, between Delancey Street and Rivington Street in Manhattan's Lower East Side. Close to the New Museum, the neighborhood unites residents of the art world and non-traditional spaces, offering an engaging and dynamic contemporary art scene. Close by, there are acclaimed galleries such as 11 R, 47 Canal, Bridget Donahue, Bureau,

> Canada, CRG Gallery, Eva Presenhuber (coming soon), Gavin Brown's Enterprise, Jack Hanley Gallery, James Cohan, James Fuentes Gallery, KARMA, Lehhmann Maupin, Marinaro, Miguel Abreu Gallery, Nathalie Karg Gallery, Nicelle Beauchene Gallery, Pierogi Gallery, Ramiken Crucible, Salon 94, Shoot The Lobster, Simone Subal Gallery, Spencer Brownstone Gallery (coming soon), Sperone Westwater Gallery, and Rachel Uffner, among others.[3]
>
> Only a 15-minute walk away, people can visit galleries and institutions in SoHo and Tribeca, like the magnificently restored Judd Foundation, the Swiss Institute, the Drawing Center and Artists Space, one of the oldest alternative spaces in downtown New York. Walter de Maria's 'Broken Kilometer,' commissioned and maintained by the Dia Art Foundation since 1979, can still be seen at 393 West Broadway as a public art installation, as well as his 'Earth Room' in a nearby loft on Wooster Street. Amid the abundance of restaurants, cafés and shops, people can also visit major galleries like Alexander and Bonin, Jeffrey Deitch, Peter Freeman Inc., Postmasters Gallery, Ronald Feldman Fine Arts, Bortolami Gallery (coming soon), Storefront for Art and Architecture, Team Gallery, and many others.
>
> Perrotin New York is pleased to join the Lower East Side neighborhood, a wonderfully dynamic community, rich in history and cultural diversity.
>
> *Perrotin, The Invitation Book*, April – August 2017, p. 18

Any real estate agent intending to accentuate a neighborhood's desirability would certainly not repudiate this presentation. It is clear that the goal is to make a mass showing by citing galleries that are very well known alongside others that are much less so. However, some galleries that were not deemed to be of a high enough status were not included on the list. This qualifying effect is sought by being associated with other renowned contemporary art galleries and institutions based on the principle of the "collection effect." However, while the gallery emphasized the success of its New York location on Madison Avenue in the chic Upper East Side at the beginning of its presentation, it later contradicted this statement by opening a new location in an environment with very different social and artistic characteristics, resulting in an about-face that would normally have been associated with a repositioning in the field (Bourdieu, 1980). Logically, a successful trajectory would have involved migrating from the Lower East Side to the Upper East Side, not the inverse (Bourdieu & Delsaut, 1975). In this instance, the tactic is only effective because its "backwards" direction is compensated by having a much larger space, as well as the fact that Perrotin New York's new location contrasted starkly with the bourgeois environment where it began. It was in reality a repositioning in the urban space that was more suitable to the gallery's artists and image in terms of gallery conventions.

Perrotin made a similar attempt to qualify its location when opening a space in Tokyo:

> New gallery: Perrotin Tokyo opens in Roppongi, June 7, 2017.
>
> Following Paris, Hong Kong, New York and Seoul, Perrotin is pleased to announce the opening of its Tokyo space on the ground floor of the Piramide (sic) Building at 6-6-9 Roppongi, Minato-ku, Tokyo. This will be the seventh space that Emmanuel Perrotin has opened in 27 years. [. . .] Nestled in the heart of Tokyo's dynamic Roppongi neighborhood, the Piramide building, built in the 90s, hosts established galleries like the London Gallery, Ota Fine Arts, Wako Works Of Art, YKG / Yutaka Kikutake Gallery and Zen Foto Gallery. The building next door, 'Complex 665,' recently opened with ShugoArts, Taka Ishii Gallery and Tomio Koyama Gallery. Prominent galleries are located only a three minute walk away (p. 54).
>
> "The gallery is based in the heart of the Roppongi area, a cultural and vibrant neighborhood that gathers a large number of museums and galleries, such as the Mori Art Museum, the Suntory Museum of Art, the National Art Center, Kaikai Kiki Gallery, Taka Ishii Gallery Photography / Film, Take Ninagawa, amongst others" (p. 56).

Here as well, Perrotin has gone out of its way to report the multiplicity of competitors, which illustrates the social and commercial quality of the space as a contemporary art gallery district, even though it is far from the concentration that New York is known for, and the Lower East Side is much calmer than Chelsea (Halle & Tiso, 2014).

Hence, market players (here, gallerists) develop their location strategies based on both objective and subjective dimensions. When studying the case of the city of Barcelona, Joaquim Rius-Ulldemolins noted that the neighborhoods or districts with high concentrations of galleries did not reflect structural factors of an economic or social nature, or even related to the general dynamics of urban development, so much as both individual and collective strategic choices (Rius-Ulldemolins, 2012). These strategies reinforce the permanence of certain neighborhoods, as well as the emergence of new districts.

The shifts that have occurred throughout the particular history of galleries and their lifecycle are coupled with the transformations of the urban space, as it is a living entity (Grafmeyer & Authier, 2008); gallery districts also roam, and the establishments that exist within them are obliged to follow, support, and contribute to these evolutions, even if they may have preferred to remain in a given location. In New York, 303 Gallery's successive relocations reflect the general history of the art market's various shifts within the city's urban space. Lisa Spellman founded 303 Gallery in 1984 at 303 Park Avenue South, in an area that was at the time fairly removed from other galleries in the city. Soon after, in 1987, it moved to a contemporary art gallery district in the East Village; an area which was, however, already on the decline. Not wasting any time, in 1989 the gallery moved once again to 89 Greene Street in the heart of SoHo. In 1996, Gallery 303 was one of the first galleries to move into Chelsea, which was still up and coming as a gallery district; and in 2016 it consolidated its presence in this neighborhood by inaugurating its current space at 555 West 21st Street (in a building that was designed by the famous architect Norman Foster). Gallery 303 stands as an example of an institution that, after having made some unfortunate preliminary choices in terms of location (Halle & Tiso, 2014), was progressively able to correct them through a series of trial and error before eventually finding the "right" location and putting down its proverbial roots.

The qualifying function of the urban space is widely acknowledged among players on the art market, as evidenced by the conversation that I had in the autumn of 2010 with the director of a famous international gallery (with a large space in New York) that is very active in the secondary market when it had just opened a space in the Marais neighborhood in Paris:

- *Me: I'm a little surprised that you moved to this neighborhood, given your level of activity in the secondary art market. I would have thought you would go to the 8th arrondissement instead of the Marais.*
- Him: But the space here is really great, don't you think? And you know, we decided to focus on the primary market in Paris. Sometimes we'll put on exhibitions with pieces from the secondary market, but most of our lineup is going to be primary market, so your comment is apt.

This interview excerpt shows that one's geographical location is not neutral, even for galleries that sell contemporary art; depending on the level of activity in the primary and secondary markets, not all addresses or neighborhoods are on equal footing, and choosing to settle in a particular area constitutes a conscious decision and sends a message as to their positioning (cf. Bourdieu & Delsaut, 1975).

Another geographical rationale that affects a gallery's development is the radical increase in its number of locations around the world. Nowadays, the best example of this is the famous gallery Gagosian. Founded in Los Angeles, it then made New York the center of its empire, and expanded into several countries and many cities around the world. Today, the gallery has locations in the United States in Los Angeles,[4] and in New York (with its two massive Chelsea spaces on West 24th Street and West 21st Street, its three spaces—one of which is a boutique that sells editions—on Madison Avenue in the Upper East Side, and on Park Avenue), in the United Kingdom (with three spaces in London), in France (with two spaces in Paris and one in Le Bourget), in Switzerland (in Geneva and Basel), in Italy (in Rome), in Greece (in Athens), and in Hong Kong. The gallery therefore has 18 locations in no fewer than seven countries, making it a veritable, unparalleled empire. However, some of the other most famous galleries have also begun to adopt this expansion model of internationalization more broadly. Gagosian's Swiss rival Hauser & Wirth currently has locations not only in Zurich, but also in

Los Angeles, London, Somerset, Hong Kong, St. Moritz, Gstaad, the Spanish Balearic Island of Menorca, and New York—which has become one of its operational headquarters—along with its London location. In 2023, they also opened a location in Monaco and in the chic 8th arrondissement of Paris before opening a gallery in Basel and one in SoHo, in New York. It is therefore present in seven countries, just like its rival, Gagosian. Other galleries that did not get their start in the Unites States (or transplant their main operations there) have also expanded internationally to a considerable extent. For instance, the French gallery Perrotin currently occupies three spaces in Paris, as well as others in the United States (in New York, now in the Lower East Side as previously mentioned and now also in Los Angeles), Hong Kong, South Korea (in Seoul, now with two spaces), Japan (in Tokyo), and China (in Shanghai), with an overall presence in half a dozen countries.

For the last few years (and the trend is only becoming more pronounced), all of the most prominent galleries, particularly the largest ones, are opening locations in several countries—or at least, those of consequence on the international art scene (Quemin, 2001, 2002, and 2006) in the interest of controlling the market. In their pursuit of expansion, a growing number of contemporary art galleries seem to have come to the same conclusion: they have to go abroad to gain more influence. At the beginning of 2018, several galleries announced within weeks of each other that they were opening new outposts around the world. The Pace gallery, which already had eight spaces in various continents, announced the opening of a branch in Geneva in March. Likewise, David Zwirner, which already had three sites in New York and one in London, had just invested in its first Hong Kong space, then followed up this internationalization campaign by inaugurating another location in Paris.

As is evident from the cities listed above, the geographical strategies that facilitate a gallery's rise are frequently manifested and implemented via the diversification of locations across several countries (different galleries will often choose the same ones), to the scale of a given country with a multi-faceted contemporary art scene; or even in different neighborhoods of the same city. This is mainly the case in New York, where many influential galleries expanded into the Upper East Side while still maintaining their primary spaces in Chelsea. More recently, the New York neighborhood of Tribeca became an attractive area for the city's galleries, particularly for the possibility of opening a second space. Above all, for galleries that did not originate in the main city for the art market in their own country, there is a common drive to reinforce their assimilation into their original neighborhood or city, or their new location, once the "right" area has been found. This particularly aims to maintain the social quality of its environment by investing financially and symbolically in it. Hence, it is important that a gallery avoid the risk of being disqualified due to the activities that take place in their neighborhood. This involves a sort of mobilization that is both individual and collective, so as to control its development. The works of

Michel Pinçon and Monique Pinçon-Charlot—which were conducted in France but the conclusions of which could easily be transposed to other countries—shone a light on the rather common struggle between competing social or professional groups (Pinçon & Pinçon-Charlot, 1992, 1996, and 2016) for the same social space. This goes far beyond the phenomenon of gentrification (Glass, 1964) which, when their works were published, largely monopolized the attention of urban sociologists.

The previous approach of geographical expansion blending scopes of local, national, and international magnitudes was perfectly illustrated during the considerable development of the gallery Blum & Poe, which was created in 1994 in Los Angeles. The gallery's relocation and integration into Los Angeles itself were paired with a national and international expansion strategy, with the opening of a second space in Tokyo and a third in New York. They did not, however, abandon local efforts; on the contrary, Blum & Poe were the first to move into an LA neighborhood—La Cienega, which was not yet an art gallery district—where they took over an immense space. Once this new neighborhood became established on the local art scene, the gallery was quick to expand its presence even more by leaving its initial space for one four times larger, in the same area, in 2009.

Since the urban space is constantly transforming, it is difficult to control its evolution when a gallery does not occupy a position of influence or dominance. But even in these cases, it is generally crucial to associate with those that share the same interests in order to reach its professional goals (Pinçon & Pinçon-Charlot, 1992). Failing that, it is better to wait for the first signals indicating the emergence of an attractive neighborhood before committing to anything. With that in mind, it is interesting to note that even the Gagosian gallery did not make "the right turn at the right time" (Halle & Tiso, 2014) when it was too quick to make its first move into New York's Chelsea neighborhood on West 23rd Street in 1985 (it is often forgotten, as it was a failure at that time and the space was ultimately closed down). Gagosian eventually made its triumphant return much later—in 1999—this time on West 24th Street. In the interval, Chelsea's urban environment had begun to change, and it ultimately became a gallery district.

The fact that it is more prudent to wait for clear trends to emerge before committing to a choice of location is illustrated in this excerpt of an email that an artist sent me:

> My gallery in London closed its downtown space because it got too expensive, but for the moment it's not going to open another location in the city. It's going to wait a bit to see which neighborhood will evolve and attract new galleries before jumping on the bandwagon. London is a very expensive city for real estate, you have to be really careful.

I will further analyze how a contemporary art gallery's space is largely organized based on the principle of grouping and the formation of clusters by regarding several important cities for contemporary art galleries, which themselves would not exist as they are, were it not for the presence of these establishments within them. Before doing so, it is necessary to address a particular case: that of galleries that exist outside of these international hubs. I have already mentioned the very particular minority group of "fair" galleries that can avoid spatial limitations when choosing their location. Given their position, they are not required to select a major city and set up shop in a gallery district. However, they do have to contend with another spatial constraint, in that they must generally compensate for their relative isolation by having a much larger space than if they were located in a more central area in terms of the international art market. Incidentally, there is a positioning that allows such establishments to operate outside of the main metropolitan areas that have contemporary art scenes, particularly in vacation resorts that are often frequented by an affluent clientele; especially when the activities available in such places leave these people idle for a large part of the day and evening. This gallerist was able to launch his career and develop his client base in a Swiss ski station by receiving upscale visitors:

> I started to work in a gallery in Crans-Montana in Switzerland that had just opened, which was an exceptional opportunity for me. I came from a small town in Italy,[5] and I had to build up a network of collectors. I didn't have the means to travel everywhere, and wasn't presenting at the big fairs yet. Collectors weren't coming to me yet, so I had to go to them. It was a place where the collectors had the rarest thing of all: time, they were totally relaxed. Today, collectors see a hundred stands at an art fair, two minutes per gallery, stop and talk with three dealers, possibly bid on two or three paintings. On vacation, they can browse through a book, look for a painting, go for dinner. . . That's how I was able to build my network of collectors in Italy, near Milan, where I opened a gallery in 1995.
>
> Interview with Michele Casamonti, director of the Parisian gallery Tornabuoni Arte, in *La Gazette Drouot*, issue no. 14, April 7, 2017, p. 23

In order to approach the same kind of affluent clientele in identical conditions, the following galleries have opened outposts in wealthy resorts or small mountain towns: Karsten Greve Gallery in St. Moritz (in addition to Cologne and Paris), and Hauser & Wirth also in St. Moritz and Gstaad. This influential Swiss collector notes amusingly: "It's astounding how in only a few years, so many galleries have come to St. Moritz. The spaces aren't that big, there's not a whole lot to do, but it's St. Moritz, it's the right clientele, and they're ripe for the picking." Of course, some of these small towns—apart from the ski resorts—may accommodate tax residencies for wealthy art lovers; but in this instance as well, the artistic inactivity in these remote spaces provide an opportunity for galleries to turn a profit. In essence, collectors who live in such places have a lot of time on their hands, and are on the whole particularly invested in the sociability that accompanies art, even more than those who reside in metropolitan areas, where the selection of activities that they can enjoy is much broader.

Thaddaeus Ropac used a similar model to become one of the most famous galleries in the world. The gallerist inaugurated his first space in 1983 in Salzburg, an Austrian city with a population of just over half a million people located near the German border. At the time, the city had practically zero outlets for contemporary art; however, Ropac managed to capitalize on the annual Salzburg Festival of opera, classical music, and drama, which was established in 1920 and draws visitors from all over the world (over 200,000 today). The festival is known for its elegant attendees, who for the most part don eveningwear, even during heat waves or for morning performances. Often coming from very affluent social backgrounds, they pay particularly high prices to attend the performances. As the city of Salzburg offers few diversions beyond the festival calendar, the Thaddaeus Ropac gallery offers music lovers a veritable suite of activities—again, at times when they have nothing else to do (Veblen, 1899)—and they are therefore even more receptive to the visits and invitations on offer. Based on the theory of gifts and reciprocity masterfully interpreted by Marcel Mauss (Mauss, 1966), the gallery's guests were then transformed into clients, thus opening Ropac to the international market. Following this initial location in Salzburg was a second branch in Paris, which opened in the Marais in 1990. This did not entail any kind of disengagement in Salzburg; on the contrary, the gallery inaugurated an immense space of 27,000 square feet in 2010. As we saw in the previous chapter, in the same vein, in 2012 the Thaddaeus Ropac gallery also opened a mega-space of 55,000 square feet in Pantin. This was followed by a massive London space of over 16,000 square feet, in the luxurious Mayfair neighborhood; before the launch of a space in Seoul, South Korea, in 2021. The example set by this gallery demonstrates the notion of development via a geographical location that is initially peripheral to the contemporary scene, but that nonetheless regularly receives cultured, wealthy art enthusiasts; and later delineates a strategy for development and building a presence in major cities, which have the highest concentration of the most prominent contemporary art galleries.

After establishing that the urban space is not neutral, and that it is subject to galleries' appropriation and strategies, this point can now be illustrated using examples from various metropolitan areas around the world. We will see that the gallery district model is widespread on an international scale, but that it by no means constitutes a static relationship with the urban space (quite the contrary, in point of fact). For each case, the situation at a given time is clearly the result of a historic evolution pertaining to the successive qualifications of the region.

The Paris contemporary art gallery scene: The central position of the Marais

I will begin by analyzing the French (i.e., Parisian)[6] contemporary art gallery scene, both because it is one of the three most important in the world, along with London and the undisputed leader, New York; but also because it is the city with the longest history. As a matter of fact, there have consistently been many galleries and gallerists in Paris since the era of Paul Durand-Ruel (whose pioneering role was explained in the foreword of this book devoted to the historical development of the occupation of gallerists).

Historically, at the end of the nineteenth century, when the role of "gallerist" first emerged, Parisian galleries were heavily concentrated in the 9th arrondissement. Most were located near the auction house Hôtel Drouot and the nearby area around rue Lafitte and the Opéra neighborhood.[7] However, at the beginning of the twentieth century, the art gallery market progressively shifted to the 8th arrondissement, around rue La Boétie. It was only during the interwar period when the opposition between this district on the Right Bank of the Seine[8] and the Saint-Germain-des-Prés neighborhood on the Left Bank truly materialized. Over time, particularly during the 1960s, galleries on the Left Bank developed more of an avant-garde reputation than those on the Right Bank. From this, it is clear how spatial oppositions have contributed to propagating and reflecting other oppositions in the artistic domain (Bourdieu & Delsaut, 1975).

The geographer Tatiana Debroux and the historian Julie Verlaine have put together a series of maps that show the locations of the member galleries of the Comité Professionnel des Galeries d'Art (Professional Committee of Art Galleries, CPGA), from 1948, when the committee was founded, and then from 1956, 1966, 1975, 1986, 1994, and 2016 (Verlaine, 2017, p. 156).[9] This source can be cross-referenced with previous research: in the annex of *The French Art Market*, Raymonde Moulin presents the list of the CPGA's members and gives the address of the organization's headquarters circa October 1962. Since the list of the CPGA's active members was published with their addresses, I was able to calculate the distribution of these different locations: most members were situated in the 8th arrondissement (44 in total), as well as—to a lesser extent—in the 6th (31) and 7th (11) arrondissements. The 8th arrondissement alone has a higher concentration of galleries than the two main districts on the Left Bank combined. Furthermore, discounting four galleries located outside of Paris (two in Cannes on the French Riviera: one in Fontainebleau, a city that during the nineteenth century and the Second Empire came to be and has remained very bourgeois; and one in Oran, Algeria, a former French colony), all of the other galleries were situated on the Right Bank of the Seine (three in the 1st arrondissement, and one in each of the 2nd, 4th, 16th, and 17th). As a matter of fact, the migration toward the Saint-Germain-des-Prés neighborhood by most of the galleries, especially toward the Left Bank, is ripe for analysis: at the beginning of the 1960s, the Right Bank (more precisely, the 8th arrondissement) was still home to the majority of Paris' galleries. The members of the CPGA had premises in the 8th more than anywhere else, thereby cementing the neighborhood's dominance (Bourdieu, 1987) in the Parisian gallery space (Moulin, 1987). In every respect, the 8th arrondissement was the prevailing leader. This contradicts Tatiana Debroux's assertion that highly overestimates the importance of the Left Bank: "Since the interwar period, there have been two major poles in the geography of art galleries in Paris: one in the 8th arrondissement, centered around the rue la Boétie; the other in the Left Bank, in the 6th arrondissement, centered around the rue de Seine. After the Second World War, it was the latter pole that took dominance" (Debroux, 2017, p. 153). This assertion may be surprising, even though it also comments on data concerning CPGA members. The notion that the Left Bank dethroned the 8th arrondissement and became the dominant district for art galleries is also refuted by the addresses listed for the 10 remarkable Parisian galleries (one of which was located in the suburbs) from the beginning of the twentieth century up to 1970 in the brochure *Galleries of the 20th Century: France 1905–1970*, produced by the Centre Pompidou[10] for their eponymous exhibition that took place from 2019 to 2020. The brochure listed the following galleries as being located as such:

Ambroise Vollard: 37, 39 and 6 rue Lafitte, Paris 9th (1893–1914)

Daniel-Henry Kahnweiler: 28 rue Vignon, Paris 9th (1907–1914) / 29bis rue d'Astorg, Paris 8th (1920–1940)

A l'étoile scellée: 11 rue du Pré-aux-Clercs, Paris 7th (1952–1956)

Galerie Cahiers d'art: 14 rue du Dragon, Paris 6th (1934–1970)

Jeanne Bucher: 3 and 5 rue du cherche-Midi, Paris 6th (1925–1932) / various locations (1932–1935) / 9ter boulevard du Montparnasse, Paris 6th (1936–1960)

Daniel Cordier:[11] 8 rue de Duras, Paris 8th (1956–1959) / 8 rue de Miromesnil 75008, Paris, 8th (1959–1964)

Denise René: 124 rue de la Boétie, Paris 8th (1944–1977)[12]

Louis Carré: 10 avenue de Messine, Paris 8th (1940–1966)

Alphonse Chave: 13 rue Isnard, Vence, Alpes Maritimes (1947–1975)

Galerie de France: 3 rue du Faubourg Saint-Honoré, Paris 8th (1942–1981)

Iris Clert: 3 rue des Beaux-Arts, Paris 6th (1956–1961) / 28 rue du Faubourg Saint-Honoré, Paris 8th (1961–1971) / 3 rue Duphot, Paris 1st (1971–1979) / Le C.A.R.A.T, 19 rue Madeleine Michelis, Neuilly-sur-Seine (1980–1986).

Before the Marais neighborhood began to flourish as the new contemporary art gallery scene in Paris as of the 1970s, it was the 8th arrondissement, not the Saint-Germain-des-Prés neighborhood, that retained its dominance after having usurped the title from the 9th arrondissement at the turn of the century. Of course, the galleries of the Left Bank later became the competitors of the 8th arrondissement, but this district had not lost its influence.

Starting in the 1970s, the Marais began to attract a growing number of contemporary art galleries, some of which still exist today, including the Galerie Templon, which settled in its current location at 30 rue Beaubourg in 1972 (Verlaine, 2016). The Galerie du Luxembourg[13] was one of the first to join the neighborhood, at 98 rue Saint-Denis, also in 1972, along with the Galerie Beaubourg (Saint-Raymond, 2011) at 5 rue Pierre-au-Lard in 1973, and the Galerie Françoise Palluel at 91 rue Quincampoix in 1974. At the time, the neighborhood was still somewhat squalid, but was destined for a significant requalification due in particular to cultural urban redevelopment (Rodríguez Morató & Zarlenga, 2018). In 1966, this area of Paris was known as the Plateau Beaubourg, and was selected for the construction of a public library with direct access to the books, which had not yet existed in Paris. The project then evolved substantially, and in December 1969 the French Council of Ministers decided to build a monumental complex comprising not only a massive museum of paintings and sculptures, but also special departments for music, records, and even cinema and theatrical research in the same building. Although the plan had initially been to build a library, it became a secondary consideration as the new focus of the project took on the notion of having at least one section dedicated to the arts. In July 1971, two young and rather inexperienced architects—Renzo Piano and Richard Rogers—won the competition to design what would later be named the Centre Georges Pompidou, and construction began in May 1972, with the building ultimately being inaugurated on January 30th, 1977 (Dufrêne, 2000). Erecting such an emblematic building with a radically avant-garde aesthetic prompted a complete transformation of the neighborhood, making it a cultural hub due to the presence of a flagship institution that would sustain an entire ecosystem, particularly one centered around the arts. Contemporary art galleries began to flock to the neighborhood, especially since the area was positively brimming with much larger spaces and had much lower rents than the Saint-Germain-des-Prés neighborhood where the most innovative up-and-coming galleries had previously been located. Choosing a location near the National Museum of Modern Art that would soon be opening in the iconic Centre Georges Pompidou paved the way for local art lovers to explore private galleries in the neighborhood. From 1975 to 1985, the Marais was the prime destination for galleries intending to open new spaces (Moulin, 1992). It was fueled by the announcement and eventual establishment of the Centre Pompidou in 1977, and later by the opening of the Picasso Museum in 1985 into the Hôtel Salé just a few streets away, which strengthened the neighborhood's cultural identity.

The appearance, not only of the Marais but also of the galleries within it, was profoundly refreshed, in part because the former artisan or small industrial workspaces were much more spacious than in the Saint-Germain-des-Prés neighborhood. Daniel Templon explained that he had been drawn to the massive space (as it looked at the time) that would become his gallery on rue Beaubourg, which he discovered when it was still a former hat factory. Its glass roof provided the proper overhead lighting, and its metal columns evoked gallery spaces in SoHo, for those people, especially collectors, who already traveled regularly to the United States (Verlaine, 2016). Another important change for the neighborhood: it was "no longer possible for an art lover to stroll along a street of display windows (be it avenue Matignon or rue de Seine), it was now the path of the initiated" (Moulin, 1992, p. 187) with several galleries that were now hidden behind a courtyard. As a gallerist explained in Raymonde Moulin's book: "Our art is too difficult for the average pedestrian" (cited in Moulin 1992, p. 188).

"During the 1980s, there was an increase in the number of Parisian galleries displaying contemporary art, and as they moved to the east of the city, they adopted the New York model of spatial organization and the expansion of foreign galleries" (Moulin, 1992, pp. 184–185). Moulin reported that the number of galleries paying contributions to the Maison des Artistes (the entity that represents French visual artists) doubled during this decade. As for the Professional Committee of Art Galleries, which is very selective, the number of member galleries increased by 15 percent between 1962 and 1990 (reaching 133 galleries in 1990).

At the very beginning of the 1990s, Raymonde Moulin laid out the schematics for the four art neighborhoods of Paris: "Right Bank,"[14] "Left Bank," and two more recent areas, "Beaubourg," and "Bastille." In *L'artiste, l'institution et le marché* (*The Artist, the Institution, and the Market*), she reported statistics based on the list of galleries paying contributions to the Maison des Artistes[15] on behalf of their roster (totaling 529 galleries in Paris city limits in 1988)[16] (Moulin, 1992). These establishments far exceeded the limits of contemporary art galleries alone, as some of them operated more in the market of chromos. I will nevertheless analyze these statistics for lack of a better dataset. They paint a picture of the situation at the end of the 1980s as an auspicious period for contemporary art in France. The domain was well supported throughout this decade, during the "Jack Lang years," named for the Minister of Culture when left-wing François Mitterrand was elected president of the Republic in 1981:

> The increase in the number of galleries, all genres included, varies according to the neighborhood. From 1988 to 1989, the number of 'Left Bank' galleries (5th, 6th, and 7th arrondissements) rose (from 193 to 212), but the percentage compared to the total number of galleries in Paris remained more or less stable (35 and 36%). The number of 'Right Bank' galleries (8th, 9th, and 17th arrondissements) hasn't changed much (from 123 to 133), and the percentage of these galleries compared to all of the galleries in Paris dropped from 23 to 21%. The number of 'Marais-

> Beaubourg' galleries (1st, 2nd, 3rd, and 4th arrondissements) has risen sharply (from 112 to 177), with a percentage going from 21 to 29%. The number of galleries in the Bastille neighborhood (10th, 11th, 12th, 19th, and 20th arrondissements) went from 19 to 30—it will surpass 40 in 1990. The rate of growth is strongest in this neighborhood, even though the percentage compared to all of the galleries in Paris is still low, from 4 to 8%.[17]
>
> Moulin, 1992, pp. 241–242

Rounding out this data, Moulin indicated that in 1990–1991, "the distribution of contemporary art galleries in the neutral sense of the term" (sic) was approximately as follows:

> Left Bank: 40%
> Beaubourg-Marais: 29%
> Right Bank: 19%
> Bastille: 8%
> Other districts: 4%"
>
> Moulin, 1992, p. 189

Tatiana Debroux highlighted the rise in influence for the Marais neighborhood during the 1970s and 1980s:

> The 1975 map, and even more so that of 1986, shows the embryo that today constitutes the primary concentration of member galleries (of the CPGA) on the border of the 4th and 3rd arrondissements, connected by rue Quincampoix. In the Saint-Merri neighborhood in 1994, and again in 2016 in the Archives neighborhood, the proportion of members was somewhere between 10 and 20% out of a total that has increased drastically. The emergence and subsequent consolidation of the 3rd arrondissement reflects the creation of a third pole of galleries in Paris, along with that of the 8th (relatively weaker) and the Left Bank (at a comparable level of importance).

It was really after 1986 that the Marais considerably increased its influence, and the phenomenon was further accentuated after 1994 (Debroux, 2017) to the point of becoming central today:

> This new gallery district, which is now indispensable, is the result of a radical transformation in this part of Paris, which previously was not very visible in the city's artistic geography. In 1977, the opening of the major cultural institution, the Centre Pompidou, and the promise that it brought in terms of cultural clientele, along with an easier geographical accessibility than the prior concentrations of galleries, explains why

> several establishments rushed to the area, and were joined by many other galleries during the following years. Currently, the 3rd arrondissement is home to 42% of the member galleries of the Committee (CPGA), far ahead of the 6th arrondissement (20%), and the 8th arrondissement, which for a long time was the leader, but today has only 11.5% of the CPGA's members in 2016.
>
> Debroux, 2017, pp. 153–155

It is, however, important to note once again that these numbers refer to all CPGA members, not only those that pertain solely to contemporary art.

It would be incorrect to assume that today, with the roaring success of the consolidation of contemporary art galleries in the Marais, the choice of settling there was obvious. Even today, though so many art galleries reside within this part of the urban space, it has a sort of hindrance compared to the 8th arrondissement in that it does not have any large luxury hotels with a wealthy client base who are visiting Paris, and it is further away from the more bourgeois districts (Pinçon & Pinçon-Charlot, 1992, 1996, and 1997) in which most French art collectors reside. However, the image of an art gallery district paired with a mass influx is likely to attract potential buyers. As observed by this employee of a historic gallery specializing in contemporary art previously located in the 8th arrondissement before eventually moving to the east into the Marais:

> When collectors come into the gallery, even though we're in the middle of the Marais and we really have a very beautiful space, one of the first things that they say is 'Really, it's so far away! When are you coming back to the 8th? It was such a better location.' But you know, we're like most contemporary art galleries, if you look at the gallery's customer base, nearly all of them live in the 8th, the 16th, or the 7th arrondissements.

Solely taking into account the category of galleries that sell "real" contemporary art, their concentration in the 3rd arrondissement (which in reality contains most of the Marais' contemporary art galleries) would be much higher, even though the art district is split between the 3rd and 4th arrondissements. Thus, the Marais today comprises the district of contemporary art galleries *par excellence*. Most of the French galleries that participate in the FIAC art fair (which was replaced by the Paris+ fair by Art Basel in 2022, then Art Basel Paris in 2024) are located in this neighborhood, those whose contemporary nature is indisputable. Below is the geographical distribution of the 48 gallery spaces existing in Paris in 2019 that participated in the FIAC, which was the most selective French art fair:

Number of galleries per district, among the galleries participating in the 2019 FIAC fair

Marais: 28
Saint-Germain-des-Prés: 8
8th arrondissement: 4
Belleville: 4
9th arrondissement: 2
13th arrondissement: 1
18th arrondissement: 1

The importance of the Marais is indeed astounding,[18] as this neighborhood alone is home to more galleries than all the other art districts or locations combined, and the gap between it and the next in line, Saint-Germain-des-Prés, is enormous.

Admittedly, the criterion applied here of having participated in the FIAC determines a group of all the galleries that can claim to be truly contemporary, of which there are over 50 in Paris, as mentioned in the foreword of this book. The FIAC selection committee certified that the galleries in question were well and truly contemporary (Moulin & Quemin, 1993), and also attested to the quality (Misdrahi Florès, 2013) of their event calendars. Given the connection between the Marais' environment and the level of the galleries therein, it is not surprising that the concentration of this district is strengthened by the application of this criterion in order to identify galleries that are both acknowledged as undeniably contemporary and deemed to be the best in their field, at least when considered collectively. This hypothesis is confirmed if we examine the 31 galleries in Paris that participated in 2019 in Art Basel, the largest contemporary art fair in the world, which is held in Switzerland, with the following distribution of gallery spaces by district:

Number of galleries by district, among the galleries participating in the 2019 Art Basel fair

Marais: 22
Saint-Germain-des-Prés: 4
8th arrondissement: 4
13th arrondissement: 1
(Note: the other districts, which were outliers in the previous list, were no longer represented).

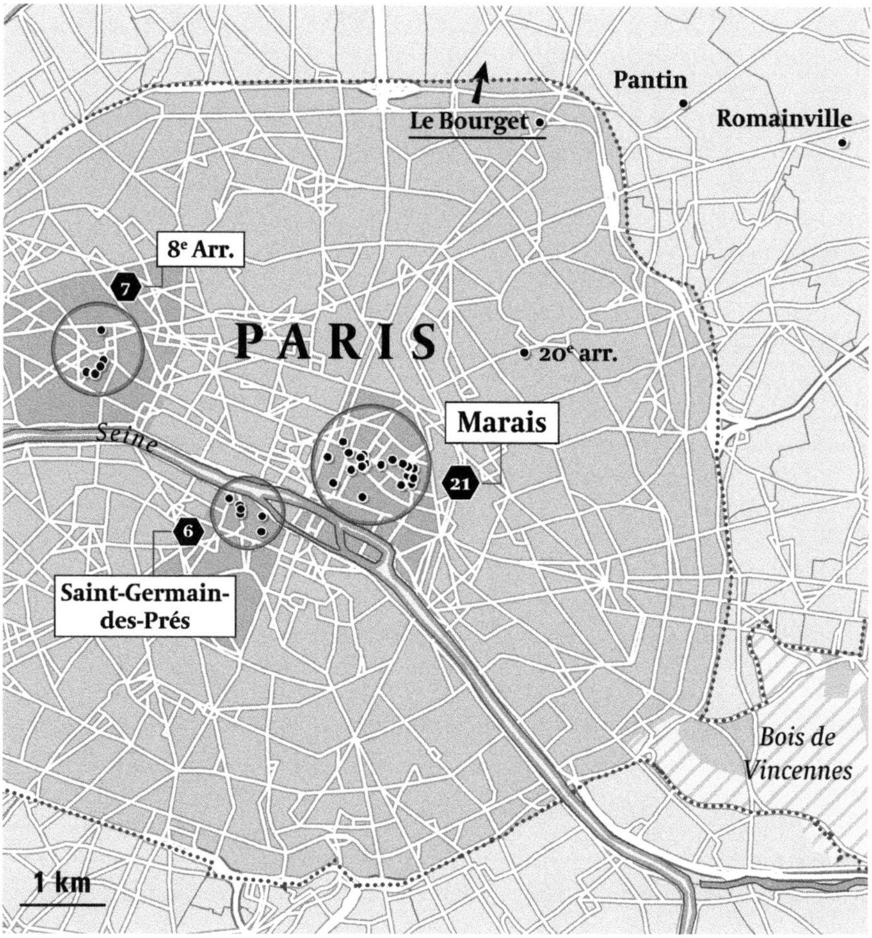

Location of contemporary art galleries established in Paris that participated in the "Galleries" sector of the Art Basel fair in 2019.

Today, understanding the geographical distribution of contemporary art galleries in Paris is to underscore the undeniable leading role of the Marais. For established galleries, this is hardly worth questioning: it is essential to have a branch in the Marais, with two exceptions: the mammoth Gagosian settled into the bourgeois 8th arrondissement, very close to the auction houses Christie's and Sotheby's; and the famous gallery, Lelong, on rue de Téhéran, which opened a second space nearby on avenue Matignon in 2018, thereby consolidating its integration into the neighborhood. In 2023, the leading international gallery Hauser & Wirth also opened a space in the 8th arrondissement. As for Saint-Germain-des-Prés, Mennour has retained his three tightly clustered spaces—the last of which was opened in 2020—as well as a small ancillary space on avenue Matignon; Georges-Philippe and Nathalie Vallois (who also opened a second space on the same street in 2016), and Galerie Loevenbruck have also maintained their spaces in the district. Having a location on the Left Bank today is considered atypical, and appears to be a resolute stance made by the various galleries therein (Bourdieu & Delsaut, 1975).

Since the 1970s, the Marais has only grown larger. Although the attempt to colonize the Bastille area, its neighbor to the southeast, was a misfire, the integration of contemporary galleries into the Marais has considerably strengthened, particularly around the two main geographical poles. Historically, it was important to be located to the west of the neighborhood, around the Centre Pompidou; however, this district ("Beaubourg") has been weakened due to the evolution of its urban planning.

The successive relocations of the Galerie du Luxembourg (later called Galerie Alain Blondel) in Paris is a perfect example. In 1972, as previously mentioned, the gallery was established at 98 rue Saint-Denis in the center of the city, close to Les Halles,[19] a former traditional wholesale food market in the capital. Following the closure of this market, there were immense premises available with very affordable leases, and so a former banana warehouse was transformed into the gallery's new space. Although the gallery had, up to that point, specialized in art from the first half of the twentieth century, the roster was then expanded to include contemporary artists. As Alain Blondel, one of the gallery's directors, explained:

> You can't imagine today the hope that this neighborhood carried at the beginning of the 70s. The galleries, the most trendsetting antique dealers, bookstores, cafes ... they all saw a future that somewhat resembled the transformation in the New York neighborhood of SoHo. At the time, the public followed this migration very well; before it was demolished, the Pavillon Baltard was a semi-permanent exhibition space. Between '72 and '74, we brought the sincerest art lovers to our gallery on rue Saint-Denis, which was already quite popular. But the illusion only lasted three years... in 1974/75, a 'mixed economy' commission was installed [...] and in the span of a few months, the neighborhood was transformed into a giant sex shop. So we moved into a new location under construction on the [nearby] Plateau Beaubourg before the Centre Pompidou was even finished.

As such, in 1977 the neighborhood's evolution obliged the gallery to move to 4 rue Aubry-le-Boucher in the Beaubourg neighborhood, right next to the esplanade of the future Centre Pompidou, which was inaugurated that same year. The directors of the gallery went their separate ways in 1978, and the gallery was renamed "Galerie Alain Blondel" in 1979. It stayed at that address until 2003, before ultimately being obliged once again to change locations. The gallerist explained:

> We had signed a lease for some unfinished premises that were close to an HLM[20] (this organization had occupied two sides of the square bordered by

> rue Aubry-le-Boucher). The leases were initially reserved for businesses with an art-related activity, and so our neighbors were the Galerie Beaubourg (Pierre Nahon and Patrice Trigano were the partners), another gallery whose name I forget, and the bookstore Le XXe Siècle & Ses Sources (which we had shares in). We stayed there for 25 years, and even though we were exceptionally visible, little by little the pressure of 'making the street lively' (protests, acrobatic performances, demonstrations of all sorts that sometimes blocked our doors) made it impossible to maintain our business. We often reminded the institutions that should have been involved (the town hall, Centre Pompidou, local administrative offices, etc.) of the contract that originally brought us there, for the 'artistic' mission of the area. We were only met with disregard [...]. We were simply an impediment to the stranglehold that 'brands' wanted to have on the neighborhood, so in 2003, after all our colleagues had already left, we signed our lease over to Starbucks ... The neighborhood's metamorphosis was complete.

The transformation being described here is fairly analogous to that put forth by David Halle and Elisabeth Tiso regarding SoHo in New York (presented later in this chapter) (Halle & Tiso, 2014). In 2004, Galerie Alain Blondel moved into another space in the Marais, a little more to the east than its former space, at 128 rue Vieille-du-Temple. It stayed there for eight years, before occupying new premises at 50 rue du Temple in 2012.

Since then, galleries have seemed to move more generally to the other side—the east side—of the Marais. To this day, there are four market heavyweights within a small area located at the intersection of rue de Turenne and rue Debelleyme: Almine Rech, Perrotin, Karsten Greve, and Thaddaeus Ropac. However, the Beaubourg neighborhood is once again showing strong signs of vitality. In May 2018, Galerie Templon, which had been located at 30 rue Beaubourg since 1972, opened a larger second space on rue du Grenier Saint-Lazare, a stone's throw away from the first. Rue Beaubourg (also called rue du Renard further along the street) and the streets intersecting it are home to one of the strongest concentrations of galleries in Paris, with the galleries Jérôme Poggi (which left the Gare du Nord neighborhood in 2014), Ceysson & Bénétière (since 2009), and Nathalie Obadia (with two longstanding spaces on rue du Cloître Saint-Merri and rue du Bourg-Tibourg),[21] in addition to Templon. On the corner of rue Beaubourg, the streets rue de Montmorency and rue Chapon are teeming with galleries, including Betrand Grimont, which already had two adjacent spaces (one small, the other midsize) before opening this third larger space that had been vacated by the Galerie Anne de Villepoix to create a larger space that would host art and events. Between rue Beaubourg and rue de Turenne, the network of galleries is very dense: Art: Concept, Eric Dupont, Christophe Gaillard, Max Hetzler, Marian Goodman, David Zwirner (who succeeded VnH in its space on rue Vieille du Temple), Xippas, Mor Charpentier, Denise René (until its closure), Suzanne Tarasieve, Praz-Delavallade, Lahumière. There are so

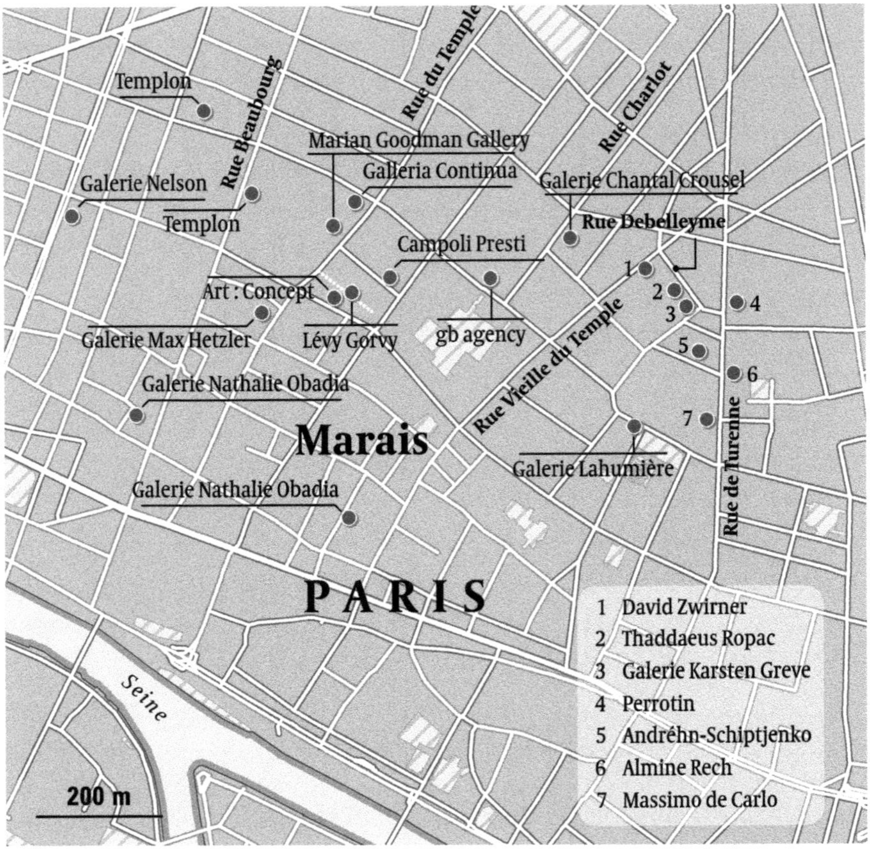

Location of contemporary art galleries established in the Marais neighborhood that participated in the "Galleries" sector of the Art Basel fair in 2019.

many venues that it is impossible to name them all. Leaving Ivry, Galerie RX moved into a former typical Parisian mansion in 2016. Nearby, the galleries gb agency (before closing in 2024) and Chantal Crousel both expanded their exhibition spaces in 2019 by annexing a small extra room in a neighboring building. Extension is a fundamental trend in Paris, especially in the most in-demand neighborhoods, along with the trend of opening a second space near to the first one. In the context of the more unstable establishments being forced to close down, expanding one's space constitutes a display of power, which necessitates the right choice of location.

Outside of the Marais, the 8th arrondissement, and Saint-Germain-des-Prés—the three traditional gallery districts—other spaces, which are endlessly different, have been attempting to emerge in Paris for the past 30 years.

It is important to note the remarkable initiative led by the local authorities: rue Louise Weiss, which was originally situated in an underdeveloped urban neighborhood next to the railroad tracks in the 13th arrondissement on the

Left Bank of Paris, was designed to accommodate new, cutting-edge galleries and stand as complementary to the gallery district in the Marais, which was globally perceived as being more established (Bourdieu & Delsaut, 1975). Inaugurated in 1988 as a gallery-friendly space, rue Louise Weiss was a significant area for French contemporary art for several years. Quite a few galleries flourished in this "trailblazing" environment, such as Perrotin, Almine Rech, Fabienne Leclerc, Jousse Enterprise, Air de Paris, and Kréo. However, as they grew in prominence during the 2000s, these galleries began to leave the neighborhood one after the other; the spaces that had been designed to accommodate these new galleries had become cramped, and art lovers rarely frequented the neighborhood outside of exhibition openings. Although the gallery Air de Paris initially expanded into the former premises of its now-departed colleagues (who had left for the Marais), it also ultimately left rue Louise Weiss in October 2019 and moved into the Komunuma complex in Romainville, a northeast suburb of Paris. With the relocation of Air de Paris, the final holdout establishment that had been sustaining rue Louise Weiss, the death knell was sounded for this former contemporary art district.

The working-class Belleville neighborhood represents another zone of Paris that, for a while (and not without some fanfare), intended to challenge the pivotal role of the Marais in the Parisian gallery market until 2018, when this ambition was dealt its final blow. Galleries closed one by one, including Bugada & Cargnel (the only one to have a large exhibition space) on rue de l'Equerre in the 19th arrondissement, and Samy Abraham (which had cut its teeth on rue Louise Weiss), not far from Bugada & Cargnel on rue Ramponeau in the 20th arrondissement. Hardly any galleries remain, other than the gallery Jocelyn Wolff, which has also had a location in Romainville since 2019, as well as Crèvecoeur and Marcelle Alix (but these are only small outfits). The other establishments' miniscule spaces and the distance between each of them did not bode well for their future, and in June 2020 the gallery Antoine Lévi announced that it was leaving Belleville to move into the outskirts of the Marais on rue de Turbigo.

In an undoubtedly shrewder maneuver, the galleries Paris-Beijing (that was later renamed Paris B) and Backslash moved onto rue Notre-Dame-de-Nazareth on the periphery of the Marais (the latter into a 2,700-square-foot space). Paris-Beijing later moved to a nearby location on rue de Turbigo, a major artery in the North East of the Marais where galleries did not traditionally venture. A dozen (often small) galleries have now hung their shingles in this sector, where being in close proximity to other establishments is more favorable to the development of an artistic ecosystem.

The most recent prospects are, however, now located outside of Paris. As established in the previous chapter, the gallery Thaddaeus Ropac led a veritable symbolic revolution in 2012 by allowing contemporary galleries and art lovers to break through the mental boundaries between the city limits of Paris and the larger region of Ile-de-France. Since then, thanks to Ropac's immense, magnificent space, Pantin has been on the contemporary Parisian map. In

January 2017, the Centre national des arts plastiques (the National Center of Visual Arts, CNAP) announced that it was moving to Pantin; Thaddaeus Ropac's gallery had laid the groundwork so well for the visual arts in this section of the urban space that an eminent public French institution was then motivated to follow in this leading gallery's footsteps (Citerni, 2018; Ansaloni, 2020). Energized by this dynamic, it is the bordering commune of Romainville that is now attempting to emerge as an environment conducive to contemporary art (galleries in particular). In October 2019, the galleries Jocelyn Wolff (created in 2003), In Situ—Fabienne Leclerc (created in 2001 and itinerant for a long time, and later totally isolated in the south of the 18th arrondissement), Air de Paris (created in 1990, and the last to leave rue Louise Weiss in the 13th arrondissement), and Vincent Sator (created in 2011, which has nevertheless retained its initial space on the impasse des Gravilliers in the Marais), amassed in the same complex, Komunuma. With a surface area of 120,000 square feet, the site was developed by a corporate foundation, Fiminco. A sure sign of the times, where the rue Louise Weiss was the result of a public initiative, the new site in Romainville is the product of a private initiative; however, the project does not appear capable of generating a real dynamic that would challenge the importance of the Marais for Parisian art galleries.[22]

In 2021, the Galerie Nathalie Obadia opened a branch in the 8th arrondissement following the lead of its fellow gallery, Perrotin (which already had an annex in the area and later opened a space (for two years only) with two other partners to develop its secondary market activity), and Almine Rech, both of which had done so not long before. However, each of these cases constitute smaller branches of galleries whose primary spaces remain in the Marais. With the emergence of a gallery district laid out along avenue Matignon but composed of galleries that have preserved their main space in the Marais, Paris is emulating—on a much smaller scale—the New York model, where one neighborhood (in this case, Chelsea) has the majority of galleries' primary spaces, but the largest institutions have frequently felt it necessary to reconnect with the urban space wherein the collectors reside: the Upper East Side. In Paris, a functional equivalent might be the 8th arrondissement, where certain gallery clients live, and which also borders the 16th, 17th, and 7th arrondissements, which are also traditionally bourgeois neighborhoods in the French capital that are home to most of the city's art buyers. It is the New York model that will be analyzed next.

New York and the triumph of the West Chelsea neighborhood

Retracing the history of how New York contemporary art galleries have developed is practically impossible without summarizing their successive relocations to different, clearly defined neighborhoods (Molotch & Treskon,

2009) up to the triumph of the district of West Chelsea, which today is heavily populated by galleries (Halle & Tiso, 2014).

Salvador Dalí, who is famous for having been a provocateur and megalomaniac, decided to designate the train station in the southern French city of Perpignan (which is very close to the Spanish border) as the center of the world (clearly, an arbitrary declaration). Although the fantasy implicated in this choice may be laughable, as the surface of the planet patently cannot have a center, the same cannot be said for contemporary art. While France and Paris were for a long time the center of this social world, it has incontrovertibly been repositioned in the United States (more specifically, in New York)[23] (Guilbaut, 1985; Quemin, 2001, 2002, 2004 and 2006; Obadia, 2019). This center is located even more precisely in West Chelsea, an extremely dense hub with hundreds of contemporary art galleries, most of which are very well reputed, and some of which are undeniable market juggernauts.

The Chelsea gallery district encompasses a geographical rectangle bordered by 10th Avenue to the east, 11th Avenue to the west, and stretching essentially north to south from West 27th Street to West 18th Street. In actuality, Chelsea extends to either side of 10th Avenue, which spans both the north and south sections of the neighborhood. However, in the contemporary art world, when players talk about this district, they are nearly always talking implicitly about its western segment, without always saying "West" before "Chelsea." The east side of the district, which is traditionally residential, is another de facto universe. Here, it is once again clear how an objective space is reinterpreted by individuals who appropriate it literally and symbolically (Chombart de Lauwe, 1956) based on what they do with it.

The West Chelsea neighborhood is now so strongly associated with the incredibly dense concentration of contemporary New York galleries that one might almost believe that is has always been the case. However, the New York art market has developed over time by successively relocating into the neighborhoods that became home to the most galleries at a time. The work produced by David Halle and Elisabeth Tiso provides the best in-depth analysis of the various geographical movements and rationales that allowed West Chelsea to emerge as we know it today (Halle & Tiso, 2014).

In the 1950s, the heart of the New York contemporary art market was located in Midtown, on 57th Street. However, as of the end of the 1960s, the SoHo neighborhood, which is further to the south of Manhattan, progressively supplanted this space (Kostelanetz, 2003). The district, which at the time had a poor reputation, nonetheless attracted artists with its low rents, its industrial architecture and its massive lofts (Zukin, 1982). In order to benefit from these enticements, Paula Cooper made the particularly daring but ultimately fortuitous choice to be the first to open her gallery in this neighborhood in 1968. Until the end of the 1990s, SoHo was the heart of the New York art gallery market (Molotch & Treskon, 2009), even though there were attempts to introduce new districts, like the East Village in the 1980s (which did not last long in this respect).

The simultaneous decline of SoHo (Kostelanetz, 2003) and development of Chelsea are due in essence to the real estate market (Halle & Tiso, 2014). The successive arrival of artists and then galleries in SoHo—attracted by the initially low rents—triggered a gentrification (Glass, 1964) in the neighborhood and an upswing in social quality. This in turn attracted fashion brands, prompting a spectacular rise in the price of commercial leases. The galleries, nearly all of which were tenants, were thus forced to withdraw; hence, West Chelsea quickly became "the place to be."

Like SoHo had been for a long time, before art galleries began to move into the neighborhood, thus initiating a process of spatial and social requalification (Grafmeyer & Authier, 2008), West Chelsea seemed very unappealing (Molotch & Treskon, 2009). Fairly isolated from the rest of Manhattan, with no subway lines nearby, the dilapidated urban space ran along disused elevated train tracks called the High Line. The neighborhood, which was composed essentially of garages and warehouses in immense spaces, could be dangerous at night. While it lacked any residents (like its neighbor, the Meatpacking District), prostitution and drug trafficking were rife. Socially disparaged and quite unattractive, the area was characterized by very low real estate prices for buildings with massive square footage. In 1985, and later in 1987, two nonprofit centers—the Kitchen, and later the larger Dia Foundation, both having originated in SoHo, moved successively to Chelsea; thus, they laid the groundwork for a roadmap that galleries could then replicate. If they came *en masse*, this would surely change the appearance of the neighborhood and draw the attention of collectors. Interestingly, Gagosian had opened a location on West 23rd Street in West Chelsea in 1985, which is a fact that is often overlooked; it was, however far too soon, and the gallery was not able to entice its peers to come to this new area, and eventually had to shut down. This failure illustrates the concept of the "wrong turn" as posited by David Halle and Elisabeth Tiso (Halle & Tiso, 2014): when galleries move into an urban space, they must choose not only the right place, but also the right time, or else their geographical strategy could fail. Despite this setback, Gagosian made another attempt at integrating into the neighborhood, and in 1999 it opened a location on West 24th Street, which was a resounding success. But in the meantime, the district had begun to change, and Gagosian was not the only gallery to descend upon it.

Matthew Marks was in fact the first to move to Chelsea to open a gallery permanently. Having launched his business in 1990 in a small space in the Upper East Side, the leases in SoHo had already become too expensive when he was looking to expand. He took the daring initiative of buying a space on West 22nd Street in the middle of Chelsea in 1994, which elicited a decent amount of misunderstanding among those close to him, as West Chelsea seemed to many observers unsuitable for the development of an art gallery. However, this new occupation was successful for two reasons. First, leases in SoHo, where practically all galleries were tenants, had risen sharply. Second, with the arrival of contemporary art galleries, the area had become "cutting edge," then more and more in vogue, drawing an increasing number of clothing stores. This new competition for urban spaces (Pinçon & Pinçon-Charlot, 1992, 1996) automatically drove rent prices higher than ever before, obliging galleries in the area to seek new, cheaper neighborhoods that could accommodate them. Incidentally, Matthew Marks quickly convinced his "star" (Quemin, 1993b) gallerist friends from SoHo, Paul Morris and Pat Hearn, to join him on the same street a few months after he moved to West Chelsea. Nearly one year later, in 1995, Paula Cooper (also very prominent) opened a space on the nearby West 21st Street. This arrival was all the more important symbolically speaking, given that she was the one who had discovered and inducted SoHo as a gallery district (Halle & Tiso, 2014). By leaving SoHo, she led the charge toward Chelsea that was likely to be successful, as it was legitimized by a professional whose quality as a pioneer in launching new gallery districts had already been established. This influx of heavyweights contributed to a bandwagon effect (Leibenstein, 1950), which was escalated by the number of galleries being chased out of Soho (when it came time to renew their lease) in the second half of the 1990s (Molotch & Treskon, 2009; Halle & Tiso, 2014). Despite Chelsea's environment originally being perceived as inhospitable, since the garages and warehouses initially continued to operate alongside the galleries, and it was too far from public transportation, even the gallerists who for a long time were reticent to move into this urban space ultimately made the leap, as was the case for David Zwirner[24] in 2002. There is one fundamental change worth highlighting: in Chelsea, many galleries that had learned from their experiences in SoHo came to understand the importance of owning their space, and bought their premises as soon as possible.

Chelsea underwent a meteoric rise from 1998 to 2004, thus becoming the dominant district for galleries in New York. It not only replaced the previous neighborhoods; it reached a degree unmatched by anything that had come before. In 1996, 12 galleries moved into Chelsea, which already had a total of 70 at the end of 1998, 231 in 2007, and 410 at the end of 2013 (Halle & Tiso, 2014). Today, the total number of galleries is around 300.[25]

However, as of the middle of the 2000s, tensions began to arise in Chelsea as the neighborhood was also becoming increasingly gentrified with the (previously unthinkable) construction of luxury condominiums, some of which were designed by the greatest international architects. After having a persisting adverse reputation in the New York urban space, the neighborhood has become extremely desirable due to the advent of these contemporary art galleries, which led to garages and warehouses being evicted on most streets. The installation of the High Line, an elevated greenway on former railroad tracks, which traverses Chelsea and winds through the Meatpacking District all the way to Hudson Yards, also helped to re-characterize everything surrounding it (Halle & Tiso, 2014; Rothenberg & Lang, 2017). Once West Chelsea became the dominant district for galleries, newer neighborhoods doubled down on their attempts to challenge it via a specific dynamic of the artistic field that notably manifests itself under geographical dimensions (Bourdieu & Delsaut, 1975). The Lower East Side seemed to be a reasonable alternative, and continues at least in part to do so, but to a much lesser degree. Perhaps more

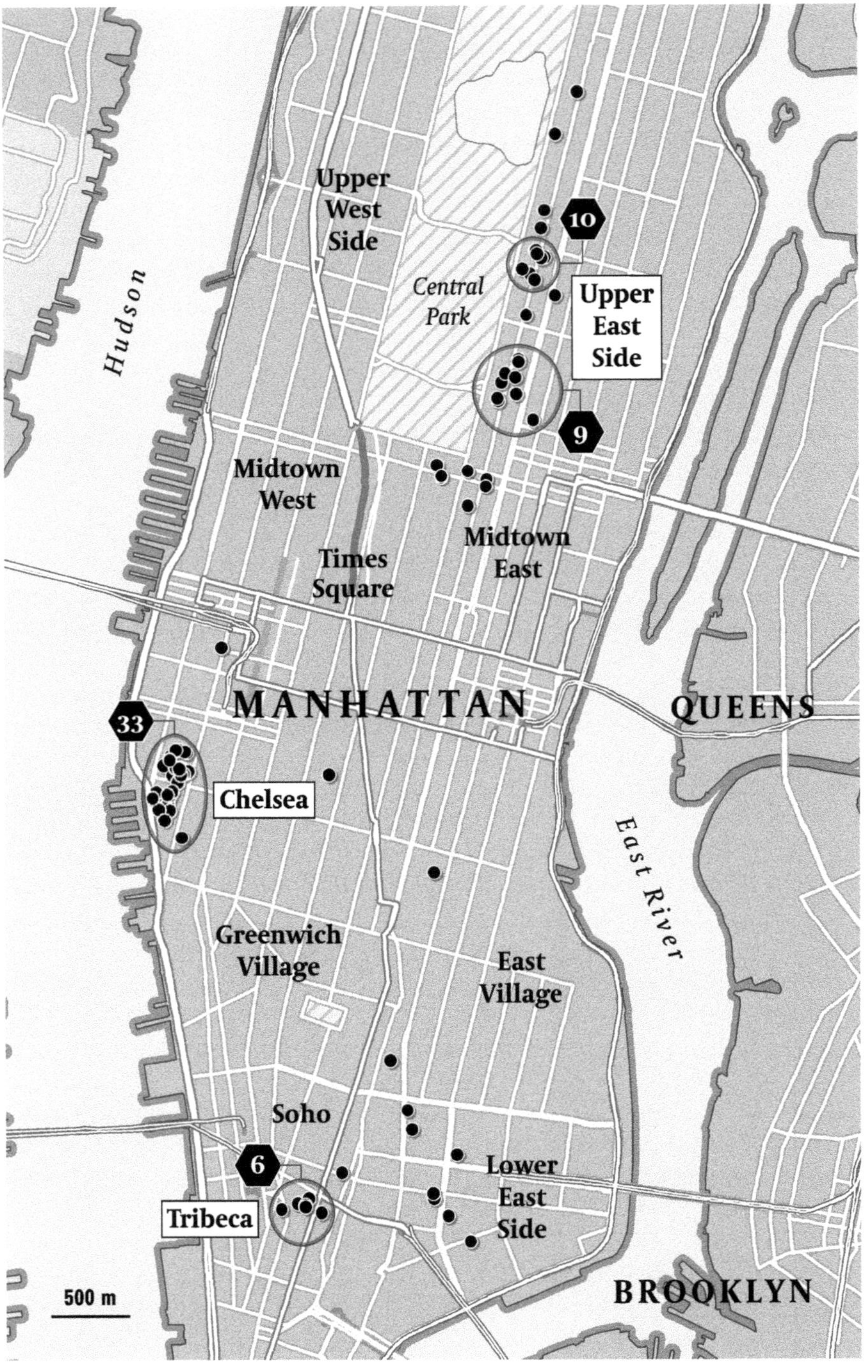

Location of contemporary art galleries established in New York that participated in the "Galleries" sector of the Art Basel fair in 2019.

unexpectedly, the very chic Upper East Side has been making itself more appealing to contemporary art galleries for the last few years. The most prestigious establishments have been inaugurating locations in this neighborhood, but more often than not these are secondary spaces, as the galleries have maintained their primary location in Chelsea. Outside of Manhattan, Williamsburg was just a flash in the pan; the neighborhood's potential to rival Chelsea evaporated in 2004. Another Brooklyn neighborhood, Bushwick, was hailed for a while by its ardent supporters as the new Mecca for contemporary art that would dethrone Chelsea (Zukin & Braslow, 2011); however, there as well, these hopes were quickly definitively dashed. This space is largely reduced to a parcel of land for emerging galleries to occupy or, at a push, is little more than an area where a gallery can open a second space to complement its primary premises in a more central location, which was almost certainly in Manhattan. Likewise, the Flower District already represents a bygone possibility, and the promise of Harlem—which had also been designated as a new possible area for investment—did not come to fruition.

Currently, in addition to the complementary neighborhoods of the Lower East Side and the Upper East Side, it is the neighborhood of Tribeca, further south than West Chelsea, that has the best chance of standing as a worthy challenge.[26] The Postmasters Gallery, created in 1984 in the East Village, moved to SoHo in 1989, then to Chelsea in 1998, before finally investing in a 6,500-square-foot space in Tribeca in 2013. Its directors explained their successive relocations by the pressure they felt due to the gentrification that progressively took place in each of their former neighborhoods (in "This Is the Toughest Challenge My Business Has Ever Faced. But Here's Why Small Galleries Like Mine Will Come Out Alive," *Artnet News*, April 27, 2020). However, it is clear in the following extract how this other gallerist—Stefania Bortolami, who was a pioneer in building Tribeca up as a gallery district—decided to open a second space in this exciting new area. She chose her location first and foremost for its spacious interior, but also for the neighborhood's characteristics, which were quite enticing. Notably, she elaborates on the comparison between the Lower East Side and Chelsea, which is still the prevailing model:

> *You recently moved your gallery from Chelsea to Tribeca. Was this a logistical or strategic decision?*
>
> – Well, I had to move from my space, so I met with a real estate agent and he came to me with a pile of spaces. I wanted to pay more or less the same amount of money that I was paying, and he showed me spaces in Chelsea, Harlem, and Midtown that were not what I was looking for. And then he showed me a picture of this space. The picture was very different [from seeing it firsthand]. The space required a total gut renovation. It looked terrible. But I fell in love.
>
> This is the first space we came to see, and it happened to be in Tribeca. And when I thought about it, it made sense. It's not the Lower East

> Side, which is a bit crowded. Tribeca has plenty of beautiful homes with lots of walls—walls that will need things on them—and plenty of new construction happening nearby. It's very easy to reach by subway from the East, West, and Brooklyn. It's got the history of all the artists living in the neighborhood, and it has a little bit of the nostalgia of SoHo. So for me it ticked all the right boxes.
>
> I was quite happy to be out of Chelsea, to tell you the truth. Chelsea is going in a specific direction, which is luxury—in terms of both the condo and office developments—and the mega-galleries are picking up more and more real estate. A gallery like mine will not be able to compete in terms of space, and I don't want to. So it felt like it was not the right spot for me anymore.
>
> Stefania Bortolami in *Artnet News*, July 7, 2017

Nowadays, Chelsea's appeal is indisputably without equal, and it has reached dizzying heights in all respects. The galleries that lined the north side of West 24th Street, between 11th and 10th Avenues from west to east in 2018 was mind-boggling: Gagosian (which takes up nearly a third of the street!), Mary Boone, Pace (its second space), Luhring Augustine, Andrea Rosen (which had nevertheless announced that it was closing), Matthew Marks, Metro Pictures (which has since closed), Barbara Gladstone, Marianne Boesky (and Boesky East!), and finally Bryce Wolkowitz which is the only gallery behind the others in terms of prestige. Beyond this single street, which remains packed with galleries—especially prominent ones and mostly on its north side—due to the exceptional number of establishments that have flocked to the area, Chelsea boasts a level of gallery concentration that is utterly unrivaled in the world. This stimulates certain kinds of competition that exist in the urban space like nowhere else. Each of the "big four" galleries—those with the most financial control—now have mega-spaces (which I addressed in the previous chapter). Following Gagosian's lead, David Zwirner, Hauser & Wirth, and Pace now have at least one gallery in Chelsea each, which are exceptional resources for their business, and this further testifies to their universally acknowledged position. This rivalry between the four giants of Chelsea has manifested in a symbolic marking and sharing of the urban space, each of the four competitors having figuratively and literally appropriated a different street to develop their brand. Gagosian created the first enormous space, which at the time was totally unequalled, on the corner of West 24th Street and 11th Avenue; its longstanding main rival, Pace, took over West 25th Street. The gallery's ambitions to rival the other major market players who also had locations in Chelsea had grown too much to stay in its original space, but it stayed on "its" street to build its superb mega-space, which was inaugurated in 2019. Having experienced a tremendous rise over the last ten years, David Zwirner and Hauser & Wirth had to assert themselves in Chelsea to mark their territory both in terms of the geographical space of contemporary art as well as on the market. After initially taking over a former roller rink on West 18th Street (as previously mentioned),

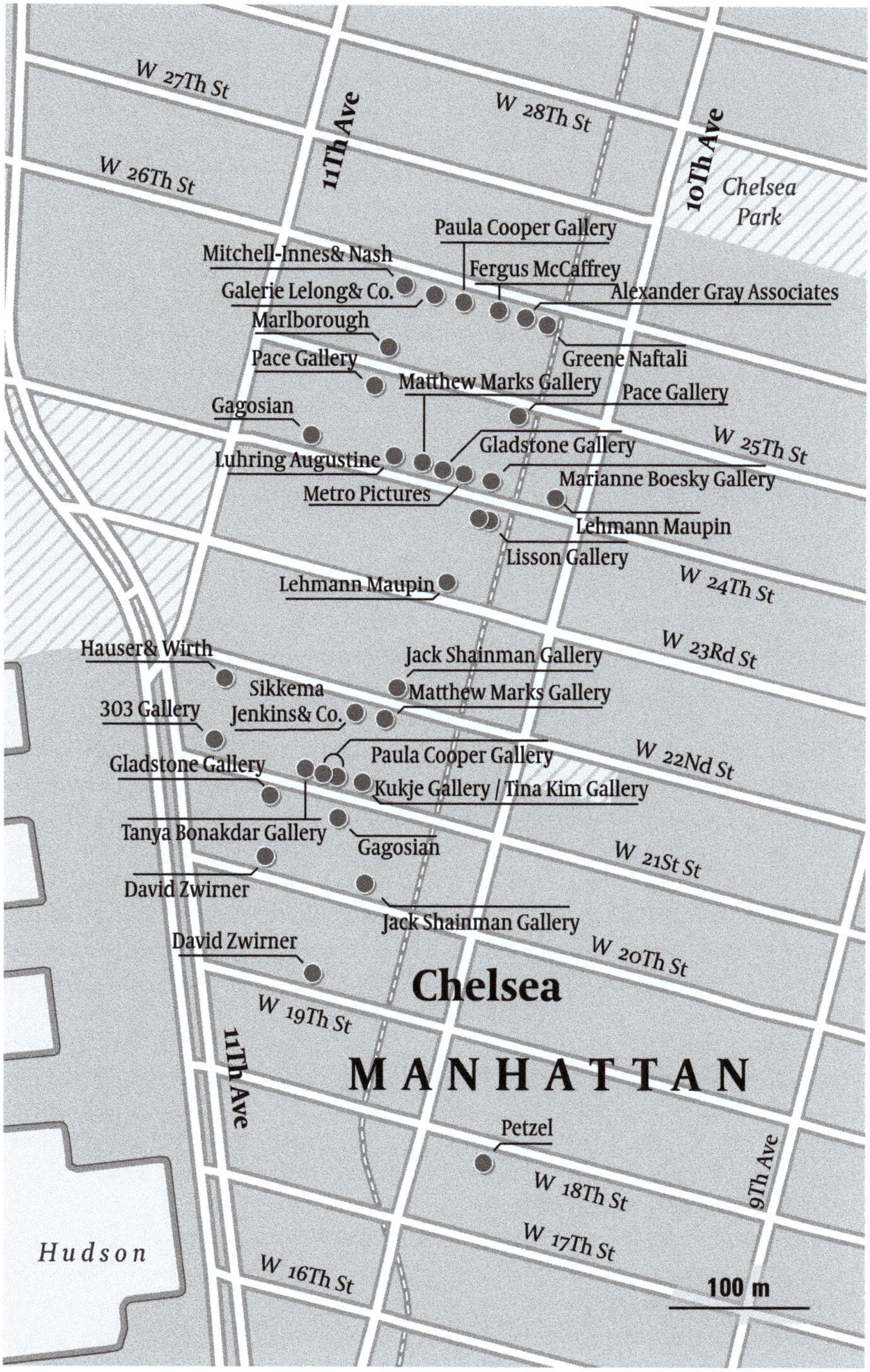

Location of contemporary art galleries established in Chelsea neighborhood that participated in the "Galleries" sector of the Art Basel fair in 2019.

and later moving into a five-story building that used to be home to the Dia contemporary art center on West 22nd Street, Hauser & Wirth also had a magnificent new building constructed on the same street. In 2013, their competitor David Zwirner also had an exceptional five-story building erected on West 20th Street, and later also commissioned a sumptuous new building on West 21st Street to complement the first gallery on West 20th Street.[27] In doing so, David Zwirner ventured outside of "its" traditional emblematic street, albeit only a short distance away; transitioning to a major thoroughfare where none of its main competitors had yet made its mark. At the end of this series of maneuvers, moving north to south, West 25th Street, West 24th Street, West 22nd Street, West 21st Street, and West 20th Street had all been claimed by a mega-gallery's flagship location.[28] Each of these spaces constitutes the primary address of each of the galleries mentioned above, representing each gallery's highest symbolic value (Pinçon & Pinçon-Charlot, 1992 and 1996). Of course, all of these galleries have additional locations on other streets in Chelsea[29] and/or New York, as well as in other cities.

Will Chelsea's hegemony endure? While this district's decline is constantly being announced (and has been for years), particularly by market players who are trying to promote other parts of the urban space, there is no reason to give credence to this dark prediction. Unlike SoHo, which underwent an inevitable decline after its golden age of contemporary art galleries, most of the establishments that moved into Chelsea own their premises (as previously mentioned), especially those that arrived early on, when property prices were still very low (Halle & Tiso, 2014). Insofar as they had learned their lessons from practically being evicted from SoHo due to the sharp increase in rent and the impossibility of preserving the qualities of the neighborhood (Pinçon & Pinçon-Charlot, 1992), which would supposedly have designated the area for art lovers rather than fashionistas, gallerists did not make the same mistake in Chelsea. Furthermore, over the years, galleries have been bestowing themselves with magnificent spaces, which are major investments; essentially, most gallery spaces were either totally redesigned or built from scratch with luxurious standards. In this neighborhood, any gallery worth its salt must respect the codes that are in effect in the contemporary art world: immense rooms, high white walls and spot rail, polished concrete floors, often superb wood or metal carpentry, overhead lighting, and immaculate finishing touches. With its unsurpassed density and the luxurious design of the galleries, the neighborhood's artistic offerings attract collectors and art advisors, particularly because the spaces are always of an excellent caliber. Chelsea benefits from a social qualification that does not exist anywhere else in the world; a Chelsea address alone distinguishes and designates galleries as being—at least potentially—part of the best contemporary institutions and awards them some degree of certification. All of these factors together result in galleries having no reason to leave a district that they collectively control (Pinçon & Pinçon-Charlot, 1992), especially one that has greatly contributed to the success (or even accolades) (Quemin, 2013b) of many of them.

Not counting the real estate risk, there is a potential danger as to how the district and its spaces will age, the outcome of which could cause these galleries and their locations to fall under the category of "historical" contemporary art, not unlike the Saint-Germain-des-Prés neighborhood in Paris, which in the 1970s lost its strong association with the art of its era, to the benefit of the Marais. Hence, even though the biggest galleries in Chelsea may display and sell paintings (and to a lesser extent, sculptures) at a staggering rate (Halle & Tiso, 2014), in order to maintain their place as market leader, they alternate between their more frequent exhibitions of these mediums and others with less of a commercial intention that grants much more (positive) attention to the gallery's location and environment. This allows them to cultivate and conserve their image as true contemporary galleries. This desire to include videos, performances, and "talks" with the artists in their lineup has been completely integrated into the interior design of these mega-galleries. The stratagem is now oriented much more toward symbolic positioning than market posturing (Bourdieu & Delsaut, 1975). Likewise when new, established and leading galleries alike add young artists to their roster, it is not only a case of paving the way for their future, but also a question of image. This is because, even for the largest galleries—which play a central role in certifying the value of art (Moulin & Quemin, 1993)—there is always a risk in purporting to lead young artists to inevitable success. It is always the safer bet to add artists to their list of represented talents if they already have reputations that were previously built by other, lesser-known galleries. The risk, which is both unavoidable and very high at the beginning and even the middle of a gallery's operations, is therefore generally externalized to less significant galleries. However, conversely, major galleries are required to cultivate their image as a "real" hyper-contemporary art gallery, and they cannot discount the younger generations—even in an artistic milieu where, since the 1970s, the most famous artists tend on the whole to be older (Quemin, 2013b)—which is why galleries now occasionally include very young artists on their rosters.

While Chelsea is the undisputed center of the gallery scene in the United States (and the world), care must be taken to manage this resounding success, particularly by maintaining a gallery's image in such a way that it does not become antiquated and lose its truly "contemporary" status.

London: a similar scene to Paris in terms of the impact of contemporary art galleries

I decided not to go into detail on the current London contemporary art gallery scene in this book, because it shares a fair number of characteristics with the Paris scene. Moreover, Brexit's effect on the London scene has had the effect of considerably augmenting the influence of its historical rival,

Paris. In terms of international impact, the two cities of London and Paris are far behind New York; and all three are miles ahead of Berlin, if we take the influence of a city's galleries into account rather than the mere number of them. In this regard, Berlin therefore has the undisputed fourth most significant international gallery scene. Here, I will give a brief overview of how the London gallery scene has developed, as well as its current main hubs, to compare London's dynamic with that of Paris and New York.

As previously stated, while the largest galleries in Paris are now concentrated in the Marais and, to a lesser extent, in the 8th arrondissement (with a few vestiges in the 6th arrondissement), it is the chic neighborhood of Mayfair that is home to most of London's most famous galleries. The area surrounding the emblematic New and Old Bond Streets, Dover Street, and Cork Street is the center of the local art market, particularly in regards to contemporary art galleries.

As a very influential international gallerist intimated to me before inaugurating his London location: "If you move to London, you have to go to Mayfair. Elsewhere, it's not really worth it when you're an international gallery." Small and midsized establishments (particularly the new ones) are more spread out, but they tend to be located in the east and northeast of London; just like in Paris, where some galleries got their start on rue Louise Weiss in the 13th arrondissement before moving to Belleville or the outskirts of the Marais (and some later ventured out to Romainville, also to the northeast of Paris).

The history of Mayfair (Citerni, 2018), and especially that of its main road, Cork Street, is inseparable from the Mayor Gallery, which was opened by the pioneer Fred Mayor in 1925. He was among the first (and in several cases was the first in London) to hold exhibitions featuring works by Paul Klee, Max Ernst, Alexander Calder, Joan Miró, and Francis Bacon. The art market then developed and condensed in the upscale district of Mayfair, when a significant evolution came about in the mid-1980s with the emergence of a new slate of galleries. This includes that of Maureen Paley in the East End, a traditionally working-class area of London where it would previously have seemed incongruous to open an art gallery. The American-born gallerist was thus perhaps more willing to push the symbolic boundaries of an urban space that was new to her. As Mayfair nonetheless increasingly became a location for established galleries, other areas such as Bethnal Green, Hackney, and Hoxton in northeast London gradually emerged as alternative locations.

When the YBA (Young British Artists) movement took off in the 1990s,[30] Hoxton Square in the northeast of London quickly became the epicenter of the city's creative scene. The gallery White Cube, founded by Jay Jopling, became a trailblazer in the field by representing the new generation of turbulent artists who would soon explode on the international scene.

Furthermore, in the neighborhood of Bethnal Green—a fairly industrial part of the East End—galleries boldly situated on Vyner Street gave rise to a dynamic environment in East London. The first to open a space was Stuart Shave, founder and director of the Modern Art gallery.

Like all major metropolitan areas, London's East End did not escape rising real estate prices, due in part to the Olympic Games held in 2012 in London. Located in the East End, this event led to an extensive requalification of this part of the urban space, which thus rose in social value and caused an increase in property prices. While some galleries managed to retain their locations, others left for the Fitzrovia neighborhood in the West End.

While, throughout the decades, alternative districts tended to shift around within the city, Mayfair (which was sometimes deemed to be too classical by detractors, who advocated for a more "cutting edge" conception of contemporary art) nevertheless managed to maintain its dominant position (Bourdieu & Delsaut, 1975). Mayfair's unarguable central position was consolidated by the advent of the biggest international galleries. The four

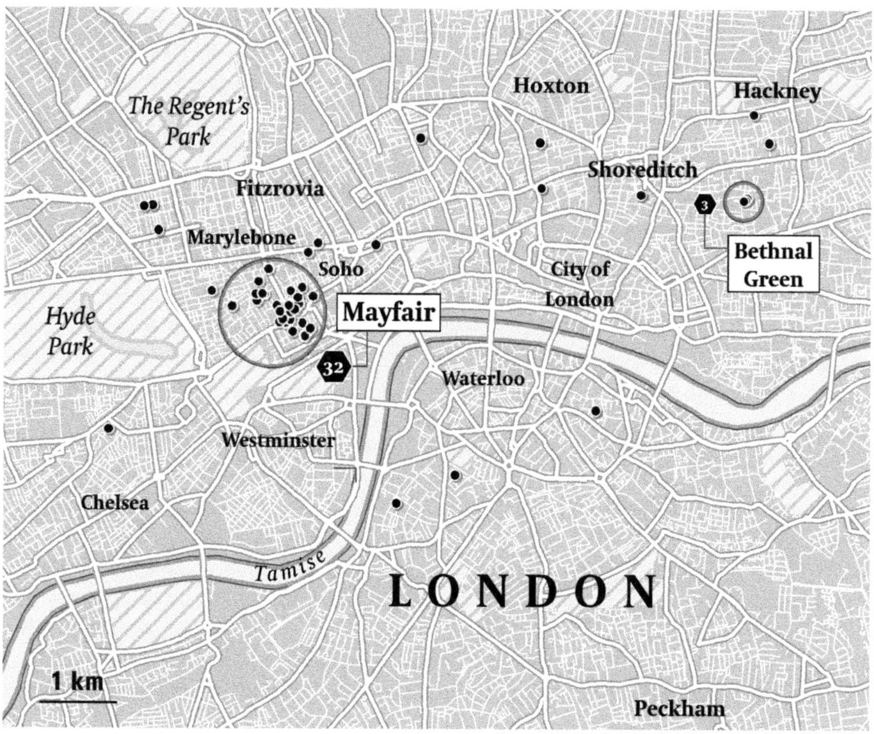

Location of contemporary art galleries established in London that participated in the "Galleries" sector of the Art Basel fair in 2019.

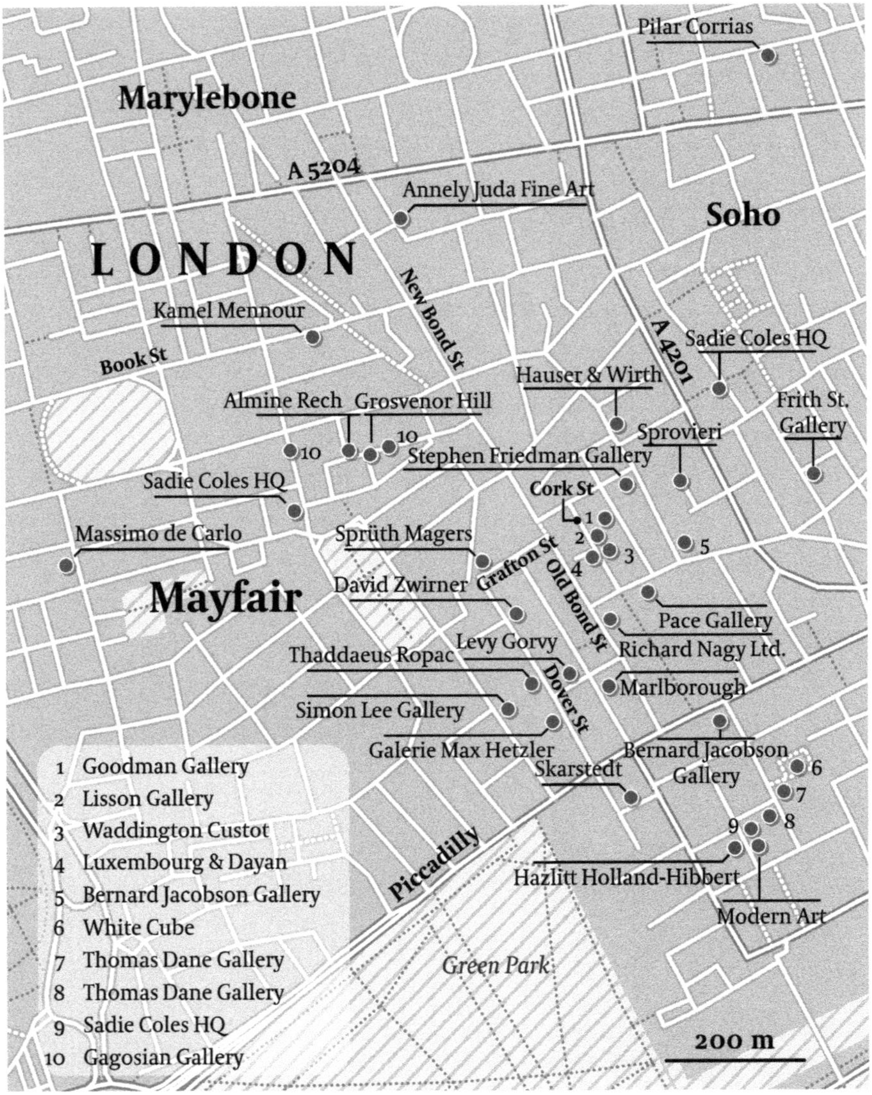

Location of contemporary art galleries established in Mayfair in London that participated in the "Galleries" sector of the Art Basel fair in 2019.

giants that run their British outfits from their Chelsea headquarters—Gagosian, Pace, David Zwirner, and Hauser & Wirth—joined the ranks of such prestigious London galleries as White Cube, Lisson, Victoria Miro, and Blain/Southern (until this last gallery closed in 2020). They were later joined by European heavy hitters like Thaddaeus Ropac, Sprüth Magers, and Almine Rech. Unlike the Marais in Paris, Mayfair is also home to the headquarters of major auction houses. In recent years, Mayfair has only further reinforced its dominant status. In November 2020, even though it was based in Burlington Gardens in London, an address shared by the Royal Academy of Arts since 2012, the Pace gallery (which got its start in London on Lexington Street) announced in autumn 2021 that it would take over the former premises of its colleague Blain/Southern (which, as previously mentioned, had closed). Thus, it extended its influence by occupying a space of 8,600 square feet, still in the heart of Mayfair.

The recent evolution of the London scene is also characterized by a new popular peripheral settlement of galleries. It is not in the east of the city—as it had been for many years, nor is it in the west—but it has now, for years, been in the south. The alternative district for budding galleries on everyone's lips is that of the Peckham district; it is no coincidence that a journalist for the *New Statesman* entitled his piece covering the 2012 opening of Ropac's gallery in Pantin "the Peckham of Paris" (Citerni, 2018).

A possible indication of how the most unquestionably contemporary London galleries (those that are most integrated into the art scene) are currently concentrated and spatially distributed, is attempting to identify them based on their participation in art fairs. Valeria Gemelli did as much by taking a census of all the galleries in London—72 in total—that in 2016 or 2017 participated in at least one of the following events: the three fairs organized by Art Basel at the time (in Basel, Miami Beach, and Hong Kong), Frieze, Art Brussels, and Art Cologne[31] (Gemelli, 2020). The London conurbation was then divided into five main zones: the center, east, west, north, and south.[32]

Strikingly, most of the galleries included in the study—52 out of 72, three quarters of them—were located in London's central zone, with the highest concentrations in the neighborhoods of Mayfair, Soho, and Marylebone. The second most represented zone was East London, with 15 galleries (20 percent of all London galleries). In this traditionally working-class environment (one of the poorest areas in the entire city), urban regeneration has given rise to neighborhoods such as Shoreditch and Hackney, which have now become fashionable, after which establishing a contemporary art gallery in these areas would no longer appear incongruous in the slightest. The central and east zones alone represent 90 percent of the galleries included in the study; the five remaining galleries were all located in the south zone of London, with the west appearing merely to be a mirage, with entities that did not have access to international fairs (or at least those taken into account for the study).

As in the two examples of Paris and New York that were previously analyzed in more detail, there is also a high concentration of galleries in London's urban space. Over time, the city has had a clearly identified and particularly stable artistic center, (i.e., Mayfair) with outlying districts that regularly change locations; however, nowadays the East End seems to have managed to earn its place on the London gallery scene as an alternative location, mostly for smaller galleries.

Berlin: a gallery scene that is relatively behind compared to other major international cities

As with London, I decided not to go into great detail regarding Berlin's art scene; essentially, this is because, unlike the three prominent cities presented above—Paris, New York, and London—Berlin is part of a much less monocentric national scene that characterizes Germany. Of course, there are many other cities, outside of New York, in the United States with a real contemporary art scene—Los Angeles being foremost among them—however, even in this case, there is an extremely pronounced imbalance between Los Angeles and New York, whose influence is overwhelming.

While the United States (and New York in particular) has the highest concentration by far of preeminent contemporary galleries in the world, in Europe it is Germany that is home to the highest number of distinguished galleries. However, the trajectory of the art market was severely shaken by the Second World War, whose effects were catastrophic in more ways than one. Not only was the national economy devastated after the war, but the country lost most of the great art dealers of the time, most of whom were of the Jewish faith (Zwirner, 2019). After the war, galleries gradually began to emerge once again in the Ruhr area; however, the reunification of the country after the fall of the Berlin Wall in 1989 caused the tables to turn. Many major galleries were founded in Berlin, or existing establishments left the towns where they originated to move to Berlin, or else opened a second branch in the capital city. Since then, Berlin has cemented itself as being essential for sales on the primary art market, and its influence extends beyond national borders. During the 2017 Art Basel fair, the number of Berlin galleries amounted to 21 (even more than the Parisian galleries, which totaled 19). This impressive turnout of Berlin galleries may seem paradoxical; essentially, while Berlin has no fewer than 6,000 visual artists, it would appear that the city is nonetheless largely devoid of collectors. As this Swiss gallerist confided to me during the COVID-19 pandemic: "I'm fairly pessimistic about the model that fairs are following, and even more about the future of the galleries that make their living off of them because they don't have a local client base, particularly Berlin galleries. It's not even worth listing off names, it's going to hurt." With the exception of the important Hoffmann and Boros collections (the latter is on display in a converted former bunker), Berlin has few significant collections (it is important to keep in mind that the German capital is a poor city). The market is characterized by a large number of galleries—some of which are famous—but with a weak presence of international heavyweights, and an anemic local clientele.[33]

Unlike the Marais in Paris, Chelsea in New York, or Mayfair in London, there is not a single district in Berlin that is home to the city's main contemporary art galleries; the city is notably more polycentric. Traditionally, art galleries were located in the central historic neighborhood of Mitte, which has retained a considerable number of its galleries along with Berlin's main center for contemporary art: the KW. However, there are currently two other areas that compete directly with Mitte: its main rival, the neighborhood of Kreuzberg, in the south of the city; and the more recent Potsdamer Strasse in Schöneberg to the west, very close to the Neue Nationalgalerie. Finally, in the elegant neighborhood of Charlottenburg, even further west, there is a handful of other galleries. As Berlin is a city with surprisingly fluid vehicular traffic, residents often travel by car, and most galleries therefore have parking spaces. Galleries are often located a fair distance from one another, which can be a deterrent for pedestrians; especially since people literally have to get lost in the labyrinth of back alleys to find them, as very few look out onto the street. When the spaces are not located on a courtyard (sometimes they are tucked into the back of a building through second or third courtyards), the space is occasionally located on an upper floor of a building, making it virtually impossible for non-insiders to access.

Of the 20-odd "major" Berlin galleries, four of them—Sprüth Magers, Konrad Fischer, Koenig, and Judin—stand out due to their truly spectacular spaces. Sprüth Magers has a remarkable space in the middle of the Mitte neighborhood, including a cavernous main room. Much more isolated from its counterparts, the Konrad Fischer gallery occupies the entirety of a small building. Also well away from the rest of the galleries is the Koenig gallery, situated in an unprepossessing area filled with social housing; the gallery took over an old church with brutalist concrete architecture and an immense nave that was transformed into a magnificent exhibition space. However, in order to justify the size of this space, the gallery needs to feature artists that produce works in very large formats. Until the closure of the Blain/Southern gallery in 2020, its Berlin branch shared the space in a former printing press with its fellow gallery, Judin, which had equally impressive proportions (especially the height of the ceiling).

However, it is worth pointing out one particularity of the Berlin gallery scene: more than anywhere else in the world—especially in New York, London, or Paris—galleries often organize exhibitions "for their image," displaying artworks that are difficult to sell. This is even the case during the Berlin Gallery Weekend, during which collectors are much more likely to come to the city, especially those coming from further away. Essentially, in Berlin, given the lack of strong local demand, many establishments are de facto "fair" galleries: their main objective is to continue to be selected for the most important international art fairs in order to be in contact with buyers, who are not in abundance on a local level. For instance, the famous Esther Schipper gallery makes no secret of the fact that fairs represent more than 60 percent of its annual income (it participates in around 10 fairs every year).[34] This explains the general care afforded to the interior design of exhibition spaces (high, perfectly white walls and spot rails, overhead natural lighting, polished concrete floor), as it is a question of winning over other professionals in the artistic sector. Ultimately, the Berlin gallery scene presents itself as a mix of characteristics shared with the other main international cities in terms of galleries; and an urban space with weak local demand, which is singular and somewhat paradoxical for a large metropolitan area that is home to many artists. It tends to present attributes that are similar to those of "fair" galleries in small towns, which completely bypass the necessity of strategic geographical location thanks to the demand that is essentially generated outside of their own space.

A few notes on the spatial concentration of galleries in cities outside of the West or in the Southern Hemisphere

I could have wrapped up this overview by also developing other examples outside of the Western world or in the Southern hemisphere in detail; however, the local scenes are much smaller than in the previous cases. In Russia, Moscow stands as a good example of geographical gallery distribution on a scene and market that are both peripheral[35] and embryonic; here again, the principle of clustered contemporary galleries is prevalent; as evidenced by the brownfield of Winzavod, created some 15 years ago. Very close to the center of Moscow, right next to a metro station, it is nestled in between railroad tracks in an urban space utterly devoid of charm. While the agglomeration claims to have 11 contemporary art galleries in a small leaflet (published in Russian and English and offered free of charge), some of these spaces are in reality more involved in the chromos market. Very few institutions meet the prevailing presentational standards for the international scene, and their positioning evokes that of Berlin's alternative galleries. This testifies to the extreme weakness of the local market. In reality, despite the city's cluster, the two galleries that are much more contemporary than all the others, Pop/off/art and Regina, are quite isolated among less properly contemporary establishments.

Another case that could have been developed, here due to the dynamism of its national gallery scene, is that of Brazil. São Paulo has long been a dynamic metropolitan area for contemporary art galleries. Somewhat surprisingly, it is the Vila Madalena district that is most associated with this kind of activity, even if few galleries are situated there (with the exception, however, of the famous galleries Millan and Fortes Vilaça, which later became Fortes d'Aloia & Gabriel, until it abandoned its space for the very peripheric district of Galpao), all of which are more or less on a main thoroughfare, Rua Fradique Coutinho. In reality, it is the upscale neighborhood of Jardins that is home to most galleries (including the historic Luisa Strina). As this district's social image has already been associated with a bourgeois environment for a long time (both commercial and residential), its nonetheless objective association with contemporary art galleries is manifestly less strong than in the previously mentioned neighborhood, whose image was more malleable. Here as well, it is clear how the objective urban space is reinterpreted in a subjective manner (Chombart de Lauwe, 1956), not only individually, but collectively as well. Other than the two previous areas, there is a multitude of more isolated entities in many parts of the city. As far as Rio de Janeiro is concerned, over the past 10 years, the gallery scene has been shifting toward the lagoon (having previously and for a long time been fragmented) in the neighborhoods of Ipanema, Leblon, and, above all, Gavea and Jardim Botânico, with the jockey club site.

In Hong Kong, the H Queens tower, designed by the famous Hong Kong architect William Lin in the heart of the Central neighborhood, was deliberately created to accommodate artistic establishments, contemporary art galleries in particular. The concentration of these galleries is such that the tower is sometimes referred to as the "Vertical Chelsea." The biggest international galleries—like David Zwirner, Hauser & Wirth, and Pace, as well as other famous establishments like Pearl Lam Galleries, Whitestone Gallery, and Tang Contemporary Art—flocked to the building. Close by, the Gagosian and Lehmann Maupin galleries moved into spaces in the Pedder Building. Other major galleries are concentrated, for the most part, not far from this area. Again, it is the model of concentration that prevails, especially in a city as constrained as Hong Kong in terms of property.

Conclusion

My previous analyses of the biggest metropolitan areas for contemporary art galleries—New York, London, Paris, and to a lesser extent, Berlin; with some additional observations on more marginal or peripheral scenes—demonstrate that, as long as the city is important enough, a model tends to come into effect. There is generally a center that is clearly identified as the most desirable and the most legitimate, which tends to have the highest concentration of galleries that want to establish and cultivate their social qualification as noteworthy establishments. This area is fairly stable over time, even if it emerged as the result of a historical milestone. Often, smaller galleries that take more radical positions in order to stand out will try to find a social space away from this artistic nucleus that is simultaneously relatively affordable and capable of representing their avant-garde stance in the domain (Bourdieu & Delsaut, 1975; Bourdieu, 1987). However, it is clear that these attempts are accompanied by a significant amount of instability, for two main reasons: first, these organizations are often in a precarious situation, and if they were to disappear they could bring about the end of a potential new contemporary art gallery district that would have competed with the dominant neighborhood. Second, for the galleries that do manage to succeed, they generally tend to eventually migrate toward the dominant neighborhood, but not before frequent attempts to disqualify it as being too established, too conformist (when the gallery did not yet have the means to settle there) (Bourdieu & Delsaut, 1975). A gallerist interviewed at the turn of the millennium, when his gallery was located on the outskirts of his city (and who today runs a large international gallery) exemplified this point:

> Really, I have no interest in moving to the [dominant neighborhood], I'm not interested in what they do there. I'm not saying it's not good, or that it's not as good as what I do, but I just wouldn't feel like I belonged there. It's very conventional, I shouldn't say that, but I think it's very bourgeois, what they sell there.

Some years later, due to his success, this professional nevertheless ultimately migrated to the neighborhood that he had previously denigrated, and opened a superb space (the peripheral area where he had previously developed his business has since disappeared as a gallery district).

If we review all of the successive analyses of the spatial phenomena that prevail in the cities studied in this chapter, a structuralist model seems to best represent how contemporary art gallery scenes operate on a metropolitan level. There is a recurring opposition between a center that is home to most of the established institutions (and other, smaller galleries that are looking to benefit from this proximity by settling in the same urban space as the most legitimate establishments), and galleries located on the periphery of the main neighborhood that are largely built in symbolic opposition to the center. Outside of the gallery, which is fundamental and presents strong permanent traits, the neighborhood itself matters slightly less, at least in the sense that it can shift. This is clearly evidenced by the successive migrations of art districts, particularly those that are geographical outliers, and which appear much more vulnerable and transitory than the centers; another common characteristic among the various cities that were analyzed in this chapter.

3

Galleries and international art fairs: The success of a relatively deterritorialized system

While biennials are the old guard of artistic events, with the Venice Biennale[1] (the oldest of these events) dating back to the 19th century, art fairs are much newer, in existence since the 1960s. Today, these two kinds of events are quite different from one another. Unlike fairs, biennials are not commercial exhibitions;[2] however, this was not always the case. Essentially, when it was created in 1895, the Venice Biennale had a sales office. When studying this topic after the Second World War, at a time when the office was directed by the gallerist Ettore Gian Ferrari, Clarissa Ricci discerned the origin of fairs that later appeared in Europe in the past commercial activity of the principal biennial in the world. This office, whose commercial function was denigrated during the events of May 1968 (when a group of predominantly young people led protests throughout France to criticize the capitalist system), nevertheless managed to survive until 1973. This was due to the fact that the Italian art market had been, in part, sustained up to that point by the dynamic created by the transactions made at the Venice Biennale's sales office (Ricci, 2010).[3]

However, it was not until 1967 that the first art fair in the world to specialize in modern and contemporary art was created in Cologne, entitled Kölner Kunstmarkt or Kunstmarkt Köln, according to various sources (Oberste-Hetbleck, 2014; Zwirner, 2019). The event was launched by the Verein progressiver deutscher Kunsthändler (the Association of Progressive German Art Dealers). The aim was to promote Germany's art sector and its artists, and to establish a new center for the art market in post-war Germany (Zwirner, 2019). As the fair had been reserved solely for members of the organizing association, it quickly faced competition from other initiatives in the same region, i.e. the Ruhr (Oberste-Hetbleck, 2014). Even more significantly, in 1970, the city of Basel in Switzerland reproduced the initiative, later becoming the number one event in the world; even to this day, Art Basel is the uncontested leader in a domain that has become practically indispensable for contemporary art galleries.

A method of organizing fairs that is sometimes overlooked

Somewhat surprisingly, even for art enthusiasts, fairs are still sometimes confused with biennials and their respective organizational procedures are often obscure.

While biennials generally take place once every two years and last for several months, fairs are annual and last four to five days (including the first day, which is reserved for professionals and other VIPs). Every year, in each city, they are organized at the same time of year.

Biennials feature artists who are chosen by one or several curators, whereas for fairs it is the galleries that are selected. As a rule of thumb, these galleries must first pay a few hundred euros (often around €400 or €500) to submit their application to the fair, which will be reviewed by a selection committee that is typically composed solely (or mostly) of gallerists designated by the commercial entity that manages the fair. This peer selection method guarantees an excellent familiarity with the professional domain, but it can entail some conflicts of interest. Hence, as explained by this European gallerist during an informal conversation about what goes on behind the scenes of certain selection procedures:

> For one year, we participated in Art Brussels, then [X, the director of an international gallery] joined the selection committee, and the problem is that we have an artist in common [Y, a superstar of contemporary art], but they have to pay 10% of their sales to [X]'s New York gallery, while we're not required to do that, because we have a history with them. So we can sell the artist's pieces for a slightly lower price than they can. For him, obviously, he's worked it somehow so that we wouldn't be selected anymore, because if we were both at the same fair, he wouldn't have any chance of selling this artist's work. That's how it goes, these selection committees are the judges, and they're being judged. Me, I could easily get onto the fair's selection committee in my city, and I could make a deal with galleries not to block them as long as they grant me access to fairs where they are on the selection committee. But it's so much work, it takes time to do all that.

Another gallerist mentioned these same competitive relationships—here referring to the past—to explain why a gallery was not participating in a fair in its own city, even though logically it should have been included:

> [S], her gallery is really good, it has a super roster of artists, she makes the effort to really display them, it's not just to boost her website. Her gallery's space isn't bad at all, and in a really good area . . . well, there's absolutely no reason for her not to be accepted [to the biggest fair in her city], except that once, she made herself an enemy of a fellow gallerist who can now directly intervene in any selection committees that follow. In fact, she had poached one of the other gallerist's main collectors, who regularly bought pieces from her, and who was vital for the gallery's success. One day, he went to go make a purchase at [S]. Just between us, I'm sure that that's why [S] was rejected by the fair, because other than that there's no reason. And then, applying a certain amount of arbitrariness when choosing galleries, for people who are a little devious, they say that it's good, it reinforces their power by scaring galleries and telling them that they'd better not make any wrong steps.

Whether or not it is true, this analysis demonstrates that the selection procedure, similar as it is to a competitive context, is not exempt from interferences that cause it to deviate from the selection criteria normally in effect.

If we disregard the previous influences, the decisions are nevertheless supposed to be based on the components of the application: the gallery that wants to participate in the fair presents its identity, i.e. its "line"; the roster of artists that it represents, and the presentation that it wants to display during the fair, with the creators that will be featured, and the manner in which the booth's space (with particular emphasis on the picture rails) will be arranged.

The judgment issued by the selection committee (Misdrahi Flores, 2013) may seem harsh for the galleries whose applications are rejected, especially if up to that point they had regularly been accepted for the event, and are later turned away in favor of new choices. The tense relationships that this produces between galleries and fairs is clearly illustrated in the following press release issued via email in October 2019, a few days before the opening of the FIAC art fair in Paris. The French gallery in question, which is shown to have been rejected, breaks the news by trying to reframe the matter: naturally, it would not be able to participate in the fair that year, as it insisted on not being made to go against its values. It also took care to highlight its investment in an art scene outside of France (in California, renowned internationally for its creativity):

> **FIAC 2019: Praz-Delavallade will not participate in the 2019 FIAC fair at the Grand Palais.**
>
> Our absence can be explained by our refusal to change our initial presentation despite Jennifer Flay's[4] mediation. It was a difficult decision to make, attached as we are to the French scene, but our reorientation (particularly toward California) has allowed us to explore other artistic scenes. We are proud to support artists of many generations, some of whom are internationally recognized, others who are still on their path

> toward greatness, and the youngest among them who represent an exhilarating continuum. We have therefore decided to reserve our energy and our resources for other activities to promote our new recruits, and we will be highlighting several of them in the 2019–2020 season.

A gallery being rejected by a fair in which it had participated in previous years is all the more brutal since, in general, the admission process is simplified when a gallery has already been accepted for that fair before. Typically, the gallery merely announces what it will be presenting, with very little oversight, making the first admission very important. Sometimes, a gallery may be placed on a waiting list as a kind of first step before being admitted to the main sector of the fair.

The galleries selected by the committee will then pay a fee that is usually proportionate to the surface area of their booths. The rates are highly variable depending on the event. The general price per square meter for a booth was around €300 in 2017 at Art Cologne, making it a very affordable fair, while the cost was nearly €700 for the FIAC in Paris; however, this is in turn far less than the $1,000 for the Armory Show in New York (these last two events are much more expensive, but grant access to the most dynamic segment of the art market).

The buildings hosting the various fairs can accommodate booths that are more or less spacious, which also has an effect on the prices. At the fair in Bologna, which is a fairly modest event, a booth costs around €20,000. At Art Stage Singapore, a lower-ranking fair with a mostly "regional" audience (Quemin, 2001 and 2002), the average price in 2018 to rent a booth ranged between €20,000 and €35,000. At the major fairs, the rates are much higher. In 2017, the largest booth at the Armory Show cost $77,500, and the largest booth at Art Basel Miami Beach or Art Basel Hong Kong was around $100,000. In Basel, the booths were also around €100,000.[5] When the price for a booth is very high, galleries cannot really afford to take any risks, and visitors to these fairs have virtually no chance of discovering young artists; moreover, the presentations are generally oriented around artists and conventions that are already recognized on the market, so that the gallery may break even.

Recently, fairs were alerted to the sometimes prohibitive expense of participating in their events for galleries whose financial resources were limited. This runs the risk of resulting in a certain amount of monotony in the art being featured; as such, in 2018, the FIAC reviewed the gallery pricing policy for its 45th fair, ultimately becoming less financially demanding for small and midsize galleries. As Jennifer Flay, the event's artistic director, explained in a press release:

> The FIAC brings together exhibitors from different sectors of the market. There is a significant gap between the possible benefits for prominent galleries that are featuring successful artists, and the smaller galleries that

support less established artists. We are aware of this difficulty, which is only made more acute by the constrained market context for this emerging sector, and we have conducted a review throughout 2017, resulting in this modification. It is our intent to maintain this modification. Much remains to be done to fortify the future of our participating galleries.

In broad strokes, the price modulation was as follows:[6]

- For booths with a small surface area, the FIAC lowered its cost per square meter by 5 percent. The price for this category became €550/sq.m. (€55/sq.ft.) in 2018.
- For larger booths, the FIAC raised its cost per square meter by 2.2 percent on average. The price for this category reached €650/sq.m. (€65/sq.ft.).
- For up-and-coming galleries, the cost per square meter in the Lafayette Sector remained the same, at €290/sq.m (€29/sq.ft.). This very preferential rate was made possible thanks to the patronage of the Galeries Lafayette Group[7] ("Lafayette Sector").[8]

The price differences between the small booths (intended for the less developed galleries) and the large booths may seem altogether minimal, but it is important to keep in mind that, in general, it is in the fair's best interest to attract the largest galleries, as this will broadcast a statement as to the event's quality. The objective to ensure a certain amount of diversity among the exhibitors, especially with lesser-known galleries, is therefore secondary. However, the tendency toward modulating the costs for booths by making them slightly more affordable for less established participants is beginning to spread, as leading fairs including the Armory Show (in spring 2018) and Art Basel Miami Beach (in December 2019) also implemented a pricing system similar to that presented above, to be more accessible for small and midsize galleries.

It should be noted that differential pricing also allows fair organizers to influence what will be exhibited during the fair beyond the selection phase of rejecting or accepting applications. The establishments that agree to display what is expected from them by the fair's selection committee can sometimes receive a preferential rate. Such was the case at the 2018 Armory Show for the Focus sector, which was dedicated to presentations with one or two "less known" (sic) contemporary artists, presenting pieces within the theme "Art and Technology." This sector was curated by Gabriel Ritter, from the Minneapolis Institute of Art.

The cost of participating in fairs is an important element to consider, as it tends to directly influence the presentations (both the artworks and the design of the booth), as indicated by this international gallerist in 2017 during the Armory Show (which, as previously mentioned, is a particularly expensive fair):

> I think it's great that the debate on the direct consequence of the cost of booths on the quality of the presentation has been raised. Basically, we're always likely to display more audacious pieces at less expensive fairs. But it's not just a question of renting the space, it goes beyond that. The cost of lighting is also something that directly impacts the presentation, since at the Armory Show we don't tend to order enough lighting fixtures, and we can't even use our own spotlights, it's forbidden. It's the law in America with the unions, they're the ones who have to provide us with all the spotlights, and it's astronomically expensive! So obviously, galleries tend to light their stands less to save money.

Moreover, the price of booths (and the compounded costs of designing them), which is already a significant amount on its own, is hardly the only expense of participating in fairs. Beyond the travel and accommodation costs for a gallery's staff, participating in these events can incur additional expenses, especially shipping the artworks (along with the insurance of this shipment), particularly when the fair takes place in a distant location.

This small Parisian gallery reported the collective costs of these fairs: "All in all, Art Paris[9] cost me something like €50,000, including the price of the booth, insurance, and transport. This year, I wanted to do a satellite fair in Miami Beach at the same time as the local Art Basel fair, and that tallied up to €70,000."

As this Paris professional who manages to attend fairs indicates, thanks to his gallery's audacious image: "For a small-to-midsize gallery like mine, a fair calls for a budget of around €50,000. That's not nothing, especially when you participate in more than one per year, as I do."

However, more than the price of the booths—or even more precisely, the sum of all the costs of participating in a fair—it is essential that these events turn a profit. Even in the small fairs whose exhibitors are mostly from the country hosting the event (or even the same city), some gallerists discuss the risk of participating in these events: "This year, at the [G] fair, there was no one. It's tough when you pay €12,000 for the booth and then you have to sell €24,000 worth of art!"[10]

"Breaking even" is an expression that is closely associated with this line of work. This Parisian gallerist explained it thus: "We don't do Art Brussels, even though it's a good fair and it would align with our objectives, since Belgian collectors are very faithful to their galleries. But it costs around €25,000, it's doable, but we wouldn't sell very much and it would probably take us four or five years to break even."

This famous gallery, with locations in Paris and Brussels, gave a similar rationale in terms of profitability:

> The fair where the gallery makes its highest profit margin is the FIAC, because the associated costs are fairly low for us, for Parisian galleries, since we're already here and we sell well at that fair. We also have many

> of our main collectors here. The second most important fair for us is Art Basel, since we can sell really expensive pieces there, and sometimes we earn more there than at the FIAC, but it's more random, we work with really high prices. After that is the Armory Show, but it has the disadvantage of being a very expensive fair. The rest of the ranking is kind of unstable, we have pieces that are fairly unique with prices that can be quite high, so it's somewhat random, the difference of selling one or two works can make a big difference, and we might sell a lot or not a lot at the same fair in different years.

While the decision to participate in some fairs may seem like a foregone conclusion, for others the choice is much riskier. It is clear from this interview extract that not all fairs are necessarily the best choice for all galleries (with the possible exception of Art Basel) (Quemin, 2013a).

In addition to the elevated costs of fairs, and the risk that comes along with some of them—especially for galleries that feature artworks at a lower price than their more established fellows—participating in fairs also entails significant human costs, particularly in terms of fatigue and impact on one's private life. This director of one of the largest international galleries explained:

> When I joined the gallery, I was very clear, I had to negotiate. Since I have two young children, I made sure that I wouldn't be sent to a lot of fairs, because that's a never-ending job, I wouldn't be at home very often, and this part of the job, I must say, isn't very compatible with having a family. You're always away from home if you work for a major gallery and if you do fairs. You don't have any private life, no more family time.

A former associate director of another gallery even mentioned the substances that some employees would take to cope with the exhaustion caused by fairs—something that I heard about on several occasions—and asserted that this would affect people with families much more, as they have a hard time maintaining the pace of participating in fairs non-stop:

> The professional life when working for a gallery can seem very glamorous, but it's hard. There's a real tension, especially when you do a lot of fairs, you never stop, it's year round now. That affects so many people, especially those with a family, they have to try to balance it with their job, and when you're participating in fairs you don't have much of a choice. Some of them have to do coke because if they don't, it's really hard to keep up the pace.

It is often the frenetic speed that is emphasized when discussing fairs, as illustrated by this European gallerist during a conversation in 2017:

> I mean, it's a hellish speed, this art world calendar with fairs that are so massive and so close together! It never ends. I think that more and more, people will choose events, fairs, and exhibitions, and then ultimately only participate in a handful of cherry-picked social events. I would bet that only the local events, or the super qualitative ones, will remain.

Unlike a gallery's usual image to the general public, the fact of being in charge of its sales functions is often presented as a physical undertaking, and attending the fair (even if traveling abroad and experiencing the exciting, intense dynamic may be a kind of compensation) is often reduced to "dirty work," to borrow the term coined by Everett C. Hughes (Hughes, 1984). As this comment regarding fatigue was regularly brought up during my conversations with professionals who participate in fairs, and as I mentioned in the foreword of this book on methodology, I followed the same frenetic pace as the staff of several major international galleries and attended a dozen fairs in the span of one year. This fieldwork was intended to allow me to physically experience what my interviewees went through.[11] It became clear to me that, in essence, one must have an iron constitution in order to participate non-stop in fairs, some with very short intervals between them, and some of which take place on different continents (for instance, the ARCO in Madrid and the Armory Show in New York, which take place over two successive weeks). After receiving visitors and negotiating with potential buyers over the course of five days, some gallery staff may even be obliged to stay longer to oversee the disassembly of the booth, or to go almost immediately to the next city to supervise the installation of the next one! If it is necessary to return home in the interval between fairs, this requires two plane trips,[12] with the possibility of jet lag, and each fair requires people to work in confined spaces (often without natural light, which exacerbates the fatigue even more). Frequently, women wear high heels, experiencing additional physical strain. However, gallery staff must always welcome clients with a smile, and switch between different languages at a moment's notice.

Nevertheless, despite the high financial costs and intense organizational and human tolls, fairs have become vital for galleries. As this contemporary art gallery veteran stated: "Fairs cost us excessive amounts of money, but it's a necessary element of our business." (Daniel Templon in "Les Templon, father-son gallerists," *La Gazette Drouot*, issue no. 2, January 17, 2020, p. 161). Another French gallerist, who has a location outside of Paris, and whose local demand is inevitably limited, made the same observation: "It's simple: today, when you're a contemporary art gallery, especially a midsize or a big one, you can't get away with not doing commercial expos or fairs anymore."

Finally, this German gallerist confirmed the previous comments:

- *What market evolutions have impacted you the most?*
- The most flagrant evolution is obviously the globalization of the contemporary art market. During the financial crisis in 2008, a lot of

> us thought that the first thing to disappear would be contemporary art fairs, they're too expensive. But the complete opposite ended up happening: we have to be present across all the markets.
>
> "Esther Schipper, gallerist: 'Berlin is less accessible to young artists, so it's gentrifying'", *Le Journal des Arts*, no. 524, May 24, 2019

This excerpt shows that even an economic crisis like that of 2008 did not put an end to fairs; on the contrary, they continued to prosper.

Why should galleries participate in fairs? When they were created at the end of the 1960s, and in the years that followed, fairs were designed, among other reasons, to combat the development of auction houses and to stop clients from abandoning galleries (Adam, 2014) by continuously being in touch with them. When galleries believe that they can potentially make significant sales at fairs, they see these events as important (or even essential); this is the case for some galleries more than for others. Issue number 1,470 of *Le Quotidien de l'art* (Art Daily) from April 4th, 2018 bore the headline "46% of sales at fairs,"[13] a number that must be considered with extreme reservation, like all transactions that take place outside of auctions. It can, however, constitute a very general order of magnitude, as some galleries admit to making 70 to 80 percent of their revenue at fairs, either during the event itself, or directly after having made new contacts during the event.

Alongside the sustained increase in the number of fairs, it is also and above all the gallery's involvement in these events that has seen a spectacular growth over the past 20 years, and particularly in the past 15 years (Quemin, 2013a).[14] As such, in 2008, the all-round champion of participating in fairs was the Viennese Galerie Krinzinger, which made 12 annual presentations. Its fellow French gallery, Yvon Lambert, came in second with nine fairs. Fifteen years ago, these two numbers were extremely impressive; at the time, only five galleries participated in over seven fairs during the 41 events of a certain caliber that I included in my research, and only 101 of them were involved in at least five fairs during the year (Quemin, 2013a). Generally speaking, the massive American galleries participated in at least three events, as they felt obligated to maintain their position on the market; however, they were not the most active out of all the galleries, assuming that their own spaces would be sufficient to sell their pieces and reach new clients. The space itself and its geographical location (discussed in the first and second chapters of this book, respectively) seemed to be adequate resources to justify declining the opportunities offered by fairs. Nowadays, the previously mentioned numbers hardly seem conceivable; today, nearly all of the largest international galleries participate in at least 10 or 12 fairs per year, or even 20!

Over a span of 10 years, fairs have in fact literally imposed themselves on the international contemporary art scene, and have become a foundational element of (and completely intertwined with) a gallery's operations, now regularly punctuating their event calendars and representing a major component of their sales strategy. Fairs are the best way to find new clients, and they play a decisive role in developing the range of contacts and operations that ultimately results in the sale of artworks. This director of a large gallery with locations in Paris and Brussels explained:

> In 2002, when I started working for Gallery [X], we did three fairs per year: the FIAC, Art Basel, and Chicago, that was all. Today, the fair system is completely internationalized, the schedule is designed with all the fairs in mind, and it's now almost impossible to compare two very good fairs with each other, to say where a sale was concluded: we make a new contact at one fair, and that can turn into a transaction at another fair or in one of our galleries in Paris or Brussels (...). We did 15 fairs last year, we're going to do 12 this year. It's a real system that helps us stay in contact with collectors.

Fairs have now become so crucial for a midsize or large gallery's business that it is increasingly difficult to evaluate their impact in terms of sales. As this director of a large gallery confirmed:

> It's very difficult to say what percentage of our business is accounted for by fairs, even though we do around 15 per year and we're very present in this domain. I would say that generally, very generally, it's a 50/50 split between fairs and sales in our own spaces. But there are clients who we see or who we meet at fairs who don't buy anything at that moment, we sell them a piece later on. And conversely, there are other clients who regularly come to our galleries who never buy anything, and then one day they come to one of our stands at a fair and then they buy something!

This associate of a midsize gallery concurred: fairs spread awareness of her gallery and help her reach new potential clients, but she does not necessarily make any sales during the event:

> Fairs expect galleries to take risks, to put on solo shows, to entrust their booths to curators. Our colleague [X] keeps putting together his booths like we did in the 1990s, showing what he wants to sell, a little of all his artists, one piece only from each, even though booths are becoming more like a display case for the gallery, it allows us to cultivate an image. We don't necessarily sell anything at the fair, but we need to arouse interest so we can sell pieces later.

Fairs are first and foremost ideal opportunities to access the market. They also thrive on the fact that (at least for some galleries) they can generate a different kind of sale, particularly those with higher prices, by affording smaller and midsize galleries access to more well-off collectors. When they are selected, they are therefore in contact with clients of the largest establishments, thanks to the proximity of the various booths. As this French gallerist explained in 2017: "A midsize gallery like mine, we do 7 or 8 fairs a year, it's essential, especially when we can sell pieces at a fair for a higher price than to collectors who come into our gallery."

The nearly indispensable nature of fairs for galleries (or at least, for those that do not intend to remain very small), is particularly evident in the closure of the large gallery Blain/Southern in February 2020, even though it had a clearly international scope, with locations in London, Berlin, and New York. It had been founded 10 years earlier by two experienced partners: Harry Blain—who remained the head of the gallery until its closure—and Graham Southern—who had left the previous autumn. One of the reasons that the gallery failed may have been its inability to gain access to fairs, as its founders had previously presided on the board of the Haunch of Venison gallery, which was excluded from fairs due to its financial connection to an auction house,[15] having been bought out in 2007 by Christie's.[16] The causal relationship between a gallery's closure and the responsibility of the fair system is also illustrated in the following example, though at a much lower level of the market: in June 2019, this gallerist who was working at the time in Lyon, the second-largest city in France, and fairly isolated from international fairs, was forced to close down his business. He explained that he lost his clientele because of the fair system that virtually depleted local markets: "I was offering affordable prices, with popular artists. And yet, I couldn't turn a profit. Collectors are mobile, they buy a lot at fairs, and they're hard to pin down." (Paul Ripoche, in *Le Journal des Arts*, December 16, 2019).

The following interview with a gallerist whose business got its start in Los Angeles, and who now has a second space in Paris, clearly shows that fairs are a crucial means of supplementing local demand by granting access to a larger pool of collectors; it does, however, also emphasize the risky nature of fairs:

- *How is the market in Los Angeles doing?*
- There are far more collectors now than when we started. But intrinsically, Los Angeles is facing the same problems as all the other cities. The operational costs like rent, salaries, etc. are getting very high. Galleries can't make a living from their natural catchment area alone, so they must imperatively grow larger. This means participating in fairs or opening new spaces. Since the market is global, you can't rely solely on local collectors.
- *Does that mean that you'll definitely have to expand into other countries?*
- It means that you have to constantly take risks, make new bets. You know, even though we took a reckless risk by opening a second space, when you stop and think about it, it's the same as participating in a fair. The annual rent for a space in a major city is identical to the

> price for a midsize booth at any fair. (...) Galleries are jeopardizing their existence if even a single fair goes sideways for them.
>
> Robbie Fitzpatrick, *La Gazette Drouot*, no. 16, April 20, 2018, pp. 14-15

A certain sense of reservation is perceptible in the following remark from Paula Cooper, a prominent New York gallerist[17] whose activity has never evolved to mega-gallery status. Even though she has been very successful, she has not developed her business in a manner that would suggest purely commercial aims:

> Contemporary art fairs have proliferated. They are essential nowadays. It's a real problem right now, since they eclipse galleries, and collectors tend to concentrate on fairs more than on galleries. When I started, I didn't participate in any art fairs. I visited Art Basel on my own, and it was marvelous just to be able to walk around. I participated in the first FIAC (Foire Internationale d'Art Contemporain [International Contemporary Art Fair]) in 1974, and 15 years later I'm participating in Art Basel. All in all, we went to three or four fairs every year: Art Basel in Basel—which was the most successful—Miami, and the FIAC. This year, for the first time, we're trying Art Basel Hong Kong with a selection of artists from the gallery, including Cecily Brown and Atsuko Tanaka, since the Hong Kong scene is very active, especially with the arrival of galleries like Perrotin, David Zwirner, and Pace.
>
> "Paula Cooper 'The competition has become extremely tough, overwhelming, maddening,'" *Le Journal des Arts*, no. 520, March 29, 2019

As the following international gallerist indicated in 2019, fairs are conducive to sales because they create an effect of concentrated supply,[18] which attracts an internalized demand, but also because they induce competition between buyers;[19] a phenomenon that is further reinforced by their short-term nature:

> This year, at the FIAC, we sold really well. But it's clear that, more and more, businessmen and CEOs don't have the time to run around and visit all the galleries, to see all the vernissages, they're paying more and more attention to what fair booths offer. If you feature good pieces, they buy them quickly. If they don't buy it, they know that another collector might!

Many gallerists report that vernissages at fairs bring competition to a fever pitch, and collectors are therefore more encouraged to decide quickly and not to negotiate the price as much! As this director of one of the largest galleries in the world explained:

> There could obviously be exceptions, but in general, at fairs, we sell quite well during the first two days, it's the most important time for us because we can sell at high prices. The last day is different; we still make sales, but it's people who have come to take a stab at proposing their own prices for the pieces that haven't been sold yet! Clearly we can't tell them that these pieces will go quickly because they're in demand, and they know that shipping them back to our country will be expensive for us, so they sometimes make bids that are fairly aggressive in terms of price. But the first two days at fairs, those can be periods of really intense sales. And we also make a lot of contacts.

Not only are fairs the best means of staying in touch with one's collectors because they allow galleries to take advantage of the incentive effect of cultural events (which was identified long ago in the context of museums [Bourdieu & Darbel, 1997]), but they are also the best place to reach new clients. This international gallerist emphasizes the function that allows him to further build his list of contacts: "As a shop window, it allows you to reach a broad and very diverse public who wouldn't necessarily come into your gallery—one of the fundamental aspects of an art fair is meeting people who you can later go see and create a relationship." (*Artnet News*, "Former Christie's Rainmaker Brett Gorvy on How He's Creating a New Power Center in the Gallery World," June 12, 2017).

Similarly, at the end of 2020, this gallerist with locations in three countries highlighted the gap in the market caused by fair cancellations; explaining how essential they were in acquiring new clients:

> We have been missing fairs a lot since the beginning of the COVID-19 pandemic. We're doing well, we're selling a decent amount, but we're not expanding our clientele, and with a business like ours you need a client base. We have to constantly be in search of new clients, expanding our clientele if possible, because inevitably, we always lose some of our clients, so we have to replace them if we don't want to lose momentum. In previous years, we increased our client base by 10 to 20%, but with the pandemic, that's no longer the case, and one thing is clear: we're not meeting any new clients any more, like none. Fairs were essential for that. And it's a big problem for a gallerist's business.

This established French collector explained how she got her start in the year 2000, and indicates that it was at a fair that she first made contact with a gallery, of which she later became a regular client:

> Before, I took my family to galleries on the Left Bank [of Paris] every weekend, but I didn't really buy anything. And then, at some point, I wanted to buy a piece by Garouste, so I went to Templon's gallery, and he invited me to have dinner with him and his life partner[20] in New York.

> Later, I bought pieces from both of them. As I became more familiar with contemporary art and galleries, I discovered the existence of the Ropac gallery and how great it was, but I didn't really dare to go there. Who was I to try to buy anything from them? We finally became acquainted at an art fair with one of their directors, who wanted to sell me a sketch. After that, I bought regularly from them, the prices were already pretty high, but still not as much as they are now, seeing how they've grown, what with the development of their artists' careers.

Furthermore, fairs have become indispensable for many establishments, as they generate an effect of qualification by certifying (Moulin & Quemin, 1993) the credibility and quality of participating galleries. However, it is important to note that this qualifying function is bilateral: what is a good gallery? Today, broadly speaking, it is an establishment that participates in the best fairs. Conversely, what is a good fair? It is essentially an event that hosts the most renowned galleries. It is for this exact reason that artistic directors for international fairs travel the world each year attempting to convince the best (Misdrahi Flores, 2013) galleries to participate in their event. There is a real sense of canvassing, and not all potential clients are considered equal. Fairs can therefore agree to the conditions set by potential participants that they hope to entice, such as reduced booth prices or the promise of being assigned the best booth locations, in order to ensure their presence. Essentially, while the price per square foot is generally homogenous, some locations inside the exhibition hall are more sought-after, as they offer better visibility and are more desirable. As such, booths on the corner of the central aisles are generally particularly coveted, whereas the stations situated on the edge of the building hosting the event are less desirable. Galleries are fully aware of this fact,[21] and this plays a role in the overall process of negotiation. As this associate of an international gallery put it:

> Fairs and galleries, it's a little complicated because, even for a fair like Frieze New York, it sends an image about participating galleries, but at the same time, this image is constructed by the participants. This fair is expensive, and at the same time, we don't sell much after the first two hours of the opening, so more and more people are having a hard time deciding whether to go, or may not even go. For us, the fair's director called us five times to ask if we would be coming back, but why would we go to Frieze New York if we're not good enough for Frieze London? We explained that we want both, or nothing at all! Fairs provide the best conditions for the galleries that they want. You have to negotiate for a really good location or a massive discount. We galleries also bring something to fairs.

The relationship between galleries and fairs therefore appears broadly to be one of power, or even of force.

Fairs are even more crucial for galleries located in cities or even countries where the local contemporary art market is weak (Fournier & Roy-Valex, 2002; Gabriel, 2007). In this case, galleries are therefore often obliged to accede to all of a fair's demands. This explains how the Viennese gallery Krinzinger found itself (as previously mentioned) at the head of the ranking mentioned in this chapter on the galleries that were most active in the main contemporary art fairs of the world that were held in 2008 (Quemin, 2013a). In essence, the galleries with the deepest pockets (particularly those located in the largest international contemporary art centers, foremost of which is the Chelsea neighborhood in New York) are much less dependent on fairs, and for a long time they showed a certain amount of disdain for them. Participating in fairs to a limited extent also allowed them to flaunt their influence; however, as these events continued to grow, market heavyweights had a change of heart and began to invest extensively in fairs. As such, in 2018, the gallery Gagosian returned to the Armory Show after having been absent since 2013, and its fellow gallery, Perrotin, did the same for the first time since 2011; as did (to a lesser degree of renown) Regen Projects, which had last participated in 2015. In a previous study conducted in 2008, I found that galleries in general participated in (far) fewer fairs and that the largest institutions, the mega-galleries (particularly those with a flagship gallery in New York) were not the biggest investors in fairs (Quemin, 2013a). However, the situation has greatly evolved since then. These major institutions believed that they already had sufficient access to the most dynamic market in the world, thus leaving the smaller galleries, especially those that operated within the secondary market, to devote more of their energy to international fairs in order to expand their market. Today, it is a completely different scenario, and the most influential galleries no longer keep the same distance from fairs as they did even at the end of the first decade of the millennium. Nowadays, they are very present on the fair scene; but that is also because they are extremely desirable for fairs—which typically withhold the best booth locations for them—as the presence of the most prestigious and influential galleries is particularly useful for these events. In essence, these galleries certify (Moulin & Quemin, 1993) the fair's level of excellence, and by their presence alone draw their own collectors to the event, whom every single exhibitor is hoping will visit their booth. However, it should be noted that some of these large galleries do not "play the game," as they are well aware of the benefit of their mere presence for fairs. In such situations, they do little more than present a disappointing booth that is underwhelming given their capabilities. This once again allows them to prove the distance that they can maintain between themselves and the event, to demonstrate that they, not the fair, are in the dominant position. Additionally, this allows them to avoid competing too much with their own exhibition spaces. Whereas midsize galleries are virtually required to "give it their all" when they can participate in fairs of a certain standing, the largest galleries are not subject to the same pressure.

Generally speaking, gallerists resent having to acquiesce to a fair's decisions—be it from the selection committee or the artistic director—when they intervene in a gallery's presentation. However, this is somewhat graciously accepted when the event is of a very high caliber: "[At fairs] we're quite free, except a few recommendations from Art Basel, which encourages us to make aesthetic choices, not just commercial ones. It's more or less a good thing." (Daniel Templon in "The Templons, father-son gallerists," *La Gazette Drouot*, no. 2, January 17, 2020, p. 161). However, in reality, everything depends on the gallery's reputation and influence. A fair's requirements of their exhibitors must be proportionate to the level of legitimacy of each party involved, or else relationships could become tense and the collaboration could cease.

While the balance of power between fairs and galleries has generally been fairly stable over time, it can occasionally reverse with no warning. The best example of this phenomenon is Art Basel Hong Kong, which is usually highly selective and has been even more so in recent years, thanks to the growing enthusiasm for Chinese contemporary art and the upsurge in Chinese collectors on the international art market. However, after the uprisings that affected Hong Kong in 2019, this Parisian gallerist commented at the end of that year:

> Usually, Art Basel Hong Kong kind of looks down on us, it's more distant. But with the shambles that's taking place in the city right now, they came to visit us at the FIAC to be sure that we were planning on applying. So all of a sudden, they're being very considerate. But it's still a long way away, we have the time to see what happens before we decide. We won't get involved just to make them happy, and this year they're not in a position to impose their conditions on us.

The onset of the COVID-19 pandemic at the beginning of 2020 drastically undermined the power dynamic that up to that point had played in the fair's favor.

In order to be continuously attractive to the top galleries, fairs must also do their utmost to ensure that sales are sustained, both by encouraging the largest galleries to apply (and then selecting them), as well as guaranteeing the presence of institutions and the best collectors, without which the best galleries—who have the most agency—would neglect to participate in the event. As this international gallerist explained:

> Currently, we do a dozen fairs per year, and what counts isn't so much managing to make a profit at each one, but the fair as a whole. We're not going to devote a lot of energy to fairs that we know don't work, we have enough choice. There are fairs that we're never going back to, like Cape Town, we sold really badly. Düsseldorf was really bad as well. We sold one of our German artists, but even though he's well known, he's not very expensive because he produces a lot of pieces, and we didn't even manage

> to sell our other German artists. That's the fundamental problem with that fair. We're not going back there either. There are other fairs where we sell really well, why should we spend our energy on some of them that don't work well, or just aren't for us?

In several respects, fairs have become indispensable events for the contemporary art world. Fair attendees engage in interactions—and transactions— far beyond the four walls of the fair; and even professionals whose galleries were not present at fairs frequently come to them, as these events have become highly attractive. Over 15 years, there has been a large increase in the number of contemporary art galleries participating in fairs, which is paired with an increase in attendance on the part of other galleries, even when they do not have a booth. Gallerists who direct these establishments will sometimes come to the fair simply as visitors and buy pieces from their colleagues, or hope to run into some of their own clients in the aisles and thus remain in contact with them—or even make appointments outside of the fair—knowing which of their collectors will be in attendance. As this associate gallery director explained: "When we go to a city for a fair, we make the most of it by making appointments at the same time, always." This German gallerist also explained: "During fairs, I'm not always at my booth, I do lots of lunches and dinners, I make appointments, it's as important as the booth itself." This director gave a similar remark, but with more detail:

> M. [the gallerist] moves around a lot for fairs, but in general, he only stays at his booth on the day of the preview, especially during the time slots reserved for the very important collectors. After that, he stays in the city, but he spends most of his time at lunches, dinners, and cocktail receptions, he meets our most important collectors either by making appointments or with invitations, or else he goes to the previews that are organized at the same time as the fair, when he knows that he'll run into all the most important collectors.

Clearly, galleries are very proactively pursuing sales, even at fairs (this point will be developed further in the next chapter). A booth functions as a shop window that demonstrates to everyone that the gallery is present, enabling them to reach new potential clients. Sales (especially sizable ones) are often concluded during the VIP preview, but they can also begin there and continue outside of the fair, particularly for the largest galleries, which have the most extensive little black books of collectors.

The explanations given in this chapter so far show clearly that, on the whole, fairs have had a resounding success over recent years. That is, up to the outbreak of the COVID-19 pandemic in 2020, which brought their development to a sudden halt. However, since the pandemic has abated and made the notion of "returning to normal" possible, business has resumed steadily. It is because the influence of fairs has considerably increased, especially during the 2010s, that they now constitute an obligatory point of passage for any midsize or large gallery.

Galleries are more invested in fairs than ever, but with less enthusiasm

The previously mentioned severe financial and organizational constraints that fairs now impose on galleries have fomented criticisms and concerns. Among the most active galleries, which nonetheless participate in renowned events, there is a distinct desire to "calm things down." François Ceysson, the co-owner of the gallery Ceysson & Bénétière (which got its start in Saint-Etienne, a midsize city in France, but now also has locations in Luxemburg, Paris, New York and Tokyo),[22] explained:

> We're wrapping up 2019 with 14 fairs under our belt, as opposed to 17 in 2018; that includes small fairs like Upstate in the Hamptons, Camera Camera, Approche, Vilnius, etc. Our strategy was to cement our place in big fairs like the FIAC and Art Basel Miami Beach, but other fairs that seemed prestigious on paper turned out not to be appropriate for us, and we decided to stop going, or at least to take a break, despite the recognition that they bring to the gallery. They were Frieze New York (after doing two shows), the Armory Show (after three shows), and Frieze London Masters (after one show). Beyond the disproportionate cost of the stand, the cost of transportation and especially the amount of energy required from our staff . . . it was too much. We'll try to cap ourselves at 6 fairs in 2020 . . . or under 10, in any case, even counting the small fairs.
>
> in *Artension*, March–April 2020, p. 59

The gallery's reprioritization was even more understandable, as it already had a "mega-space" in Luxembourg, and was in the process of inaugurating a second mega-space in the following months in Saint-Etienne, the gallery's birthplace.

This director of a major gallery gave a more candid summary of another problem that many galleries are currently facing: "Basically, fairs have become essential for galleries. Once an opening is over, many galleries don't have any visitors anymore. But we still need a place where we can receive the people who want to see our pieces; in fact, thanks to fairs, gallery spaces are more and more for our image."

While fairs have developed greatly, they nevertheless have certain limits nowadays. Of course, they have helped to offset the influence of auction houses by adding galleries to an event calendar that is more likely to arouse the interest of art lovers (Bourdieu & Darbel, 1997), as well as bringing galleries together *en masse* to expand their collective offer (Adam, 2014). However, due to their success, fairs now tend to compete directly with gallery spaces. Even though fairs were conceived to counteract the downward trend of clients visiting galleries (and therefore being difficult to reach), their almost unexpected success has only exacerbated the phenomenon.

For this associate of an international gallery that is established in France and has a large provincial client base, it was important to modulate the scope of fairs:

> Fairs have become super important, but even so, the fair system has its limits. It's not as indispensable as they'd like it to be. Out of the 10 primary clients that keep our gallery alive, I would say that half of them are completely outside of the fair system, they never set foot in a fair, and don't really even know that they exist. I'm sure that for some of them, even Art Basel wouldn't ring a bell, or the FIAC would be very vague, so telling them that we're participating in such-and-such fair, really, for them, it doesn't mean anything.

This gallerist, who runs an international gallery, wondered if—at the end of 2020—fairs had not already lived out their moment of glory: "This year, even Art Basel Miami Beach, it was ok, but not at all as good as what everyone expected. It's simple: today, there are too many fairs, collectors are pulled in too many directions. We'll go back for sure, but I think we can expect the craze of fairs to be behind us." She is joined in her observation by a fellow German gallerist, who sent me the following remark in an email at the beginning of 2020: "It's pretty general, galleries, Berlin galleries in particular, they stake everything on fairs . . . but because the supply of fairs has greatly exceeded the demand for the last two or three years, they're not what they used to be."

Before the COVID-19 pandemic broke out at the beginning of 2020, the notion of an excessive supply of fairs was being increasingly acknowledged, not only because collectors are more in demand and cannot therefore spend as much money in a growing number of fairs, but also because, in order to attract these highly sought-after visitors and keep them in the city where the event is being held for a longer amount of time, fairs are increasingly likely to propose a series of activities outside of the event, thus emptying the fair's aisles of visitors, especially collectors. However, it should be noted that they are, in reality, hoping to impede those activities that are outside of their walls and beyond their control. This American gallerist regretted that fairs themselves are less frequented by the collectors who nevertheless make the journey to the host city: "Today, there are too many fairs that compete with each other, and in order to attract collectors, they organize VIP programs that drive people out of the fairs. So the collectors spend less and less time in the aisles and at the booths!"

However, while the press releases issued at the end of the fairs regularly report "strong sales" in a "vibrant market," and "new, booming markets" with "record sales" in an "exceptional year," and while galleries often feel obliged to confirm these declarations—in the hopes of once again being selected for future fairs, and also to sustain the belief in the quality of their artists (Bourdieu, 1987)—the reality is sometimes another case entirely. Once all the costs associated with fairs have been deducted, it is not uncommon for galleries to have to wait weeks, or even months, after the fair ends for their participation to start paying dividends. It is sometimes simply the fact that galleries feel obliged to participate in certain fairs to stay in touch with the local collectors and show interest in their national art scene and market. For galleries with limited financial means, other kinds of events such as gallery weekends or a temporary exchange of exhibition spaces are much less expensive and sometimes constitute alternative projects.

More recently, it is the "online" fairs that have started to show their cracks. During the first year of the COVID-19 pandemic, in 2020, several galleries and online fairs purported that these virtual events were a satisfactory alternative to their physical counterparts. However, even though these claims were cycled through the media in an attempt to impose the idea that online fairs were effective, little by little the illusion proved difficult to maintain. At the beginning of 2021, in a bid to guarantee the success of its Hong Kong show—the dates of which were scheduled in May instead of the traditional slot in March, in the hope that the COVID-19 pandemic would have abated by that point—Art Basel proposed a brand new option to its exhibitors: "ghost booths." In the event that gallerists and their employees were not able to travel to Hong Kong for the fair, the organizers offered the possibility of renting a booth of 150 to 200 square feet for $9,500, or one of 200 to 250 square feet for $11,500. For each booth, the fair took it upon itself to recruit an assistant that could welcome visitors and put collectors in touch virtually with a gallery staff member during the opening hours of the event. It is clear how such an initiative aimed to inject more materiality or physicality into fairs held during the period of the COVID-19 pandemic, and the online versions of these events have already shown their limits. This is despite the enthusiastic discourse that was mostly meant to legitimize online fairs and maintain confidence in the health of the market.

An explosion and internationalization of fairs, which remain geographically entrenched

The augmented impact of fairs was very pronounced during the 2010s, but it is in reality the next phase of an expansion pattern that had begun many years earlier. Once these events had been created and were well established, they could only grow in magnitude. Even though, as mentioned at the beginning of this chapter, the earliest fairs took place at the very end of the 1960s and the first half of the 1970s, the number of fairs has risen considerably in recent years, and new events of significance have appeared.

Art Basel, the number one fair in the world due to its major impact on the market, currently features nearly 300 exhibitors—230 of which are galleries in its main sector—selected from a total of 800 applicants. The competition is therefore fierce and, moreover, many galleries that would like to participate in this prestigious event eliminate themselves by not even submitting an application. Because this fair generates so much publicity (and even more sales), it alone represents more than 50 percent of the annual income for some galleries. As part of Art Basel's international development—and even though it seemed for a long time that it would rule the entire art world on its own—its parent company, MCH Group, first created two satellite events; followed more recently by a third in 2022. The first took place in the United States, in Miami Beach, where it has taken place almost every year[23] since 2002 (the first show, scheduled for the end of 2001, was canceled due to the September 11 terrorist attacks). Since 2013, the Art Basel brand has also extended into Asia, with another fair organized in Hong Kong. Every year, MCH Group has ensured that these two satellite events would not compete with its main fair, but would rather reinforce its influence. As such, Art Basel Miami Beach (which aims to have more control over the North and South American market) is organized each year in December, six months after the Swiss fair, which is held yearly in June.[24] As for Art Basel Hong Kong, it was created in 2013 in the wake of the rapid development of the Chinese art market during the 2000s (Quemin, 2013c) and is scheduled to take place every March,[25] in the middle of the other two events organized by Art Basel's parent company. Finally, in 2022, the first iteration of Paris + by Art Basel took place in the French capital, as MCH Group had managed to secure the October time slot that had, up to that point, always been reserved for the FIAC in the Grand Palais (Ephémère exhibition hall)[26] in Paris.

In the United States, Art Basel's main competitors are Expo Chicago—created in 1980 under the name Art Chicago (and later changing its name in 2012)—and the Armory Show, which was created in 1994 in New York. Frieze New York was established in the same city in 2012, itself an offshoot of its parent fair Frieze, which was created in London in 2003. A yearly show under the Frieze banner was later organized in Los Angeles in 2019 (it was forced to cancel its 2020 show); and another in Seoul, South Korea, was created in 2022. The very first iteration of this Korean show was an immediate success. An additional event on this list of noteworthy fairs was the top French fair, the FIAC—Foire Internationale d'Art Contemporain (International Fair for Contemporary Art; this name was not adopted until the fair's second year)—created in 1974 in Paris and held annually until 2021. Initially taking place in the former Bastille train station, where the second Paris opera house currently stands, it moved into the prestigious Grand Palais in 1976, before leaving it in 1994 due to restoration work for tents erected at Quai Branly (near the Eiffel Tower), and later for the unattractive Parc des Expositions on the border of the southern working-class area of Paris. After returning to the Grand Palais in 2006, the fair was once again forced to temporarily leave the space after its 2019 show, and in 2020 the event was canceled due to the COVID-19 pandemic. Due to the aforementioned renovation of the Grand Palais, its subsequent iterations moved to a massive marquee erected in front of the Ecole Militaire (also close to the Eiffel Tower), where the structure was planned to stay until 2024. Among the other events of importance are Madrid's ARCO (dating back to 1982); Art Brussels (whose origins date all the way back to the end of the 1960s); SP Arte in São Paulo (created in 2005); and Rio Art Fair (2011) (Stocco, 2016). Also significant are the three largest Italian fairs—in Turin (Artissima, 1994), Milan (Miart, 1996), and Bologna (Arte Feria, 1974)[27]—as well as those of Dubai (2007) and Abu Dhabi (2009). All in all, there are ample events. The founding years cited above after the name of each fair testify to a continuous process of introducing new events of this caliber over the decades.

As previously indicated, fairs have not only grown in number since the end of the 1960s; their role has also become considerably more important, whereas for a long time they occupied a narrow portion of the international art market. It should be noted that Raymonde Moulin hardly mentioned fairs in her two major books, published in 1967 and 1992 (Moulin, 1967 [1987] and 1992). This is because, even at the beginning of the 1990s, these events still played a limited role on the art market. This is in strong contrast with their current indispensable status.

Today, the total number of fairs held around the world each year is well over 200; the number is sometimes reported to be 260. In its March 2, 2016 issue, *Artnet News* estimated the number of art fairs in the world to be approximately 270, and declared that there had been "around 68" in 2005. In addition to the primary events previously listed, are the many events in the more marginal cities on the international art scene (Quemin, 2001, 2002, 2006, 2013a and b; Van Hest, 2012; Obadia, 2019). Additionally, there are several satellite fairs that take advantage of the high concentration of collectors drawn by the primary fairs in an attempt to attract these potential clients with a competing event—albeit on a smaller scale—organized at the same time in the same city. As such, no fewer than 10 "fringe" fairs are organized simultaneously with Art Basel's main event.

Moreover, as the fair system has intensified, the main metropolitan areas are teeming with initiatives throughout the year. To give an example, there is a continuous series of fairs in Paris: beyond the FIAC (which became Paris + by Art Basel in 2022, then Art Basel Paris in 2024) there is Paris Photo—another international event with a prestigious reputation—as well as other current or recent fairs such as Art Paris, Paris Internationale, Bienvenue, Drawing Now, Young International Art Fair, AKAA (Also Known As Africa), Asia Now, Art Elysées, among others. This list is not exhaustive, as it does not include events of smaller magnitude. Altogether, there are 10 or so fairs in Paris alone specializing in art that is more or less contemporary; in France, several events also take place each year outside of the capital. The fair system has generated a veritable abundance of opportunities for galleries (and organizers of these events).

However, the number of international art fairs that were *truly* contemporary (i.e., featuring a significant proportion of foreign exhibitors and presenting a real diversity in the national origins of exhibitors, not just from two countries) was much lower in 2008 (Quemin, 2013a). At the end of the 2000s, I tallied only 41 during my research on this topic. With many galleries engaging in several fairs, the number of fair participants reached 4,113, for a collective 2,322 contemporary art galleries in the world in 2008. Although generally speaking the contemporary art world likes to present itself as being entirely globalized, there are still extremely pronounced indicators of geographical concentration (Obadia, 2019). Hence, whether referring to the places where the fairs are organized or the countries of origin of the galleries that are most involved in these events, the United States, Germany, the United Kingdom, France, Italy, and Switzerland are perennially present; and the rest of the world often represents a minimal percentage (Quemin, 2013a). Of course, during the 2000s in particular, fairs began to materialize in more marginal spaces around the world (Stocco, 2016) but these events remain, on the whole, second class, and the galleries in the countries organizing them have not developed by leaps and bounds. Thus, even though Art Basel Hong Kong has established itself as a dynamo on the international scene, this is thanks in particular to the power[28] of the Swiss group that owns it, and the remarkable international proliferation of its events did not incite a surge in popularity for Chinese galleries or those with a special geographical association. In the Middle Kingdom, even today, the most famous institutions come from the West (Quemin, 2013c). Likewise, while the first Frieze Seoul fair in 2022 was particularly successful, it is still a European group (this time, of British origin) that owns it.

Fairs have undoubtedly been able to grow to such an extent these days, in part, because they have been able to adapt their operational model. In his book, *The Art Fair Age*, Paco Barragan offers an interpretation of this transformation (Barragan, 2008). He asserts that it is not the giant Art Basel that created this new kind of fair that has progressively established itself around the world, but rather the Madrid fair ARCO, which was created at the beginning of the 1990s under the auspices of its then-director, Rosina Gómez-Baeza. She transformed art fairs, which had previously been simple commercial happenings, into veritable cultural events, wherein the lived experience was drastically enhanced. The pioneering Gómez-Baeza introduced the notion of spotlighting a particular country, solo shows, and more specific sectors during fairs (some of these sectors were even curated); these features went on to be widely reproduced by competitors. In the mid-1990s, she also experimented with panels and talks. All of these innovations occurred simultaneously with vernissages of Madrid's museums, sometimes with exhibitions related to the fair's country of focus, as well as private dinners and evening festivities. Up to that point, the fair model had consisted nearly exclusively of presenting artworks at booths; and, after the event had shut down for the day, the gallerists, collectors, and artists had a private dinner together. It was necessary for the ARCO fair to innovate because the Spanish market lacked contemporary art collectors who were as engaged as those in Germany, for example. Spain also suffered from the absence of great contemporary art museums, until the inauguration of the Reina Sofia Museum in Madrid in 1992, and later the MACBA in Barcelona in 1995. ARCO therefore filled a hitherto largely vacant space for contemporary art in Spain and, as it is publicly funded, it has always sought to attract a large audience. This is in contrast to other events that, on the contrary, complain about the influx of "curious" attendees. As the fair was organized by Spanish local authorities via the Municipality of Madrid and the Chamber of Commerce, communications addressed to the general public quickly became an important area of development (Barragan, 2008).

Even though today, contemporary art galleries can be very international organizations, they still bear the unmistakable seal of geographical affiliation. The most obvious incarnation of this factor is physical location, as illustrated in the previous chapter. Galleries are almost inevitably compelled to settle in particular districts, even in the age of the Internet and art fairs, both of which could have considerably reduced the influence of geographical factors.

Furthermore, fairs have retained significant geographical affiliations in many other respects. Nowadays, the primary global fairs all take place in Western countries and in the northern hemisphere (Quemin, 2013a). The only two exceptions to this rule are Art Basel Hong Kong and, very recently, Frieze Seoul. Both of these (as previously indicated) belong to a Swiss group and a British group, respectively. Moreover, as I have repeatedly established in my previous works, the Western space in which the contemporary art market operates is by no means homogeneous; on the contrary, there is a very pronounced hierarchy of countries within it. The United States, Germany, the United Kingdom, France, Switzerland, and Italy (Quemin, 2001, 2002, 2006, and 2013b) occupy much higher positions than any other country, and even among these there are significant differences in influence.

While fairs present themselves as international and, to a large extent, "deterritorialized" events, geography plays a massive role, as there is almost systematically a premium for galleries from the host country. This is true to a lesser extent for Art Basel than for other events, which is what makes this fair the most authentically international of its kind. However, at practically all fairs, and this is particularly the case in Italy—especially in Milan and Bologna, less so in Turin (Quemin 2013a)—galleries located in the same country as the fair, and sometimes even the same city, are often highly overrepresented.

Beyond the host country itself, there are affinities and networks between certain countries, which means that it is not in the best interest of all galleries to prioritize the same fairs. While commentators nearly always emphasize the internationalization or even globalization of the art market, this in no way means that the geographical dimension has disappeared; it would in fact be a mistake to ignore it. This is evident in the following remark made by the director of a large gallery that was founded in Paris (with an additional location in Brussels) and is involved with a dozen fairs around the world each year:

> Well, for us, two fairs are the most important in terms of results: the FIAC and Art Basel. After that, the third is Art Brussels. But we sell just as well at Art Paris. I would say that the other important fair for us is Art Genève. There are a lot of French and Belgian visitors, so we know them, they know us, it's great for sales.

It is clear that only Art Basel has managed to almost completely detach itself from its geographical limits, and all the other fairs mentioned illustrate the influence of the geographical/"local" factor. On the other end of the spectrum of fairs in which this gallery participates is Art Paris (a less established fair). This constitutes an effective means of making sales because it is located in an area that is largely controlled by the gallery.

This spatial influence is further reinforced by the region's impact on the content featured in the booths, both in terms of the host country and a gallery's country of origin. Very often, galleries present a greater selection of artists from their own country than what is offered by other establishments from different countries. As such, in October 2019, 35 percent of the artists featured by the 40 French contemporary art galleries participating in the FIAC (the premier Parisian fair at the time) were French. The proportion was even higher for the following galleries, all of which originated in France: Nathalie Obadia (5 artists out of 12), Templon (6 out of 15), Loevenbruck (five out of eight), and Ceysson & Bénétière (all of their artists, thanks to a booth dedicated to the Support/Surface movement). In addition to the French-born artists included in the figures cited above, there were other artists who were foreign-born residents of France; however, *Le Journal des Arts* featured the headline "FIAC 2019, 35% of French artists in French galleries. The French galleries present at the FIAC exhibit predominantly foreign artists" (in lejournaldesarts.fr, October 21, 2019). In discussions that have arisen in reaction to these numbers, some wondered whether French galleries were doing enough to support the artists from their own country, maintaining that their presence in national galleries was low, even though it was already at 35 percent. In essence, these already high figures would probably be even higher in art scenes wherein artists occupy more established positions in the international market than creators in France, (i.e. Germany, the United Kingdom, and the United States in particular), because the premium for national creators is associated with unequal positions on the contemporary art scene and is even more pronounced when the country holds strong international positions (Quemin, 2001, 2002, 2006, and 2013b).

When it comes to the foreign artists they represent, galleries generally tend to highlight those from a few specific countries (especially the United States, the United Kingdom, and Germany) that are seen as being more "international" than the others. For the rest, participating galleries typically make an effort to be in alignment with the country in which the fair is taking place. This can also be illustrated by the Templon Gallery, which has locations in Paris and Brussels (as well as a recent addition in New York). The gallery has a very diversified artist roster in terms of nationality and country of residence, and it usually presents booths with many of its creators. Thanks to this diversified roster, the gallery can feature its American artists (and those who live in the United States) James Casebere, Gregory Crewdson, Jim Dine, David LaChapelle, Ivan Navarro, Philip Pearlstein, George Segal, and Kehinde Wiley at American art fairs. For German fairs, it can feature its German artists Franz Ackermann, Norbert Bisky, and Jonathan Meese; and its Indian creators Anju and Atul Dodiya, Jitish Kallat, and Sudarshan Shetty are more heavily featured in the Middle East, as the market is oriented more toward these artists. Even though the contemporary art market is often portrayed as being globalized, this certainly does not mean that national factors have zero impact. This is confirmed by the following French gallerist, who explained the double role that nationality plays: "Our gallery has not participated in Art Cologne for a very long time, but this year we decided to go back. It makes total sense for a gallery like ours: we have a lot of German artists, and a lot of our collectors are also German." Galleries frequently highlight artists from the country where the fair in which they are participating is taking place, and they often do so instinctively, as it is in their best interest: people who visit the event—a significant number of whom generally come from the host country—are more inclined to buy pieces produced by national artists. It is, however, also because fair organizers frequently encourage galleries to feature artists from the host country, as they know that doing so will appeal to local visitors and collectors. In the following excerpt, it is clear how regional and national circumstances have a massive impact, even in a setting as international as that of major contemporary art fairs. Upon his return from Art Brussels, a Swiss gallerist friend of mine sent me the following email in 2017:

> Got back from Art Brussels Monday evening . . . the fair went well, at least with the Belgian collectors who share a certain amount of enthusiasm for . . . Belgian artists! We sold well (a Belgian artist, a Swiss one, and an American one), and we're still waiting for [two very well-known Belgian artists] ... It's a little more difficult for the more expensive pieces. French people came to the fair too, but just like at Drawing Now Fair, we picked

> up on their hesitation. The French [presidential] elections aren't helping us, there's a contagious uncertainty spreading all over the country.

This excerpt demonstrates that the context in question is undoubtedly cultural in nature, but also political. During my field observations at fairs around the world, I was surprised to notice that the participants, be they gallerists or collectors, closely followed the news in their countries and spoke with each other about it quite a bit, even if they were thousands of miles away from home.

Another element of fairs that is influenced by the spatial factor is the position of different countries on the international art scene (Quemin, 2001, 2002, 2006, 2013b; van Hest, 2012; Obadia, 2019), which also impacts the placement of the booths reserved for galleries from these countries at the event. For instance, at the FIAC, as with most fairs, it was clear that the areas around the central aisles—especially the corners—were the most coveted spaces, as they offer the best visibility; they were consequently primarily reserved for market juggernauts from the United States and a handful of very large, extremely international galleries, all of which came from a very small number of countries.

Despite this trend toward so-called globalization, there are still specificities for certain countries, cities, and even buildings that host fairs; and these are not fully interchangeable. As this German gallerist indicated when asked about the strategy that she has adopted for the 10 or so fairs in which she participates every year:

> Fairs represent over 60% of the gallery's revenue. Strategies differ from one event to another; it's a matter of numbers. Putting on a monographic exhibition affords a huge amount of visibility that we can't accomplish in our gallery, but at the same time, it's always a long-term investment. We have to think about it a lot. In the past, we worked on a strategy of complementarity between the FIAC in Paris and Frieze in London. At Frieze London, we have big booths designed to look like group exhibitions to give an idea of the breadth of our program. At the FIAC, where the booths are smaller, we have often put up monographic exhibitions, such as Ann Veronica Janssens in 2018, or Tomás Saraceno in 2017. The Grand Palais is an extraordinary backdrop, with a particular light. All of this makes you want to develop special projects, and that corresponds with what collectors are looking for.
>
> "Esther Schipper, gallerist: 'Berlin is less accessible to young artists, so it's gentrifying'," *Le Journal des Arts*, no. 524, May 24, 2019

All of the above clearly demonstrates that, while fairs clearly take place in an extremely internationalized market, the impact of the geographical factor remains highly pronounced on multiple levels.

Art Basel: a long-triumphant model of geographical expansion with some recent ups and downs

Out of all the art fairs, Art Basel in Switzerland—whose parent company (as previously mentioned) is the MCH Group—currently holds the undisputed top global position. It would therefore be appropriate to accord this event a special place in this analysis. The fair was founded in 1970 by the Basel gallerists Trudl Bruckner, Balz Hilt, and Ernst Beyeler; with the latter being a driving force in its creation (Zwirner, 2019). The first occasion of this event took place under the name "Art 1'70"[29] in 1970, one year after the seminal exhibition "*When Attitudes Become Form*" by the Swiss curator Harald Szeemann, held at the Kunsthalle in Bern in 1969. During its first show, either 60 or 113 (depending on the source) contemporary art galleries from 10 countries were present, thus attracting over 16,000 visitors. At the end of the 2010s, the event hosted nearly 300 galleries from 35 countries, and around 230 of these galleries were in their main sector, "Galleries," with the other participants being separated between the sectors "Edition," "Feature," and "Statement." In 2017, the fair welcomed nearly 100,000 visitors (82,000 in 2023); a far cry from the 16,000 visitors in 1970.[30]

The event was able to grow to such an extent due in particular to the fact that it focused on collectors from the very beginning. Ernst Beyeler understood that if he managed to attract the most important collectors to his fair, the best galleries would inevitably follow. Another major area of development was that, from early on in its existence, American galleries were involved in the fair. Such was the case for André Emmerich, who featured a Pop Art presentation during the very first show. In many respects, the Basel fair constituted a bridgehead for the American art market in Europe. Thanks to its judicious strategic choices, the event has also managed its growth perfectly. In essence, fairs are characterized by a certain tendency to expand (and even, in recent years, by a race toward immensity); however, if they feature too many exhibitors in proportion to the size of their market—which depends directly on the number of buyers that they manage to attract—the quality of the participating galleries is likely to decrease, and the best galleries may see their sales figures decrease due to the heightened competition, meaning they may no longer apply to participate.[31]

In 1975, a few years after its first show, the number of exhibitors at Art Basel had already risen to 300; this was not an excessive amount, as collectors were almost immediately drawn to the event. In only five years, the fair had reached its maximum capacity, as the number of exhibitors has not changed since. At the same time, the fair has always tried to innovate, especially by proposing new sectors dedicated to young artists. In 1974, the "Neue Tendenzen" ("New Trends") space was created, wherein the galleries featured new artists. This sector was replaced by the "Perspective" platform in 1979. The fair encountered its first challenges in the 1980s, as it had to differentiate itself from such competitors as the FIAC in France, Art Chicago in the United States, and Art Cologne in Germany. At the time, Art Basel had a selection committee with representatives from each participating country; this model changed with the arrival of a new director, Lorenzo Rudolf, who remained at the head of Art Basel for nine years, from 1991 to 2000. In 1992, the selection committee was reduced to only three members, thus remedying the phenomenon of decision dilution. In 1995, the fair gave pride of place to the medium of video with its "Art Video Forum" and introduced its "Art Statement" sector; the latter being an exhibition reserved for young artists. That same year, Samuel Keller, then a director of communication, launched the fair's website; the first virtual platform for an art fair in the world.

It was, nevertheless, in the 2000s that Art Basel had the most pronounced period of development, under the impetus of Samuel Keller. He had been promoted to director of the fair in 2000, and stayed in that role until 2007. He was greatly inspired by ARCO's model—previously presented in this chapter (Barragan, 2008)—which he borrowed and adapted to galvanize the leading fair in the world. Keller worked to create the "Unlimited" sector, which was and is still dedicated to monumental artworks and, as of its introduction to the fair, has competed with biennials in terms of the kinds f spectacular, often monumental pieces being presented. Keller also put the finishing touches on the first offshoot of the event, Art Basel Miami Beach. As previously mentioned, although this was originally scheduled for December 2001, it had to be pushed back a year because of the September 11 terrorist attacks. This Florida iteration was constructed as a very festive international fair, with renowned evening events that somewhat eclipsed the artistic element and contrasted with the seriousness of its parent fair, which is more austere and formal. The event also made an impression with the originality of its "Positions" sector, wherein galleries displayed pieces by young artists in containers placed on the beach. Practically since its inauguration, the Miami Beach fair has been on the calendar of major international events. In 2004, Art Basel launched a series of talks, called "Art Basel Conversations." By the time Keller passed the torch to his successor in 2007, Art Basel had seen its aura grow considerably brighter.

The fair then continued its geographic expansion, this time in Asia (Yun, 2021) with the creation of Art Basel Hong Kong in 2013. The political, economic, cultural, and artistic emergence of the Asian continent inevitably fueled the MCH Group's desire for expansion and innovation, and the event enjoyed increasing success for years. With its three locations (at the time), the various Art Basel fairs were able to control the highest market segment on the three most important continents for the art market (Europe, the Americas, and Asia), without competing with the "mother fair," which remained at the center of the ecosystem. For years, the strategy applied by all market players has been to "complement" Art Basel, and its parent company, MCH Group, has managed to achieve this very well.

Essentially, with Art Basel Miami Beach, the objective was to control the market in North and South America. For 10 years, Art Basel Miami Beach was the only satellite fair of its parent company that could put considerable energy into its development. The Florida event has swiftly established itself as the uncontested leader of art fairs in the Americas. With a six-month interval from the Swiss version of the fair, it was clearly the only event capable of drawing the most influential European collectors away from their own continent; even more so because, in the United States, the Chicago fair was on the decline and the Armory Show in New York had been snubbed by the city's largest galleries. Art Basel Miami Beach could also count on a strong attendance of art lovers from Latin America, as well as visitors from Asia to a lesser extent.

Over time, and particularly due to the creation and subsequent growth of Art Basel's other satellite fair—Art Basel Hong Kong—the American version of the fair underwent a transformation. Today, it has taken on a strongly American tone; with a staggering presence of paintings and pieces that are often very colorful, sometimes in the Pop Art genre, and less materialist or expressionist. Though initially created above all to cater to collectors in North and South America, the fair has been attracting more and more art lovers from the United States, as it aligns with their expectations. As Nathalie Obadia (who has galleries in Paris and Brussels) explained when commenting on Art Basel Miami Beach: "Here, not many buyers come from New York, New Yorkers are already satisfied, they don't need this fair. But we reach a lot of important collectors from cities in the middle of the United States, who are very close to the local museums in their cities" (*La Gazette Drouot*, no. 2, January 17, 2020, pp. 162–163).

Art Basel Hong Kong has traditionally been one of the most popular fairs. Despite the scarcity of space in the city, it attracts great numbers of visitors as the event is part of a project to promote contemporary art in Asia. It quickly took the market by storm: including collectors as well as the general public. The latter is a major component of the event, and tickets are generally sold out before the event even begins. This is because the Hong Kong fair was able to take root locally, and also position itself as a hub for all of Asia, thus capitalizing on the curiosity about this continent from the rest of the world and satisfying the local public. It has also benefited from the lack of both import and export taxes, and the organizers have gone to great pedagogical lengths, educating their participating galleries on how to adapt to the local scene, and encouraging exhibitors to feature Western artists, as well as Eastern ones. Over a few years, the fair has literally imposed itself on the international art scene, rising to the level of its Floridian counterpart.

However, as of June 2019, the context has grown more somber. Hong Kong, as an autonomous territory of China, experienced a popular protest movement on an unprecedented scale since it was handed over to China in 1997 by the United Kingdom. Several festivals were either disrupted or canceled, and sales at the Fine Art China fair, which took place in October, were affected by the political upheaval. Conversely, sales at the auction houses, Christie's and Sotheby's, that also occurred in October did not appear to suffer from the situation. A few galleries defected from the fair, initially due to the turbulent political context, before it was eventually canceled due to the COVID-19 pandemic that broke out at the beginning of 2020. One might posit that the pandemic was something of a benefit for organizers, who were in danger of falling out of favor with the local authorities if they did not manage to guarantee their exhibitors' presence, which would result in empty booths during the event. A few weeks prior, at the end of the Miami Beach fair, MCH Group announced an exclusive attractive pricing scheme for its upcoming exhibitors in Hong Kong. This was all the more necessary, as the turnout at the Florida fair was unusually lackluster, due to a downturn in the art market in 2019. Notwithstanding, the essential hypothetical alternative for Hong Kong was thus: even if galleries had rallied and made the effort to come to the event in order to remain in good standing with the organizers, would the collectors have attended as well?

The COVID-19 pandemic therefore solved this problem by obliging the fair's organizers to cancel the 2020 Art Basel Hong Kong show for both economic and health reasons. Instead, they held a simple "virtual" fair. The 235 participating galleries were reimbursed 75 percent of the price of their booth, with the remaining 25 percent being reserved to maintain their virtual booths. What was originally only intended to be an online preview of the fair's booths became the event itself. Out of necessity, the Art Basel Hong Kong Online Viewing Rooms became the first 100 percent digital art fair. In addition to being held online, the event's duration was also modified, with the dates being extended. After a two-day VIP preview on March 18 and 19, the show was opened to the general public for six days, from March 20 to 25. The presentation of the website was nothing original; each gallery had its own identical Viewing Room: a bench[32] was placed in front of a white wall, on which all of the artworks were displayed. After a paragraph presenting the selection, a maximum of 10 pieces were displayed on a virtual photo carousel. In a rare decision, prices for the works were listed on the website, some of which were fairly high. Interested collectors could then contact the gallery by clicking on a link for each piece to a virtual inbox. Still, the event resulted in limited success, thus aligning with the more general level of performance of online art sales, which I would assert that galleries tend to overestimate, even to this day.

Before the shutdown in 2020, encouraged by the previous success of its substantial international initiatives, MCH Group wanted to continue its policy of dominating the market. With three continents under its control, its focus then turned to buying out local fairs to further reinforce its influence by refining its network. This race to develop and expand perfectly reflects that of galleries that open locations in other countries, but it has gone far beyond the simple framework of the market, and involves all branches of contemporary art[33] (Quemin, 2020a).

At the beginning of 2017, MCH Group acquired 25 percent of the capital from art.fair International GmbH—the organizer of the Art Düsseldorf fair—as well as the India Art Fair in New Delhi. For the first time, the parent company of Art Basel intended to engage in fairs that are neither global nor continental in scope, but rather are more national or "regional" (Quemin, 2002). In December of the same year, the company continued its expansion by acquiring the majority (67.5 percent) of the London fair, Masterpiece. The event—which specializes in art, antiquities, design, and jewelry—was the first of its kind to be acquired by MCH Group, which up to that point had concentrated on contemporary art.

At the time of these acquisitions, the fair landscape was in the midst of a rapid restructuring. This coincided with Art Cologne, the oldest fair in the world, simultaneously announcing that it was creating a new commercial venture—Art Berlin, in concert with the contemporary art fair ABC Berlin—with the goal of reviving and expanding this event. Berlin had not had a large contemporary art fair since the closure of its previous event, Art Forum, in 2010. The alternative fair, ABC, had failed to draw international collectors to Berlin, as they preferred the format of the Berlin Gallery Weekend, held every year in May. The Art Berlin fair, founded in 2017 and taking place every September in the hangars of the former Tempelhof airport, aimed to operate in symbiosis with the Berlin Gallery Weekend. Incidentally, both events had had the same director, Maike Cruse, for the last two years. The fair hosted around 110 galleries, many of which were, of course, German; including famous establishments such as Sprüth Magers, Konrad Fischer, Esther Schipper, Eigen + Art, Kewenig, König, Nagel Draxler, and Georg Nothlefer. The third iteration of Art Berlin took place in September 2019 during the Berlin Art Week; a six-day cultural event that occurs each autumn. However, in December 2019, Kölnmesse (the organizer of Art Berlin) announced that it was canceling the fair definitively after only three years. The company had not been able to reserve space at the Tempelhof airport for 2020, the lack of support from the city was keenly felt,[34] and the revenue from previous years was not satisfactory.

Before Art Berlin was discontinued, the relationship between MCH Group and the smaller company, Kölnmesse, had been strained. In 2017, Daniel Hug, the director of the Art Cologne fair, butted heads with the Art Basel fair, accusing it of "colonialism" in its strategy of investing in several countries, with its participation in the Art India and Art Düsseldorf fairs. He contrasted this expansion model to that of Art Cologne, the latter of which, he claimed, aimed to promote and develop the German art market. Marc Spiegler, the director of Art Basel, was obliged to defend himself by arguing that the danger for galleries and for the art market was not rooted in inter-fair competition, but rather that from auction houses.

However, just like its moderately-sized regional competitor, Kölnmesse—whose expansion in Berlin came to an end with the discontinuation of the local fair—MCH Group quickly began to withdraw from fairs that existed solely on a national or regional level. In November 2018, the group sold its shares in the Düsseldorf, New Delhi, and Singapore fairs, as they had lost 60 percent of their value in the course of one year.[35] Not only did MCH Group sell the shares that it had held in India Art Fair and Art Düsseldorf since 2017, it also backtracked by giving up a stake in the new fair, Art SG, which was scheduled to take place in Singapore in November 2019. Ultimately, in the art domain, in addition to the various iterations of the Art Basel fair (which totaled three at that time), the company has retained only Masterpiece, the London antiques show that it acquired in 2017, and for which it was planning to create an offshoot event in Asia. Another major development was that the company Lupa Systems (owned by businessman James Murdoch, son of media magnate Rupert Murdoch) acquired a stake in MCH Group in August 2020 with an $80 million investment. However, this initiative came under fire for a time, as other shareholders attempted to oppose the maneuver.

Another initiative launched by Art Basel ended in a crushing failure. Entitled "Art Basel Inside," it was set to take place in Abu Dhabi, with entrepreneurs in the art world and cultural leaders coming together for a three-day conference in February 2020. Tickets were announced at $15,000 per person. The event was abruptly canceled in 2019 without any real clarification. This reversal tarnished the image of the fair and its organizing company, for whom everything had seemed for a long time to be successful.

While, on the whole, the Art Basel fair's trajectory since 1970 paints the picture of a resounding success that has led the event to occupy its current undisputed top international position, the last few years have shown riskier industrial choices have been made within the group that owns the fair. The new economic order brought about by the COVID-19 pandemic and the turmoil that it wrought on several markets, followed swiftly by the war that broke out in Ukraine in February 2022, only exacerbated the uncertainties that have clouded the company's future, which up to that point had seemed so irreversibly bright.

However, MCH Group's prospects have started to take a turn for the better with the "coup" that occurred at the beginning of 2022. Although it had always seemed impossible, the Swiss group managed to secure the Parisian space that had been hitherto claimed by the FIAC each October, ousting it from the Grand Palais Ephémère (the temporary exhibition space while the historic building closer to the center of Paris was being renovated through 2024). The group was able to launch its own fair, Paris + by Art

Basel (that was renamed Art Basel Paris in 2024), thus considerably strengthening its position on the international art market by ousting a competitor from its usual location and ultimately eliminating it. This success has bolstered the group, which must nevertheless manage the significant risk of decline for Art Basel Hong Kong due to the political instability of the region. The ensuing weakening of the Asian fair gave way to the establishment of a competitor on the same continent, Frieze Seoul in South Korea, which was successfully inaugurated in 2022.

This is all the more concerning for MCH Group, as Frieze now not only controls a dynamic art fair on the Asian continent, but in the summer of 2023 it was announced that Frieze also acquired two other art fairs in the United States: Expo Chicago and the Armory Show (in addition to Frieze New York, which had been created in 2012). The new dynamics between these three significant American fairs, now that they are controlled by the same company, could threaten the current leading position of Art Basel Miami Beach on the American continent.

In this section, I have developed the example of Art Basel and the company that owns it, MCH Group, insofar as it is the most successful case of its kind; despite its recent setbacks. It is also the best illustration of how the market has become internationalized (Quemin, 2002 and 2006). During its resounding success, it offered a model that other fairs could replicate, particularly in terms of expanding into other countries. This is how the London fair Frieze, which was created in 2003, had as previously mentioned launched an American offshoot (Frieze New York) in 2012; then a new (initially smaller) fair in Los Angeles, Frieze LA in 2019; before repeating this feat once again in South Korea with Frieze Seoul in 2022. With this recently created fair and the additional acquisition of two renowned American fairs, the Frieze group has recently experienced a pronounced degree of development. This clearly illustrates the tendency of concentration in the international art market that I frequently underscored in the French version of this book that was published in 2021 (Quemin, 2021).

Elsewhere, the Reed Expositions Group—which has owned the two primary French fairs, the FIAC and Paris Photo, for a long time—has always failed in its attempts to internationally expand. It managed to create Photo London in 2007, but was forced to discontinue it after a single show. As for Photo Los Angeles, which was launched in 2013, the event came to an end after its third year. In the same year, 2016, the FIAC project in Los Angeles was also abandoned, as had been the 2015 fair in Saint Petersburg. It would therefore be incorrect to apply the success of Art Basel and, to a lesser extent, Frieze, to the widespread pursuit of fair internationalization. Fairs have retained, for the most part, their geographical affiliations (Quemin, 2013a); even though they try to branch out into other countries (which is, moreover, only the case for a handful of them).

Conclusion

In just over a decade, fairs have become absolutely essential for contemporary art galleries. This is true for the galleries themselves—whether they are moderately or highly integrated into the international scene—as explained throughout this chapter; but it also applies to more marginal establishments, whose positioning between true contemporary art and "contemporized chromos"[36] is sometimes more blurred, or that may actually belong solely to the second category. Very often, they reproduce the model of participating in fairs and expos (at a more modest scale). However, for each event, even if it is possible to reach new buyers, they tend to compete with the gallery's own space, as already established in the first chapter of this book. Thus, as fairs grow in influence, they call into question (at least in part) the very core of the business practices conducted by the establishments that bring fairs to life. These events were hit hard by the COVID-19 pandemic, with a long series of postponements and cancellations. As this director of one of the largest galleries in the world put it in April 2020: "In my opinion, we're not going to have fairs for the next two years. A fair's success relies on an international public and high attendance . . . two aspects that are just unimaginable right now." After this period of interruption, or even chaotic continuation—with multiple postponements taking place while the COVID-19 pandemic was in full swing in 2020 and 2021—fairs have on the whole resumed the pivotal role that they had previously occupied on the international art market. The fact of having been effectively shut out of the art world for two years did not put an end to their hegemony, and the market has in no way shunned these actors in an attempt to recalibrate itself.

PART TWO

The occupation of gallerist

4

Sales: A fundamental undertaking

In the most common sociological approach to work, there tends to be a distinction between everything relating to organization, a sector that is more often studied within the sociology of professions (Dubar, Tripier, & Boussard, 2012); and everything relating to tasks, a domain that is traditionally central to the sociology of work (Stroobants, 2016). The latter—though it has been present since the origins of sociology, notably with the writings of Karl Marx (Marx, 1887) and Emile Durkheim (Durkheim, 1997 [1897]) in the nineteenth century—developed significantly in countries such as France after the Second World War. However, at the time—in the midst of reconstruction and the revival of production—the industrial sectors were those that were researched the most. Historically, the domain of sales has not been of great interest to sociology; perhaps due in particular to the fact that it has been studied by a different discipline—management sciences—in the larger field of marketing. This does not, however, mean that the sociological perspective is incapable of analyzing this subject; the proof of this is provided in brilliant fashion by Henri Peretz, in an article on the sale of ready-to-wear luxury clothing (Peretz, 1992). The sale of works of art—in this case, contemporary art—can be just as much the subject of a sociological perspective (Hughes, 1984), which is notably inspired by the interactionist approach, among others. In the artistic sector, sales are similar to the field of clothing, studied by Peretz, insofar as it is also related to the domains of private life and of personal taste (Bourdieu, 1987). Here as well, the seller has to be an expert in their domain of activity, and the customer must be prepared to reveal their preferences to him or her. This is by no means easy for those accustomed to maintaining social interaction relationships that are typically characterized by a position of superiority (Pinçon & Pinçon-Charlot, 1997 and 2016). In the context of purchasing artworks, particularly contemporary pieces, one must accept that they will potentially be judged based on what they like, as tastes are ranked and subject to judgment (Bourdieu, 1987). The seller must ensure that this does not cause any discomfort, which could end the sales relationship.

Running a gallery: to do what, and under what conditions?

It is important to note that, since the beginning of their existence, galleries have cornered the market for newly produced artworks. Why should an artist work with these establishments? Essentially, partnering with a gallery is largely an imperative for artists who intend to make a living from their art; that is, those who are the most professionally integrated. Today, there is a general model in place that is virtually generalized in the contemporary art market: that of entrusting one's creations to a gallerist. The competing model of a gallery purchasing pieces, which was the former standard (Moulin, 1987), has all but disappeared. There are very few who still follow this model, like this influential German gallerist:

> I work in a very particular way. Almost always, what I show in my gallery belongs to me. I buy from artists and then resell, it's a model that barely exists anymore. I buy a lot and I can store everything. Before, there were more dealers who operated like this. I remember once, [a fellow gallerist] wanted to buy 20 pieces by Josef Albers from me, I had around 50 in stock, so it wasn't a problem for me to sell him so much at once, they were mine.

Conversely, according to the model that has now become widely accepted (Moulin, 1987 and 1992), the artist entrusts the works to be sold to a gallery, and the final selling price is split (usually in equal shares) between each of the parties. In total, 50 percent goes to the artist in repayment for their creation, and the same amount goes to the gallery to cover its costs (salaries, rent, etc.) and its promotional work (Moulin, 1987). However, when the artist is a star (Quemin, 2013b) for whom any promotional work is no longer truly necessary (or requires much less effort) and whose works can fetch a much higher price than a less established artist, the division of earnings is no longer equal, and the artist may receive up to 60 percent of the sale.[1] This percentage is generally accorded to star artists by galleries that are heavyweights on the market.[2] By using the services of an agent, Frank Dunphy—who counted several other Young British Artists such as Tracey Emin, Rachel Whiteread, and the brothers Jake and Dinos Chapman among his clients Damien Hirst even successfully secured a higher share in all sales. Although he was being represented by the most renowned galleries in the world, he managed (by all accounts) to negotiate with them to receive a share of 70 percent or even 90 percent on the sales of his works, when he was at the height of his glory (cf. *ArtnetNews*, "Frank Dunphy, the Bullish Business Manager Who Helped Damien Hirst Amass Millions, Has Died," August 28, 2020).

These unusually advantageous conditions for the artist have made it possible to minimize the risk that they will leave one gallery for another one where they would benefit from better financial conditions. Note that the case of star artists clearly invalidates the very romantic conception of the condition of the artist that still largely prevails today (Moulin, 1992), wherein the creator is often perceived as being exploited by the dealer. As a matter of fact, in the case of renowned creators—especially those whose work sells for the highest prices—it is apparent that the balance of power between artist and gallery plays in favor of the former. Yet even these artists continue to rely on galleries to sell their productions. If they do so, and if they agree to pay very high amounts to their galleries, it is because these establishments perform a promotional function (Moulin, 1995) of which the most experienced artists are fully aware. The only real example of a star artist who decided to bypass galleries in order to sell his works directly is, again, that of British artist Damien Hirst during the auction, *Beautiful Inside My Head Forever*, orchestrated by the Sotheby's auction house in September 2008 in London. The sale was a resounding success, as the Gagosian gallery, which up to that point had represented Hirst, bid on some pieces, as did White Cube and Harry Blain, co-founder of the Haunch of Venison gallery, and later Blain/Southern. Safe to say, this sale, though it bypassed galleries completely, benefited from their fervent support, as it was in their interest to consolidate Hirst's stature and prices to enhance the value of their stock. In the months and years that followed, however, the price of Hirst's work fell sharply. After ending his collaboration with galleries, Hirst eventually made his way back to them, and he is once again represented by the famous galleries White Cube and Gagosian. Far from being a long-lasting challenge to the role played by galleries on the primary market, the emblematic *Beautiful Inside My Head Forever* auction sale was only a dead-end occasion of an artist thumbing his nose at galleries, despite the fact that he was so famous and in demand on the market. Though it is often cited, the 2008 sale was merely a blip on the primary market, and even the most famous artists (or those who are most in demand) understand that they need a gallery's support. This is vital on many levels—particularly when it comes to looking for prospective clients in order to conclude sales—but also in terms of the very fact of being publicly represented by a gallery, especially when the gallery is acclaimed, thereby producing a qualification effect. The astronomical prices on the primary market for the works of Anselm Kiefer, one of the most expensive artists in the world, is an apt example. The Thaddaeus Ropac and White Cube galleries sell many of his larger works at around €1,500,000 each. As for the paintings of exceptional dimensions (over eight meters long), which were exhibited at the Gagosian gallery in Le Bourget (in the northern suburbs of Paris) at the beginning of 2021, each was priced at €2,200,000. It should be noted that the star artist, whose extremely high prices indicate a very strong market, continues to work with three of the largest galleries in the world and does not sell any of his pieces directly, even since his rise to fame.

Even in the 1960s, Raymonde Moulin noted that a gallery's support was essential for artists who wished to be fully recognized as such:

> Either by following the prevailing taste and interpreting an existing demand, or shaping the taste and creating the demand that he needs, the dealer's function is to integrate the painter into the market. Even if artists manage to secure their material existence by dealing directly with clients, they are condemned to remain on the sidelines of a system in which the dealer is the keystone.
>
> Moulin, 1987

The gallery is therefore a practically obligatory point of passage for contemporary artists if they wish to sell their creations. One of the most internationally recognized French artists explained:

> At one point in my career, I found myself without a gallery. I had a gallery in Italy that had behaved badly with me, they stole works from me. I wanted to sell my works directly, but that only lasts for a certain amount of time. For a while, you sell to the people you meet, but then you realize how much work it actually is. If you want to make a living from what you create, you have to turn into a real sales rep, and this is to the detriment of your creation, of your production. You sell a few pieces to the people you meet when you go out, but you have to do it all the time, and even then it dries up pretty quickly. It is therefore absolutely necessary to have a gallery, you don't have a choice. And when you meet people, they immediately ask which gallery you're with, and if you respond that you're not with anyone, it goes over like a lead balloon, you've literally shot yourself in the foot.

Generally, galleries dedicate an individual exhibition to their artists once every two years on average. This calendar, which has historically generated very irregular revenue for artists, now includes a second type of exhibition in the form of participating in fairs, as illustrated in the previous chapter. As the largest galleries frequently participate in 10 or 12 fairs throughout the year (and sometimes up to 20), sales tend to become more regular. As (more or less) conducive as the place of sales is to transactions, so is the context. This relates not only to general economic activity, but also to market cycles, or the timing of the interactions that may lead to a sale. Fairs in general, due to their limited duration and the competition between collectors, promote transactions which, as I emphasized in the previous chapter, are then frequently finalized more quickly.[3] At fairs and galleries alike, openings are particularly important moments, whether contacts are made for future transactions or sales are immediately concluded. While, during certain openings, the exhibition is "sold out," it is not uncommon for only four or five pieces to have been bought, out of the 15 or 20 that are available. But it is important that art lovers (and especially collectors) show their interest at this time to ensure sales over the four, six, or eight weeks of a gallery exhibition. Openings are particularly conducive to sales because they intensify the competition between collectors, which benefits the gallery, and therefore (thanks to the principle of sharing the profit of a sale) the artist.

Individual sellers: interpersonal skills and long-term relationships

Who sells the artworks? This task falls to the gallerist and, if there are any, other sales associates. These individuals are more or less specialized in sales, but not everyone is appointed to this task. This staff member of one of the largest galleries in the world jokingly described the sales practices of one of his gallery's competitors, which are not at all the same as his own: "At [X], everyone does sales, it's a very strange model. Even the gallery staff joke about it, they say that, for them, even the cleaning lady can make sales!"[4] Sales associates have a special status, as they are the ones who must monopolize contact with collectors, and must be visible to potential buyers more than anyone else. Although the relationships between staff members and collectors may seem fairly relaxed, they are in reality very organized and structured, and everyone must be sure to stay in their respective lanes. As this former intern of one of the largest galleries in the world explained:

> When I did my internship at [X], at first, I made mistakes. When clients talked to me, I had conversations with them. My manager explained to me that we shouldn't do that, we had to limit our conversations with clients as much as possible. The salespeople are the ones that should be in contact with them, you shouldn't speak with collectors when you're not in sales.

During a field observation session in a very large international gallery, I was able to witness a moment of conflict between one of the gallery's staff members and a couple of potential buyers, who wanted to know the price of a piece hanging on a wall and asked the young woman standing in one of the exhibition rooms. Instead of answering them immediately, the young lady asked them to wait for a few moments, and went to find one of the directors. When she returned a few minutes later, the potential buyers were very unpleasant and loudly expressed their disapproval that the staff member in the room was "not even able" to give them a price. With a remarkable amount of professionalism, the director apologized to them and explained that her colleague was only familiar with the gallery's administrative aspects, and it would be better to deal with a person who knew the artist's work inside and out and would be the best source of information. It was above all a question of immediately directing potential buyers to one of the gallery's sales specialists, as being proficient in this area constitutes a real skill.

In a professional and social environment that is very prone to euphemisms, it should be noted that the title of salesperson—which may seem too trivial—is sometimes used to designate the function, but not the profession associated with it. Collectors sometimes talk about "their" dealer, as do gallery staff amongst themselves, but this disappears when discussing the official title of the profession. As this assistant jokingly pointed out: "At the gallery, all the sales staff have the title of director, director this or director that. And besides, we call the clients collectors. In both cases it's more flattering, it's more chic, but I mean, they're still salespeople and clients!" Essentially, in galleries, most salespeople are designated by the more illustrious title of director, assistant director, or associate director. If there is a hierarchical superior, that person generally bears the title general director or executive director. It is more gratifying for collectors to deal with *directors* than with *salespeople*. The term[5] is a more general euphemism for the sales relationship; the main function, which is commercial, should not be overemphasized. It is necessary to constantly regulate the gallery's commercial image, or risk symbolically discrediting the organization (Bourdieu, 1996). Galleries whose market objective is not sufficiently veiled in such euphemisms are thus criticized for being too commercial; even if, by their very nature, all private galleries are indeed mercantile, commercial establishments.

Hence, as I emphasized in the first chapter, everything in a real contemporary art gallery's exhibition space is laid out so that it more closely resembles a museum than a shop. Furthermore, the visitor is left to move around freely without a salesperson immediately approaching them and trying to sell them artworks. (The situation is very different with art fair booths, whose spaces are more cramped and whose commercial aim is evident and accepted by all). As I myself am very familiar with "real contemporary art galleries," I am always somewhat uneasy when, on occasion, I visit a gallery that does not really belong to this social world and does not respect its codes. It is therefore uncomfortable when someone from the gallery whom I do not know follows me throughout my visit and does everything possible to initiate and maintain a conversation to explain the work of the artist(s) on display, in the hopes of concluding one or several transactions.[6]

Sales may be the sole function of some staff members, or it may be associated—as is often the case—with that of "liaisons." The term refers to managing the gallery's relationships with some of the artists it represents. The liaison is their regular contact, relieving the gallerist of this relational and organizational work. As this gallery staff member who performs both functions puts it: "Unlike here, in our gallery in [a foreign city], we have people who only do sales, they're not liaisons, but I find that, well, the work is less interesting. Because being a sales associate while also interacting with the artists, having close relationships with them, makes the work and even the sale much more interesting."

In the milieu of galleries, as in the general luxury market—and unlike in the mass market—the sales relationship is generally very personalized (Peretz, 1992). Occasionally (though it is rare), a single person will be able to sell certain specific artworks, as the director of one of the largest galleries in the world reported:

> At the FIAC, one of our clients came to see me at our booth, he was interested in a piece for sale by one of our fellow gallerists, who is known for being a bit difficult. I went to his booth and asked one of his staff members who's been with the gallery for a long time what the price of this painting was. On her price list, there was indeed a number for all the other pieces, but for that one there was just the initials of the boss, no price, you absolutely had to go through him to be able to buy the [T].

Much more often, like in the luxury sector, whenever a client becomes a "regular," they are assigned a specific sales associate (Peretz, 1992). However, the fact that sales tasks and liaison tasks are frequently associated with one another can result in a vague understanding of how faithful clients may be assigned a sales associate for a new purchase. A sales associate was asked:

> When you sell pieces at the gallery, do you break up your client portfolio based on the relationships that each salesperson has with the artists, do you direct the client to artist's liaison, or do you make sure that each person works with their regular clients?" She replied: "Absolutely, that's exactly how it works, but it's not very clear whether we should favor one of those methods over the other. In fact, we combine them and decide which one to do according to the situation. In our gallery in [a city in another country], things are simpler, all the staff are salespeople.

This young woman, who works for a large gallery and is both a sales associate and a liaison, mentioned a gaffe that she made at the start of her career. She did everything possible to conclude a sale, but she had not understood that she should make sure not to encroach on the territory of her colleagues:

> When I started at the gallery, I was very young, I had no experience, but I wanted to do sales. At the beginning, I made mistakes, I behaved badly with my colleagues, because I didn't know how it worked. When I saw clients, I really wanted to sell to them, I didn't ask if there was already someone taking care of them at the gallery. It's actually very organized, a client has a regular sales associate, and you shouldn't take clients from your colleagues, it's very personalized.

This division of labor can even interrupt a possible sale in the negotiation phase so as to respect the assignment of clients to sales associates. For instance, when I was observing a fair booth in the company of an artist from the gallery, the director addressed her thus: "One of our clients is very interested in this piece. I think it will happen. But I just started the sale, the gallerist is going to take over, she's one of his clients." The notion of personalizing the sales relationship makes sense, particularly because it is useful to know the clients and their personalities and tastes (Peretz, 1992), but also in order to create an emotional attachment, as will be analyzed in the next chapter.

Building this link often calls for salespeople to share common traits with their regular clients. These two employees of a large gallery, who both perform sales and liaison functions, comment on the attitude of a gallerist who runs another large gallery. Without going so far as to question the entire principle, they state that they find it excessive to pair clients and sales associates based on the individual characteristics that they have in common. Their reservations are focused particularly on the bluntness with which these pairings are systematically established:

> Well, we know her, she sometimes says things very candidly. She once said in front of me that it was perfect that I was gay, because that way I could take care of gay customers, or [L] could take care of Jewish clients because she was Jewish. She also has a gay salesperson for her gay clients, and she takes care of the Jewish clients because, in a way, she also has this Jewish identity, and she also has Jewish salespeople. But for us, this idea of breaking up the clientele according to the characteristics of the sales associates, it's not at all our way of seeing things, at least not in such a mechanical way.

His colleague agrees:

> Yes, here I'm often referred to Jewish clients, especially the Sephardic ones, sometimes Arab people, as my family is from North Africa, but so what? I don't see why that means that I'm the one who should take care of Jewish or Arab clients, at least not every single time.

The preceding statement provides an opportunity to indicate that, as noted by Henri Peretz regarding the sale of luxury or high-end clothing, homosexual salespeople are highly represented (Peretz, 1992), no doubt for several reasons related to the skills that they supposedly possess, which broadly stem from a reversal of a previously held stigma (Goffman, 1986). Not only is the professional artistic field more tolerant than other sectors, but taste is one of the traits that is often ascribed to homosexual men, a stereotypical assumption in and of itself. Moreover, identifying with a minority sexual orientation generally requires an ability to manage it, and the individualized means of doing so depends a great deal on one's position in relation to others (Pollak, 1993). The skills that can result from this experience (which initially develop in one's private life) can then be utilized in the context of a sales function. A decent portion of sales-related work consists precisely of knowing how to maintain the right distance (Lemarchant, 1999) with clients. I have gleaned this thanks to long visits to galleries where I could observe the interactions (Peretz, 1992) between collectors and gallerists or their staff. This manifests in particular through the level of formality used in a conversation, what is or is not appropriate to ask about the client's marital or private life, and the jokes that are made or not made. Observing the communication (which is verbal as well as physical) between sales associates and clients over the long term is proof enough that these exchanges do indeed constitute a real level of effort and a proper competence, even if it is not very visible (or is on the whole invisible) (Strauss, 1959). In reality, they are crucial in order to forge a relationship with a client, which must be personalized if it is to stand the test of time. Erving Goffman offers an enlightening analysis on the occupational domains in which customer service professionals, who have a lower social status, sell a good that represents a symbol of their clientele's higher social status (Goffman, 1951, p. 303).

The previous point raises the question of the social origins of gallery staff who are assigned the role of sales associate, which in reality exists on a very broad spectrum. Unlike many paid occupations that are generally unthinkable (or at least, undesirable) for members of the wealthiest social categories (Saint Martin, 1993; Pinçon-Charlot, 1996 and 2016), working in a gallery is an acceptable employment option for people in the upper class, particularly women. As a matter of fact, the high level of social legitimacy in the art domain combined, moreover, with a system of fairly strong incentives, distinguishes the sector from other, "ordinary" occupations. Furthermore, these staff members, who often come from a very privileged social background, are an important resource for galleries, especially the largest ones. Thanks to their upbringing, they have access to the social circles that are most likely to buy art, especially contemporary art. Even before they enter the sector, they may already be in contact with people who will become their "natural" clients (before committing to selling artworks), but they are also familiar with the social codes that will allow them to effectively evolve in this social environment. Among these characteristics are, for example, having good manners or being well traveled, along with having an extremely full little black book of precious contacts. As this collector confided to me:

> My sales associate [one of the directors] at the gallery, she's perfect. She never forgets my birthday, every year she has flowers delivered to me, she's always very attentive, I pay a lot of attention to that. She also knows exactly what I need, she doesn't annoy me by offering me pieces that

> aren't for me, and when I want something, she finds it for me, even if it takes several years.

It is clear here how the sociology of professions often benefits from linking one's occupation to one's private experience (Quemin, 2002b) even if, too often, the discipline tends to dissociate these two dimensions. Thus, among gallery staff members who are assigned to sell contemporary art pieces, especially within the largest establishments, many of them come from dynastic families (Pinçon & Pinçon-Charlot, 1996 and 2016); be they aristocratic, industrial, or political. For the members of these families, their surname largely functions as a brand that amplifies the prestige already associated with the name of the gallery. Their colleagues of less exclusive social backgrounds are more frequently referred to in the art world by their first name alone, along with the name of the gallery for which they work. If a sales associate's social background is (more often than not) very upper class, it can also extend to other upper (or upper middle) classes. There is something of a homology (Bourdieu, 1987) between a salesperson's social background and the level of the gallery at which they are employed. By contrast, it is very rare for sales associates to come from a working-class social background. For several years, a large French gallery employed a person who stood out in the civilized environment of galleries; although he was French, his first name was Anglo-Saxon in origin—a detail which, in the French context, denoted a social background that was out of step with his colleagues (Besnard & Desplanques, 1986)—and he made a big splash in the social world of major galleries.

For collectors, the fact of maintaining a privileged relationship with a sales associate in a gallery is often accompanied by the habit of denigrating the other salespeople working for the establishment (being too pushy, badly brought up, uncultured and uninteresting are the most commonly used reproaches), as if they could only have formed and continued this harmonious relationship with a single person. The ideology of the elective, "charm offensive" relationship is easily perceptible, as it frequently follows an exclusive model: there are often qualities that people wish to possess themselves that they find in (or project onto) "their" sales associate. Social and interpersonal skills in particular are essential, but collectors frequently expect additional qualities "of the heart," this is because the sales relationship is extremely personalized, and often extends (at least for the best clients) beyond interactions that are strictly related to purchases and transactions. However, it is not uncommon, after a few years, for a sales associate to fall out of favor with "their" collector, who may decide to make their purchases through one of their colleagues.

The lasting relationship between sales associates and their clients prolongs the duration of the sale. In fact, it would be appropriate to emphasize the temporal dimension of sales "in progress." It most often involves forging a medium- or long-term relationship (see the next chapter) between the buyer and the salesperson; independent of this, agreeing on the price of an artwork can take time, partly because the gallery may need to seek the artist's approval if they are considering a significant price reduction. As such, it makes little sense to hire short-term workers for an art fair booth; the sales associates need to know the gallery and the artists' work very well, and need to be able to stay in contact with interested buyers.

The domain of sales gives rise to active client canvassing, when "sales associates" contact their clients to make "offers." In order to be this enterprising, salespeople need a certain amount of proximity to their clients, otherwise the interaction would be perceived as being too intrusive, and would have very little chance of concluding successfully. It is therefore necessary to start by considering the clients' "tastes" and the "need" that the sales associate hopes to fill with their proposal.

"Salespeople" between competing galleries frequently know each other[7] (and the reputations of their peers). This associate director, who is widely recognized for his talent as a salesman, disapproved of a gallery director who often goes too far and leans into aggressive commercial practices:

> [C], she's terrible. The other day, I was chatting with one of our collectors and I saw her, she was circling us like a hyena, she was ready to pounce. As soon as I finished chatting with the collector, she jumped on him, he didn't have a chance, she was going to do anything and everything to sell him something immediately.

The deliberate intention not to display a gallery's commercial dimension, but rather to maintain the illusion of pure artistic selflessness (Bourdieu & Darbel, 1987) is also perceivable via the discretion that characterizes the system of sales incentives or commissions made available to salespeople. As the associate director of a gallery explained: "We may be friends, you and I, but we are absolutely forbidden to talk about bonuses." Some galleries pay a percentage on sales of 2–5 percent, or up to 7 percent in the world's largest establishments. In a major Italian gallery, the rate goes up to 10 percent. There are sometimes other incentive systems to drive sales; for example, instead of offering a percentage of each sale, a gallery may give an annual quota: in a large gallery, a salesperson could be paid a bonus if they make €1.2 million in sales.[8] Often, especially in large galleries, salespeople are chosen for the network of collectors or potential clients that they would bring to the gallery upon joining the staff. This network may be constructed of social and family connections, as previously stated, or come from previous professional encounters. The gallerist referred to in the following statement suffers from a bad reputation, as he competes with his own sales team, even those whom he selected so that his gallery could benefit from their personal networks: "[X] is much too hard, he recruited [Y] because he knew that he has a great network of collectors, both through his family and through his previous position in an auction house. But, to avoid having to pay him a commission on sales and to make sure that [Y]'s clients would stay with the gallery if ever he left, he's been trying to steal his clients from the start. It's pathetic, he shouldn't be doing that." As another type of incentive, this general manager of an international gallery has a share in the profit of all of the sales her gallery makes, which prevents her from being tempted to compete with her directors (who are also her subordinates, as was the case with the previously cited gallerist).

Controlling sales and clients

To whom do galleries sell contemporary artworks? Contrary to a commonly held belief that stems from an ill-informed spontaneous association between contemporaneity and youth (Quemin, 2013b), contemporary art collectors are mostly people from older generations. Typically, among a gallery's most important clients, people over 50 or 60 years old are highly represented, especially for the most famous galleries. Collectors are also, fundamentally, self-employed, CEOs, top executives, or in lucrative liberal professions, much more often than they are "standard" salaried workers (Mercier, 2012). They generally buy works from only a handful of galleries, where they are, more or less, loyal clients. It is in this context that they come (as previously mentioned) to be assigned a dedicated sales associate, usually only one per gallery. These professionals then compete with their counterparts in other galleries to make transactions.

As has been previously established, from the salesperson's point of view, the domain of sales is extremely personalized, and it is therefore necessary to know any client, even potential ones, as well as possible. Fred Davis and later Lewis A. Mennerick, having taken an interest in various commercial fields, have demonstrated that it is always important for the salesperson to be able to characterize their client in order to conclude a transaction (Davis, 1959; Mennerick, 1974). This associate director recounted her employer's embarrassment during an interaction of which she suddenly lost control, no longer knowing with whom she was dealing:

> In our field, it's very important to recognize people. My boss is usually very good at this, but I remember one time when she made a mistake, we had lunch with a man she thought was a gallerist, and after a while she realized that she had made a mistake. She said to me in a low voice, "Damn, it's not him, he must be a collector, make him talk so we know who he is."

It is therefore essential to know "who is whom," to situate the person as precisely as possible in the social space which, according to the principle of intuitive sociology, can provide initial indications of that person's tastes

(Bourdieu, 1987). It is then a matter of developing this point by becoming more familiar with loyal collectors. As Henri Peretz notes: "The time devoted to a client also results from the desire to develop a bond with loyal customers whose tastes and habits the salespeople know" (Peretz, 1992, p. 55).

In a more prosaic sense, to recognize the client is to show interest in them. Paradoxically, the outbreak of the COVID-19 pandemic in 2020 both complicated and facilitated the relationship with clients, as explained in 2021 by this director of a major gallery:

> The collectors that we've already worked with, they want us to recognize them, it's a very strong expectation on their part. At the moment, as we're required to wear a face mask, sometimes we really don't know who we're dealing with, and it's very embarrassing, it makes us very uncomfortable.

One of his colleagues who was also involved in the conversation added this clarification:

> Yes, but at the same time, it gives us a built-in excuse, we can say that it's the mask's fault that we don't recognize them, so it's less embarrassing. But in normal times, when you're at a fair booth and someone who has already bought pieces from you shows up and you don't recognize them, it's really not an easy situation to manage.

Clients are vital in any enterprise with a fundamentally commercial nature. It is therefore necessary not only to find buyers, but also to win over the *right* clients; a condition that does not necessarily exist in other business sectors, thus making the gallery sector more complex. The "right" client must all the more be identified as such; as they will then receive special, preferential treatment, even if they buy less than other clients of the gallery. In this context, it is not only the number of artworks purchased or how much is spent that counts.

By applying the perspective of interactionist sociology (Hughes, 1984), we may identify some of the characteristics of a good client: someone who buys artworks without wasting too much of the sales associate's time, and who also does not negotiate the price (or at least, only does so to a conventional extent). This gallerist explained: "Well, of course, at this fair, there are buyers who come and come back two or three times, sometimes even four times before making a decision, but there are also good collectors, who know what they want, and they decide right away." Good collectors are also those with whom a relationship of trust can be developed and, in particular, with whom there is no indication that they will resell the works shortly after having acquired them, for capital gain. As this collector, who is also an art advisor for clients in many countries, told me during a dinner organized by one of the premier galleries in the world:

> Me, I'm honest with galleries, whether it's me, or my clients. We do not sell the works at auction but [our host] has been tricked by buyers before. I'm thinking in particular of a Swiss man who resold quickly after buying something from him to turn a profit. Nothing could be done, even the greatest gallerists aren't immune to this. He has insane artists, some of whom can cause a real speculative fever. [G]'s works are offered here for 1.1 million, but they're worth 3 million at auction. For each piece, there are easily 10 clients, it's the gallery that chooses between them.

An essential part of a gallerist's work[9] consists of regulating demand; whether this involves stoking it—in the case of little-known or undervalued artists—or controlling it, by selectively choosing buyers when the demand is too high.

Controlling demand involves a series of singularities for contemporary works of art that does not exist in the classic economic model. The undertaking of galleries selling artworks does not strictly follow the law of supply and demand. In the segment of the market that corresponds to contemporary art, it is necessary to create demand from a predefined supply, according to the model established by Paul Durand-Ruel at the end of the nineteenth century (as outlined in the historical foreword of this book).

In the very particular contemporary art market, it is the supply that comes first; it is very rare for a gallerist to dare to question the work of their artist by refusing to exhibit a series, or even by directly influencing the development of the artist's work and giving input during the creation process. Contemporary galleries operate, in fact, in a supply-side economy, and it would be poorly received to adapt production in order to meet demand. However, by choosing whether or not to represent an artist, a gallerist plays a part in determining the later development of the artist's production; and, as inappropriate as it would be to influence the development of artworks in general, the gallerist has more capacity to intervene in the *production* of pieces. Insofar as the gallery commits its financial capital, there is reason for it to facilitate a profitable return on investment.

Controlling demand can also involve channeling it between the gallery's various artists. At all levels of development, gallerists tend to orient requests from their clients between the artists they represent. As this professional at the head of a small gallery explained:

> [A] thought that I wasn't good enough for him and that I wasn't supporting him well enough, but he left a year ago now, and he still doesn't have a gallery in Paris. At a fair recently, his works were displayed by a small-town gallery, but he sold practically nothing, whereas I sold his works pretty well. In fact, he was in competition with another of my artists, [B], but [B] brought a lot to the gallery. [A] was my most popular artist, just after [B], but [B] really has something exceptional, he's very

> popular with collectors. But his prices are insanely high compared to the other artists in my gallery. So when people were interested in [B] but I realized that it was beyond their means, I redirected them to [A]. As they saw that [B]'s prices had increased a lot, they told themselves that it would be the same for [A], so it was beneficial for him.

This colleague mentions the same strategy:

> [X], I had linked him to [Y]. When collectors were interested in [Y], I tried to give them [X]. There are people who weren't really interested in his work, but who wanted to support the gallery. That's how it goes with some collectors. I gave them [X]'s work on several occasions, because they still like it.

Another major departure from the general economic principle is that the salesperson often operates by *choosing* the buyer, at least in the galleries that are sufficiently established and recognized. As this director of one of the largest galleries in the world recounted in this interview excerpt:

- This artist, we could sell him for much more, we sell his paintings at between €200,000 and €300,000, but at auction, he almost always makes around €500,000. He's even made up to €800,000, which isn't normal, it's speculation. It bothers us a lot, it bothers the artist too, we have to be very careful who we sell to.
- *You don't want the buyers to 'screw you over' and quickly or even immediately put the piece up for auction or sell it to someone who would, is that it?*
- Yes, and we know that it can be very tempting. But we don't want that, we can't accept that.
- *If one of your clients did it, would you blacklist them?*
- Yes.

Not only can the contemporary art gallery choose the buyer, but it can also decide what it will sell to them. Contrary to classic economic theory, the question of price stems from the restricted accessibility of the good, or goods (here it is more precise to use the plural). In essence, in order to be able to acquire an artist's work, certain clients are almost forced to buy pieces (one or several, generally by other artists) that they do not want, either beforehand or at the same time. This practice is especially widespread among the largest American galleries, but is much less so in Europe, where it is less culturally accepted.

The notion of choosing one's buyers is particularly prominent in the case of "waiting lists." The famous New York gallerist Mary Boone (who is strongly associated with the flamboyant 1980s) is considered to be, if not the inventor of the principle of the waiting list in the world of galleries, at least the one who largely cemented it.

> The concept seems straightforward: When demand for an artist's work outstrips supply, interested collectors place their names on a list kept by the gallerist. As the artist completes new works, the gallerist theoretically works down from the top of the list, offering each freshly produced piece to the next pre-registered client.
>
> The Dealer Will See You Now: Why Gallery Waiting Lists Are the Ultimate Art-Market Paradox," *Artnet News*, June 22, 2017

It would, however, be appropriate to clarify how waiting lists actually work. Interested clients are not served based solely on the order in which they gave their names. Gregor Staiger—from the eponymous Zurich gallery—discussed the relationships of acquaintance between collectors, which could at first glance indicate a mere routine or affective dimension:

> Although he can't regulate secondary market forces outside of his control, [Staiger] notes, he can prioritize clients he trusts. 'We've had the best experience working with collectors who are otherwise invested in the gallery's program,' he explains.
>
> "The Art Market is Having a Party About Nicolas Party. Here's How the Playful Young Art Star Got So Hot, So Fast," *Artnet News*, August 19, 2019

However, even more fundamentally, potential buyers will be served according to the *interest* they present, both in the eyes of the artist and, even more so, of the gallery. It is the gallerist's responsibility to draw up lists, but also to decide who can buy the works once they become available[10] by adopting a strategic approach:

> However, the reality is that waiting lists are often not as democratic as they sound. [. . .] anyone who has a reputable private (but open to the public) museum, like Eli Broad in California, or the Rubell family [are served first]. They're followed by those who've built private collections [. . .].
>
> First, the waiting list simultaneously guarantees sales and boosts an artist's prices. Its pure existence signals to interested collectors that someone else is already poised hungrily in the shadows, ready to pounce on any piece they might pass up. (...) This quirk of human nature minimizes the odds that any collector on the list will decline the opportunity to buy once it is granted. Furthermore, the waiting list also automatically justifies any asking price the gallerist chooses by implying

> that a standing offer already exists at that price. As a result, collectors on the list essentially forfeit all bargaining power to the gallerist.
>
> But the second reason for the waiting list actually extends to almost all high-end gallery sales: (...) a self-reinforcing system of value. Selling an artist's work is important to elevating his (...) standing on the market, but not as important as selling it to 'the right collectors,' meaning those already held in high regard within this socioeconomic niche.
>
> "The Dealer Will See You Now: Why Gallery Waiting Lists Are the Ultimate Art-Market Paradox," *Artnet News*, June 22, 2017

As a matter of fact, when it comes to the best galleries, the largest and most renowned, a piece of contemporary art is not so much "sold" as it is "placed." Access to the works themselves is therefore a product in and of itself. This is what economists call a "matching market"; it is not only a question of initiating a transaction, but it also involves a sort of pairing. Matching markets, which were studied in particular by the economist Alvin Roth (Roth & Vande Vate, 1990), constitute special markets wherein buyers cannot simply select whatever they have the financial means to buy, they must also themselves be chosen. In the case of contemporary art galleries, these establishments are even prepared to give up part of the profit they could have immediately made as, in the long run, the work of the artist will appreciate in value if it is properly placed, which could take more time. It is a long-term venture, and the return on investment made by this temporal protraction will ultimately be beneficial for both the artist and the gallery. A good gallery will also often prefer to sell a piece at a lower price to a prestigious institution, such as a major museum, than to sell it for a much higher price to a buyer who has no particular legitimacy. Here again, it is clear that the works and the players on the art market and in the art world mutually qualify each other (Moulin & Quemin, 1993).

A basic principle that applies to all galleries, and even more so to the largest among them, is therefore to place artists in the best possible collections, both public and private. As this associate director of one of the largest galleries in the world, with locations in several European cities, explained:

> Well, some of our artists are so in demand that we really choose who we sell them to. First are the major museums, then the large private collections, then our loyal collectors. Recently, a couple of collectors wanted to buy two paintings by [K], but no, the rule was only one per person. They tried to play up the fact that they wanted one each, that they were two different people, but no, they can only have one as a couple. It would have been an easy sale for 3 million, but with them it was only 1.5 million.

The same ranking of priorities exists everywhere in the world:

> After receiving a PDF blast about a gallery's forthcoming show of a new artist, San Francisco-based collector and arts publicist Florie Hutchinson replied to ask about prices. 'Thanks so much for your interest,' came the response. 'Just to warn you it is fairly unlikely there will be a painting available as we have a lot of people waiting for work and the priority is museums, then clients donating the works to museums. We're also taking into consideration how long clients have been waiting and bearing in mind how much support those clients give the wider gallery program.'
>
> "The Cost of Price Transparency: Why Some Dealers Would Rather Alienate You Forever Than Reveal the Price of an Artwork," *Artnet News*, June 11, 2019

The following excerpt—taken from an interview with the associate director of a major French gallery—also reveals that the notion of selling to an intermediary induces reluctance, as it does not allow gallerists to control the "quality" of the final purchaser. Such a transaction could therefore cause someone to be lower on the waiting list. The potential client does not manage to secure a sale, to her great disappointment, even though selling artworks to her would ensure a large number of pieces sold at high prices:

> She is an advisor and she trades artworks, she buys several pieces from the same artist and then resells them to her clients. She has been wanting to buy works by [O] for a while, but she always comes too late. When we were at a fair, we sold everything, and she was unhappy because she told us that we knew she wanted to buy from us, but we prefer to place [O]'s works with very good collections, in museums or with excellent collectors, or with clients who are important to us because they regularly buy from the gallery.

While this mechanism of placing works with the right collections represents a basic principle for gallerists and their professional sales associates, it is also perfectly mastered by many artists. As this important gallerist reported when talking about a superstar artist: "During his exhibition in New York, it seemed that [K] wanted above all to sell to clients who were committed to making donations to museums, he didn't want just anyone to be able to buy his works, and he wanted them to go to American museums."

Collectors themselves also believe that the act of purchasing art is determined by the quality of the buyers. Incidentally, this is why press releases (to which collectors have access during exhibitions) generally indicate which artists are represented by which major collections. This constitutes a guarantee of quality of their work, and ensures that the value (both aesthetic and financial) will endure over time (Moulin, 1992). This art lover—who has a very beautiful collection—criticized a gallery from which she has nevertheless regularly bought pieces in the past, before later changing her mind:

> I don't buy from them anymore, it's actually a bad gallery. They sell to bring in money without worrying about who is buying from them, they don't refuse anyone because their collection isn't good enough. They're traders.

Retail price: a determining factor

In addition to the partnership of buyer and seller, who come together around the artwork, price is another important element of the sale. It is not widely advertised in the gallery world, as the strictly commercial dimension of this sector is largely euphemized, or even hidden. Incidentally, pricing has not been widely studied by art sociologists, with the exception of the works of Raymonde Moulin (Moulin, 1987) and Olav Velthuis (Velthuis, 2002 and 2005). The former adopted a *de facto* interactionist position by explaining that reputations and prices depend on the judgments produced by the art world (Becker, 1982) on a set of beliefs shared by a community of market players. Pierre Bourdieu provides a similar analysis in terms of the economy of symbolic goods wherein the value of art, far from having an objective material basis, resides in a set of beliefs (Bourdieu, 1996).

In their own sales spaces, galleries that belong to the social world of contemporary art (Becker, 1982), and have mastered its code: never list a price next to the artwork; even at fair booths the practice remains very uncommon. A small number of galleries even refuse to give prices to people they do not know, be it at fairs or in their own spaces. This important collector recounted a misadventure that occurred when one of the largest international establishments inaugurated a location in France:

> I went to this gallery once, shortly after they opened. I asked a young woman from the gallery who was nearby for a price and she replied, "Ma'am, we don't give out prices!" No doubt they wanted to be very chic, but I found that so crass! Suffice it to say, I have not set foot there ever since.

Pricing is fairly simple in the secondary market,[11] since there are already established price levels that are widely accepted. The artwork is compared to others with which it shares a maximum number of characteristics in order to determine the price at which it can be purchased, as well as the price at which it can later be resold. The identity of the artist, medium, dimensions, year of creation, and rarity (Moulin, 1995) are all criteria that are generally taken into account.

On the primary market, pricing the work of one's artists is a delicate task. The gallerist typically goes about it intuitively, taking their various individual experiences into account. If the artist has already been exhibited in their gallery (or in another gallery), the previous prices become a point of reference. Diana Crane shows that, in the case of new artists, as the "product" is too new to have a clearly established price (Crane, 1987), the gallerist generally proceeds instinctually. They apply a price point that is comparable to that of artists of the same age, and modulate (based on prior experience) according to the anticipated demand. The same criteria as in the secondary market are considered, with the exception of the artist's identity being less important, as it largely remains to be constructed. A similar problem can arise for established artists even if, in general, the new price points are broadly determined from past prices (Frey & Pommerenhe, 1989). As such, this collector reported an unsuccessful initiative by one of the largest galleries in the world (of American origin) when it opened a location in a new city in Europe:

> When he opened his new gallery in [X], [Y] couldn't find anything better to do than to offer [Z]'s works on paper at prices that nearly reached a million dollars! It's downright insane. For almost the same price, four or five years ago, you could have gotten large, magnificent paintings by the greatest German artists of our time. You would have to be crazy to agree to pay such prices for an artist who's much less recognized than them, and for simple pieces created on paper. Frankly, to arrive on the scene like that, it was quite arrogant.

As the gallerist in question was very experienced, one could presume that the asking price was motivated by the desire to reproduce the Veblen effect, wherein the very high price indicated is intended to make the works more desirable (Veblen, 1899). However, it would appear that it did not work as expected, and instead harmed the gallery's image, which was perceived as excessive in its valuations. Conversely, I was able to witness conversations suggesting that artists might have been priced too low, in a decision stemming from the same uncertainty, but this time in the other direction. The following comments made by an assistant director of an international gallery with a location in Paris reflect this:

> There, for [X], we sold everything even before the opening. We wanted to adopt a reasonable price point, because it was his first solo exhibition in a gallery in France, between €30,000 and €80,000, it was good. [The gallery head] wanted us to set higher points, and then he told us we should have listened to him, but we, the team, we preferred to stick to that point—and he listened to us. And I still think it's better for the future.

As a matter of fact, the essential is not so much the prices in absolute terms; what matters even more is how they evolve, which must be in an upward trajectory. In general, the commonly applied principle consists of gradually increasing the price point throughout the artist's career (Moulin, 1987; Velthuis, 2005). In the 1960s, Raymonde Moulin recorded the following statement, which remains just as relevant today, of a gallerist: "You understand, for prices, you can never go backwards (...). We take advantage of an exhibition to revise our prices; we don't even revise them every year" (cited in Moulin, 1987 [1967]). The gradual increase in price will be maintained in order to guarantee the quality (Misdrahi Flores, 2013) of the artist's work. As a gallerist interviewed by Olav Velthuis summarized in an extremely concise statement: "I just make them go up" (Velthuis, 2002, p. 60).[12] Auctions are rejected by galleries because they disrupt their price control strategies. While these public sales can lead to rapid price hikes in the short term, they are accompanied in the longer term by a high probability of dropping prices, which is detrimental for the artist market, as professionals intend to adjust supply and demand themselves. In the Western art market, when demand exceeds supply for an artist, galleries typically establish a waiting list (as previously noted in this chapter) and select collectors whom they serve first, instead of increasing prices (Velthuis, 2005). Conversely, on the Chinese contemporary art market, galleries have often considered it fairer to adjust supply and demand through a sort of bidding system. In this system, the collector wanting a work of art enough to pay the highest price will acquire it. Chinese galleries have tended to think that the best artists would stand the test of the market. However, after having been widely adopted by Chinese galleries, this practice has broadly shown its limitations.

Stopping a price from climbing beyond its appropriate level is all the more important, as it then determines transactions. In general, collectors do not like to emphasize the motivation behind (or even the simple financial dimension of) their purchases. However, the financial aspect is not totally absent, and it sometimes emerges spontaneously; in particular, by inquiring how an artist's prices evolve. I witnessed the following exchange in which a gallery director came to greet a couple of collectors at a vernissage, after their hostess had introduced the artist and his work in a few words:

- Ah, but you know, we already have one.
- You have one of his drawings?
- No, no, a painting.
- Ah, I didn't know that.
- We bought it about 10 years ago. Has the value gone up much since then?
- [the director, obviously uncomfortable] No, not really, all the pieces in the exhibition, which span his entire career, are between €150,000 and €300,000 . . .
- Oh, well then yes, it has gone up quite a bit, we paid much less than that.

During this interaction, I could feel the collectors' relief of being reassured about both the financial and aesthetic value of their work (and more broadly, about the artist's work) as they appear to be intrinsically linked (Moulin, 1987 and 1992). The gallery director herself seemed to share this sentiment; having to announce that prices had fallen (or not risen) would have been an admission of failure. When an artist does not find success, rather than lowering their prices, a gallery may prefer to apply larger, more general discounts. This allows it to preserve the belief in the value of the work created by the artist whom the gallery represents. The practice of "discounts" will be analyzed later.

Another element that affects how an artwork is priced is the existence of threshold effects. These exist both in absolute terms—in the general art market—and at the gallery level, as not all establishments operate within the same market segment. As this French gallerist put it:

> We other 'normal' contemporary art galleries know very well that there are thresholds. Up to €5,000, it's quite easy to sell, let's say you can go up to €8,000, after that it becomes so much more complicated. Then there's a new level around €30,000 or €50,000. Between this amount and €300,000, transactions are really rare. Beyond that, it becomes easier again, people no longer need to count, they don't look at what they're spending.

It is clear that the gallerist is talking about fairly clear price points that largely prevail on the market but, at the same time, he takes care to specify that this concerns the majority of galleries ("normal," as he describes them). There are, in fact, other galleries that operate at much higher price levels and are not subject to the levels previously indicated. Galleries are characterized by average price points that can vary quite a bit; some frequently reach amounts that are inaccessible to their fellow establishments. Galleries generally have no trouble positioning themselves in a price range, as the following interview excerpt shows:

> Where does the gallery stand compared to market prices? To borrow an expression from the financial world, we are in the 'upper middle market,' with artworks up to €50,000. Then, some of my artists want to keep prices fairly low, and thus continue to be collected by buyers who don't necessarily have deep pockets. The works by Alexandre Hollan,[13] for example, who was supported from the beginning of his career by poets, academics, and artists, vary between €650 and €20,000, even though he is internationally recognized and is collected by several institutions of renown. Jean-Bernard Métais[14] as well, his sculptures and outdoor installations can reach several million euros, he also exhibits pieces with prices starting at €3,000.
>
> "Marie-Hélène de la Forest Divonne, a Breath of Fresh Air," *La Gazette Drouot*, no. 32, September 21, 2018, p. 23

Note that the gallerist indicates a price range that may seem surprising and significantly out of phase with the recognition that these artists have. By contrast, the lower price points that she mentions appear to be much more in line with the artist's reputation beyond their gallery alone.

This collector jokingly discussed the exceptional price at which she acquired a piece from one of the largest galleries in the world; a purchase that she knew was completely atypical:

> So we, me and my husband, it makes us laugh a lot, we bought a piece by [X] for barely a few thousand euros. At the time, he was practically a kid, and what he creates isn't what lends itself the most to the market, and he had just started with the [Y] gallery. It's one of the most famous in the world, and it very often holds exhibitions in which most of the works exceed a million euros! But we only paid a few thousand euros, I don't think they even remember that they were able to sell his pieces at such low prices! It's very chic when we say that we're clients of theirs [she laughs].

Price points, in fact, largely segment the market at all levels: artists, galleries, and collectors; and they directly determine the domain of sales in terms of the networks in which a sale could take place. This director of one of the largest galleries in the world explained:

- Before, I worked in Germany in one of the best galleries in the country. It was really an exceptional experience. Then I came to work in France, and again I really liked it. At the time, it was one of the biggest galleries, I really built myself a large client base.
- *But were you able to keep it when you came here later?*
- No, of course not. Price points really had nothing to do with this place. I think that when I was recruited, it was because I had good sales experience, even international experience, I know how to behave with clients, what to do in order to sell a piece. But you see, even me, although I already knew the environment well, I was surprised to find that, with my previous clients, I wasn't really able to keep more than a few, even though I liked them a lot, I know that they were satisfied with my work, that some of them would obviously have loved to buy works by artists at my new gallery. It's just that in terms of financial means, they couldn't follow me.

This excerpt clearly shows that within the same social world (that of contemporary art galleries), there are very different prices of entry that help to segment this universe and delineate the sub-spaces that are fairly impermeable in terms of collectors.[15] This collector explained that one's financial means determine which galleries they can buy from:

> We started a collection of minimalist art about 30 years ago. There are artists that we weren't able to buy at that time because we were just getting started, and there are some that we can't buy today because their prices have gone up too much. Even the galleries, there are some, you can hardly buy anything there, they're too expensive for us, even if we have nearly 300 pieces, including some from very well-known artists.

This art advisor also reported threshold effects based on prices:

> Well, I take my clients to galleries, Galleries [X], [Y], and [Z] for example, that have a certain price point, often with pieces around €50,000, for example. The Ropac gallery, it's excellent, I would love to be able to take them there to make purchases, because it has some great artists, but it doesn't match my clients' price points, it's way too expensive.

When integrating a new artist, a gallery may sometimes adapt the artist's prices in order to make them more compatible with their own. As this collector explained:

> [A] doesn't really have the clients for €5,000 pieces. So, since she doesn't have the market for it, when she brought [X] to her gallery, she didn't beat around the bush, she raised the price of her smallest pieces to €10,000 overnight!

There are also psychological effects that intervene in determining prices, which are not limited to the mere fact of being perceived as reasonable by collectors. The rivalry between artists also comes into play, especially if they are represented by the same gallery. It may therefore be unacceptable for some artists to claim that their work is being promoted less than that of their peers. As this director of one of the largest galleries in the world explained:

> At the previous exhibition, [B]'s paintings were listed at €800,000 or even €1 million, and then he learned of [A]'s prices, which were significantly higher than his, and he therefore demanded that his prices be raised. Now, at this exhibition, [B]'s paintings are listed at 1.2 million.

According to the Veblen effect, the highest price effectively guarantees the best possible quality, and can reinforce the works' desirability among collectors (Veblen, 1899). As a result, it can be difficult for a star artist to accept that a peer from their own gallery would be sold at even higher price points than their own.

The market segmentation by price point that prevails between galleries produces similar effects at the city level, when an entire local market is similarly subject to threshold effects. Thus, as in the case of the previous gallery director who had to completely rebuild her client portfolio after changing employers, since her new gallery operates at much higher price points than her former one, certain marketplaces are—as a whole—subject to analogous patterns. This gallery weekend manager in a European city that is fairly marginal on the art market explained:

> Well, here, it's not New York, London, Paris, or even Berlin. The galleries all sell in a price range that goes from a few thousand euros to around €50,000. Recently, I know that [X] Gallery, which also sometimes offers somewhat historical pieces, made a sale for around €150,000, but that's very exceptional for this area. Us, what we're targeting, the collectors that we have to try to bring in during our gallery weekend, are those who buy pieces for up to €50,000, they're the best targets for our galleries.

Price modulation: the practice of "discounts"

The price of artworks is therefore a benchmark and a considerable constraint for galleries. However, as previously explained, price is by no means invariable; on the contrary, it is personalized according to the client (and the client's desirability), since they qualify the work just as much as the work qualifies them once it is acquired, or even as soon as they express their intention to buy it. Although it is never presented as such, the price of art is, in reality, merely indicative. It is then subject to a degree of modulation—generally downwards—taking into account the importance that the client represents, both for the artist's career and for the gallery.

In his thesis on prices in the contemporary art world, Olav Velthuis mentions that discounts are used to close a sale (Velthuis, 2002, p. 89), but they have not been the subject of a very thorough analysis. However, it is the practice that has the greatest impact on the price point once it has been determined prior to a transaction. As a matter of fact, even if not all galleries do it systematically, they often grant a 10 percent price reduction as soon as it is requested. The best clients therefore typically seek to deal directly with the gallerist, or with the gallery's general manager—rather than with other sales associates—believing that they can obtain the best reductions, and therefore the best final prices. Some galleries will even give a 12 or 15 percent discount to their best clients, or to those with whom they wish to make a sale. They may even grant greater discounts still; this is particularly true for museums, whose acquisition budgets are very limited, but whose capacity of certification (Moulin & Quemin, 1993) by acquisition is widely sought by galleries and artists. There are also "museum quality" private collections that—while they do not always admit the general public—also award the gallery and the artist a label and therefore constitute strategic placements, especially if they are known for easily lending out their pieces in the context of exhibitions. This staff member of a major American gallery explained:

> This piece [by a great, now-deceased artist] is a work on cardboard. We offered it at a fair for €250,000, but ultimately we sold it at 200,000 because it was very particular. It's a corporate collection from the same country as the fair and the artist. We wanted it to be a part of their collection, so we made a big commercial gesture.

Art market players other than gallerists also understand how useful it can be to give a discount, be it the standard 10 percent or even higher. But this is sometimes less well understood than it is among gallerists and their sales associates. As a now-deceased artist's daughter—who is very involved in managing the stock left by her father—explained:

> The other beneficiary has a hard time understanding that it's normal to give collectors a 10% discount. Even more, when you want to add a piece to a good collection. The piece by my father that was displayed at Art Basel Unlimited was listed at €190,000, but in the end, the gallery sold it for €150,000 because the collection was worth it. I was very happy with this sale, even though the reduction was considerable.

Discounts, though very often applied and sometimes quite substantial, consistently tend to be minimized, particularly because they call the idea of a fair initial price into question. Moreover, the artist's work should not be devalued by presenting the reduction of the initially announced price as being self-evident. However, although the 10 percent price reduction is widely recognized, several galleries more or less frequently make an "effort" of going up to 15, or 20 percent, or even more. This is only because these discount levels are generally no longer systematic. On occasion, galleries have assured me that they never go beyond reducing the advertised price of a piece by 10 or 15 percent (and they were categorical on this point); and later, some collectors claimed that they acquired works from these galleries at a 20, 25, or even 30 percent reduction! However, the commercial policy of offering (too) high discounts is generally frowned upon in the profession. As indicated by this art advisor, who had acquired a piece from a gallery that had assured me they never granted a discount of over 10 percent: "Recently, I had one of my clients buy this painting for €400,000. It's by a very prominent artist. But since I'm an art advisor, I negotiated for the client and I got a little more than 10% [off]. And the gallery also paid me my 10% commission." However, it is not only works in a gallery's high price range that are affected by substantial discounts. Another art advisor explained: "This drawing [by a very prominent, in demand artist], it was offered for €7,000 by [a Swiss gallery], but I wanted it for my personal collection, and

I negotiated it down to 5,000."[16] I was amused, upon learning this fact, to share it with the Swiss gallerist, who is a good friend (without mentioning the identity of the buyer): a reduction of 28 percent went far beyond anything he had told me up to then. However, despite having been discovered—and without denying the reality of the number that I had given him—he defended himself: "For institutions and collections that are very large or have great potential, we sometimes offer a 20% price cut. And the trick is that in Switzerland, we sell on behalf of a third party, [the artist] who is not taxable for VAT purposes, so we don't include it on the invoice, which is a big discount!" Still, the sale price was much lower than the advertised price.

Clearly, from the previous examples, the question of price and possible discounts is a very sensitive subject, and it is hardly possible to study it from the gallery perspective alone, as Olav Velthuis did in his research on how contemporary art prices are determined. Simultaneously analyzing the situation from the buyers' side sheds light on the practice of sales in a totally different way. It is likewise very revealing that Velthuis hardly mentions discounts, even though they occupy an important, or even central place in the sales strategy (Velthuis, 2002).

On both sides of the sales relationship, agreeing to a discount (or not) and how much it will be is subject to expectations that can on occasion diverge sharply. As such, a French gallerist told her entire team not to give any discounts during the 2019 FIAC art fair, since the event was shaping up to be auspicious (and incidentally lived up to its promise). However, the gallerist earned a bad reputation following this decision, with collectors reproaching her for her commercial intransigence in an environment where "gestures" are the norm. The practice of discounts, which are normally seen as gifts given to the customer, is framed by normative expectations that make them almost obligatory (Mauss, 1966). As this international gallery director indicated:

> For the FIAC, [the gallerist] had decided that we wouldn't give any discounts, as many clients come to the FIAC and like to buy from us, since we're a French gallery, she made this choice. But maybe it was a bit too radical. There are artists we share with other galleries, and collectors can get comparable pieces by the same artist from another gallery, but 10 or even 15% cheaper. So they may have felt that we were scorning them a little bit, or that we weren't recognizing or valuing them enough. And then, these are the people who may have bought lots of other works from us, and who we lost as clients at that time, because the relationship of trust is very important.

This practice of discounts, which gives the impression of giving a gift to the client, is so widespread that this collector is annoyed when a gallerist does not agree to do so: "[X], she's very tough in business. All the gallerists give me a reduction of 10%, sometimes even 15%. I always negotiate, but with [X], the price is the price, she doesn't make any gestures."

The practice of discounts is so widespread that some galleries have even integrated them into their management software for upcoming sales. *Artnet News*, when reporting on the presentation made by a famous international gallerist at one of the "Talking Galleries" symposiums in Barcelona, explained:

> However, Perrotin also demonstrated how integral technology has become to his organization. In one of the symposium's buzziest moments, he walked the audience through the custom software he uses to manage his web of six international galleries, which collectively house over 100 staff members. He explained that he first began building the software at the tender age of 18 and now employs 12 engineers to maintain and refine it. The program acts as the central nervous system of the gallery, allowing him to set deadlines and follow up on priorities with employees, as well as see all works currently on reserve to specific clients (including at what price, and at what size discount).
>
> *Artnet News*, "Here Are the 4 Major Conundrums That Will Define the Art Market of the Future, According to Experts," January 29, 2019

The principle of granting discounts to clients is so integrated into the sales relationship that not asking for a discount (when the buyer clearly does not know that there is a possibility to do so, or how to do it) can confuse the sales associate. As this associate director of an international gallery jokingly reported:

> The other day, I sold a painting to a collector, and I told him the price, and when it came time to buy, he didn't even ask for a discount. He paid the price and apparently he was very happy. And then, a few days later, he contacted me again . . . to buy two more pieces! And even then, he still didn't mention any discounts that we could give him. Well, it bothered me, so I told him that, since he was buying three pieces from us, I was going to take 10% off on the two new ones. But, just between us, I even wondered if I shouldn't also take 10% off the first one. But I didn't, I was a bit of a snake. But not that much, actually, because if I hadn't offered to take the 10% off the two new pieces, I'm sure he wouldn't have even asked, and I could easily have saved that discount.

It is clear in this excerpt how different levels of what is fair or not in terms of commercial practice can clash, and how the price reduction offered to clients is broadly a given . . . without being invariably so.

To summarize the previous developments, when it is not implemented in a more individualized way to place pieces with particular collections, discounts generally allow galleries to facilitate the conclusion of the transaction (Velthuis, 2002), as well as to develop the client's loyalty to the gallery.

Reaching clients, then selling to them

How are contemporary art pieces sold? While the transaction is structured by the various players and parameters presented in the previous section (to wit: the seller, the client, the pieces, and their price levels), it is also the subject of codified cultural practices. The process of purchasing a work of art is not the same as for other products. To illustrate this, I will begin with an anecdote of a young woman who, after having built her career in the French banking sector, intended to settle in Asia and open a contemporary art gallery to fulfill her personal passion for art. However—as she was largely external to the art world, its uses and conventions (Becker, 1982)—she naively thought that it would be enough to rent a space, hang her shingle outside it, and display works so that clients could come in spontaneously.[17] In fact, sales largely work in this manner for galleries that sell chromos (Couture, 1981; Moulin, 1992), even if they often try to boost their sales by adopting techniques to attract and retain clients who are accustomed to the techniques utilized by contemporary art galleries. It should be noted that these chromo establishments very rarely present themselves as such to their clients who, moreover, are usually unaware of the codes and boundaries that are particular to the social world of art as a whole, as well as its different segments.

While the contemporary art sector has its singularities in terms of sales practices (the primary one, as previously mentioned, consists of the choice of buyer, at least for the most established galleries), it nevertheless shares common traits with other sectors. As is the case everywhere, one must first successfully make contact with the prospective client; only then will it be possible to make the actual sale.

In the case of contemporary art galleries, and contrary to what people who are not familiar with these establishments may believe, they do not wait for clients to show up to buy artworks.[18] Sales constitute a proactive activity; art galleries are in no way shops which clients can "drop by" with a clearly identified need. Even more than in many sectors, it is a question of teasing out this need; of building it up. The field today is a far cry from the time of Daniel-Henry Kahnweiler, who explained that his work as a gallerist consisted of acquiring works and then waiting patiently for collectors to come to buy them (Moulin, 1987).

There is an entire range of techniques to encourage art lovers, and especially collectors, to circulate; be it within the confines of the gallery itself, or at its booth during an art fair. Galleries sometimes even go so far as to show clients artworks in their own homes; it is therefore the works, not the collectors, that are mobile.

The next chapter will analyze how invitations constitute an essential springboard for sales, even more so because they seem to present access to the world of galleries free of charge. Broadly speaking, this is true, with the convention of exhibition previews to which the gallery's supporters are invited; but there is also a host of other, more personalized occasions. For instance, the gallery allows the client to bypass paying an entrance fee for a fair by sending them an invitation, or offers access to a talkback, a cocktail reception, a dinner, or a museum that it has privatized. The gift of free entry is enhanced by the added benefit of privileged, exclusive access. However, according to the analyses of Marcel Mauss in his *Essay on the Gift*, this lavishness contains in itself the gesture that will be paid back in turn (Mauss, 1966); here, in the context of buying works of art.

An important element of a gallery's work also consists of canvassing museums and individual collectors to offer them works available for purchase by sending them files presenting the works. This involves direct contact, particularly by telephone, and sending emails with visuals of the works. Even before openings or fairs, it is not uncommon for works that will be displayed to already have been sold. As this art advisor explained:

> Art Basel is crazy, we have five minutes, or let's say half an hour to make a decision. Obviously, the galleries send us visuals of the works they're going to display at their booth in advance. It's fine for me, because I'm a personal collector, and I advise five collectors, two in the United States, in New York, two in Switzerland, and one in the Netherlands. So I regularly buy from certain galleries, so they can keep some works aside for me that will therefore be sold even before the fair opens.

These very active and fairly intrusive practices are only tolerated thanks to the long-term relationship between the salesperson and the collector. Far from being presented as a commercial procedure, the initiative must be presented as a means to help improve a collection.

As always, this must be practiced in moderation. This director of a major gallery criticized the overly aggressive methods used by a competing gallerist:

> It's crazy, she called friends of mine, some of my closest friends, who are collectors, to offer them an artist, but she doesn't know them at all. But that didn't stop her, she called them. But it doesn't work like that at all, she knows that, but it doesn't bother her, she's pushy, she goes in all guns blazing. And she puts an enormous amount of pressure on her sales associates to do the same.

Excessive pressure is, in fact, often poorly perceived by collectors. One such collector explained:

> Me, when they offer to come to my home to present artworks, in general, I don't like it. It's very intrusive, it's difficult to send works away once they've been brought over, but I always do it. I always say immediately that I don't like it, and that I've never bought anything like that, but it's

> sometimes difficult to stop the person that you're close to in the gallery from coming to present a work to you.

The desire to reach collectors explains why gallerists or their employees are present at any occasion where they could be in touch with potential buyers. This is particularly the case for openings in museums or art centers, especially when a gallery's artist is included in the exhibition. It is then customary to send a staff member of the gallery, who certainly fulfills their role as "artist liaison," but who can also take advantage of the opportunity to maintain contact with (or even sell to) collectors who will be present. Gallerists and their teams are also frequently present in large numbers at openings and "professionals"[19] days at biennials, even though these are not (officially at least) commercial events. As this Italian gallerist put it: "At the Venice Biennale too, the market is there, but it's more underground." As the following associate director of a British gallery explained, also in reference to the Venice Biennale:

> In the biennials that matter, it's normal, if you're a big, serious gallery, you have to be there, like with the openings of its artists, as well as the first days, during the pro or VIP days. We see everyone go by, we rekindle our contacts. Here, there are four of us from the gallery, we form a kind of hedge right in the middle of the Arsenale building, people can't get past us without being blocked! And you know, it works, we haven't stopped selling since the beginning!

However, a French gallerist disapproved of this way of doing things, which she finds too overtly commercial:

> Ah, but I don't stand in front of my artists' works at the biennial. It's not my way! But if you go to the Hirst exhibition,[20] you'll see, Jay Jopling is always around, he's there to catch collectors. Me, I don't work like that, I wait for people to come to me. Also, what my artists show here aren't really things for sale.

It should nevertheless be noted that this gallerist mitigated her disapproval by conceding that she does not proceed in this way herself because the works produced by her artists are less suitable for sale in such a context. Outside of the biennial, transactions can also be pursued, as this Swiss gallerist confided to me during the same event: "Our two directors came for the biennial's opening, and I can assure you that they have appointments with collectors practically every half an hour during the preview days. They keep selling!"

Not all artists and works are sold with the same ease; they are, after all, not standardized products. The same gallery can alternate between exhibitions wherein it will sell all of the works—sometimes as of the evening of the opening (with some works having been sold even before this, as previously indicated)—while, at other shows, only 20 to 30 percent of the works will be sold. This principle is true for even the largest galleries in the world. For a given gallery—especially if it is situated in a high segment of the market—it is often the most expensive artists who are the easiest to sell. As this French gallerist indicated:

> Here, my exhibition of [M], everything has been sold. I was sure that it would be the case and I'm very happy, because we sold a lot to French collectors. Since [M] is American, I told her to send me her works, that I would sell them for her. And it's also important for collectors, they see that, when a job is good, you have to make your mind up right away. If you wait too long, then there'll be nothing left.

It is clear how exhibiting "good" artists who are in high demand makes it easier to sell artists who are less highly rated, less in demand, as collectors will then fear missing out on a purchase by learning from their experience with another artist from the gallery.

This highlights the importance of the roster, which must therefore include enough artists whose works sell fairly easily, and who will thus drive all transactions upwards. As this American gallerist put it: "Very divisive artists aren't a problem. In any case, we won't sell to everyone. The hardest thing is the artists who arouse a middling interest among everyone."

To proceed to the actual sale, there are general, fairly simple techniques. First of all, it is not simply a question of selling a piece; there is a whole accompanying discourse that gives it meaning, which Americans in particular designate by the term "narrative." This associate director of one of the largest international galleries explained: "I can't really sell to the same clients in my new gallery, because the price of the works is higher. People can't really follow, but I can use the same sales techniques. I know that to make a sale, you have to tell a story, you have to intellectualize, that's how I sell . . . and it works." In this other high-level gallery, it is the establishment's owner, who is very involved in sales, who is the first to become involved in the interaction. As one of her employees explained:

> When [N] presents a new series by an artist, she first talks with them and asks 'What's the story?' Then, when she's with the clients, in a way, she embellishes, but she starts from that, she can easily talk about the artists that she presents, it's one of her strengths.

Clearly, the role of the artist is to produce "quality" works (Misdrahi Flores, 2013), but also to know how to talk about their work, to give it meaning. In order to capitalize on this discourse produced by the artists themselves, certain galleries organize a pre-opening for their staff—especially their salesforce—at which the artist is also present. It is a question of better understanding the work, and for the sales associates, of developing a narrative that is likely to motivate transactions, or else of preparing the best responses to questions that collectors may ask; this is because the conversation, the discourse, is essential.

This associate director of another large gallery reported the difficulties that can occur with one of the artists—for whom he is the liaison—when it comes to making a sale, if he finds himself directly in the presence of potential buyers:

> I think he's a very good artist, he does a very good job on the works, but then when he has to interact with collectors he's . . . how can I say it, he's borderline. Recently, he was there when a collector was looking at one of his paintings, which depicted a woman with a handbag under her arm, and he explained, 'the handbag is the power, and around it there is the world.' And he didn't say anything else. I had to take over to sell the painting, to build a discourse around it, and frankly, I struggled. I love his work, but that doesn't help.

On occasion, it may even be necessary to divert the potential buyers' attention away from the subject being represented by the artist. As this associate director of an international gallery explained:

> It's true that we've been talking with [the gallerist] for a while about this series of works about Palestine, and we were quite worried. This kind of subject isn't very successful. Like everywhere else, we have a lot of collectors who are of Jewish origin. We try not to push the political dimension [when we present the works], even if it's obviously very present.

In some galleries, depending on their profile and that of the collectors, it may even be necessary to resolutely anchor the discourse in art history in an even more accentuated way than is generally done. As this employee of a major German gallery pointed out:

> Many of us at the gallery have studied art history. Mr. [X], [the gallerist], he doesn't expect us to sell to clients who say they love the piece, who buy and then leave. There are galleries like that, but this isn't our case. Mr. [X] thinks it's normal to talk about the artist and their work, that's what he's like, and our collectors too, we have to be the same. Our collectors aren't young people who have made a quick buck, they're fairly old, they don't make purchases in the same way, they don't have the same relationship with art, so knowing art history, it's added value.

All people who work in sales report using very elementary techniques, which may amuse even the salespeople themselves due to their simplicity, but these tactics nevertheless prove to be effective. They provide interesting parallels with those studied by Henri Peretz in ready-to-wear luxury clothing sales (Peretz, 1992). This associate director of an American gallery explained:

> Generally speaking, to make a sale, you mustn't contradict the clients when they talk about the works, you have to go along with them . . . even when they're wrong and talking nonsense, it doesn't matter. Correcting them can cause you to miss out on a sale.

This daughter of a photographer who often receives collectors, quips about the ease with which it is possible to make a sale as long as the previous principle is applied: "In fact, it's not very difficult to make a sale, you need to make the buyers believe that they understand the artist, you always have to go in their direction. Even after the sale is concluded, you have to tell them that they bought the best piece." She continued: "You have to tell them what they want to hear, make them believe that they understand the artist's work." Even after the sale is finished, it is not uncommon to continue to reinforce the client's conviction that they have made a wise choice. To that end, the sales associate will take the time to send the buyer a congratulatory email, or will state during a future meeting that the price the client obtained was particularly good and that the prospects of seeing it go up are significant. For the client to be loyal to the gallery in the long term, it is important that they be completely and lastingly satisfied with their purchase.

This aim explains a practice that is sometimes employed by galleries: the exchange. In *The French Art Market*, Raymonde Moulin makes mention of its existence (Moulin, 1987). When a collector no longer wishes to keep a piece that they acquired from a gallery, the "good" galleries are supposed to offer an exchange by taking back the initial work at its acquisition price. This is, in a way, a kind of insurance offered to buyers, even if the fact of valuing the work at its acquisition price demonstrates that the gallerist has not properly carried out the work to ensure the upward pecuniary progression that was expected by all parties involved.

However, even among the world's largest galleries, exchanges are not as easy in practice as they are in theory. The fact that some gallerists drag their feet, or even refuse to comply, sometimes results in a heightened sense of enmity, of which I have heard several instances. Without explicitly stating as much, this collector—whom I met during a lunch organized by one of the primary galleries in the world—recounted:

> In our collection, we have nearly 300 works. We've been collecting for more than 30 years, so inevitably there are things that we like less today. And from time to time, we want to sell pieces, but it's always very complicated. Galleries don't like buying pieces back at all, it's almost impossible. At best, they'll agree to take back a piece from one of their artists in exchange for another, but even that isn't easy. Even for a well-

> known artist. We have a big [K] [a famous conceptual artist] that we don't want to keep, but here, the gallery has explained to us that there is no market for him. They always say that. We could put it up at auction, and we'd get a pretty low price, but if we want to sell it discreetly, in fact, we really can't. We gave them a painting several years ago, officially, the gallery has to sell it for us, they agreed to take custody of it, but we understand that it's just a polite way of refusing to buy it back from us or to exchange it. If you have a large Baselitz, of course, everyone will agree to take it off your hands. But it's always the same artists. But you, you'll tell me, we know that now, but we're still going to keep buying [she smiles].

However, gallerists may also use more complex techniques to facilitate sales. In essence, it is always a question of inciting curiosity and interest in the gallery and in the work of its artists. This international gallerist with locations in three countries thus reported fairly elaborate practices:

> This artist, I'm going to present her in Europe for the first time here in Paris, but my aim is more to target collectors from [another European country]. I could certainly have shown her in my gallery in this country, that would have made more sense, but the collectors are sometimes snobs, they often like to discover an artist while abroad, to buy pieces far from their home, so I'm exhibiting her here, in Paris. In the same way, I sometimes do risky things so that nothing is self-evident in the eyes of the collectors, I want to intrigue them. Once, I organized a vernissage on December 29th, in a small town. Obviously, you would think that on the 29th, everyone is already busy, what with New Year's Eve and New Year's Day, but the fact that it seems risky, that helped to highlight the artist.

Doubtless because galleries do not highlight the commercial dimension of their business, as they tend to constantly euphemize it, this domain has not often been studied by the social sciences in the artistic sector. Pierre Bourdieu performed an in-depth analysis of how, in artistic fields, the economic dimension is both constantly denied and delegitimized; it could even be considered to be a fundamental trait of these fields (Bourdieu, 1996). In the domain of symbolic goods, contesting the economic dimension makes it possible to accumulate symbolic capital which, over time, can be converted into economic capital; it is therefore a matter of protracting production. Galleries thus occupy a paradoxical position, as they must resolutely operate within the market without allowing the economic dimension to undermine the production of symbolic capital. They must develop their mercantile (or dare I say, commercial) activity without being accused of being "commercial." This constitutes one of the almost "magical" social operations that, in reality, are rooted in the symbolic sphere, as Bourdieu and Yvette Delsaut established in the domain of *haute couture* (Bourdieu & Delsaut, 1975). It is because it manages to prove its symbolic excellence, as well as that of the artists—and more broadly the (especially aesthetic) value of the art that it represents—that the gallery manages to escape the prosaic world of commerce, even though we have seen that the sale of works of art sometimes calls for relationships and techniques that are just as applicable to luxury goods in general, or even those relating to the mass market.

Conclusion

The sale of artworks is the central focus of the gallerist's profession, and galleries are largely structured around it. Though it has been so little studied up to this point, it is undoubtedly due to a lack of access not only to the milieu, but also to the business aspect itself; both of which are quite closed. While—as already emphasized in the foreword of this book—it is practically essential to have a great amount of familiarity with galleries in order to be able to study their social world, this is even more the case for sales; to be able to study it as closely as possible, to go beyond the framework of mere appearances (Velthuis, 2002, 2003, and 2005).[21]

At the beginning of this chapter, I showed why galleries are essential players in the art market, if only by specializing in transactions; I then analyzed the role of sales associates and clients who come together in their agreement on the very possibility of making a transaction. Each party must recognize the legitimacy of the other, so that the exchange can occur; thus taking the interaction far beyond the mere act of establishing a given price. Furthermore, I thought that it would be interesting to explain how this is determined by including an essential practice (that of discounts), which has not been sufficiently studied by sociologists and economists of the art market. To fully understand the activity of sales, when all is said and done, it is important to situate it within a set of social relationships that goes beyond the simple framework of transactions. This point will be reviewed in the next chapter, with a focus on the role of friendship and how it is forged and maintained through sociability in order to facilitate sales.

5

Sociability and friendship: Resources for the gallerist occupation

As I indicated in the previous chapter, while the sales function outweighs all other operations within contemporary art galleries, it is by no means the only one, as we will see in this chapter. There is one overriding characteristic in this sector, as well as in the social world in which it exists: far more than in other domains—and particularly in mass markets—sales cannot be separated from long-term relationships (Peretz, 1992), which generally extend beyond the framework of each transaction. The sale of contemporary artworks involves a specific and fundamental sociability that must be initiated and cultivated in various ways. This requires a specific resource: friendship. While it is usually considered a disinterested value (Bidart, 1997), in this context it is utilized as a professional resource. Without emotional relationships, especially friendship, a great deal of the contemporary art economy—particularly as concerns private transactions[1]—would be seriously jeopardized. A significant share of a gallerist's professional skills calls for possessing and nurturing a good interpersonal or friendship-based network in the art world, specifically among collectors. It is virtually impossible to go into this field successfully without developing the skills to gain entry into this social world and to establish relationships. Beyond gallerists themselves, this aspect is also important when galleries recruit sales staff, directors, associate directors, or (to a much lesser extent) assistants. As I stated in the previous chapter, it is necessary to have the "right network," gained by previous professional experience and/or by social relationships in a private setting, as the professional space takes advantage of the resources produced by the private sphere (Quemin, 2002b).

Relationships with collectors: taking advantage of their motivations

Gallerists organize social occasions to put themselves in contact with new clients and maintain contact with the existing ones. Some French gallerists choose a vacation resort on the Mediterranean seaside or in the Luberon region during the summer, or in the mountains in winter (Pinçon & Pinçon-Charlot, 1996 and 2016) (places collectors are most likely to frequent). Their leisure activities can also be motivated by similar considerations. As such, this gallerist complained about one of his fellows: "I see her regularly at the opera, but what she likes best about the opera is the intermission. It might be surprising, but I've noticed that she always leaves after it [he smiles]." The intermission serves as an intense social opportunity during which it is possible for gallerists to meet many collectors, whether to reestablish connections with those they already know and who buy artworks at the gallery, or to meet potential new clients. This type of occasion is even more crucial because these moments create a sense of society around supposed common interests. However, they are branded with an apparent sign of disinterestedness (after all, they are not taking place in a commercial setting) even though the gallerist who derided his colleague's behavior doubted her devotion to the opera, as she was apparently there only for professional interests, with a commercial aim. On each occasion, whether it is a question of leisure activities or a resort, the goal is to reach collectors in a setting that suggests the sharing of common tastes (Bourdieu, 1979). Moreover, sharing these social occasions with one's clients is a means of getting to know them better and ascertaining their tastes.[2]

Another way to maintain regular contact with one's clients is to play to their motivations. Collectors come in several types (Mercier, 2012); one of their motivations is the possibility of making a financial investment, but this is not advocated by the most respectable galleries. When I asked the general director of one of these galleries: "Do some collectors emphasize the financial aspect, the desire to make a good investment, or even the possibility of making some money when they buy?" She answered: "It's quite rare. It does happen, but if it occurs, I reframe the issue: I explain that it is not possible to buy contemporary art like that". A second motivation has to do with a collector's need to stand out (Bourdieu, 1979), especially in contemporary art, which tends to be very class-dependent and has long been associated with the upper classes (Bourdieu & Darbel, 1969). The interactionist approach developed mainly by Erving Goffman uses a different theoretical angle. He suggests classifying such occupations as that of the gallerist as "curator staff," which would enable the upper social categories to assert their status: "Starting from when a class's symbolic equipment becomes elaborate, curator staff can be developed; its job is to build and maintain this statutory machinery" (Goffman, 1951, p. 303). Raymonde Moulin, in her study of the 1960s art market, noted that some interviewees explained that owning a collection was an element of their "standing" (Moulin, 1967, p. 191). She went on to say: "Possession of recognized and costly paintings satisfies the individual's desire for power, and it has the capacity of conferring a social rank on the individual" (p. 204).[3] In addition, the most expensive works were often acquired by an international elite made up of first- or second-generation upstarts who asserted their new social status through art.

One mode of searching for distinction can be seen in imitating a social group above one's own so as to attach oneself to it symbolically (Besnard & Desplanques, 1986). The explanation is given by this midsize gallery's director:

> As the collectors who are part of VIP programs are invited to the biggest collectors' homes in the city where the fair is organized, this produces an effect of imitation. A collector wants to have the same artists as those the bigger collector has. It's just that without the same means as the bigger one, they'll buy works by the same artist, but smaller ones!

In the 1960s, Moulin noted the same phenomenon: "the dealer knows very well that the collector becomes the champion of 'his' painters in society and contributes to creating an environment of snobbery around them" (Moulin, 1967, p. 139). Galleries actively cultivate the need to stand out, even more so when combined with their own interest in setting the stage for their artists' work:

> Sometimes we lend works to clients because a photo shoot of their collection is organized at their home. It's flattering, and they're happy to give the impression of having more than they really do, and for us it gives us the chance to speak about our artists. It puts their works in appropriate settings in beautiful apartments.

The desire for distinction can also be found in the following two forms of motivations, even if this dimension may appear secondary.

First, several collectors spoke of a support system. Buying contemporary art means helping artists and even galleries (Mercier, 2012).[4] This company director and collector clearly illustrates this motivation; while he always pays for the works he buys, he does not always bother to pick them up! And the amounts in question are not trivial:

- I buy to support an artist, a gallery, and to be able to say that I participate, that the artist should continue, but sometimes I don't even pick up the works.
- *What price point do you go up to when you don't go to pick up the paintings?*
- I'm thinking of a time about three years ago, I bought a painting and

> didn't go get it, but there are others. There was a work I bought five years ago during the Frieze show in London. I wouldn't dare try to pick it up now. The first one, I remember very well. I paid €8,000.

Hence, galleries have to formulate strategies so that they can benefit from collectors' spending. This Swiss gallery director has been able to create an emotional bond with a number of her regular clients, and explained:

> We're lucky, our gallery. We have collectors who buy works at practically every exhibition. They really like us and support us sincerely. That is their aim. Yet we are in a city where people travel a lot, they can afford it, so they could look elsewhere, even abroad, but they regularly buy at our gallery.

Another recurrent motivation for buyers that galleries can take advantage of is access to the social world of contemporary art (Becker, 1988), which is enabled by purchasing artworks. This functions all the better as it is a highly valued and gratifying social world. The best way to ensure regular purchases is to take advantage of the integration and socialization that contemporary art galleries can offer to their clients. The previously mentioned company director and collector, who spoke of his selfless support for artists and galleries, conceded, however, that buying contemporary works of art also enabled him to have access (and subsequently belong) to a social world into which entry is restricted: "When I began to collect, when I bought my first work, I thought 'finally, I've paid my way'. It was very exciting, I had taken courses on contemporary art at the Jeu de Paume [a contemporary art center in Paris], I was still an outsider, and then I entered that world." This associate gallery director shared a similar analysis:

> We have collectors who are lawyers, CEOs, traders. They've got money but if they didn't collect, they wouldn't have access to the world to which buying contemporary art can open doors. They get VIP invitations to art fairs thanks to us; they're blown away by the people they meet. Take [X], who has already bought pieces at the gallery, but smaller things. He made a big purchase, and was invited to one of our dinners [at the gallerist's home]. That really impressed him. He wouldn't stop thanking me; clearly, for him that represented something really important.

Another collector made a similar remark, asserting that it is not only the artists and their works that inform the attraction of acquisitions: "There are one or two artists whom I'd like to buy at the [P gallery], but when I go there, I feel it's not for me. I'd be lost among their collectors, no one would pay any attention to me; they wouldn't take care of me like here where I'm regularly invited to events, so, no, I don't buy." During a small party that a major collector organized at her home, I overheard the following—

astonishingly lucid and frank—analysis. She explained to the companion (who works in the luxury sector) of a gallery manager:

> OK, to be clear, when you're a collector, it's often because you are interested in contemporary art, let's say that's the best scenario, but it's also to support artists, or even more precisely one or two galleries—you most often buy from the same galleries. But there's a reason for that. Let's not beat around the bush, if you collect, it's also to be courted, to be invited to cocktail receptions, events, dinners in places that are out of the ordinary. If you had to organize that yourself it would take a lot of time and wouldn't have that special touch, that special feel, so it's something you're very sensitive to.

This director of a Belgian gallery clarified the above statement, while confirming the general notion:

> Art Geneva is a special fair largely because of its Swiss collectors. There are quite a lot of people who come and buy works, but they prefer not to be identified as collectors, they don't want to receive invitations all the time, they couldn't care less about the social relationship side, the snobbish side that other collectors seek. But then again, some collectors want to be cared for, to be remembered all the time.

To be invited to events, and then to be invited regularly, is to belong to a community (Tönnies, 2010), for one's own image and in the eyes of others. As this gallerist said during the 2017 Venice Biennale: "Here, since the beginning of the biennial, people spend their time asking those they meet if they're going to one of the two Pinault dinners. If some people were invited in the past but not this year, they feel downgraded."

This gallerist, who has a branch in a chic Swiss resort town, emphasized how simple the events he organizes are, fully aware that some people may expect him to play the glamor card, but that is not the case: "Even if I have a gallery in a very chic town, I don't put on big events, nothing like that. It doesn't correspond at all with my gallery, so even if some collectors expect that of a gallery, and I know very well that many of them would do it in this situation, it's just not me." It must be pointed out, however, that this gallerist does regularly organize very tasteful dinners for openings.

The entire contemporary art world, and that of galleries in particular, is thus organized around a sort of sociability that makes it possible both for this social world to exist as such; but also, more prosaically, for contact between collectors and gallerists to develop. It is worth repeating that it is rare for collectors to arrive spontaneously in a gallery to buy contemporary art. The gallery has to *invite* them, while at the same time playing into their expectations. There is also the "experiential" model of art fairs, as discussed in chapter 3, which veered away from the prevailing model (i.e., mainly selling booth space to galleries). ARCO, and later Art Basel, made sure that their fairs became more and more of an experience, but one that was largely social. Today, all the big fairs have had to adopt this established model, at least to some extent (Barragan, 2008). As this gallerist, who has locations in two European countries, stated:

> Today the art market is more and more events-driven. Openings—many collectors live for this kind of event. It's a kind of artistic tourism; you reserve for Venice, Basel, Basel Miami, Documenta, and so on and so forth, the fairs and auctions. People say 'I'm going to Frieze;' they don't say I'm going to London any more. And when they say they're going to Basel, everyone knows that they're going to Art Basel. They wouldn't ever go to Basel outside of the fair, even though there are great museums there.

While fairs have considerably developed their special events for collectors, which then allows them to offer a whole area of sociability and a feeling of belonging, the same is true for galleries. The need to provide collectors with entertainment is completely integral to their work, as this art professional stated:

> It's changed a lot though. When I started the gallery, entertainment didn't really exist like it does today. There was the opening, and then there was the closing. Everything was more artist-based then. You would go to people's houses. Now it's almost like galleries need to open up an entertainment division! [laughs]
>
> "How Does a Gallery Stay in Business for 35 Years? Lisa Spellman on 303 Gallery's Staying Power and the Hardest Part of Being a Dealer," *Artnet News*, July 19, 2019

A staff member for a large gallery made a more disillusioned and less humorous remark:

> Sometimes I wonder what I'm doing in this sector. I wanted to work in contemporary art to be in touch with artworks and artists, but this is becoming quite rare in my job. That's the liaisons' job. I spend most of my time organizing pre-pre-openings and pre-pre-pre-openings for very rich people and for even richer people.

Showing interest in a gallery, or in the work of one or more artists and, even more so, making a purchase means embarking on a relationship that—in spite of its strongly commercial dimension—will include "entertainment"[5] through offering seemingly free invitations and supposedly purely selfless gifts. However, in point of fact, selflessness does not really exist (Caillé, 2005). The art gallery world is one of only seemingly free gifts, with intertwined systems of obligations (Mauss, 2007). As this collector stated:

"We're regularly invited by several galleries whose invitations we accept so that afterwards we're practically obliged to buy from them if we don't want to be crass, and if we have the bare minimum of manners." There is no clearer expression of gifts and counter-gifts, and how the former feeds into the latter.

A large part of a gallerist's work then inevitably revolves around cultivating the link that connects them to collectors, and that is precisely the aim of these regular invitations. The presence that these invitations can lead to (if clients accept them) is an asset in developing sales directly, but even when this is not the case, the simple fact of communicating and having a thought and/or gesture nourishes the link. As this gallery director stated:

> €3,600 to participate in the Paris Gallery Weekend is not very expensive; it's reasonable compared to the cost of having a booth at a fair. The most important thing is that it keeps contact with collectors open, showing them we think of them even if they're not in Paris at that time, if they can't come. It provides an opportunity to contact them, to remind them of our existence.

Keeping in touch with collectors helps to satisfy the integration function that is specific to the social world of contemporary art.

Sociability, cocktail receptions, and dinners: supposed gifts as a breeding ground for the sales relationship

Among all of the social occasions that galleries offer their collectors, openings[6]—in their most enticing form to a general public—prevail, whether they are at the most basic level, or are followed by a cocktail reception or dinner. These occasions create and support links with both confirmed and potential clients. The opening is a special moment in the life of a gallery—a strong moment—but it has not been deemed of great interest to social scientists, and has not been the subject of exhaustive analyses (Verlaine, 2009). One gallery director, fully aware of the importance of these events, told me that she thought that they were sufficiently important to be the object of a sociological approach: "You should really write a book on openings and dinners, because you go out a lot, you meet lots of people, it's very interesting. The problem is that you'd have to find the right tone."

Outside observers see only a superficial moment, when in reality these are occasions that make a lot of social sense (Pinçon & Pinçon-Charlot, 1996), and also constitute a significant professional opportunity. In addition, on the gallery side, this type of event accounts for a significant financial and organizational investment. In all serious galleries, the guests are not there by chance. Those invited (other than gallery staff), are essentially collectors (especially the gallery's most faithful clients), the artist whose exhibition is beginning (and their potential employees), and often other creators whom the gallery represents, museum professionals and curators who may include the gallery's artists in their lineup, journalists, and critics who can highlight these creators' work by providing visibility and legitimacy. The largest galleries make a point of inviting figures in politics, the arts and culture in general[7] and also sometimes in fashion; they bear witness to the broad symbolic legitimacy of the gallery.

The practice of post-opening dinners is an extension of those organized with collectors and artists. Louis Carré, an important French gallerist of the twentieth century, liked to say: "good business calls for a good meal!" Today, cocktail receptions and (when collectors are in the picture) dinners for openings are fairly common. Depending on the establishment and the occasion, the dinners take place in the galleries, at the gallerist's home, or in a restaurant. These occasions can appear somewhat superficial to the outside observer, merely society *soirées*, but they perform a social function: they provide an opportunity for the group to exist symbolically as such (Pinçon & Pinçon-Charlot, 1996). They reveal who is or is not part of the group, and they reinforce its cohesion. This is true, first, in the eyes of the participants themselves: they are validated *vis à vis* their peers by successive festive events that take place, or even might have taken place. The guests ask each other if they have been to see this exhibition or that; if they attended this event, if they attended that reception. Thus, during the 2017 Venice Biennale, participants of the opening and "professionals" days frequently asked their interlocutors if they had attended Documenta in Kassel before the biennial. The question came up frequently in conversation. Participants in these events are not fooled by this classist aspect (Bourdieu, 1979). Cultural practices—what they are and how strong their impact is—play an essential role in this. The simple fact of being invited is perceived by the guests as a social certification of belonging to the peer group, with all the social qualities that it implies. When I shared my astonishment at always being invited to the dinners and cocktail receptions hosted by the largest art galleries with an art advisor, she answered: "Yes, I can understand. I'm not rich either like most of the people here are, but you know, it's simple: if you didn't have the codes, you wouldn't be invited."

These status attributions (Bourdieu, 1979) of inclusion and exclusion go beyond the occasions themselves via photos, especially as today they are often posted online, particularly on the website *Say Who,* which is devoted to society events. One must be photographed, but also identified, with one's name clearly labeled on the photo. Being photographed (and identified) attests doubly to the interest one produces; it signals that one has a proper place in this social world. Some photos feature anonymous people (though not many), because they are of less interest. These people "merely" accompany those who count for something in the photo and its selection by the site. In this case, the social function resembles that analyzed by Michel Pinçon and Monique Pinçon-Charlot of when elites stage themselves, during balls for example, showing themselves off to all as they arrive (Pinçon & Pinçon-Charlot, 1996). This self-staging generally presents a sartorial aspect. The galleries' staff—particularly the women who work in sales—and the female guests, usually wear dresses and heels. Recognizing the performance aspect that these occasions entailed, a female associate director laughingly greeted me with: "Today, it's an opening, so I washed my hair!"

However, it would be a mistake to designate the function of these occasions as being solely symbolic. This element has been carefully analyzed in sociological terms (Pinçon & Pinçon-Charlot, 1996 and 1997). These invitations also provide the participants with an opportunity to socialize and discuss with their peers, knowing that their social quality has been certified by the event's organizers. Since access to these occasions—which are generally held in the evening—is by invitation only, guests are assured that the people they meet there rightly belong in this social world; thus providing the foundations for the event to which they have been invited. Much more than conversation takes place: business cards, telephone numbers, email addresses are exchanged, all of which extend the contact after the meeting. This type of occasion also has many professional uses, even if at first sight they present all the characteristics of being free, since one does not pay to participate (on the contrary, one is invited). These invitations must be situated in a larger framework: gallerists constantly offer gifts to collectors and do things for them such as giving catalogues and other expensive books, little presents when clients buy several works, studio visits allowing them to meet the artists, and many invitations to various events (Velthuis, 2002). When it is the galleries that extend an invitation, they honor their guests who, in exchange, will be likely to reciprocate the gift that has been given to them (Mauss, 2007). For collectors, it behooves them to buy artworks from their host. As this collector stated (and his wife, who was also present for the interview, agreed): "For us, we don't go to the dinners very often because there are gallerists who are very insistent. They invite you once and as soon as they see you again they practically ask you when you're going to buy something. And you see very quickly that if you don't buy regularly, you're not invited anymore." The intermingled obligations of gifts and counter-gifts are also perfectly represented in the comments made by this other collector: "I buy from them fairly often, but here I'm not invited to their dinner. I keep thinking about it. I might stop buying from them."

Besides these invitations organized by a gallery itself, other occasions can be used for professional pursuits. At the end of a dinner in May 2019—organized during the Parisian Gallery Weekend—which brought together several of these establishments and collectors, a gallery staff member sent me an email along with a photo taken and published by the website *Say Who* and asked me who was at my side. Like me, she had identified this newcomer in the Parisian art world as a probable collector: she was trying to find out who was there, to add to her database of potential clients.

For those who take obvious and intentional professional advantage of these occasions, it is difficult to qualify them as socialite events—given the generally superficial nature usually associated with this term, and to think of oneself personally as being part of "high society"—since these gatherings are categorized as work events.[8] As this general manager of an international gallery (who has already been cited in this book) explained:

> Are we socialites, me or even you, I would say yes. We go out a lot, we meet important people whom we didn't necessarily know before; I would say that we don't think of ourselves as socialites because there is a major professional dimension to our activities, but seen from the outside, I think that yes, people perceive our sociability, our relationships, as high society.

It stands to reason that belonging to the social world of contemporary art galleries in a professional capacity goes along with having certain social skills, such as being at ease during these *soirées*, being willing to meet many unknown people, and knowing how to speak to them (in English or in a foreign language). Thus, as I noted in a previous chapter, among the gallery directors and staff who are in sales, there are many aristocrats or members of the bourgeoisie who, at an early age, have been socialized with the values of the social elite (Saint Martin, 1993), and privately acquired the skills that they will develop and utilize later on in a professional framework (Quemin, 2002b).

Generally speaking, these *soirées* take place in a fairly homogeneous circle; however the dinners are determined by class to an even greater degree. Sitting down to dinner introduces a new dimension: dining at the same table and sharing a meal is tantamount to really belonging to the same world, albeit symbolically; but it also shows that one has passed the test, as table manners embody social class and are socially discriminating (Le Wita, 1988). Opening dinners are social rites for the elite. In the most prestigious French galleries, the well-to-do of French society mingle with each other. This includes the CAC 40 (the French equivalent of the Dow Jones in the United States) business people and wealthy heirs; the elite of the entertainment industry, especially cinema; as well as the most prominent politicians, notably ministers in the current and past administrations. While there are far more right-wing elected officials, it is not uncommon to find personalities from both sides of the political aisle socializing at these dinners. There is a core group of guests often seen at these events, even though they may vary in size between galleries, or even for the same gallery, according to the circumstances. The rate of overlap is higher between directly competing galleries: they often share the same guests, sometimes to quite a large extent. In such cases, these people may have to make a choice when events organized by several galleries occur on the same evening. I have at times crossed paths with the same guests at dinners held on consecutive days in galleries of comparable price levels, especially at the top of the Parisian gallery hierarchy. Collectors may come in couples; other guests are generally invited alone when their involvement in the art world is professional. Even if people are invited as friends of the gallery, it is obvious that this "friendship" is directly determined by the guests' roles in relation to the gallery.

The guests most likely to be more peripheral to the social world in the broadest sense are some of the gallery staff (who are, nevertheless, fully integrated in the professional world), as well as journalists and critics. Still, it is often the case that for these people, one of the factors expediting their inclusion into the gallery world is to have a social background that affords them a more legitimate place than most of their fellow journalists and critics within this universe. Some, even among the collectors, can occasionally be shockingly bereft of manners; they are included only because they have great financial clout, which does not offset the misgivings they bring to the fore.

The opening cocktail reception or dinner is presented as a simple festive and convivial occasion, but everyone must adhere to their role, as these occasions are socially formatted. This can clearly be seen with the participants in whose "honor" the event is organized. They have to *do their job*. I was at an opening where the artists being exhibited spent the early evening in the street outside the gallery drinking beer and smoking, while the collectors were together inside the gallery. The gallerists did not appreciate such behavior from their artists, and the regular attendees of these openings took it as a breach of professionalism. Conversely, there are other occasions when experienced and highly recognized artists were stationed next to their biggest collectors or VIP guests; or they table-hopped, making sure to exchange a kind word with all of the guests, each one noting that they were "doing their job." The two preceding examples clearly show how being invited to an event (and therefore seeming to share a simple moment of conviviality), and the professional dimension (which is always underlying) are intertwined.

For seated dinners, the seating plan must be scrupulously worked out ahead of time.[9] Just like invitations and how often they are sent out, seating plans are determined by each person's usefulness to the gallery, but they also have to take into account what each guest can expect (Mauss, 2007) depending on the importance they think they represent for the gallery; whether their contribution is strictly economic or more symbolic. Directors and associate directors generally know who all the guests are, and they take care to weigh each aspect of the event. I have often seen a certain very well-off collector in some of the largest galleries in France who had a bad reputation because of her bad manners and her demands. As this gallery director explained:

> She is really pathetic: she calls us before the dinners to which we've invited her to know what table she's being seated at. We know that if she's not seated at [the gallerist's table], she won't come. She's a very

> important collector; we know that she buys a lot from our main competitor, but we don't know if she behaves the same way with them. She is well known in these circles for being such a pain, gallerists and other collectors, everyone will say the same thing. But she buys very expensive artworks, so we have no choice.

This collector's behavior is particularly resented because it reveals a reality that should have remained hidden: she takes certain attentions for granted, whereas this social world covers itself with an aura of giving these for free (Caillé, 2005).

As Thorstein Veblen so astutely analyzed, the table should honor the guests (Veblen, 1899). Whether the dinner takes place at the gallerist's home or in a restaurant, the setting must showcase the guests, as must the setting of the table. At the very least, it must align with the image that the gallery wants to put forward and the price points that it features. The menu has to be of the same caliber: the most prestigious galleries offer a sumptuous menu (for example, lobster salad, farm-bred chicken with morels, raspberry *mille-feuille*), but it must not be heavy either. Particular attention is given to alcoholic beverages, whose social and class function is very significant (Bourdieu, 1979; Pinçon & Pinçon-Charlot, 1996 and 1997). Being invited, warmly welcomed, and honored by a quality wine all attest to the seriousness of the gallery and its respect for its clients. This cements the relationship, as this collector explained:

> There are galleries you enter, the people look down on you, it can be terrible for new collectors. These gallerists think that because these collectors have money they're necessarily stupid, ignorant. I buy from two galleries for the most part, sometimes a third. [V] too, he's become a friend; he's really nice. His artists' prices are lower, but he really knows how to entertain. He serves very good wine at his dinners and all the collectors know that. I always tell him: 'Remember, don't skimp on the wine; that doesn't save money. People talk to each other.' Since he entertains very well, everyone knows how seriously he takes his clients.

Alcohol is important as a symbol because it is associated with festive occasions, and the most expensive of its products are directly correlated with prestigious affairs. It must also be drunk with pleasure and in sufficient quantities to make the guests feel more at ease. During French dinners, I have frequently observed that the participants generally use the formal "*vous*" form to address one another when they meet, but with alcohol consumption and the feeling of being among peers (Pinçon & Pinçon-Charlot, 1992, 1996, and 1997), it is not rare that they later begin to use the familiar "*tu*" form,[10] particularly when they are approximately of the same age. This is especially true because the seated dinner will have placed people next to each other who are likely to get along.

One alcoholic beverage stands apart from all the others. Almost inevitably, at least as of a certain price point, champagne is *de rigueur*—if not during the whole meal and evening, then at least for the cocktail hour—it serves as a social marker (Pinçon & Pinçon- Charlot, 1997). The following two interview extracts illustrate the virtual necessity of being lavishly generous (Mauss, 2007) and, in the second one, champagne serves as a symbol of this extravagance. This major French gallerist criticizes the stinginess of one of her fellows: "Her opening dinners—many collectors who are invited don't go. The ambiance is off, the meals are cheap; there are no second helpings, and you feel like everything is being counted. In these circles, this leaves a very bad impression." Another gallerist apologized to me because she wouldn't be hosting an opening dinner, although directing a gallery virtually requires a certain amount of generosity and entertaining if they want to keep their status (Caillé, 2005). Champagne's function as a symbol is obvious: "Well, you know, there won't be a real opening dinner this evening because the fair is open late tonight, and there have been so many things in Paris these last two weeks, but there will be champagne at the opening tonight and we'll do a dinner another time for this artist and, of course, you'll be invited." Some galleries with a lower status make the effort to announce that champagne will be served when they send out their invitations (which sometimes turns out to be ordinary sparkling wine).

Champagne acts as a social lubricant. During an evening event organized by a major gallery established in Paris, during which champagne was flowing, one of the sales consultants—who had just about spent his whole evening with a particular couple—returned to a group of salespeople with whom I had been chatting for a moment. It was a gallery known for its excellent work relationships among colleagues:

- Well, I did it. I just sold them their first work! [clearly excited]
- *Me: Their first work from the gallery or by [X] [the artist being exhibited that day and whose opening it was]?*
- No, no, no: their first artwork!!! They've never bought any before! And things really seem good. Look: they said they've been interested in contemporary art for a few years but they were still hesitating because they don't have the social codes and needed help [he puts on a theatrical tone], I said: I think you have come to the right person! [the whole group bursts out laughing].

During this evening in honor of an artist, sales were rife, and while they may have seemed to be overwhelmed by the gallery's extravagance, commercial strategies were at work. Many sales were made during this evening, and many others began that were wrapped up later on. Entertaining in a convivial framework creates relationships of trust that endure and develop revenue, while at the same time planting the seeds for future sales. Alcohol (champagne, in particular) is far more than a festive or opulent symbol; it has a practical function, which is to promote conviviality. Human relations become warmer more quickly and less formal during the evening, and it also encourages negotiations on sales, or even helps to carry them to fruition. As this pair of gallerists from Dubai told a magazine that asked a much less relevant question than the answer given:

— *Does hot staff help selling better?*
— No but alcohol does.

Interview with Nadine Knotzer and Kourosh Nouri, directors of Carbon 12 Gallery in Dubai, in *The Art Gorgeous*, issue no. 6, 2019, p. 88

Nevertheless, there are limits to the system of invitations to cocktail receptions and dinners. The onset of the COVID-19 pandemic at the beginning of 2020 complicated this practice. As this gallerist, who runs an establishment with locations in three countries, said at the end of 2020: "Openings, they can seem a bit high society, but with COVID-19, which kept us from organizing them, you can see that they're really super useful. If people hadn't had three glasses of champagne, there are tons of works I would never have sold! It also gives them the opportunity to go out." The preceding comments really confirm that exhibitions and events, in the words of the professionals themselves, reinforce cultural practices by adding them to a social calendar (Bourdieu & Darbel, 1969), and also that gifts lead to counter-gifts (Mauss, 2007); one is greeted with pomp—symbolized by champagne—and one must reciprocate the gift. Moreover, because of its disinhibiting character, alcohol (especially when it is a drink that one "cannot turn down") opens the door to transactions.

Furthermore, the system of cocktail reception or dinner invitations is also subject to the limitations that result from the other offers received by the most courted collectors. Here, this gallerist who runs a midsize gallery in London stated: "It's really tough to get people to come to dinners or cocktail parties if you're a midsize gallery; everyone wants to go to Zwirner, Hauser & Wirth or White Cube, the big galleries. The smaller ones—that doesn't interest them."

Finally, even when they attend an event, the most desirable guests are often the most critical. This participant of François Pinault's grand dinner at the 2019 Venice Biennale judged the evening harshly: "Clearly, the dinner last night was boring. It's impossible to host 1,500 people well. In addition, it was cold and very marketing-oriented. Pinault has to entertain all of Christie's important clients. There were very few artists, in fact, few intelligent or cultivated people. It really wasn't cultural." This is a textbook example of distinction by detachment (Bourdieu, 1979), which can always plague events *vis à vis* their guests.

It is clear that over the past few years, the number of special events has increased among contemporary art galleries:[11] cocktail receptions, dinners, and other entertainment occasions proposed to collectors became more and more important, and sometimes more sophisticated. Some large galleries pushed this phenomenon to the point of investing in the "lifestyle" domain. The largest galleries reinforce their presence even more, so as to be closer to their clients. Contemporary art (and specifically that promoted by the gallery) thus becomes a way of life that can become part of collectors' lives in the long term. In March 2018, the Hauser & Wirth gallery announced its plan to open a 48-room boutique hotel at the end of the year in Braemer, Scotland; like a luxury brand. They followed the example of the *haute couture* fashion designer Giorgio Armani who, during his industrial development, had previously expanded the scope of his business to the hotel industry and thus into the "lifestyle" category. The Hauser & Wirth hotel opened in December 2018; that same month, the gallery also launched a quarterly magazine, *Ursula*, which published essays, interviews, portfolios, and photos of artists. This initiative was similar to the Gagosian gallery's magazine, *Gagosian Quarterly*. The website for this publication speaks of its first issue, published in spring 2017, with these headings: essays, interviews, studio visits, photo essays, philanthropy, books, lifestyle, and videos. It should be noted that while "lifestyle" is given as a specific heading, the whole magazine embodies this category. The aim is to familiarize readers with the gallery and its artists, and not to publish reviews of shows of other creators, as art magazines normally do. Considering previous analyses, it can be said that these magazines back up the brand image of the galleries involved, but they are also a means of influencing the lifestyle of the super-rich by becoming trendsetters in questions of taste (Bourdieu, 1979).

Friendship: a professional resource

Emotional links have long been one of a gallerist's resources. As early as 1967, in *Le marché de la peinture en France* (*The French Art Market*) (Moulin, 1987), Raymonde Moulin included statements from various gallerists who made specific mention of the level of friendship:

> The gallery's activity is founded on friendly relations. We work together. [. . .] Art lovers who are interested in the gallery are friends. Friends become clients: clients become friends. [. . .] We have worked hard to create an atmosphere, a circle.
>
> Moulin, 1967, p. 139

Yet there has not been much research on this point. This is partially due to the recent nature of the sociology of emotions in relation to the much longer history of the discipline as a whole. Moreover, when social scientists have studied affects, they focused more on *emotion* (that is, on temporary manifestations) more than long-lasting effects, or *feelings*. One of the pioneering works dates back to the 1980s, with Arlie Hochschild's study of stewardesses having to smile on command.[12] She developed the notion of emotional work, and paved the way for the sociology of emotions (Hochschild, 1980). It should be noted that this relatively recent field in the broader history of sociology in general remains less mined than other areas of the discipline, and that feelings still remain largely unexamined. Claire Bidart, however, conducted an important study on friendship (Bidart, 1997); but she analyzed this feeling more as something selfless, without financial implications, that can turn out to be useful (though essentially indirectly). Bidart showed that friendship functions largely as a sort of capital in higher social categories, but she did not really analyze its use in professional situations. My position is that the feeling of friendship should be considered as a real resource that can also be used in professional circumstances, but can also entail sentimental work,[13] like emotional work does (Hochschild, 2017). In point of fact, it requires a great deal of effort to generate such feelings, especially as positive emotions must last and take place in a more general framework: that of the friendly relationship. This approach differs from that produced by Aurélie Jeantet on emotions in the workplace. While this perspective holds that in a professional setting, emotions are socially constructed, they are considered to be fundamentally distinguished by unpredictability; they cannot really be utilized intentionally, and they have a tendency to play tricks on those who manifest them (Jeantet, 2018). Yet the way gallerists analyze and then put friendship to work shows that this feeling is consciously managed to produce long-lasting commercial relationships. Gallerists clearly have an interest in cultivating friendships with their clients, as it encourages loyalty and leads to sales. Collectors are just as desirous to develop such a relationship, which certifies their passion for contemporary art in everyone's eyes.[14] As such, it is not unusual for gallerists to be invited to the weddings (or second weddings) of their clients or their clients' children, or to attend funeral services as "real" friends would do.[15] This epithet is awkward to use; it simply avoids using a reductive term to acknowledge how different this type of friendly relationship that links gallerists to "their" collectors is, to point to feelings that do not belong to any kind of professional relationship. The link can be considered as less pure—as it is branded as self-serving—but that would overlook the fact that friendship, in general, constitutes a relationship in which everyone can "benefit", regardless of how.

During my fieldwork in recent years, just like Raymonde Moulin when she first began her research, many professionals spontaneously expressed notions that referred to an affective dimension so as to qualify the relationship that connects art galleries and collectors. This is not surprising in a field of extremely personalized activities. It is particularly revealed in the eponymous dimension of the business, as most contemporary art galleries go by the name of their founders, and they keep that name very often; even when the founder hands the establishment over to a successor.[16] As this director of a British gallery stated: "It took a lot of work to get where we are today. My boss created a real community around the gallery. It really is just that, a community that's at the heart of the gallery's operations, and that must constantly be kept up."

Some galleries often use the family metaphor to designate relationships among their members above all else, as is clear in this interview extract:

> The Pace gallery is a family, a family of about 200 employees spread out over the four corners of the world. The owners, Arne Glimcher and his son, give the local directors free rein for their own projects, which are then validated collectively.
>
> Valentina Volchkova, Pace Gallery staff member, in *la Gazette Drouot,* no. 14, April 6, 2018, p. 22

Other galleries also portray an almost familial dimension that furthers the staff's relationships with their collectors. In Elisabetta Negroni's analysis, this is the case at the Italian Galleria Continua (Negroni, 2017). This gallery's specific positioning hinges on highlighting its emotional connections with its collectors; its competitors are well aware of this, as the director of a French gallery with international influence stated:

> Our Instagram account is pretty mild. We feature the works and the spaces of our galleries. But if you look at Continua's account, they go all out for personalization, you constantly see pictures of their directors. Their positioning is really cool, and it has kind of become their brand image. Us too, as far as [the gallerist] is concerned, in his own way, he's very close to his collectors, but we don't show it off as much.

Another example of the family approach used in this professional universe occurred in April 2020; in an attempt to combat the COVID-19 pandemic, the major international gallery Hauser & Wirth announced the sale of works created by the gallery's staff, as well as their immediate families.[17] Even the director of the Opera Gallery—an establishment with a less clear-cut contemporary positioning, whose secondary market operations far surpass those of the primary market—refers to the family model: "This notion of 'family' matters a lot to us, and besides, it's the gallerist's job!" (*La Gazette Drouot*, no. 42, December 6, 2019, p. 257).

Like the Galleria Continua, albeit not with the same international scope, the gallerist Kristin Hjellegjerde—who has locations in London and Berlin (and for a time also had one in Norway, and now has one in Palm Beach in the United States)—gives a personal touch to her relationships with her contacts, especially collectors, highlighting their familial dynamic. Her Instagram account features artworks and photos of her various spaces, and also pictures of her family: herself, her husband, and her children. Family and emotions are the central foci of her communications. For example, the gallery issued this press release in April 2018 to declare new artist representations: "We are proud to announce the inclusion of Audun Alvestad & Cristina Banban in our gallery's family." The term "family" was chosen over that of "roster," which is generally used to designate the list of artists represented; a more neutral and distant, even cold, word. This same gallerist ends all of her Internet newsletters "with love." She sent her season's greetings on December 21st, 2019: "Season's greetings / Kristin Hjellegjerde Gallery / London Bridge / Wandsworth / Berlin / With Love / Kristin & the gallery family." Everything is included here: the use of the first name without the last name, implying a greater proximity (Besnard & Desplanques, 1986), reference to the family dynamic, and use of an emotional expression to reinforce the link with the gallery's patrons. While Hjellegjerde clearly has a particularly warm personality, this behavior is not unusual in the world of galleries, albeit in a less pointed way and more in the context of interpersonal relationships. Even the major gallery David Zwirner, one of the most influential in the world, sent an email in April 2020 with "Hello Friends" at the beginning, and signed "the David Zwirner team."

The gallery manager of this major French establishment explained how emotional relationships have impacted the client database:

> Recently, we reorganized our database and found three big categories: artists, collectors, and journalists. But there were also people who didn't fit in any of the three categories. At first, we called them 'other' and then [M] said: but in fact, we should call all these people 'family and friends' and we really liked that. We decided to keep that title! And then, because there are people we like a lot who were in the other categories, we took them out and put them in that new one.

While collectors are generally presented as friends of the gallery there is, in point of fact, a spectrum as not everyone qualifies as the same kind of "friend." But that does not mean that amicable or familial relationships do not exist; quite the contrary, as the previous example shows.

Another analogy of galleries with a family aspect: the widespread practice of celebrating anniversaries, at least the benchmarks (for example, the gallery's 10th or 50th anniversary). Just like for a family, this maintains the emotional link, and creates or extends the feeling of belonging to a community (Tönnies, 1887). Collectors and their family and friends are always invited to these anniversaries, and the staff as well, signaling to the first two groups that they are all part of the same gallery history.

However, it is the notion of friendship that is the most emphasized in the world of galleries, as they often send emails to all of their contacts starting with "Dear friends", or "Dear friends of the gallery." This is the most prevalent notion when gallerists evoke their links to collectors. During an art fair, I was quite astonished to hear a gallerist from the United States speaking to a fellow gallerist and refer to "a friend slash collector," an almost perfect synthesis of the cohabitation and manifestation of these two universes, one generally belonging to the emotional domain, and the other to the professional. Both exist together: a relationship of a professional nature (here commercial), is reworked in another register, that of feelings. Hence, in the context of selling contemporary art, there is a real effort made on the emotional side and as the sales component takes place over time, it is less impersonal and infrequent than for many other common items of consumption.

As previously mentioned, even more attention is paid to cultivating friendships, as they prolong the link and consolidate trust; this is essential so that the buyers do not sell their works at auction when prices tend to rise, since the gallery has to keep control of the supply (Moulin, 1967). The gallery must also be sure that it can count on continued purchases from its clients, hence why personalized relationships are so vital. Each salesperson has to be able to develop a special relationship with their clients (Peretz, 1992). In the words of an associate gallery director: "We try to make sure our clients continue to buy from us and not from other galleries, but also, if possible, we try to build their loyalty personally to develop sales, and for that there has to be an emotional link." Friendship, in a way, forges links of dependence so that for many collectors it is almost unthinkable to buy artworks from anyone but their special interlocutor. This reiterates what I asserted at the beginning of this chapter: the relationship between collectors and gallerists is singular in that the former show their tastes, even though they are not necessarily experts, and are aware that these tastes are classist, especially as pertains to social dynamics (Bourdieu, 1979). Expressing one's tastes (in this case, in art) means giving of oneself, sharing of one's personality.

The sales team understands that personalizing relationships contributes to the final sale, and they can become irritated when their employer does not allow them to benefit from that relationship to the fullest extent. In the words of an annoyed associate director:

> At the gallery—this is classic—we have to reach out to our client database before the art fairs. We say how happy we are at the idea that we'll see them soon, that we'll be there for them personally, and then at the last minute other colleagues are sent to the fair, not us!

This extract shows that having a relational and personalized aspect is important, but ultimately, whether the usual salesperson is present or not, clients must be able to expect a personalized interaction. Be it the case or not, this simple prospect might be enough to attract the clients to the booth. During a dinner with a gallerist (who claims not to be very active on the secondary market), a collector explained to me:

> For me, it's clear: I'm so attached to the gallery and to [X] that if I wanted to buy a work by Combas, I just tell him and he has a look for me. I prefer to buy from him rather than going to auction houses or to another gallery.

Friendship is a constant theme in gallerists' comments, and even more so in those of their core staff. This relationship revolves heavily around the gallery owner(s) even more than the rest of the sales team, who benefit from it, of course, but to a lesser extent. This gallerist clearly links his practices to the emotional sphere:

> I don't really have a relationship with the art market. I sell the works of the artists that I exhibit to collectors who are basically friends of the gallery. We share a passion for what I show, what I explore, and they value my work and my commitments
>
> Philippe Godin, in '*Galeristes, une exception culturelle*,' *Libération* online, *La diagonale de l'art*, December 1, 2018

Friendship seems to be fortified by long-term association. As this general director of a large gallery said:

> Even with my colleagues who do the selling at the gallery, it is sometimes difficult to get them to understand why I want to keep certain clients, and to take care of them myself. After many years, some have become friends, even if they are professional contacts. We talk about very personal, even intimate things, about our families.

A collector had this to say during an exhibition opening:

> It's true that when one begins to collect regularly, one expects to be well treated, to be considered as a friend. I have lunch several times a year with [D], we tell each other things, I've known him for 15 years.

The importance of time (substantiated by sociological research on friendship) comes up again and again in my interviews. Claire Bidart's work shows that a friend is a person one can count on when things are tough, and this strengthens the relationship (Bidart, 1997). In an email during the COVID-19 pandemic, this gallerist with whom I am close said:

> We did a lot of business, very discreetly. No discounts, no online shows, just simple, regular, friendly calls to our collectors who often came to us themselves to ask if we had anything interesting. Certainly, for some of them, sales were triggered by the desire to support us.

Similarly, during the first COVID-19 lockdown in France in spring 2020, several gallerists—some of whom are the most important on a national, or even global scale—called me personally for news. Of course, I was very touched by this sign of friendship, even though I was aware that they were going through their little black books to keep their professional contacts active.

Friendship is so important in the contemporary art gallery world that the way it is staged can sometimes seem excessive at first, because the relationship is brief (Bidart, 1993). Thus, this gallerist (Francisco Rovira Rullán, from the Puerto Rican Roberto Paradise gallery) congratulated the Art Dubai fair organizers and was delighted that in just a few days he made so many new friends. "Almost all our sales came from new collectors of the United Arab Emirates, who quickly became more than clients, friends" (*La Gazette Drouot,* no. 14, from April 6, 2018, p. 28).

People make new contacts so readily during these contemporary art-oriented occasions that it may at first be disconcerting, since this contradicts sociological research (Bidart, 1993). During my first gallery dinners, I was taken aback by an invitation to spend a weekend in a collector's country home in the Luberon region, even though I had never met him before. I originally thought it was just said out of politeness, to show interest. But the collector insisted on the invitation, which indicated that he was serious, and it was a proper invitation; and in this social *milieu* it was neither inappropriate nor hasty. Another time, I was again invited on a vacation in Corsica during an opening dinner by someone at my table (who later became a close friend).

The blossoming of friendly relationships that did not require a long maturation and familiarity born of time can even surprise professionals themselves, even if they have been fully integrated into this social world for years, to the point of comical misunderstandings. A London gallery director recounted:

> I had a client, with her husband, they were a pretty young couple, around my age; they were very warm towards me. One time we happened to meet, me and my husband, and they really insisted that we go to their house in the country. I felt like they were far more invested emotionally in the relationship than I was, and I didn't really want to go, but they were important clients for me, and we really didn't have much choice. To tell you just how strange the situation was—my husband and I wondered if they weren't planning on partner-swapping! [she laughs]. Even though I work in a gallery, this invitation just didn't seem natural. In the end, there was nothing sexual, we were relieved, but they spent their time smoking pot. For my husband and me, that's not our thing, so it was a pretty lousy weekend, but I really couldn't have said no.[18]

While interactions can sometimes develop quickly and even lead to misunderstandings, it is because some people involved in the gallery social world tend to create very strong emotional attachments in their relationships, more than some of their interlocutors. Moreover, given the reassuring nature of the fact that people evolve in a rather homogenous social world, due to the certification capacity of the social network in which they evolve, it becomes easier for them to let strangers into their private lives. People thus invite new acquaintances very easily to dinners at their home, or for a weekend in their country house.

Beyond the anecdotes given previously—which nonetheless make sense from a sociological point of view—it is possible to provide examples of initiatives that galleries have taken to nourish friendship, clearly showing that this is a matter of a deliberate effort pertaining to feelings (Hochschild, 2017, Jeantet 2018). This can be seen in the most visible part of this work during occasions of sociability (analyzed earlier in this chapter). They are all geared to create a gift that will call for a counter-gift[19] (Mauss, 2007; Caillé, 2005), but also to maintain a sense of familiarity with collectors, who are all potential clients. There is also invisible work at play that consolidates the friendly relationship with collectors.

As such, this young woman, assistant to the director of a major international gallery in Italy, explained that she often answers the director's emails but is careful to make it seem as though he is the one responding. The relationship has to appear personalized, so she resorts to subterfuge to create the illusion:

> I've been the personal assistant of [X] for a year now, and I'm getting to know him well. I answer his emails and write them pretending to be him. People don't realize. I have some tricks to make it sound like [X] is the one writing. When he's texting on his phone he's often a bit clumsy, and even on his computer. He doesn't always put his glasses on. I notice he often has too many spaces between words. So when I write pretending to be him, I do the same thing. I add spaces so that it really looks like emails from [X]. People think he's the one who's writing, and it's important for them.

The assistant continued, saying that personal relationships are at the heart of the link between her employer and his clients, and she has to make sure to take that into account. In reality though, in terms of interpersonal relationships, a third person intervenes in the conversation, and the other person has no idea of her involvement: "Sometimes [X] tells me that a collector has had health problems. So the next time I write, I ask about it, even though I'm writing in [X]'s place. But [X] is very human, and it's really something he'd do himself. It's just that I'm writing as if I were him."

Because relationships have to be as personalized as possible to create a feeling of familiarity and closeness, some galleries go even further in maintaining the fiction that email messages were written by their interlocutor at the gallery, particularly by the gallerist. Although I am fully integrated in the social world of contemporary art galleries, I had never heard of these practices until June 2017, when I received an email that seemed to be perfectly in line with my relationship with the gallerist (for example, the use of my first name in the greeting, the use of the familiar "*tu*" form in French, the invitation to an opening, etc.), until I reached the closing of the email, which was too formal given our close relationship. This clue was enough to make me deduce that the entire email, which had initially seemed genuine, was in reality automatically composed by a software program that had been pre-programmed with various parameters. The only giveaway was the closer, which did not correspond to what had been used in our many exchanges, written by the real person! I told my interlocutor about my discovery; he thought it was amusing that he had been unmasked. During a private dinner, I told another international gallerist with whom I have a close relationship about my earlier discovery, and he responded:

> I shouldn't say this, but we jot down everything that people say when they tell us about themselves, their birthdays, their wives' birthdays, etc., and we then send pre-written emails that are personalized with this information, but people aren't aware of it. We have a software program that allows us to decide if we want to use '*tu*' or '*vous*', if we're writing to a man or a woman. My gallery has grown in part because of this. We gather statistics, we see how much they spent in our gallery in recent months and how much they spent a year earlier. All of this is accounted for, what they bought before, and we suggest precise works based on all that. But they're convinced that we really wrote to them ourselves, and that's very important!

The previous quote shows that if interpersonal relationships fit into a framework that clearly falls under the umbrella of friendship (Bidart, 1997), though this feeling guides the interactions between gallerists and collectors, there is then at the same time a professional and commercial use for the relationship. The professional and private spaces are totally entwined (Quemin, 2002b).

This executive director of an international gallery puts into perspective the generally held discourse on friendship that supposedly links galleries and their staff to their clients:

> Relationships with collectors are a bit complex. Lots of them think they're friends of ours. In our sales role, there is a relational dimension that is very important, even emotional sometimes; it goes so far that things can become blurry, but they are a particular type of friend.

However, it should be kept in mind that these reservations are made by a director, and not by a gallerist, for whom interpersonal relationships based on friendship are rarely questioned.

It is obvious that, as in all friendly relationships, those that link gallerists or their staff with their clients (in spite of all the work produced to make this attachment last) can nevertheless come to an end. Such is the case, as mentioned earlier, when a salesperson leaves one gallery for another with higher price levels that are inaccessible even to longtime collectors, who were sometimes counted among their faithful clients, as this special type of "friend."

This is also the case when a collector turns their back on a gallery of which they had been a faithful supporter, by no longer buying works. In general, the friendly relationship wanes progressively, and ultimately stops. When this is caused by a client's regular purchases from a competing gallery, it can bring about deep resentments on the market, with some gallerists going so far as to claim that a competitor "stole" one of "their" collectors, depriving them of one of their "friends." This does not occur too often, and there are many cases of long-lasting relationships among gallerists and collectors.

Among gallerists there is sometimes a sort of nostalgia for a bygone era when relationships were supposedly characterized by selflessness and emotion, when friendship was more present. The gallerist Farideh Cadot, when she closed her public space in 2017, said:

> My collectors from back in the day, who still follow me today, are people who buy with their hearts, their heads, with whom there has always been an intellectual exchange, a friendship, a link. We spent whole afternoons in the gallery talking, the aim was not only to make a sale. It's all changed now. I wrote a manifesto in 2011 on this subject in which I foresaw this decline. Today when one reads about the opening of a Foundation in Mexico, the coverage only talks about people, their clothes, the party, but never what was on display. In this context, art is disappearing [. . .] We also used to have fun; we don't have fun anymore.
>
> "Farideh Cadot, Gallerist in Paris: 'Art Is Disappearing,' "
> *Le journal des Arts,* no. 483, July 7, 2017

This husband of a prominent international gallerist also notes a decline in friendship in the art world, but he inverts the meanings of the words "friend" and "buddy" to note the degree of emotional closeness and greater selflessness in relationships among "buddies"; the term friendship seems so clichéd to him, and paradoxically associated with professional aims: "Thirty years ago, there were real buddies in the art market but today everyone is everyone's friend, and it's just not the same thing anymore."

Conclusion

While sales are still the primary task of the gallerist occupation (as outlined in the previous chapter), it cannot really be expressed directly, since a gallery that is perceived as being too commercial loses its credibility for that sole reason. It therefore becomes essential for sales to take place in another register; essentially that of shared love for art (Bourdieu & Darbel, 1969), either for the artworks or for the social world organized around art if one is coming from the collectors' vantage point. Gallerists seem to be obliged to claim to embrace values inspired by the world of feelings, be it the same love of art or friendship that leads them to share their interest for certain artists, those whom they represent, with their close contacts. In an expression by Pierre Bourdieu, interest in disinterestedness is twofold (Bourdieu, 1992). It is necessary to demonstrate a certain distance from the market, the commercial dimension of the profession, but it is also important to note that the gallerist is never as convincing as when they sincerely believe in the artists whose work they represent. Emphasizing the sociability that surrounds the art world and the importance of emotional relationships in no way means that the ultimate goal of galleries is not commercial or market oriented. It would be naïve to hide this reality. But it is important to recognize that the affective dimension, sometimes with artists but more often with collectors, especially the main ones, is also strong, particularly because it is involved in attaining commercial objectives, and it permeates the galleries' *modus operandi*. More than any other feeling, friendship—with a vested interest,[20] admittedly, but which nevertheless shares many of its characteristics—is an important element of the contemporary art gallery domain. It largely determines sales when they become regular and consequently, much work is required in order to nurture it.

6

Beyond sales: The other activities of contemporary art galleries

Of all the activities performed by galleries, the domain of sales is both the primary and most emblematic among them. As such, it tends to eclipse other, equally important tasks that shape the occupation of gallerist, in all of its diversity. Professionals in the sector are amused and somewhat annoyed by the superficiality and simplicity that is, incorrectly, ascribed to their profession even by collectors, their business partners, who are nevertheless in regular contact with them. This general manager of a large European gallery reported:

> It's pretty crazy, people don't realize at all what it is to be a gallerist. We have clients telling us all the time that they'd like to change jobs and do what we do because they love art, they don't see everything we do, that it's real work. For example, I have a collector who told me (it happens all the time), that she's going to go into semi-retirement, and that she could see herself opening a gallery. So I said kindly: What is your job, you're a dentist? It's a little bit like if I said: the day when I decide to shut down the gallery, I'd like to become a dentist, just like that, late in life. And even then, I could only do a little bit, small things like cleanings! [She laughs] But being a gallerist is a real job, just like dentistry, you have to learn it,[1] and you can't do it halfway.

The profession of gallerist, in fact, covers a wide range of tasks that are intended to support artists and contribute to their success in a more general way.[2] As such, in France, according to the code of ethics set forth by the Comité Professionnel des Galeries d'Art (Professional Committee of Art Galleries, CPGA) currently in effect: "the gallerist is appointed by the artist or his successors in title to promote, distribute, and sell the artworks." "The gallerist has the role of an intermediary between the artist and institutional or private collectors and art professionals. He can promote contacts with journalists and art critics. This way, the gallerist improves the artist's visibility, putting him or her in touch with all professionals likely to contribute to his or her fame."

In some extreme cases, a gallery's mission can extend even further. This extract from a press release issued in March 2018 by the influential gallery Hauser & Wirth clearly shows the extensive diversity of the work that can take place in a gallery to support its artists, reaching far beyond the activity of sales alone:

> **Hauser & Wirth announces worldwide representation of Zeng Fanzhi.**
> We are delighted to announce worldwide representation of leading Chinese artist Zeng Fanzhi. Hauser & Wirth looks forward to further developing the artist's international profile through a series of major exhibitions, public programs, publishing projects, and through the commissioning of new scholarship. Together the gallery and the artist will launch initiatives that place a strong emphasis on education and academic pursuit—in addition to representing the artist, Hauser & Wirth will establish an ongoing collaboration with the Fanzhi Foundation, which supports and promotes art and culture-related events in conjunction with a range of institutions worldwide.
>
> Hauser & Wirth's first exhibition project with Zeng will take place in fall this year. A number of academic events—including international symposia—are also being planned to coincide with the publication of a comprehensive catalogue raisonné of the artist's work: Volume 1, documenting the first 20 years (1984-2004) of Zeng's career, will be released in summer 2018. In addition to an in-depth collaboration with Hauser & Wirth, the artist will continue a relationship and professional exchange with his existing galleries.

While this example may seem extreme, insofar as Hauser & Wirth is probably (at least among all the most prominent structures) the gallery whose work most closely resembles that of museums, it only accentuates the tendencies that are widely reproduced among contemporary art galleries today.

Without necessarily going as far as to declare it explicitly, it is commonly accepted that the work of "good" or "real" gallerists must extend far beyond sales, and this is what justifies the gallery retaining a large part of the sale price (generally half, as established in chapter 4). This large variety of tasks makes the occupation of gallerist unique when they operate in the primary market. The following professional, who runs a midsize gallery, expressed her irritation at the lack of distinction that is made between galleries that do their work properly—in all of its diversity and assuming all of their responsibilities—and other galleries, whose involvement seems to her much more superficial:

> It's been like that for years. You have to be hype, promising, finger on the pulse. No one cares, journalists most of all, whether galleries close, if they

> take good care of their artists, if they pay them correctly and if they invest in the long term, with regular solo shows in a place suitable for their image, with publications, if they have several loyal collectors, if they're really present on the market . . . what counts too much, since the end of the 90s, is doing trendy fairs and having 'hot' artists. Promising galleries are constantly coming and going, it's not very interesting. For me, what matters is actually persisting and supporting my artists, whose work I consider necessary and important. That's already a lot to do.

As this British gallerist who runs another midsize gallery explained:

> It's frustrating when we have to compete at fairs with galleries that don't do the same job as us, that only get their stock from the secondary market, and that put together a booth dedicated to an artist that we represent. But they don't do the same job as us, they don't support artists, they don't do all the work that we do with collectors, as well as the press, critics, and institutions. It's really something else.

It is not only a question of distinguishing good professionals from bad (Hughes, 1984); they simply would not do the same job.

The same diversity of tasks performed by some galleries more than others is also clearly illustrated by this French visual artist:

> Usually, the gallerist acts as an agent, usually . . . he prepares your dossiers for you, he sends [them] to foundations, he looks for sponsors. He's even supposed to do applications for you, to send your file to institutions, art centers, submit you for competitions or scholarships . . . but it depends on the gallery. The ones that work well, that want to make some cash, it's in their best interest to promote their artists, they do that. Because for them, being able to say 'artist selected for the Marcel Duchamp prize' is great for the gallery! Usually, the gallery takes 50% because it does this work, it invests a lot of money in you, you go to participate in Art Paris, it costs them €20,000 between renting the space and transporting the pieces. Well, mine takes that percentage, even though it doesn't do all that work.
>
> Sinigaglia-Amadio and Sinigaglia, 2017, p. 89

As a matter of fact, all of the above hardly differs from what Raymonde Moulin presented in 1967, over half a century ago, to characterize the role of the gallery and its owner:

> Having chosen 'his' artists, the dealer organizes their 'launch' or their 'showcase' [. . .] He includes the painter in group exhibitions, organizes personal exhibitions for him, supports the price in public sales according to his possibilities and interests, displays him at international events," "As

> a supporter with a personal investment, he helps the artist to overcome the trials that punctuate a painter's international career
>
> Moulin, 1967 [1987], p. 125

However, it is important to note that, in order to be able to honor its commitment to each artist as previously explained, and to do so in the best possible way, the gallery must first ensure its survival; and if possible, its development. There are therefore three main foci that can be identified among the gallery's activities: those that contribute to its own development, those that maintain relationships with artists, and the promotional work for these artists, which constitutes a sort of preparation for sales.

Managing the development of the gallery and its image

While art galleries constantly highlight the support of their represented artists as the end goal of their commercial operation, this necessarily takes place via the pursuit of their own existence and, if possible, their growth. In *The French Art Market*, Raymonde Moulin traces the contours of the dealer-entrepreneur model (Moulin, 1967 [1987]), which was first established by Paul Durand-Ruel, and which illustrates the Schumpeterian analysis that underlines the importance of innovation (Schumpeter, 2008). Moulin later provides a synthesis in *The Artist, the Institution, and the Market*:

> The keystone of the system is the dealer-entrepreneur, in the Schumpeterian sense of this term (i.e., innovator) [. . .]. He can [. . .] attempt to maximize his profit in two different ways: either by storing paintings acquired at relatively low prices and waiting, by selecting his clients; or else by creating a temporarily favorable situation (by capitalizing on the artist's aura, the clientele's enthusiasm, and the upsurge of speculative bets), sell a lot and raise prices very quickly. This last strategy [. . .] has dominated the contemporary art market over the past 30 years [. . .]. This new strategy, taking place over a shortened timespan, calls for a socially and geographically expanded space of action.
>
> Moulin, 1992, p. 46

> In each major commercial space, the contemporary art sector is structured around a limited number of leading galleries that are capable of introducing new products and [. . .] setting prices [. . .]. Top galleries show artistic leadership by helping to determine the dominant trend.
>
> Moulin, 1992, p. 47

Note, however, that the dealer-entrepreneur model created by Durand-Ruel was somewhat challenged at the same time as the monopoly contract (transferring ownership of the painter's works to the dealer). The formula of the simple sales agent/dealer who takes paintings on consignment without any guarantee of selling them has become almost systematically adopted today; for those who do not follow this model, most of the practices sketched out by Durand-Ruel (Patry, 2014) presented in the first foreword of this book remain in effect.

In *The Artist, the Institution, and the Market*, Moulin distinguishes the two main dealer models: dealer-entrepreneurs and dealer-traders. Dealer-traders specialize in the secondary market and minimize the dual risk of aesthetic and financial gambles. In the order of transactions, they succeed dealer-entrepreneurs (Moulin, 1992); I am more interested in the latter here.

In order to succeed, galleries must fully embrace their commercial dimension:

> The contemporary art market is one in which the uncertainty of aesthetic appreciation is at its zenith, where connoisseurs themselves do not agree on a unanimous judgment and are not independent of the economic system, where coalitions of interests that rely on extra-aesthetic factors intervene to accelerate the pace of profits and losses. Contemporary works that have recently been introduced on the market constitute highly speculative values insofar as their artistic quality is not guaranteed by the judgment of time. They depend, in the immediate future, on the opinion that the dealer and the buyers have of their future prospects.
>
> p. 483

She continues: "Monopoly and speculation are constituent elements of the art market." (Moulin, 1992, p. 484).

The attempt to control prices in the long term is accompanied by managing the market of represented artists; as shown in the chapter on sales. In 1967, Moulin noted: "the rational calculation of the dealer-entrepreneur who tries to associate financial value and aesthetic value thus avoids speculative practices. In the same vein, galleries strive to place the works 'in stable hands' and not with 'collector-dealers'" (p. 181). Moulin provided the following excerpt from an interview with a gallerist:

> I monitor public sales, but there are very few of our artists who go on public sale in Paris. It's very rare. It isn't difficult to place orders, if I want to buy the piece or bid higher [. . .] I do not sell to just anyone. The collectors to whom I have sold pieces and who want to resell, which is rare, have the courtesy to tell me (gallery director, Paris).
>
> Moulin, 1967 [1987], p. 181

As previously mentioned, the extent of the difficulty for contemporary art galleries lies in not appearing to be too commercial (or even not being commercial at all), although they are by definition commercial entities. It is therefore their artistic legitimacy that must be highlighted and cultivated. Its longevity is also an important source of legitimacy; experiencing commercial or mercantile success is not perceived as a problem when it has been deferred, if it was not sought in the short term. Approval is additionally granted when long-term strategies have been adopted, or when commercial success develops over the long term, with the artists that were supported from the outset initially generating little demand before the market was interested in them. There is an evident parallel that can be drawn with the analyses of Pierre Bourdieu on the success of the short term, which is less legitimate in the artistic fields because it is marred by the commercial prosperity that soon follows it. Bourdieu clearly outlines how it is nevertheless long-term success that will ultimately produce the real best sellers, but much later, which is socially more acceptable (Bourdieu, 1996).

The occupation of gallerist does indeed constitute a commercial undertaking, even if this dimension must be blurred; it is a question of controlling a market as much as possible, and to do so, some believe it to be useful to denigrate their closest competitors because: (1) not all galleries belong to the contemporary art world, only some do; and (2) among these, there is a segmentation that depends both on the average price of the works for sale, and the type of art being offered; particularly in terms of the dominant medium, with the place of painting constituting a major division (Halle & Tiso, 2014). In the case of Paris, most truly contemporary galleries sell pieces with average prices of a few thousand or a few tens of thousand euros, but the largest galleries offer a price range of a few hundred thousand euros. In France, like in many other countries, this threshold is rarely exceeded. Few galleries—other than Marian Goodman, David Zwirner, Gagosian, White Cube, Hauser & Wirth and Thaddaeus Ropac—repeatedly approach or exceed the million-euro benchmark with several works in many exhibitions (even non-historical ones).

Like all businesses, galleries are often driven by the objective of increasing both their revenue and their profit. Revenue and profit can sometimes seem fairly high for small and midsize galleries that have, at best, only a few staff members; however, large galleries face high fixed costs. In particular, they often employ a few dozen staff members or more (the largest galleries often have barely over 100 staff members; those whose payrolls go beyond these numbers are extremely rare and the number of staff rarely exceed 300 people in any gallery worldwide). For instance, a certain large gallery of French origin must make €600,000 in sales per month to cover its fixed costs. This German artist also indicated: "The international gallery that represents me is one of the biggest in the world, it seems like it has to reach three million in sales each month just to cover its fixed costs, it's absolutely insane." The French gallery Ceysson & Bénétière is one of the rare establishments that openly publicizes its revenue; as François Ceysson explained: "Our gallery makes between €8 and 10 million in revenue annually, but what matters is . . . the profit, not the revenue!"

Even if, as we will see in the third part of this book, we must always consider data relating to galleries' turnover with the greatest of caution, the following news source is pertinent as it indicates a strong segmentation of French galleries from this point of view:

> At a time when the Professional Committee of Art Galleries (CPGA) released a study by the economist Clare McAndrew conducted on its members, we dedicate an article to the economic model of contemporary art galleries, with the youngest and most prospective among them struggling to establish their financial viability in the face of market behemoths, which ultimately amass the most-sought after artists on the market. The figures produced by the CPGA study, previewed by the *Journal des Arts*, are based on data from 145 respondents (the professional organization has 241 members). By extrapolation, the overall revenue of these respondents was around €480 million in 2015, with an average at around €2 million per gallery. But this amount does not reflect the diversity of the respondents' situations, with 34% of galleries making a revenue of less than €220,000, and at the other end of the spectrum, only 4% reaching between €17.7 and €26.5 million. Figures that shed light on the situation in France, those cited in the article were taken from the 2016 Art Basel and UBS Global Art Market Report, also written by Clare McAndrew.
>
> *La Gazette Drouot*, no. 18, May 2017, p. 3

In order to determine orders of magnitude, it is important to note that in France, galleries are often considered "small" if they make under €500,000 in revenue, "midsize" if their sales are between €500,000 and €3 million, and "large" if they exceed the latter. These orders of magnitude are regularly mentioned in the French press. In Germany, the Institute for Strategy Development (IFSE) published a report at the end of 2020 that classified galleries according to their revenue as follows: small galleries earned up to €400,000, average galleries earned between €400,000 and €1.5 million, and "top" galleries earned above €1.5 million (IFSE, 2020).[3]

There is generally an overall correlation—a homology, to use the terminology of Pierre Bourdieu—between the recognition of represented artists and the "size" of the gallery, wherein the latter must elevate its artists to its own level. Their progression in terms of recognition also allows the gallery to grow in return.

The following excerpt shows as much:

– *How have the prices of Alina Szapocznikow's works increased since you began representing her estate?*

– Over eight years, the prices have multiplied by five on average, whereas 20 years ago you could still find her pieces at flea markets! This economic valuation is interesting to analyze and can be explained by the events that have taken place: around 20 exhibitions in institutions, including the Centre Pompidou in Paris and the MoMA in New York, the production of five monographic catalogues, etc. Increasing prices in order to limit the demand and thus preserve the estate's funds has allowed the beneficiaries and the gallery to retain a series of works in order to be able to easily show and share this work.

Hervé Loevenbruck, Contemporary Art Activist,
in *La Gazette Drouot*, no. 35, October 18, 2019, p. 186

In addition to the financial income, managing the gallery's image is also an imperative, which especially involves the organization of the events mentioned in chapter 5, as well as other activities. In essence, galleries must maintain a clear mission statement, both *vis-à-vis* collectors and other partners of the gallery. This is very apparent in cities where the local market is limited. During the Berlin Gallery Weekend in May 2016, many galleries presented works that were difficult to sell, such as installations. In a city with a weak art market (some might even say it is a very weak one), the main issue actually stems from the image being presented at a time when a maximum number of potential clients, as well as art professionals, were in attendance. It was a matter of attracting critics (whose influence nowadays is nevertheless limited), as well as curators and directors of institutions and, more importantly still, fair organizers and selection committee members. It was essential to win over the latter above all, because being admitted to fairs is truly vital for galleries, as this is where collectors can come to buy their works. From that point on, a good number of galleries have doubled down on the radicality of their "proposals" so as to leave no room for doubt as to the "contemporaneity" associated with the gallery's quality (Misdrahi Flores, 2013). This is especially true for Berlin galleries, which must live up to enormous expectations in that respect. This particular scene is a perfect example of how accurate the notion of "interest in selflessness" ("*intérêt au désintéressement*" in French), coined by Pierre Bourdieu (Bourdieu, 1996) is; here staged primarily to draw the attention of professionals within the art market, as well as collectors to a lesser or secondary extent.

These image construction strategies are directly determined by the segment of the art market in which the gallery is positioned, with the previous example highlighting the geographical element in particular. The Berlin context produces specific practices that are very different from those employed in New York, especially in Chelsea, the district with the highest concentration of contemporary galleries in the world. This was particularly evident in the case of the four global leaders in terms of economic influence, all of which (as previously noted) have locations in Chelsea. The Berlin Gallery Weekend, in

June 2016, offered a strong contrast with the Armory Show art fair held in March 2017. Here, unlike in Berlin, the primary goal was to sell artworks in galleries' own spaces, which have been constructed and designated as a legitimate environment. During the period of the two major New York contemporary art fairs—the Armory Show in March and Frieze New York in May at the time (just like the rest of the year, incidentally)—these galleries are much less subject to the rationales of fairs, as they already have access to a very active local market. In this case, it is much more a question of selling artworks directly to clients in their own space (or beginning the process there). Even when they participate in fairs, galleries sometimes flaunt their disinterest for them.[4]

As such, while participating in the Art Cologne fair in April 2017, the giant Gagosian, which had one of the two largest booths, displayed a grand total of . . . four pieces. Three paintings, radical in their heightened degree of minimalism, were hung on the exterior picture rails, while the interior of the booth featured a lone work abandoned in the middle of the booth. The space, which may have seemed wasted, actually helped to directly express the gallery's detachment from the commercial purposes of fairs, which have become absolutely vital for many galleries today. Similarly, one of the direct competitors of Gagosian—the Pace gallery—was the only one of the largest establishments in New York to have a booth at the 2017 Armory Show. However, its space featured a single solitary work (from Project Drift): a huge block that seemed to be made of concrete and hovered above the booth. There again, it was a question of expressing the gallery's detachment from commercial objectives; all the more so in a fair where the price of booths per square meter is among the highest in the world (see chapter 3). Visitors could not help but wonder if the event's organizers had not invited the gallery at all, due to its prestige. In the case of these two mega-galleries, established in particular in Chelsea in massive spaces at the very heart of the global art market (both of which have opened subsidiary locations in several cities that are important in the international market), the strategy of making sales in galleries and participating in fairs is the exact reverse of that employed by Berlin galleries, which occupy a clearly peripheral space in terms of the local or exterior market. It is therefore not only a question of adopting the right positioning, but also, in cases where it can serve the gallery's brand, of making it obvious.

The origin of capital and the discreet role of backers

In the 1960s, in her pioneering book, *The French Art Market*, Raymonde Moulin noted that in the art market some galleries had financial partners (Moulin, 1987). Today, like in the past, support from these players most likely involves only a limited number of galleries, but the fact that their support is almost always discreet, if not completely secret, can fuel certain suspicions and rumors.

In 1967, when discussing "dealer-entrepreneurs," Moulin highlighted the various solutions available to them when they were getting their start: "The solutions for young dealers today are manifold: obtaining (at least temporarily) financial support from their family, if they can afford it; adopting a 'trader' role and keeping a selection of good paintings in the back of the gallery for art lovers; accepting consignments of pieces from artists without any advance payments; or resorting to having sponsors"[5] (Moulin, 1967 [1987], p. 120). At the time, Moulin mentioned the role of banks that supported galleries by specifying: "there are many financiers, industrialists, bankers who, in a private capacity and because they are themselves collectors, finance galleries" (Moulin, 1967, p. 121). She also mentions the reluctance of gallerists to engage in this model, for fear that their financial partners encroach on their freedom to choose their artists.

The term "backer," which designates a financial partner,[6] is now widely used in the gallery world; even though, paradoxically, it can only concern a few galleries (or even none of them, according to most professionals). It should also be noted that the term is used rather loosely, and that the kinds of involvement for these financial partners in galleries—when they exist—are fairly variable. This gallerist, who runs a midsize gallery, explained:

> When she heard that I was going to take over her old space, [X] called me, sweet as honey, and she asked me if my backer had supported me in this move. In fact, she wanted to know if I had a backer. But no, I have a partner, but that has nothing to do with this plan, which will pay for itself.

These privileged business partners are often major collectors for their partner gallery. Their support for contemporary art galleries is by no means automatic; far from it. As Moulin notes in an excerpt cited above, in the era that she studied, dealers could do without the support of a financier simply by accepting works on consignment instead of acquiring them, thus reducing their need for capital. As this model has become practically exclusive nowadays, the use of a financial partner has become much less necessary. However, insofar as it increases a gallery's resources, it can be useful; but it is rarely (or at least, is only incidentally) publicized. As this other gallerist confided to me when he learned that one of his colleagues was going to vacate her space: "It's a pity that she didn't tell us that she was leaving and giving up her space, we could have done something with a few collectors so that I could take it over."

When clients strongly support a few artists, and if they have significant financial means, they can in fact become involved with a gallery, especially if the latter will then advocate for their preferred artists. In that case, it is then difficult to refuse an artist who occupies an important place in the partner's collection. Financing a gallery represents a cost, but it is also a means of supporting the financial value of the works owned by the collector, because an artist who is not supported by a gallery will quickly see their works depreciate in value. In 2017, this gallerist who runs a midsize gallery explained to me:

> When I took this new, more central and more expensive space, I needed to have more capital, especially to do renovations, so I contacted the five or six collectors who follow me the most and I told them about this opportunity for a new space. I asked them if they could buy more works to help me with this move, of course I gave them a special price. But it's a win-win, the fact that I have this new space, it's given the gallery more credibility, so that also enhances the value of the works made by the artists they collect. Well, now I'm seriously thinking about expanding, either by finding a second space very close to here, or by leaving for a single space, but much larger. My problem is that I now have about 15 artists, and to dedicate regular exhibitions to them, even with a very fast tempo of putting on an exhibition every month or so, it's difficult, especially when I've brought in two new artists this year, and when people have met me at the fair booths and when they come, they see that my location is very good, but they're surprised that the space isn't bigger.

It is often when this question of growth arises that galleries may need to call on their capital resources without always going through banking institutions.

Even outside of their own circumstances, gallerists do not like to mention the fact that some of their colleagues may rely on backers. This important French gallerist stated quite concisely: "We talk about backers, but it's very rare. In Paris, there's only one gallery that has them, it's [X] [a midsize gallery]." This assertion is, however, false, as another gallerist to whom I am close has intimated to me on several occasions that the gallery has a financial partner that it makes no attempt to hide.

Collectors speak much more freely about these associations. This important French collector, who is very integrated into the international contemporary art scene remarked: "I am always surprised when I learn that a gallerist whom I have known for years and years actually has a financier behind him, who may also be a friend of mine. People are so discreet about it. But it's not exceptional, you know." During a dinner, another collector confided to me: "It seems that there are Chinese financiers behind Gallery [X]."[7]

Among all the businesspeople likely to support galleries, one such person who regularly sparks rumors on the art market is François Pinault, who is unquestionably one of the major international players on this market. His possible involvement with one or a few galleries is notably associated with the fact that, in 2007, Christie's auction house (which he owns) acquired a gallery, Haunch of Venison.[8] However, the venture was cut short, as the gallery was then refused access to fairs; the other galleries accused Pinault of unfair competition due to his connections with an auction house. From that moment on, Pinault has not officially maintained financial ties with any galleries. Yet, it would not be absurd to posit that Pinault has interests in one or two galleries, as this art market journalist analyzed:

> François Pinault had wanted to buy a gallery when he acquired Haunch of Venison, but when he did so openly, he lost access to fairs, which are nevertheless decisive today. But when a rich man wants something, he obviously gets it, even more so if he's extremely rich, as rich as François Pinault is. So it makes sense to look at international galleries, especially French ones, all the more so if their development seems much too extensive in proportion to the reputation of their artists.

The press naturally listed the names of his potential partners:

> Pinault relies on gallerist friends to support his protégés. All of Paris is talking about his financial relationships with two stars. First, Emmanuel Perrotin, who was booted from the Basel fair in 2007 for sneaking Pinault into the fair before the opening [. . .]. He denies any direct financial support, even though he confirms that "Pinault is an important collector for the gallery." Second, Kamel Mennour, who supported Philippe Parreno, Adel Abdessemed, and Martial Raysse. Renowned for his pieces from the 1960s, the painter Martial Raysse struggled to attract clients with his recent works, which were bought *en masse* by the billionaire. "It was the artist who contacted me, François Pinault didn't ask me anything," protests Mennour. "I was not supported by anyone, he likes my lineup, that's it." The gallerist organized charity sales with Christie's, where people could win a trip to Venice, with a private visit of the Palazzo Grassi led by Pinault.
>
> in "François Pinault, the Godfather of Contemporary Art," by David Bensoussan, *Challenges*, no. 559, March 29, 2018, p. 78

As previously stated, Pinault managed to gain access to the Art Basel fair several times before it opened thanks to the complicity of a gallerist to whom he is close (Fredet, 2017). This other player in the art market explained:

> Emmanuel Perrotin had taken the risk of letting François Pinault into the Basel fair before the opening, and he's not stupid, he must have suspected that, if he were caught, he would be kicked out of the fair. We can't take this kind of risk for a client, even if he's one of the gallery's most important clients, since being able to participate in the Basel fair has enormous

> financial outcomes. But he took that risk. And what's interesting is that the Basel fair didn't even blacklist him permanently, so I think there was pressure from Pinault to let Perrotin come back. But well, if it were just to bring back one of the many gallerists from whom he buys, Pinault really wouldn't have cared to weigh in, it seems to me to point to much stronger relationships. But of course, we can't prove that.

As highlighted in this excerpt, the facts referred to in the conditional tense should be taken and considered with extreme caution. Rather than drawing certain (or probable) conclusions from one or two special cases, it is better to recall that market players often hint at the presence of backers, and that their covert support is the subject of recurring rumors. Moreover, it seems likely that their intervention is currently limited to a rather small number of galleries only.

Crucial partners for galleries: the artists

Just as much as collectors, whose relationships with galleries were reviewed in the previous two chapters on sales and sociability (with a particular focus on friendship), artists constitute absolutely crucial partners.

The first step in representing these people and in supporting their work is finding "one's" artists. Practices have not changed much since the end of the 1950s. As Raymonde Moulin noted in the 1960s: "Rarely is a painter chosen because he approached the dealer. One could even say that it never happens. There is a word-of-mouth complicity on the topic of an artist in a certain milieu. That is what counts" (Moulin, 1967 [1987], p. 127). Even nowadays, the introduction rarely takes place in the context of unsolicited applications. Gallerists tend to dread this kind of approach, as they can be time consuming and awkward, and they only pay off very occasionally. As this director of a large French gallery explained:

> It's terrible, these artists who send us emails to let us know about their work, or even who come into the gallery to present their work to us. They're already shooting themselves in the foot just by doing that, they show that they don't know that it doesn't work like that at all. The worst are the ones who come to our booths at fairs and think that we have time to take care of them, when it's actually the worst time to get in touch with us! And then, the few times that I had a look at their work because they had come to the gallery, it was really a disaster, so it's very embarrassing.

However, there are a handful of exceptional cases in which such an introduction goes well. This French gallerist who runs a small establishment explained:

> [X] naively came to see me at Art Paris art fair, and of course I was overwhelmed, I told him to come to the gallery instead on another day, and then I completely forgot. When he came back, I had no idea what it was going to be like, but as soon as he started showing me his work, it was like, whoa!

Gallerists sometimes search for artists by visiting the senior exhibitions of art school students or by visiting studios, during fairs that the gallerist attends either as a simple visitor or as an exhibitor, and by attending exhibitions; but very often, these occasions are not entirely chance encounters, and they are partly guided by word of mouth. Being highly assimilated into the art world makes it equally possible to be discovered and to play the role of intermediary, and clearly shows the relevance of the concept of informal academies that can confer the title of "artist" (Becker, 1982; Moulin, 1992). It is therefore all the more important for artists to be able to be discovered. Martin Fuller demonstrates how artists, especially when they are young or not well known, will try to find more opportunities to socialize with gallerists (as they cannot apply directly); for instance, by attending openings and visiting galleries with reputations of being welcoming to up-and-coming artists (Fuller, 2015). It is also important for creators to maintain a supportive network in the art world, with contacts who can recommend others to take an interest in their work. Within this network, other artists (their peers) help them to be discovered early, as formalized by Alan Bowness in his model of successive circles of recognition (Bowness, 1989).[9] The same goes for gallerists: for them as well, having a network capable of identifying "good" artists and directing them toward the gallery is also a valuable resource. While it is common to emphasize how important being represented by a gallery is for artists, it would be a miscalculation to state that the partnership is inessential for galleries. Not only do they necessarily need artists, but they also need "good" (Misdrahi Flores, 2013) ones. For gallerists, the pressure is therefore just as strong. As this important American gallerist put it at the beginning of 2020: "Right now, there's a lot of competition for artists. You have to decide very quickly, otherwise another gallery could do it." Gallerists are very attached to the role of discovering and choosing their artists; however, they are not in the best position to do so. While the most active gallerists travel quite a bit (which is a very useful means of training their eye, as they can encounter the most diverse forms of creation possible), they are often going to and from art fairs. In such instances, they hardly have time to discover the works exhibited at their colleagues' booths at their own pace, not to mention the possibility of visiting interesting local galleries and major institutions.

Insofar as choosing their artists to develop a roster constitutes a strong act of identity for the gallery, some gallerists do not appreciate being advised, or that it be made public. As this director of an international European gallery explained, in reference to the gallery's owner:

> She doesn't like being given advice on artists to represent because she doesn't want to owe anything to anyone, and she wouldn't like people to say that they were the ones who guided her choices. With us, it's different, she sometimes asks us or listens to us. Me, for [X], I had to insist several times. What made her reconsider was that I pointed out to her that several of our collectors had already purchased pieces by this artist, when we didn't represent him yet. It was relevant to the taste of the gallery, and it was going to make those buyers happy to see that we were going their way. And then there was a time when we didn't really have a sculptor anymore, but it's useful to have one, especially for designing fair booths, so that ended up convincing her to take [X].

Integrating a new artist necessarily involves taking many factors into account, including the artist's work and how it aligns with the gallery's "vision." It can be a more or less pronounced interest in painting, for "conceptual" approaches; i.e., for a given generation of artists, for certain national or ethnic backgrounds, for women, etc. Depending on their choice, galleries can decide to specialize (relatively speaking) in an area or, conversely, to opt for diversification, which is generally seen as presenting a certain complementarity. The market from which an artist can benefit in the long term, or from which they already benefit, must also be taken into account. As this French gallerist reported: "Gallery [X] has just taken on [Y] as an artist. It's obviously a good choice, we know that François Pinault collects this artist, a lot even, so he will support him, offer him many opportunities. It's all very good for the gallery, there's even a waiting list." However, more broadly, the ideal situation is one in which the new artist has a similar level of reputation to that of the gallery, or slightly higher. While it is not generally beneficial to integrate an unknown artist, unless the gallerist believes strongly in their potential, an artist with a reputation that is much larger than that of the gallery can prove difficult in any attempts at making further progress. As a matter of fact, the easiest relationships to manage are those between gallerists and artists of comparable levels of reputation, because they are the most balanced. It can be difficult for a small gallery to have an artist who is much more famous than the others; and it can be just as delicate for an artist to have a lower reputation than that of their gallery, or their peers who are also represented therein. This is why there is generally a homology effect (Bourdieu, 1996) between the middle-ranking artists of the gallery and the reputation of the gallery itself.

Artists whose reputation or market strays too far from that of the gallery's may find themselves in a more difficult situation. As this German artist explained:

> I heard that my main gallery in the world would have to make three million in sales each month to cover its fixed costs! They have incredible premises, they have a big staff, they do a lot of fairs. Obviously, it therefore needs

> expensive artists to cover its costs. You have to be reasonable, I understand what my position in the gallery is, even though it represents me. I started with this gallerist, he's progressed a lot and he's become a star, but my personal market isn't at the same level. I occupy a very marginal position in it. Even if, for me, it's very chic to say that the gallery represents me, it's very good for my image, but I'm not like the other artists.[10]

In general, provided that the gallery has the means (i.e., that it is on the same level of recognition in the gallery world as the position occupied by the artist in their own social world or space) and the more recognition an artist already has, the more beneficial it would be to represent them. This is how the French visual artist Laure Prouvost came to be supported by the MOT International gallery in the United Kingdom until the gallery unexpectedly closed in 2016. While many artists find themselves in a delicate position after such an upset and must endure somewhat long periods in which they find themselves without a gallery to represent them in a given country, Prouvost (who remained represented by the Nathalie Obadia gallery, with locations in France and Belgium, and by the Carlier-Gebauer gallery in Germany) quickly joined the Lisson gallery. One of the largest British galleries—also with a location in the heart of Chelsea in New York—it represents many highly renowned artists, and in fact offered a new progression to Prouvost's career by affording her better access to the British market and a new presence on the American market.

The superstar Cindy Sherman experienced a similar situation in March 2021, when the major New York gallery Metro Pictures (which had represented her for a very long time and for which she was the most recognized artist) announced that it was permanently closing. A single day after the announcement that this gallery was disappearing, *Artnet News* revealed that Cindy Sherman had promptly joined the massive international gallery Hauser & Wirth. Of all the renowned artists from Metro Pictures (in addition to Sherman, it represented Louise Lawler, Robert Longo, Trevor Paglen, Camille Henrot, and Isaac Julien) she was the most famous, and the first to join a new gallery; taking advantage, moreover, of the occasion to integrate a particularly famous and prestigious establishment.

Though it is widely accepted that artists will migrate toward larger galleries while simultaneously building their reputation, the galleries that make a practice of poaching artists whose early careers were constructed by their fellow galleries are generally condemned. Those that specialize in this strategy are often described as predatory, as they benefit directly from previously performed promotional work (Moulin, 1987) without having borne the cost. Here again, this is a phenomenon that existed over half a century ago, when sociologists began to study the art market:

> Dealers easily 'poach' artists when they have the financial means. They compete for renowned painters much like football clubs compete for

> great players. [. . .] The painter-dealer relationship is based on a balance of power: the dealer is all-powerful vis-à-vis a painter who has a limited reputation and no social ranking, but a painter who has made a name for himself can tyrannize his dealer.
>
> Moulin, 1967 [1987], p. 129

Among the various artists likely to be represented by galleries, there is a particular place for estates—the bodies that manage the interests of artists who are now deceased—and these are particularly desirable. Generally, a gallery's share in estate sales is much lower, but it is more a question of prestige and image. Additionally, as the artist's production is now finished, the stock of their creations is easier to manage. Finally, estates generally make the act of representing these artists more stable over time; as this gallerist says: "They are more reliable than artists, it's simpler."

It is important to reiterate here that while in the domain of social representations artists are perceived as being highly dependent on their gallery, it should not be ignored that the relationship of dependence is in fact a two-way street. Although the romantic ideology of the artist being a victim of their gallerist remains the most ingrained social image (Moulin, 1992), relationships are much more balanced in favor of artists than common sense would suppose. Galleries invest in their artists, whose potential departure can have significant, even devastating financial and reputational consequences. This is particularly apparent in the event of separations. As this gallerist at the head of a small French establishment explained:

> When I lost [A], it was very hard for me, very abrupt. He left me at the last minute, a few days before the opening of the exhibition that we had scheduled, it put me in danger. I had already pre-sold almost everything based on photos, so I had to explain to them that I was no longer working with him. I begged him to do that last show with me and to leave afterwards. No one would have known, could have guessed how much he actually hated me, and how much I held it against him for doing this to me. He hurt me a lot, he caused some collectors to turn their backs on my gallery. When I cross paths with them at fairs now, they make out like they don't even see me. He said that I didn't pay him and that I owed him money, but it's false, I pay my artists.

During my numerous field observations, I myself witnessed situations in which gallerists were, in a way, taken hostage by one of their artists, as in the case of this other painter who for some years had been in high demand on the market. At the last minute, the artist delivered a series that was almost entirely slapdash and of poor quality, which the gallerist and his employees did not discover until the night before the exhibition began. As it was impossible to cancel at the last minute, the gallerist had to sell this series that, nevertheless, harmed both the artist's work and the gallery's reputation.

Another practice—feared by galleries—that can be detrimental to them is that artists may sell their works directly to clients without going through the gallery that represents them, so as not to pay the commission that would be deducted.[11] As Raymonde Moulin indicated in the 1960s, galleries are therefore sometimes reluctant to inform artists who is buying their works, for fear of being "double-crossed" and the artist leaving with a list of collectors if ever it occurred to them to change galleries. In order to facilitate sales, however, it is in the gallery's interest to put collectors in contact with artists, because: "At the heart of the art world is the artist, and it is the contact with the creator itself that constitutes a sense of supreme gratification" (Moulin, 1967 [1987], p. 220). While the gallerist must generally know how to organize this meeting in order to facilitate sales, it is therefore not without risk. It is clear how two interests can contradict one another.

While it is very rare today for gallerists to pay their artists a monthly stipend, it is not uncommon for them to invest in other, non-monetary ways, even beyond the simple professional framework. The following two gallerists expressed similar ideas: "What we do for our artists can go really far. We had an artist who was in a really difficult financial situation, who owned his house with his studio but who couldn't make ends meet. We're the ones who found a buyer for his property." As this colleague who runs a midsize structure indicated:

> Having 12 artists is already a lot of work, we practically babysit some of them. There are some artists, we're completely at their service, we may put on turnkey exhibitions of their works, like the one we organized for [X], which was shown by a bank. We try to find artist residencies for them, we put together dossiers for institutions, we present them for prizes and awards, and then there's the fairs and the regular operations of the gallery . . . it's a lot of work! But we also provide them with much more personal services.

The duo of artist and gallery helps to boost sales—as explained in the two previous chapters—once the works have been created, as well as by the initial choice to represent the artist (as previously indicated). From a sociological perspective, the latter could give the impression of a sort of co-creation, wherein the person who presents the work on the market (Becker, 1982) is equally involved with the person who produced the physical work. It is even more obvious when the gallerist is involved in the production, even though this is far from being the norm. Simply visiting an artist's studio while they are creating a work can carry the possibility of influencing their choices, for instance by asking the artist for pieces in a specific format, of one kind rather than another; or it can even pave the way for more intrusive practices. This employee of one of the largest galleries in the world recounted an anecdote that illustrates the harmonious relationship between the gallerist and their artist, which aims to adapt the work to existing demand:

> I remember once, our boss was with [a star artist], and he wanted to put a snake in relief on one of his paintings. An assistant was there with the box of snakes [she laughs] and our boss said that collectors wouldn't really like having that in their home, that objects in relief don't help to sell works, especially snakes. And the [star artist], he just put the snake back in the box. He's a star, he could have taken offense, but he's smart, he understands that he creates, but afterwards the gallery has to be able to sell it!

Another example in which the gallerist sometimes intervenes directly in the artist's process; this professional recounted a moment when she stepped in so as to obtain a more visually striking work: "I had asked [X] to think about doing an installation for the skylight, I was really surprised by what he made, and when I saw it, I told him: I like it a lot, but add more hair, add more hair!" [she laughs]." The responsibility of directing the artist's production to better respond to future demand can also fall to the gallery liaison with whom the artist is in contact, without being explicit. It is more a question of carrying out invisible work (Strauss, 1959) that involves largely informal interactions. Once the artist has been assimilated into the gallery, most of the relationship between them and the establishment goes through the "liaison" assigned to them, who will often act as the privileged salesperson of their creations. Detailed knowledge not only of the artist's work, but also of their market and clients, can also on occasion guide production. As this gallery director, who is known to be an excellent salesman, explained:

> Well, [X] [an artist], he left to continue his previous series, to build on the same theme, the same motif. We had sold his pieces very well, because in any case he's a painter who is very successful with collectors, but we could see that in the end, nearly all those who could buy this type of painting had done so. So I told him nicely that it would be good if he moved on, because ultimately we were going to start struggling to sell his work.

Though the relationships that unite galleries (and gallerists) and their artists are usually long term, they are rarely formalized by contracts, contrary to what one might expect from this continuous collaboration. In *The French Art Market*, Raymonde Moulin gives examples of real contracts in the appendices of the book, but these were already old examples at the time of publication, signed by Daniel-Henry Kahnweiler and the Bernheim Jeune gallery between 1900 and 1920. The other contracts, which were redacted, date back to 1957 and the beginning of the 1960s, well before the book was published (Moulin, 1967 [1987], pp. 544–557). In the book, Moulin distinguishes between on-sight contracts, where the dealer chooses which works they will take; and exclusivity contracts, with the regular purchase of paintings or the consignment of paintings with regular advance payments (the amount and pay period of which are usually irregular), or else the payment of a monthly stipend considered as a down payment on future sales. However, she notes that the distinction between purchase and consignment contracts was not always clear. Gallerists such as Paul Durand-Ruel and Ambroise Vollard (whom I wrote about in the historical foreword of this book) bought works in bulk and then resold them whenever they liked, at the prices that they determined. They often followed a *pro forma* payment system, depending on the dimensions of the painting, which at that time was a very commonly used system (Moulin, 1987). When he was a simple sales agent, the dealer theoretically received 33 percent of the price, but if he took on the responsibility of advertising and exhibitions, as is now systematically the case (at least, in theory), his percentage increased. Contracts existed in both written and verbal forms, and lawsuits were rare. A quarter of a century later, in *The Artist, the Institution, and the Market*, Moulin no longer gave examples of contracts between galleries and artists in the appendices of her book (Moulin, 1992); in the meantime, contracts had most likely on the whole ceased to be utilized.

Today, most galleries only use tacit and temporary contracts with artists. The gallerist takes the works on consignment and keeps 50 percent to cover the gallery's costs and the promotional work. This important French gallerist, who has been active for over 50 years, brusquely dismissed the notion of contracts: "Contracts are useless. In any case, if the artist or the gallery no longer wants to collaborate, even if we were locked into a contract, we couldn't do anything. It's a moral commitment, that's all. If one of the two parties is acting in bad faith, it becomes impossible to stay together. Why insist?" This German gallerist explained from his point of view: "Personally, I don't have a contract with my artists. My kind of contract could be a letter like the one that [X, a star artist] sent me, he wrote to me . . . that he wanted to keep working with me for many years! [he laughs]."

A previously cited fellow gallerist, who runs a small Parisian gallery and does sign contracts with her artists, recounted a major disappointment that occurred with one of them. Two weeks before a highly publicized opening, he backed out of entrusting his works, many of which had already been pre-sold, to her. She concluded: "In fact, with artists, there's no point in signing contracts. If they don't want to continue, there's nothing to be done. I had really done a lot of work for [X]."

Contracts therefore only occupy a marginal place in the relationship between gallerist and artist. This director of one of the largest galleries in the world responded in surprise at one of my questions on this subject:

> In fact, it bothers me a little to have to tell you this, but honestly I don't know at all if the gallery has contracts with their artists, and I'm sure that my colleagues don't know either. Whether our boss has signed representation contracts with his artists, and if so, if that's the case with all the artists or just some of them, really, we don't know anything at all.

Contracts that bind galleries to their artists are so rare or ineffective that in December 2017 in France, there was an attempt (that ultimately was not very successful) to set forth a model for a contract between both parties. The CPGA drew up a template for a written representation contract that would offer a minimal contractual basis, with the aim of making the situation easier for galleries and securing their relationships with artists. The CPGA had taken a similar initiative in the 1970s by distributing several models of artist–gallery contracts to its members. In the new contract, the general principle of splitting the sales price in two between both parties is set forth, even though it had already been widely adopted in practice. The prior recuperation of production costs before this division—a frequent source of misunderstanding, or even contention—was also established, and the same applies to the commonly accepted use of a potential 10 percent discount on the sales price.[12] However, this new contractual resource has not led to any real evolution of market practices.

The promotional work performed by a gallery

A gallery's sales practices inevitably go hand in hand with promoting its artists' careers, insofar as a contemporary art gallery's business model is centered around creating demand for works that it does not yet have (White & White, 1965; Moulin, 1987). To do so, it is necessary to constantly strive to increase the visibility and recognition of its artists in the broadest possible way (Quemin, 2013b). As Raymonde Moulin analyzed in *The Artist, the Institution, and the Market*:

> The emblematic artist of our time is the contemporary artist whose career is international. This label, which constitutes one of the major challenges of artistic competition, is the product of a mode of organization implemented by a network of cultural institutions and promoting galleries. [. . .] Access to the international art world must go through a prescribed route. The artist is invited by juries of contemporary art specialists to participate in events where selection, validation, and international accolades all take place.
>
> Moulin, 1992, p. 354

Emphasizing the collective dimension of promotional work, Moulin continues:

> "The support of an internationally influential gallery, or even better, of a 'cartel' of galleries, the patronage of a museum director or an international curator, the recommendation of a collector or of an artist who is himself

> international… these are but a few highly favorable factors" (p. 355). "The highest level of artist ratification takes place via informal academies. Elected artists derive their ultimate qualification from places where their work is presented, and from the internationalization of their reputation"
>
> (Moulin, 1992, p. 356).

Moulin gives a rough outline of a professional progression that strongly resembles a *cursus honorum*, which parallels the ascent through the phases of recognition, as described by Alan Bowness (Bowness, 1989).

An initial form of support for artists in the gallery, which differs from sales, involves controlling their prices; in essence, it is necessary to convince buyers that prices are "fair." As established in chapter 4 of this book, which is devoted to sales, an opening strategy aims to select buyers so as to ensure that they will not put the works up on the secondary market, especially as concerns auctions (which are all the more dangerous as sales prices are public and can therefore serve as a reference). Failing this, it therefore becomes necessary to intervene on the secondary market, in particular by buying back the artists' works (often at public sales), as reaching a price lower than that available in a gallery could cause some to doubt the fairness of the gallery's pricing scheme. As Moulin notes:

> The price dictated by the dealer, who distills supply and stimulates demand, can immediately be called into question on the 'parallel market' or in public sales: its arbitrary nature emerges as soon as the 'short-term' stage is over, and demand among those prepared to pay such high prices becomes scarce (or disappears altogether)—unlike individual demand, collective demand is in fact elastic in terms of price.
>
> Moulin, 1967 [1987], pp. 482–483

Even today, artists are frequently sustained by defending the price level set by the gallery: works that are presented on the secondary market can then be bought back. The prestigious New York gallery Paula Cooper won the respect of the contemporary art community thanks to its founder's personality (and her commitment to minimalist art in particular), but also by her refusal to play the "market" game too much. As such, she has always refused to contribute to speculation on her artists' prices. Yet, this has not resulted in an absence of the auction market, which is on the contrary used to stabilize the prices of the artists represented by the gallery. As Cooper explained:

> Another development is the growing impact of auction houses, which affects all galleries, and this can be extremely problematic. They don't pay enough attention to young artists, who sometimes end up hurt. Published figures are the tip of the iceberg: transactions that take place in galleries are part of the private domain. For an artist to be sold in an auction house, they need a solid reputation. When a work is

priced down, the artist's market value is affected. We've never sold a piece at auction. We do buy from time to time though, sometimes to support our artists.

Paula Cooper, "The Competition Has Become Extremely Tough, Overwhelming, Maddening," *Le Journal des Arts*, no. 520, March 29, 2019

It is also important for galleries to structure the market for their artists by collaborating with other establishments, or at least finding their place among them. Thus, they may form a network with other galleries that are likely to represent the artist in other countries. In the past, the best example of this was the Leo Castelli gallery, whose international expansions were noted within the framework of such agreements in the historical foreword of this book. The best thing is for the artist to be represented by galleries of comparable prestige, otherwise the relationship between them can become difficult to manage. This is also true in a national context, with some artists being represented simultaneously by several galleries in the same country; a situation that is not always free of tensions. Such is the case for a well-known French artist who is represented by two French galleries, both of which are influential and international, but are at different levels in their development. One is now fully established and has a historic status, the other is clearly on the rise. One of the directors of the former gallery explained:

> Well, gallery [X], with which we share representation of [Y], we know that it gives discounts of around 25 to 30%, whereas we never go beyond the 10% that's common in the industry.[13] So of course, everyone knows, when clients want to buy [Y], they now go directly to [X]. Last year, we sold a piece by [Y] for €20,000, they sold for 1.2 million! We keep him on our roster out of loyalty, and because our boss sincerely likes his work, but obviously we can't sell anything, from a commercial perspective, it makes no sense.

This situation gives a wonderful illustration of Pierre Bourdieu's concept of a "field" (Bourdieu & Delsaut, 1975; Bourdieu, 1987; Bourdieu, 1996) and the effects that result from the position occupied by each agent (to use Bourdieu's terminology) within it. Those who are in a dominant position have an interest in symbolically maintaining the status quo of prices, and at the same time, their ranking in the eyes of potential buyers. Conversely, those who aspire to occupy a higher position in the field and to take the place of those agents who control it have a greater incentive to adopt transgressive behaviors. It is evident how the contrasting positions occupied in the field of galleries lead various players to adopt different behaviors, as each practice is, in effect, adapted to its own position, and directly generated or determined by it.

Inter-gallery collaborations also result from the collective advancement of their artists' careers. The term "parent gallery" generally refers to the one that launched the creator's career. This artist may sometimes work with other galleries, mainly abroad, while continuing their partnership with the establishment that has been following them for a long time. Generally speaking, recognizing the work that was done to launch an artist justifies the payment of a commission—frequently 10 percent, at least for a while—by any subsequent galleries to the original gallery. As this professional who runs a midsize establishment explained:

> When an artist is already represented by a gallery that launched their career, and for a long time assumed the cost with no real immediate return, if a new gallery in another country then represents that artist, it will often pay 10% to the parent gallery. We represented [R] from the start, we were the only ones, we're his parent gallery. Now he has other galleries that pay us 10% when they sell his works, but that's normal. We also think it's fair to pay 10% to galleries that secured the very beginning of an artist's career, that's the hardest part.

The proportion is considerable: insofar as the gallery making the sale generally receives half of the sale price, it therefore gives up 20 percent of its own share. This beneficiary of a deceased artist's estate, however, mentioned the tensions that can arise regarding the commission paid to the parent gallery:

> My father's work had great visibility during his lifetime, and then he was kind of forgotten. It was [X], who runs a midsize gallery in his country, where my father lived for a long time, who rediscovered him. It was also in [X]'s gallery where [Y], whose gallery is in Paris, later noticed him. The first few times, she paid him a 10% commission on her sales, it was normal, he'd taken a risk and it was really him who made this rediscovery. But well, [Y] runs a much larger gallery, its scope is much more international, and it participates in the biggest fairs around the world, it supports much more prominent artists. Which means that my father's work has gained a lot of recognition thanks to her. After a while, [Y] kindly explained to [X] that continuing to pay him a commission on her sales was no longer justified, she had fully assumed her share of the promotional work, which now clearly benefited him in turn. Truly, she's doing a lot of work, it makes sense that she stopped paying her 10%, even if, of course, at first, [X] was disappointed.

In addition to the work conducted with their fellow galleries, another form of promotion is oriented toward institutions, museums, and contemporary art centers. In *The Artist, the Institution, and the Market*, Raymonde Moulin clearly analyzes how the value of contemporary art is constructed as museums and the market grow in influence (Moulin, 1992). In France, at the end of the 1980s and during this period of a very heavy state-led support of the arts (Saez, 2004; Poirrier, 2010), institutions played an important role in promoting contemporary art (Moulin, 1992; Moulin & Quemin, 1993). Moulin tended to indicate an analogous influence between the two segments.[14] Over the past 30 years, the function of certifying the value of contemporary art has clearly moved from the institutional sphere to the commercial sphere (Quemin, 2020b). However, aesthetic certification still influences market value; as a result, even today, it is important to maintain good relationships with curators, who are particularly courted by galleries. Moreover, those establishments with significant financial means are, in return, equally valuable partners for curators, because their generosity can prove decisive in enhancing collections, and their support (both logistical and monetary) is essential for organizing exhibitions (Quemin, 2020b). One way to win over curators is to regularly invite them to cocktail receptions and dinners hosted by the gallery—where they are the VIP guests—and they are therefore the favored targets of sociability tactics and friendly relationships, as analyzed in chapter 5 of this book. Large galleries often request articles, catalogue texts, or press releases (for a fee) from them that are distributed during their exhibitions. This kind of positive relationship carries the possibility of securing exhibitions by these curators for the gallery's artists in return. Whatever the means used to recruit its allies, it is widely accepted that it is the gallery's responsibility to promote its artists' exhibitions in institutions in order to increase their visibility and their legitimacy, which will benefit their careers and their market prices. As this artist explained:

> I may live in this city [in France], but it wasn't my French gallery that got this important solo show for me here. It was the director of my Swiss gallery, who did a wonderful job. She really fought for me to exhibit in my city's museum.

The following artist, Julie Mehretu, who is based in the United States and is one of the most renowned creators of her generation, was quick to pay homage to the work of her gallerist, the American Marian Goodman, which led to a prestigious commission from a large museum that afforded her the best possible conditions:

> The artist [Mehretu] says her two monumentally scaled paintings installed this fall in the atrium of the San Francisco Museum of Modern Art (SFMOMA) would not have happened without Goodman. The museum originally approached Mehretu with an offer to pay for the production of the paintings, but would not commit to buying them until after they were complete.

Goodman was firm with both the museum and artist: The project would consume at least a year of her life, and there should be a commitment from the start to purchase these enormous paintings, which would not easily find another home.

'I walked away thinking, what museum buys something without knowing what it will be?' says Mehretu. But SFMOMA's leadership came back six months later with a commitment to buy the works. 'It was a challenge for San Francisco but I think it helped structure how they will go forward with their commissioning program. That was really Marian's negotiation and brilliance.'

Artnet News, "On Her 40th Anniversary, Artists Share How Marian Goodman Became the Art World's Least Pretentious Power Broker," December 20, 2017

Another example of the close relationship between galleries and curators took place in 2019, during the Venice Biennale. The international selection of curator Ralph Rugoff (director of the Hayward Gallery in London), which had only 79 artists, featured no fewer than five artists (Michael Armitage, Liu Wei, Christian Marclay, Julie Mehretu, and Danh Vō) who were represented by the London-based gallery White Cube! The overrepresentation of artists from this gallery was absolutely staggering; comparatively speaking, White Cube featured only two artists in the national pavilions (Ibrahim Mahama was one of the six artists presented in the Ghana pavilion, and He Xiangyu was among the four artists featured in the China pavilion). Meanwhile, the overall number of artists presented in national pavilions was much higher than that of the international selection that year. As another point of comparison, the Thaddaeus Ropac gallery, which is at the very least on a par with White Cube—also with a location in London, but originally created in Austria and later developed primarily in Paris—was only represented in the international selection by a single artist (Lee Bul). This example clearly illustrates the effect that networks have on heads of institutions and curators on the one hand, and galleries on the other, on both a geographical and interpersonal basis.

Another showcase offered to their artists, which complements the exhibitions held on their own premises, is the promotional work that galleries generally try to perform for their artists through publications. Traditionally, this involves catalogues produced by the gallery itself (smaller establishments make do with simple booklets) or purchasing advertising spaces. This kind of artist promotion is therefore based on art criticism and the press. Art criticism as we understand it today really emerged in the second half of the eighteenth century with the publication of reviews in newspapers. The French philosopher Denis Diderot is seen as the first great art critic; he commented on the artistic events of his time and bet on the future, whereas his predecessors tended much more often to reflect on the past. However, it was in the nineteenth century in particular—the great century of both French painting and art criticism—that the latter truly took off (Bourdieu, 1996). Artistic events, high-circulation press that covers artistic news, and specialized magazines have developed and grown in number concurrently.

While today art criticism has become fairly marginal in terms of influence, it played a much larger role in the 1960s. In *The French Art Market*, Raymonde Moulin speaks more of propaganda—the term then preferred by players in the *milieu*—than of advertising, as this term is considered negatively (Moulin, 1987). Contrary to today, where major galleries almost always have a position dedicated to public relations and the press, Moulin indicated at that time:

> Painting galleries do not have a specialized public relations department, but rather receptions organized by the dealer, or by one of the gallery's official collectors, that perform the same function: vernissage cocktail receptions, social gatherings, parties with a splendor that evokes the patronage of years gone by but where munificence cannot in the current situation be dissociated from the utilitarian objective.
>
> Moulin, 1967 [1987], p. 445

"Propaganda" also existed in the texts written by art critics and specialized journalists with whom it was useful for a gallery to have good relationships in order to promote the work of its artists. Moulin notes that, unlike the gallerist or the artist, the art critic was already the poor member of the proverbial family, due in particular to their low pay. Additionally, they suffered from a moral devaluation of art criticism that resulted from compromising behavior within the market. In the 1960s, Moulin made the distinction between "informative criticism" and "celebratory criticism," even though she highlighted the versatility of the players who contributed to both. Though the artist was most often noticed by their peers first, critics seem to have been the second to intervene; Moulin confirms these first two phases of the artistic recognition process, which was later developed by Alan Bowness (Bowness, 1989). In the writings that Moulin analyzed, she notes recurring terms that aimed to enhance the artists' work (metaphysics, ontology, phenomenology, transcendental, dialectic, beyond, vision of the world, etc.) which today sound very dated. This is because the vocabulary of art criticism has changed a great deal since then. Currently, unlike the terms that Moulin noted in the 1960s, the critical texts that I regularly read more often use expressions such as see, interrogate, question, subtle, interpersonal, humorously, modernity, post-modern, narrative, and commodification (the latter is mostly used by English language texts), which have become recurrent terms in writings about art.

Today, although communication is still important in terms of supporting artists, its iterations have greatly evolved. Catalogues and advertising spaces have taken on more importance, in particular due to the possibility of printing in color, which has likely contributed to the decline of the written word. Today, richly illustrated catalogues and advertising spaces have become all the more important and strategic as they can generate other publications, as expenses often constitute investments for future printed communications. The authors of these catalogues are not chosen randomly; they may be recognized intellectuals whose name alone will reinforce the artist's legitimacy, and galleries may just as well solicit authors who also write for the press. Securing the favor of such contributors means that galleries can hope to encourage more writings in return from these players, who will then exemplify the interest of contributing material for no additional cost from the gallery, since they will be doing so as part of their journalistic pursuits. Moreover, producing editorial content leads to better promotion, since it gives the appearance of being neutral and financially impartial, rather than simply purchasing advertising spaces. Critics and journalists who have written catalogue texts for the gallery (or brochures that are distributed during exhibitions) are, however, entitled to remuneration. The prevailing expectations for galleries *vis-à-vis* authors are identical to those regarding the media. Purchasing advertising space is a direct cost in order to immediately achieve better visibility; but each of the parties involved—be it gallery, newspaper, or magazine—is well aware that such financial support will almost necessarily imply devoting more editorial content (with a complimentary tone) to loyal advertisers. While nothing is strictly codified, it is enough that these relationships of gifts and counter-gifts (Mauss, 1966) deviate from the mutual expectations of the parties involved for the relationship that binds them to be seriously disrupted.

Some media sources do not follow this pattern, such as the general press, which is far less dependent on galleries than the art press when it comes to advertisers; but also (in France) in the specialized art press, *la Gazette Drouot*, as it has the advantage of near-captive advertisers: auction houses that communicate most of all about their upcoming sales. This magazine therefore does not need to solicit external advertisers from the auction field in order to be economically viable; it is, in point of fact, very profitable. Then again, other press establishments, particularly those with specialized foci on the visual arts, are very dependent on their advertisers and can hardly take the risk that their most regular clients withdraw their support should they print articles that are too critical. This is all the more delicate since the number of media sources devoted to art (and more specifically the art market) has exploded in the span of a few years. As such, in France, whereas the bimonthly magazine *Le Journal des Arts* enjoyed a monopoly in the niche of press specializing in art market news for a long time, this niche (along with its advertisers) is now shared with two daily newspapers: the French-language version of *The Art Newspaper* and *Le Quotidien de l'Art*.

This journalist and art critic is well aware of the interest he represents for galleries, which varies according to their market and their level of development:

> Even large galleries are very keen on having reviews of their exhibitions in the press. But it's not so much because it would have an impact on their sales, as may be the case for small galleries; it's mainly in relation to the secondary market. When we talk about one of their exhibitions of an already very well-known artist, it designates them as THE gallery for this artist, and that brings them works that they can sell, the salespeople come to them, so that's where the stake is for galleries. And I'm not naïve, I know that when they come to me for a catalogue, they want to curry my favor for the future.

The art press tends to pass off the costs associated with a journalist's work to the gallery, which then practically becomes a *de facto* sponsor. As this journalist, who specializes in the art market, indicated:

> Even here [a very influential newspaper, especially among collectors], we can't cover events independently, we have to find funding linked to the events that we cover, and we're therefore hampered by that, we can't be critical. Even for meals, the newspaper wants us to convince others to treat us, and people who understand this and who have the means to do so will cover absolutely everything. From a journalistic point of view, it still poses a problem.

This other journalist, who also writes for a very influential newspaper among collectors and who is not a freelancer (which is rare among those who write about art), continued: "Personally, I haven't gotten a raise for eight years. It's really tough, even more so because I'm constantly around people who make millions." This art critic and journalist reported the same financial constraints for the profession: "It's hard to have to beg to write two or three pages, especially since it doesn't pay well. In reality, I make a living by writing prefaces for catalogues and, above all, by curating exhibitions, mainly abroad, because there are countries where you're well paid for that."

The dependence that journalists' and art critics have on the art market is all the more intense as there is a real excess of supply, with people who write about art frequently being seen as entirely substitutable, thus causing pay rates to be lowered. Over the years of my being an art critic, I have seen that experience and competence are only minimally taken into account. As this veteran of the sector lamented: "Today, critics have practically no impact, the market crushes everything. It's the galleries, the art advisors who have the power. We've become negligible. We influence nothing in the shadow of the market, and we're largely dependent on it because the media doesn't pay decently." In order to avoid being too dependent, it is better to be an employee (as a last resort) or to have a second, more lucrative occupation. In some cases, which are rare, people may present themselves as journalists or critics, but also engage in art trading to ensure the comfortable incomes that they would not receive from their publicly advertised professions. As this gallerist, who has locations in several countries, explained: "[X] is supposed to write about art, but he also makes a lot of sales... and he makes a very good living from it. For us, last year, he made over a million in sales, we give him 10%, he made more than €100,000 in commissions with our gallery in one year, it's still very comfortable." In this instance, the role of journalist and art critic is used as a business card, and as a means to access another, much more profitable occupation.

In addition to the traditional media, there is now communication on social media in the form of posts. Galleries, which are now often on Instagram and/or Facebook, broadcast their news, as well as that of their artists. Still today, it is essentially a question of image, and sales generated by social media are still rare; most often, this mode of communication is simply a first approach to raising awareness of an artist and their work. As this American gallerist conceded: "We talk about Instagram a lot, some fellow gallerists report sales through it or via their website, but it's mostly a bluff to make themselves look trendy. With very rare exceptions, collectors want to see what they're buying." This head of a Swiss gallery confirmed: "I'm very disappointed by the race to digitalize art . . . all galleries, without exception, are gobbling it up, but without any real results. With the COVID-19 pandemic, it will be even more pronounced, but it's not real, we're not selling anything." Though in public, some gallerists emphasize the benefits of using social media to boost sales, most agree in private that the shares from digital remain low. It is much more a question of image with the aim of adding the sheen of avant-gardism to a gallery.

Conclusion:

While sales, even today, tend to be the most emblematic activity within galleries, it by no means encompasses the many aspects of their work. The task of promoting the artists that it supports takes on different facets, all of which aim to boost their reputation and increase their recognition (Quemin, 2013). Due to the close link that exists between the two forms of enhancement (aesthetic and reputational on the one hand, and economic on the other), the market dimension, though it tends to be increasingly reinforced, has everything to gain from relying on reputation and legitimacy. According to the conception inherited from the romantic period, as previously mentioned, gallerists are sometimes suspected of unduly lining their pockets at the expense of their artists. At the level of smaller galleries and those less integrated into the international contemporary art scene, it is certain that artists find themselves in a weakened position relative to the gallery, as they are largely substitutable for one another. By contrast, at the top of the contemporary art world and market, despite being very powerful, the great gallerists appear to be extremely dependent on their artists As long as the extreme singularity of those is pronounced and recognized. It is noteworthy that even in the absence of representation contracts, relationships between artists and galleries are, in fact, just as long lasting. This simple observation will likely lead players in the industry to significantly modify or even reconsider the sometimes unfavorable image that the general public may occasionally still associate with a gallery's business practices by shining a light on all of the work that they perform to support artists throughout the development of their career.

7

Recent trends: Evolution in the gallery sphere and in the gallerist occupation

In the second part of this book so far I have presented and analyzed different fundamental, permanent features of a gallerist's occupation, as well as the environment in which it takes place. It would be appropriate here to focus on certain recent developments that have, at least in part, transformed how professionals operate, as they move away from their traditional practices, and as they continue to form the basis of business practices in this sector. In essence, over the last few years there has been an advent of new trends, which have caused a sharp acceleration of developments that until recently had been more gradual. This chapter will analyze these trends.

Increased competition, gallery concentration/ expansion, threats to second-tier galleries: a market that is increasingly controlled by "mega-galleries"

The most striking feature of the 2010s is likely the *exacerbated level of competition* resulting from the complementary effects of a *higher concentration of galleries* and *growth* with the expansion of various galleries, both within their own cities (by opening additional spaces and/or enlarging their premises), and internationally (by opening subsidiary galleries abroad). Though I will present the various points successively, it is important to note that they are, in reality, tightly intertwined.

The following interview extract effectively recounts the complete transformation that has been taking place since the 1960s, when the French art veteran Daniel Templon began his career as a gallerist:

- *Q: is your occupation more difficult nowadays?*
- Daniel Templon: Yes, it's definitely more complex. You have to be informed about everything. The market is global and terribly competitive, even though in the 1960s it was limited to the United States and a few countries in Europe. At that time, England played a very small role, it had about 30 galleries of significance. What's also new nowadays is that four galleries, Gagosian, Pace, Zwirner, and Hauser & Wirth, monopolize 50% of the market, making things really difficult for many young galleries.

"The Templons, Father-Son Gallerists,"
La Gazette Drouot, no. 2, January 17, 2020, p. 159

As his fellow veteran gallerist Paula Cooper (from New York) indicated in 2019 on the occasion of her 80th birthday and the 50th anniversary of her gallery:

> The competition has become extremely tough, overwhelming, maddening. I try to stay focused and pay attention. There is a gross lack of professionalism; it's representative of the world today, where people are greedy and ruthless. You have to stay positive and do everything you can to avoid it

Le Journal des Arts, no. 520, March 29, 2019, "Paula Cooper, 'The Competition Has Become Extremely Tough, Overwhelming, Maddening'"

This former German gallerist, who has since become a curator, provides a similar observation by emphasizing the intensification that she perceived in the occupation in recent years:

> A few years ago, I had a gallery in New York, it was a crazy life. You really had to work all the time just to pay the rent. Now, the fairs are endless, I had to sacrifice a relationship that was very important to me, because I was traveling constantly. Being a gallerist, it's a job that looks glamorous, but it's exhausting. It's really endless work, and the working conditions have gone downhill recently. We're always under pressure, you have to run around constantly.

It should be noted that, among all the contemporary art gallerists whom I have been visiting diligently for some 20 years now, none of them have given a single indication that they disagree with the notion of accelerating/intensifying their pace of work and the lifestyle associated with it.

Even though, as the three previous interview excerpts show, the profession has evolved a great deal with its intensifications and accelerations, it is because the market in which contemporary art galleries operate has changed considerably since the 1960s. It has had a particularly spectacular growth and a notable change in scale, especially since the 1990s. Lisa Spellman, who has directed the 303 Gallery in New York since 1984, gives a perfect overview of this evolution simply by mentioning price levels, which immediately evoke very different issues. In the 1980s,

> most of the works we sold were $2,500 to $12,000. Now, $50,000 is the new $2,500 [of this era]
>
> *Artnet News,* "Has the Great Depression Struck Galleries? Kenny Schachter Ventures Among the Art Hobos at Armory Week," March 14, 2018

An absolutely fundamental fact is: the profession of gallerist has become increasingly capitalistic, which historically it was not (or at least, not very much). The main galleries are now held captive in a race toward enormity, so that both galleries and artists can keep their competitors at a distance; because the latter do not have the same resources (particularly financial) as the most established players. All galleries, without exception, that intend to "stay in the game" are now under intense pressure to continuously grow, both to attract more renowned artists and to avoid having their most desirable artists (the most prominent and/or expensive ones) poached from them by their competitors, particularly by the largest galleries. Nowadays, establishments must grow in order to survive, to not fade away; we are witnessing an ever-growing division in the market between increasingly massive entities and other galleries.

Essentially, the gallery market increasingly operates according to the "winner takes all" economic model, which is characteristic of the "star system" economy (Rosen, 1981). While small and midsize establishments assume the risk of launching artists who are still unknown, they are also in danger of having their artists poached by more prestigious galleries that have more financial means once these artists begin to grow in demand. The only way to make the most out of an artist's departure for a larger gallery—apart from the critical recognition of having discovered new talent—is to build up a stock of this artist's works, which can later be profitable due to their increased value when they join a more established gallery with wealthier clients. However, many midsize (and especially smaller) galleries have little capital, and building up a stock is therefore very difficult for them. Consequently, the departure of an artist whose reputation—and market value—is on the rise constitutes a net loss, at least in the short term; and the first gallery's previous investments in the artist's career and renown are reduced to nothing, since the prior risk-taking is not remunerated in the slightest (if no stock could be retained). The largest galleries thus prosper by capitalizing on the work of smaller establishments, which may even shutter their doors after the departure of some of their more successful artists.

Nevertheless, these small galleries will be replaced by others, thus maintaining the influx that ultimately benefits the largest galleries. This is a common model in the cultural industries—which is becoming ever more significant in the contemporary art gallery sector—that has been studied by economists under the name of fringe oligopoly (Benhamou, 2003). A handful of very large establishments dominate the market and reap the benefits, while a fringe made up of much smaller organizations take risks and bring innovations to the market, generally acting as new talent scouts. Once the market notices this new talent, they will generally be completely absorbed by its most powerful players.

Today, it is not the position of these very small players that is becoming the most challenging to maintain; it has always been difficult for them. It is the middle segment of the market that, in the current system, has become the most complex to make profitable. Classically, small galleries are created and are then closed, without doing too much damage, because their costs remain stable due to the fact that they have limited resources. Conversely, at the intermediate level, players must necessarily invest substantial sums to offer a quality lineup that will attract a wider audience and thus allow them to "cover their costs" and generate profits. Midsize galleries find themselves crushed by the race for growth, which creates an untraversable schism between them and the main galleries on the market, where previously there was much more of a continuum. Today, these midsize galleries (more specifically those on the smaller side of the "average" spectrum), which already have high costs, are the most vulnerable; their position is therefore particularly fragile. In France, a notable example of this was the Galerie VnH, created in 2014, which had from the outset intended to position itself in the segment of "midsize galleries," without having previously started as a small gallery as of its inauguration. Its two partners, who had already been active on the art market via their previous experiences, had raised enough capital to move into a large space with a perfect location in the Paris district of the Marais. However, this experience only lasted five years, as the gallery never managed to develop. More generally, midsize galleries are particularly vulnerable as they can still be refused access to fairs, even when they have participated in some of them for years, and are most at risk of having their most prominent artists poached, those with the greatest potential for joining star galleries (Quemin, 2013b).

The significance of the acquisition model for talent who were initially supported by small and midsize establishments in the gallery world is clearly exemplified through the words of this gallerist who runs a large establishment; when I asked him if the artist whose exhibition he was visiting at the same time as myself would join his gallery, he jokingly replied: "It's a bit early. We're going to let him go to [A], and in a few years, we'll steal him from her [he laughs]!" The smaller galleries are practically incubators, and prepare the market for their larger competitors. A few rare galleries manage to grow with their artists, but most of the others are weakened by the departure of an artist, who then progresses without the former gallery by joining more established competitors.

The previously mentioned competition and artist migration have led to the emergence of a particular kind of gallery model, the "mega-gallery," which is imposing itself more and more within the market. Although they are clearly in a dominant position and they benefit directly from the work undertaken by smaller establishments, these galleries are also subject to very potent limitations. In essence, with the sole exception of the entity at the top of the heap, one gallery is always the smaller competitor of another gallery. Therefore, the dynamic that is specific to this sector pushes galleries to constantly grow in order (ideally) to avoid the threat entirely, or at least to grow enough to weather any potential attacks from the smallest possible number of competitors. This is why, over the last few years, there has been an exponential growth in investments, thus widening the gap between the largest galleries, which want to protect themselves from each other (and can afford the ever-more staggering costs) and the other galleries. Large or midsize establishments that cannot or do not wish to invest even more are sometimes forced to close. Such was the case in France in 2013, when the large Parisian gallery Jérôme de Noirmont (which at the time represented international artists as famous as Jeff Koons and Shirin Neshat)—with a location on the chic Avenue Matignon in the 8th arrondissement, and active for 19 years—shuttered its doors. Its owners explained that they could no longer remain in business and continue to work as they had before without having to make very large investments. Because the art market is now like a game of poker, what was the case in 2013 has only become even more strongly accentuated since then. When direct competitors put more money on the table, those who intend to stay in the game are forced to follow suit, otherwise they must withdraw. In July 2020, Gavin Brown—the founder and director of the New York gallery Gavin Brown's Enterprise—also announced that he was closing his gallery and joining another renowned New York establishment, Gladstone, as a partner, bringing with him some of his artists. As I will develop later, its location in north Manhattan was no longer tenable following the cancelation of fairs after the COVID-19 pandemic had broken out. To compensate this, and in order to continue supporting his artists—and to sell their works—he would practically have had to move into the heart of Chelsea, and therefore make a very large investment if he wanted to have the same square footage of exhibition space. Brown preferred to close his gallery and join another that was already firmly established in the Chelsea neighborhood.[1] The maneuver resulted in the instant creation of a mega-gallery, which was now capable of competing with market heavyweights. In the third part of this book, we will also see that, for many years, the Pace gallery has lost ground in comparison to its direct competitors, by dragging its feet in making large investments over a long period.

Similarly, in February 2021, it was announced that the influential New York gallery Metro Pictures would close at the end of the year. However, this gallery represented star artists, and even a super star of the artistic scene: Cindy Sherman. In addition to her, the roster included Louise Lawler, Robert Longo, Trevor Paglen, Camille Henrot, Olaf Breuning, and Jim Shaw; all of whom were already extremely well-known artists. However, the gallery did not have a space that could stand up to the market heavyweights and the new standards that they set.

The influence of the spatial factor is further reinforced with the increased competition between galleries. I will not go into detail on geographical reconfigurations, both at the local and international levels, as they have already been addressed in two previous chapters; but they relate—at least in part—to the phenomena of growing galleries, competition, and concentration. Recall that galleries will compete with each other by opening increasingly large spaces, or even several spaces in the same city or urban area; as such, the industry is becoming more and more capitalistic. The same goes for their ambition of internationalization: the largest "truly international" galleries now often try to gain a monopoly on the representation of their artists on a scale of either continental Europe, all of Europe (including the United Kingdom) or all of North America. International development in its most successful formats can now even help a gallery to provide the artists it represents with complete international coverage.[2] The best example of this extensive internationalization is illustrated by the influential Gagosian gallery, which today has nearly 20 locations in seven countries; a dispersion with no equivalent, either today or in all of gallery history. Another of the largest galleries, Thaddaeus Ropac, started its internationalization by participating in fairs[3] and shifting from operating solely in Austria, where the art market is very limited—but where it had access to a European, and even worldwide clientele via the Salzburg music festival—to a much more European scope by moving into Paris.[4] It then reinforced its European expansion by opening a new space in London in 2017, in a magnificent building located neighborhood in the city for art, Mayfair, where fixed costs are extremely high. In 2021, it inaugurated another gallery on the Asian continent, in Seoul.

There is therefore a clear shift away from the traditional performance of the role of gallerist, which until the rise of the Gagosian gallery, and later the emergence of its rivals, was (with some rare notable exceptions) a profession with low capitalistic intensity. Over the last few years, this capitalistic intensity has grown considerably stronger. Galleries that wanted to gain access to the coveted circle of the most influential establishments—those that represent and attract the most successful artists—must now have ever-larger spaces that, moreover, cannot be just anywhere. This spatial demarcation is absolutely fundamental in this industry, as geographical location must reflect one's position in the space (or in this case, field) of galleries (Bourdieu, 1987), which itself is linked to the aesthetic positions that are adopted (Bourdieu & Delsaut, 1975). This is particularly the case at the heart of the international art market, in the New York neighborhood of Chelsea, where the "big four"—Gagosian, David Zwirner, Hauser & Wirth, and Pace[5]—enter into competition with each other in terms of space that would have been truly unthinkable 10 years ago. Each has "its own" street,[6] a stone's throw from the others, which they symbolically control. Gagosian, which had long dominated without any real challengers, left its mark on all of West 24th Street, where it opened the first mega-space in 1999, and remained unrivaled for many years.

Likewise, in July 2020, it was announced that Gagosian would take over part of the space of the former Marciano Art Foundation in Los Angeles. The foundation, which had been housed in a former Masonic temple that spanned over around 90,000 square feet on Wilshire Boulevard, closed abruptly in November 2019 when the employees announced that they wanted to form a union. The owners of the private museum (also the creators and owners of the brand Guess jeans) Maurice and Paul Marciano then retaliated by immediately closing down the institution. The building, which had already been redesigned to reflect truly museum-level characteristics, was to be the second location of the Gagosian gallery in Los Angeles, in addition to its long-standing location in the heart of the very chic Beverly Hills neighborhood. The opening of the new premises was announced for January 2021, but was delayed due to the COVID-19 pandemic, which broke out at the beginning of 2020. When Gagosian moved into the space, it was to occupy 13,000 square feet (to begin with?); this is slightly larger than its space in Beverly Hills, which itself had been expanded in 2009. Not only was the new branch intended to allow Gagosian to double its surface area in Los Angeles, but it was meant to provide significant opportunities for expansion in the rest of the building. The location even offers prospects of rivaling the mega-space inaugurated by the Hauser & Wirth gallery in Los Angeles in 2016. This is reminiscent of the manner in which Gagosian rushed to open a huge space in 2012 in the Parisian suburb of Le Bourget, when its direct competitor Thaddaeus Ropac had opened its spectacular Pantin complex; another city in the same suburban area. It is clear here how the market leader was able to maintain its dominance in major cities that are key for the art market—and to guarantee its top position—through a real estate strategy. Gagosian's expansion announcement in Los Angeles, despite the COVID-19 pandemic, also shows an acceleration of competition at the top of the hierarchy of the largest galleries; and an ever-increasing expansion/concentration, the economic context notwithstanding, which at the time may not have seemed favorable.

In the same way, in the model that has gradually been implemented over the past 10 years, it is more essential than ever before to have locations abroad; but then again, these locations cannot be just anywhere; not in any country, city, or neighborhood. This also demonstrates to what extent, even in the era of supposed globalization (Quemin, 2002, 2013a, 2013b), geography is by no means neutral. Internationalization always exerts a pressure on galleries to set up shop abroad, and has in no way erased the qualifying and limiting nature of the spatial factor. This is also perfectly illustrated by Gagosian's numerous branches, which (apart from its establishments in Rome and Athens, which are located in cities that are fairly marginal for the international art scene and the art market) are situated in the most important cities and countries for the market. Another mega-gallery that was initially closely tied to its Zurich-based presence, Hauser & Wirth, has also gradually taken an international position. Although Switzerland already occupies a prominent place on the international scene, Hauser & Wirth's owners have notably established themselves in two countries that are even more central to the art market: the United Kingdom and the United States. Additionally, they opened a branch in Paris in 2023 when the city had become more central to the European art market following Brexit and the weakening of London's art ecosystem.

Inter-gallery rivalry now takes place in the pursuit of "world representation," even though—contrary to what the expression might suggest—this does not necessarily imply exclusivity. This is clearly demonstrated in this press release issued by the influential gallery Hauser & Wirth in March 2018. The email was entitled "Announcing the worldwide representation of Chinese artist Zeng Fanzhi," and the body of the message was again entitled "Hauser & Wirth is delighted to announce worldwide representation of leading Chinese artist Zeng Fanzhi." However, after enumerating the long list of activities that the gallery was planning to promote the artist's work, the press release later mentioned: "In addition to an in-depth collaboration with Hauser & Wirth, the artist will continue a relationship and professional exchange with his existing galleries."

Note that, a few years previously, the prominent gallery Thaddaeus Ropac, for its part, had defended its decision to only represent its artists in Europe, not in North America, explaining in particular that it could not fulfill a service of creating relationships with museums to equal effect on all continents; however, the gallery seems to have recently decided to change its stance. This reversal has, to a large extent, become inevitable, insofar as its direct competitors—the other largest international galleries—have managed to secure global representations, and could thus place themselves in a position of strength in relation to Thaddaeus Ropac, in order to win the representation of artists (living or deceased, in the form of estates) who would prefer to work with a single (leading) gallery for the whole world.

Another manifestation of the frantic race for international expansion is the frenzy of fairs, which has grown to such proportions that it has, as I have observed, on occasion become problematic. As mentioned in the third chapter, in 2008, the all-around champion of participating in fairs was the Viennese gallery Krinzinger, with 12 annual representations. Its fellow French gallery Yvon Lambert came in second with nine fairs (Quemin, 2013a). Fifteen years ago, the two preceding numbers seemed highly impressive; only five galleries at the time participated in over seven fairs, and only 101 were involved in at least five fairs during the year. Generally speaking, and as was previously mentioned, the very large American galleries participated in at least three events; as it was above all a matter of maintaining their status, but they were not the most active in this area, since they believed that the space of their galleries would be sufficient to reach new customers. Fifteen years later, these figures hardly seem believable. Just before the outbreak of the COVID-19 pandemic, almost all of the major international galleries participated in at least 10 or 12 fairs, if not 20! The most prestigious events, Art Basel being in the forefront, are clearly oriented toward the profession's aristocracy, and have become essential for all other galleries that have a chance of reaching the upper echelons. For most participating galleries, being accepted for the Art Basel fair in Switzerland, which is now generally accomplished after a *cursus honorum* of first participating in Art Basel Miami Beach and Art Basel Hong Kong, represents the golden ticket to also being selected for other fairs that are now held in many cities around the world; the largest of which are essentially in the northern hemisphere (giving another indication of the limits of globalization, which results in zero geographical homogenization on a worldwide scale).

For years now, the strategy used by all players, consisting of "cordoning off" or locking" the market, has been adopted by Art Basel. Furthermore, the fair is very successful, covering the three largest continents for contemporary art: Europe (in Basel and also Paris as of 2022), North America (in Miami Beach), and Asia (in Hong Kong); thus preventing any possibility for a real competitor to emerge.[7] As we saw when analyzing the role of fairs, MCH Group (the conglomerate that owns Art Basel) later bought out local fairs to further strengthen its presence via a tighter network, at least until it began to experience serious setbacks; up to that point, this strategy seemed to be self-evident, and would inevitably be declared a success. But the group found its way back to success in 2022; managing to oust the FIAC fair from Paris, and launching its competing fair, Paris + by Art Basel (later renamed Art Basel Paris in 2024). This new development certainly made it necessary for Frieze to develop in a massive way if it wanted to stay into the game. Hence, it created Frieze Seoul in 2022 and, just a year later, bought both the Armory show and Expo Chicago in order to reinforce its North American presence, which up to that point had been limited to Frieze New York.

At the gallery level, the race to enormity, combined with high (even staggering) costs, results in increasingly expensive entrance tickets for those of them that want to belong to the exclusive group of very large establishments. This generally shelters insiders from vague threats of rivalry between most of their potential competitors, which provides them with two ways of controlling the market with more certainty: because they send collectors a very clear signal of their power—and therefore of their supposed excellence—but also because they can offer artists the best possible conditions for exhibitions. Thus, they attract the most desired, and especially the most recognized among them. These gallerists with huge financial means can also fund artists in the production of increasingly expensive works, which, similarly, also protects star artists from having to compete with possible rivals and newcomers to the field (Bourdieu & Delsaut, 1975; Quemin, 2013b). In essence, the competition between galleries—which necessitates ever-increasing amounts of capital—is sometimes reproduced among creators. Star artists are thus the only players in a position to create projects that sometimes incur considerable costs, which will effectively enable them to create impressive and highly expensive works that are likely to maintain and consolidate their reputation. The best example of this is most likely the colossal exhibition for the British artist Damien Hirst in Venice, in the two spaces owned by the mega-collector François Pinault (Quemin, 2020b) in the spring of 2017, at the same time as the Venice Biennale. Everything seemed to have been done in order to guarantee that the presentation would have maximum impact in the international contemporary art world, with the characteristics of spectacular works and the very high production costs, and their staging in terms of perfectly mastered space design. Furthermore, the location and dates that were selected ensured that the biggest players in the art world could not miss this demonstration of power; a veritable logistic and financial *tour de force*.

Not only did the double monographic Damien Hirst exhibition that was held in the massive spaces of the Punta della Dogana and the Palazzo Grassi in Venice occupy a very large physical surface area (both horizontally and vertically), but additionally, some of the exhibited works were immense, even truly colossal. When artists conceive of such monumental works, the costs associated with their production, the expenses pertaining to the technical aspects of their creation and to their transportation, as well as the infrastructure required to accommodate them are all exceptional. Only artists who have reached true fame (Quemin, 2013b) can afford to do such a project and raise the necessary funding. By joining the race for enormity, they are clearly holding all other competition at bay. In this case, the absolutely enormous production costs effectively prevented most artists from competing with Damien Hirst to produce such financially and technically ambitious works.

During my field observations at the Venice Biennale that year, Hirst's spectacular double exhibition was brought up in every conversation, largely overshadowing the biennial itself. The many gallerists with whom I spoke or whom I overheard in conversation all mentioned the production costs, sometimes along with comments pertaining to the source of the funds for this project. The following French gallerist, who runs a midsize establishment, specified: "Well, the immense 60-foot-high sculpture by Damien Hirst isn't made of bronze. I heard that the production cost was 42 million. But hey, even without taking the support of his dealers into account, it must be said that Hirst has a fortune of 270 million." An Italian gallerist, who runs a midsize gallery, indicated another production price of 50 million for Hirst's exhibition. During a different conversation, yet another gallerist who runs an international establishment told me: "The production cost is reportedly 80 million, but it's certainly more than that." Throughout the biennial's opening week, gallerists whom I met thus spontaneously posited costs of 40 million, 42 million, 50 million, 60 million, and 80 million (specifying that this last amount was probably underestimated). The currency—euros, dollars, or British pounds—was most often not even specified, as if it hardly mattered given the immensity of the sum. In all of these conversations, it was clear that the creation, the work, was inseparable from the staggering production cost.

Even though Hirst has a very large fortune that regularly places him among the richest in the British population, such an exhibition would not have been possible without the direct support of a few pivotal players in the market: the mega-collector François Pinault, owner of the auction house Christie's, as well as the Palazzo Grassi and the Punta della Dogana in Venice (as of 2021, he also owns a third exhibition space, the Bourse de Commerce, in Paris), as well as the support of the two influential international galleries, Gagosian[8] and White Cube. As this French gallerist, who runs a midsize establishment commented: "This exhibition in Pinault's space, it's a solo show for Hirst, but not quite. It's also an expo of Pinault, Gagosian, Jay Jopling, and Mougrabi!"[9] He then added:

> And Hirst too! But not only as an artist. I remember, a client told me in 2008 that Hirst could no longer buy works from me, inexpensive things, because he'd bought pieces that cost an arm and a leg in his own auction. But the client explained to me that Hirst didn't really have a choice, he was obliged to support the market so that his collection and his prices wouldn't collapse. Hirst is a real businessman.

Essentially, in this system where the costs of running a contemporary art business are ceaselessly rising and now reaching new heights, it is those who occupy the dominant positions—gallerists and artists alike—who directly benefit from the situation, even though they still have to make investments that are significant (to say the least).

What applies to the production and organization of exhibitions also applies for the invitations, which constitute another aspect of the event. The example of Hirst's exhibition also illustrates this notion. In every instance, it is a matter of cordoning off the industry in order to prevent competition. As this journalist, who is familiar with the art market, indicated: "Here in Venice, it's very obvious. Pinault has it locked down. There are three possible evenings for receptions during the biennial's opening; Pinault organizes dinners on two evenings immediately, and now there's not enough room for the others." As another visitor to the biennale indicated: "Pinault invited 1,500 people for dinner. It's a lot of people, it's difficult for the others to receive interested parties when someone has scooped up the invitations so extensively."

My analysis of these previously cited groups of players in the world of visual arts (especially gallerists), their growing polarization, and the strategies at work (which indicate a fierce competition), illustrate Pierre Bourdieu's theory; wherein he explains:

> In a field, and this is the general law of fields, those who hold the dominant position, who have the most specific capital, are put into opposition via a host of relationships with new entrants (I'm intentionally using a metaphor borrowed from economics), newcomers, latecomers, upstarts who do not have much specific capital. The former have conservation strategies intended to take advantage of a gradually accumulated capital. New entrants have subversion strategies oriented toward a specific accumulation of capital, which suppose a more or less radical reversal of the values chart, a more or less revolutionary redefinition of the principles of product production and appreciation, and at the same time, a devaluation of the capital held by the dominant parties.
>
> Bourdieu, 1980 [1992], pp. 198–199

Here, it is a question of accumulating economic capital to an unprecedented degree, but we will see later that this is accompanied by a display of cultural and symbolic capital. In the preceding observation, Bourdieu identifies a general law that affects all creative fields, with the first domain for which he gives an extremely thorough analysis being that of *haute couture* (Bourdieu & Delsaut, 1975), then literature (Bourdieu, 1996), and finally the visual arts (Bourdieu, 2017). It is notable that, in the art market, economic capital has become particularly strategic, in a domain (i.e., the visual arts) where, generally speaking, it was historically more symbolic capital and cultural capital that were predominant (Bourdieu, 2017). Of course, in the era of Paul Durand-Ruel, financial capital favored success and recognition, but it did not occupy as central a position as it does today. Furthermore, since then, the practice that has been implemented for gallerists of taking artists' works on commission, instead of buying and storing them (sometimes for a long time) before selling them, revolutionized the field in financial terms. Yet in recent years, not only has the economic rationale been considerably reinforced with the emergence of major players with huge financial means, but it has become particularly difficult for new entrants to challenge established positions. The stakes (aesthetic, symbolic, and financial) have become so important that it is now very difficult to unseat the dominant positions and those who occupy them. We will see that some of the largest galleries take inspiration directly from museum-level institutions (Quemin, 2020b) and thus display their detachment from the objectively commercial purpose of their operations. Consequently, it has become practically impossible to contest these galleries—which are often some of the most influential—by asserting that the commercial dimension, while still directly associated with their success, is too strong. Although this notion should leave them wide open to criticism, they know exactly how to protect themselves against such attacks from their competitors, who could attempt to challenge their supremacy by denouncing their economic success. These kinds of remarks call for an adjustment of the previous analysis provided by Bourdieu, who conceives of fields as systems that are, naturally, marked by a structure's continuity—in a very structuralist model—but are generally considered to be highly dynamic. In the case of the social field of galleries, the competition is now largely static;[10] it is essentially the retirement or passing of the founder of a major gallery that can "change the game," much more than internal forces in the field. Moreover, in this domain, which appears broadly to be cordoned off, reconfigurations are more likely to take place as a result of *ad hoc* alliances between different players (or agents, to use Bourdieu's terminology), rather than a collective reversal of positions.

In addition to a dynamic that is specific to the field of galleries, which nowadays is not conducive to frequent reversals, due to the successful solidification of the market implemented by dominant agents therein, the effects of economic context are also noticeable. In today's society, which is characterized by increasingly mobile art lovers and collectors, who exchange ever-greater quantities of information faster than ever before (with the exception of the duration of the COVID-19 pandemic at its worse), the contemporary art world also exists within this frenzy. In order to stand out in the flow of information and in an increasingly fierce competitive context in a market that incorporates more and more suppliers, establishments must be able to distinguish themselves by being memorable; however, this necessitates the ever-increasing mobilization of resources. This general progression has given rise to a new hyper-competitive model that generally affects all market players. The COVID-19 pandemic may have temporarily slowed things down, but has not derailed this fundamental evolution.

As a direct consequence of the contemporary art gallery market's transformation (which has already been described and analyzed in this book), the art gallery world had been talking about a "gallery crisis" long before the serious health and economic crisis that resulted from the COVID-19 pandemic, which hit the market in the beginning of 2020. The term—which began to circulate recurrently in 2018—designated how difficult it was for small, and midsize galleries in particular, to survive, following the profound shift of concentration and increased competition that took place in the 2010s. It also referred to the decline in visitors in gallery spaces. The term "gallery crisis" thus gained traction over a few years.[11] It now clearly has a structural dimension beyond the circumstantial economic crisis that resulted from the COVID-19 pandemic.

The traditional economy for contemporary art galleries—at least those that do not belong to the highest segment in the market—has been weakened by a shrinking clientele due to the gradual decline of the reservoir of highly committed "young collectors" visiting and supporting them. Contrary to a commonly held idea, contemporary art collectors are most often of a fairly advanced age; some of whom are in their fifties but even more are in their sixties and seventies. Before reaching these age groups, it is difficult to collect expensive works, due to the life cycle that is particularly typical of upper-class households. It is possible to link the scarcity of young collectors to a certain stagnation of income, paired with the constantly increasing costs of living in large cities with the rise in real estate prices. Furthermore, this phenomenon is accompanied by the fact that today people receive their inheritance later in life, due to longer life expectancy of their elderly family members. The pool of young collectors with sufficient financial means to buy contemporary art is also therefore restricted, especially since the boom in contemporary art, when price levels in galleries generally increased; and it is very difficult to introduce artists at lower price levels without running the risk of discrediting them, as price is a supposed indicator of quality (Moulin, 1987). Note that the same problem of solvency occurs in the real estate market in the largest international cities; it has, however, been partially resolved by the practice of extending credit with longer durations. For instance, real estate loans, which historically lasted for a period of 12 to 15 years (in France, at least) are now often increased to 18, or even 20 years. Yet people rarely buy contemporary art on credit, and certainly not for such long periods. Independent of the effects of the COVID-19 pandemic, which I will review at the end of this chapter, the galleries whose sales are not focused on the wealthiest populations are directly impacted by these general evolutions. This tends to further widen the gap between mega-galleries and other establishments.

Gallery closures, mergers, and associations: a reconfiguration of the field

Gallery closures can be caused by different factors. This may be due in particular to the fact that collectors' tastes have changed. This is what New York gallerist Francis Naumann posited when he shut down his gallery in October 2019, after nearly 20 years of business. He explained that it was becoming more difficult to sell twentieth-century art, as the younger generation of collectors were only interested in artists from their own time. Another recurring reason for closure is the passing of gallery founders, in a *milieu* where the leader's personality is vital. Experience shows that contemporary art galleries are very generally created and directed by charismatic founders, whose qualities are difficult to transfer to their successors. The cessation of business is very common when there is no offspring (especially a son) to take over.

Nevertheless, it is not only certain market segments (in terms of specialization) that are now threatened, and closures pertaining to the passing of gallery founders have gone up in recent years. Gallery closures were a notable trend at the end of the 2010s, well before the onset of the COVID-19 pandemic and resulting economic crisis. They were common in the art market in Europe and the United States alike, which shows that this phenomenon was not strictly connected to national contexts, nor to the COVID-19 pandemic.

In July 2017, the London gallery Breese Little—founded seven years earlier by Josephine Breese and Henry Little in the Clerkenwell neighborhood, and later located in Bethnal Green—announced that they were definitively ceasing operations. After the closure of the Limoncello Gallery a few months prior, this dynamic new player in the London middle-market scene that had championed emerging artists called it quits.

In January 2018, the Zurich gallery Katz Contemporary—created by Frédérique Hutter 10 years earlier—also announced that it was closing its space, and would continue to operate to a lesser extent in a different format. This decision came on the heels of the closure of other Swiss galleries, such as RaebervonStenglin in 2016; as well as the Rotwand, Herrmann Germann Contemporary, and Freymond-Guth galleries in 2017.

In March 2018, the Bugada & Cargnel gallery shut its doors after nearly 12 years of business in the Belleville neighborhood of Paris.[12] While its directors indicated that it was only a "see you later," they have not resumed any gallerist functions or any other activity intended for the market and the art world since this closure.

On the other side of the Atlantic, in the United States, the gallery Elizabeth Dee (which at the time only represented a dozen artists, including John Giorno, and presented a list of 40 other artists whose works were for sale) announced in March 2018 that they would be closing their space in Harlem barely two years after moving into the neighborhood.

In addition to closures due to the passing of some gallery owners, other gallerists who have terminated their own independent businesses later joined the ranks of other heavyweight galleries, thus accentuating the polarization that exists in the market. Foremost among the success stories is the influential David Zwirner gallery. In November 2018, Steven Kasher—a gallerist who specialized in photography—closed his own establishment in order to become an employee at David Zwirner, thereby reproducing the actions of many people before him. Previously, in New York, in February 2017, the gallerist Andrea Rosen—who ran a major establishment on West 24th Street, the most prestigious street in Chelsea—announced that she was closing her own gallery in order to devote herself to managing the Félix Gonzàles-Torres estate, and would now be working for the mega-gallery David Zwirner, with which she had previously shared representation of the deceased artist. Even before that, in 2013, Christopher D'Amelio had also closed his Chelsea gallery to then become a senior partner at David Zwirner. This phenomenon of integrating smaller competitors who were forced to terminate their business is not limited to the New York branch of the Zwirner gallery; shortly before Steven Kasher, the Shanghai gallerist Leo Xu had closed his eponymous gallery to direct the operations of David Zwirner in Hong Kong. The same prevailing strategy of onboarding a pre-existing gallery or hiring its manager was employed when Zwirner recruited Victoire de Pourtalès in 2019 in its attempt to establish itself in Paris. The American heavyweight even incorporated her structure by taking over her premises and employees after she closed the VnH gallery, which she had founded in 2015 with her partner Hélène Nguyen.

Gallery closures therefore go hand in hand with the phenomenon of concentration, and heavily contribute to it by simultaneously causing midsize establishments to close, and by participating in the growth of the most influential galleries. Those who previously managed their own establishments later join galleries larger than those they used to run as salaried staff members.

It was nevertheless the following closure, which took place after the onset of the COVID-19 pandemic, that most amazed players in the international market: in July 2020, the New York gallerist Gavin Brown—who had run Gavin Brown's Enterprise for 26 years—suddenly announced the cessation of his business in order to become a partner of the influential Gladstone Gallery;[13] with its flagship space in the Chelsea neighborhood. Gavin Brown's nomadic gallery, which was created in a small space in West Soho in 1994, moved below Chelsea onto West 15th Street, then to Leroy Street in the West Village. Finally, in 2016, it took over a huge space: a former brewery with three floors located in Harlem, on 127th Street. Although the gallery had unquestionably launched the careers of star artists such as Peter Doig, Urs Fischer, and Elizabeth Peyton, it had always been located outside of the central neighborhoods of the art market. The move to Harlem in particular was a "wrong turn," in the sense that David Halle and Elisabeth Tiso mean it (Halle & Tiso, 2014). At the time, by moving into a huge space, the gallery hoped to generate a dynamic in the district of Manhattan that was best known in the visual art world for housing the Studio Museum, dedicated to artists of African descent; however, no large-scale commercial entity had been established there, and it failed to attract significant fellow galleries to the neighborhood.[14] As long as the Gavin Brown's Enterprise gallery had access to fairs, the contacts that they made during these events could compensate for the low number of visitors to its isolated space in Harlem. Yet, once the COVID-19 pandemic struck, the gallery found itself cut off from its clients and potential new buyers. As soon as the gallery announced that it would be closing, Brown specified that he would be joining the Gladstone gallery and that some of the artists whom he represented would be joining him in this new establishment: Alex Katz, Arthur Jafa, Joan Jonas, Rirkrit Tiravanija, Mike Leckey, Frances Stark, Rachel Rose, LaToya Ruby Frazier, and Ed Atkins (all of whom were among the gallery's most recognized artists in different age groups).

Brown's departure for the Gladstone gallery also resulted in the abandonment of his massive Harlem space—which was not taken over by any new galleries—thereby acknowledging the fact that in 2020, Harlem was no longer on the contemporary art map as a possible gallery district. Furthermore, the Gladstone gallery already had three New York spaces, including two in the midst of Chelsea, at the heart of the New York, and indeed the international, art markets on West 21st Street and West 24th Street (the third location is in the Upper East Side). Conversely, the Gladstone gallery planned to keep the Rome space that Brown vacated in 2015 as a complement to its other European location in Brussels.

With Brown's arrival, along with his most desirable artists, the Gladstone gallery was now in a much better situation to compete with its four neighboring mega-galleries in Chelsea: Gagosian, David Zwirner, Hauser & Wirth, and Pace. The very prominent artists who came along with Brown thus helped to flesh out an impressive roster, which had already included Matthew Barney, Alighiero Boeti, Keith Haring, Thomas Hirschhorn, Cameron Jamie, Sarah Lucas, Robert Mapplethorpe, Mario and Marisa Merz, Wangechi Mutu, Shirin Neshat, Philippe Parreno, Elizabeth Peyton, Ugo Rondinone, Rosemarie Trockel, and Banks Violet, among others. It is worth noting that, among the most recognized artists represented by Gavin Brown, the "market darlings" were even more present on its roster than those initially on the Gladstone gallery's roster; some of whom were more oriented toward museums than to the market (Moulin, 1992). The Gladstone gallery's absorption of part of Gavin Brown's Enterprise is a remarkable example of the art market's recent evolution, with a race for enormity that involves the amalgamation of two influential players in order to gain access to a much higher level of impact. The notion of growth or consolidation is clearly a "win-win" operation that distinctly increases the influence of the new entity on all levels.

The Gladstone gallery's integration of Gavin Brown and many of his artists strongly resembles the pioneering maneuver performed much earlier by the two German gallerists Monika Sprüth and Philomene Magers, who joined forces with their respective galleries to create Sprüth Magers in 1998.[15] At a time when the market was increasingly encouraging galleries to grow,[16] the union of Gavin Brown's and the Gladstone gallery's assets consolidated the business of the latter, which consequently grew much stronger, especially since Barbara Gladstone was born in 1940 and her advanced age at the time—80 years old—ran the risk of weakening the gallery. Brown's arrival promised a partner who was both very experienced and much younger, who would invest in the gallery and also strengthen it by virtue of his younger age (Gladstone died in 2024).

Another announcement that stunned the market was when the influential New York gallery Metro Pictures declared in March 2021 that they had decided to close at the end of the year. Admittedly, its two leaders were older, but the decision may also have been partly motivated both by the competition's structural growth and the COVID-19 pandemic, which affected galleries that up to that point had been quite successful.

Without going so far as to merge, other galleries have developed partnerships that were hitherto completely unheard of, giving rise to establishments of considerable influence. As such, mega-galleries have become so powerful that, if a few were to join forces, they could even compete directly with the largest auction houses.

In 2017, a number of observers reported a clear shift in the art market by dealers and art galleries toward private sales, to the detriment of public auctions. The main reason for this increase in activity among dealers and galleries was derived from collectors' desire to maintain a certain degree of confidentiality pertaining to their transactions, as this need for anonymity had become more difficult to preserve during a public auction.

In February 2020, three New York market heavyweight galleries—Acquavella, Gagosian, and Pace[17]—banded together to disperse the large collection of David Marron, the late financier and former chairman of the board of New York's Museum of Modern Art. All told, it was nearly 300 works, with a total value of around $450 million. Given its size and importance, the collection initially seemed inevitably destined to be sold by one of the two star auction houses, Christie's or Sotheby's; however, a very unusual plan was quickly put into place that would thwart the appetites of these major players on the art market. Marc Glimcher, the director of the Pace gallery, had heard that the Marron family was planning to put their collection up for public sale. He then called Larry Gagosian to present an alternative proposition to the family. The two men then contacted Bill Acquavella, who also had a long-standing relationship with Donald Marron; the latter having built his collection in large part thanks to the Pace, Gagosian, and Acquavella galleries.

From April 24 to May 16, 2020, the Pace and Gagosian galleries presented a joint exhibition of key works from Marron's collection, notably by Pablo Picasso and Mark Rothko, in their massive Chelsea spaces. These pieces were supplemented by selected works lent by institutions, which highlighted them even more. In addition to this exhibition, the collection was celebrated with a book ("not a catalogue," Glimcher was careful to specify, thus distinguishing it from auction catalogues that include price estimates) produced by the art publisher Phaidon. After selling Marron's collection, the art press reported other provisions of the agreement that had enabled the three partners to finalize the agreement with the Marron family, beyond the exhibition and communications conditions that were particularly gratifying. While the two main auction houses had agreed to guarantee the collection for $300 million, the three market heavyweights—Acquavella, Gagosian, and Pace—together were able to present a counter-proposal of $350 million, thus sealing the deal. Another element of the agreement's appeal may have been the discretion and speed that the galleries could offer. If a work did not immediately find a buyer on the market at the time, it would not be made public, the failure would remain discreet and would not permanently disqualify the work, as would inevitably occur at an auction sale due to its public dimension. Maintaining the same concern for the discretion that is common for private transactions, Glimcher explained that the galleries would neither publicly disclose which works would or would not be available for sale, nor would they disclose a price estimate for the collection. Finally, most if not all of the pieces attracted buyers in advance. It is clear that, when deprived of their traditional *coup de grâce* to guarantee a minimum price at the highest level, even the largest auction houses could in no way compete with the offer put forth by this triumvirate of power gallerists. It is impressive that galleries (at least leading ones when they join forces) can now occasionally provide a superior guarantee to the traditional art market heavyweights Christie's and Sotheby's.

Following the success of this operation, which was initially designed to be a one-off, the three partners announced in September 2020 that they would carry on their collaboration under the name of AGP Ventures, once again to disperse massive collections. The foundation of this new entity in no way led to the dissolution of the pre-existing galleries.

It should be noted that the sale of the Marron collection by the three enterprising and influential gallerists was not an entirely new initiative. In 2008, the sale of artworks worth several hundred million dollars that belonged to the late, great gallerist Ileana Sonnabend had already taken place in private sales,[18] for which Larry Gagosian played a key role in the agreement that was implemented. Antonio Homem, one of Sonnabend's two heirs, told the *New York Times* in April 2008 that the estate had agreed to sell "two blocs of works" with a staggering combined estimated value of $600 million (about $750 million today, accounting for inflation). While this amount is much higher than the estimated $450 million for the Marron collection, it is important to note that it was a matter of dispersing what constituted both the private collection and (probably) the stock that Sonnabend had amassed as a gallerist. The circumstances were therefore singularly different from Marron's collection, as he was only a collector; were he a dealer, the works that he owned (if the practices that had prevailed up to that point were replicated) would logically have fallen to one of the two major auction houses, Christie's or Sotheby's.[19]

In addition to the spectacular initiative that took place in 2020, detailed earlier, the massive investment on the part of the largest international galleries in the secondary market—an area over which the powerful auction houses have historically ruled without any real challenger—is also reflected in the recruitment rationales of the main galleries and the careers that they offer. At the very beginning of 2020, Brady Doty joined the David Zwirner gallery as Senior Director of its New York office in the Upper East Side. A specialist in art from the 1980s to the present day, and a former Gagosian employee, she had previously co-directed the Skarstedt gallery, which at the time had locations in London and New York, and for which she developed the secondary market focus. It was for the precise reason of implementing this same ambition that David Zwirner invited her to join his team. In essence, the secondary market now presents a real stake for major contemporary art galleries, whose extensive expansion is no longer reflected solely by the upsurge of locations around the world. The race to represent the estates of the great twentieth century artists also proves this notion. Doty worked jointly with Koji Inoue, another eminent recruit for David Zwirner, who had poached her at the end of 2018 from the international management team for contemporary art at Christie's, for the same purpose of strengthening its position on the secondary market.

Art advisors who are increasingly present

Symmetrical to the growing concentration of supply that is distinguished by a limited number of ever-growing galleries, demand (at least on the highest segment of the market) is also tending to become even more concentrated, with the increasingly pronounced involvement of art advisors. The English title of the profession is even used in non-English speaking countries, partly because it is gender-neutral; in reality, most art advisors are women.

During my continuous participation in the field over a dozen years, I have noted that art advisors are more and more often in attendance at opening dinners, especially the extremely selective ones that are organized by the largest galleries with a broad international scope. Art advisors are increasingly present on the contemporary art scene, especially with very large galleries. To give an idea of their influence, they are privileged partners of the largest galleries: Gagosian, David Zwirner, White Cube, Thaddaeus Ropac, or, in the French case, even galleries of a lesser stature like Lelong and Templon. This is particularly true for works that are sold for several hundreds of thousands of dollars or euros, sometimes even over a million.[20] In essence, it is above all collectors with strong or very strong purchasing power who hire these professionals to buy works for them. Still, art advisors are also tending more and more to be present in notable galleries that do not belong to the exclusive group of leading establishments in the world.

However, the galleries to which this most often applies are generally those that have the most "international" rosters; i.e., those that mainly feature American, German, and British artists (Quemin 2001, 2002, 2006, and 2013b), because they are often the most requested artists. For galleries whose list of artists is essentially limited to a national scale and does not heavily feature artists from the previously listed countries, the presence of art advisors becomes much more infrequent.

The gallerist Lisa Spellman, who runs the 303 Gallery in New York, believes the growing influence of art advisors to be one of the main features of how the landscape of collectors and clients has evolved since she started in the business:

- *From your perspective, how has the landscape of collectors evolved over 35 years?*
- There were maybe 50 collectors when I opened the gallery. The stakes seemed higher then. Everything is so global now; everyone's richer. The risk is diluted in a way, spread out. I love dealing with collectors themselves. But the role of the art advisor has grown to a whole other level. There are a lot more advisors now than there were 35 years ago.
- *How do you feel about that?*
- I really appreciate the work that they do, because it's time consuming to educate collectors and show them work from all over the world. When they bring in a prepared client, it makes the experience that much more enjoyable. Whereas back in the old days, you would practically have to hold seminars on what appropriation and institutional critique were. Still, I love New York City collectors because I feel most of them are still old school. They come to the gallery themselves. They look at the work.

Lisa Spellman in "How Does a Gallery Stay in Business for 35 Years? Lisa Spellman on 303 Gallery's Staying Power and the Hardest Part of Being a Dealer," *Artnet News*, July 19, 2019

Historically, art advisors have not necessarily been in good standing with galleries because they are professionals who disrupt the supposedly selfless friendly relationship that is important to the gallerist occupation. Furthermore, by aggregating a larger number of purchases than if collectors had been dealt with individually, these professionals can negotiate more advantageous conditions than different buyers could on their own. As this director of an international gallery explained:

> Today, there are plenty of art advisors who are odious. You meet a collector, she tells you that she likes a piece, then when we're about to discuss the price, the collector steps back and it's the art advisor who negotiates. She'll ask you for a 10% discount for her client and 10% for her, for her commission. For us, that's a direct no, so afterwards, it becomes a back-and-forth of haggling, she tries to get 8% for her client and 6% for her, or vice versa. I hate those kinds of negotiations.[21]

It is also the financial dimension of purchases for which art advisors are very often reproached. As explained by this former gallerist who gave up the profession, which she had done for several years with some success before experiencing a downturn, and who now devotes herself solely to private home sales:

> Nowadays, when we come back from Art Basel on the train, it's full of art advisors who are accompanying their clients. Many are alumni of

> Christie's and Sotheby's, they see works of art as financial assets, they advise their clients to buy 10 or 15 works by an artist. And then you have to sell four or five of them to make a profit, that's what the art market has become.

In the art world in general, players frequently express reservations about the occupation of art advisor, precisely because it calls the notion of the love of art into question (Bourdieu & Darbel, 1997) by openly acknowledging the element of trading.[22] There is even a caricatural tone conveyed in the words of this journalist:

> Art advisor is a title that isn't regulated, there are plenty of people who claim to be art advisors because it's chic, but they don't have any skills. The other day, I was with one of my friends, an older gentleman, and we see two young girls go by, in high heels, and he says to me, 'You'll see, every time, those two girls, they're art advisors.' So we go to talk to them and my friend asks them, 'Ladies, are you art advisors?' 'Yes, yes,' they were obviously so happy to be recognized as such. But you know, we also recognize these young women by the fact that they claim to be art advisors, they've sometimes studied a little art history, but that's all. They only have a limited role in transactions, they're mainly there to meet rich men and to get married.

The following gallerist who runs an establishment with locations in Paris and Brussels explains that they work with a dozen or so art advisors at most, including a large proportion of Asian professionals (one Korean and three or four Chinese women). They help the gallery reach a clientele that would otherwise remain largely inaccessible. Thus, the larger discount given on the sale price is justified, since without the contribution of these intermediaries, the bulk of the transactions within the gallery simply would not take place.

From the perspective of their clientele, art advisors fulfill several functions. The use of their services is a way for collectors who have the means but do not fall into the category of mega-collectors, and have not (yet?) been identified by galleries as owning first-class collections, to recalibrate the balance of power with the largest galleries. This can help to convince them to sell their most prominent, most requested artists to these clients. Where these collectors would have had no chance of achieving their goals if they introduced themselves alone, they can, in a way, be socially certified by the art advisor who is working for them. The involvement of art advisors therefore represents not only a much larger number of transactions being concluded, but it can also guarantee that an art advisor's clients respect the implicit standards of the market, including the strongest expectation that galleries have, which is that the client will not resell the work immediately (or too quickly), especially at an auction.

Since the title of art advisor is in no way regulated, anyone can claim it, and it is certain that their level of integration into the gallery world (and legitimacy therein) is extremely variable among these market players. Today, there are undoubtedly more and more art advisors who have managed to establish themselves as not only credible, but even important go-betweens for clients and galleries, especially for the most influential among them. The image of the occupation has significantly improved, particularly among gallerists. While some people may still hold certain prejudices about this group, most gallerists develop relationships of respect with "their" art advisors; that is, those with whom they work regularly. Thanks to the shifts that have occurred due to regular interactions with them (especially as regards negotiating prices), relationships have become more peaceful, and are now more often a matter of cooperation.

Relationships with one's artists: the effects of growing competition

As I will develop in greater length in the last part of this book—which will explain how I constructed the international ranked list of galleries that is provided—artists are absolutely central for galleries, particularly the most influential among them, as the most recognized artists are not easily substitutable, and the number of star artists (Quemin, 2013b) is limited. Through the words of this director of a major international gallery, it is clear that these establishments are highly subject to the demands of the artists whom they represent:

> Artists today are asking for a very international presence. If the big galleries are opening more and more spaces, it's not so much a commercial race, it's much more a means of retaining artists. The market being what it is, the big names are very sought-after
>
> Valentina Volchkova, staff member of the Pace gallery, in *La Gazette Drouot*, no. 14, April 6, 2018, p. 21.

Making the right choices and succeeding in keeping artists is therefore a particular strategy for large galleries. It is also important that they know how to take advantage of market evolutions and new emerging trends.

Today, the obvious trend is worldwide representation, especially with the estates of deceased artists, and with artists on the road to stardom, because it is still difficult for galleries (even the most prominent in the world) to oblige artists to have only one gallery, even in a given city. This is how, nowadays the largest galleries—even when they have locations in one or more of the same cities—can share several artists, who are generally stars (Quemin, 2013b).

In 2019, the intensification of this trend thus led this European gallerist, one of the most important in the world, to completely contradict the comments he had previously made to me by announcing the worldwide representation of the estate of a deceased artist, when two years earlier he was critical of this possibility. As he argued then:

> Personally, I'm opposed to representing an artist for the whole world, I don't think it seems like a good thing for the artist. We're a very recognized gallery, we have connections with all the major museums, all the major art centers throughout Europe. It's a lot of work, we couldn't provide the same service to our artists in the United States, it's quite simply not our area. [For an artist,] one gallery for Europe, another for America, that really seems to me much more desirable than having worldwide representations. That's not what we want.

The largest galleries in the world sometimes try to obtain exclusive representation of their artists, especially the youngest, who want to join them in order to gain access to their network of very wealthy collectors and to benefit from the gallery's promotional work (especially exhibitions), which smaller establishments cannot provide.

However, some artists who are on the rise are trying to escape such a degree of control. This European gallerist mentioned the decision made by one of his artists after winning a very prestigious international prize:

> [X], after winning her prize, several of the biggest New York galleries in the world contacted us to offer to represent her, as she didn't have a gallery in the United States yet. She had a choice of half a dozen excellent galleries. She preferred not to go to one of the big ones, but to [Y], which mainly has one star artist, the others are less prominent. She wanted to choose a gallery that would really support her rather than being lost among dozens of artists who would have been the gallery's priority. There, she's sure that her gallery will give her the time of day.

This other important French gallerist mentioned the same decisions made by artists, including one who clearly puts his galleries in competition with one another:

> [X] is very clever, he's super prominent, he's one of the most talked about artists of his generation. He could easily go to one of the biggest galleries in the world. But no, he's chosen to stay with four very good galleries in Europe and the United States, just not any of the giants. As a result, he puts us in competition to have his works and to get the best conditions. We're the ones who have to ask him for his paintings. Like, he's going to make me one or two for a fair, I have to thank him. And then, normally,

> we pay once the works are sold, but he's going to ask me to pay him in advance. I can't say no! He's playing the game well, he when I started to feature his paintings, they cost $15,000; today, he's up to $350,000. His rating has gone up quite a bit, and he's kept his freedom.

Just like in the past, the choice of artists is the primary component of a gallery's strategic goals (Moulin, 1987), particularly as pertains to its "mission" and its most loyal collectors (and their expectations). Any decisions made must also take market evolution into account. Over the last few years, it has become good practice to bank particularly on artists who have been treated unfairly by the market for too long, women being foremost. This is why, of the half-dozen new artists for whom the influential Thaddaeus Ropac gallery has recently announced representation, most are women. Admittedly, the gallery was very much lagging behind in this respect, but it is evident that the gender dimension is now clearly recognized, and that the gallery has taken care to correct its significant imbalance between male and female artists. Artists of African descent, whom the art market has also overlooked for too long, are now benefiting (in the same way) from a clear attempt to rectify past neglect.[23] Another strong trend in recent years is that many galleries have rediscovered older or even deceased artists, following a process of historical contextualization that aimed to increase the market value of the artists in question. While previously, it was highly unlikely for a contemporary artist who had not experienced real success during their lifetime or who had been forgotten to rise to prominence later on (Milo, 1986), many rediscoveries have come about recently. Therefore, being old or deceased is no longer an impediment to having one's work recognized; nowadays, it can even be considered an advantage. As the following French gallerist who runs a midsize gallery joked: "For some time now, it's been the big thing, everyone wants to have a few older artists who otherwise would have been neglected. As soon as we see each other, it's a joke between gallerists, we ask each other, 'So, have you found your old guy?'"

Yet at the other end of the generational spectrum, the opposite trend has also recently emerged, especially with the largest galleries. For many years now, there has been a particular *cursus honorum* that did not exist in the 1970s (Quemin, 2013b), and has been implemented for those on track to become a star artist. The typical age of an established artist has gone up considerably since that era. However, as competition has greatly increased between leading galleries, which are at the top of the international market, it has recently become necessary (if not essential) to now integrate very young artists into even the largest galleries, lest the directly competing galleries attract them. These young artists are also a means for the most established galleries to assert their position in the most essential form of contemporary art (the newest of the artistic genres). This avoids the risk of being called into question in this domain, which could happen if they only represented artists in their sixties and even, as has become increasingly the case over the years, in their seventies and eighties. As an effect of the competition between major galleries, the integration of very young artists—which was practically unthinkable only seven or eight years ago—has become a prominent feature of the relationship between artists and the most influential galleries.

To give an example of a gallery at a lower level of recognition than the mega-galleries that consistently tend to be affected by the phenomenon, I will cite the case of the painter Julie Curtiss, who was born in 1982. She benefited from heavy media coverage when her works reached the half-million dollar mark in auctions, which was about ten times their in-gallery price. This amount is surprising, to say the least, for an artist who was at the time not even in her forties. She joined the Anton Kern gallery, which, during the Art Basel Miami Beach fair, agreed to sell one of her paintings to a collector, on the condition that they would donate it to a museum within 5 years ("'The Vultures Are Circling': The Market for Young Artists Is White-Hot Again – But Can They Get Out Alive?", *ArtnetNews*, December 6, 2019).

However, the best example of a considerable gap between a gallery's level of prestige and the age of the artist joining it is probably the partnership between Avery Singer and Hauser & Wirth. At the end of 2019, the New York painter Avery Singer, who was born in 1987 and at the time was only 32 years old, joined the mega-gallery, which already represented other artists hitherto perceived as very "young,"[24] such as Amy Sherald (born in 1973) and Nicolas Party (born in 1980). There is hence a considerable shift toward youth in terms of recruiting new artists. Singer, who was already very prominent when she was being represented by Gavin Brown's Enterprise in New York, left this gallery at the beginning of 2019 without immediately joining one of its competitors. Such an attitude is generally strongly discouraged for artists; however, in her case, the art market and world were immediately abuzz with rumors that she would be joining one of the largest galleries in the world (Gagosian, David Zwirner, or Hauser & Wirth). These were galleries to which some of her pieces had previously been loaned, all of which most likely approached her. It was ultimately the last of these galleries that she chose. It should be noted that Singer managed to preserve her representation by the Berlin gallery Kraupa-Tuskany Zeidler, which is nevertheless no match for the economic weight of her current main gallery. When she joined Hauser & Wirth, some commentators asserted that she had been offered a bonus of $1 million, which the gallery was forced to deny. In private transactions, some of Singer's works have reached the million dollar mark, while in auctions one of her creations was sold in May 2018 for $735,000; more than six times its estimated price. Already extremely popular with the market and collectors, Singer was just as popular with institutions; she had already had solo exhibitions at the Kunsthalle in Zurich in 2014, when she was only 27 years old (!), at the Hammer Museum in Los Angeles in 2015, at the Sandretto Re Rebaudengo Foundation in Turin in 2015, at the Stedlijk Museum in Amsterdam and the Vienna Secession in 2016, and at the Ludwig Museum in Cologne in 2019. In addition to the previous prestigious institutions, her work had also been presented at various biennials, including the Venice Biennale in 2019. The international selection of the latter for that year, however, only offered its picture rails to an exceptionally limited number of artists.

A year earlier, Hauser & Wirth had recruited two former Christie's employees who specialized in the impressionist and modern periods, thus suggesting an accentuation of its activity in the secondary market. However, the influential gallery clearly had no intention of abandoning the contemporary segment, and had succeeded in securing a collaboration with such a young artist, who was already exceptionally renowned.

As I mentioned at the beginning of this chapter, the accentuated competition between various galleries, especially the largest among them, is thus clearly exerting its effects on many levels, particularly in the domain of artist representation.

Museums: increased influence for galleries and a new level of competition with institutions

Although aesthetic and financial values have mutually supported each other for a long time—at least since Raymonde Moulin studied them in the 1950s and 1960s (Moulin, 1987 and 1992)—the market has now largely taken over as the driving force behind value creation, and its influence is consistently growing. Currently, leading galleries (and primary collectors) play a major role in the art world (Quemin, 2020b). Institutions—museums and art centers—are now often relegated to the background in the domain of contemporary art. They are used to the benefit of the market (and its interests) in different ways, whether they involve the most important collectors or the largest galleries.

The first way is certainly rare but reveals all the same how galleries make use of museums resources. When they launched their careers as gallerists, the associates of the French gallery Ceysson & Bénétière skillfully capitalized on the name of the former's father, who was a very well-recognized professional in France, having directed the Museum of Contemporary Art in Saint-Etienne in its heyday, and the National Museum of Modern Art—Centre Georges Pompidou in Paris. The repute of this well-known name working with these institutions was then transferred to the market space.

More broadly, contemporary art galleries often tend to set up shop near museums and art centers, so as to benefit from the foot traffic that they generate. As such, the New York neighborhood of Chelsea in particular, as previously seen, was taken over by galleries due to the presence of an influential contemporary art center, the Dia, which was there prior to their arrival. In Paris, the symbiosis with the Centre Pompidou and its National Museum of Modern Art heavily influenced the attraction of the Marais neighborhood as a gallery district (and still does). These establishments began to flock to the area when the project to create "Beaubourg" became publicly known, and they first gathered in the part of the Marais that was closest to the future building. The district's appeal for galleries has not waned since then, and it is not limited to the singular desire of attracting collectors. As this Parisian gallerist, who for a long time had a location near the gare du Nord and was then situated on rue Beaubourg, explained: "Now that I'm on rue Beaubourg, everything has changed for me: the curators come in a lot more."

Galleries are also increasingly involved in how institutions operate, as they often have a major interest in collaborating with them. Important gallerists—just as much as (mega-)collectors, for that matter—are now essential partners for institutions. Today, major contemporary exhibitions need their support, both to finance them (in part) and to loan out the works from their private collections. It should therefore be noted that the most influential galleries in the world appeal to major institutional exhibitions on a massive scale for the artists they represent. With the emergence of a few major players onto the contemporary art gallery scene, the power of granting renown to artists is now concentrated among a very limited number of galleries, and it uses the largest contemporary art museums and centers as a support system. In 2015, *The Art Newspaper* published a study showing that 30 percent of the main solo exhibitions organized by the most famous American museums—including the Metropolitan Museum, the MoMA, the Whitney Museum, the Guggenheim Museum, and the New Museum—between 2007 and 2013 were dedicated to artists represented by only five contemporary art galleries (the overrepresentation was outrageous, as the newspaper estimated that the city of New York was home to more than 1,400 galleries).[25] The five galleries in question were all based in New York: the four mega-galleries Gagosian, David Zwirner, Hauser & Wirth, and Pace, as well as Marian Goodman. It is noteworthy that the latter has not adopted such an intensely strong capitalistic model as its previously mentioned peers, and it has always kept its distance from the Chelsea neighborhood, retaining its location on East 57th Street (a stone's throw from the MoMA) until recently announcing a relocation to Tribeca in 2024. However, the renown of the artists that it represents nevertheless makes it one of the most prestigious galleries in the world. This simple figure of 30 percent clearly shows the influence of these leading galleries, which monopolize a significant portion of the lineup for the largest museums; in particular because, due to their financial means, they can cover certain exhibitions costs (Quemin, 2020b).

The Art Newspaper commented on the fact of only five galleries corresponding to 30 percent of major solo exhibitions, as follows:

> The figure raises questions about the growing influence of a small number of galleries in a rapidly consolidating art market – especially when they often offer logistical and financial support for exhibitions. At the same time, some wonder whether museums are doing enough to expose the public to art they would not otherwise see.
>
> According to Robert Storr, the dean of the Yale University School of Art, "Curators are abdicating and delegating their responsibilities . . . to more adventurous gallerists who, aside from the profit motive and in some respects because of it, seem in many cases to be bolder and more curious than their institutional counterparts."

The same survey revealed that more than 9 out of 10 (11 out of 12, in fact) of the major solo exhibitions organized by the Guggenheim Museum in New York between 2007 and 2013 were devoted to artists represented by the same five previous galleries. However, a spokeswoman for the Guggenheim was quick to point out that the representing gallery had never been taken into account, and that the choice was made solely on the basis of the "excellence"[26] of the artists selected. Even the New Museum, despite its commitment to offering the New York general public exhibitions of artists that it could not discover in other institutions, devoted 40% of its main exhibitions to artists represented by one or more of the previous five major galleries. Some people criticized the acute overrepresentation in some museums' choices of a limited number of around 300 artists and estates. However, the same article mentioned an artist population of around 200,000 in the United States alone (according to a 2011 report from the National Endowment for the Arts) and more than 250 galleries had been selected by Art Basel Miami Beach in the year preceding the publication of the study. Museums in New York were even more likely than those in Los Angeles to devote an exhibition to artists from the five prominent galleries, clearly showing the influence of this reticular network and its geographical dimension. It is important to highlight the fact that four out of five of the preceding galleries were created in the United States (Hauser & Wirth, for its part, was initially founded in Zurich, Switzerland, but now operates mainly in New York and the United Kingdom). They are all, moreover, notably associated with New York, even though the contemporary art world often likes to think of itself as being "globalized" and to willfully ignore the notion of national borders (Quemin, 2001, 2002a, 2002c, 2004, 2006, 2013a, 2013b, 2023). The article emphasized the importance of the financial support provided by galleries for organizing exhibitions, the most influential among them therefore having the best chance of seeing their artists exhibited by renowned museums. It also indicated that, given the impact that such museum exhibitions can have on sales, financing these events to the tune of several hundred thousand dollars provided an excellent return on investment. In a way, one could say that the most influential galleries have transformed museum exhibition spaces into an extension of their own premises (admittedly temporarily, but recurrently). All evidence indicates that, since the year this study was carried out, the situation has barely changed; museums and contemporary art centers can hardly do without the support of the largest galleries, which moreover tend to have a significant concentration of "museum-quality" artists (Quemin, 2020b). Nowadays, the public funding being made available to institutions to organize exhibitions is becoming rarer. At the same time, the largest galleries more often find themselves in a position to contribute to such exhibitions; they can therefore participate directly in financing public institutions, even when they themselves do not organize "museum-quality" exhibitions.

This tendency of the largest galleries to make use of institute resources is all the more effective as museums and contemporary art centers also benefit from them. By maintaining positive relationships with influential galleries, institutions increase their chances of receiving donations from them that would enhance their collections, or that would encourage collectors to do the same. Major galleries can thereby both authorize and practically require certain clients to buy two works, generally by the same artist, on the condition that they donate one of them to a museum (and the gallery commonly acts as a guarantor for the choice of work). Since museum acquisition budgets, especially for public institutions, are often extremely small compared to the price of the works created by the most recognized artists in the contemporary art world—those whose productions are specifically intended to join these collections—institutions have little choice but to maintain excellent relationships with both collectors and gallerists, if they hope to successfully and satisfactorily enhance their collections. While visiting the massive exhibition dedicated to the star artist Damien Hirst in the two spaces owned by the collector and businessman François Pinault in Venice in 2017, I was stunned to hear a visitor ask her tour guide a question, and the frankness of the response. Were the displayed works intended to go to museums after the exhibition? "No, no, the works won't go to museums, they don't have the means. They'll go to private collectors."

This is because today, institutions are placed in a largely ancillary position due to the frequent reduction of their budgets, which is concurrent with the explosion of resources available to the largest galleries; and this is the case in all countries. Competition is not particularly in the institutions' favor. Relationships with museums have been redefined by the advent of mega-galleries, which increasingly tend to monopolize their resources (Quemin, 2020b). During the 2010s, the number of major collections (especially those open to the public) has grown drastically around the world, especially in China and the Arabian Peninsula. To attract the general public, they tend to favor a limited number of star artists (Quemin, 2013b) being represented by a handful of very large galleries, who have therefore benefited primarily from this very selective market, and whose works may elude museums that are less well endowed.

Although they are commercial establishments, mega-galleries now sometimes organize exhibitions in which very few works, or occasionally no works at all, are for sale. These are intended solely to develop their image, or to promote a museum, for the relevance of the presentation. Hence, leading galleries appropriate part of a museum's power of certification, which was previously derived from the monopoly that they had held in that domain. These galleries show that they can organize very high-level exhibitions, on a par with museums, and they cherry-pick works from the best collections to do so. This also allows them to know precisely where the works are, and then track them so as to make significant profits on the secondary market when the time comes to put them back up for sale.

The situation is similar for spaces, especially exhibition rooms. Historically, commercial galleries have had small premises that manifestly prevented them from competing with museums; today, the most influential galleries have extremely large spaces that allow them to compete with many museums and art centers. This is particularly evident in the case of the prominent gallery Hauser & Wirth, whose museum aspirations are unambiguously evident.

Today, the largest galleries are no longer in competition with midsize galleries, nor do they have a rivalry between their peers. They are (in terms of lineup) in competition with the museums with which they directly compete; this would still have been unthinkable a decade ago. As of the end of the 2010s in particular, the elites in the gallery sector have been replicating museum conditions more and more by presenting successful historic exhibitions of Picasso and other deceased colossuses; many of which are produced by former or current curators of prestigious institutions. Even their integrated publishing houses rival (and occasionally surpass) their counterparts, producing catalogues in illustrious museums and other non-profit organizations; and often on a much shorter schedule, with highly superior firepower. Whether in North America—with the Gagosian and David Zwirner galleries—or in Europe—with the Thaddaeus Ropac, Hauser & Wirth, White Cube, Sprüth Magers, and Almine Rech galleries—the exhibitions offered by these establishments can compete with the top museums, be it by the spaces that they occupy, the layouts that they design, or the works that they display. Some easily manage to do all three.

During the months of May and June 2012, the Gagosian gallery, which for a long time was far in the lead on the market, organized a spectacular Lucio Fontana exhibition in its flagship space on West 24th Street in New York, two years before the major retrospective dedicated to the same artist mounted by the Musée d'Art Moderne de la Ville de Paris from April to August 2014. As this curator explained to me in the interim between the two events:

> The Fontana exhibition at Gagosian, you could say that it's museum quality, it's not clichéd. The works are truly amazing. He managed to get pieces that are absolutely exceptional, and in any case practically nothing is for sale, it's a prestigious exhibition. It'll be difficult for the Museum of Modern Art in Paris to do better with their show later. Fortunately, they have ceramics that don't often travel due to vibrations. We can have them in Paris, Gagosian couldn't bring them to New York for that reason, but otherwise this exhibition is both magnificent and very complete.

More recently, other major prestigious galleries have also managed to regularly organize high-level exhibitions that can compete with museums (Quemin, 2020b). An example of this is the various exhibitions that the influential Thaddaeus Ropac gallery has devoted to Joseph Beuys, including "Utopia at the Stag Monuments," which took place in London from April to June 2018. The presentation was curated by Sir Norman Rosenthal, the former director of the Royal Academy of Arts in London, and was introduced by a press release that highlighted the exceptional nature of this exhibition. The announcement presented a clear comparison of the works on display to those of London's most prestigious museum of contemporary art (and one of the most legitimate institutions in the world)—the Tate Modern—hinting at the superiority of the work exhibited by the gallery, being an original and not merely a reproduction.[27] "Most important exhibition," "over a decade," "major sculptures," "legendary exhibition," "first time since its creation"; the superlatives and laudatory comments used to describe the event were plentiful, in a gallery that is nevertheless generally associated with a more sober tone:

> The most important UK exhibition of Beuys' work in over a decade.
>
> Reuniting most of the original elements of Beuys' seminal Stag Monuments for the first time since its creation.
>
> A version in bronze of the eponymous environment is currently on view at the Tate Modern, but this will be the first time that the original elements will be displayed in London.
>
> Galerie Thaddaeus Ropac, London, is pleased to present *Joseph Beuys: Utopia at the Stag Monuments*, the most important UK exhibition of Beuys' work in over a decade. Curated by Norman Rosenthal, who worked with Beuys on many exhibitions from 1970 onwards, the exhibition brings together pivotal works from various stages of the artist's life. The exhibition spans the years 1947–1985 and can be seen through a retrospective lens, featuring major sculptures and rarely seen works, which cumulatively reveal the extent to which the artist's ideas and idiosyncratic iconography were clearly defined from the very beginning of his career. The show's title originates from *Hirschdenkmäler* (Stag Monuments), the environment Beuys created for the legendary 1982 Berlin exhibition *Zeitgeist*, co-curated by Christos M. Joachimides

> and Rosenthal himself. Notably, for the first time since its creation most of the original elements of *Stag Monuments*, including *Ofen* (Oven), will be reunited in the Library Gallery at Ely House.

All of this rhetoric clearly emphasizes the exceptionality of the presentation, and far from anchoring it in the commercial sphere, places it, on the contrary, on a truly museum-caliber level. It was not the market that was in the spotlight; it was art history.[28]

Practically at the same time as the previous London presentation by Thaddaeus Ropac, its fellow gallery Almine Rech organized another exhibition with the same star curator, Sir Norman Rosenthal. Entitled *A New Spirit Then, A New Spirit Now, 1981–2018*, it took place from May to June 2018, and was presented in the following manner in the press release:

> Almine Rech Gallery is pleased to present *A New Spirit Then, A New Spirit Now, 1981–2018*. Curated by Norman Rosenthal, this exhibition reconstructs and reinterprets *A New Spirit in Painting*, a seminal presentation of 20th-century painting at the Royal Academy of Arts in London co-curated by Rosenthal with Christos Joachimides and Nicholas Serota in 1981.
>
> In *A New Spirit Then, A New Spirit Now, 1981–2018*, Rosenthal reassesses this defining moment in his curatorial career with nearly 40 years of hindsight. The original show challenged painting's status as a 'conservative' medium by presenting a self-aware relationship between the artist, painted image, and reality. Rosenthal pushes this investigation even further in his new presentation, questioning the role of personal and collective memory in our conception of this moment. The majority of the artists presented in the exhibition are living and working today. *A New Spirit Then, A New Spirit Now, 1981–2018* is staged across two of Almine Rech Gallery's spaces, and features artists who were included in the seminal 1981 exhibition at the Royal Academy. In New York, the exhibition presented historical paintings from the 1980s. In London, the exhibition expands with works made by the same artists after the year 2000.
>
> List of exhibited artists: Frank AUERBACH, Georg BASELITZ, Francesco CLEMENTE, Rainer FETTING, Per KIRKEBY, Maria LASSNIG, Markus LÜPERTZ, Malcolm MORLEY, A.R. PENCK, Pablo PICASSO, Susan ROTHENBERG, David SALLE, Julian SCHNABEL.

Whereas in the 1980s, Rosenthal organized his major exhibition in an institution (The Royal Academy of Arts, which is highly recognized), it was in a gallery—a commercial entity—nearly four decades later that he proceeded to resume this presentation, going even more in depth in his commentary (a point that the press release highlighted). The gallery therefore made it possible to go even further than an influential institution. Furthermore, while the initial presentation had taken place in only one city (London), the new dual exhibition was shared between two top-class metropolises for the contemporary scene and its market: London and New York.[29]

The final example that I will mention here (although the list could go on and on): in 2019, the Chillida Foundation in the Spanish Basque Country was able to reopen, as the influential international gallery Hauser & Wirth started representing the artist's estate, and thus invested in promoting his work. By fighting to attract estates, mega-galleries now in fact no longer leave room even for institutions in the "historical contemporary" segment. The Chillida Foundation, which was once again accessible thanks to Hauser & Wirth's financial support, was added (along with the establishment's commercial premises in the major art capitals and in resort towns frequented by an affluent public) to a vast gallery located in Somerset, in the English countryside, as well as the immense complex in downtown Los Angeles, thus taking it beyond the notion of being a simple "gallery." It preceded the next "mega-space" that was to open in Spain, in the Balearic Islands, right off the coast of Menorca. In this last environment, given the characteristics of the locale and those of the building, it was evident that the exhibition space's purpose was very much designed to resemble a non-profit, institutional ambiance, and that the retail space was fairly secondary.

The rationale of putting up museum-level presentations is not limited to specific exhibitions or places designed essentially on the basis of that purpose, which is distinguishable from the main sales spaces in galleries. When it finally came Pace's turn to take the plunge to open a mega-space in Chelsea at the end of 2019, it was also strongly influenced by the museum model (in this case, with a significant experimental element). From the outset, it chose to integrate the possibility of presenting art forms that are still largely in the making, and whose market is still very limited.

This "museumification" of the exhibition spaces that galleries use to present their artists is also remarkably illustrated by the fact that after having collaborated with architects who specialize in designing their spaces—the most famous of this group being Annabelle Selldorf—galleries can now reach out to architects whose reputation is associated with proper museum spaces. Thus, for the interior design of its two spaces in Paris, the Templon gallery called on Jean-Michel Wilmotte, who is famous for his numerous collaborations with museums, including the Louvre. Additionally, David Zwirner turned to the star architect Renzo Piano to design a new building in Chelsea, before he ultimately had to abandon the project in the summer of 2023.

Thanks to the new premises that they now have, along with their considerable financial resources, galleries can now organize exhibitions that are not only museum-caliber, but also that can attract large crowds. Hence, they directly compete with institutions for the public in terms of attracting visitors, whom galleries can incite to become more demanding (especially since, in the context of gallery shows, visitors do not pay entrance fees). To illustrate how gallery exhibitions are able to siphon considerable audiences away from institutions, I will cite the exhibitions that the David Zwirner gallery devoted to its artist Yayoi Kusama. In 2019, its presentation *Every Day, I Pray For Love*, organized in New York in its West 20th Street space, was planned to accommodate 100,000 visitors. Before that, another exhibition that the gallery dedicated to the Japanese superstar, entitled *Festival of Life*, which was also held in Chelsea in its space on West 19th Street in 2018, welcomed no fewer than 75,000 visitors. On some days, the waiting time to view the exhibition was around six hours, and the gallery was obliged to limit the time spent in certain rooms to a single minute in order to regulate the flow of visitors. The exhibition, which lasted 23 days, admitted on average more than 1,500 people per day; by comparison, the blockbuster exhibition at the Hirshhorn Museum in Washington DC—dedicated to the same artist—received 2,000 visitors per day. Daily attendance of Kusama's exhibition at David Zwirner (which was, admittedly, exceptional) exceeded the exhibition that the Met Breuer, a large museum in New York, had dedicated to Nasreen Mohamedi for its inauguration in 2016 (1,300 daily admissions), or that organized by the Broad in Los Angeles, also in 2016, for another superstar artist: Cindy Sherman (1,200 admissions per day).

Another sign of the unprecedented new investment on the part of galleries in the domain of exhibitions; they are hiring more and more professionals who previously worked in museums as curators, or even as directors of these institutions. Another significant advantage, in addition to their curatorial skills and the prestige that they bring with them to major galleries, is that these new recruits can also give them access to networks of collectors with whom they collaborated in their previous positions. Over the past few years, the tendency to hire former staff members from prominent museums and art centers has gone up drastically. The end of the 2010s heralded a veritable procession of the most influential international galleries recruiting high-ranking employees from major museums and contemporary art centers. Among the most notable transfers were the following. In the United Kingdom, Dame Julia Peyton-Jones—one of the most prominent British curators of contemporary art—after a brilliant career as the head of the Serpentine Galleries in London, and now retired, joined the British branch of the Thaddaeus Ropac gallery in 2017.[30] This enlistment was announced as follows in a press release:

> **JULIA PEYTON-JONES TO JOIN GALERIE THADDAEUS ROPAC AS SENIOR GLOBAL DIRECTOR**[31]
>
> Dame Julia Peyton-Jones has been named Senior Global Director of the Thaddaeus Ropac Gallery. The former director of the Serpentine Galleries for 25 years, Peyton-Jones will begin her role as ambassador and curator starting on September 1st, 2017, and will be based in London, where the gallery opened a new space in Mayfair earlier this year.

> During her tenure as director of the Serpentine Galleries from 1991 to 2016, Peyton-Jones worked with many of the world's leading artists on exhibitions, trainings, public programs, and groundbreaking projects, transforming the Serpentine in London into an internationally renowned visual arts institution. [. . .]
>
> Having won numerous awards and honors for her achievements at the Serpentine, Peyton-Jones was appointed an Officer of the Order of the British Empire in 2003, and a Dame Commander of the British Empire in 2016. Peyton-Jones now sits on the board of numerous public and non-profit institutions.

That same year, in 2017, after 20 years spent at the reputed Museum of Contemporary Art in Los Angeles (MoCA) as a curator, Paul Schimmel joined the mega-gallery Hauser & Wirth as director and co-founder of its Los Angeles branch. Of course, due to his prior roles, he had acquired great expertise in presenting high-level exhibitions, as well as developing close ties with the greatest collectors in California. It is important to note that professionals from the world of museums who are recruited by galleries are systematically assigned to the city in which they performed their previous roles, even when the galleries they join are located in different areas. This is easily explained: it is in the city wherein they operated as curators that they have the richest network of relationships with collectors. This shows that it is not only their museum skills, or the prestige associated with their previous roles, that galleries are seeking; it is also their access to the market through the connections that they maintain with collectors.

In 2018, it was the influential British gallery White Cube that, in order to reinforce its presence in the United States, recruited Eric Shiner as the artistic director of its New York branch. In 2016, he began working as senior vice president of contemporary art for the auction house Sotheby's but prior to that he was director of the Andy Warhol Museum in Pittsburgh. As a new staff member of White Cube, he brought with him solid skills pertaining to Andy Warhol and contemporary Asian art, as well as the networks of collectors associated with these two domains.

The following is the final example that I will give from this influx of highly qualified art center and museum staff joining influential commercial entities (Quemin, 2020b). In 2019, Amira Gad joined the Lehmann Maupin gallery—which has locations in New York, Hong Kong, and Seoul—as artistic director. She was also poached from the Serpentine Galleries in London, an institution for which she had been one of the very prominent curators[32] since 2014. In her new role, she was charged with developing the artistic calendars for the Lehmann Maupin gallery, both in Great Britain and in continental Europe. She was also meant to participate in the opening of the gallery's fifth space, scheduled for spring 2020, in the London neighborhood of South Kensington. Her two employers, Rachel Lehmann and David Maupin, counted on their new recruit to infuse their curatorial department—which was created in 2016—with her *savoir-faire* on exhibitions, as well as to allow the gallery to benefit from her institutional network, and most likely to develop its contacts with the collectors she had hitherto met in a non-profit setting.

To conclude on this trend of staff transferring from institutions to galleries, I will note that the movements of personnel between these two poles are not one-way, from the former to the latter. The largest galleries have grown a great deal in legitimacy, and the vocations that they perform have both been inspired by the museum model and gone on to influence it. As a result, it is now entirely possible, even at a very high position in the hierarchy, to move from a gallery to a museum or an art center. Working as a gallerist can then provide access to management roles in institutions; in February 2018, the largest Scandinavian gallery—the Galerie Forsblom in Helsinki—announced the recruitment of a new director, Katarina Siltavuori, as her predecessor Kiira Miesmaa had just been appointed Senior Curator of the Kunsthalle in Helsinki.

The economic crisis resulting from the COVID-19 pandemic, and how contemporary art galleries have adapted to the new market context

As good health is generally considered to be the natural state of the human body (while the fact of the matter is that humans are, in reality, equally naturally afflicted by disease) the notion of the art market being naturally prosperous is also an illusion. Crises are part and parcel of the functioning of the market, even if they often tend to be perceived as external accidents. Whether exogenous or endogenous, crises punctuate the history of the art market and, as Raymonde Moulin noted in her first works, contemporary art galleries are in general ill-equipped to resist them (Moulin, 1987).

The painting market experienced a period of great prosperity during the 1950s, lasting until 1962. Although growth had already been sustained from 1945 to 1950, it then accelerated even more, due in particular to regular forecasts of improved activity. With the art market crash of 1962 following the Wall Street Flash Crash of the same year, dealers kept prices high, but demand petered out. The debacle was aggravated by the widespread resale of speculative collectors and dealers shutting down their operations, thus flooding the market with their works being offered *en masse* at auction. The crisis was further exacerbated as the American market became more autonomous and self-sufficient in the post-war era, with the United States increasingly becoming its own supplier. The crisis also eventually made its way over to the European market.

All over the world, the crisis impacted innovative art rather than conservative art, which better suits the taste of the majority of buyers. Dealers then adapted by offering more young artists and smaller formats (Moulin, 1987). What lessons can we learn from this major crisis? It seems to me that, in rereading Raymonde Moulin and given the current context, it is the following dual fact that should be kept in mind: stock market difficulties have mainly affected the most speculative sector of the market, and "these are the galleries situated in the intermediate zone of the market, above the 'test clubs' and below the galleries devoted to recognized values, which seem to be the most vulnerable" (Moulin, 1967 [1987], p. 470). This observation offers a striking parallel with the current era: it is the midsize galleries, particularly the mid-to-large ones, which are the most vulnerable today. In addition to a sort of fragility that has become structural for this type of gallery, there is now a second, cyclical fragility.

Among the more recent crises, there was another, particularly brutal one for the art market in 1990. As the French market veteran Daniel Templon explained during the *Talking Galleries* symposium in Barcelona in January 2018, his sales fell by two thirds during the 1990 crisis, which lasted for several years. Whereas, up to that point, he had sold around 40 works per year, the number of transactions fell to around 14 once the crisis hit[33] ("5 Disruptive Trends Art Galleries Need to Understand If They Want to Survive," in *Artnet News*, January 30, 2018). Marion Papillon, the president of the French Comité Professionnel des Galeries d'Art (Professional Committee of Art Galleries, CPGA), recently recalled that in France, no fewer than 46 percent of galleries had to close between 1992 and 1995, clearly showing the extreme severity of the 1990 crisis.

Comparatively, the effects of the 2008 financial crisis were much less harsh, in particular because new market players, first and foremost being China (Quemin, 2013c), as well As other countries, in the Middle East, broadly offset the decline in demand.

The 2020 economic crisis, which brought a large part of society to a standstill, and affected the art market following the outbreak of the COVID-19 pandemic, effectively put an end to a very long phase of prosperity.

The onsets of these crises serve as a reminder of the full impact of macroeconomic factors in the development of the art market, as well as the extent to which its soundness can influence the repercussions of a crisis. Almost until the end of the 1970s, there was hardly a market for contemporary art. It was really during the 1980's, sometimes described as the years of "money is king," that the game truly changed. Subsequently, the number of millionaires rose sharply in the world's population from the late 1990s into the twenty-first century, leading to a significant increase in demand for goods that symbolize social success. Owing to an evolution in taste, contemporary art has become a product that is in great demand; and due to this new solvent clientele, its market has grown considerably, both in volume and in price, with the Veblen effect (Veblen, 1899) therefore in full effect here. While, as Artprice data shows, artists born after 1945 accounted for 0.8 percent of the auction sales in 1988, this percentage soared to 13.7 percent in 2017–2018 (Artprice, 2019b) and 17.6 percent in 2021–2022 (Artprice, 2022). Another sign of this very significant expansion of the market is that the number of contemporary art fairs has greatly increased in the twenty-first century, as mentioned in a previous chapter. A market in rapid expansion in the medium term does not, however, mean that it is sheltered from economic crises; the warning shot from the onset of the COVID-19 pandemic at the beginning of 2020 serves as a reminder of this. While the market had already slightly waned in 2019, it was much more severely impacted in 2020. The following year saw the global auction market drop by 21 percent[34] according to Artprice, for a new total of $10.57 billion (Artprice, 2021).[35]

Before the sudden outbreak of the joint health and economic global crisis in recent years, it was the prospect of Brexit that occupied many people's minds. In essence, the art market (like all markets in general) does not appreciate uncertainty. With the onset of the 2020 economic crisis after COVID-19 struck, Brexit suddenly found itself relegated to the rank of a somewhat trivial event. A German gallerist made this comment in May 2019, which only a few months later, what with the COVID-19 pandemic having surged, sounded strangely dated:

> – *In your opinion, what will the next major developments in the contemporary art market be?*
> – The evolution of the market is always dependent on social evolution, as well as political and economic changes, on a global level. One doesn't go without the other. I have a lot of questions about Brexit. In particular, there's a lot of uncertainty about its impact on the evolution of the European market. We're living through a moment of extremely important transformations, and it's difficult to predict the future.
>
> "Esther Schipper, Gallerist: 'Berlin is less accessible to young artists, so it's gentrifying'," *Le Journal des Arts*, no. 524, May 24, 2019

With the 2020 economic crisis, it was logical to anticipate a decline in average prices (or at least, a much more limited increase). A sharp drop in prices is always difficult for contemporary art galleries to implement, as it tends to send a signal of lower quality regarding the artists' production (Moulin, 1987). Above all, crises generally reverse the balance of power between galleries and collectors, with the latter taking advantage and being able to negotiate much more.

In order to maintain trust, which is an essential dimension in all markets, gallerists generally tend to exaggerate their level of activity (even more so in times of crisis). However, people to whom I am especially close have told me about the difficulties they experienced due to the slowdown (or even sharp decline) of the market, especially during the periods of confinement experienced by a country like France; with the worst of them being that of spring 2020. As this gallerist, whose establishment has locations in three countries, conceded: "Here, we're keeping up the fight . . . a few sales here and there, we're working on future releases, but to be honest, business is very slow, and collectors are more concerned about their short-term future than about the next painting or the next work to buy."

Also in 2020, a fellow gallerist with whom I am very close wrapped up the email he sent me with a humorous "Hey, you wouldn't like to buy a painting from me, would you?", expressing the decline in business during this period of crisis, and the pressing need to make a sale.

Among all the consequences of the COVID-19 pandemic, the sudden cancellation of fairs was likely the most brutal for all international galleries, particularly major ones, especially since it was accompanied by a drop in visitors in the galleries' physical spaces due to social distancing measures and lockdown. It was, however, more generally physical encounters that were severely impeded, along with the sudden interruption of dinners and cocktail receptions, and the evaporation of exhibition openings during the months following the outbreak of the pandemic; this is despite (as I have previously detailed) how important they are for developing sales. In spring 2020, many art fairs around the world were postponed,[36] and then canceled (Art Basel, which was first postponed from June, to September 2020, was ultimately called off in June) or simply canceled outright (in July 2020, Frieze announced the cancellation of its shows scheduled for the following October in London) and they were often replaced by a simple online version. The impact was all the more potent since, as I have already established, fairs have become a major cog in the art market for contemporary art galleries. In response to the pandemic, fairs (just like galleries) attempted to develop their online "viewing rooms."

At the end of spring 2020, this important French gallerist made a distinction between the various fairs, in the hopes that those with the deepest roots in their national markets could be held despite all other circumstances: "The FIAC (in Paris) could take place, it works a lot with French buyers, it's sustained by the local market, which isn't the case with the Art Basel fairs. In Basel and Hong Kong, you need visitors who travel, and the context doesn't lend itself to that as long as COVID-19 is present." This is why the FIAC organizers took much longer than their competitors to resolve to cancel their event for 2020, and the hopes of the aforementioned professional were therefore dashed.

With the scheduling of the primary fairs being shifted to the fall of 2020, there was a risk of heavy congestion for the art calendar at the end of the year. As this Swiss gallerist feared: "Regarding fairs, I don't see how next autumn will be able to fit all the events . . . collectors will have to choose between around 20 important events over two months . . . if they all end up taking place, I think it's going to be carnage." The problem did not ultimately arise, as the pandemic had not abated by that time.

The COVID-19 pandemic caused an almost total shutdown of the art world from March to May 2020 in France, and it had heavy repercussions for the art market the world over. Given the unfavorable economic context that had impacted galleries in various ways, they have had to attempt to react and adapt to this new environment.

Among the consequences of the COVID-19 pandemic were gallery closures, layoffs, staff furloughs, and lower wages. On April 1, 2020, *Le Journal des Arts* in France ran the headline: "Emmanuel Perrotin: 'Many Galleries Will Close'." At the beginning of the same month, also in France, the Professional Committee of Art Galleries raised the alarm about the state of the gallerist occupation. The moment that public places were locked down by order of the French government on March 16, 2020, the professional body carried out a study among its members to assess the impact of COVID-19 on their economy in the short- and medium-term: a third of respondents indicated that they feared not being able to sustain their business in the second half of the year. In France, galleries utilized the furlough system extensively. At the same time, the press was also echoing similar concerns about the survival of galleries abroad, especially in Los Angeles.

I have already mentioned the closure of the major New York galleries Gavin Brown's Enterprise in 2020, and then Metro Pictures in 2021; other prominent establishments partially closed down. The Finnish gallery Forsblom announced in March 2020 that it would give up its Stockholm location due to the pandemic, but would keep its space in Helsinki. In a similar approach, the Marian Goodman gallery vacated its London space in the fall of 2020, retaining only its locations in New York and Paris. In each case, it was a matter of galleries reducing their costs during a period wherein the economic context had become notably more difficult.

It should be noted that even the most influential galleries were affected. In April 2020, Gagosian announced that it would be furloughing its part-time workers and interns, and declared that it was lowering the wages of the rest of its staff. Those earning under $150,000 per year received a 10 percent pay cut, and those earning over $200,000 lost 20 percent of their income. Its competitor Pace put half of its New York employees on unpaid leave, while the Lévy-Gorvy gallery laid off a significant percentage of its workforce.

Another effect produced by COVID-19 was that some (large) galleries reacted to the pandemic by (unexpectedly) opening new branches so as to reach out to clients via these new physical spaces.

In the United States, several major galleries quickly sought to reconnect with their wealthy clients who had fled the New York lockdown by settling in their second homes in the Hamptons, at the eastern tip of Long Island, for the long-term. Such was the case for Gagosian, Pace, Skarstedt, Lisson, and Hauser & Wirth (the latter had already opened locations in two leisure resorts, Gstaad and St. Moritz in Switzerland, so this kind of maneuver was not a novelty).[37] It was not always clear if these premises would remain after the pandemic, or if they would only be short-lived.

In Florida, Pace, Acquavella, and Lehmann Maupin also moved into the upscale seaside resort of Palm Beach (as did Sotheby's). Shortly after these galleries, Paula Cooper, who until then had always refused to expand outside New York, joined the migration (although she only signed a short-term lease).

In the new context of a crashing market, galleries also sought to liven up their spaces, which had become less attractive due to the new health and safety measures, and less conducive to sales. They therefore adopted joint initiatives to that purpose. In France, at the end of the first lockdown in the spring of 2020, nearly 45 Parisian galleries in the Marais district decided to open on some Sundays. This collective plan made it possible to celebrate their reopening. These galleries also launched the free application—Marais. guide—intended for contemporary art lovers. It listed 90 galleries in the Marais, offered customizable routes, and could make personal appointments. In doing so, they illustrated how the location and existence of gallery clusters have been transformed into resources, thus confirming my analysis from the first part of this book.

Additionally, some galleries expanded their lineups with exhibitions of lesser economic impact. In France, the Perrotin gallery launched "Restons Unis" (Stay Together), an initiative that consisted of opening its spaces to smaller establishments (26 in total), exhibiting the artists of six or seven galleries for two weeks at a time between May and August 2020. Fellow galleries were graciously invited, and Perrotin made no commission on any sales.

As for the Thaddaeus Ropac gallery, it announced in May 2020 that it would open its massive Pantin space in September for an exhibition that would feature around 60 young artists and emerging galleries selected by the Jeune Création non-profit association. Here again, any profits from sales went entirely to the artists and their galleries. Furthermore, the sales team at the Thaddaeus Ropac gallery was made available to the exhibition, and the gallery's collectors were invited to attend. Lastly, the Ropac gallery took it upon itself to acquire some of the exhibited works offered by invited galleries.

Nevertheless, the art world's biggest reaction to the COVID-19 outbreak was the slew of new endeavors to develop and augment online transactions; even before 2020, galleries had been trying to enhance their sales through this channel, but the context of a sharp reduction in physical interactions due to the pandemic led them to ramp their efforts up.

Since the market was effectively paralyzed, many hopes were transferred to online sales, which at best represent only 10 percent of gallery transactions, and (at least for the moment) are only suitable for inexpensive works (priced under $10,000, or sometimes $5,000) or for artists who are already very established and are already in high demand, especially on the secondary market. However, even in this case—as shown in the chapter on sales—

the mutual acquaintanceship (or friendship) between gallerist and client, as well as providing sociability, generally plays a major role in finalizing a sale. Despite these significant limitations, the Internet has taken on a new dimension with the COVID-19 pandemic, as this medium has made it possible to avoid physical contact.

Following Art Basel Hong Kong, most of the fairs that had been cancelled in 2020 proposed a virtual replacement. The Internet has helped these events to maintain a certain amount of continuity, despite the fact that their physical version was not able to take place. In spite of the consistently favorable press releases, transactions remained limited overall. As Anne-Claudie Coric, the general manager of the French Templon gallery, explained: "So far, these online fairs haven't really worked" (in "Art Paris Digital confronted with the anger of several exhibitors," *Le Journal des Arts*, June 2, 2020).

Collective initiatives with the intention of boosting the market also attempted to use the Internet as a resource. As the Parisian galleries, Perrotin and Thaddaeus Ropac, had opened their physical spaces to accommodate smaller establishments in a gesture of solidarity, the New York gallery David Zwirner invited a dozen other, smaller galleries to be featured on its website.

In April 2020, the auction house Sotheby's announced a new "Sotheby's Gallery Network" initiative that consisted of hosting eight prominent contemporary art galleries on its website: Gavin Brown's Enterprise, Lehmann Maupin, Jack Shainman Gallery, Luhring Augustine, Kasmin Gallery, Petzel Gallery, Sperone Westwater, and Van Doren Waxter. The nature of the initiative indicated that the number of galleries could easily be raised. The works presented could only be purchased through the website, with Sotheby's receiving a fixed commission on any sales made. The pieces (between three and 10 per gallery) were classified via their associations with various partner galleries, and offered at prices starting at a little more than \$10,000, and going as high as around \$1 million. Up to \$150,000, transactions could be finalized via the Sotheby's site; for any price higher than that, buyers had to contact Sotheby's staff to complete a transaction. The galleries benefited from Sotheby's image, and from those of its clients who visited the site, thus finding a new outlet for art; but they did not have control of the buyers, even though this is usually an essential element of their business.

At the end of April 2020, the launch of another initiative was announced in the United States: an online platform hosting 60 galleries based in Los Angeles, GalleryPlatform.LA, to be made available on May 15 of that year. Each week, the shared platform would feature 12 galleries, with each scheduled to return every six weeks. Initiated by Jeffrey Deitch—the gallerist and former director of the Museum of Contemporary Art in Los Angeles—the project aimed to unite a vast spectrum of galleries (provided that they offered truly contemporary art), thus allowing them to expand the range of prices in particular. The organizing committee was, however, run by some of the most influential galleries on the Angeleno scene: Blum & Poe, Bel Ami, Château

Shatto, David Kordansky, François Ghebaly, Gagosian, Jeffrey Deitch, Jenny's, Make Room Los Angeles, Matthew Marks, Nicodim, Regen Projects, Residency Art, Sprüth Magers, and Various Small Fires. Admittedly, not all of these galleries could be considered "the most influential," but—with the notable exception of Hauser & Wirth—virtually all of the most recognized establishments in the city were included on this committee.

Finally, on a more individual level, galleries escalated the efforts they had already been making for several years on their websites, often with limited success.[38] Before the pandemic, the challenge was essentially not to take the risk of allowing a segment of the market to develop that could later slip through their fingers.

Hence, in 2018, the influential David Zwirner gallery hired a new staff member, Elena Soboleva, to manage the sales of its virtual space, considering it as a sixth sales space in its own right. This included making use of sales that could occur via social media.

However, to date, the digital sphere still has not generated many sales for galleries; even though they have a common tendency to overestimate it for reasons of image, in order to portray themselves as innovators. Younger, more digitally focused collectors are predictably more receptive to online purchases, albeit at relatively low price points. Conversely, more experienced collectors who are aware of the possible pitfalls of the condition and origin of an artwork remain wary, yet it is their spending habits that essentially fuel the art market. Digital is now a very important vector of information more than a mode of transaction. As this gallerist, established in the United Arab Emirates, conceded:

> – *How many works did you sell via an Instagram post?*
> – We love Instagram but use it fairly little for sales. . . myself, I only sold a few works via this addictive tool.
>
> Interview with Nadine Knotzer and Kourosh Nouri, directors of the Carbon 12 gallery in Dubai, in *The Art Gorgeous*, no. 6, 2019, p. 88

More recently, however, galleries have made significant efforts in this domain in light of the COVID-19 pandemic, particularly by crafting their online viewing rooms with more detail. The largest galleries are producing more and more audio and video content, while at the same time publishing print magazines.

Currently, the online exhibitions held by some galleries are only accessible to visitors after they have provided their contact information; especially their email address. This could eventually allow galleries to have a better understanding of their clients' tastes, and to identify these individuals and ultimately reach out to them with personalized offers (types of works and artists, price range, etc.) based on how they navigate around the site (taking which pages they visit and how long they spend on each of them in particular into account); alternately, an algorithm could guide these visitors in their navigation if their anonymity were to be preserved in order to respect certain legal provisions.

It is, however, interesting to note that the galleries that most readily embrace new technologies generally tend to use them as an element of their brand image, and therefore have every interest in exaggerating their real impact.

In April 2020, just days after the mega-gallery Hauser & Wirth revealed its ambitious plans to develop a new virtual reality platform called ArtLab,[39] its competitors (the British Lisson and the Italian Massimo de Carlo) announced in turn that they would be launching their own e-commerce virtual reality platforms. Although it is clear that COVID-19 has accelerated initiatives for online transactions, the Internet still represents an underwhelming sales channel for contemporary art galleries.

Conclusion

While, in the context of this book, I have sought to identify the principal, fairly permanent features of the gallery environment and the gallerist occupation, it seemed necessary to me to specify certain recent transformations by integrating the impact of the COVID-19 pandemic, which dealt a hard blow in 2020 and 2021, primarily. I first exposed the fundamental, strongly interconnected trends of the increase in competition, of concentration, of gallery expansions and the growing threats to second-tier galleries. Nowadays, the market tends to be increasingly controlled by mega-galleries, and the economic model of the "fringe oligopoly" is even more pronounced. With gallery closures, mergers, and associations, a certain recalibration of the field has been taking shape, but most of the transformations have already occurred, and the new configuration that has been implemented is now largely long-lasting, with the overwhelming influence of a handful of leading galleries. I have indicated the same trend toward a concentration of demand with the augmented presence of art advisors, especially with the largest galleries. Relationships with artists have also been affected by the evolution of the market, which is now producing stars (Quemin, 2013b) who are clearly not interchangeable, and over whom major galleries are fighting. As for the relationships that galleries maintain with museums, the considerably reinforced influence of the largest galleries is tending to place museums in an increasingly ancillary position.

COVID-19 threatened the market across the board. Galleries very quickly attempted to react to this new, particularly unfavorable situation. While the most media-friendly initiatives involve new investments in the Internet by developing online viewing rooms, it seems to me that the prospects offered by online sales today (despite the recent, yet enduring pandemic context that has been calamitous to physical sales) have not fully realized their potential, and do not offer real perspectives of making sales, at least in the near future.

PART THREE

Analyzing the hierarchy among galleries

8

Understanding the gallery hierarchy: How to construct a ranked list of the main contemporary art galleries in the world

Since I have studied the art market for over 30 years, my experience has made me more sensitive to how my work is received by the social world that I analyze. Generally, when an author writes a book, it is customary to consider that the reader will start at the beginning of it, and continue through the pages in order. However, in this instance, I would not be surprised if many people reading this book were to begin by consulting the table of contents and immediately choose to read this part—which is devoted to the classification of galleries—given that quantification and ranked lists hold a special attraction (Spoerhase, 2018; Mennicken & Nelson Espeland, 2019), or even fascination in social life in general, and in the art world in particular (Quemin, 2013). Some people will probably not even be able to resist instantly consulting the table of ranked galleries, without bothering to understand how the list was constructed beforehand, even though this information has an impact on the results obtained. This is why I wanted to develop the most rigorous methodology possible, but also to indicate the inevitable choices and potential biases that I have taken care, if not to eliminate completely, at least to limit as much as possible (Quemin, 2019 and 2020a).

This section of the book—which will discuss the hierarchy that exists in the world of contemporary art galleries, even at its highest level—is likely be the one that will elicit the most reactions, particularly because it refers to existing issues in the social world being studied. As I elaborated earlier in this book, there is now a strong incentive for growth, which is increasingly necessary for a gallery to be "major". This grandiosity is also expressed in the quality of the artists that they represent. This is why the research that I have conducted on contemporary art galleries will likely prompt the same reactions as those that resulted from previous research that I conducted in France some 20 years ago on the place of contemporary French artists on the international art scene (Quemin, 2001 and 2002). Some readers were not particularly satisfied to see that I had revealed the weak position held by French artists. Though they did not always go to the trouble to properly (or even briefly) review my previous work, they put forward two rebuttals (largely contradictory, moreover) which they were quick to associate with one another; and they did not stop there. My results were thus declared false because they could simply not be true. However, these results were also described as being accurate—by the very same detractors—but so well known that it was not necessary to discuss them. It is easy to imagine that those who, upon seeing the classification of the galleries that I will present later in this part of the book, will not be satisfied with their placements, will quickly denounce a scientific instrument whose results "couldn't possibly be true." Upon learning about my project to create a ranked list of the most influential galleries in the world, a Swiss gallerist friend replied to me in an email in 2019: "I'm delighted to read this, but you won't only be making friends." As previously occurred at the beginning of the 2000s, my critics will not fail to initiate a domino effect of comments to denounce a "science which disturbs," to borrow the phrase coined by Pierre Bourdieu (Bourdieu, 1993), if only due to its independence. In the early 2000s, the players who felt most directly implicated by my results had no hesitation in trying to shoot them down, both in the worlds of art and social science research; most often by attempting to deploy people in less established professional situations (or even hardly established at all), whose positions were better suited to play the role of infantrymen for their backers.

Essentially, revealing objective positions calls part of the opacity that characterizes the art market into question, and therefore threatens some of the interests at stake in a system in which each player is well advised to exaggerate their real impact. This is because, in a universe that is tightly bound to the rationale of symbolic capital (Bourdieu, 1987)—as in many other social worlds—only the rich get richer (in other words, success begets success), and the "Matthew effect" is in full swing (Merton, 1968). There are similar effects between the gallery, collector, and artist levels. For each context, the financial implications are significant. For example, the overall level of their artist roster makes it possible (or not) for galleries to take on new artists, depending on the reputation and recognition that the galleries already have. This is how Sean Scully—a highly recognized artist (in January 2021 he was ranked 73rd in the world by Artfacts) who was already represented in the United States and in France by the influential Lelong & Co—was occasionally exhibited by the Almine Rech gallery (a major establishment) and eventually also joined the Thaddaeus Ropac gallery, which is among the elite of the gallery world. For such a prominent artist, a new collaboration could only have been envisaged with a gallery that had an outstanding reputation; he thus joined a group of artists that is among the most recognized in the world.

The issue of classification is all the more crucial for those players who appear on the list; not only does it have the objective assessment function that I have just mentioned, thus revealing a reality of their situation, but ranked lists also have a performative dimension. With these two factors combined, it is easy to understand why players do not appreciate being subjected to their rationale, especially if they believe that the results are unfavorable toward them.

In the domain of social sciences, Pierre Bourdieu was probably one of the first authors to draw attention to rankings, through the analyses he devoted to the "hit parade of intellectuals" (Bourdieu, 1984). He did not, however, conceptualize such instruments himself with a view to sociological knowledge. The same remark could be made for all the authors who went on to emphasize the interest of rankings as an area of study for the social sciences. Researchers have generally highlighted the growing influence of quantification and classification undertakings (Mennicken & Nelson Espeland, 2019), especially in art (DiMaggio, 1987), and predicted their future development (Blank, 2007). Other authors have investigated the consequences of ranked lists, and have particularly indicated their capacity to induce anxiety (Bowker & Leigh Star, 2000; Esposito & Stark, 2019). It should be specified here that social science research on ranked lists has focused primarily on the education system, particularly higher education (Gioia & Corley, 2002; Rindova, Williamson, Petkova & Seyer, 2005; Espeland Nelson & Sauder, 2007; Wedlin, 2007; Sauder & Espeland Nelson, 2009; Hazelkorn, 2014; Espeland Nelson & Sauder, 2016; Brankovic, Ringel & Werron, 2018; Erkkilä & Piironen, 2018; Welsh, 2020), especially business and law schools. Presumably, researchers have been challenged by the growing influence of these instruments on their own existence as academics. It should be noted that, outside this area of higher education, research on rankings remains limited; even though ranked lists are ubiquitous in social life today.[1] Furthermore, not only do social science researchers pay little attention to these social facts that have become very widespread, but they limit themselves to analyzing existing classifications, they do not take on the task of developing these lists themselves so as to use them as proper instruments for knowledge.

As part of this research on gallerists and galleries, I wanted to take advantage of the heuristic capacities of ranked lists, but I also wanted to take the fact that the art world—and more particularly the contemporary art world—is very fond of rankings (Quemin, 2013a) into account. This is especially apparent in the case of artists; the most famous of the ranked lists for artists being the Kunstkompass (Verger, 1987; Quemin, 2001,[2] 2002, 2004, 2006, and 2013; Buckermann, 2016). The first edition of this indicator dates back to 1970, practically at the same moment as the emergence of the contemporary art world. This ranking of the 100 most prominent international artists, which has been published almost every year since, appeared in two German magazines successively: first *Capital*, then a brief stint in *Manager Magazine* before returning to the columns of the former. The fact that, despite a fairly obvious bias in favor of German artists, it has persisted since the 1970s, shows that the art world does indeed accord it a certain amount of credit. Moreover, the artists that it presents as being the most venerated are, for the most part, undisputedly some of the most important creators of our time. Following the departure of the Kunstkompass director, *Capital* has published another indicator as of October 2008,[3] the "Capital Kunstmarkt-Kompass." This competing ranked list is produced by the company Artfacts.net, which since 2003 has developed the "Artfacts.net Artist Ranking" (Quemin, 2013b; Bellavance et al., 2018), and as of 2008 has been more widely publicized thanks to a collaboration with *Capital* magazine. Bolstered by its success, the Artfacts ranked list is also regularly published in France by *Le Journal des Arts*,[4] which offers its readers the opportunity of discovering both the list of the 100 most visible artists in the world, as well as another ranking dedicated exclusively to French artists, or artists living in France.

In all rankings, the result obtained depends on the qualifying operations and their weighting. How does the Artfacts classification function?[5] Given the extent to which I will use this data, it is important to clarify this point.

Unlike the Kunstkompass, which excludes events pertaining to the market and which only considers three main types of qualifying occasions (solo exhibitions, group exhibitions, and articles in major contemporary art magazines), the Artfacts ranked list uses a much broader set of qualifying criteria by adding those associated with institutions and pertaining to the market (Moulin, 1992): public institutions with or without a collection, biennials and triennials, other temporary exhibition spaces, contemporary art galleries, fairs, auctions, "art hotels," art magazines and newspapers, publishing houses, art schools, festivals, non-profit associations, art management institutions, and private collections. The whole is, as we can see, quite vast. Without being absolutely exhaustive, this wide-sweeping review of information helps to minimize some risks of possible bias; especially national ones, such as the principal pro-German bias that clearly affects the Kunstkompass (Quemin, 2001, 2002, 2004, 2006, and 2013). While some criteria are more central in the construction of reputations, others are fairly (or even completely) marginal. It is therefore important that the coefficients assigned to these various effects reflect these disparities. To this end, Artfacts has developed an algorithm that assigns them a weight pertaining to the reputation of the artists associated with them. Basically, they receive "network points" (any artist collected by museums and represented by galleries is attributed these points, which are then conferred on the institutions that collect or represent the artists; these points thereby reflect the reputation of a given institution). At each exhibition in a museum or gallery, or during any of the occasions mentioned above, an artist accumulates points. One fact deserves to be underlined: it is not only the qualifying events of the past year that are taken into account; the Artfacts indicator goes far back in time and also assigns a (lesser) weight to older events.

In a press release issued in March 2018 ("ArtFacts.Net's Contribution to Art Basel's Report: 'The Art Market 2018'"), Artfacts was presented as such:

> ArtFacts.Net was founded by Marek Claaßen, an awarded Internet entrepreneur in 2001. Its database currently lists approximately 800,000 exhibitions, 40,000 galleries and institutions, and more than half-a-million artists from 192 countries. ArtFacts.Net monitors artists by providing each with an algorithmically calculated rank derived from quantified criteria such as gallery representation, collecting institutions, institution type and international reach. The ArtFacts.Net ranking makes it possible to compare artists where minimal or no sales data is available. Based in Berlin with a global network of editors, the ArtFacts.Net team represents a unique body of commitment and expertise.

In July 2024, Artfacts referenced more than one million artists worldwide.

The ranking system awards "network points" to artists and "institution points" to galleries and museums based on their level of renown. The scores influence one another; the more renowned the museum or gallery, the more points the artist obtains after an exhibition, and conversely, an influential artist will bring additional points to the museum or gallery if they begin to be associated with it. An algorithm assigns values based on what we call the attention economy. While it may seem confusing logically that institutions and artists mutually influence each other's weight or ranking, sociological analysis has essentially made it possible to show that, in the contemporary art world, artists and galleries (as well as gallerists), just as much as artists and institutions, mutually contribute to each other's reputations and qualification (Moulin, 1992). It is the specific interest of the Artfacts' method to attempt to account for this particularity in the contemporary art world. Unlike other methods—such as the Kunstkompass, in which the significant degree of subjectivity in selecting the predetermined coefficients can introduce considerable bias (the very high representation of German institutions and their excessive impact contribute directly to the highly-placed, likely overestimated, German artists) (Quemin, 2002)—the coefficients that Artfacts attributes to locations are not fixed and subjective. Conversely, they are produced and regularly updated every week by an algorithm according to the certification (Moulin & Quemin, 1993; Moulin, 1995) that they confer on the artists with whom they are associated. Unlike the Kunstkompass, in which the coefficients are fixed and are only modified very occasionally, when the production method of the ranked list is overhauled, the coefficients for Artfacts' classification system are constantly changing.

It should be noted that this primary ranked list is established according to the points accumulated since the creation of the indicator in 1999, but this does not ultimately have as considerable an impact as one might imagine if it is compared to the result that artists would get if only the points that they accumulated in the previous year were retained; as with the Kunstkompass, success leads to success, as the "Matthew effect" dictates (Merton, 1968; Fraiberger et al., 2018). More fundamentally, the very extensive breadth of the database is an essential dimension of this classification.

It may be annoying for some that Artfacts, a private company, does not disclose how it constructs its algorithm in great detail and shields itself behind the tenet of industrial secrecy, as certain other sources do. It should be noted here that I have nevertheless managed to reconstitute a portion of the coefficients attributed to institutions, which seemed to me to be entirely relevant. However, in the absence of perfect transparency on each of the criteria from which it results (but with an essential knowledge of the overall procedure that I believe to be in effect),[6] a method can also be estimated by the result it produces. Furthermore, in the case of Artfacts, the website appears to be a satisfactory source of information for its ranking of artists, especially those at the top of the list.

Prior classifications of galleries or gallerists

There are already sources that aim to summarize the impact of various prominent international galleries in an orderly fashion, and which, in a certain way, constitute prerequisites for the classification that I will present in the next segment of this part of the book. Among these, the best known is the Power 100. In my previous work, I strongly emphasized the caution with which the positions that are meant to be reflected in this indicator must be considered (Quemin, 2013).

The Power 100, published annually since 2002 by the British magazine *ArtReview*, covers a wider population of players in the contemporary art world than gallerists alone. In essence, this indicator extends the classification process far beyond these professionals, and includes the various players within the art world (understood here in the sense of contemporary visual arts and, at the beginning of the indicator's existence, of architecture).[7] These are ordered from the most powerful, which is ranked first, to the 100th position. The Power 100 does not comment on reputation, but on influence; or more precisely, on power.

What legitimacy does the Power 100 have in the contemporary art world? The very important gallerist quoted below, whose name regularly appears on the Power 100 list, has adopted a very critical position toward it:

> The Power 100 is a joke. The ranking mixes artists with dealers, I find that really weird. [. . .] The Power 100 is stupid vanity, you only look at it for fun.

Note, however, that he concedes that, even if it is a distraction, it is possible to consult the ranking in a lighthearted way.

Two delicious anecdotes give an effective overview of the Power 100's influence in the international contemporary art world and the way in which, despite its obvious limits, players can use it to market themselves. The contemporary São Paulo art fair SP-Arte, created in 2005, announced its 2013 edition by presenting itself as the third largest fair in the world behind Art Basel and Frieze Art Fair, which did not fail to surprise. As a matter of fact, the best criterion for classifying fairs would undoubtedly be the revenue that they generate, either at the fair itself or over the weeks that follow, thanks to contacts made during the event. However, there is no data on the transactions that are carried out, which are private and therefore discreet. Another ranking criterion could be suggested in the form of the number of exhibitors, as a large fair can accommodate a decent number of participating galleries because the market generated by it is considerable due to the influx of many very active collectors. In this respect, SP-Arte came in far behind the other two art fairs on the ranked list in 2013 (all three of which took place only weeks apart). SP-Arte had 122 exhibitors, as opposed to 201 galleries for ARCO, the Madrid fair (which is only of midsize impact), and the more than 300 at Art Basel 2013, the domain leader.[8] How then could the São Paulo fair come out with the astonishing claim that it occupied the third-highest position in the world, which is entirely contradicted by its number of participating galleries? The fair asserted that it had hosted the highest proportion (after Art Basel and the Frieze Art Fair in London) of gallerists listed in the Power 100 ranking of the most influential personalities in the art world published by *ArtReview*. One would have to be very naïve to be totally convinced by this rhetoric, but it is revealing of the reputation and a certain legitimacy of the Power 100 that it was thus deployed for communication purposes, as if it could provide an objective assessment of the impact of fairs, even though the reasoning was highly debatable, to say the least.

In the same way, more recently, at the beginning of 2021, the Perrotin gallery issued a communiqué based on the 2020 Power 100. It stated that it could be considered the fourth largest gallery in the world (in 2020, Perrotin was ranked 50th on the Power 100 list, behind Larry Gagosian, David Zwirner, and the partners of the Hauser & Wirth gallery, who placed—I will return to this point later—29th, 30th, and 31st, respectively). However, this edition of the ranking should have, even more than the previous versions, elicited many reservations as to its seriousness; the gallery had suddenly introduced a mass of personalities of African descent to compensate for their significant absence theretofore! A person reading the Power 100 in 2020 would have gotten the impression that the most internationally renowned gallerists had suddenly ceased to exert their power on the contemporary art world, which was clearly not the case. However, the Perrotin gallery was quick to step into the spotlight and accord itself an exaggerated importance on the international art market, based on this very debatable ranked list.

But how is the Power 100 constructed, and how much credit can the social sciences lend to this indicator? In its November 2012 issue, *ArtReview* presented the Power 100 in the following terms:

> The *ArtReview* Power 100, published each year in the November issue of *ArtReview* magazine, is an extensive census of the most powerful figures in the contemporary art world. Entrants are classified according to a combination of the influence exerted on the production of art internationally, their purely financial influence (although, nowadays, this is no longer such an important factor) and according to their activity during the previous 12 months—a criterion that concerns artists, of course, but also collectors, gallerists, and curators. Regular appearances are also made by those who run the primary art fairs, by the directors of museums and foundations, and even occasionally by critics.
>
> *ArtReview*, November 2012

In 2009, the magazine indicated:

> "the *ArtReview* Power 100 ranks the most powerful artists, collectors, curators, and critics in contemporary art."[9] "The Power 100 constitutes an attempt to sketch the contours of the general tendencies and forces that shape the contemporary art world, and, this is particularly important, to give them a degree of transparency that they would not otherwise have" (p. 74).

As I briefly mentioned when first broaching the topic of the Power 100, every year in November since 2002,[10] *ArtReview* has published the hierarchical list of the 100 supposedly most powerful personalities in the international contemporary art world; it would actually be more accurate to say the 100 most powerful "positions," as many of the placements in the ranking are occupied by two people, sometimes three, and exceptionally four. The Power 100 therefore assembles well over 100 people every year. The ranking presents brief biographies of the personalities listed, emphasizing their recent or upcoming news; this is generally accompanied by a photo portrait, sometimes in full-page format.

What exactly is the methodology that has been implemented, and how are the positions assigned in the ranked list? The magazine stated in 2009:

> The Power 100 ranking is decided by a panel of international experts that includes the editors and contributors of *ArtReview*, and a large and growing number of players in the art world who prefer to maintain anonymity for obvious professional and social reasons
>
> *ArtReview*, November 2009, p.74

That same year, the authors explained that, like in each edition, art advisors and art reviews were deliberately excluded from the ranked list. The former because it was difficult to know how power is shared between advisors and collectors; and the latter because it would create a conflict of interest, insofar as it would pass judgment on the place of *ArtReview* in the ranking. In each edition, the main focus is on the distinguished players' influence during the

12 months preceding the ranking, and that which they are likely to exert in the immediate future, hence a fairly high turnover of the personalities selected. In my previous analyses of the Power 100, I calculated renewal rates from one year to the next that are generally around 25 percent, but can be as high as 35 percent (Quemin, 2013b).[11]

Despite the lack of precision on the methodology, like all indicators, the Power 100 claims a certain rigor, which here is supposed to be ensured by the use of "observation" and not "judgment": "the list is based on observation more than judgments as to who is best and who is worst" (in *ArtReview*, November 2012). It should, however, be underlined that the nature of the methodology used to produce the Power 100 is very imprecise. It is perfectly conceivable that the newspaper would involve its own employees, but nothing is known about the mysterious outside personalities who are potentially associated with the ranking process (not even their number—if they do indeed exist—or any of their characteristics) nor what forms the ranking criteria that ultimately lead to annually published ranked lists. It is quite paradoxical that the Power 100, which is meant to reveal a concealed power in the art world (indeed, it is not coincidental that on at least two occasions, the covers of *ArtReview*'s November issue introducing the annual ranked list were adorned with motifs evoking Masonic symbols) does not prove to be more demanding of itself in terms of transparency.

Moreover, certain indications cast doubt on the fact that a significant number of outside experts are truly consulted, and that their opinion is then taken into account and added to that of the other participants (Quemin, 2013b). We can therefore reserve some skepticism about the methodology that would consist of contacting a diversified panel of experts and taking all the opinions received into account each year to establish the ranking by following the answers collected down to the letter. As such, all contemporary architects were removed from the list on the same year. This seems to be more an editorial decision than an aggregation of judgments collected separately. The same applies to institutions (Deutsche Bank and UBS), which simultaneously disappeared from the ranking to make way for individual personalities (alone or in groups); even though their connections to qualifying institutions were often strong. Similarly, in 2006, Google appeared on the list, but in 100th position; this certainly could be a coincidence, but it could also be due to the desire to include this company on the list of entities that exert power on the art world, while conceding the liminal nature of the site in question in this universe. Similarly, while in some years women have featured in much larger numbers—seemingly out of the blue and most likely expressing an editorial statement—the 2020 edition of the ranked list, which was still meant to reflect *power* in the contemporary art world, suddenly featured (as I previously mentioned) a high number of personalities of African descent; a totally trivial maneuver for those who have an intimate knowledge of the contemporary art world. In reading the 2020 edition of the Power 100, one could say (provocatively) that it would have even been urgent to implement public policies to prevent people of African descent from accumulating so much power; it could have even been considered necessary to take action so as to allow people with European heritage to be more integrated into the contemporary art world! More seriously, this overestimation of the power of people of African descent in the contemporary art world and on the market was, in fact, totally superficial; one could imagine that it did not result from the aggregation of answers obtained from multiple experts outside of the newspaper, but that it basically resulted from a decision of the editorial board, both to factor in the "Black Lives Matter" movement and to generate buzz.

The preceding observations show that we have every right to doubt the reliability of an indicator that only reveals its methodology in an extremely vague manner; and for which I have shown that the elected panel, who supposedly hold some power (though not *the* power), see high renewal rates from one year to the next, or strong variations in positions in the rankings (Quemin, 2013b). However, real power should theoretically already entail the ability to stay on the ranked list due to the controlling function that is hypothetically exerted on the art world. It is difficult to see how power could vary so drastically and so abruptly over such a short time, when the social sciences have clearly shown that reputation—which may seem more unstable than power—actually has a remarkable amount of permanence over time.

Although public attention to people or their visibility has generally long been considered to be highly volatile (Belle, 2007; Boorstin, 1961; Cowen, 2000; Kurzman et al., 2007), a more recent and more rigorous empirical approach studying the phenomenon (van de Rijt, Shor, Ward & Skiena, 2013) based on the recurrence of names in the media demonstrated that at high levels of prominence visibility remains very stable over time. My research on contemporary art superstars has fully confirmed this (Quemin, 2013b). My empirical data was also able to corroborate that, as common sense generally dictates, it is often the case that "success begets success"; a perfect illustration of the "Matthew effect" (Merton, 1968; Huber, 1998). An artist is all the more likely to be considered worthy of interest, and even classified as a star in a given year, if they were already considered as such in a previous year. The most accurate factor of predicting success—let alone stardom—is the level of renown or visibility that they had already reached, as shown in another domain of study by Jeffrey Evans Stake (on law school rankings) (Stake, 2006). This can be explained by many factors, including the following: rankings—here in the domain of contemporary art—are influenced by various effects such as the bandwagon effect (Leibenstein, 1950), and self-fulfilling prophecies (Nelson Espeland & Sauder, 2007).

Because of this, it hardly seems possible to me to use the Power 100 as a scientific instrument without smoothing out the strong annual variations that neutralize a large part of the indicator's relevance through its successive editions. Moreover, as it reflects impressions of supposed "experts," much more than objective positions, the classification seems to me to shed light above all on rather vague reputations; these can sometimes turn out, in reality, to be very disconnected from the positions of power that these people actually occupy.

However, even though we can criticize the Power 100 from a researcher's point of view, the fact remains that this list has a relative legitimacy, or at least that it arouses a certain interest within the art world, since it has been published for over 20 years. Additionally, its results are often reproduced by other media outlets or are mentioned by players in the art world. Finally, the social sciences exist to remind us that an instrument can present biases—and even occasionally very significant biases, as is the case with the Power 100—without dismissing its interest from a sociological point of view. However, it is absolutely necessary to keep the existence of these biases in mind, to attempt to identify them, and to control them as much as possible. This then allows for the use of such rankings, imperfect though they may be, in a sociological context.

One of the uses for the Power 100 is demonstrated in the following. In my previous work, I showed that, during the period of 2006–2012, gallerists represented 19.5 percent of personalities from the art world referenced by the Power 100, behind artists (24.9 percent) and collectors (20.7 percent), but far ahead of curators (14.4 percent), museum directors (8.8 percent), critics (4.2 percent), fair directors, auction house managers, and architects (1.7 percent each) (the remaining 2.5 percent of the functions represented refer to a diverse series of activities other than those listed here) (Quemin, 2013b). However, if we take only the 29 personalities who appeared continuously on the Power 100 from 2006 to 2012 and who—by virtue of their systematic appearance stood out as being, in reality, the most powerful, since they had the power to stay in the ranking year after year—the proportion of gallerists increased very significantly (12 personalities out of 29, or more than 4 out of 10). The American gallerist Larry Gagosian therefore appeared at the top of the ranking. Among the top 10 personalities on the ranked list, with this filter applied, were no fewer than six gallerists. In addition to Gagosian, who held the first position, were: the Swiss Iwan Wirth (the third-highest ranked personality, who was constantly on the list); as well as Americans David Zwirner, Marian Goodman, and Marc Glimcher (director of the Pace gallery), who appeared in 5th, 8th, and 10th positions, respectively; and finally the British Jay Jopling (head of the White Cube gallery), who also ranked 18th. Beyond the highly fluctuating data of the Power 100 over the years, when we analyze the people who are most often featured on the ranked list, this clearly demonstrates the power of gallerists. This is despite the fact that in general, as I must repeatedly reiterate here, the indicator is unreliable for a given year. With only five positions each for collectors and artists, these two groups placed far behind gallerists if we considered the 29 players who were continuously featured on the Power 100 (Quemin, 2013b). When approached from this second angle of the regularity of presence, the indicator clearly reflects the strong influence of the market within the contemporary art world (Quemin, 2020b), which was much less the case in the 1980s (Moulin, 1992).

What place have gallerists had on the Power 100 over the past 20 years; which professionals have been featured, and what positions do they occupy? I have studied these points for successive years. In 2002, when the indicator was created, then 5 and 10 years later, and finally, in recent years (2018–2022).

Gallerists listed in the Power 100 of 2002, 2007, 2012, and 2018–2022, and the rankings they occupy:

2002	2007	2012
12. William Acquavella	2. Larry Gagosian	2. Larry Gagosian
18. Jay Jopling	8. Jay Jopling	4. Iwan Wirth
19. Arne Glimcher	10. David Zwirner	5. David Zwirner
23. Larry Gagosian	14. Iwan Wirth	17. Marc Glimcher
26. Nicholas Logsdail	16. H. Blain & G. Southern	18. Marian Goodman
28. Anthony d'Offay	21. Marian Goodman	20. Jay Jopling
33. Victoria Miro	22. Marc Glimcher	24. Barbara Gladstone
39. Ernst Beyeler	27. Matthew Marks	29. Nicholas Logsdail
44. Marian Goodman	33. William Acquavella	34. Tim Blum & Jeff Poe
54. Enrico Navarra	36. Barbara Gladstone	38. M. Sprüth & P. Magers
64. Andrea Rosen	37. D. Lévy & R. Mnuchin	39. Matthew Marks
74. Leslie Waddington	42. Sadie Coles	40. Gavin Brown
76. Harry Blain & G. Southern	43. Victoria Miro	49. Sadie Coles
78. Matthew Marks	54. Jeffrey Deitch	50. Daniel Buchholz
	64. T. Blum & J. Poe	51. Toby Webster
	74. Maureen Paley	55. Michael Ringier
	84. Nicolas Logsdail	62. Emmanuel Perrotin
	95. Javier Peres	66. Thaddaeus Ropac
		71. Luisa Strina
		73. J. Kuri & M. Manzutto
		79. Massimo de Carlo
		82. « team Continua »

2002	2007	2012
		89. Gisela Capitain
		90. Carol Greene
		91. Franco Noero & P. Falone
		94. Maureen Paley
		97. Victoria Miro
		99. Johann König
		100. Gregor Podnar

2018	2019	2020
1. David Zwirner	3. Iwan & M. Wirth	29. Larry Gagosian
6. Iwan & M. Wirth	5. David Zwirner	30. David Zwirner
21. M. Sprüth & P. Magers	23. Marc Glimcher	31. Iwan Wirth & al.
22. Larry Gagosian	27. Larry Gagosian	50. Emmanuel Perrotin
26. Gavin Brown	33. Jay Jopling	57. José Kuri & M. Manzutto
27. Marian Goodman	39. M. Sprüth & P. Magers	58. Nicholas Logsdail & al.
29. Marc Glimcher	42. Marian Goodman	60. Marc Glimcher
32. N. Logsdail & al.	46. Nicholas Logsdail & al.	64. Lorenz Helbling
34. J. Kuri & M. Manzutto	48. Gavin Brown	65. Liza Essers
39. Jay Jopling	52. Emmanuel Perrotin	83. Hyun-Sook Lee
43. Sadie Coles	57. Thaddaeus Ropac	86 – Prateek et P. Raja
48. Daniel Buchholz	59. José Kuri & M. Manzutto	89. « Mendes Wood team »
52. Esther Schipper	60. Hyun-Sook Lee	92. I. Lorenzo & R. Rillo
54. Emmanuel Perrotin	67. Esther Schipper	93. « Continua team »
57. Lorenz Helbling	69. Daniel Buchholz	94. B. Gladstone & G. Brown
64. Thaddaeus Ropac	70. Sadie Coles	
68. Hyun-Sook Lee	74. Almine Rech	

2018	2019	2020
79. Luisa Strina	75. Lorenz Helbling	
82. « Continua team »	84. Luisa Strina	
86. Almine Rech	94. « Continua team »	
89. Tim Blum & J. Poe	96. Massimo de Carlo	
91. Massimo de Carlo	97. « Mendes Wood team »	
93. Tim Neuger & B. Riemschneider	100. David Kordansky	
96. Vanessa Carlos		
98. « Mendes Wood team »		

2021	2022
23. David Zwirner	9. David Zwirner
25. Larry Gagosian	17. Iwan Wirth, Manuela Wirth & Marc Payot
26. Iwan Wirth, Manuela Wirth & Marc Payot	20. Larry Gagosian
32. Marc Glimcher (& Mollie Dent-Brocklehurst)	23. Marc Glimcher
52. Emmanuel Perrotin	30. Monika Sprüth & Philomene Magers
66. Monika Sprüth & Philomene Magers	46. Emmanuel Perrotin
67. Marianne Ibrahim	64. Liza Essers (Goodman gallery)
74. Liza Essers (Goodman gallery)	65. Prateek & Priyanka Raja (Experimenter gallery)
76. Prateek & Priyanka Raja (Experimenter gallery)	75. Hyun-Sook Lee (Kukje gallery)
97. M. Cristiani, L. Fiaschi & M. Rigillo (Galleria Continua)	85. José Kuri & Monica Manzutto (Kurimanzutto gallery)
	91. Isa Lorenzo & Rachel Rillo (Silverlens gallery)
	93. Atsuko Ninagawa
	94. Barbara Gladstone

Based on the sample years that I have selected, during the 2000s there was a strong observable upswing in the power of gallerists (Quemin, 2020b). In 2002, there were still only 14 who were featured in the ranking, and the highest ranked among them—William Acquavella (from the United States)—came out in 12th position; in 2007, there were 18, and Acquavella's compatriot Larry Gagosian rose to 2nd place in the ranking. At the beginning of the 2010s, gallerists represented nearly a third of the personalities featured on the Power 100; and they occupied, moreover, particularly high positions (2nd, 4th and 5th, occupied by Larry Gagosian, Iwan Wirth, and David Zwirner, respectively, in 2012). In 2018 and 2019, the proportion of gallerists fell sharply, to around a quarter of the personalities referenced on the Power 100, and the positions occupied tended to decrease somewhat. In 2020, the drop was much more pronounced, with only 15 gallerists now being featured on the list. Their number fell all the way down to 10 in 2021, before rising slightly to 13 in 2022. Additionally, the positions assigned to gallerists now placed them much lower than they were during the 2010s. This double decline, however, seems to me to reflect less of a real loss in power for gallerists in the contemporary art world than the ever more assertive desire of those responsible for *ArtReview* to give a more intellectual and political dimension to their classification (Quemin, 2013b). This "zeitgeist" is also reflected in the fact of ensuring greater geographical (and ethnic) diversity of the gallerists represented, not unlike (moreover) for all of the personalities appearing in the ranking. In reality, it expresses the *power* suggested by its name less and less—as well as the power highlighted in the editorials that the indicator presents—and it refers more to *influence*. Hence, as I have already mentioned, in the midst of the "Black Lives Matter" movement in 2020, the magazine awarded an astronomically high placement to personalities of African descent and placed them at the top of the ranking, which did not correspond at all to their real power. The number of gallerists then plummeted to only 15 and, in order to leave the top positions to the new personalities that were suddenly being promoted, these professionals suffered a spectacular drop in their rankings. As such, in 2019, the first half of the list still had no fewer than nine gallerists, including two in the top five positions; in 2020, the first half of the list only featured four gallerists, and the highest-ranked of them—Larry Gagosian—only came in at number 29. In 2022, however, the number of gallerists in the first half of the ranking rose to six, and the highest of them—David Zwirner—reached 9th position.

The previous developments seem to me to clearly indicate how much caution we should use when considering the information compiled by the Power 100. From the various publications of the ranked list, we can, however, retain a group of gallerists—and galleries—that regularly appear in recent editions, with rankings that indicate an elevated position in the gallery hierarchy. These include Gagosian, David Zwirner, Hauser & Wirth, Pace (Marc Glimcher), Marian Goodman, and Gavin Brown (recently affiliated with Barbara Gladstone) for the United States; White Cube (Jay Jopling) and Lisson gallery (Nicholas Logsdail) for the United Kingdom; and Sprüth Magers, Emmanuel Perrotin, and Thaddaeus Ropac for continental Europe. Each gallery named here was associated with their main or original area of operations.[12]

Even though I have repeatedly emphasized the extreme caution with which the different editions of the Power 100 and the ranking associated with the personalities being referenced must be considered, given the very serious doubts surrounding the methodology adopted to develop the each year's winners, one could nevertheless expect that the gallerists who have appeared most often in recent years would also feature in a ranking constructed with more methodological rigor, and that would also focus on the elite within the profession. In my work on star artists (Quemin, 2013b), I was able to verify that when analyzing the highest levels of renown, methodology tends to exert little impact on the results that are obtained (Nelson Espeland & Sauder, 2007), whether a complex or less elaborate methodology is used. This is what I was able to demonstrate by revealing and emphasizing the close proximity of the rankings of artists who were placed at the very top of the ArtFacts and Kunstkompass lists in a given year. That is, even though the former includes more than one million artists in the world (in 2024), and the latter only publishes the top 100 positions, the differences between the two lists could be monumental. However, the two rankings are very similar at the top of the respective lists. Even when it comes to a simple aggregation of opinions, as is the case for the Power 100, the star galleries and gallerists are so recognized that their names tend to be suggested as soon as members of the art world raise the question of how to construct a classification system; or they appear quite invariably, no matter the method used to produce a ranking. Some methods, since they are more refined and rigorous than others, can provide more reliable results. However, when considering the most prominent individuals in a social world, even the most rudimentary methods can provide fairly accurate results. Conversely, the further down the rankings one goes, the more the impact of the methodology being applied is felt.

It is also possible to mention other prerequisites for the ranked list of galleries that I will offer here (that have previously been published), this time focusing exclusively on gallerists.

As a direct consequence of the omnipresence of ranked lists in the contemporary art world (Quemin, 2013b), for its 500th issue in 2018, the French magazine *Le Journal des Arts* rewarded its readers with several "ranked lists" to commemorate this anniversary. Among these was the "Top 10 prescriptive galleries."[13] Despite the tantalizing title, this "top 10" was unranked and no methodology was mentioned. While the title advertised prescriptive galleries, the introduction specified: "These establishments embody the revival of Parisian galleries where the public can discover young French and international art. Open to the world, they reflect the dynamism of the French scene," as if prescriptive galleries were not, obviously, the largest of them all. Moreover, somewhat surprisingly, this "top 10" gave the place of honor to galleries in the Parisian neighborhood of Belleville, even at a time when, several months prior, the closure of two out of the three most impactful galleries in the area had already been announced. At the time Belleville, which for a while had attempted to compete with the central district of the Marais, was already in the midst of a total loss of momentum. Finally, a large proportion of the galleries selected had participated in the small fringe fair Paris Internationale; as if this criterion seemed, strangely, to have been employed so as to define what a prescriptive gallery was. The establishments listed were as follows, almost all accompanied by their date of creation: Marcelle Alix (2009), Galerie Allen (2013), Anne-Sarah Bénichou (2016), Crèvecoeur (2009), Antoine Lévi (2011), Freedman Fitzpatrick (created in 2012 in Los Angeles, then moved to Paris the previous winter), High Art (2013), Mor Charpentier (2010), Joseph Tang, Sultana (having opened in Paris in 2010, in the Marais, then moved to Belleville in 2014). The inappropriate title of the various lists, and the complete disregard in terms of methodology once again merit a reminder of the interest generated by ranked lists (Blank, 2007) in the art world. Their mere existence is sometimes sufficient to justify them.

The fact that *Le Journal des Arts* took the initiative to publish ranked lists (or that they referred to those lists as such) is not surprising, given its owner and editor-in-chief's sensitivity to the social sciences. As I have already mentioned, this same media outlet has regularly published rankings of the most prominent artists, both international and French creators, based on Artfacts data. It also incorporated another precedent of ranked lists of contemporary art galleries via the one that I myself had developed to classify established galleries in France. While proceeding in an exploratory manner to conduct the research that ultimately became the provenance of this book, I drew up a ranked list of (French) galleries and was eager to share it widely, particularly among professionals, in order to hear their feedback. *Le Journal des Arts* then published my classification—along with its methodology—in several successive issues in the fall of 2016, the first of which was during the main French contemporary art fair at the time: the FIAC. This specific publication and the emphasis placed on the French art scene led me to integrate elements that reflected how players had been assimilated into said scene, such as the nominees or winners of the Marcel Duchamp Prize (the French equivalent of the Turner Prize in the United Kingdom), or the purchases of works from galleries by national authorities such as the Fonds National d'Art Contemporain (National Contemporary Art Fund). This would be much more difficult, if not impossible, to fit into an international framework. I had also already integrated the data on artist classification produced by Artfacts, a point to which I will very soon return.[14]

Constructing a ranked list of galleries: a sociological perspective

As a result of my long-term familiarity with the very numerous classifications of artists (Quemin, 2013b), once I began down the path of constructing a ranked list of contemporary art galleries, the question of designing a relevant methodology that could substantiate the positions occupied by the various galleries immediately arose.

I decided to develop a classification of galleries in an attempt to synthesize and evaluate information on these establishments (Quemin, 2019 and 2020a). From this perspective, the rankings that can be produced by sociologists do not fundamentally differ from other tools that are often created and used in the social sciences, such as social mobility tables. These instruments are so common in sociology that no one would question their scientific dimension, and their dual function of synthesizing and assessing information is widely accepted. The very fact that rankings exist (and preexist) in the "ordinary" social world does not disqualify them as appropriate tools for sociological analysis, even though the scientific approach is (too) often conceived as being radically different from common (empirical) knowledge of social phenomena (Bourdieu, 1992). In point of fact, the circumstances are more subtle. This can easily be illustrated by mentioning other methods that are widely used in the social sciences. For example, there is a continuity—with no distinct gap—between the ordinary observation of social situations and the specific use of observation by the social sciences in general, and by sociology in particular as a scientific method (Beaud & Weber, 1997). The same can be said for everyday conversations and interviews as another specific method for the social sciences (Blanchet & Gotman, 2007; Kaufmann, 2016). Of course, in the two previous cases—observation and interviews—there is a strong difference between the two opposite poles of the practices (the ordinary and the "purely" scientific). However, it is quite impossible to distinguish a point at which ordinary practices disappear to the "pure" benefit of those pertaining to science. It should not be underestimated that ordinary knowledge plays an important role in the social sciences (Passeron, 1991), especially since any type of knowledge includes an element of scientific thought. This point is not far removed from the quip often made by the sociologist Howard S. Becker in private conversations, when he asserted that "if it's interesting, it's sociology." Deciding to use an instrument that is more spontaneously associated with a non-scientific perspective, and that is often used in journalism—among other social contexts than that of research—does not disqualify it from being an appropriate scientific tool; that is, at least if the methods used to construct it are both rigorous and transparent (i.e., they can be criticized and debated by others [Passeron, 1991]; this is a dimension that many classifications lack when they are produced outside of a scientific context, as non-scientific art world rankings clearly demonstrate).

Having worked as an art critic and art journalist for 10 years, I became familiar with the many rankings that exist in the art world. Having then decided to study them from a sociological point of view in one of my previous books (Quemin, 2013b), I became fully aware, not only of their interest in generating knowledge about the social world that produces them, but also the limitations of many of them in terms of methodology. It therefore became particularly interesting for me to try to work out a classification that would satisfy scientific requirements in terms of rigor better than the "ordinary" or "lay" classifications.

In essence, it is particularly useful and perhaps even essential to evaluate the occupied positions, especially through the use of rankings; as representations can be distorted or skewed, in particular by communication. Hence, this Belgian gallerist with whom I have a friendly relationship told me how surprised he was upon learning to what extent the Thaddaeus Ropac gallery constitutes a major player on the French and international markets:

> To be quite honest, I wasn't even aware of how much of a heavyweight Ropac is on the Parisian market. Obviously, everyone knows him. We all know, without really knowing it, incidentally, that his gallery is one of the biggest in the world, but I thought it was kind of, an Austrian passing through Paris who invested very little in this city. I let myself be fooled a bit by his competitors, who spend a lot of money on communication, advertising, and whom I would have thought were more important in France. If you're a bit outside of the art world, or if you're abroad, of course, you can be fooled.

Therefore, constructing one or more ranked lists in the social sciences means resorting to objective assessment so as to better understand the structuring and hierarchy of a social world by breaking with preconceptions (Durkheim, 2011).

The false approach to classification based on gallery revenue

Quite obviously, an initial approach open to analysts would consist of ordering galleries according to their economic impact, based on their revenue. Although it comes to mind almost spontaneously, this way of proceeding is an aporia. Raymonde Moulin—whose pioneering role in the socio-economic analysis of the art market I have frequently referenced—proposed an examination of the role of gallerists in the promotion of art, by investigating the strategies that they utilize. However, she never sought to study the organization of this social world as such by analyzing the factors of its segmentation; neither in 1967 in *Le marché de la peinture en France* (*The French Art Market*), nor later in *L'artiste, l'institution et le marché* (*The Artist, the Institution, and the Market*) (Moulin, 1967 [1987] and 1992).

In fact, this lack of attention to the hierarchy of the gallerist profession can be explained by the fact that Moulin warned against the difficulties, or even impossibility, of knowing the reality of artistic transactions that take place in the form of private sales, as well as their amounts. In the third part of *The French Art Market*, entitled "Transactions," she highlights the following: "it is difficult to know the prices from private sales, as is the quantity of paintings sold" (p. 366). She continues: "To study the market of private sales, as to study the black market during the war years, there is no other way than to aggregate the observations and to try to identify an overall impression, with all the necessary reservations" (p. 367) (Moulin, 1967 [1987]). It should be particularly emphasized that Moulin was speaking at the time only of *impressions*, and definitely not *estimations*, and is thus in an antithetical position to recent economists, who have generally shown a great amount of negligence in this matter. In her later book, *The Artist, the Institution, and the Market* (published in 1992), that also regards the (mainly French) art market, she continues: "it is impossible to accurately assess the number of sales made in the artists' studios and through galleries. The evaluation method proposed here is based on extrapolation, using the only available statistics, those of foreign trade and the Professional Committee of Art Galleries" (p. 233). Suffice it to say that, while she ventured to produce figures and even to use the term "evaluation," she preferred to entrust the responsibility to sources other than herself. When, despite her previous approaches, she grew bolder in estimating the amount of exports of contemporary art sales in France to be 70 percent—and tax evasion to be a minimum of 30 percent[15]—she nevertheless concluded: "My assessment of the volume of transactions remains, in all likelihood, well below the reality, as the art trade is characterized by its non-transparency" (Moulin, 1992, p. 235).

In light of the previous admonitions, one can therefore only be surprised at the naivety of the media, which regularly publishes figures on artistic transactions even though an elemental familiarity with the art market would suffice for one to be convinced that they have no credibility, except for those who want to believe them. This is because, when it comes to the art market, like many other domains, figures are fascinating (Lamont, 2012; Spoerhase, 2018; Mennicken & Nelson Espeland, 2019), and they frequently function as shields; simply due to the fact of being produced, they too often prevent us from questioning their accuracy. Furthermore, rare are the authors who are sufficiently scrupulous to account for both their precise method of development and the possible limits that may characterize their classification. In point of fact, it seems to me that the more debatable the figures are, the less their authors go to the trouble to caution against all the uncertainties that surround them.

Of the two segments that comprise the art market, public sales and private transactions, the former is by far the most transparent.[16] However, even in this domain, there can be uncertainty about what a change of owner during an auction actually entails, or about the actual amounts, even though sales prices are public. For example, it is well known that not all auctions in China are systematically followed by a sale, as the practice of "irresponsible bidding" is particularly widespread compared to in the West. A percentage of transactions concluded at auctions in China are then not paid by the buyers, and an unpaid good is then able to be put back onto the market and sold (for real this time) at a lower price. Even outside of China, regarding some ultra-publicized record prices, the market is not lacking in rumors that the advertised prices have not been paid. This French gallerist confidently asserted to me: "In the case of the sale of Damien Hirst in 2008, the exceptional price that his skull sculpture reached, it was just hot air. The price was, in fact, never paid. Several people in the industry have assured me of this." The following collector, who is the former department head of an auction house (also married to an art advisor, and therefore well integrated into the various roles that exist in the art market), also confided to me:

> The *Salvator Mundi* by Leonardo da Vinci, which was advertised everywhere as having been sold for \$450 million, was supposed to be loaned in 2017 as part of an exhibition, and its insurance value wasn't declared at \$450 million, but at . . . \$175 million! But then, what price was actually paid? And the person who orchestrated the sale, and who was presented to us as practically a genius for having reached such a staggering amount, he left the auction house very soon after. Officially, it was of his own free will, but I think he was pushed out the door. Since then, we haven't heard from him at all, it's as if he's been forgotten.

In the two previous examples, it is not possible to determine the veracity of the transaction prices, although they were made public, specifically because certain rumors would indicate that these sales might have been manipulated. However, these comments were made by art market insiders, whose positions allow them, if not to definitively guarantee the accuracy of the facts reported—which should also be taken with a grain of salt—at least to express a skeptical point of view that therefore seems credible in the eyes of some professionals themselves.

This demonstrates that even auctions, although they remain known in a largely reliable manner by simple virtue of their public nature, remain afflicted by a degree (admittedly reduced) of opacity or scheming. This applies in particular to the largest transactions, which are likely to set new price points.

The analysis of public transactions is always more pertinent than the sales market in galleries, whether the transactions take place in their own spaces or within the framework of a fair. In this case, neither the number of works sold nor the prices are generally made public. Even when both are advertised, there is little means to verify the veracity of each transaction. The fair reports that are widely published in the specialized art press, which indicates transactions as well as prices (neither of which can be verified), are therefore somewhat amusing. They actually reflect a lack of seriousness on the part of the journalists or editorial staff who request this information, as it is almost impossible for them to acquire it reliably.

Generally speaking, unless a gallery has sold extremely poorly at a fair in a given year and does not wish to apply for the same fair the following year—which may lead it to take revenge by making very harsh comments about the event—gallerists always claim to have sold well. This is because, like all markets, the art market is based on trust. Sending it a signal of a reversal of fortune, or even a simple slowdown, carries the potential of shooting oneself in the foot. Gallerists therefore almost always express a sense of satisfaction that is, if not complete—which is not at all uncommon—then at least comfortable. On more than one occasion, gallerists have told me of their great satisfaction when I (even discreetly) asked them about their performance at the end of a fair, claiming to have sold very well; then, months later, no longer remembering having made such declarations to me, these same professionals conceded that their sales had been disastrous, and that they had therefore given up on participating in the same fair the following year. In a similar way, this gallerist who runs an establishment with locations in two European countries made fun of the information communicated by one of the directors of a competing gallery, with whom he maintains cordial ties, while being even closer to the owner of the gallery for which this director works. The following interview extract clearly shows that, in general, the information being transmitted aims to produce an impression (which is sometimes false) of success:

> When I ask [P] if a fair worked out well for them, he almost always answers that business was very good, that it went very well. But often, some time later, I meet with his boss, who's a close friend of mine, and when we talk about it, he tells me without watching what he's saying that the fair was a disaster for them [he laughs]. It's part of the game.

I am well aware that, if I had not maintained close relationships with many gallerists for a very long time—some for 20 years; and some of whom I even knew as teenagers, before they became gallerists, from being invited to the houses of their parents who themselves worked in the art market—I would probably never have had access to such confidences, which are reserved for "insiders" (Becker, 1963). The following point should also be emphasized: essentially gallerists, like all players in the art market, often say that you have to buy when the market is in a period of euphoria, because it is flourishing; and that you have to buy in times of crisis, because it is the best time to do business. This persistent yet excessive optimism extends from the market situation to individual transactions, and even the art press (part of which maintains a certain proximity with galleries) serves as a relay for the always exaggeratedly optimistic assertions. In the same way that the sales made by galleries at fairs often tend to be overestimated, it is amusing that the press almost invariably reports, year after year, that fairs are still moving upmarket. The only times at which galleries acknowledge disappointing results are when they seek state aid, as these circumstances have led them to seriously rethink their usual discourse.

The sale of da Vinci's *Salvator Mundi* in 2017 was not the only event that threw the media into a tizzy because of the staggering price that had initially been reported. Two years earlier, in February 2015, the private sale of a painting by Paul Gauguin, *Nafea Faa Ipoipo* (1892), was widely covered by the media. The *New York Times* in particular reported a price of $300 million, which made it the most expensive work of art ever sold. At the time, the information was broadly reproduced by the media, most often without indicating the slightest doubt as to the transaction's amount. However, since the intermediary Simon de Pury had not received the commission that he was due, he appealed to the Swiss justice system to recover the $10 million that he was owed. In this case, the real price was then necessarily revealed and it appeared that, far from $300 million, Gauguin's painting had been sold for $210 million; meaning that the media had overvalued its price by 43 percent! In addition to this considerable discrepancy with the advertised price, which had been very widely broadcasted without the slightest hesitation, it is worth highlighting another essential piece of information provided by the legal procedure: the work had indeed been sold. Since the transaction had taken place in a private setting, it could just as well have been the case that the sale, although announced, never actually occurred. This simple example of a singular transaction with a huge discrepancy between the announced sales price (or the price that the media had believed) and the actual transaction price should encourage the greatest caution when commentators consider the segment of the art market that pertains to private sales.

It is therefore all the more regrettable that, despite such cases—which are absolutely indisputable—some authors still indulge in producing figures presented as "estimates" of the market (whose superficial dimension is nevertheless vital to highlight given the false reflections that they impart). Another example: in 2000, the prestigious art fair TEFAF began publishing an annual report on the global art market with a year-by-year "estimate" of the total amount of all art sold internationally. As of 2008, the work was performed by the economist Clare McAndrew. However, in 2016, she accepted an offer from Art Basel—which specializes in contemporary art—and its partner, the Swiss bank UBS. McAndrew's departure forced TEFAF to entrust the production of its annual report to another author: professor of finance Rachel Pownall. For a year, two competing reports were thus published, both with the intention of making an estimate of the global art market. For the year in question, 2016, for which two "estimates" were produced by two competing economists, the difference in results turned out to be enormous. The McAndrew/Art Basel/UBS estimate (McAndrew, 2017) ($56.6 billion in revenue for the entire art market in 2016 (-11 percent variation compared to 2015) / 296,315 private sellers worldwide) listed $11.6 billion more, and was 26 percent higher than that produced by Rachel Pownall (Pownall, 2017) ($45 billion in sales in 2016 [up 1.7 percent compared to 2015] with an estimate of only 51,000 private sellers worldwide, almost six times less than McAndrew). Despite these considerable differences in the "estimates" produced by these two authors, there was absolutely no possibility of determining which of the various figures given were the most correct (or the least false), and it was not even possible to confirm whether some of them were relevant to at least some extent. It should be noted that the difference in appreciation of the private transactions market was all the more enormous as the amount reached by the auction market had to be identical for the two authors; according to Artprice, it amounted to $12.45 billion in 2016 (Artprice, 2017). If we subtract this amount from each of the estimates by McAndrew on the one hand, and Pownall on the other, the former must therefore have estimated private transactions to be at $44.14 billion, the latter at $32.55 billion. McAndrew therefore believed she could indicate an amount generated by private transactions that was over a third higher than that calculated by Pownall.

Faced with the worrying lack of rigor thus flagrantly demonstrated by the comparison of the two reports and the totally divergent figures from 2016, TEFAF immediately decided to refrain from publishing future annual reports with an estimate of the global art market, including both public and private sales. Art Basel and its partner UBS were then able to continue their publications on the art market without any competition that could contradict them (or, more precisely, that could reveal the inherent vanity in claiming to be able to seriously estimate a market whose flows are, by their very nature, discreet). Although this demonstration makes it difficult to dispute that the figures provided to "estimate" the global art market (including private transactions) are totally lacking in rigor, the problem was partly solved by TEFAF immediately ceasing to produce its own figures. Wisely, the fair quickly made the following announcement: it would now concentrate on producing "very in-depth and focused reports that would now cover a variety of topics." However, Art Basel, UBS, and McAndrew did not seem fazed by the huge difference in estimates with their former competitor, and they continued to publish their annual report with renewed "estimates" of the global art market year after year.[17] Nevertheless, the least that can be said is that the discrepancy between McAndrew's and Pownall's results raised relevant questions about the ability to measure an opaque market; it is highly regrettable that the (small) debate sparked by the publication of two radically different "estimates" ended before it had taken on proportions that would have been worrying for their authors. Still, such a debate would have been perfectly legitimate. Some commentators (though too few of them) occasionally warn against published data that claims to reflect the entirety of the art market, indicating their highly unreliable nature. As such, in his editorial in issue 14 of the French art magazine *La Gazette Drouot* of April 7, 2017, entitled "Prices and Reports," the editor-in-chief Sylvain Alliod asserted: "Nothing other than the evaluation of the global art market marks a difference of $11.6 billion, no less! For Rachel Pownall, it is up 1.7%, but down 11% for Clare McAndrew. It could almost be funny, if the problem of this volatile data did not prevent public authorities from taking a fairly opaque market more seriously" (p. 3).

My highlighting the extreme limitations of these art market "evaluations" is in no way unfounded. I have provided two illustrations of these limitations; from different private sales and from reports claiming to encompass the entire market. As previously indicated, it is impossible to know whether either of the two figures produced in the same year on the art market was even remotely credible. It could even be that either of the two "evaluations" were totally superficial, as all estimates that claim to reflect an essentially discreet market inevitably are.

I feel it necessary to mention and build on the previous point in order to emphasize that, even in the case of aggregated data on the art market, and although they include auction sales (which do not vary between authors, since the sales prices are made public), the differences that can be found in various estimations are, quite simply, enormous. Nevertheless, it should be mentioned that in addition to a considerable difference in the estimated total, the detail of the amount that corresponds to each gallery, or even each sale, could be even greater; and that disparate errors may partially offset one another when the amounts are added together. Estimating the global art market by including private transactions and each gallery's proceeds is a pipe dream, since private sales can never be known with any precision. As previously mentioned, it is often said in the art world that two of the largest galleries in the world, Gagosian and Pace, have been selling over $1 billion worth of artworks annually for years. Once again, it is impossible to verify this information. The very fact that many leading galleries in the contemporary art world have branches in different countries makes it more difficult to appraise the scope of their business, as well as to know where the works are actually sold. This is not always reflected, even in the figures that galleries provide when they pay their taxes. Anyone who is sufficiently integrated into the art market and who is a real insider also knows that not all sales are declared.[18] Although referring to the respective economic results of contemporary art galleries could have been considered as the best way to proceed in developing a ranked list of these establishments, my knowledge of both the existing data (and their indisputable limitations) and the social world of galleries has convinced me that it was, in fact, impossible to do so on the basis of sales or revenue. When it comes to private sales organized by galleries, researchers must be wise and honest enough to admit that it is impossible to produce satisfactory data concerning this segment of the art market.

My consistent presence in the domain, and the close relationships I have maintained with many gallerists, have only confirmed the previous point. The following conversation with an important French gallerist with whom I have maintained a very cordial relationship for 20 years illustrates that anyone who is truly familiar with the art market cannot run the serious risk of producing an evaluation that includes transactions carried out by galleries:

- *Me: [P] states that he has a revenue of 80 million. 80 million is still very high. How much do you make?*
- Her: It's none of your business.
- *Me: But if someone were to ask you in an anonymous survey, would you answer?*
- Her: No, of course not. But if I did answer, it would be so imprecise that, in any case, it wouldn't be usable.

This simple extract exemplifies the total lack of seriousness (or cynicism) on the part of economists or sociologists who think or maintain, even if they may not have any conviction, that galleries will honestly disclose their sales figures. In a similar way, the conversation that I had in 2019 with this gallerist who manages an establishment with locations in three countries (over two continents) illustrates that it is hardly possible to consider gallery revenue as a means of classification:

- We're growing at full throttle, but we're still far from certain fellow gallerists with whom we share artists. Last year we made €8 million in revenue, [X] made 30.
- *Me: And anyway, that's the declared figure, he probably made a lot more . . .*
- Him: Yes, it's true, and he surely declares certain sales as having been made in [another country where the gallery also has a location] when they were really made in France in order to reduce his revenue here. But there are also, of course, all the sales that may have been "forgotten" [he smiles].

The same lack of accuracy and transparency in declared sales figures is evident in the words of this collector:

> Once, I wanted to send a work back to [X, an influential international gallery of French origin] for a refund so I could buy a new one, so I had to pay a lot in taxes. My husband and I talked about it, and we found a solution. I then went to see my contact at the gallery and the accountant with my husband, and he explained the plan to them. We changed the sale price and the purchase price that would be declared, it didn't make

them lose anything, but for me it made a significant difference. The same thing then happened with [Y, an influential establishment of foreign origin with a prominent location in France]. We agreed on both prices, but they're the ones who immediately suggested that I declare other amounts so that I could pay less in tax.

The principles adopted for constructing the ranked list of the best galleries that I have developed

Utilizing artist rosters to qualify galleries: a mirroring qualification

Insofar as it turned out, in reality, to be generally impossible to rank the most important galleries in the world based on their revenue—as I have just shown—how else could I proceed? Essentially, I decided to consider gallery rosters, as the quality (Misdrahi Flores, 2013) of the gallery's artists is directly linked to the quality associated with the gallery itself. To put it in other terms, there is a structural homology (Bourdieu, 1992 and 1996) between the level of the gallery and the level of its artists, with both qualifying each other mutually. There is therefore a reciprocal, "mirroring" qualification of galleries[19] and the artists they represent. So what is a "leading" gallery? It is fundamentally a gallery that represents prominent or leading artists. Symmetrically, what is a "leading" artist? It is an artist who is represented by a leading gallery. For establishments, representing recognized artists is a privileged means of attesting to their quality and their truly contemporary nature. It should be noted that, while it is important that they attract and/or retain artists who have achieved significant levels of renown, for a given degree of recognition, galleries generally prefer to work with the most sought-after creators in the market; that is, those whose price points are high and for whom demand is greatest. There are very well-known artists whose works sell poorly (Moulin, 1987), but this lower market value is usually relative. Moreover, including this type of artist on a gallery's roster and in its lineup can help it to avoid an overly "commercial" label. An artist's reputation (Quemin, 2013b) is therefore highly prized, regardless of the more or less commercial segment (Moulin, 1992) on which creators have positioned themselves, in spite of the general preference among gallerists for artists who sell best.

The qualifying power of the most influential galleries draws attention to the artists who join their roster, and helps to promote their success by creating a phenomenon of certifying the value of art (Moulin & Quemin, 1992) via the "collection effect." For example, this Swiss gallerist with whom

I have a friendly relationship explained the success of an artist who had recently joined the ranks of the Gagosian gallery—one of the heavyweights on the market—with the "collection effect" thus evolving to its ultimate iteration in the form of the "Gagosian effect":

> Everyone is talking about [this artist] basically . . . but it's the Gagosian effect . . . pure speculation . . . and his show at [X] during Art Basel last year was also a catastrophe, but hey, Gagosian represents him now, so that gives him the space, the credit, he benefits from the machine.

It also seemed appropriate for me to base my ranked list of galleries on the recognition of their represented artists insofar as artists are absolutely essential to the gallery sphere, as I emphasized earlier in this book. As the French gallerist Jean-Gabriel Mitterrand explained: "in a gallery, you operate from day to day: you run after a certain kind of success, that is to say after renowned artists. Then you have to take care of them, know how to sell them (or else they leave you), help them set up big exhibitions in museums" (*Le Journal des Arts*, no. 522, April 26, 2019, "Jean-Gabriel Mitterrand, Gallerist: 'We Want to Work with Established Artists'"). It is clear from these comments that success for galleries is highly dependent on the artists, and even collectors are secondary to them. Attracting leading creators will thus drive buyers to engage with their gallery.

The absolutely central role of the artist roster for a gallery is also evident in the case of the Blain / Southern gallery which, as previously mentioned, was forced to close its doors in 2020. The gallery was created in 2010 by Harry Blain and Graham Southern, the former partners of Haunch of Venison, an establishment that they had sold to Christie's in 2007. Thanks to their previous experience and their contacts in the sector, the two partners were then able to attract important, already recognized artists, such as Mat Collishaw and Bill Viola, right off the bat. After the departure of one of the two partners, Graham Southern, in the fall of 2019, no fewer than five artists left the gallery: Henning Strassburger and Rachel Howard, but especially the highly reputed artists Mat Collishaw, Jake & Dinos Chapman, and Sean Scully.[20] In February 2020, Harry Blain announced that he would be closing his three galleries in London, Berlin, and New York. While other problems may also have existed, these defections of their most recognized artists inevitably put the final nail in the coffin for the gallery. A gallery's ability to maintain massive spaces that are well situated in the largest art metropolises and employ many staff members—other factors that bespeak its power—is only possible if it has a roster of artists whose works are likely to sell highly enough to cover these fixed costs.[21]

The following is another example. A director of one of the largest galleries in the world also emphasized that artists are absolutely essential in the gallerist profession, at least at the highest level, and all the more so because the most recognized artists are not substitutable:

> The difficulty, when you want to start a gallery, is fundamentally to have artists, the right artists, especially those who are already recognized, and not having to start from square one. Even if, like me, we have a very good network of collectors, even if we have significant financial support thanks to a backer, and I wouldn't have any trouble convincing some of our collectors to support me, but convincing renowned artists, or even ones who are still on the rise, to join my gallery, it would be practically impossible. That's why I'm not branching out on my own. People tell me that I should, but they don't understand that what is central to our profession is the artists. The right ones.

Gallerists and artists therefore qualify each other, and the methodology that I have developed aims to reflect this essential aspect.

The use of Artfacts artist data

Given the familiarity that I have acquired with ranked lists of artists in my previous work (Quemin, 2013b), I decided to start with data taken from Artfacts (more specifically, from their lists of artists). However, in the French version of this book (published in 2021), I had to specify a fact that may, on first sight, have been surprising. Whereas Artfacts is mainly known for its ranked list of artists, in terms of its data pertaining to reputation or visibility, it also produced quantified data on galleries. Thus, a lesser-known fact is that galleries are also referenced by Artfacts, and are even assigned a ranking. Nevertheless—somewhat surprisingly—while it would have been very simple for Artfacts to aggregate all the galleries in a numbered tabulation in order to have a full ranked list, the company had never undertaken such an initiative at the time. When we acknowledge the appetite of the contemporary art world for a wide variety of classifications, not only of artists (Quemin, 2013b), this was by no means surprising. The explanation undoubtedly lay in a major aberration in the data that Artfacts produces on galleries; namely, the top position, which in 2021 was attributed by the algorithm to the Leo Castelli gallery. This establishment which at the beginning of 2023, was still ranked in third position, was in fact the most influential in the world from the 1960s to the 1980s (and even up to 1990) (Cohen-Solal, 2009). However, although it still exists—having survived the passing of its founder—it occupies an extremely secondary position on the international art market. The top position, which for a long time was attributed to the Leo Castelli gallery but very clearly harkens back to a bygone era, stemmed from an effect of hysteresis (Bourdieu, 1992). Even its recent third position placement at the beginning of 2023 was extremely exaggerated. Much more than a piece of information pertaining to a real ranked list of galleries, such a placement clearly testified to the indicator's inertia. It was an aberration that even a minimal amount of familiarity with the contemporary art world would immediately decry, as the Leo Castelli gallery has become completely auxiliary on the contemporary art scene. This case is a useful reminder that in the age of "big data," it is not enough to produce data; we must also think about how it is constructed, as well as its relevance. In addition to the quality of the data, the ways in which it is utilized and subsequently interpreted are essential stages in research. The Leo Castelli gallery's totally confounding position, which was a result of poorly thought-out data, and had not been subject to any kind of critical examination so as to correct an obvious bias produced by this method, negated all credibility from such a ranked list. This is certainly why Artfacts had never put forward such a classification.

Note, however, that while the top position occupied by the Leo Castelli gallery in 2021, or even its number three ranking at the beginning of 2023, completely invalidated any ranked list that was produced based on rankings attributed to the galleries by the Artfacts website, the other positions were on the whole much more credible, especially at the top of the list. The following galleries in particular could be found in the rankings (as of February 2023): Gagosian, first; Ropac, second (it was ranked third in 2021, and in 2019 was only awarded 10th position by Artfacts!); Leo Castelli, third (i.e., a truly aberrant position given its low current impact, making it the only real oddity at the top of the list); Hauser & Wirth, 4th (in 2021, this gallery was only ranked 18th by Artfacts); David Zwirner, 5th; Sprüth Magers, 6th; White Cube, 7th (surprisingly, this highly recognized gallery was ranked only 39th in 2021); Lisson, 8th; Pace, 9th (it was ranked 4th in early 2021).

Between 2021 and the beginning of 2023, the Artfacts top 10 seems to have grown in global relevance and, as we will see, the initial 2023 positions were much more similar to the international ranking of galleries that I published in 2021. At the start of 2023, the Artfacts ranking continued as follows: Perrotin, 13th (this ranking is surprisingly favorable given the low overall recognition of the gallery's artists); Almine Rech, 14th (the gallery was ranked 24th at the start of 2021), Lelong & Co, 16th; Continua, seventeenth (this gallery came in at only 37th in 2021); Chantal Crousel, nineteenth; Massino de Carlo, 23rd; Esther Schipper, 25th; Marian Goodman, 27th (such a low ranking is undoubtedly very surprising for one of the most recognized galleries in the world); Templon, 31st; Nathalie Obadia, 40th; Kukje, 47th; Gladstone, 61st; Victoria Miro, 88th; Paula Cooper, 91st (surprisingly, as she was in the 69th position in 2021). Note that Xavier Hufkens, Konrad Fischer, and Greta Meert only placed in 152nd, 172nd, and 478th positions, respectively, in February 2023; which may seem like very low rankings for these well-known galleries. Finally, unexpectedly, the Mennour gallery, which had placed in 30th position in the Artfacts ranking at the start of 2021, fell to 77th in February 2023. Meanwhile, Fortes d'Aloia & Gabriel fell from the 23rd position to 523rd, which could only result from a gross error on the site.

Although Artfacts attributed rankings to galleries on its website, it had never published a proper list of rankings; this could be explained by the fact that the position of the Leo Castelli gallery could not be justified, and tended to discredit any attempt to construct such an indicator. However, things suddenly changed in the summer of 2023. For the very first time, Artfacts sent a newsletter to its subscribers presenting its brand new ranked list of galleries. Its methodology remained very obscure, however; the newsletter only indicated:

> The gallery ranking is created using an algorithm which incorporates the following 4 factors to quantify their performance:
>
> 1 Talent discovery—the number of top artists a gallery has shown within the artist's first year of their career
> 2 Talent representation—the number of trending artists a gallery has shown over an extended period of time
> 3 Fair participation—the gallery's footprint at international art fairs
> 4 Exhibition programme—the gallery's exhibition programme and the ranking of their artists.
>
> in *Artfacts Newsletter*, June 13, 2023

As Artfacts had created its own proper gallery ranking out of the blue—without a single explanation—the ranking of the Leo Castelli gallery, which had been named the third-best gallery in the world just a few months before, suddenly dropped to 445th. Moreover, all the previous positions held by the historic gallery were recalculated without mention. For instance, without any justification, its position for the year 2019 suddenly became 398th, and it was 356th for 2021.

The ranking that was presented by Artfacts was fairly similar to the one that I published in 2021, and even more so to the one that I present later in this book for the year 2023—with some very notable exceptions—and it demonstrated a very clear bias toward galleries with numerous locations in the world, even if their list of represented artists was not as strong:

1 Gagosian[22]
2 Hauser & Wirth
3 Thaddaeus Ropac
4 David Zwirner
5 Pace
6 Galleria Continua
7 Perrotin
8 Almine Rech
9 Lelong & Co

10 White Cube
11 Lisson
12 Marian Goodman
13 Sprüth Magers
14 Marlborough
15 Goodman
16 Massimo de Carlo
17 Michael Werner
18 Max Hetzler
19 Nathalie Obadia
20 Kamel Mennour

Rather surprisingly, some galleries (though not all of them), were associated with one city that was probably considered their main location; However, it was not always the one in which they had been created. I mentioned earlier that the Leo Castelli gallery had all of a sudden been downgraded, and that its long-standing presence at the top of the Artfacts ranking was a clear occurrence of a hysteresis effect (Bourdieu, 1992). The Marlborough gallery's very high position (14th) in the recent Artfacts ranking is problematic, as this establishment, which in the past was considered a leader in the field, only plays a minor role on the contemporary art market today. In April 2024, the Marlborough even announced that it was closing. Its position in the Artfacts ranking of galleries clearly expresses another patent case of the hysteresis effect (Bourdieu, 1992). Still, as the information provided on the construction methodology of the ranking remains quite vague, it is impossible to understand how the algorithm could arrive at such an unlikely conclusion, and it casts doubt on the previous ranking in its entirety.[23]

Artfacts data: the quality of data as pertains to artist rankings

Insofar as I have just indicted that it is—unfortunately—not possible to rely on the rankings that the Artfacts website associates with various galleries (this would have saved me a great amount of work in processing quantitative data), it is important to consider the quality of the data produced by Artfacts on artists, since it is their rankings that I used to construct my own indicator. What credit should be accorded to the data produced by Artfacts in this respect?

It would be appropriate to highlight the following dual fact: the artist rankings present, on the whole, a genuine reliability that an intimate knowledge of the art world and market can corroborate; but in some rare cases, the data presents certain limitations. I have shown in my previous work that artist rankings are generally very reliable at the top of the list, and the method adopted (as long as it shows a degree of consideration and is formalized) ultimately does not matter very much (Quemin, 2013b). However, the rankings become less reliable at the bottom of the list. This can be explained in particular as follows: when an artist is highly recognized, they are associated with institutions that are themselves very prominent, and that present little risk of escaping the observer's sphere of knowledge. Furthermore, the artist is so visible that, among the multitudes of places where they could be featured, even if some were to be neglected—which is unlikely—the great number of their other presentations would largely compensate for this limited deficiency.

Among the artists with the highest rankings on Artfacts, one of them seemed to me to be egregiously out of place; the case is exceptional enough that it deserves mention. According to the website, Olga Kisseleva was, in February 2021, the 128th most prominent artist in the world (and the 85th if we only consider living artists). This fact could be all the more surprising for a French audience, as this artist lives (at least for part of the year) in France, where her reputation remains limited. As such, she came in on the Artfacts ranked list behind Kader Attia (22nd), Christian Boltanski (57th), Daniel Buren (88th), Pierre Huyghes (101st), Laure Prouvost (111th), and Sophie Calle (124th). However, she was supposedly more recognized than Mounir Fatmi (129th), Philippe Pareno (149th), Camille Henrot (159th), and Ito Barrada (199th). The ranking that the algorithm assigned to Annette Messager was also terribly low compared to that of Kisseleva; Messager coming in at 279th position. Moving even further down the ranking of French artists, one could see that ORLAN was ranked only 810th. It was particularly interesting to compare ORLAN's Artfacts ranking with that of Kisseleva, insofar as they are two women artists living in France, and whose work incorporates the capacities of new technologies (even if ORLAN's work, which spans six decades, extends far beyond this qualification). Despite the fact that ORLAN is an internationally renowned artist to whom a large number of monographs have been dedicated—and who features in a great many books all over the world that analyze performance, body art, and even new technologies—this was in no way reflected in her Artfacts ranking, which is nevertheless intended to reflect creator visibility. She has had several international exhibitions, and is represented by the Ceysson & Bénétière gallery, which has locations in France, Luxembourg, the United States and Japan; with a grand total of six main spaces. ORLAN's Artfacts blurb mentioned the three artists with whom she is most often exhibited as being Cindy Sherman, VALIE EXPORT, and Marina Abramovic; three superstars of the international scene. On the same ranked list, the page dedicated to Kisseleva mentioned that the three artists with whom she was most often exhibited were AES +F . . . ORLAN (!), and Lucy & Jorge Orta. It was evident that these creators were of less renown than those who were associated with ORLAN. The discrepancy between the rankings of these two French visual artists, as I have just indicated, is all the more disconcerting as it has persisted (in a broadly inexplicable manner) for several years. Note that this striking aberration in the respective rankings of these two artists has since been corrected. Thus, in February 2023, Kisseleva was ranked 1,131st, and her past rankings have dropped quite a bit (her ranking in 2021 was then rectified to the 1,213th position), while ORLAN jumped to the 615th place.

Another telling example is that in August 2019, the very prominent Swiss artist, Nicolas Party, was represented by the influential Xavier Hufkens gallery in Brussels and by the heavyweight Pace gallery in New York (he had joined the latter several weeks earlier); as well as by the Kaufmann Repetto gallery in Milan, the Modern Institute in Glasgow, the Galerie Gregor Staiger in Zurich, and the Karma gallery in New York. Despite this, his Artfacts blurb only mentioned two galleries (they were admittedly indicated as merely a selection, but on what basis?): Kaufmann Repetto and Gregor Staiger. One could presume that his Artfacts ranking (2,214th) was directly affected by these astonishing omissions.[24]

More generally, the Artfacts data on artists sometimes permanently disregards certain exhibitions—including individual ones—or even the names of certain galleries that represent an artist, which can significantly affect an artist's position. However, as I have already mentioned, the more an artist has a star-level status (or is close to achieving it), the lower the risk of such an oversight; as their renown takes on so many forms that, even if certain events are not listed, the whole is so rich that it is much less affected. It is also for this reason that—with a few exceptions—the higher the artists are ranked (therefore with a numerically low number on the Artfacts list), the less their renown is subject to skepticism.

Additionally, the more acclaimed a gallery is, the lower the risk that its artists will be victims of an undervaluation of their recognition. This more often affects the artists represented by small and midsize galleries—and particularly the smallest establishments—which in any case are by no means those on which my international ranked list intends to focus.

Another point merits being highlighted: the Artfacts data on artist rankings is far from being free of permanent omissions or even, on occasion, factual errors, but one cannot expect data that has not been produced within a scientific framework to be perfectly accurate. As Guy Bellavance and his co-authors explain: "In the end, the platform therefore presents itself above all as an 'argument.' It is based on discursive logic. Similar to a Bourdieu-esque logic, its legitimacy derives from the trust accorded to it by its actual or potential users, from the belief shared by cultural circles in the value of the instrument" (Bellavance et al., 2018, p. 86).

Moreover, despite its limitations, this data can be used in a well thought-out manner, taking care to control for the biases associated with it, and attempting to limit their effects. In the social sciences, we can use biased data; the fact that it is imperfect does not make it unusable, we just have to identify the biases associated with the data and find a way to reduce them as much as possible (or even eliminate them); or when this is not possible, to address any limitations in the analysis. I previously reported this in my past works based on the Kunstkompass (Quemin 2001, 2002, 2004, 2006, and 2013b). I showed in particular that, even if this indicator has an obvious bias toward German artists, it was perfectly possible to use it in my research by taking this limitation into account in my synchronous analyses; and that the effects of this bias became negligible when a diachronic country-by-country analysis was completed.

While social science researchers obviously wish to have as much high-quality data as possible, it should be emphasized that it is not only the quality or the relevance of the data that is important; it is also the way in which it is used, and how it is interpreted.

I have just exposed here, in complete transparency, certain limitations of the artist data produced by Artfacts, while nonetheless indicating that it is possible to use it from a social science perspective by taking care to adopt a method that can—as we will soon see—restrict the negative effects. There is no doubt that those who will be bothered by the results of my ranked lists, since they will not occupy the positions that they believe should be ascribed to them, will take up the criticisms that were presented at the beginning of this chapter—likely without citing the source—and surely neglecting to keep the following in mind: despite the limitations of the initial data (or at least of the few cases that I have indicated, which essentially constitute counter-examples), these can indeed be used in a scientific approach if we remain vigilant (as I will attempt to do) in applying a method that reduces data biases as much as possible.

Finally, it should be noted that the use of Artfacts data was made possible insofar as, quite fortunately, there are very few homonyms between artists, despite the extent of my data and database. In the rare moments when this problem arose, I could identify the artist who actually corresponded to the gallery being studied by referring to the list of the creator's exhibitions in their Artfacts blurb.

Which galleries should be ranked? Primary market galleries that participated in Art Basel in 2019

The market of gallery sales is actually made up of two segments: the primary market—works are available for sale for the first time—and the secondary market, in which works that previously belonged to another owner are once again for sale (Moulin, 1987 and 1992). I have chosen to limit the analysis here to galleries that are active on the primary market for the most part, even though there is some overlap between the two domains. As the following two journalists rightly indicated: "Between the primary and secondary markets, the boundaries are often porous [. . .] A gallery can be part of the primary market and sometimes will sell works from the secondary market. A secondary market gallery can also represent primary market artists." (Granet & Lamour, 2018, p. 97).

Even though the fact of considering a gallery to be mainly active in the first or secondary market may seem somewhat arbitrary given the lack of transparency that typically characterizes transactions, I have combined information that I obtained from the websites of these galleries (particularly as concerns the birthdate of the represented artists, as some galleries regularly or exclusively mention artists who are deceased) with my own knowledge of the market, which I have obtained either via my own experiences or by asking the opinions of other insiders.

The objective, within the framework of this research, was not to classify all of the approximately 2,200 contemporary art galleries in the world (Quemin, 2013a)—which would prove to be very tedious and perhaps even impossible—as the number of galleries in all the world is very high, and the boundaries of defining truly contemporary art can become blurred when one moves away from the center of this universe. However, I wanted to be sure that I included the largest galleries in the world on my international ranked list. A point of observation quickly emerged: participation in Art Basel. As I explained in the chapter dedicated to international fairs, Art Basel is the undisputed champion of its sector (Quemin, 2013a and b). The financial stakes are such that no gallery that has the possibility to participate can refuse this windfall of an opportunity. Over recent years, the number of galleries that participate in Art Basel has remained fairly stable, as has the number of galleries appearing in its main "Galleries" sector; the most prestigious and competitive of them all. As such, in 2020, out of a total of 288 galleries participating in the various sectors of the event, 232 were announced as exhibitors in this sector[25] (compared to 222 galleries in 2019). In 2022, there were 234 in the "Galleries" sector alone, out of a total of 289 participants.

It should be noted that, while Art Basel ensures that none of the largest galleries in the world will be neglected, the fair also features establishments of a much smaller scale. The international ranked list that I have drawn up tests this hypothesis, as well as the explanations that are sometimes given by players in the art world to account for the wide variety of sizes for the galleries that participate in Art Basel. Thus, as this Swiss gallerist explained to me in 2019, when I told him about my project of creating a ranked list based on participation in Art Basel: "A gallery's size isn't entirely relevant when participating in Art Basel . . . There are the Basel galleries that are present, specifically because they're from Basel, but are of no particular importance (Gisele Linder, Nicolas Krupp, von Bartha . . .) [. . .]. And I would say that the most powerful of all of them isn't even there: Bruno Bischofberger . . ."[26] My method, which I will explain in greater detail later in this chapter, makes it possible to verify whether the rosters of these galleries are particularly weak compared to non-Basel galleries, or even whether Swiss galleries can in fact benefit from the simple bonus of their geographical and/or reticular proximity with the fair.

Among the galleries participating in Art Basel in 2022 in the main "Galleries" sector, I have determined that the following galleries belong mainly to the secondary market, and therefore do not appear on my international ranked list.

List of galleries participating in the Art Basel "Galleries" sector in 2022 operating mainly in the secondary market (and indication of their nationality):

Acquavella Galleries (US)
Applicat-Prazan (FR)
Di Donna (US)
Hazlitt Holland-Hibbert (UK)
Edward Tyler Nahem Fine Art (US)
Bernard Jacobson Gallery (UK)
Helly Nahmad Gallery (US)
Galerie Thomas (DE)
Galleria Christian Stein (IT)
Luxembourg + Co (US)
Gray Gallery (US)
Richard Nagy Ltd. (UK)
Tornabuoni Art (IT)
Van de Weghe (US)

Each time a determination takes place, an element of arbitrariness can marginally taint the decisions; it is therefore important that this element remain very limited.

Which artists should be considered from each gallery? The decision to only include the "best" artists

From the moment that I decided to qualify galleries by their artists, the option that most naturally came to mind was to qualify each gallery by all of the artists whom it represents, then to calculate their average ranking. I ultimately ruled out this way of proceeding, as I deemed it more relevant to calculate the average ranking of the top 10 artists represented by each gallery using data from the Artfacts.net website (Quemin, 2019 and 2020a). I chose this number of 10 artists particularly because some galleries represent fewer than 20 artists (this is fairly rare among the most influential galleries in the world). This may also seem surprising, as a prominent gallery's size is generally associated with an extensive roster that can go far beyond the norm—which is around 30 artists represented by truly international galleries. However, the most established and influential galleries sometimes report a considerable number of artists—Gagosian has long indicated no fewer than 120–130 artists on its website.

Since there are galleries with a very limited number of artists, it was therefore not possible to calculate the average Artfacts ranking on the 20 most prominent artists for each gallery. However, it should be noted that the average ranking of the top 10 artists is often indicative of the entire list of artists, and I was able to verify that considering the top 10 or 20 "best" artists of each gallery only marginally affects the classification.

The fact of considering the top 10 artists from each gallery is also justified by the fact that many galleries admit to making the majority of their revenue from the sales of only 10 artists: the bottom of their roster has much less of an impact on their business, both in terms of the visibility/identity of the establishment and its financial results. As this international American gallerist stated:

> Apart from Gagosian, which carefully selects most of its artists, because almost all of them can be sold at very high prices, all the other galleries make most of their sales and profits with a very limited number of the artists that they represent. Sometimes it could be five, other times it might be 10 or 15, but the full list of artists, or even a significant portion of it, is never what's at stake for us in our business.

Moreover, for a very successful gallery, the notion of expanding its artist roster beyond star artists, who nowadays are very often in their sixties, seventies, and eighties (possible even in their nineties) (Quemin, 2013b and 2020b) can act as an incubator for young future talent. However, in general young artists who are, at best, on their way to fame, have a higher number in the reputational ranked list than their elder peers (that is to say that young people are lower in the classification). One such investment in the future is very evident in the case of the French gallery Mennour, which knows (potentially better than any other) how to lead very young artists to much greater visibility (or even acclaim) in the span of a few years. Including young artists in the calculation of the average ranking that is attributed to each gallery would have the effect of raising their assigned number, and therefore lowering the position of the galleries in the classification, whereas this is a strategy with the potential to guarantee future success.

The fact of calculating an average from 10 artists—the "best"—also helps to improve the quality of the data taken from Artfacts. By considering only the highest-ranked artists, the focus then becomes those whose rankings are the most reliable, as my previous work has already established (Quemin, 2013b). If, additionally, one of the artists in the selection is less rigorously scored by Artfacts, this has less of an impact on the result obtained than by concentrating on a single individual.

It should be specified here that the fact of including only 10 artists from a gallery's roster seemed to me to be a satisfactory way of proceeding in all cases since, as I have mentioned, almost all galleries make the majority of their sales from the upper part of the list of the artists whom they represent. That is, all except one: Gagosian, which follows a business model that has no equivalent in the contemporary art gallery world. Whereas other galleries, even the best of them, capitalize on a limited number of their artists, Gagosian has managed to bring together a considerable number of artists with very high profiles (and a solid reputation) to a degree with which no gallery can directly compete. To put it in other words, even though the rare elite gallery may have managed to overtake Gagosian in terms of the average ranking of their "frontrunners" (whose ranking will therefore be slightly lower), Gagosian no doubt compensates by expanding its collection of the most desirable artists like no other; which all (or most) galleries would like to dispute. As this gallerist who has locations in several countries pointed out:

> Gagosian's roster is simple: you take all the artists who go for the highest prices at auction, they're almost all with him. Not just one or two, it's an incredible number. When there are young people, well, generally not that young, but let's say younger than his other artists, who start to break into the auction market, when the money starts flowing, Gagosian brings them into his gallery. He's the only one doing this. He doesn't bother building careers, he comes in out of the blue when the market is ready.

This quite singular positioning is surely linked to the fact that, originally, Larry Gagosian worked a great deal in the secondary market. When he decided to shift to the primary market, aware of the significant profits that could be made there, he did not do so by promoting new talents himself, but by "poaching" artists from other galleries, some of which are very influential (Velthuis, 2002, p. 116). It was precisely to convince the most desirable artists to join him that he needed to outfit himself with a totally exceptional space on West 24th Street in Chelsea, which for a long time remained without any rival in the world.[27] It should also be reiterated that Gagosian has an unequaled number of locations in the world, and that the gallerist has even created a multinational corporation of art that has no equivalent throughout the history of the market segment in which he operates.

The following conclusion can be drawn from the above information: although the Gagosian gallery will be included in my classification, since it unquestionably belongs to the same professional group and the same market sector as all of the galleries that will appear on this international ranked list, the prevailing rationale in its business operations is absolutely unique, which can blur its proper placement in the classification. Its position may therefore be portrayed less precisely than that of other galleries. However, given that this establishment represents an incontrovertible and rarely disputed heavyweight in the gallery world, it is to be expected that the ranking it receives based on the methodology that I have conceptualized will place it among the very best galleries in the world.

While, as I have just indicated, no establishment can directly compete with the Gagosian gallery in terms of the breadth of its roster of star artists, especially the stars who perform exceptionally well on the market—even more so than the artists who are most popular among institutions (Moulin, 1992)—it is certain that appetites among other galleries have grown more voracious as Larry Gagosian, the current emperor of the art market, has aged (he was born in 1945). Although, for a long time, it was the Pace gallery that stood as a potential challenger; more recently, the Hauser & Wirth and David Zwirner galleries have emerged as Gagosian's most dangerous rivals. The three competing galleries came to challenge Gagosian's stronghold in Chelsea, New York, at the heart of the international art market. Larry Gagosian has long reigned supreme in his West 24th Street mega-space, to which no other structure could favorably compare. It is not without reason that his three most direct competitors—Pace, with a noticeable delay—have, in turn, outfitted themselves with remarkable spaces that are absolutely necessary to attract the greatest number of wealthy collectors possible but, more importantly, to entice the most venerated artists.

It should also be noted that, in order to produce the most accurate ranked list possible, I have not systematically selected the 10 highest-ranked artists from each gallery. On the contrary, I have submitted the choice of these 10 "best" creators (Misdrahi Flores, 2013) to an additional condition: that they be living or, in the case of deceased artists, that the gallery represent their estate[28] (or any organization of the same type) (Quemin, 2019 and 2020a). This was to avoid any instances of galleries falsely acknowledging or implying collaboration with deceased artists on their website along with the artists whom they really represent, even though they had obviously chosen them from among the most prestigious artists in order to boost their own image (despite having no real connection to them).

While, in general, I relied on the website of various contemporary art galleries to find the list of artists whom they represent, I have therefore once again proceeded in a well-reasoned manner by examining each list to ensure that there was indeed a relationship of partnership with the artists; either directly with them, in the case of living artists, or with their estate, in the case of deceased artists.

Using gallery websites was possible due to the fact that today, almost all real contemporary art establishments (and even those that exist outside of this single segment of the art market) have a website; except the French gallery Pietro Sparta.[29] Among the items offered by the drop-down menu on the gallery's homepage is almost always the tab "Artists," leading to its roster, which necessarily attests to the gallery's contemporary nature and expresses its mission statement. In general, this list grows along with the longevity and impact of the gallery. While the smallest, strictly contemporary establishments can make do with a dozen artists, the most influential can border on 100 artists. In February 2021, if one considered the rosters of the four competing heavyweights in Chelsea, it was the Pace gallery that listed the most names (111), ahead of Gagosian (92)[30] and Hauser & Wirth (91), which are practically on a par with one another; then David Zwirner (72) who, from this point of view, seemed to be bringing up the rear compared to its predecessors. In February 2023, the same four previous galleries totaled 124 artists for Pace, which is still clearly in the lead from this point of view, then 103 for Gagosian, 94 for Hauser & Wirth (58 artists and 38 estates) and 78 for David Zwirner.

One convention largely prevails: the "represented artists" are those with whom there is a long-term relationship, and who are regularly displayed, both within the confines of the gallery (where they generally benefit from a personal exhibition every two or three years) and at fairs. With them, there is a lasting, if not exclusive (or at least very privileged) connection with only a handful of galleries. In this, they differ from the mere "artists" whose names appear under this label alone, or who are introduced by the inscription "Works By." Among the largest galleries, this convention is broadly respected. If we consider the case of galleries with locations in France, the Marian Goodman and Nathalie Obadia galleries only cite their own artists, those whom they really represent. The Templon and Chantal Crousel galleries both display a main list, supplemented (in different ways) by another, with the introduction "Works By." Almine Rech does the same with three separate lists: "Artists" (specifying the estates or successions), "Projects," and "Exhibited." One is led to understand that the connection between the first group and the gallery is the strongest. Mennour separates its artists into three categories: "Artists," "Estates," and "Works By." As for Lelong & Co, it distinguishes between its artists and those of its editions (i.e., printed multiples).

There are therefore variable practices, which can nevertheless lead to the separation of different groups when necessary. However, today artists and galleries are very rarely bound by contracts (Moulin, 1992), which makes the relationship uniting them less clear, and some galleries do not hesitate to play up this vagueness; on their "Artists" list, they combine creators with whom they maintain a relationship that falls under the banner of *representation*, and others whom they *present* only occasionally or whose works they simply have in stock. In this case, the link is very tenuous, and one could still be surprised to discover that galleries muddy the waters in such a way. As this employee of a large gallery conceded: "Yes, it's true, we mix up everything on the gallery's site, the artists we represent and others with whom we have no real representation. It's not a lie, since we haven't stated that we represent them all, but it's obviously the impression that we're giving. Let's just say that we're embellishing reality." When questioned, this associate director of another major international gallery tried to explain, and to put the confusion generated among visitors to the gallery's website into perspective:

> In reality, even we don't really know who's represented or not. I really think that here, our boss is the only one who knows. We see that artists return regularly to our exhibitions, others don't. I don't know if there are contracts, and to tell the truth, until your question, I had never really thought about it! It's true that all this lacks transparency.

Is this less scrupulous approach connected to mega-galleries? The Gagosian gallery makes a fair distinction between "Artists" and "Artists in Current [Gagosian] Exhibitions," with the lack of precision in the term being highly notable. One of the other colossuses, Pace, similarly presents a single list; also that of its "Artists." However, if we look at the websites of their two direct competitors, David Zwirner displays a single list of "Artists," all of whom seem to be well represented, and Hauser & Wirth takes care to distinguish between its living "Artists" (55 in total) and those represented via their "Estate" (36 other creators) (the figures here relate to the year 2021).

As I have become increasingly familiar with galleries, I discovered that they tend on occasion to cheat somewhat as concerns the list of artists whom they represent. Contrary to what one might think, it is not the smallest establishments that are the least reliable; the symbolic stakes are so high at the top of the gallery hierarchy that some of the most influential among them try to introduce a certain amount of confusion by mixing up their own artists with creators with whom they do not actually maintain any privileged connection. Surprisingly, after making this discovery, I realized that most gallerists were unaware that some of their competitors were engaging in such a practice.

One artist in particular caught my attention: Pablo Picasso. To be able to boast of being the gallerist for the absolute genius of the twentieth century is to add much more than another pearl to one's crown; it is to add a veritable diamond. While browsing the websites of the major galleries, I discovered that Picasso's name appears on the artist list of both Gagosian and Pace. Would the artist (or in this case, his estate) be represented by both galleries? Is he represented by only one of them? Or neither? I then contacted the Picasso Administration and received an answer that was as clear as it was firm: "The Picasso Administration has no representation agreement with any gallery." It is therefore regrettable that the websites of two of the most influential galleries in the world can so easily mislead people by hinting at a representation that does not, in fact, exist. The gallerist Almine Rech, in her private life, is married to Bernard Ruiz-Picasso, the artist's grandson. Along with her husband, she runs the *Fundación Almine y Bernard Ruiz-Picasso para el Arte*. As a result, one could legitimately think that she is one of the best-placed people (if not *the* best-placed) to find works by Picasso for sale. However, she has the grace to include Picasso in the "Works By" section

("Exhibited") of her gallery's website, thereby demonstrating more transparency than her fellow gallerists, who prefer not to distinguish any category.

At the end of this development, it seems that the websites of contemporary art galleries, while they are generally good sources of information on the lists of artists whom they represent, must nevertheless be taken with a certain amount of reservation, since transparency is not always the order of the day. This is why, considering the Artfacts ranking of the artists who qualify each gallery, I have limited myself to living artists only; or, when they are deceased, the gallery website must mention an estate (or equivalent entity). Insofar as certain leading galleries tend to misleadingly include artists on their roster so as to enhance their prestige and legitimacy, this precaution that I have introduced affords a better degree of reliability to my results.

This lengthy development is intended to present the characteristics of the data that I used and the methodological choices that I opted for in complete transparency, so as to attempt to produce a relevant ranked list (Quemin, 2019 and 2020a). Although I relied primarily on the data produced by the Art Basel fair for the list of participating galleries—as well as that generated by Artfacts and that made freely available by galleries on their websites—the use of all of this data was well thought out; the product of many stages of selection throughout the development of my methodology.

It is therefore necessary to have real skills in the social sciences, derived from a detailed knowledge of the art market and the gallery world, to be able to establish a relevant classification of the latter by avoiding and correcting any biases as much as possible. In this context, it would be ill advised to oppose quantitative and qualitative methods.

I must once again emphasize that using the artists rankings provided by Artfacts.net, as I have done here, is especially relevant because I have only included the largest galleries; limiting my analysis to the elite within the profession, the galleries selected by the prestigious and unrivaled Art Basel fair, and because I have, moreover, focused on the most recognized artists (the "top 10") of each gallery (who are actually *represented* by them). As previously stated, my previous work on reputation and acclaim (Quemin, 2013b) demonstrated that at the highest level of artistic recognition, the possible biases associated with the various instruments and methods utilized to identify the subjects of this acclaim only have a minimal effect. For important artists, especially for the stars of contemporary art, the method that I have adopted has, in reality, only a minor impact on the rankings revealed in the upper section of the list, which my analyses comparing the rankings according to the Kunstkompass and Artfacts.net rankings have been able to establish (Quemin, 2013b). I then averaged the result obtained for each primary market gallery based on its top 10 most prominent represented artists. While I decided to proceed from internal data, it has been subjected to a specific analysis procedure, which is characteristic of the domain of the social sciences.[31]

9

The international ranked list of the "best" contemporary art galleries

Now that I have described the methodology that I used to compile my ranked list of galleries in great detail (see previous chapter), I can present the list itself and interpret the results. Since I also generated a similar ranked list in 2019 following the same methodology, I will be able to elaborate on the evolutions that have taken place in the four intervening years.

Restricting my classification to the galleries that participated in the main sector of the Art Basel fair in 2022, I chose to focus solely on the galleries for which the primary market is their principal occupation (or at least comprises a significant portion of their business). As I mentioned in the previous chapter, I decided to discount all of the galleries that operate exclusively or mainly within the secondary market. I was therefore left with a grand total of 213 galleries (as opposed to 200 in 2019) to classify, present, and analyze.

An initial commentary on this ranked list consists of examining some galleries individually. This is without doubt the approach that will most interest readers who are familiar with the contemporary art world; those who are most integrated into it.

However, before doing so, it would be a good idea to reiterate the fact that I mentioned while detailing my methodology: when I began to consider the best way to classify galleries based on their artist roster, realizing that I would have to do so in order to present the hierarchy between various galleries as impartially as possible, I concluded that the Gagosian gallery, given its completely unique business model, could not be judged using the exact same criteria as its competitors. What is essential in the social sciences is that we report the reality being studied in the most relevant way possible; this means not only establishing rules pertaining to how we gain knowledge, but also knowing how to recognize their potential limits, as they may not apply in very specific circumstances. The fact that there are exceptions to the rule does not in any way invalidate said rule, as long as we are able to justify this deviation, as I have done here.

I previously explained that Gagosian did not end up in the top position when I used the classification system that was based on a general model, even though it should have had a very high ranking (it was in fact the only gallery whose placement seemed to be a true discrepancy). When applying the classification principle that was systematically utilized for other establishments, my calculations show the Gagosian gallery is rightfully placed in 6th position (it was ranked 5th in 2019), which confirms that it undoubtedly ranks among the most important and "best" galleries in the world[1] (Misdrahi Flores, 2013). Nevertheless, given the singular extent of its roster of very highly ranked artists, which extends well beyond its top 10 creators, Gagosian's 6th-place ranking is still somewhat low. One could easily posit that its extensive roster of star artists would justify its being put on a par with the very few galleries ahead of it, as there is only an average of 10 points between some of them. By contrast, the average score that separates the first gallery in the ranking, Thaddaeus Ropac, from its immediate successor, Sprüth Magers, shows a much more pronounced gap than that which separates the other galleries in the top six: there is a considerable 22 points between them, as opposed to the 15 points between Sprüth Magers and the trio of David Zwirner, White Cube, and Hauser & Wirth; who are virtually tied in terms of the quality of their artist roster. Gagosian comes in a full 10 points lower. I will revisit this point of the top position in the ranked list later, as it is fairly important, symbolically speaking. Although it is impossible to provide an irreproachable solution to determine who, between Larry Gagosian and Thaddaeus Ropac, runs the "best" gallery in the world; the considerable lead held by the Thaddaeus Ropac gallery is significant enough to indicate its extreme singularity, even among its elite contemporaries at the very top of the ranked list. This analysis can, in point of fact, be approached in terms of artistic "quality" (Misdrahi Flores, 2013), as I referred to the reputation or recognition of the artists that they represent as a means of qualifying the galleries (Moulin & Quemin, 1993). The art world, just like general common sense would maintain, is on the whole permeated by the idea that the most influential gallery in the world—the one with the most (often luxurious) exhibition spaces—should automatically be the best. I will address this point by referring to the work produced by Pierre Bourdieu on the concept of autonomy (Bourdieu, 1996).

The 213 best contemporary art galleries in the world in 2023

Name of the gallery	Rank in 2023	Average rank of the 10 best living artists or estates in 2023
Thaddaeus Ropac	1	22.6
Sprüth Magers	2	45.1
David Zwirner	3	49
White Cube	4	49.8
Hauser & Wirth	5	49.9
Gagosian	6	59.6
Konrad Fischer Galerie	7	70
Skarstedt	8	71.4
Marian Goodman Gallery	9	73.4
Lisson Gallery	10	80.2
Galerie Chantal Crousel	11	88.8
Galerie Rüdiger Schöttle	12	106.6
Gladstone Gallery	13	114.9
Galleria Continua	14	122.1
Galleria Christian Stein	15	125.3
Mennour	16	132.7
Esther Schipper	17	150.7
Regen Projects	18	151.5
Pace Gallery	19	158.2
Kukje Gallery	20	161.9
Lia Rumma	21	177
Almine Rech	22	186
Galerie Max Hetzler	23	199.5
Xavier Hufkens	24	205.3
kurimanzutto	25	207.4
Galerie Greta Meert	26	213.8
Alfonso Artiaco	27	218
Galleria Massimo Minini	28	224.5
Goodman Gallery	29	234.2

Galleria Raffaella Cortese	30	236.4
Bernier/Eliades	31	248.5
Kewenig	32	252
Massimo De Carlo	33	253.3
Sadie Coles HQ	34	254.2
neugerriemschneider	35	259.7
Galerie Krinzinger	36	262.1
303 Gallery	37	269.3
Perrotin	38	291.4
Tanya Bonakdar Gallery	39	295
Sean Kelly	40	297.8
Taka Ishii Gallery	41	303.9
Galerie Lelong & Co.	42	319.6
Galerie Eva Presenhuber	43	337.9
Lehmann Maupin	44	344.4
König Galerie	45	353.1
Galerie Gisela Capitain	46	366.2
Galleri Nicolai Wallner	47	370.9
Galería Juana de Aizpuru	48	371.6
Simon Lee Gallery	49	373.2
Matthew Marks Gallery	50	378.2
Tucci Russo Studio per l'Arte Contemporanea	51	379.3
Victoria Miro	52	381.6
Petzel	53	406.5
Galerie nächst St. Stephan Rosemarie Schwarzwälder	54	410.7
Galerie Peter Kilchmann	55	420.8
Sfeir-Semler Gallery	56	427.3
Galeria Luisa Strina	57	430.5
Thomas Dane Gallery	58	430.9

(continued)

Name of the gallery	Rank in 2023	Average rank of the 10 best living artists or estates in 2023
Paula Cooper Gallery	59	433
Fraenkel Gallery	60	433.9
KOW	61	445.6
Galerie Buchholz	62	448.8
Luhring Augustine	63	449
Templon	64	449.7
Stampa	65	458.5
Anton Kern Gallery	66	459.9
Gió Marconi	67	476.7
Galerie Pietro Spartà	68	482.1
Frith Street Gallery	69	493
Galerie Nagel Draxler	70	493
Sperone Westwater	71	502.6
Stephen Friedman Gallery	72	502.9
David Kordansky Gallery	73	506.6
kaufmann repetto	74	507.5
Contemporary Fine Arts	75	511.7
Air de Paris	76	515.2
Mehdi Chouakri	77	524
Jan Mot	78	524.9
Maureen Paley	79	529
Peter Freeman, Inc.	80	534.6
Jack Shainman Gallery	81	552.9
Galerie Tschudi	82	588.3
Mendes Wood DM	83	608.5
carlier gebauer	84	621.7
Galerie Thomas Schulte	85	624.2
Cristina Guerra Contemporary Art	86	642.3
Galleria Franco Noero	87	657.9

Pilar Corrias	88	658.7
Vielmetter Los Angeles	89	666.8
Galerie Bärbel Grässlin	90	679.5
James Cohan Gallery	91	682.2
Galerie Neu	92	702.4
Sprovieri	93	733.4
Mai 36 Galerie	94	745.9
Galerie Francesca Pia	95	762.9
galería Elba Benítez	96	775.5
Cheim & Read	97	798.5
Reena Spaulings Fine Art	98	798.7
Blum & Poe	99	801.6
Andrew Kreps Gallery	100	811.2
The Modern Institute	101	826.9
Bortolami	102	838.6
Greene Naftali	103	863
Stevenson	104	863.4
Meyer Riegger	105	872.1
Barbara Wien	106	881.3
dépendance	107	890.8
Nicolas Krupp	108	898.8
Galerie Nathalie Obadia	109	902.7
Fortes D'Aloia & Gabriel	110	910.4
Annet Gelink Gallery	111	926.6
Galerie Barbara Weiss	112	961.7
Gray	113	965.1
Modern Art	114	969.8
ProjecteSD	115	986.1
gb agency	116	1033.6
Galerie Nordenhake	117	1057.2
Wentrup	118	1058.9

(continued)

Name of the gallery	Rank in 2023	Average rank of the 10 best living artists or estates in 2023
Mitchell-Innes & Nash	119	1068.1
Galerie Thomas Zander	120	1096.4
Cabinet	121	1123
Buchmann Galerie	122	1131.5
Sies + Höke	123	1151.3
Art : Concept	124	1177.3
Galerie Isabella Bortolozzi	125	1188.4
Casey Kaplan	126	1193.3
Galería Elvira González	127	1207
Sikkema Jenkins & Co.	128	1234.9
Campoli Presti	129	1257
Edwynn Houk Gallery	130	1269.8
Vitamin Creative Space	131	1272.9
Rodeo	132	1326.8
P.P.O.W	133	1327.4
ZERO...	134	1340.5
Galerie Jocelyn Wolff	135	1435.4
Ben Brown Fine Arts	136	1440.2
von Bartha	137	1442.7
Karma International	138	1483.2
Galeria Pedro Cera	139	1531.1
ShanghART Gallery	140	1561
Marianne Boesky Gallery	141	1624.6
Foksal Gallery Foundation	142	1635.8
Galerie Martin Janda	143	1645.7
Nils Stærk	144	1662.8
Annely Juda Fine Art	145	1700.4
Standard (Oslo)	146	1702.8
galerie frank elbaz	147	1710.8

greengrassi	148	1715.1
Gregor Podnar	149	1727.8
Labor	150	1728.8
Zeno X Gallery	151	1773.5
A arte Invernizzi	152	1809.3
OMR	153	1822.2
Tanya Leighton	154	1859
Miguel Abreu Gallery	155	1894.2
Layr	156	1945.2
Anthony Meier Fine Arts	157	1960.3
Herald St	158	1967.9
Kiang Malingue	159	1976.5
Michael Werner Gallery	160	1981.6
Travesía Cuatro	161	2005.4
The Approach	162	2028.5
Kerlin Gallery	163	2063.1
Skopia / P.-H. Jaccaud	164	2064.8
Galerie Eigen + Art	165	2069.6
Alexander Gray Associates	166	2129.1
Kate MacGarry	167	2142.5
BQ	168	2220.7
ChertLüdde	169	2233.7
Experimenter	170	2258.7
Antenna Space	171	2360
Kadel Willborn	172	2361.3
Magazzino	173	2388.7
Essex Street/Maxwell Graham	174	2457.8
Galerie Vera Munro	175	2460.2
Galerie Guido W. Baudach	176	2500.8
Galerie Urs Meile	177	2505.7
Andréhn-Schiptjenko	178	2514.7

(continued)

Name of the gallery	Rank in 2023	Average rank of the 10 best living artists or estates in 2023
Hollybush Gardens	179	2708.2
Galeria Plan B	180	2899.5
Balice Hertling	181	2904.9
Société	182	2969.4
47 Canal	183	2969.7
Galerie Karsten Greve	184	3022.6
Chemould Prescott Road	185	3049.4
Galerie Georges-Philippe & Nathalie Vallois	186	3075.9
Alison Jacques	187	3126.4
Peres Projects	188	3137.8
David Nolan Gallery	189	3184.9
Carlos/Ishikawa	190	3256
Take Ninagawa	191	3797.2
Galerie Gregor Staiger	192	3829.4
Catriona Jeffries	193	3843.8
Canada	194	4050.4
K-T Z	195	4189.8
mother's tankstation limited	196	5103.3
A Gentil Carioca	197	5380.4
JTT	198	5814.1
Casas Riegner	199	6278.2
Mariane Ibrahim	200	8137
The Mayor Gallery	201	8982.6
Galerie Gisèle Linder	202	9124.3
Jenkins Johnson Gallery	203	9904.6
Galerie Lahumière	204	11460.3
Galerie Max Mayer	205	12149.6
Fergus McCaffrey	206	13314.2
Daniel Blau	207	13509.4

Tokyo Gallery + BTAP	208	15009.8
Galerie Carzaniga	209	15297.6
Jeffrey Deitch	210	17289.7
Gomide & Co[1]	211	58619
Ecart[2]	212	x
The Breeder[3]	213	x

[1] Less than 10 living artists or estates [2] x: No site or list of artists available [3] x: No site or list of artists available

The top 10 galleries in the world

Interpreting ranked lists generally elicits a dual reaction: readers pay very close attention to individuals or institutions at the top of the ranking, and they are also looking for information about the people and establishments that interest them the most, those with which they feel they feel the closest affiliation. Since the latter dimension is more personal and based on individual taste, I will pay special attention to the galleries at the top of the list, in particular by listing the top 10 artists of their rosters, who are the reason that these galleries have such high placements.

The top 10 galleries in the world in 2023, as determined by the average ranking of their 10 best artists (according to Artfacts)*

Gallery	**Ranking**	**Average Artfacts ranking of its Top 10 artists**
Thaddaeus Ropac	1	22.6
Sprüth Magers	2	45.1
David Zwirner	3	49.0
White Cube	4	49.8
Hauser & Wirth	5	49.9
Gagosian	6	59.6
Konrad Fischer	7	70.0
Skarstedt	8	71.4
Marian Goodman	9	73.4
Lisson	10	80.2

* Note: See the comments above, as well as in the previous section, regarding the Gagosian gallery's disparate ranking.

As we will see when analyzing the breakdown of the top artists on the "best" galleries' rosters, the artists who have achieved success (especially the most well-known among them) are frequently represented by several galleries around the world; sometimes two or three, or even half a dozen (but rarely more than that). This multi-representation allows them to be present in the principal regions of the world in terms of market activity (Quemin, 2013b). An artist of a given level is almost always represented by galleries that correspond to a commensurate level, meaning that they almost always share the same degree of impact and renown; clearly illustrating a principle of structural homology (Bourdieu, 1992).

1. The Thaddaeus Ropac gallery

The Thaddaeus Ropac gallery was founded in 1983 in Salzburg, Austria; a midsize city (its current population is around 150,000) that was far from the contemporary art circuit at the time, and primarily known internationally for its Mozart festival, which was created in 1920. In Salzburg, the Thaddaeus Ropac gallery's presence is divided between two spaces: the elegant Kast villa, a historic building dating from the nineteenth century in the heart of the city, and the Halle, an immense converted former industrial space located on the outskirts of town and opened in 2010.[2] In 1990, the gallery opened a space in Paris, in the Marais neighborhood, and since then it has gradually taken over the many floors of its current location. In 2012, it achieved a veritable "symbolic revolution" (Bourdieu, 1996) by breaking out of the Paris city limits; with surprising audacity, it occupied a huge decommissioned industrial complex made up of three main buildings in Pantin, an inner suburb of Paris. The gallery also expanded into London in 2017, in the very chic Mayfair neighborhood, moving into Ely House, an elegant five-story mansion. For some time, the gallery also had salespeople in Asia, but did not own any property on the continent itself; however, it opened a branch in Seoul at the end of 2021, banking on the rapid development of this major city on the international art scene.

Although today, the Thaddaeus Ropac gallery is primarily run out of Paris, its history is deeply anchored in the DACH region (Germany, Austria, and Switzerland). Salzburg is, of course, located in Austria, but it is only a few miles from the German border, and is therefore much closer to Munich than to Vienna.

As of 2023, the Thaddaeus Ropac gallery has one of the most extensive artist rosters in the world, with 72 artists. It is also one of the most famous galleries.[3]

The Thaddaeus Ropac gallery: Rankings[4] of its top 10 artists, according to Artfacts (average ranking: 22.6):

Artist	2023 Artfacts ranking
Joseph Beuys Estate	3
Georg Baselitz	7
Robert Rauschenberg Foundation	11
Erwin Wurm	15
VALIE EXPORT	23
Arnulf Rainer	26
Imi Knoebel	27
Alex Katz	30
Harun Farocki Estate	39
Anselm Kiefer	45

It could be interesting to compare the results from 2023 with those from 2019. Even when different artist names appear on the list for a given year, they are still placed very high on the list.

The Thaddaeus Ropac gallery: Rankings of its top 10 artists, according to Artfacts in 2019 (average ranking: 27):

Lawrence Weiner	10
Erwin Wurm	12
Robert Rauschenberg Foundation	14
Georg Baselitz	16
Harun Farocki Estate	21
VALIE EXPORT	28
Arnulf Rainer	32
Alex Katz	41
Anselm Kiefer	44
Imi Knoebel	49

The Thaddaeus Ropac gallery's excellence is apparent from its top 10 artists, which includes some of the greatest artists from Germany,[5] Austria, and the United States. Even the rankings of the artists immediately following the top 10 associated with Thaddaeus Ropac are particularly low, numerically speaking, meaning that they are placed very high on the Artfacts ranked list: Sean Scully (61st), Tony Cragg (74th), Gilbert & George (77th), the Donald Judd and Robert Mapplethorpe Foundations (79th and 107th, respectively). Additionally, as well as the deceased artists whose foundations are represented, the gallery also displays striking works by Marcel Duchamp (33rd); however, he was not included in calculating the gallery's average ranking, as his estate is not officially represented by the gallery.

The Thaddaeus Ropac gallery's greatest strength lies in the fact that it has managed to gather together artists who are heavyweights on the market and have amazing visibility, thus combining the two elements involved in establishing the value of art (Moulin, 1992). This group includes Georg Baselitz (7th), Robert Rauschenberg (11th), Alex Katz (30th), Anselm Kiefer (45th), and Sean Scully (61st). The gallery has rounded up practically all of the great painters of our time, especially those of German origin, and the great Austrian and Swiss artists can also be found in this prestigious gallery. However, in a veritable *tour de force*, in addition to the most recognized Europeans, the gallery has also been able to attract some of the most important American artists, and to flesh out its roster with the elite of non-Western artists. While traditionally, Thaddaeus Ropac has not represented many female artists, their number has been increasing spectacularly as of the end of the 2010s. This is because the gallery reacts quickly to emerging trends in the history of contemporary art, and it also contributes to them.

How does one account for the gallery's resounding success? Very early on, Thaddaeus Ropac was close to the artist Joseph Beuys, who introduced him to his peers after Ropac became a gallerist. He therefore quickly made artists central to his development strategy, which turned out to be very wise; with the structuring of the contemporary art world, artists who were still largely interchangeable at the beginning of the 1970s (when the contemporary art world began to emerge [Quemin, 2013]) have gradually become less and less substitutable between each other. Real star artists have emerged over time, and little by little a series of obligatory benchmarks has taken shape, which these artists must navigate with the guidance of one or several galleries. Note that, although his initial introduction was mainly facilitated by Joseph Beuys, Ropac was able to distance himself from working with "conceptual" art alone and take an interest in figurative painting (particularly by German artists) at a time when it was not in high demand (Zwirner, 2019). The triumph of German figurative painting on the international scene in the decades following the Thaddaeus Ropac gallery's creation was complemented by the parallel triumph of one of the movement's leading gallerists, who made this success possible through his support.

Ropac made the most of having been widely introduced into the business and sponsored by Beuys by becoming an "artist's" gallerist, and he was particularly attentive to his relationships with his artists, offering them excellent representation conditions. He therefore benefited enormously from the rise in artist popularity and market demand that took place around the turn of the millennium in particular. Gallerists have become central figures in the art market and in the world, but they could hardly exist without the support of the most recognized artists. Today, the greatest creators are less directly dependent on Larry Gagosian or Thaddaeus Ropac than the artists who were championed by Leo Castelli (Cohen-Solal, 2009).

The city of Salzburg also plays a critical role in Ropac's triumph. Many important artists were already represented by a gallery in Germany, a country in which these establishments were very influential, particularly in the Ruhr region. If a German gallerist were to request national exclusivity from their artists, all of their colleagues were denied access to them. However, as the Thaddaeus Ropac gallery was located in Austria, but only a few dozen miles from the German border, it avoided these restrictions while still having easy access to the German market due to its geographical proximity. When Ropac started his career, he was therefore able to develop his business away from the competition while circumventing the restrictions imposed by the most influential gallerists on any competitors who had a chance of overshadowing them by also being located in key cities for the international art scene. At the time, even though it was not explicitly acknowledged, a single leader of the profession (or two at most) controlled an artist's market, and since they had the right of first refusal, they decided what they were willing to leave to their competitors who were operating in other countries. This is how Pace in the United States and Bischofberger in Switzerland still largely controlled the art market even if they did not exhibit a certain artwork. At the time, as Ropac was located in a country whose scene and market were fairly secondary – especially since he was not in Vienna, but in a city that was barely worth mentioning on the international contemporary art map – he easily sidestepped this system wherein only the most powerful gallerists could control the market (Cohen-Solal, 2009).

Thanks to the Salsburg festival, the Thaddaeus Ropac gallery came into contact with a very international and art-savvy clientele who needed to pass the time while in the city. With the help of Eliette von Karajan, the wife of the famous conductor and a personal friend, Ropac was able to make contact with this privileged world and eventually build up his client base; facilitated by his easy access to a group of top-tier artists. For the rest of the year (when the festival was not taking place), since the city of Salzburg did not have a real market for contemporary art, the gallery had to resort to art fairs early on in its existence; fairs have since become increasingly essential in the gallery domain (Quemin, 2013b).

Another element that played a major role in the Thaddaeus Ropac gallery's incredible development was its expansion into Paris. Ropac himself has never hidden the fact that his decision to open a branch in France was largely intended to satisfy his artists, who are always attracted to the charms of Paris, as well as its cultural aura. This second location reproduced a notable characteristic of its Salzburg space: being in a location that has less intense competition than London and New York. Even though in these cities (especially the latter), the most influential galleries in the world have invested in the kind of massive spaces that would make them fierce competition, facing off directly with one another for the representation of the best artists and thus depriving their competitors (at least in part, as double representation by two major galleries is not exceptional nowadays, but artists are rarely represented by more than two galleries in the same city), it is possible for galleries in less competitive metropolitan areas to develop higher-quality rosters with less effort. Once their roster is substantial enough, collectors are eager to come to vernissages, even from abroad. Furthermore, art fairs can largely compensate for the fact of being located in a smaller metropolitan area. Only after the Thaddaeus Ropac gallery had become one of the most influential establishments in the world and therefore able to compete at the highest level with its British and American competitors did it open a third location in London, thus diving directly into the upper segment of the London art market.

By opening its Paris gallery in 1990, the up-and-coming Thaddaeus Ropac gallery highlighted very prominent American artists such as Sturtevant, Peter Halley, and Jeff Koons (ranked 3,802nd, 121st, and 94th, respectively, by Artfacts in 1990). These were very enviable rankings for a gallery that had only been in operation for seven years and was in the process of expanding its representation beyond its own zone of cultural affiliation into a more competitive space, while not relocating right in the center of the international contemporary art world—which would have been New York—or the most high-profile city in Europe, which would have been London.

Although Thaddaeus Ropac's dazzling success, as revealed by my ranked list, may be surprising to people who are familiar with the art market—as they are often convinced that Larry Gagosian is the undisputed, unbeatable frontrunner—a major event sent a strong warning signal throughout the world of European and international art, though it was probably not recognized for what it was at the time. In 2012, Thaddaeus Ropac was the first to cross the symbolic barrier of the Parisian ring road (the highway that encircles the city of Paris) by inaugurating a mega-space in Pantin, an inner suburb to the northeast of the city. A few days later, the then-undisputed behemoth Gagosian followed suit, opening a massive gallery in Le Bourget, a northern Parisian suburb. The mere fact that the world leader of contemporary art gallerists found himself in the position of following in the footsteps of another gallerist was an almost unimaginable first.

The Thaddaeus Ropac gallery—just like Ropac himself—tends to exhibit a certain amount of reservation, which is why players who are familiar with the art market are sometimes surprised at its first-place position in the ranking. An example of this reservation is its manner of expanding internationally, although it does not do so very often, and generally takes place without any real fanfare. It was only in 2021 that the gallery expanded outside of Europe, opting to open a branch in the city of Seoul. Before that, the following gallerist, who was already one of the most influential gallerists in France when Ropac opened his gallery in the Marais in 1990, spoke of a fairly inconspicuous arrival, and clearly emphasizes the crucial role that artists have played in the gallery's development:

> We already knew of Thaddaeus Ropac when he moved to Paris, his name wasn't unknown. We knew that he was living in Salzburg and that he organized a lot of dinners during the Mozart Festival, every day, it gave him access to a lot of very important collectors. And then, he had an amazing stroke of luck, he represented Kiefer, a major artist who ultimately carried his gallery. When Ropac came to France, we weren't really keeping an eye on him, he went low profile, it wasn't an event. Little by little, he began to grow to what he is today.

This French collector (who is a part of the European aristocracy) confirmed this point of view: "Of course we knew who Ropac was, but his arrival in Paris was really discreet. He was closely followed by his collectors, but outside of that circle his impact was limited."

Another prominent French gallerist expressed a different perspective:

> The moment Ropac moved to Paris, I knew that something was going on. He arrived, and he hosted an incredible evening in the courtyard of the Opéra Comique. We already knew him from Salzburg, we knew that he entertained people during the festival, but when he opened his space in Paris, his collectors made the trip for the occasion. There were people from the aristocracy, both German and European, very wealthy. If I recall, there were the Thurm and Taxis, the Thyssen-Bornemiszas, Louise Blouin must have also been there, from Canada, she's fallen completely off the map now but at the time she was very important. Organizing such an evening was a great indicator of what was going to happen. And again, anybody who's anybody was there, but it wasn't what he's become since then.

Today, Thaddaeus Ropac is one of the few galleries in the world that can regularly present solo exhibitions, even in its largest spaces, in which most of the works on display reach or exceed €1 million in price (works by star artists can go as high as 1.5 million). Moreover, these price points are in no way questioned or criticized by collectors, as the legitimacy of the gallery and its artists is unequivocal.

The gallery has another strong point: Thaddaeus Ropac was born in 1960. Unlike some other galleries at the top of my ranked list, whose futures are nebulous due to the advanced age of their founder, the Thaddaeus Ropac gallery has a substantial advantage in that respect.

It is difficult today to determine whether the Thaddaeus Ropac gallery is more Austrian, French, or British, even though it is mainly run out of France. The gallery's configuration is complex, given its undeniable roots in the DACH region, and its close association with the German figurative painting movement. In the words of this influential French gallerist: "Today, Ropac is the biggest German gallery. He has really slid into the position of the greatest German gallerist. Even in Germany, with the exception of one or two competitors, there's no one left, at least at that level. Ropac is sort of the only one!" I, however, would slightly amend this assertion. Another adjective seems to me to be more accurate in describing the Thaddaeus Ropac gallery and its success: as the title of "German gallery" accurately describes neither its national origin nor its breadth, and even though it has recently expanded into Asia, it is above all else a *European* establishment.

A dead heat between the four galleries vying for the ranking's second position: Sprüth Magers, David Zwirner, White Cube, and Hauser & Wirth

Even though each position on a ranked list tends to be precisely numbered, it should be noted that the average rankings of the 10 best artists from the Sprüth Magers (45.1), and even more so David Zwirner, White Cube, and Hauser & Wirth galleries (49, 49.8, and 49.9, respectively) are very close; while the Sprüth Magers gallery's second-position ranking is 22.5 points away from the number one gallery, Thaddaeus Ropac, there are only about 4 points separating the three galleries immediately after it, which themselves practically share the same average score. We could even consider these four galleries as a pool, since their rankings are so close, even though Sprüth Magers has a slight lead. Given how this data is produced and the inevitable effect that approximation will have (as I previously emphasized), it would be appropriate to assert that the David Zwirner, White Cube, and Hauser & Wirth galleries, in reality, share the same position in the ranked list, rather than considering them in close succession.

These four galleries should be examined as a homogeneous group since, in addition to their very close, or even practically identical average rating, they all experienced similar growths between 2019 and 2022, benefiting from the very pronounced competitive advantage that mega-galleries currently possess. Sprüth Magers moved from 4th to 2nd position, David Zwirner rose from 7th to 3rd place, White Cube from 6th to 4th, and Hauser & Wirth from 9th to 5th.[6] In doing so, all of these galleries overtook and ousted other galleries that, although very high-level, do not operate under the mega-gallery model.

The Sprüth Magers gallery

The Sprüth Magers gallery was founded in Cologne in 1998 with the merger of the individual galleries run by Monika Sprüth and Philomene Magers,[7] who both had specific specializations. Before they joined forces (and continuing on afterward), Sprüth was more interested in the aesthetic influence of emerging female contemporary artists, whereas Magers was more focused on artists of the generation prior to that explored by her business partner. The gallery therefore underwent a dual phase of growth, from their initial specializations (at a more modest level), then building up to a synergistic complementarity following their merger. It also demonstrates a particular interest in visual photography, with German artists such as Andreas Gursky and Thomas Ruff, or Americans such as Cindy Sherman. Today, Sprüth Magers has spaces in Berlin's Mitte district (since 2008), London's Mayfair (since 2007, on Grafton Street), and on Los Angeles' Miracle Mile, just across the street from the LACMA (since 2016). Additionally, they have offices in their original city of Cologne, and in Hong Kong.

Sprüth Magers gallery: ranking of its top 10 artists according to Artfacts (average ranking: 45.1):

Cindy Sherman	5
Thomas Ruff	10
Rosemarie Trockel	16
Ed Ruscha	20
John Baldessari estate	36
Jenny Holzer	54
Andreas Gursky	60
Gilbert & George	77
Kara Walker	85
Louise Lawler	88

My ranked list reflects the fact that Sprüth Magers has become one of the most influential galleries in the world today, not only due to the extent of its roster, but also the incredible recognition factor of its main artists. The rest of its roster, which, incidentally, is quite long (with 72 artists as of 2023), boasts rankings that are consistently low numerically (meaning that the artists are at the top of the ranking). In addition to its judicious artistic choice—in particular the emphasis that it placed on female artists at a time when they were widely neglected, and the focus on visual photography, which subsequently became a highly recognized field—the Sprüth Magers gallery developed rapidly on account of the fusion of the two pre-existing establishments. This combination took place at a time when there was not yet a strong push for growth, and the two partners therefore were among the first to benefit from this joint development. Just like the Thaddaeus Ropac gallery, because Sprüth Magers had invested heavily in the quality of its roster (which has become all the more essential in recent years) and because star artists (Quemin, 2013) are seeing much less fluctuation in their rankings, the average score of Sprüth Magers' top 10 artists dropped between 2019 and 2023 (also like the Ropac gallery's artists). This means that the recognition of the gallery's main artists has further increased, thus allowing the gallery to rise from 4th position in 2019 to second four years later, as I have already indicated.

The David Zwirner gallery

David Zwirner is originally from Germany and descended from an artistic lineage, as his father, Rudolf Zwirner, was a German gallerist who notably co-created the first contemporary art fair in the world, Art Cologne (Oberste-Hetbleck, 2014; Zwirner, 2019). However, contrary to some interpretations of this information, the David Zwirner gallery is in no way German; it is wholly American. Zwirner has spent his entire visual arts career in the United States, and he founded his eponymous gallery in New York in 1993 in the SoHo neighborhood (Halle & Tiso, 2014). In 2002, after this area fell out of favor as a gallery district, the gallery then moved to Chelsea, in a space on West 19th Street. For a while, from 2000 to 2009, Zwirner also had a partnership with Iwan Wirth, creating the Zwirner & Wirth gallery based in the Upper East Side and operating in private sales. After 2009, Zwirner devoted himself solely to his own gallery. In the cluster of three galleries, whose average ranking of their 10 best artists are incredibly similar, David Zwirner is closer to Hauser & Wirth due to their shared history; but also (as we will see) to the relative newness of both establishments. This is a trait that they also share with the White Cube gallery, which (along with David Zwirner) was founded in 1993. Incidentally, although Iwan Wirth had created his first gallery in 1986, he founded his second establishment, Hauser & Wirth, in 1992, at almost the same time. The three galleries are therefore remarkably new given the positions that they occupy at the top of the ranked list.

The David Zwirner gallery currently owns impressive premises in Chelsea, New York, with two beautiful buildings on West 19th and West 20th Street. Furthermore, since 2007, its presence in New York has expanded thanks to a location on the Upper East Side, and more recently a space with a less clearly commercial status in the Tribeca neighborhood; Zwirner therefore has a total of four spaces in New York. The plan to build a brand new gallery in the Chelsea district, designed by the esteemed architect Renzo Piano, had been on the cards for several years, but it was eventually scrapped in the summer of 2023. As for London, the David Zwirner gallery has had a space in the upscale district of Mayfair since 2012, and it opened a branch in Hong Kong in 2017. In Paris, where its space was inaugurated in 2019, Zwirner did not opt for the very bourgeois 8th arrondissement, but for the Marais neighborhood. In May 2023, the gallery announced that it would be opening a new space in the Melrose Hill district of Los Angeles that same month; consisting of two adjacent buildings and 16,000 square feet of exhibition space. Although the David Zwirner gallery's expansion has for a long time taken place primarily in New York, particularly in the Chelsea area, it has grown considerably outside of the city in recent years. In order to be placed so high on the ranked list, it must also necessarily have an excellent roster:

The David Zwirner gallery: ranking of its top 10 artists according to Artfacts (average ranking: 49):

Gerhard Richter	4
Wolfgang Tillmans	9
Thomas Ruff	10
Yayoi Kusama	19
Francis Alÿs	28
Richard Serra	46
Isa Genzken	49
Marlene Dumas	84
Rirkrit Tiravanija	112
Barbara Kruger	129

Note that, despite his German origins, David Zwirner has in no way served as a bridgehead for German artists in the United States. Admittedly, some of his most established artists are Thomas Ruff and Isa Genzken, but for a long time the David Zwirner gallery has not displayed any works by the greatest German painters, nor by the Düsseldorf School of Photography; with the exception of Ruff. This persisting absence of representation of the greatest German painters was masterfully rectified in 2023 when the star artist Gerhard Richter, who had been represented for a very long time by the Marian Goodman gallery, left it to join David Zwirner's roster. Naturally, such a major "get" caused the David Zwirner gallery to rise on my ranked list (and to decrease the ranking of Richter's former gallery's). To be sure, an artist as lauded as Richter could only have joined a very limited number of galleries; being a star artist, he had no other option than to join a star gallery. It was therefore the David Zwirner gallery, an establishment of commensurate prestige, that benefited from Richter's migration.

The White Cube gallery

Founded in 1993 in London by the incredibly wealthy Jay Jopling, the White Cube gallery has been closely tied to the dazzling success of the YBAs (Young British Artists), foremost of whom is Damien Hirst, who is still represented by the gallery. Today, White Cube is more focused than its competitors of equal standing on British artists, at least at the top of its roster (however, it has recently considerably expanded its lineup). With a handful of exceptions, it mainly represents artists (around 50 of them) with very significant reputations, some of whom have achieved star status.

White Cube gallery: ranking of its top 10 artists according to Artfacts (average ranking: 49.8):

Bruce Nauman	6
Georg Baselitz	7
Imi Knoebel	26
Mona Hatoum	34
Anselm Kiefer	37
Christian Marclay	57
Andreas Gursky	61
Damien Hirst	72
Gilbert & George	85
Danh Vo	113

The list of artists represented by White Cube inevitably evokes that of its fellow galleries Thaddaeus Ropac and, as we will later see, Gagosian, with some of the most recognized artists of our time entrusting their interests in North America to the Gagosian gallery, to White Cube in the UK, and the Thaddaeus Ropac gallery in continental Europe. White Cube currently has two massive spaces in London: one in the central district of Saint James, close to Mayfair, and the other in Bermondsey; which is further away from the center of London, south of the Thames. In addition to these two galleries, White Cube has had a third location in Hong Kong for several years and later opened a space in Seoul in the autumn of 2023. White Cube had only an office in New York City for a long time, on the chic Madison Avenue in the Upper East Side, but it opened a new gallery in October 2023 in the same district. It also opened a space in West Palm Beach, in Florida. In Paris, White Cube has an office on the elegant Avenue Matignon in the 8th arrondissement. The gallery's international development in terms of new spaces has clearly accelerated in recent years as a consequence of the growing competition between market leaders and of the necessity to be increasingly present internationally.

The Hauser & Wirth gallery

It would be pertinent to spend more time analyzing Hauser & Wirth than the previously discussed establishments of comparable level because it has adopted a very particular model in the world of the great international galleries.

As I briefly mentioned previously, Iwan Wirth inaugurated his first gallery in Zurich in 1986, before founding another gallery, Hauser & Wirth, in the same city in 1992 with his wife Manuela, and her mother, Ursula Hauser, who had amassed a large fortune by owning and running department stores, and who largely acted as a backer. In 2000, the three partners were joined by Marc Payot, who later became co-president of the gallery. Like its fellows David Zwirner and White Cube, the gallery is notably young given the position that it holds on my ranked list, but it was able to turn Ursula Hauser's fortune into an opportunity for accelerated development. In 1998, only six years after its creation, the up-and-coming gallery participated in the Art Basel fair for the first time, no doubt benefiting from a certain advantage accorded to Swiss galleries.

Hauser & Wirth, which is now no longer run out of Zurich, but primarily out of the United Kingdom and New York, attests to its impressive growth with a staff of over 250 people worldwide. Thanks to its geographical expansion, it has become the only gallery that is truly capable of competing with the international expansion of its rival Gagosian, which I will present next. In Zurich, its city of origin, the gallery occupies a space on Limmatstrasse, in a former industrial district that has since attracted several contemporary art galleries. It has another location in downtown Zurich, on Rämistrasse. The gallery was able to expand its reach throughout Switzerland by opening branches in the upscale ski resorts of Saint Moritz and Gstaad in 2015. At the same time, the gallery has had substantial international development, often in spectacular spaces. It opened a location in New

York City in 2009 in the very heart of the art market, the Chelsea neighborhood; after taking over an immense former roller rink, and later an entire building previously occupied by the Dia Art Foundation, the gallery later commissioned a building to be built on West 22nd Street, as well as another location on the Upper East Side. In October 2023, Hauser & Wirth announced that it would soon open a third New York branch in the district of SoHo, in a former garage that had previously been home to the Gagosian gallery before it left in 1999 for its current Chelsea location on West 24th Street. Following the COVID-19 pandemic, Hauser & Wirth inaugurated an annex space in the Hamptons; a favorite vacation spot for wealthy New Yorkers. The gallery has also been active in Los Angeles since 2016, where it occupies a massive space that, in many respects, comes across as more of a museum than a commercial gallery (Quemin, 2020b). It was, however, in the United Kingdom that the gallery made its first international venture. Its British presence is split between London, where it opened a branch in 2003 in an enormous, very well-located space on the prestigious thoroughfare of Saville Row, in the art and luxury neighborhood of Mayfair, and a huge, bucolic complex in the Somerset countryside, which was inaugurated in 2014. The gallery succeeded in transforming the small town of Bruton into a specific destination for art lovers.[8] Additionally, the gallery has had a space in Hong Kong since 2016. Finally, in 2021, the gallery opened a spectacular new 16,000-square-foot space in Spain on Illa del Rei, a small Balearic island situated opposite Port Mahón in Menorca. Once again, the space appears to be a cross between a commercial gallery and a museum. It should also be noted that the Hauser & Wirth gallery, which represents the estate of the Chillida Foundation, also manages the deceased artist's huge sculpture park in the Spanish Basque country. It later opened branches in Monaco, in the SoHo neighborhood of New York and in Paris, in the elegant 8th arrondissement, in 2023, and in 2024, in Basel, in Switzerland. To date, Hauser & Wirth manages a total of 16 galleries located in seven countries. It has developed an original model that combines elements taken directly from the best commercial galleries, with certain characteristics borrowed from museums, and it benefits from an impressive legitimacy and high symbolic capital due to its original positioning. As the gallery explained in a press release when announcing its intention to create a space in the Balearic Islands: "the artists and estates represented by the gallery have contributed to shaping its identity over the past quarter century, and are the inspiration for Hauser & Wirth's diverse range of activities relating to art, education, conservation, and sustainability."[9]

Hauser & Wirth has clearly managed to build an image that breaks from the traditional commercial aspect of its economic sector. It is the inclusion of a large number of artist estates, including star artists, on the gallery's roster (no fewer than seven estates out of their 10 best-ranked artists) that is unequivocally the most original facet of Hauser & Wirth's model in terms of artist representation.

Hauser & Wirth gallery: ranking of its top 10 artists according to Artfacts (average ranking: 49.9):

Cindy Sherman		5
Louise Bourgeois	estate	7
Dieter Roth Estate	estate	42
Jenny Holzer		52
Isa Genzken		55
Alexander Calder	estate	58
François Morellet	estate	59
Maria Lassnig	estate	61
Mike Kelley Foundation for the Arts	estate	77
Estate of Günther Förg	estate	83

In its extensive artist roster of 97 (a very high number, which is made possible thanks to its numerous exhibition spaces), Hauser & Wirth thus represents 59 living artists and 38 estates of deceased artists (the latter group is even identified as such on the gallery's website). Among its living artists, the gallery supports fewer artists who are superstars on the art market than its direct competitors (Gagosian, David Zwirner, and Thaddaeus Ropac); instead, it tends to favor more conceptual artists whose work does not sell as well, and who are more popular with institutions than collectors. When the American gallery Metro Pictures, which had represented Cindy Sherman for a long time, closed at the end of 2021, Sherman had no choice but to join a leading gallery; she ultimately chose Hauser & Wirth. On top of the continuous representation of already-renowned artists, this very notable transfer caused Hauser & Wirth to rise significantly between the 2019 and 2023 versions of my ranked list (from 9th position to 5th).

The Gagosian gallery

The Gagosian gallery occupies such a truly singular place on the international contemporary art market that it would be unthinkable not to delve into its analysis in detail.

As I have already indicated and emphasized, the Gagosian gallery's ranking in comparison to the other best galleries in the world is not as well reflected by the method that I have elaborated as that of its competitors. However, although my methodology is not particularly well suited to this very peculiar case, it clearly indicates that Gagosian belongs among the elite of the field. The rankings of its top 10 artists proves as much

The Gagosian gallery: ranking of its top 10 artists according to Artfacts (average ranking: 59.6):

Georg Baselitz	7
Ed Ruscha	20
Richard Serra	41
Anselm Kiefer	45
Andreas Gursky	59
Douglas Gordon	62
Damien Hirst	68
Harold Ancart	89
Albert Oehlen	92
Giuseppe Penone	113

As I have already explained, in the specific case of this gallery, it is not only the positions of its top 10 artists that are exceptionally high in the Artfacts ranked list; the placements of practically all of its artists are exceptionally low numerically speaking (meaning that they rank very high in the Artfacts classification). In this, it differs greatly from other galleries, even the leaders of the pack. Among the 105 artists that Gagosian represented or exhibited in 2023 (its website does not make the distinction between the two), the only artists to exceed the 8,000th position are Rachel Feinstein (8,035th), Tetsuya Ishida (8,520th), Jia Aili (9,345th), Mark Tansey (10,303rd), Anna Weyant (10,502nd), Y.Z Kami (10,892nd), and Richard Wright (11,686th). However, one fact may account for some of these ranks (which are surprisingly high in comparison to the other artists represented by Gagosian): Anna Weyant is a very young artist, especially for such a prestigious gallery, since she was born in 1995. Additionally, Rachel Feinstein is the wife of John Currin, another artist represented by Gagosian, and ranked 1,794th by Artfacts.

Larry Gagosian was born in Los Angeles in 1945 to an actress mother and an accountant father who worked for the local government, in a social environment that did not much value the visual arts. He got his start by selling posters when he was still a student at UCLA, not imagining that this would eventually lead him to become a gallerist, as he did not even know that this profession existed. He then began working in the secondary market by reselling artworks by contemporary artists. He founded his first gallery in Los Angeles in 1980, and in 1985 he opened another location in New York. As early as 1986, he began to intuit that Chelsea would become the next gallery district, and opened a second space in New York on West 23rd

Street as we already mentioned. This choice, which was ultimately before its time, is a perfect illustration of the concept of the "wrong turn" developed by David Halle and Elisabeth Tiso (Halle & Tiso, 2014), as the gallery was later forced to close this branch.

In 1989, after the Gagosian gallery had significantly grown in scope, it moved into a larger space on the Upper East Side, on the very stylish Madison Avenue, and began working more closely with the Leo Castelli gallery (Cohen-Solal, 2009). In 1991, Gagosian opened a second New York space in SoHo, the gallery district of the time, where it exhibited younger artists. In 1995, the gallery inaugurated a branch in the chic Beverly Hills neighborhood of Los Angeles, entrusting the development of the space to star architect Richard Meier. In New York, in 1999, Gagosian returned to Chelsea—this time on West 24th Street—moving into a space spanning 25,000 square feet; this time, the move was a resounding success. For the first time, Richard Serra and Damien Hirst could exhibit their monumental works in a commercial gallery space.

It was only after Gagosian put down roots in this immense Chelsea space that the gallery was able to become an international establishment, by opening a massive branch in the center of London, near Piccadilly Circus, in 2000. At the time, it was the largest gallery in all of London. A second London space was inaugurated in 2004 on Britannia Street; as it was of a comparable size to Gagosian's space in Chelsea, this new branch in turn became the largest gallery in London. In New York, Gagosian later supplemented the Chelsea mega-gallery on West 24th Street with another space on West 21st Street in 2006, which thus became the third New York location (as Gagosian had retained its space on Madison Avenue, which itself has grown to take over more floors in the building; once in 2007 and again in 2008). Also in 2007, Gagosian opened a gallery in Rome, then another in Athens in 2009, and in 2010 it opened a space in Geneva, and another in the chic 8th arrondissement in Paris.[10] In 2011, it expanded once again into Hong Kong, and in 2012 it opened a mega-space of 17,000 square feet in Le Bourget, in the northern suburbs of Paris. This spectacular gallery, which was designed by another star architect, Jean Nouvel, is located just next to an airport, meaning that visitors can come directly to the gallery from their private jets. In 2016, the gallery continued its expansion within the United States by inaugurating a branch in San Francisco, which has since closed.

Larry Gagosian, who now heads a team of about 300 people, runs his global operations from his home base in New York, where he currently manages six exhibition spaces. In addition to his iconic building at 555, West 24th Street in Chelsea, he has invested in two other spaces, both a stone's throw away and equally remarkable; one of which is located at number 541 on the same street, allowing Gagosian to further develop his domination of this major contemporary art thoroughfare; and the other within shouting distance on West 21st Street. The gallery's presence in New York is compounded by two Uptown locations: on Park Avenue and on

Madison Avenue, in the Upper East Side (the most upscale neighborhood in New York). Larry Gagosian has also maintained his space in Los Angeles, in the luxurious Beverly Hills district. In addition to the locations in these two cities, the gallery also has spaces in the top two European cities for the art market: Paris and London (on Grosvenor Hill and Davies Street, which are both located in the most elegant neighborhood of the city, and a third less central location on Britannia Street). Also in Europe, the influential gallery has even more spaces in Rome, Athens, Geneva, and more recently, in Basel. As one of the gallery directors stated:

> Of course, we have locations in some places in the world that don't really make sense vis à vis the art market. There are artists for whom it is important to have an exhibition in Rome or Athens, even though we know very well that we won't make many sales there. These spaces are really a service that we offer to our artists, and it's about image, like when auction houses send works around the world before a sale. The impact on transactions is often quite negligible.

However, the Gagosian gallery does not open spaces only for the sake of doing so, and has thus never opened a space in Berlin, which does not offer sufficient market appeal. Outside of the Western world, Gagosian only has its Hong Kong branch. In January 2021, the gallery announced that it had closed its San Francisco space, which was very close to the major contemporary art museum SFMoMA, just five years after it had opened, so as to double down on Gagosian's presence on the West Coast of the United States. However, this closure in no way indicated a withdrawal from California; at practically the same time, the gallery decided to take over the space of the defunct Marciano Museum—a former Masonic temple of more than 85,000 square feet on Wilshire Boulevard—not far from its Beverly Hills branch.

To date, the Gagosian gallery boasts an unequaled number of 20 locations worldwide (plus a boutique in New York). It operates in 10 cities and 7 countries. Additionally, its spaces are almost always spectacular, especially in regards to their size. Such an international presence can only be possible by having a roster of equally impressive artists, both as concerns their renown and their popularity on the market. Whether in terms of its recognition—and unparalleled access to the international market—or the quality of its roster, the Gagosian gallery's excellence is unmistakable. The gallery's prestige allows it to regularly organize museum-quality exhibitions; and it readily puts on shows in which, on occasion, virtually no artwork is for sale (or sometimes none at all), in order to reinforce its image even more (Quemin, 2020b).

As this influential gallerist who is based in two European countries indicated: "Gagosian has achieved something that no other gallery has managed to do. He has created a global brand, known throughout the world." Admittedly, Larry Gagosian is the successor of Leo Castelli (Cohen-

Solal, 2009), who was something of a mentor to Gagosian, and whom he replaced as the most powerful gallerist in the world. However, whereas Castelli collaborated with a network of "friendly galleries" throughout the most important art metropolises and which paid him a commission on the sales of his artists, Larry Gagosian instituted a system of direct sales outside of the United States by opening a large number of branches in foreign countries. In doing so, Gagosian demonstrated that he was no longer satisfied with a simple commission system; instead, the gallery would retain the entire transaction amount for itself. This model comes with high fixed costs that can only be covered by representing a great many artists who are highly desired on the market. Though the Gagosian gallery spares no expense on its magnificent and often massive spaces, which allows it to accommodate collections in the best possible conditions, as well as to attract the most recognized artists (who are very sensitive to the kind of high-quality exhibitions that the gallery can offer), a good part of its costs is externalized, particularly pertaining to how the gallery ensures an artist's renown (Quemin, 2013). Gagosian thereby does not contribute to an artist's early career; in general, he integrates them into his roster once their prices have risen markedly, at which point he directly participates in reinforcing the gallery world's model of a fringe oligopoly (Benhamou, 1996).

For years, Larry Gagosian has been made out to be the emperor of the art market, without any rival. Like the most powerful emperors in history, the sun never sets on his empire; however, this dominion now appears to be challenged. For a long time, only the Pace gallery seemed to be a contender for representing some of the same artists. More recently, the threat seems to be coming more from competitors David Zwirner and Hauser & Wirth; both galleries have established spaces to rival Gagosian in the very heart of his Chelsea stronghold, and have outfitted themselves with magnificent mega-spaces of their own. While Gagosian used to have something of a monopoly and could offer its artists exhibition conditions worthy of a (small) museum, its competitors have now also equipped themselves with remarkable exhibition spaces. Pace, which had been trailing behind due to its not having made the same essential investment, was ultimately obliged to do so in turn. As these now fully credible rivals began to emerge, Gagosian was forced to agree to share representation of certain star artists with his most direct competitors; nevertheless, he has most likely managed to remain in the lead, at least in economic terms.[11] My ranked list, which strives to highlight the "quality" of galleries based on the "quality" of their most recognized—or even lauded—artists, tends to indicate that there may be an alternative rationale to that associated with mere market power. In this respect, Larry Gagosian must contend with another considerable rival, Thaddaeus Ropac, who is too often disregarded because he does not have a presence in New York, the flagship metropolis of the international art market (concentrated in the Chelsea neighborhood). Finally, the Gagosian gallery faces another threat in the form of its leader's age; born in 1945, Larry Gagosian is now nearing 80 years old. The history of the art market shows that the act of passing the torch often signals a gallery's decline, particularly when their leader does not have a child (especially a son) who can succeed them. Such is the case for Larry Gagosian, who has no offspring.

From a certain point of view, the Gagosian and Thaddaeus Ropac galleries follow a similar business development model, and both are among the foremost galleries in the world today, no matter the criteria. Finally, both establishments place a particular emphasis on their artists.[12] As I previously mentioned, Larry Gagosian held an absolute monopoly for a long time, as he was the only person who could offer his artists a mega-space, which was, moreover, located in Manhattan—the heart of the art market—with its flagship gallery on West 24th Street in Chelsea (Halle & Tiso, 2014). Thaddaeus Ropac who, as previously stated, got into the profession thanks to his privileged relationship with Joseph Beuys, was introduced very early on to important and major artists, whom he immediately placed at the center of his development model. From then on, it was essential that he be able to offer them one or even several spaces that would satisfy their aspirations, with an important step being the 2012 inauguration of his mega-space in Pantin, which was particularly out of proportion to artists such as Antony Gormley, Georg Baselitz, and Anselm Kiefer, who were but a few of the gallery's long list of represented star artists. There is a notable parallel between the tremendous development of the two previous major galleries and the means by which the Art Basel fair has distinguished itself from competing events: by banking on collectors (Oberste-Hetbleck, 2014; Zwirner, 2019). While other fairs aimed above all else to satisfy their direct clients (i.e., galleries), Art Basel understood that winning over the greatest collectors would automatically attract the best galleries. Similarly, whether pertaining to the Gagosian or Thaddaeus Ropac galleries, the fact of exhibiting the most recognized artists ensures the support of the greatest collectors. This is also one of the reasons for both galleries' investment in museum exhibitions, which complement those organized in their own spaces and which contribute directly to the acclaim (Quemin, 2013b) of the artists whom they support.

Neck-and-neck for 7th place: the Konrad Fischer, Skarstedt, and Marian Goodman galleries:

The Konrad Fischer, Skarstedt, and Marian Goodman galleries are practically on equal footing on my ranked list; the average ranking of their 10 best artists is 70.0 for the first, 71.4 for the second, and 73.4 for the third. It should also be noted that the average ranking of their top 10 represented artists is significantly higher than all of the preceding galleries (the difference of their averages amounts to more than 10 points between them and Gagosian, which is just before them on the list), tending to indicate that they belong to a distinct group of galleries.

The Konrad Fischer gallery

The Konrad Fischer gallery directly benefited from Germany's growing influence (concentrated specifically in the Ruhr region) on the European contemporary art scene during the 1970s and 1980s (Zwirner, 2019) and it also contributed to this regional growth. In 1967, Konrad and Dorothee Fischer inaugurated a small gallery in the center of Düsseldorf with an exhibition of Carl Andre artworks. At the time, minimal and conceptual art was virtually unknown in Europe; many of the American artists from this wave (who are among the most established artists today) had their first European exhibitions at Konrad Fischer, and are still represented by the gallery today. By virtue of frequently inviting their artists to create their works *in situ*, the Fischers largely helped to energize the Düsseldorf art scene. The gallery was then able to expand its lineup to movements such as Arte Povera, which has also found success on the international scene; however, its later choices of artists have been somewhat less successful overall. In 2007, the gallery opened a second space outside of Düsseldorf, in Berlin. The organization is now run by the founders' daughter, Berta Fischer.

For a gallery of its impact, Konrad Fischer has a roster of average scope, with a total of 56 artists.

Konrad Fischer gallery: Ranking of its top 10 artists according to Artfacts (average ranking: 70.0):

Bruce Nauman	6
Thomas Ruff	10
Daniel Buren	65
Richard Long	74
Tony Cragg	78
Gilbert & George	81
Hans-Peter Feldmann	87
Carl Andre	90
Giuseppe Penone	100
Thomas Schütte	109

Even today, the gallery avails itself of a group of artists that it has represented since it was founded. Its excellent position in the classification is in part due to an effect of hysteresis (Bourdieu, 1992): the gallery's strength lies in its headliners, but beyond its top 10 artists, the rankings are clearly worse than those of the Thaddaeus Ropac and Gagosian galleries, for instance. As this Belgian gallerist stated: "The Konrad Fischer gallery in Düsseldorf is one of the best in the world. They introduced American minimalist and conceptual artists to Germany, at a time when almost no one knew who they were in Europe, and they were not very expensive. They're only present in one country, it's a model that you see less and less now." This fellow gallerist based in two European countries agreed: "It's an excellent gallery, they've been representing very important artists for years, and they've been able to keep them, which isn't that easy. But they haven't really been able to revitalize their roster."

In a way, Konrad Fischer is the European counterpart of the Marian Goodman gallery. Whereas the latter introduced European artists to the United States, for whom its fellow New York galleries showed little interest at the time, Konrad Fischer served as a bridgehead in Europe for American artists, who up to that point had not been much esteemed (nor exhibited) in the Old World. This proves, once again, that specialization can ultimately pay dividends.

Konrad Fischer—an excellent gallery that benefited from its wise choices over the decades—currently presents a totally atypical profile due to its only having locations in one country, and only two cities at that; neither of which has an international market as thriving as in other cities. The gallery is placed so high on the ranked list in large part due to its heritage. In 2021, I wrote that this gallery would in all likelihood eventually be relegated to operating mostly in the secondary market (Quemin, 2021). The decline that it has already experienced in the ranking, falling from third to 7th place in 4 years (between 2019 and 2023), attests to something of an erosion of its position when faced with the rise of mega-galleries.

The Skarstedt gallery

The Skarstedt gallery's position on my ranked list is liminal; in essence, it is not easy to determine whether this gallery is more involved in the primary or secondary market. While it was historically more active in the latter, it has invested more in the primary market in recent years; hence my decision to include it in the classification that I have presented here.

At this level of recognition, the gallery stands out due to its very restricted roster of only 33 artists:

Skarstedt gallery: ranking of its top 10 artists according to Artfacts (average ranking: 71.4):

Cindy Sherman	5
Georg Baselitz	7
Rosemarie Trockel	14

(continued)

Jenny Holzer	52
Martin Kippenberger*	76
Albert Oehlen	77
Thomas Schütte	114
Jeff Koons	119
Richard Prince	121
Barbara Kruger	129

*Estate of Martin Kippenberger in the US in collaboration with the Gisela Capitain gallery in Cologne.

Founded in 1994 by Per Skarstedt in New York, the gallery now has locations solely in the three main international cities of contemporary art: New York (on the Upper East Side, since it began), London (in the Mayfair neighborhood, since 2012), and Paris (since 2021). Its Paris space was initially established in the Marais district, clearly demonstrating its desire to further develop its operations in the primary market, which is highly associated with this area. However, the Skarstedt gallery very quickly left this neighborhood to set up shop in a more predictable area, given its history on the secondary market, in the heart of the bourgeois 8th arrondissement of Paris, on Avenue Matignon.

The Marian Goodman gallery:

Even before the creation of her eponymous gallery, Marian Goodman co-founded Multiples, Inc. in 1965; an organization that published prints, multiples, and art books by leading American artists such as Richard Artschwager, John Baldessari, Dan Graham, Sol LeWitt, Roy Lichtenstein, Claes Oldenburg, James Rosenquist, and Andy Warhol. From 1968 to 1975, Multiples, Inc. also published first editions of European artists such as Joseph Beuys, Marcel Broodthaers, Blinky Palermo, and Gerhard Richter; these were intended for American audiences. In 1974, after starting to work in close collaboration with Marcel Broodthaers, Goodman tried to find a gallery that would represent him in New York. She was ultimately unsuccessful, as knowledge of contemporary European art at the time was limited in the United States, due to the lack of travel, exhibitions, and sharing of information about these artists among the American audience. Goodman therefore decided to open her own gallery to show Broodthaers' works, along with those of other European artists. She took inspiration from the great Leo Castelli for her business model (Cohen-Solal, 2009).

Although Broodthaers died in 1976, Goodman did not give up on her passion project, and she founded her eponymous gallery in New York in 1977 in the heart of Midtown, on East 57th Street, where she remained until 2024. The gallery began to grow in the early 1980s, with a lineup primarily centered on European artists who were still underappreciated in the United States at the time; such as Gerhard Richter, Tony Cragg, Giovanni Anselmo, Giuseppe Penone, and Giulio Paolini (all of whom she still represents, with the exception of Richter, whom she lost in 2023).

Although the gallery never made the move to Chelsea, it expanded into Europe in 1995, which seemed logical given its orientation, and it chose to put down roots in the Marais neighborhood of Paris.[13] In 2014, the gallery opened an additional branch in London, which was inaugurated with a Gerhard Richter exhibition. However, Paris has always been its main location in Europe, and Goodman continues to oversee her network, limited in scope though it may be, from New York. As this star artist, who is represented by the gallery, stated: "Marian's principal characteristic is that she's cautious. She thinks a lot before making a decision, and she only acts if she's sure that she will succeed." Nevertheless, In the wake of post-Brexit instability, and then the COVID-19 pandemic, the Marian Goodman gallery closed its London space in 2020. In its place, the gallery introduced Marian Goodman Projects, a less costly and more flexible entity that can organize ad hoc events both in London and in other cities. It also opened a space in Los Angeles in 2023.

The Marian Goodman gallery: ranking of its top 10 artists according to Artfacts (average ranking: 73.4):

William Kentridge	6
Tony Cragg	25
Nan Goldin	50
Hiroshi Sugimoto	57
Tacita Dean	81
Anri Sala	88
Danh Vo	90
Thomas Struth	99
Giuseppe Penone	100
Julie Mehretu	138

While the Marian Goodman gallery is often associated with star European artists, it should be noted that the headliners on its roster are in fact from more diverse backgrounds. With only 50 creators, the gallery works with a rather limited number of artists for an establishment of its caliber; particularly in recent years when leading galleries have tended to expand their list of represented artists.

The Marian Goodman gallery's long-lasting resounding success, just like that of the Thaddaeus Ropac gallery, can be explained by the priority afforded to their artists, as well as a particular specialization (also like Thaddaeus Ropac). Whereas Thaddaeus Ropac initially favored German and American artists and committed to a focus on figurative painting, Marian Goodman featured the most recognized European artists at a time when her fellow American gallerists did not show any particular interest in them. However, the gallery has always been somewhat undersized in proportion to its quality (Misdrahi Flores, 2013), which is reflected in my ranked list. In 2021, I wrote that the gallery appeared to have grown weaker due to the advanced age of its founder and director, who was born in 1928 and was therefore already over 90 years old (Quemin, 2021). In 2023, the art world was rocked by the shocking announcement that star artist Gerhard Richter would be leaving Marian Goodman for its competitor David Zwirner. The downward progression of the Marian Goodman gallery's ranking in recent years clearly reflects the challenges that I wrote about in 2021. Between 2019 and the beginning of 2023, the gallery has fallen significantly in the classification, from 2nd place to eighth only. Furthermore, the recently announced departure of Nan Goldin, another star artist, for its competitor Gagosian would lead the Marian Goodman gallery to drop even further in my ranking were I to recalculate the data. My ranked list clearly reflects the dynamics at work regarding the headliners of various gallery rosters. Not having adopted the mega-gallery economic model seems to have weakened the Marian Goodman gallery. In 2023, aware of the need to react to the gallery's decline, the current management team announced the gallery's imminent move from its historic New York stronghold in Midtown to the up-and-coming Tribeca neighborhood. The opening, in a whole building, was announced for the Autumn of 2024. This proves, once again, that urban space is not neutral, and that galleries will incorporate it into their development strategies, even those that were long located in a given neighborhood, even after it began to decline as a gallery district.

The Lisson gallery, in 10th place

The Lisson gallery, originally in London, is one of the older galleries in this group of frontrunners, as it was founded in 1967 by Nicholas Logsdail, even before the contemporary art world had really emerged (Quemin, 2002 and 2013b). Nevertheless, the gallery has been able to secure a remarkable position in this segment of the art market and rise to the top of its field. Its London presence is divided between two different spaces on Lisson Street and Bell Street. In New York, the gallery opened a branch in Chelsea in 2016 on West 24th Street (but at a respectful distance from the goliath Gagosian, across the street and down the block from the flagship location of its powerful competitor). Following the COVID-19 pandemic, during which many wealthy New York collectors vacated their homes on the Upper East Side and moved into their summer residences in the Hamptons, Lisson opened a temporary annex space in East Hampton, so as to be closer to its clients. It also opened an outpost in Los Angeles in April 2023, and has a location in Shanghai, as well as in Beijing; the gallery therefore operates in three countries and four major cities. Clearly, the gallery is continuing its geographical expansion in order to "maintain its ranking" and control its market.

The Lisson gallery: ranking of its top 10 artists according to Artfacts (average ranking: 80.2):

Marina Abramović	44
Ai Weiwei	45
Sean Scully	62
Daniel Buren	67
Richard Long	71
Laure Prouvost	75
Tony Cragg	80
Anish Kapoor	102
Jonathan Monk	116
Dan Graham	140

The top of the Lisson gallery's roster features a significant number of British star artists, who either live in the United Kingdom or have been active there; thus drawing a parallel with the gallery's closest competitor, White Cube.

A unique case: The Chantal Crousel gallery

Although most rankings are based on a decimal system, I thought it would be interesting to make an exception to this unspoken rule by focusing on the Chantal Crousel gallery, which now falls into 11th place (it was in 10th place in 2019). This outcome is absolutely remarkable for an establishment that is by no means a mega-gallery, and only operates in a single country. Its business model is similar to that of Konrad Fischer, which also has locations in a single country, and only in two cities.

The Chantal Crousel gallery was created in Paris in 1980. Its founder had previously worked as a secretary in Belgium, her country of birth. After seeing a drawing by Man Ray in a shop window—a work that she later acquired—she decided to go to France to study art history, and later opened her gallery. Very quickly, her establishment expanded its lineup to artists from countries other than France and Belgium, including Cindy Sherman and Alighiero Boetti. Originally located near Beaubourg and the Musée National d'Art Moderne on the border of the Marais neighborhood, it moved to the space that it currently occupies in the heart of the same district in 2000. It had a second space in Paris for a time, near the Place de la République, a more popular district, but ultimately had to give it up. Nowadays, it constitutes an exception at the top of my ranked list; not only does it operate in only one city, but it has maintained its single midsize space, which is well below the quality (Misdrahi Flores, 2013) of its artist roster.[14] For years now, the gallery has been actively looking for a larger location in the Marais, as the intellectual neighborhood matches its identity perfectly. Since 2005, the gallery has been represented by a partner in Beijing, and would be capable of opening a space there; however, for a gallery of this quality, these two ambitions have been slow to materialize.

In 2000, Chantal Crousel's son, Niklas Svennung, joined his mother's gallery after having worked in New York with David Zwirner for four years, before eventually taking over as executive director in 2019; Chantal Crousel took on the role of consultant; and with that, the mother–son duo are now partners and co-owners of the gallery.

It would have been unfeasible to imagine the Chantal Crousel gallery in 11th position, were it not for the carefully thought-out calculation of my ranked list. The gallery represents only 35 artists, none of whom are the undisputed stars of the art market who naturally draw attention to the galleries that represent them. In an article from February 16, 2021, the online newspaper *Artnet News* reported: "Nothing predestined Chantal Crousel to become one of the most successful gallerists in Paris."[15] However, this statement ought to be rectified: the Chantal Crousel gallery is not one of the most successful *in Paris*. The level that it has reached in terms of representing some of the most internationally renowned artists elevates it to the status of one of the best galleries *in the world*.

The Chantal Crousel gallery: Ranking of its top 10 artists according to Artfacts (average ranking: 88.8):

Wolfgang Tillmans	9
Mona Hatoum	35
Heimo Zobernig	37
Anri Sala	95

(continued)

Pierre Huyghe	106
Rirkrit Tiravanija	111
Glenn Ligon	112
Danh Vo	113
Gabriel Orozco	129
Thomas Hirschhorn	141

While Chantel Crousel's roster is small (which is understandable, given its single exhibition space), it features practically zero little-known artists, with the exception of Clément Rodzielski (ranked 4,937th by Artfacts as of September 2023, but still very young, as he was born in 1979) and Moshe Ninio (ranked 16,809th by Artfacts). Discounting these two, all of the gallery's artists have rankings below 4,000. Most likely because it does not focus on the most popular artists on the market (who are mainly from the United States, Germany, and Great-Britain [Quemin, 2002, 2004, 2006 and 2013b]), the Chantal Crousel gallery presents a great diversity of nationalities among its artists, especially as concerns its most prominent creators.

Crousel explains that 70 percent of her sales are to foreign collectors, either at fairs or via remote transactions. This high proportion can be explained by the fact that the gallery has been able to establish a niche in conceptual art that is widely acknowledged on the international level. The gallery often integrates artists while they are still young, helping them build toward a stronger level of recognition, and does not seek to collaborate directly with artists who already have an established reputation.

What can we conclude from the top 10 galleries in the classification?

In light of the information presented thus far, there is an undeniable diversity of profiles for the galleries that are placed highest on my ranked list. The top 10 galleries have been in existence for varying amounts of time. The two oldest establishments—Konrad Fischer and Lisson—were founded in 1967. Although the former has not managed to compile a current artist roster that reproduces the success of its halcyon days, it has at least sustained enough prestige to keep hold of its great historical artists. By contrast, its competitor Lisson has had much more success in revitalizing its artistic offering, which may have been its key to international expansion. Another wave of galleries that would go on to become some of the best in the world began around the early 1980s; Marian Goodman opened just before, in 1977, Gagosian in

1980, and Thaddaeus Ropac in 1983. Finally, the last group of top galleries came into existence in the early 1990s: Hauser & Wirth in 1992, David Zwirner and White Cube in 1993, and Skarstedt in 1994. While the Sprüth Magers gallery is newer, as it was founded in 1998, it is in point of fact the result of the merger of two pre-existing establishments; its two co-founders were therefore active on the market long before. This data proves that establishing one of the top galleries in the world takes time. Both in the past and nowadays, artists must reach a series of benchmarks in order to be considered highly successful (Quemin, 2013b), which takes time; and the same is true for galleries. Of particular importance in this process is being accepted to various art fairs, which can both broaden the market to which galleries have access and help them attract more recognized artists by offering them better sales prospects via these fairs.

The fact of comparing the 10 galleries at the top of the ranked list also shines a light on highly varied forms of geographical positioning. There is a spectrum of circumstances, with Konrad Fischer on one end, being present in a single country (but in the two main regions of the national market, Berlin and the Ruhr), and the galleries with the largest number of locations on the other end: Hauser & Wirth, with its 16 spaces in 7 countries, is the only gallery that comes close to competing with the sheer numbers of the behemoth Gagosian, which currently boasts an unparalleled 20 galleries around the world (plus a boutique in New York) in nine cities and seven countries (Quemin, 2020b). The fact that the top 10 comprises establishments with spectacular artist rosters and locations in a limited number of cities or countries shows that there is no single formula for a successful gallery. However, the best galleries in the world (those that work with the most recognized artists) often have multiple spaces in several countries. Their economic power facilitates their development, and their geographical expansion reinforces their growth. Note, however, that these galleries that are qualified as the best in the world collectively have locations, whether in their country of origin or abroad, in a very small number of countries, which are all located in the northern hemisphere (Quemin, 2013a and 2023). With the notable exception of the Thaddaeus Ropac gallery—which was founded outside of a major contemporary art city, in a somewhat marginal country as far as the art world is concerned, but later expanded into two major art cities (and more recently into Seoul) as part of its development—all of the top establishments were created in a handful of countries: The United States, the United Kingdom, Germany, and Switzerland. As these galleries have grown, there has been a discernible shift of their headquarters toward subsequent locations, which then become the operational center for the gallery leader. The phenomenon has been particularly observable for Gagosian, which was founded in Los Angeles but is now managed out of New York; Thaddaeus Ropac, which was created in Salzburg but is now managed from Paris; and Hauser & Wirth, which began in Zurich but is now run primarily out of London and New York. Clearly, in an era that is associated with the push for "globalization" and the dissolution of borders, geographical rationales still hold sway, even for the best, most powerful galleries; those that might in theory have been exempted (at least in part) from such constraints. These very international galleries are fervently pursuing their development abroad, but not everywhere; most of the world remains, even to this day, totally ignored (Quemin, 2002, 2004, 2006, 2013a and b, and 2023).

A recurring element in all of these cases is that the galleries that have achieved resounding success have often benefited from their respective specializations, but it is difficult to determine whether they cohered into a particular strategy. Gagosian has amassed a wide array of the most expensive artists on the market, whereas Konrad Fischer bet the proverbial farm on the first generation of conceptual artists. In the latter's case, this also involved a particular emphasis on American artists, thus making it the *de facto* counterpart of Marian Goodman (as I have already indicated), which introduced many European artists to the United States. Conversely, Thaddaeus Ropac initially banked on German and American artists, as well as Austrian creators; and on a particular medium: painting. White Cube adopted a rather similar strategy to Thaddaeus Ropac (though White Cube's focus is not on Austrian artists, which remains one of the purviews of Thaddaeus Ropac), and it also shares a common trait with Lisson: they have both greatly supported British artists, and they have been supported by them. In light of the various galleries at the top of this classification, one could conclude that specialization, though always relative, has often been a wise choice.

Another influential factor that could explain how some galleries made it to the top of this ranked list is that their owners had considerable financial resources. As such, they were able to secure a great amount of money in a sector that has not historically been intensely capitalistic in nature. This helped them to stand out from their fellow galleries, as they could quickly acquire an exhibition space that gave them a clearcut competitive advantage. Hence, they were able not only to attract the attention of collectors, but also to gain the representation of the most coveted artists by offering them the best exhibition conditions. I previously mentioned the fact that Ursula Hauser's wealth was able to support the development of the gallery that she created with her daughter and son-in-law. The director of a major European gallery also indicated: "As regards White Cube, Jay Jopling is immensely rich, and he was able to develop his business very quickly thanks to his fortune, which predates his entry into the field. This kind of establishment is another kind of gallery model, they don't have the same account balancing constraints as a gallery like ours does."

Another fact that is revealed by my ranked list is that there is a recent trend of reinforcing mega-galleries' influence on the market and in the art world. The analyses that I developed in the second part of this book, and that I previously presented in 2021 (Quemin, 2021) are broadly confirmed by the evolution of my ranked lists between 2019 and 2023. In essence, the main artists who are promoted by mega-galleries have moved up the Artfacts classification, leading to a drop in the average ranking calculated for these establishments (meaning that they are climbing toward the first position) and their placements among this small group of the best galleries in the world.

The top of my ranked list could also provide material for a gender analysis, considering who founded the galleries and/or still runs them today. Unlike in other professional worlds, the elite of contemporary art galleries is not overly unfavorable to women, and is even quite welcoming toward them (Herstatt, 2008). However, gender parity is by no means imminent in this sector, and in all the countries from which these galleries are run, the largest companies in their sector are not generally directed by women. Of the top 10 galleries that managed to rise to the highest level of success, only two are led solely by women: the Sprüth Magers and the Marian Goodman galleries. Although the Konrad Fischer gallery bears the name of the husband alone, it was founded by Fischer and his wife, and is now run by their daughter. Hauser & Wirth is now run by two men and a woman, having been created by a man and two women. It is notable that the world of contemporary art galleries demonstrates a certain openness to women; or to put it differently, is less unfavorable to them than the rest of the business world.

Still on the subject of women, a second point is particularly remarkable if the analysis is extended beyond the top 10 galleries: generally speaking, in many professional worlds, the higher up the hierarchy, the more the number of women tends to decrease. In the art world, this phenomenon is not very pronounced, as shown by the proportion of women who have founded and manage galleries (at the time of their foundation and during the years that led to their growth) and who are now running the galleries with the best artist rosters.

Number of women and men who run the contemporary art galleries on my international ranked list:

	Top 10 of the ranked list	**Top 50**	**Top 100**
Men	6	29	58
Women	2	17	34
Both	2	4	8

It is remarkable that the distribution of men and women is so stable toward the top of the list. The proportions are identical between the top 100 and the top 50, and they are still close for the top 10 alone. Approximately six out of ten galleries are founded and directed by one or more men, around one-third were founded and are currently directed by one or more women, and approximately 1 in 10 is directed by partnerships composed of both genders. Note that these results are very similar to those produced in 2019 (Quemin, 2021). This is all the more noteworthy and surprising as, in general, when the financial stakes for a business are very high, women are strongly under-represented in top management roles. As such, in most economic segments, there are very few women who run major companies. Here, the fact that art is generally socially perceived as a sector that is more associated with women can, in part, compensate for the social representation of associating business management and financial matters with men.

Another element that must be acknowledged is the age of gallery owners, as it has so much influence on the future of the galleries themselves. In the case of the Konrad Fischer gallery, the matter of succession has already been resolved: as previously mentioned, Berta, the daughter of founders Konrad and Dorothee Fischer, took over from the couple. Today, the transition for leadership of the Marian Goodman gallery is imminent given the very advanced age of its founder, and the succession of Larry Gagosian has been a hot topic of conversation for years. There are some rumors on which of his staff members could step into his role, but nothing is certain at this point. In this context, Thaddaeus Ropac, born in 1960; Jay Jopling, born in 1963; David Zwirner, born in 1964; and Iwan Wirth, born in 1970, offer a relative guarantee of stability as concerns their age and their ability to continue to strengthen the development of their galleries over the coming years. This assurance can even extend into the longer term, when children work with their parents. Such is the case for Lucas Zwirner, who is the Head of Content at David Zwirner, where he oversees all of its publications. Galleries that are likely to be taken over by the offspring of the founder, particularly the sons—as the surname carries over the aura bestowed by the person who founded the gallery and led it to glory—have an asset for the future. However, history has shown that maintaining the success of the highest-level galleries is generally closely tied to their founder.

The ranked list that I have compiled also highlights a reality that is too seldom acknowledged in the contemporary art world: many of the top ten galleries have regularly been distinguished by the Power 100 list, which constitutes one of the original contemporary art world indicators (Quemin, 2013b). However, the top of my ranked list reveals how the Power 100 is, in point of fact, very dependent on the single image that is associated with the galleries. The most discreet establishments, such as the Konrad Fischer gallery, which has a long history (at least in terms of the contemporary art world), have largely been overlooked by the Power 100.[16] Conversely, the more visibility a gallery has, the more it is seen as proof of its power, and the more likely the gallery is to be featured and highly placed in the Power 100, which primarily reflects preconceptions (Durkheim, 2007). My ranked list, which nevertheless seeks to quantifiably analyze the best galleries, not the most powerful,[17] reflects a rather different hierarchy.

The main lesson to be drawn from the top of my international ranked list of contemporary art galleries is likely the following: excellence when it comes to representing artists does not necessarily go hand in hand with having the status of "heavyweight" on the art market. In other words, the galleries with the most financial resources, with the highest capital intensity ratios, or with the most locations around the world, are not automatically at the top of the ranking. There is a peculiarity of the market that, as it is a market for symbolic goods (Bourdieu, 1971 and 1996), is more complex than other markets for ordinary goods. Although the art market operates under economic principles, it is impacted by symbolic or aesthetic factors. The rationale of the artistic field permeates and directly affects the art market much more than in other economic sectors. There is, nevertheless, a certain degree of autonomy between the two spheres; my ranked list reveals the relative autonomy of the artistic field as regards the economic field (Bourdieu, 1971 and 1996). The galleries that represent the most recognized artists and can therefore be considered the "best" or most important from an artistic point of view are not systematically those with the most financial means or the most expensive exhibition spaces.

Nonetheless, the relationship between art and money is so deeply ingrained in people's minds that the discrepancy revealed by this research—even though it is limited to some cases—will naturally arouse suspicion, or even contestation, as public knowledge generally tends not to distinguish between the two dimensions. It is also in the interest of financially powerful galleries to maintain the illusion that their influence on the art market comes down solely to the means available to each establishment, omitting the fact that the symbolic dimension of the "greatness" of artists and the galleries that represent them in reality renders the situation very complex. It can even take precedence when there is a significant disconnect between the two dimensions.

Among the elite of the gallery world, the disjunction between economic influence and aesthetic recognition is particularly clear in the case of the Chantal Crousel gallery, which is why I highlighted it, even though it now falls just outside of the top 10 (the same kind of separation also exists for the Konrad Fischer and Marian Goodman galleries, though to a lesser extent); but we will see later in this chapter that it exists on many levels, including certain establishments with lower positions in the classification, which I will analyze later. Some galleries that exhibit all the signs of economic power turn out to be comparatively weak in terms of the quality of their roster. Thus, it is evident that my ranked list is not determined by a gallery's economic influence. Even though I have clearly explained that it would not be possible to produce a classification based on this factor in any case, the number of locations and assets (especially in terms of exhibition spaces) available to certain galleries testifies to their considerable financial means; they cannot, however, automatically be considered the best galleries in the world if one were to look at their artists alone. Some galleries–those that are motivated primarily by their commercial goals—do not estimate themselves as any less important than galleries with better rankings, because their artists are more famous and recognized. In a sector that conflates the economic and symbolic dimensions, success can be seen as an expression of both dimensions in multiple ways. However, it should be noted that a gallery that is remarkably successful in economic terms but is relatively low on my ranked list could be accused of being (too) commercial, which would constitute a weakness. It would then run the risk of being less esteemed in the eyes of both its peers and collectors, at least the most legitimate among them. Compiling a ranked list that assesses performance and reveals ordered positions can call the hierarchies that are based on impressions alone into question, those that typically structure the contemporary art world, like all social worlds.

Beyond the top 10 galleries: the general conclusions of this ranked list

The classification that I have constructed can help to delineate how the world of contemporary art galleries is structured (Quemin, 2020a).

Although all of the galleries that were included in my ranking participate in the Art Basel art fair, and as such can all be considered part of an elite group within their domain, there is a considerable distance between the galleries at the very top of the ranked list and those at the bottom in terms of the renown of their most popular artists. Once again, this perfectly illustrates the Matthew effect, according to which success begets success (Merton, 1968; Buckermann, 2018; Fraiberger et al., 2018), as well as the bandwagon effect (Leibenstein, 1950); both of which benefit the most recognized players. Note that I have decided to place at the bottom of my ranked list the few galleries that do not represent even 10 living or deceased artists (by being associated with their estate). Very generally, not having a very limited roster can be perceived as a sign of fragility on the market, and galleries are not immune to the departure of one or two artists, which would place them in a very precarious economic situation. Even if these galleries represent stars, the fact that they work with a small roster often means that artists who are much less recognized are also factored into their average ranking, which drops as a result. This is the case for the Michael Werner gallery (in 160th place, with an average ranking of 1,982 for its top 10)[18] which, though it certainly represents star artists, has a low placement on the ranked list, illustrating its current liminal position on the primary market; it is, in point of fact, much more involved in the secondary market. The Elvira González gallery, which also represents highly recognized artists, has an overall ranking of 127th (with an average score of 1,207), due to the fact that it only exhibits a handful of artists, ranging from the most prominent to the less recognized, all of which were included in the calculation of my average score.

Beyond the very rare cases for which it was not possible to calculate the average of the 10 best artists, and I therefore deemed it relevant to place them at the very bottom of my ranked list (in the margins, so to speak) to reflect the singularity of this configuration, I systematically calculated the average of the 10 "best" (Misdrahi Flores, 2013) artists from each gallery.

One consideration in regards to classification ought to be mentioned: that of thresholds. In general, there is a small point difference between the galleries featured on my ranked list. This is especially the case for the top positions, where the distances between two establishments often come down to only a few points, and are very rarely beyond a dozen. Conversely, further down the list, the gaps become more significant. Around the 100th position, the differences in averages between adjacent galleries on the list tend to be around a few dozen points, and these distances only escalate, both in terms of frequency and magnitude, when moving to the bottom of the ranked list, where this trend is even more observable.

It would be appropriate at this stage to review the 20 galleries at the bottom of the classification through the lens of their artist rosters, as they are so far removed from the rest of the list in terms of the recognition of their main artists, both living and deceased. The galleries ranked 190th and lower exhibit a sort of deficiency. The averages calculated for the galleries at the end of my ranked list and the significant differences with the others indicate something of a disconnect from the discourse expressed by the organizers of Art Basel, who insist on the excellence of all the galleries that they select for their fair. This excellence, in any case, is not reflected in the level of recognition of the artists on their rosters. What other rationales could therefore be in play to allow these dozen or so galleries to participate in Art Basel, despite their rosters' conspicuous disparities from the quality of the other admitted establishments?

The bottom of the ranked list designates galleries that have very small rosters with a handful of living artists, and whose presence at Art Basel is somewhat incongruent. One of the objectives of admitting such different galleries to this prestigious art fair is to diversify the geographical origins of the participants, and to integrate a few more marginal art scenes and markets; which do not in reality have much of an impact at Art Basel or on the international contemporary art scene in general (Shchutski, 2015 and 2021). The analysis indicates the strong influence of one or several geographical rationales, which manifest in various ways. Some galleries benefit from an implicit favoritism for galleries in German-speaking Switzerland; such is the case for the Gisele Linder and Carzaniga galleries, which are both located in Basel. This favoritism is also extended to German galleries, such as the Max Mayer gallery, based in Düsseldorf; and the Daniel Blau gallery, based in Munich. This partiality toward German galleries[19] whose rosters are manifestly inferior compared to other Art Basel participants, can also explain the presence of the Parisian Galerie Lahumière;

although this gallery is clearly French, its founder was German, and she always maintained strong ties to her country of origin. There is, moreover, an effect of hysteresis (Bourdieu, 1992) at work in this case insofar as the Galerie Lahumière has been involved in Art Basel since its very first fair, at a time when the selection committee was much less selective (Oberste-Hetbleck, 2014; Zwirner, 2019). This is an excellent example of the benefit of sociological analysis, and of the classification that I have compiled. In particular, it demonstrates the capacity of both, especially to shine a light on social representations and practices that are unspoken and on the whole ignored. Were it not for this ranked list, I would never have suspected the privilege afforded to certain galleries due to their close connection with the DACH region. The other participants at the bottom of the list can generally be explained by an attempt to diversify the geographical origins of the galleries admitted to Art Basel, particularly in favor of non-Western establishments or those from the southern Hemisphere. At the bottom of the list, Take Ninagawa and Tokyo Gallery + BTAP are from Tokyo, and three other galleries are from South America: Casas Riegner is from Bogotá, Colombia, and Gomide & Co is from Sao Paulo and A Gentil Carioca from Rio de Janeiro, Brazil. Admittedly, Brazil is already represented quite a bit at Art Basel, but not nearly to the same degree as the main Western countries in the Northern Hemisphere, and the participating Brazilian galleries are highly concentrated in São Paulo (Fialho, 2006). The fact of Art Basel admitting a gallery from Rio de Janeiro allows the organizers to diversify the geographical origins of their participants. The same objective of geographical variety can also come into play in Europe itself, and can explain the inclusion of the Irish gallery Mother's Tankstation Limited, which has locations in Dublin and London.

Furthermore, geographical diversification makes sense since Art Basel, which is already highly international due to the low proportion of its national (Swiss) exhibitors compared to other fairs, and the great diversity of the countries with strong representation—primarily Germany, the United States, the United Kingdom, and France, as well as Switzerland (Quemin, 2013b)—often presents itself as a "global" event. Hence, it is essential that they integrate galleries that do not belong to countries or cities that are already strongly represented. This is particularly useful as the artists from the same country as a given gallery are generally overrepresented on its roster. More broadly, these galleries very often feature a high proportion of artists from only a few countries: their own, as well as those of neighboring or culturally similar nations, and an invariable handful of countries that always convey the image of an "international" gallery: Germany, the United Kingdom, France, Italy, and especially the United States (Quemin, 2002, 2004, 2006, 2013a, and 2013b).[20] Admitting galleries from a greater number of countries also helps Art Basel to diversify (to a certain extent) the countries of origin of the artists who are presented in the booths during the event itself.

Two cases characterized by the preponderance of a gallery's financial resources over the recognition of their artists: the Perrotin and Pace galleries

Today, the French gallery Perrotin, which was created in 1990 when its founder was only 21 years old, has a large network of locations in eight cities and six countries. In Paris, Perrotin has a primary, massive space in the Marais[21] (which it has occupied since 2005), as well as a secondary space and a showroom situated a stone's throw away; its combined exhibition spaces add up to 17,000 square feet, which are among the most beautiful in Paris (this total does not include the 7,500-square-foot showroom). In the same city, the gallery has also invested in a smaller space (750 square feet) on Avenue Matignon, in the 8th arrondissement.[22] Outside of France, the gallery has its main branch in New York. After trying to open a location in Miami,[23] Perrotin later abandoned the city so he could invest in the capital of the international art market: New York. Initially located in the Upper East Side[24] from 2013 to 2016, the gallery then left this area, which was already very popular with major international galleries, to focus on the more offbeat and marginal Lower East Side, where it moved into an immense 25,000-square-foot building. Perrotin also has branches in Hong Kong (since 2012), Seoul (since 2016), Tokyo (since 2017), Shanghai, in the heart of the Bund (since 2018), and Dubai (since 2022). It is also opened a new space in Los Angeles in 2024. Perrotin's international development has been considerable, and the gallery's financial resources are significant; to date, the gallery is active in a great many countries (six, as I have previously noted). It is therefore not surprising that, given the gallery's high visibility,[25] the Power 100 often includes Emmanuel Perrotin on its list, since it is particularly sensitive to the image of the people that it features. I have already indicated that, at the end of 2020, the gallery released a statement saying that the Power 100 had named Emmanuel Perrotin as the 4th most important gallerist in the world. However, making the effort to objectively assess the positions of these galleries instead of basing them on a simple impression provides a very different viewpoint on how important the establishment is on the international scene. From this perspective, Perrotin only comes out in 38th place. If we were solely to regard galleries that participate in Art Basel and are established in France, Perrotin lands in 12th place at the national level, far behind Thaddaeus Ropac (1st internationally), David Zwirner (3rd), Gagosian (6th), Marian Goodman (8th), Chantal Crousel (11th), the directors of the Continua gallery (14th), Mennour (16th), Esther Schipper (17th), Almine Rech (22nd), Max Hetzler (23rd), and Massimo de Carlo (33rd), which are all ranked much higher than Perrotin (38th internationally). This is a far cry from the 4th position that the gallery claimed to hold at the international level. This distance in placement from the best international galleries is due to its artist roster, as very few of its represented artists approach the caliber boasted by the establishments previously presented in this chapter. This is how it came to be that Sophie Calle, Perrotin's most recognized artist, only landed in 126th place in the Artfacts artist ranking at the beginning of 2023. Its second best-ranked artists, Elmgreen & Dragset, came in at 140th place.[26]

The Perrotin gallery: Ranking of its top 10 artists according to Artfacts (average ranking: 29.4):

Sophie Calle	126
Elmgreen & Dragset	140
Bernar Venet	165
Takashi Murakami	258
Gregor Hildebrandt	292
Xu Zhen	310
Tatiana Trouvé	338
Wim Delvoye	390
Maurizio Cattelan	417
JR	478

Although Perrotin represents 69 artists (62 of whom are living, and the remaining seven are estates), Artfacts ranks six of them after the 8,000th position, and even the three lowest-ranking artists exceed the 12,000th position. This is highly atypical for major galleries.

However, it should be noted that Perrotin has made significant progress between 2019 and 2023, rising from 49th place in the classification to 28th. Once again, this is a clear reflection of the premium that has been granted to the mega-gallery model in recent years.

Nevertheless, the most striking outcome of this ranked list outside of the top group—a result that above all proves the benefit of sociological assessment, which can help to break from social representations that are sometimes false (Durkheim, 2007)—is that of the Pace gallery being in only nineteenth position. In 2019, Pace was ranked 26th, and has clearly progressed, like nearly all mega-galleries, in the intervening four years. At first sight, Pace's placements in 2019 and 2023 may be surprising since, for a long time, this gallery seemed to be the only one at least somewhat capable of competing with the goliath Gagosian. Although it is commonplace in the art world to overestimate the quality of Pace gallery[27] and to lump it in with the leaders of the domain (including Gagosian, David Zwirner, and Hauser & Wirth), it is likely due to the nature of two effects that overlap and tend to obscure the objective reality of this social world. First, there is a sort of hysteresis effect that is at play (Bourdieu, 1992), which advantageously distorts the situation in Pace's favor; the fact that the gallery once occupied a stronger position may alter the perception of its current status. Second, the financial resources available to galleries are often taken as a herald not only of their economic success, but also their quality (Misdrahi Flores, 2013); particularly the excellence of the artists whom they represent. Again, as in the previous example of the Perrotin gallery, this is not the case.

The Pace gallery was founded in Boston in 1960 by Arne Glimcher, the father of its current leader, Marc Glimcher, and named for his own father, Pace Glimcher. In 1962, Arne Glimcher closed his Boston space and moved to New York. Although the first few years were difficult, the gallery later managed to grow rapidly, and it settled on East 57th Street in the late 1960s. In 1990, Pace opened a branch on Greene Street, in the heart of SoHo, in order to follow the New York art market's shift from Midtown to this new district (Halle & Tiso, 2014) and to offer its artists the opportunity to be showcased in the center of the New York contemporary art scene of the time. As the primary gallery district migrated from SoHo to Chelsea (Molotch & Treskon, 2009; Halle & Tiso, 2014), Pace followed suit, and in 2001 it moved to West 25th Street. Today, the gallery has eight more or less permanent spaces in five countries throughout the world. The main locations include its flagship space on West 25th Street in Manhattan—a magnificent, over-80,000-square-foot building designed specifically for Pace and inaugurated in 2019—supplemented by a second space on the same street, in addition to branches in Los Angeles,[28] London,[29] Geneva, Hong Kong, and Seoul. In July 2020, following the COVID-19 pandemic that had prompted many New York collectors to relocate to their summer homes in the Hamptons, Pace launched a temporary branch in the area so as to be closer to its clients, and opened an additional exhibition space in Palm Beach for the same purpose. It should be noted that leading up to its current configuration, Pace changed the location of its spaces several times, often opening a branch for a few years and then closing it later (e.g., in Los Angeles from 1995 to 1999). In 2008, Pace inaugurated a large satellite space in Beijing that spanned over 20,000 square feet, but decided to close it in 2019, citing trade tensions between China and the United States.

Given the considerable financial resources and the remarkable exhibition spaces that Pace has at its disposal, its artist roster falls comparatively short. Only two artists are included in Artfacts' Top 100 list, which contrasts with the other heavyweight galleries on the art market. The third artist who comes close to the Top 100, Jeff Koons, only recently joined the gallery, leaving Gagosian and David Zwirner to integrate a different mega-gallery.[30]

The Pace gallery: ranking of its top 10 artists according to Artfacts (average ranking: 158.2):

David Hockney	21
Kiki Smith	24
Jeff Koons	119
Robert Longo	153
Trevor Paglen	157
Yto Barrada	158
Lynda Benglis	173
Elmgreen & Dragset	215
Hank Willis Thomas	270
Lee Ufan	292

For the past few years, although it still benefits from the aura of its history and name, Pace has not been in a position to compete with the largest galleries to attract the most prominent artists. Admittedly, for some time, its only competitor was Larry Gagosian, who had settled into the Chelsea scene two years before Pace in 1999 (after his failed attempt in 1986) by moving into his immense space on West 24th Street. David Zwirner's arrival in 2002 onto West 19th Street, also in Chelsea, initially had little consequence on the local market, as it was at that point a midsize gallery; however, it began to experience rapid growth in 2002, and eventually became a powerhouse. The advent of the very influential Hauser & Wirth in 2014, originally on West 18th Street, completely changed the game. Following the example of their predecessor Gagosian, the two previous galleries invested in very large and beautiful spaces, and they have expanded considerably ever since. While David Zwirner's rise had on the whole been gradual, the years 2013 and 2014 marked a turning point in Chelsea, when David Zwirner suddenly made an ostentatious change by inaugurating a spectacular five-story building on West 20th Street; something that had never before been done. Before this launch, Gagosian's space on West 24th Street had certainly staked its claim on the district, but not in such a vertical manner, with an unequaled horizontal architectural statement. David Zwirner intended to challenge its rival and all potential competitors by constructing an amazing concrete building in an ultra-contemporary brutalist style. The following year, in 2014, Hauser & Wirth not only moved into the district, but did so by immediately investing in its own impressive space. The gallery originally existed on a single, expansive level that had formerly been a roller rink, before it took over the entire building that had been left vacant by the Dia contemporary art center. It later commissioned its own building, also in the heart of Chelsea, on West 22nd Street. In addition to the powerful Gagosian gallery, which since 1999 had benefited from its unrivaled space in Chelsea—it was, as previously indicated, the only gallery with a mega-space capable of competing with a (small) museum, and that thus made the most of its ostensible monopoly to attract the best artists—two other competitors of the Pace gallery, almost simultaneously, considerably expanded their exhibition spaces. When Pace only had one real competitor, even though it was admittedly only a street away from the latter's main location, it still projected a strong image, especially since the Gagosian gallery only possessed one huge space in the neighborhood. However, Gagosian opened a second, equally impressive space in Chelsea, adding to the development initiated by David Zwirner and Hauser & Wirth, the two new heavyweights in the area. Not only did they take over entire buildings, but they also had completely new buildings constructed that plainly symbolized their power and that, just like Gagosian before them offered (and still offer) the best exhibition conditions for artists. David Zwirner, not content with the magnificent building that had been erected in 2013 on West 20th Street, commissioned a second building on West 21st Street; this time entrusting the design to star architect Renzo Piano. Although David Zwirner was forced to abandon this project in the summer of 2023, it had been widely publicized for years, and it contributed to reinforcing the gallery's prestige. The Pace gallery's space, whose square footage and horizontality were at the time completely exceeded by all of these initiatives that had been undertaken by its most direct competitors, found itself greatly downgraded and weakened. From 2013 to 2014, Pace was no longer able to compete with its rivals on equal footing, thereby losing a significant amount of its luster and its credit.

Despite its location in Chelsea, and the advantages afforded to players who were already established on the market, Pace has clearly paid the price for having taken its time to make the investments that have now become indispensable. As I have already stated, the current art market conducts itself like a game of poker; if a participant—in this case, a gallerist—does not want to stake the same amount as the other players of the game, they are forced to stop playing. Fortunately for Pace, its new—beautiful—five-story building on West 25th Street (inaugurated at the end of 2019) has put the gallery back in the running. Having Jeff Koons as a represented artist may have also been one of the signals of this revitalization and renewed attractiveness. However, for years before this resurgence, the gallery had by all accounts been downgraded; and it could barely compete with Gagosian, David Zwirner, or Hauser & Wirth in attracting the most prominent and desirable artists on the market, even though it had a location in Chelsea. As a result, during this time, the gallery saw its position crumble. It finally made the essential investments, no doubt so as to avoid this downturn becoming permanent; which is clearly reflected in my ranked list. It is likely that these investments were also made so that the gallery would be in a position to attract the artists currently represented by Gagosian when the day comes for its founder to step down. Were it not for its necessary upgrade, Pace would have been doomed to decline inexorably, and would have missed out on this opportunity. It remains to be seen whether these investments were made in time. The gallery's progression between 2019 and 2023 (as I mentioned previously), moving from 26th to 19th place, is still limited, although the current market context has proven to be very favorable to the mega-gallery model; and Pace still has quite a bit of ground to make up to rejoin the ranks of its most direct competitors.

In analyzing the top 10 galleries on the ranked list that I have created, I previously highlighted in my explanation of the Konrad Fischer gallery (as well as the case of the Chantal Crousel gallery, which came in at 11th place) that there was a possible discrepancy between a gallery's various financial resources as evidenced by their exhibition spaces on the one hand, and the quality of the artists that they represent on the other. Contrary to common sense, which tends to automatically link economic power with artistic success, the cases of Konrad Fischer and Chantal Crousel exemplify a clear shift in favor of the quality of the artist roster. Further down my ranked list, I felt it necessary to comment on the symmetrical cases of the Perrotin and Pace galleries, which both have numerous and remarkable exhibition spaces, but whose lists of represented artists do not reflect the same degree of success. It is often difficult to conceptualize the autonomy (Bourdieu, 1996) that can exist between economic and artistic success, especially since they are generally associated with one another (Moulin, 1992); I will return to this point later. The sociological assessment that results from my ranked list highlights an overall link between the two spheres, while at the same time identifying some particular cases that stand as exceptions to the general rule that nonetheless cannot be overlooked.

A geographical and geopolitical interpretation of gallery participation in Art Basel and their positions in the classification

Although the art world and market are frequently presented as being "global," they should not be exempt from an academic interpretation through a geographical / sociological (Quemin, 2002, 2004, 2006, and 2013a and b), and geopolitical lens. Nathalie Obadia, a gallerist who is fully integrated into this universe and whose gallery is included on my ranked list, wrote a very enlightening book on this subject (Obadia, 2019). For any social science enthusiast, it would be unsurprising that my classification shines a light on geographical rationales that are at play.

The first 10 galleries on the list show a strong geographical concentration, even though the number of these establishments is very small. If we look solely at the nationality of origin of these galleries, the breakdown is as follows:

Breakdown by country of origin of the top 10 galleries that participated in Art Basel in 2023:

United States	4
Germany	2
United Kingdom	2
Austria	1
Switzerland	1

With the exception of Austria (although the Thaddaeus Ropac gallery was created very close to the German border and thus benefited from the German market), these are countries that occupy strong positions on the market and in the world of contemporary art (Quemin, 2002, 2006, and 2013a and b). Furthermore, it is noteworthy that, among these 10 galleries that are arguably the best in the world with regard to their artist roster, only two have moved their operational headquarters to other countries during their development; this was done by devising trajectories that factored how international influence is distributed on the art market. The Thaddaeus Ropac gallery, which was originally directed from Austria, is now mainly run out of France. Its fellow gallery Hauser & Wirth, though founded in Switzerland, eventually shifted its leadership to be based in the United Kingdom and the United States. Alternately, if we consider the country from which these galleries are currently managed instead of their country of creation, the number is reduced to four: the United States, the United Kingdom, Germany, and France. These are the central countries in the contemporary art world and on the art market, which my work has consistently highlighted for over 20 years (Quemin 2001, 2002, 2004, 2006, 2013a and b).

As these numbers for the top 10 are very small by nature, it may be instructive to now consider the distribution of the top 50 galleries on the list. Naturally, expanding the selection will result in a greater diversity—which, however, is still extremely limited, with only 15 countries, a very small proportion of the 190 nations in the world (as recognized by the United Nations), even though Art Basel is often perceived as a "global" art fair—but it also reveals a very strong hierarchy between participating countries.

Breakdown of the countries of origin of the top 50 galleries that participated in Art Basel in 2023:

United States	12
Germany	9

(continued)

Italy	7
France	5
United Kingdom	4
Switzerland	2
Austria	2
Belgium	2
Denmark	1
Spain	1
Greece	1
Mexico	1
South Korea	1
South Africa	1
Japan	1

Among the first 50 galleries in the classification, the influence of the United States is massive, and clearly comes out on top, but Germany stands as a serious challenger. These two countries alone account for nearly half of the best-ranked galleries that participate in Art Basel. It should also be noted that the top 50 in the classification is composed almost entirely of galleries that are established either in the United States or in Western Europe (46 out of 50), but above all in a very small number of countries within these geographical areas: the United States, Germany, the United Kingdom, France, Italy, and Switzerland are in the lead, like every other instance where the question of how any player's nationality or country of origin impacts the art market and art world (Quemin, 2002, 2004, 2006, and 2013a and b).

Interestingly, however, there are two high-performing galleries that do not belong to the powerhouse zone, comprising the United States and a handful of Western European countries: the Korean gallery Kukje, from Seoul, managed to secure 20th place, while the Mexican gallery Kurimanzuto landed in 25th position. These two establishments have reached an unexpected level of international success because they control the lion's share of the market on their respective national scenes. Having little to no local rivals, they can represent most of the great international artists in their respective countries, even Westerners (whether they come from the Western world originally or reside in this area while retaining citizenship in their country of origin) (Quemin, 2002, 2006 and 2013b). The situation is fairly similar to that of the South African Goodman gallery (not to be confused with the American gallery Marian Goodman), which ranks in 29th place. Operating at the highest level on a continent-wide scale, it has hardly any competition except in its own country, from its fellow gallery, Stevenson (ranked 104th). If an international artist wished to have representation in Africa, they would undoubtedly hope to join Goodman (or failing that, Stevenson, as there are hardly any other high-level choices in this region of the world). Symmetrically, if an as-yet unestablished African artist wished to access the widest market possible, as well as achieve international recognition, it is also the Goodman gallery that is in the best position to help them in their ambitions (all the more so since the gallery has now branched out into the northern Hemisphere, with a location in London, in addition to its two locations in Cape Town and Johannesburg).

In this general context, looking beyond the 50th position on the ranked list, it is also worth highlighting the performance of the Brazilian gallery Luisa Strina, in 57th place. While it performs less well than the previously cited galleries, it is active in a particularly dynamic and competitive market for the southern Hemisphere: that of São Paulo. It must therefore share the most recognized artists with its rivals, foremost of which is the Fortes, d'Aloia and Gabriel gallery (ranked 110th). To date, the major international galleries have never managed to penetrate the Brazilian market by opening branches in the area, but the fairly recent arrival of the Continua gallery in 2020 could turn the tide if it establishes itself permanently in São Paulo; however, the already fierce competition between several high-performing galleries would be further intensified.

The breakdown of countries of origin for the bottom 50 galleries in my ranked list is as follows.

Breakdown by country of origin of the bottom 50 galleries that participated in Art Basel in 2019:

Germany	14
United States	10
United Kingdom	6
Switzerland	4
France	3
Brazil	2
Japan	2
India	2
Italy	1
Ireland	1

(continued)

Sweden	1
Romania	1
Canada	1
Colombia	1
China	1

The distribution in terms of country of origin of the 50 lowest-ranked galleries at the 2019 Art Basel fair shows a stark contrast with the 50 galleries at the top of the ranking. There is a total of 15 countries in this instance as well, but the distribution is very different. At the very top of the ranked list, the United States and Western Europe occupied no fewer than 46 of the 50 positions, but at the end of the rankings, this monopoly decreases somewhat, with only 40 out of 50. It would seem, therefore, that the fair's selection committee is less discriminating with galleries from countries that are more marginal to the art world, as it accepts galleries whose artist rosters are less internationally renowned. What may be surprising, however, is that the end of the list nonetheless features a majority of galleries from the countries with the highest representation at Art Basel, and which for the most part belong to the same nations that also appear at the top of this ranked list. The selection committee tends to demonstrate a certain partiality for German galleries (which total 14 out of the 50 lowest-ranked galleries); even though, in this very case, there can be no question of favoring the participation of galleries from a country that would otherwise have very little, or even zero representation at the fair. This *de facto* favoritism is most likely due to the fact that Art Basel, though held in Switzerland, belongs to the DACH region, and since it is located so close to Germany it naturally attracts many German collectors. To a lesser extent, American galleries whose artist rosters are comparatively weaker than the general level of Art Basel participants also benefit from a certain amount of indulgence; and Swiss galleries also seem to benefit from a sort of favoritism, whereas, conversely, France and Italy do not receive any partiality; they are even under-represented in the 50 lowest-ranked galleries as compared to the top of the classification.

My ranked list clearly shows that, in general, the galleries from countries that are the most marginal to the art market (which, despite all claims to the contrary, remains very Western-centric [Quemin, 2002b and 2023]) are lower in the ranking than their Western counterparts (Quemin, 2020a). Of course, all of the galleries that I included in my calculations participate in Art Basel (it is on this precise basis that I selected them), but that does not mean that all of these galleries are of commensurate quality (Misdrahi Flores, 2013) in terms of international standards, nor that they exist on an equal footing on the international market. At the bottom of my ranked list are the Indian galleries Experimenter (170th place) and Chemould Prescott Road (185th place), the Chinese gallery Antenna Space (171st place), and the Colombian gallery Casas Riegner (199th place). Even before the downturn at the very end of the classification (which I have already examined), the proportion of marginal countries on the international contemporary art scene tends to increase closer to the bottom of the ranked list.[31]

There is a small minority of galleries that manage, at least in part, to escape the influence of the geographical factor. Such is the case for a few galleries originating from marginal countries, or even those within fairly central countries but outside of the preeminent regions on the international art scene and market. Among the major international galleries, the most striking example is that of the remarkable Italian Continua gallery, which ended up in 14th place on my ranked list (it had the same ranking in 2019). Founded in 1990 in the small Tuscan town of San Gimignano, where it resides in a former movie theater, the gallery has long eschewed the major cities for contemporary art, instead reaching out to new clients through art fairs and opting for massive spaces outside of the main cities for contemporary art. The gallery opened a space in Beijing in 2004 in a former industrial building, long before the city had become a notable place for contemporary art. In France, Continua first set up shop not in Paris, daringly enough, but in the distant rural Seine-et-Marne in 2007, where it took over two huge decommissioned industrial buildings. It then continued its singular mode of development (that is, favoring immense spaces far from the major art capitals) by opening a new branch in a former movie theater in Havana in 2015. However, more recently, the enterprising Italian gallery has returned to a more conventional mode of international development in its choice of new locations. In 2020, it opened branches in Rome (on the ground floor of the Saint Regis, a luxury hotel) and São Paulo (inside a sports complex), and in 2021, it moved into a massive space in Paris in the heart of the Marais district. The gallery's recent choices have therefore opened the door to cities that are much more prominent on the map of international contemporary art. Even before its latest geographical expansions, Continua, which now has seven branches in five different countries, in spite of having made totally atypical location choices for nearly 30 years, can easily be considered the leading Italian gallery.

The composition of Continua's artist roster—comprising 64 creators in total—is fairly irregular in that the top of the list features artists with high visibility, and those at the bottom are rather numerous, with notably lower rankings. The less prominent artists on its roster affect its overall ranking much less than in the case of the Perrotin gallery, because Continua's roster is more extensive, and its most distinguished artists, whose rankings are much higher, will keep it particularly solvent:

The Continua gallery: ranking of its top 10 artists according to Artfacts (average ranking: 122.1):

Kiki Smith	28
Kader Attia	36
Ai Weiwei	40
Daniel Buren	65
Hiroshi Sugimoto	82
Anish Kapoor	103
Michelangelo Pistoletto	107
Nedko Solakov	241
Shilpa Gupta	258
Hans Op de Beeck	261

However, the following fact must be emphasized: although Continua defied geographical constraints for a long time by establishing itself far from the main contemporary art metropolises, its recent development is now bringing it on a par with the largest galleries in this respect.

What theoretical lessons can we draw from the empirical material presented above on the international dimension that characterizes the hierarchy of galleries participating in the Art Basel fair (Quemin, 2020a)? Around 20 years ago, I began to work on the international dimension of contemporary art (Quemin, 2001, 2002, and 2004); at the time, the ideology of globalization was extremely popular, both in the contemporary art world and in the social sciences. Analyses of globalization gained traction and prominence in the 1990s, and became central to sociology in the second half of that decade (Bartelson, 2000; Bellavance, 2000; Therborn, 2000b). However, very few authors took the time to test their theoretical developments against quantitative data, and the empirical approach supporting some of the leading theoretical positions was often very limited (Ohmae, 1990; Sassen, 1992, 1999, 2000; Lash & Urry, 1994; Appadurai, 1996, 2000). In the June 2000 issue of *International Sociology*, on the theme of globalization (Theborn, 2000a), and in a book devoted specifically to cultural globalization (King, 2000), there was an almost total absence of empirical data. The authors employed abstract considerations and very rarely supported their analyses with statistical evidence, effectively ignoring the fact that this data would have the capability of providing answers (or partial answers) to some of the key questions raised by theoretical explorations of globalization.

As I have already demonstrated in some of my older publications (Quemin, 2002, 2004, 2006, and 2013b), a recurring theme in the debate on the specific dynamics of cultural globalization is the extent to which this phenomenon creates or maintains different forms of inequality, and in what ways (De Swaan, 1995; Cowen, 1998; Therborn, 2000b). One line of thinking is represented by the analyses of Saskia Sassen and Zygmunt Bauman, who suggest that, when it comes to globalization, national borders are increasingly disappearing and being replaced by growing international flows (Sassen, 1996; Bauman, 1998). In comparison to sociologists who work in the Marxist tradition (Wallerstein, 1991, 2000), they pay little attention to unequal trade and national forms of domination. A second line of thinking explains how global expansion is structured more around flow patterns than pre-established entities; for example, Manuel Castells refers to flows rather than organizations (Castells, 1991), while Jan Aart Scholte emphasizes deterritorialization as a characteristic of globalization, with the increase in flows making national units less significant (Scholte, 1996).

A line of analysis that is particularly relevant in light of the material I have analyzed thus far is outlined in the works of Immanuel Wallerstein, as well as Pierre Bourdieu and Loïc Wacquant. These authors indicate an imbalance in international cultural trade and the effects that domination may have (Wallerstein, 1991, 2000; Bourdieu & Wacquant, 1999). Wallerstein argues that transnational cultural trade simply reflects the contradictions and imbalances of the global economy, in which a handful of Western economies dominate the rest of the world. However, Bourdieu and Wacquant (as well as Gisèle Sapiro [Sapiro, 2008 and 2023]) hold that the cultural sphere presents a certain kind of autonomy (Bourdieu, 1990) from the economic sphere, which is reflected, for example, through transnational cultural trade, affecting the fields of literature and translation (Heilbron, 1999, 2001). This school of thought uses quantitative data (Heilbron, 1999, 2001; Sapiro, 2008 and 2023) to highlight the fact that "imbalances (...) characterize the very structure of international trade" (Heilbron, 2001, p. 146), and that "instead of a balance between import and export, the reality of transnational trade is a process of unequal trade" (Heilbron, 1999, p. 439). The obvious conclusion is therefore the following: cultural exchanges take place in conjunction with a clearly discernible geographical center, with the periphery being distinctly separate. Even today, the most credible works that utilize empirical data to examine the functioning of cultural globalization are often centered on the field of literature (Heilbron, 1999, 2001; Janssen et al., 2008; Casanova, 2008; Sapiro, 2008 and 2023). A similar conclusion seems to be taking shape in the field of the visual arts. The largest and most legitimate galleries on the international contemporary art scene—as well as the most recognized visual artists, for that matter—still come from a very small number of Western countries (be they their country of origin or, even more so, their country of residence). This finding illustrates the specific function of cultural hegemony in this area (Quemin, 2001, 2002, 2004, 2006, 2013a and b, 2021, 2023). The data produced and analyzed in this chapter shines a light on the very hierarchical nature of the contemporary art market and world, specifically as regards galleries. Although the inclination toward internationalization is extremely intense, globalization (in the sense of equal distribution across the entire world) remains a myth.

Conclusion:

In this section, I not only wanted to criticize existing gallery classifications, which never go to the trouble of identifying the limitations of their compilation methods, but I also highlighted the biases that I myself had to contend with, and made sure to draw attention to the choices that I have inevitably been led to make. Even though I have attempted to rectify these biases as much as possible, I have clearly indicated that my ranked list is, more than anything else, an instrument for understanding how contemporary art galleries have developed and how this social world is structured; but that it does not intend to provide definitive answers on all fronts. For example, I have consistently asserted that my classification cannot accurately determine the ranking of the most powerful gallery in the world, Gagosian, precisely because the methodology based on artists rankings that I elaborated is poorly equipped to integrate and adequately process the completely atypical characteristics of its artist roster. I also went to great lengths to indicate that it is not particularly germane to consider the ranking of each gallery to the nearest digit; it would be much more sensible to examine a gallery's position at a certain level in context of the entire list. Despite these repeated warnings, I am well aware that some readers will be tempted to ignore them, as figures are so consistently fascinating (Blank, 2007; Lamont, 2012; Mennicken & Nelson Espeland, 2019). This proclivity toward figures, which I have already addressed when stressing the extent to which the financial estimates of the art market are inescapably far-fetched, is also in full effect regarding the numbers provided by ranked lists. Still, a general result appeared with this research, Thaddaeus Ropac being the clear leader, followed by a group of four prominent galleries of similar importance, Sprüth Magers, David Zwirner, White Cube and Hauser & Wirth. They are followed by another group of leading galleries made of Konrad Fischer, Skarstedt, Marian Goodman and Lisson. Gagosian is more difficult to rank and must stand somewhere between the 6th position and the first one, as I have explained before.

It was important for me to pay particularly close attention to empirical data in order to better understand how the gallery world is structured; at least for the largest galleries, which are simultaneously the most contemporary and the most international, as these two dimensions are so intrinsically linked (Moulin, 1992). However, even though these empirical elements gave rise to an initial analysis with the objective of revealing how the gallerist occupation and its social world function, I also utilized my research to test pre-existing analytical and theoretical approaches. This particularly involved testing the analyses of Raymonde Moulin, according to whom the value of art is jointly constructed by museums and the art market (Moulin, 1992). As Moulin thoroughly demonstrated, aesthetic value is determined by financial value, and *vice versa* (Moulin & Quemin, 1993). Through the various cases of the galleries that I have presented and analyzed, it is clear that there is a general link between the quality of the roster of artists represented by these assorted galleries and these establishments' economic or financial power (a dynamic that I sought to situate not through a gallery's reported revenue, which is not a reliable data point and should therefore always be taken with skepticism, but that permeates its exhibition space or spaces). However, although this general link confirms the analyses produced by Moulin, it is not systematic. In spite of the general correlation, there may be a disconnect between the aesthetic and economic spheres for some cases because, as indicated by Pierre Bourdieu, there is a certain autonomy between them (Bourdieu, 1996). Even though, in the specific case of the art market, the two dimensions are intrinsically linked, they are not the same. There are establishments in which the quality of a gallery is clearly superior to the economic means at its disposal; the Konrad Fischer and Chantal Crousel galleries are the most striking illustrations of this phenomenon at the international level. Neither has expanded outside of their home countries like one may have expected them to do given their roster of highly recognized artists, and neither of them has inaugurated the kind of immense, prestigious space that is characteristic of most of their fellow galleries at the top of my ranked list. In the case of the Chantal Crousel gallery, this is explained by the fact that, although it has managed to assemble a very high-level roster, it is not composed of a wide selection of market heavyweights.

Contrary to the two previous examples, other galleries can have very significant financial resources, as evidenced by their exhibition spaces, without necessarily representing artists who are at the level of recognition that the galleries' economic positions would seem to prescribe. Such is the case of the Perrotin and Pace galleries, which is why I wanted to discuss them, even though they are not among the top-ranked galleries in the world in terms of their artist roster. It should be noted that, when a gallery has remarkable exhibition spaces that are disproportionately superior to the quality of its artists, it is not uncommon to explain it by a strong involvement in the secondary market or for the art world to be riddled with rumors of financial partners (backers). Their support could solve the difficult problem of balancing structurally high costs due to the multiplicity of luxurious and generally very well-located spaces in several cities, as well as paying the salaries of numerous staff members, while not having any impact on controlling the market of the most prominent and expensive artists.[32] However, in this case as well, it would be a mistake to claim to understand the role that partners who support (at least some) galleries play behind the scenes with any kind of certainty. Moreover, it is generally accepted that, even at the highest level, the essential support of such financial partners[33] remains limited to a small number of galleries.

Conclusion

Although the sociology of art and the sociology of the art market in particular has significantly evolved since the 1960s (Moulin, 1987, 1992, and 1995), there had not been a book detailing the sociology of contemporary art galleries until the publication of the French version of this research. As the title of this book clearly indicates, it was my intention to study the galleries, not the gallerists, as I did not wish to enter into the sociology of professions. Had that been the case, this book would almost necessarily have included lengthy developments on the occupation's morphology, certainly including the social origin of gallerists and their evolution, as well as their demographics. Of course, I have often discussed the gallerist as a professional figure, as the people who run the establishments in question are vital in maintaining their identity and operations. However, it is the organization of the business, its underlying rationales, and its internal structure that constitute the central focus of my analysis. While it is true that I have highlighted certain gallerists, it is essentially because they have strongly influenced the gallery model as it exists today. It is this model on which I resolved to center my research.

Before presenting the primary results of my investigative work (which I carried out over a period of 10 years) throughout the various chapters that comprise this book, I began by introducing my research with a two-part foreword. I first explained the methodology that I utilized, and then outlined the emergence of contemporary art galleries by showing the historical phases of their evolution. I paid a fair amount of attention to two great figures within the occupation: the founder Paul Durand-Ruel (Assouline, 2002; Durand-Ruel, 2014; Patry, 2014) and Leo Castelli, who embodied the transition of the heart of the contemporary art market from France to the United States (Cohen-Solal, 2009). The *modus operandi* for contemporary art galleries nowadays is still marked by the major contributions of these two professionals.

My analysis then shifted to the spatial dimension of galleries in the first part of the book, which was split into three chapters. The first dealt with the physical space of the gallery itself, which most often resembles the famous "white cube"

(O'Doherty, 2000). Even though galleries today all have a website, that could entice them to move a certain amount of their operations online, their physical space remains a decisive element. According to the principle of metonymy, the very space where the activity takes place gives its name to the activity itself. The second chapter continued this spatial analysis by focusing on the groupings of galleries via districts or clusters, which emphasize the importance of geographical location in developing a contemporary art gallery's business. A gallery's commercial success is inseparable from its location in the "right" neighborhood, and is often characterized by relocations that are very much inextricably linked with spatial and social reasoning. Not only do you have to set up shop in the right place, but you also have to do it at the right moment, because the social space is constantly changing, and it is absolutely essential to avoid the phenomenon of the "wrong turn" (Halle & Tiso, 2014). I successively reviewed the positions of large central metropolises (Paris, New York, and London) on the international art scene and market—as well as a more cursory analysis of Berlin—and a few notes on the spatial concentration of galleries in cities outside of the Western world, or located in the Southern Hemisphere. The third and final chapter in this first part was devoted to fairs; before the outbreak of the COVID-19 pandemic at the beginning of 2020, these events had become essential for contemporary art galleries (Quemin, 2013a and 2021). As they help to expand the gallery's business outside of their own premises, they may seem at first glance to be exempt from geographical determinism, due to their international aspect; however, I have shown that fairs are, in reality, also subject to extremely strong spatial influences, which reiterates the previously stated notion of the absolute necessity for galleries to settle in a suitable district. Fairs were put on hold during the COVID-19 pandemic; a period during which their absence was sorely felt by galleries, but they quickly resumed and remain vital to the functioning of the contemporary art market.

The second part of this book focuses on what occurs in the gallery space and the activities that take place therein; first and foremost being sales, an emblematic function that was the subject of the fourth chapter, where I provided in-depth analyses of the salesperson and the sales relationship. Unlike most saleable goods, in the particular case of the contemporary art market, it is important not only to conclude the transaction, but also to conduct it with the "right" buyer. I also extensively studied how sales prices are determined; a subject that is still under-researched, or has been analyzed with too little precision (Velthuis, 2002, 2003, and 2005). I demonstrated that it is, in fact, essential to include the practice of giving discounts in order to fully understand how these transactions really work. The notion of granting a client a "commercial gesture" is complemented when taken in parallel with the notions of sociability and friendship, which were the subjects of the fifth chapter. I emphasized that the sociology of emotions is still a fairly new area of the discipline, and that the sociology of feelings largely remains to be established. While in France, Claire Bidart has produced very interesting works on friendship (Bidart, 1997), sociology has not extensively integrated the ways in which friendship—or other feelings—can be used for professional means. It is due to sociability that this feeling, which ultimately becomes a resource for the sales force of galleries, can be instilled and then maintained. The sixth chapter broadened the analysis to include the wide variety of activities that contribute to supporting the artists represented by a gallery, which are often invisible to the eyes of the general public. The second part of this book ended with the seventh chapter, which analyzed recent trends and current transformations in the gallerist occupation. I frequently stressed the imposition of the new, intensely capitalistic "mega-gallery" model, as well as the consequences of increased competition. The gallery world has undergone a series of rapid transformations due to gallery closures, mergers, and partnerships over the course of a few years; however, it is the fringe oligopoly model (Benhamou, 2003) more than anything else that has become the dominant trend. Increased competition has also somewhat redefined relationships with artists—or at least, with the most recognized artists—and with certain clients, such as art advisors. The onset of the COVID-19 pandemic forced galleries to adapt quickly. One of the reactions in particular consisted of exploring new, virtual possibilities; nevertheless, despite the claims, sales through online channels remain very limited.[1]

The third and final part of the book consisted of presenting a ranked list of leading contemporary art galleries. In chapter 8, I began by presenting the methodology that I employed during my research in great detail. I then presented the classification that I had developed in the following chapter, which focused on the establishments that participated in the largest art fair in the world: Art Basel, the international elite for contemporary art galleries. This fair shines a light on the very prominent hierarchy of galleries, though by the very fact of participating in the most prestigious fair in the world, the galleries are generally all held to belong to top echelons of the art world. My ambition was to situate both the professional universe that I was studying and the hierarchy that prevails in this social world and over its market. Since ranked lists are by nature heuristic, I was able to complement the essentially spatial analysis from the first part of this book and the analysis focused on how galleries function from the second part. With the help of my ranked list, which was based off of the recognition of the "best" artists (Misdrahi Flores, 2013) from each gallery, thus making it possible to distinguish the "best" galleries, I was able in particular to question the analysis produced by Raymonde Moulin, who posited that the value of art is jointly determined by museums and the art market (Moulin, 1987 and 1992). Relying on the work of Pierre Bourdieu, I also showed that there is a certain degree of autonomy (Bourdieu, 1996) between the economic sphere and the aesthetic sphere. While generally, the most influential and flourishing galleries are those with the most impressive rosters, there have been a few exceptions: galleries whose rosters of represented artists are more solid than the financial means that they have at their disposal, and others where the reverse is true.

This sociological book and the results that it has produced would not have been possible without very diligent fieldwork and considerable integration—over a 10-year period—into the social environment in question. Being an art critic and journalist has allowed me to become assimilated into the field to a degree that my other positions of academic and researcher would never have afforded me. Combining these different positions has, moreover, made my integration somewhat unique since very few players perform all of these roles within this social world. The gallery world is one of the social and professional domains that does not let just anyone into its inner circles, and is difficult to penetrate without these qualifications. Discretion is a virtue, and even a skill, in a segment of the art market where transactions are concluded away from prying eyes. It seems to me that very few researchers—or even journalists—have been able to plumb the depths of transactions and how prices are determined (Velthuis, 2002, 2003 and 2005) to the degree that I have managed over all these years. Many gallerists, especially the most influential of them around the world, are reluctant to speak publicly; the colossus Gagosian is practically mute on the matter, and Thaddaeus Ropac is also very discreet, as he rarely expresses himself in the media (at least if we compare the very limited number of his public appearances, or even the subjects that are devoted to his gallery in the various media sources, to the prominence of his establishment). Furthermore, most professionals have linguistic and social resources that allow them to control interview situations (Pinçon & Pinçon-Charlot, 1997 and 2016). This is why the qualitative method that I most often utilized was the informal interview, during which the comments made by my interlocutors were much less filtered and measured. I also made extensive use of field observations to complement my research.

Out of respect for all the gallerists who have welcomed me into their establishments with open arms—some of whom have become friends over time (or with whom I have developed an amicable relationship)—I have taken care to be as discreet as possible in concealing the identities of the people quoted in interview excerpts. On many occasions, it would have been preferable from a sociological perspective to further specify the characteristics of those whose remarks I quoted; however, in this professional and social universe where many people know each other, it would often have been easy to identify the people in question from a few social characteristics, even if, when seen from the outside, those traits may not have seemed likely to reveal the speaker's identity. Ensuring their anonymity was all the more important to me since these remarks were very often produced in an informal context, during occasions of convivial social interactions, when players in the art world spoke much more liberally than they would have done in formal, clearly identifiable interview situations. Consequently, out of consideration for my interlocutors, I decided to qualify them as little as possible; it is therefore an ethical consideration that has taken precedence in my research. While it is possible that some people may occasionally recognize themselves in the interview extracts in this book, it is highly unlikely that they will be able to determine with certainty the identity of any of the other players quoted.

More broadly still, this book would not have been possible without the use of participatory observation (or potentially "observant participation"). This alone has allowed me to gain an incredibly extensive understanding of practices used within this social world, and not to be relegated to statements that could significantly distort the veracity of the facts. The same can be said for the objective assessments derived from quantitative methods, because (as I have shown by describing the development process of my methodology in great length and with total transparency) only an in-depth knowledge of the terrain has allowed me to identify possible biases and pitfalls, and to use them as a basis for the choices that I made throughout the development process. It would therefore have been ill-advised for me to oppose qualitative and quantitative methods, as they mutually enrich each other in the context of this research. Not only would the methodology of the ranked list have been unthinkable without an intimate and long-term knowledge of the social world I am analyzing, but what I occasionally hoped to observe in this universe and develop in my analyses was sometimes motivated by the results that came from my ranking. Ultimately, I wanted to implement a sociological approach that is both highly explanatory and comprehensive, and to do so, I considered it to be a significant asset to combine various methods.

This book is therefore clearly the result of a fairly original methodology, which is a blend of several methods that are rarely associated with a single researcher, especially if we include the application of a ranked list that was specifically produced for the purpose of the analysis. In addition to the 10-year participatory observation work and the numerous interviews—which grew more and more informal as I was progressively integrated into the social world that I was analyzing—I also regularly reviewed publications on the field that I was studying (and even wrote articles for magazines that specialize in art and the art market, which justified my long-term presence in the domain even more) or produced an in-depth overview of the art media (with a particular focus on the art market) throughout the duration of my research. This qualitative approach was completed with an original quantitative analysis that particularly introduced the construction and utilization of a ranked list to the research. Regrettably, sociology is a discipline whose methodology is rarely innovated upon, and which to this day has done very little to integrate big data from the social worlds being studied. This is especially the case with the sociology of art (Bellavance et al., 2018). Until now, sociology in general has shown little interest in how it can make use of this extensive data, which has nevertheless become increasingly present, and which (at least in part) shapes the universes to which it applies. I have sought to show that it is possible to incorporate this data into current social science approaches when analyzing social subjects and phenomena. Even though the initial data was produced outside of the scientific framework, it is germane to process it for use within a properly sociological analysis, as it can help to increase our knowledge and understanding of social worlds. Even though there are indisputable biases in existing ranked lists of artists (which I have often mentioned, both in this book and in my previous work [Quemin, 2013b and 2021]) I have shown in several publications that when taking fame at its greatest levels into account, the methodologies that are utilized ultimately have little influence on the results that are obtained. Consequently, it is possible to incorporate this data into a sociological perspective so as to increase our understanding of the social world to which it pertains, especially by using it critically and judiciously to produce a ranked list of galleries that intend to promote the quality (Misdrahi Flores, 2013) of their artist roster.

The ranked list that I have proposed, in addition to its heuristic potential, and its capacity to shed new light on a whole section of the social world and the art gallery market thanks to its dual function of quantification and classification, also identifies future areas of study. This is true both of classification operations as such, and because of the perspectives that it opens up on the art market, as well as on the establishments (and their internal hierarchies) that are active therein. However, I am well aware that it is often difficult to challenge preconceptions (Durkheim, 2011), especially when the people involved have every interest in seeing themselves or the galleries to which they have an attachment assigned a better ranking.

I had previously published a classification (this one of a more exploratory nature, and only designed to include galleries with locations in France) not in a research format, but in a French newspaper intended for art lovers, *Le Journal des Arts*, in the fall of 2016, during the FIAC (the main contemporary art fair in France at the time, before it was replaced by Paris + by Art Basel, then Art Basel Paris in 2024). In a series of unusually long articles, my methodology was also published and contextualized, which I felt was an essential precaution so as to limit or prevent any misunderstandings. As a matter of fact, the presentation of this review also included an experimental dimension with regard to its reception among the players of the art world. The reactions to the published classification clearly showed how impactful ranked lists can be, in addition to causing a few misunderstandings, despite the precautions that I had taken. Several top ranked gallerists contacted me to thank me for their excellent position on the list; even though I had explained the principles that I employed to rank the galleries in great detail, and had simply implemented them, I was, in a way, held responsible for the results of the classification. Conversely, another gallerist, whose establishment placed much lower than what he had aspired to, took me to task in a public setting, raising the usual criticism often levied against sociologists when they reveal objective social facts (Bourdieu, 1993) that this was not true because . . . it could not possibly be true. Yet another gallerist whose establishment was not included on the list even called me to ask if we could "come to an understanding" so that his gallery would appear in the ranking! All of these reactions reveal a distinct misunderstanding of the objective assessment function inherent in sociology (Durkheim, 2011) and they also show the importance of rankings in the eyes of players in the contemporary art world. Essentially, these indicators reveal positions—at least in the optimal situation, when they are rigorously constructed—but they also have a clearly performative dimension (Espeland Nelson & Sauder, 2007). For these reasons, sociology is intrinsically a disruptive science (Bourdieu, 1993).

Within the framework of this book, I advised readers to avoid the temptation (tantalizing though it may be) to take the exact ranking attributed to a given gallery and consider it as an extremely precise measurement. The method that I used relies both on the quality of the Artfacts data (which, as I have indicated, is not perfect) and the way in which galleries present information on their websites. Thus, a gallery that represents the estates of star artists without clearly specifying as such would miss out on the benefit of their representation and would be placed lower in the ranking than it should be. With this in mind, however, I explained at length why the data that I have produced is, on the whole, relevant, and provides satisfactory information on the hierarchy that exists in the gallery universe.

Finally, it should be noted that the ranked list expresses a gallery's position at a given moment, but it absolutely does not ensure that an establishment will stay in its placement in the long (or even middle) term. In this case, the data that I have analyzed is pertinent for the year 2023, and was compared to the data produced for the year 2019. The comparison between these two years is appropriate, even though they are quite close together, because of the COVID-19 pandemic, which spanned 2020 and 2021, partially paralyzing the art world and market. As I have shown in previous works (Quemin, 2013b), when a ranked list is based on a formalized, rigorous scientific method, changes end up being fairly slow from one year to the next, at least when there are no exogenous factors. Here, the onset of an epidemic of exceptional magnitude was an edifying test. As opposed to the year 2019, the main changes that took place in the gallery world as of this book's writing are most likely the closure of the American galleries Gavin Brown's Enterprise and Metro Pictures, and Gerhard Richter's transfer from Marian Goodman gallery to David Zwirner gallery. In 2023, when I once again analyzed and sorted this data, the two former galleries had fallen off of the ranked list, and the closure of Gavin Brown's Enterprise contributed to the clear upward trend of the Gladstone Gallery, as it had taken on some of the most renowned artists who had formerly been represented by Gavin Brown's Enterprise. Similarly, the main effect of Metro Pictures' closure was the near-immediate integration of its superstar artist Cindy Sherman by the mega-gallery Hauser & Wirth. This transfer stands as proof that my analysis has correctly identified a strong homology (Bourdieu, 1992) between artist and gallery spaces. Few other trajectories are worth considering. I have thoroughly indicated that galleries are qualified by their artists, especially by the dozen or so of the most important or renowned among them, just as artists are themselves qualified by the gallery that represents them (this is the basis of the methodology that I have developed). As star artist Cindy Sherman joined the influential gallery Hauser & Wirth in 2019, the ranking of this establishment rose from 9th to 7th place upon the closure of its competitor, and due to the ensuing transfer. The shift was therefore significant, and it is unsurprising that a single movement can influence a gallery's ranking when it involves a superstar as established as Sherman, whose transfer was widely covered in the press. However, as we can see, this shift did not send shockwaves through the entire ranked list. Once the methodology that aims to reveal the positions of the different establishments in the gallery world is determined, one can "simply" update the data (which nevertheless necessitates a great amount of data compilation) in order to reveal how galleries evolve in their professional space throughout the years.

More generally, beyond Sherman's transfer from Metro Pictures to Hauser & Wirth, changes in the representation of star or superstar artists directly affects the ranking. Another major shift occurred in 2022 when Gerhard Richter left his long-term gallery, Marian Goodman, to join the mega-gallery David Zwirner. Another such transfer involving a superstar artist was so significant that it had an immediate impact on the ranking of both of these galleries. This should not be surprising; it is precisely the most lauded artists who epitomize the main issues on the art market in general, particularly for the galleries that represent them. When one of the most coveted artists leaves "their" gallery, there are very few competing establishments likely to take them on, and the direction of these shifts is very indicative of the dynamics in effect in the gallery world. However, it should be noted that, while a gallery's ranking is directly impacted by transfers of these very prominent artists, this does not completely throw off their position, or its order of magnitude; nor does it call into question the overall structure of the ranked list.

To conclude, I must acknowledge that I am fully aware that this book invites different levels of reading: some relating to an interest in the social sciences, others derived more directly from an attraction to the contemporary art gallery world. However, I posit that these two approaches clearly reinforce one another, and I hope that I have been able to reconcile the two levels of expectations throughout this book. This also echoes the posture that I adopted for the purpose of conducting my research, and later of writing this book: only by possessing an extensive and intimate knowledge of the area of study can a sociologist significantly increase their familiarity with and understanding of said area, thus contributing to the discipline in a truly meaningful way.

NOTES

Introduction

1 Raymonde Moulin conducted her first preliminary inquiry in 1958–1959, then the research itself in 1962–1963.

2 In this book, Raymonde Moulin begins the second section with a review of the major players in the market, whom she designated "painting merchants" (chapter 3, pp. 89–149), then art critics (chapter 4, pp. 151–187), "clients/ collectors" (chapter 5, pp. 189–263), "clients: the State, the Cities, The Church" (chapter 6, pp. 265–292), and finally painters (chapter 7, pp. 293-361) (Moulin, 1967). Twenty years after the book was first published in French, Raymonde Moulin published an adapted version with the title *The French Art Market: a Sociological View* (Moulin, 1987).

3 Note that, in its definition of contemporary art, Artprice includes the birth year of the artists, and that those who are categorized as contemporary were born in 1945 or later. This qualification does, however, pose a problem, as some of the most expensive contemporary artists on the market, who have contributed greatly to global auction revenues, were born before 1945. To name a few: Yayoi Kusama, Jasper Johns, Gerhard Richter, David Hockney, and Georg Baselitz were born in 1929, 1930, 1932, 1937, and 1938, respectively. Although they are all still active, and contribute directly to the sales income for art that is undeniably contemporary, they are all classified under the post-war category by Artprice. In Artprice's statistics, the amount listed for sales of contemporary art would therefore appear to be undervalued, while post-war art sales would seem inflated. However, in 2020, Artprice itself acknowledged that it needed to reevaluate its definition of contemporary art (cf. "Artprice by Artmarket.com: Faut-il redéfinir la notion d'art contemporain en 2020 ? » (Artprice, 2020)) (https://www.actusnews.com/fr/ARTPRICE/cp/2020/01/14/artprice-by-artmarket_com-nbsp-faut-il-redefinir-la-notion-d_art-contemporain-en-2020-nbsp).

4 The sale smashed the previous record for a pre-Modern painting by nearly €77 million, which took place at Sotheby's in London for the sale of Pieter Paul Rubens' *The Massacre of the Innocents*.

5 Greek-born French gallerist Iris Clert (1917–1986), who greatly supported the Nouveaux Réalistes, came up with the term "galerian" to illustrate the breadth of the tasks performed and how difficult it was to manage them all.

6 Having said that, the field of sociology has, over time, questioned the very notion of vocation, and demonstrated how it is, in fact, much closer to that of a social construct.

7 In the same vein, the French auction house Piasa now organizes auction sales called "(very) contemporary art."

8 In their analysis of the socio-professional world of fashion and the selection process of runway models, Frédéric Godart and Ashley Mears identified similar phenomena (Godart and Mears, 2011).

9 Paris is divided into 20 zones called *arrondissements* (districts), that serve as administrative subdivisions.

10 As we will see in this book, the data that I propose, which incidentally supports the data from other researchers, suggests a vastly different geographical layout of the spatial distribution of contemporary art galleries, in Paris and also in France.

11 *Chiffres clés 2019* was published by the French Ministry of Culture: https://www.culture.gouv.fr/Sites-thematiques/Etudes-et-statistiques/Publications/Collections-d-ouvrages/Chiffres-cles-statistiques-de-la-culture-et-de-la-communication-2012-2019/Chiffres-cles-2019.

12 A SIRET is an administrative identification number assigned by the French government to all registered companies and associations.

13 Another example of nonsensical statistical calculations regarding art galleries: economist Clare McAndrew declared there to be nearly 300,000 galleries in the world (around 130 times greater than my own estimate)! I will dedicate a portion of the final section of this book to providing a critical analysis of the conclusions proposed by this author.

14 The company Artnet, which publishes auction sales online and also operates as a marketplace for artworks, reports 39,000 artists exhibited in over 2,200 galleries throughout the world (located in over 250 cities). This number is extremely close to my own estimates.

15 The CPGA had 81 members at the beginning of 1958, and 115 members in October 1962 (Moulin, 1967).

Foreword 1: A few methodological notes—researching the art market and its social world

1 Even though she did not travel much, Raymonde Moulin was lucky enough to live and operate in France, the heart of the international art market and art world, where she conducted her first major research project in the 1950s and the first half of the 1960s. It was only during the second half of the 1960s that New York truly outgrew Paris in this respect (Guilbaut, 1985).

2 When researching how gallerists set the prices for their art, Olav Velthuis also remarked that the answers given by his interviewees were more normative when they knew they were being recorded than at the end of the interview, when they were "off the record" (Velthuis, 2002). This is a common occurrence in the social sciences.

3 My long-term immersion in the social world of a specific domain could certainly be compared to that of Loïc Wacquant, who performed comparable research on

a completely different subject: boxing (Wacquant, 2007). The practices and their interpretations of this world could therefore be more reliably portrayed.

4 I will develop this point in the third and final part of this book.

5 It is important to note here that this is not unique to galleries, especially contemporary art galleries. This practice is widespread across commercial activities.

6 Even during non-sales events, people speak fairly regularly about money in the art world—especially in the contemporary art world—particularly when collectors and gallerists are in attendance. But this topic of conversation is raised even more often in market-related events, as sharing the same interest comes with a similar relationship to money.

7 However, among the actors of the art world, there is an implicit understanding of what can or cannot be discussed freely when it comes to money. Discussing money more readily in the social world of galleries than in other social worlds does not mean that every topic is fair game; in this social world, there are simply standards apart from society in general that must be respected.

Foreword 2: The invention of the gallerist profession and its development up to the contemporary period

1 This evolution of the profession of art dealer (and later gallerist) can be seen echoed in the evolution of the market, which has taken on different forms depending on the countries and cities wherein it exists. Titia Hulst has compiled a comprehensive synthesis of this topic in her book *Art Market: A Sourcebook of Writings on Artists, Dealers and Markets* (Hulst, 2017).

2 "Paul Durand-Ruel, the Gamble of the Impressionists. Manet, Monet, Renoir," Paris, Musée du Luxembourg, October 9, 2014–February 8, 2015 (curated by Sylvie Patry).

3 Exhibition "Galleries of the 20th Century. France, 1905–1970," Paris, Centre Pompidou, Musée National d'Art Moderne, May 22, 2019–March 2020.

4 As noted in the introduction of this book, the French capital is divided into 20 districts called *arrondissements,* that constitute administrative units, and are also often neighborhoods with high concentrations of social functions and specific atmospheres.

5 In one of Raymonde Moulin's famous texts, entitled *La genèse de la rareté artistique* (The Genesis of the Rarity of Art), she showed how rarity constitutes a significant factor in legitimizing a domain or an artwork as truly artistic (Moulin, 1995).

6 "Galleries of the 20th Century: France 1905–1970" Exhibition, Paris, Centre Pompidou, Musée National d'Art Moderne, May 22, 2019 to March, 2020.

7 Ambroise Vollard was the son of an attorney.

8 "Galleries of the 20th Century: France 1905–1970" Exhibition, Paris, Centre Pompidou, Musée National d'Art Moderne, May 22, 2019 to March, 2020.

9 In the first part of this book, I will explain how the ability to follow the geographical movements of the art market proves to be an important resource for gallerists.

10 Kahnweiler, as a German national, fled to Switzerland during the First World War, leaving his assets to be confiscated by the French government. During the Second World War, in order to escape the persecution of the Jews, he took refuge in the south of France, which was not occupied by the German army. In 1941, he sold his gallery to his step-daughter and staff member, Louise Leiris, to protect his business from the aryanization of Jewish property.

11 Raymonde Moulin also wrote about the preponderance of "Israelites" between the two World Wars across all sectors of the market (Moulin, 1967).

12 The pamphlet *Galleries of the 20th Century: France 1905–1970* (previously cited), published during the eponymous exhibition at the Centre Pompidou (*op. cit.*), after outlining the foundational role that Paul Durand-Ruel played in the domain of contemporary art galleries in the nineteenth century, identifies 11 exhibition spaces: Ambroise Vollard's galleries (1893–1914), Daniel-Henry Kahnweiler (1907–1914, then 1920–1940), A l'étoile scellée (1952–1956), Cahiers d'art (1934–1970), Jeanne Bucher (1925–1960), Daniel Cordier (1956–1964), Denise René (the pamphlet lists its years as 1934–1970, but in reality René's activity continued long after), Louis Carré (1940–1966), Alphonse Chave (1947–1975), de France (1942–1981), and Iris Clert (1956–1986). In 2020, the National Museum of Modern Art – Centre Pompidou published a special edition of the *Cahiers du Musée national d'art moderne* (Revue of the National Museum of Modern Art) dedicated to the great dealers and the main galleries in France from 1905 to 1970, featuring: Ambroise Vollard, Daniel-Henry Kahnweiler, Léonce Rosenberg, Pierre Loeb, Jeanne Bucher, Christian Zervos, Louis Carré, la Galerie de France, Denise René, Aimé and Marguerite Maeght, Colette Allendy, Nina Dausset, Alphonse Chave, Paul Facchetti, A l'étoile scellée, Rodolphe Stadler, Iris Clert, Karl Flinker, and the Givaudan Gallery.

13 Mary Boone is considered to have been one of the first to organize a system of waiting lists so as to fully capitalize on the rarity of the works produced by the most sought-after artists (Moulin, 1992 and 1995), and to augment their desirability even more.

14 Leo Castelli did not have contracts with the artists on his roster, as he did not see the use in these documents. He believed that contracts between gallerists and artists were not even worth the paper they were printed on (as reported in *Velthuis*, 2002, p. 101).

1. The gallery as a physical space

1 As we will see, the Marais neighborhood is the district of Paris that presents the highest concentration of contemporary art galleries.

2 It is important to note that a website (to a large extent) does not pose any competition for a gallery's physical space; rather, it is an extension of it. As such,

the prevailing codes in designing a website typically imitate the presentation of the physical space, and almost systematically portray a stripped down aesthetic. Websites are on the whole uniformly white, with black or grey text, and color is reserved almost solely for the works of art.

3 This is the case in Europe and the United States, but not in Brazil, where the tropical light is generally thought to be too harsh.

4 An example of this is the cluster of small galleries in Paris around the Place des Vosges in the historic neighborhood of the Marais, where their arrangement is designed to draw the attention of passersby. They have large windows that look out onto the street, combined with artworks that are very often brightly colored and pleasing to look at in order to catch the eye. As such, they stand in opposition with the vast spaces favored by contemporary art galleries in the same neighborhood that lead onto a courtyard, and each kind of gallery (properly contemporary or not) is located in a different area. The most legitimate galleries are mainly located on rue Turenne and rue Debelleyme, as well as around rue Beaubourg.

5 The press release also announced three exhibitions each for Esser and Andrianimearisoa.

6 The term "roster" is often used in the world of galleries (even in non-Anglophone countries) to designate the list of artists represented by a gallery. For example, the French equivalent is *écurie* (meaning stables), a term also occasionally used in English, but it can be uncomfortable due to its unflattering connotation.

7 The Artfacts website provides a ranking of artists according to their visibility. The lower the number, the more recognized the artist.

8 Contemporary art galleries are no exception, except the French gallery Pietro Sparta! Located in Saône-et-Loire, in Chagny (a town with a population of 6,000) in the region of Burgundy, it deliberately has no website, even though it regularly participates in major art fairs like FIAC, Art Basel, and Paris+ by Art Basel. With the exception of this anomaly, a website is clearly a necessity for galleries.

9 In the same vein, Thaddaeus Ropac's keynote speech at the 2017 professional symposium, "Talking Galleries" in Barcelona, focused on the necessity for gallerists to bring collectors and the public back into their spaces, as fairs had claimed too much of their focus.

10 A beneficial effect of the COVID-19 pandemic is that, due to museums closing for months at a time in several countries, galleries saw a drastic rise in the number of visitors desiring to see works of art in person.

11 For more on openings, see the works produced by Martin Fuller and Julie Ren (Fuller & Ren, 2019).

12 While having a high rent is already problematic for galleries, the challenge is compounded when seen in relation to their low foot traffic, particularly that of collectors.

13 The gallery had invested in a former warehouse space measuring 15,000 square feet, in the heart of a neighborhood where other galleries such as Regen Projects, Kohn Gallery, Hannah Hoffmann, and Various Small Fires are located.

14 In London, the galleries that most often rent out their spaces during Fashion Week are located in the east of the city.

15 Interestingly, at this time she was planning on closing her gallery in order to sell art from her apartment.

16 During the COVID-19 pandemic that broke out in 2020, Fashion Weeks came to a halt. Several galleries found themselves destabilized as they could no longer rent their spaces out to fashion brands. This loss of revenue, combined with the suspension of art fairs, resulted in a one-two punch that dried up many galleries' financial resources.

17 Another example is the notion of gallery sharing: for a certain amount of time, a space hosts a foreign gallery and its artists, thus creating an extraordinary event with the aim of appealing to collectors and making them want to visit the venue. Such an initiative attempts to energize galleries by expanding their audience, while at the same time cutting the costs of maintaining the space. The most famous of these international initiatives is called Condo.

18 One of the two associates for Galerie VnH, Victoire de Pourtalès, was later promoted to co-director of the American gallery, and the team that she had assembled for VnH also transferred over to the David Zwirner gallery in Paris. Galerie VnH's premises on rue Vieille du Temple, in the heart of the Marais, were also absorbed into the larger gallery. After being in business for only three years, and having occupied a very risky position as a mid-size gallery from the start, Galerie VnH was replaced/assimilated into one of the largest and most powerful galleries in the art world.

19 This same phenomenon of opening multiple locations in the same area has occurred in many cities around the world. In June 2020, the influential Belgian gallery Xavier Hufkens inaugurated its third space in Brussels, preferring to expand within the same city, rather than opening a new space elsewhere in Belgium or abroad. At the same time, Eva Presenheuber inaugurated a third space in Zurich (before later expanding into Vienna, Austria), and in May, Max Hetzler opened a third location in Berlin. The notion of doubling down on one's presence in the same city is therefore indeed a strong trend for large galleries.

20 In a previous publication dedicated to the profession of traditional auctioneers ("*commissaires-priseurs*") in France, I wrote about the drama caused by the lack of (especially male) descendants in independent domains with a strong dynastic component (Quemin, 1997).

21 In 2018, the Pace gallery was introduced by one of its staff members as follows: a "family" of around 200 people spread out over the four corners of the earth, in nine locations in particular. This number was the result of a recent acceleration in its expansion campaign, with the opening of a location in Palo Alto (on the West Coast of the United States) in 2016, and another in Seoul in 2017 (*La Gazette Drouot*, no. 14, April 6, 2018, pp. 21–22).

22 In January 2018, David Zwirner celebrated his Chelsea gallery's 25th anniversary with a retrospective of its pivotal moments, and inaugurated his first space in Asia in the city of Hong Kong, with a monographic exhibition of the famous Belgian artist Michaël Borremans.

23 This term is a portmanteau of the words 'star' and 'architect.'

24 The gallery closed the location that it had also opened in China, citing the difficulties of doing business with the country.

2. The gallery in the urban space: geography and neighborhoods

1 We will see in chapter 3 that it is fairly common for galleries to make 50% or even 70% of their sales at art fairs, or thanks to contacts made during fairs.

2 The gallery was founded in Florence, Italy on via Tornabuoni in 1981 by the father of the current owner. The gallery did not stay in its new location in the Marais, as it was too far from avenue Matignon, which was better suited to its status (it eventually returned to its original space).

3 Not only did the book mention the galleries that had not yet opened in the area, but for some of them it was not made clear that the space in question was only an ancillary space.

4 At one point, the gallery had a location in San Francisco.

5 The gallery originated in Florence.

6 This does not mean that there are no true contemporary art galleries in France outside of the greater Paris area; however, beyond the French capital, there is no contemporary gallery scene in any other city. Contrary to what one might think, excluding the Paris area, it is not the size of the city that determines how many contemporary art galleries there are. In France, there are four preeminent galleries, and they have a handful of locations in very small towns: Catherine Issert has a space in the touristic village of Saint-Paul-de-Vence on the French Riviera, Pietro Sparta has one in the small town of Chagny in Burgundy, Ceysson & Bénétière has one in the former industrial city of Saint-Etienne, in the center of France (where it got its start, but later expanded into Paris, Luxembourg, and even New York; in 2021, the gallery also inaugurated an ancillary space in Lyon, the second largest city in France), and Continua has one in Les Moulins in rural Seine-et-Marne (as previously stated, the gallery, which originated in the small Italian town of San Gimignano, also has locations in Beijing, China, and in Havana, Cuba; more recently, it expanded into Rome and São Paulo in 2020, and later into the center of Paris at the beginning of 2021).

7 Annex 8, pp. 515–517 of Raymonde Moulin's *The French Art Market* includes a map of the painting galleries in Paris at the end of the nineteenth century (Moulin, 1967).

8 The Seine river divides Paris in two, the Right Bank constituting the north half of the city, the Left Bank the south half.

9 Elements of the spatial analysis of contemporary art galleries in Paris during the period of 1945–1970 also appear in chapter 5, "The Mosaic of Parisian Galleries," in Julie Verlaine's book *Les Galeries d'art contemporain à Paris de la Libération à la fin des années 1960. Une histoire culturelle du marché de l'art*

(*Contemporary Art Galleries in Paris, from the Liberation to the end of the 1960s: a Cultural History of the Art Market*, Verlaine, 2012).

10 Exhibition: "Galleries of the 20th Century: France 1905–1970," Paris, Centre Pompidou, Musée National d'Art Moderne, from May 22, 2019 to March 2020.

11 The brochure does not list the arrondissement for each gallery, it was my decision to add it for clarity.

12 As a matter of fact, Denise René continued her activity long after the date given here.

13 In 1966, Alain Blondel and three associates created a miniscule gallery that for several years specialized in art from the first half of the twentieth century: the Galerie des Quatre-Vents (Gallery of the Four Winds) was originally located on the street of the same name in the 6th arrondissement of Paris. The following year, they moved a stone's throw away, and the establishment took on the new name of Galerie du Luxembourg, for the park located nearby. After moving to the Halles-Beaubourg neighborhood in the heart of Paris, the gallery changed its focus to contemporary art.

14 "Right Bank" here is used in the traditional sense of the term, that of the conservative bourgeois Paris located to the north of the Seine (Pinçon & Pinçon-Charlot, 2016). The Marais, while also located on the Right Bank, obviously constitutes a distinct social space.

15 As noted in the introduction of this book, the galleries that paid contributions to the Maison des Artistes went far beyond the bounds of contemporary art galleries alone, as many of them sold artworks that were more aligned with the "chromos" market (Couture, 1981) than contemporary art itself.

16 The total number of galleries for all of France at the time was 848.

17 Note the surprising definition of the "Bastille" neighborhood (in the east of Paris), which has expanded to incorporate areas that have no connection with the district and in reality constitute more of an "other" category. The choice of the Bastille neighborhood itself is a very good illustration of a "wrong turn", as coined by David Halle and Elisabeth Tiso (Halle & Tiso, 2014); that is, the fact that galleries may choose the right neighborhood at the wrong time, or in this case, a neighborhood that will later turn out to be a poor choice.

18 Considering the participant list of the second largest Parisian art fair, Art Paris, reveals a greater dispersion of gallery participants throughout the city, but it is precisely because the definition of contemporary art is less restrictive, and the vast majority of the galleries selected would not be considered as being properly contemporary by the FIAC selection committee (and that of Paris+ by Art Basel) or by other fairs that are also among the most recognized on the international contemporary art scene.

19 Located at the very center of Paris, it was sometimes designated as "the stomach of Paris".

20 In France, an HLM (habitation à loyer modéré) is essentially the equivalent of social housing.

21 In 2021, Obadia left her space on rue du Bourg-Tibourg, which was somewhat peripheral to the Marais art neighborhood, to move into the bourgeois 8th arrondissement on avenue Matignon, while still retaining her primary space in the Marais on rue du Cloître Saint-Merri, close to the corner of rue Beaubourg.

22 In the monthly *Beaux-Arts Magazine*'s January 2018 issue, the publication announced the tenancy of 10 galleries in what would become the Komunuma complex. A few days before the site's inauguration, just five galleries were announced; however, the site has only accommodated four main galleries since its opening.

23 Note that while New York—West Chelsea in particular—is the uncontested center of the gallery market for both the United States and the entire world, there is a higher concentration of artists in California (not unlike Berlin in Europe, which is known for its welcoming environment for artists, even though London and Paris have bigger gallery scenes). As such, Los Angeles—or, more precisely, the Los Angeles-Long Beach-Anaheim area—is the capital of artistic expression in the United States for visual arts, with 23,941 jobs in the creative sector, as opposed to 22,746 in New York (cf. *Artnet News*, December 8, 2017).

24 Zwirner founded his gallery in 1993 in SoHo on Greene Street.

25 These sociological estimations can be compared to another source, *Crain's New York Business*, a magazine specializing in business analysis, dating from September 2015: "Crain's has data that shows that the number of galleries is slightly lower than its peak: In 2015, West Chelsea had 294 galleries (today the number is around 300), while the Lower East Side has 224; however, during Chelsea's historic peak in 2007, 362 sites were active, as opposed to only 69 in the Lower East Side. This data shows that the Lower East Side has quickly emerged as an affordable area for new spaces, as well as for new galleries, but Chelsea remains the Mecca of the New York arts scene" (http://www.crainsnewyork.com/article/20150911/ARTS/150909867/arts-not-dead). While there is a significant gap between the data provided by the two researchers cited above, it is important to keep in mind that both sources document a very high number of galleries, and the level of competition is unrivaled anywhere else in the world.

Furthermore, according to the same source: "On the whole, it is interesting to note that the city has seen a massive 442% increase in the number of galleries since 1965—from 272 to 1,475" (http://www.crainsnewyork.com/article/20150911/ARTS/150909867/arts-not-dead). The sociologist Olav Velthuis reports the number of galleries in New York at the beginning of the 2000s as somewhere between 470 and 1,294, depending on sources. Relatedly, according to the January 2002 *Gallery Guide New York*, the highest number of galleries in New York (173, or 32.2%) were located in Chelsea, followed by 106 galleries in SoHo (19.8%), 79 between 50th and 60th Streets (14.7%), and only 36 outside of Manhattan (6.7%) (Velthuis, 2002).

26 Large international galleries have opened ancillary spaces in Tribeca, like David Zwirner's alternative space, or the French gallery Almine Rech, which was able to consolidate its presence in New York after initially settling in the Upper East Side.

27 However, the project of the new Renzo Piano designed building and gallery space had to be canceled in the summer of 2023.

28 The sole incongruity to this tight-knit network is West 23rd Street; it is, however, one of Chelsea's main east–west traffic arteries, connecting the Hudson

River to the East River. It is a two-way street, which is not the case for most of the streets and avenues; the ensuing heavy traffic is not conducive to establishing art galleries.

29 Any of the "big four" galleries can certainly have a second, smaller space on a street that is "symbolically controlled" by one of its direct competitors; it is the point-blank spatial and symbolic confrontation of two flagships being located on the same street that has always been carefully avoided up to this point by all major West Chelsea market players.

30 Most of the YBAs got a BA in fine arts from Goldsmiths, University of London, between 1987 and 1990. The 1988 *Freeze* exhibition, organized by Damien Hirst, played a major role in launching the careers of several young artists whose art was displayed at this show. However, their entry onto the international scene was due more than anything else to the 1997 *Sensation* exhibition, initially held at the Royal Academy of Arts in London, before making its way to Berlin and then New York.

31 The last two fairs, smaller than the FIAC (which has since been discontinued) and Frieze New York, were included so as to diversify the list of participants, as it would have been more restricted if the only fairs taken into consideration were the most prestigious in the world.

32 The different zones correspond to the following zip codes: Center: W1, WC1, WC2, EC1, EC2, EC3, EC4 / East: all the zip codes beginning with an E, excluding those previously mentioned beginning with EC / West: all the zip codes beginning with W, excluding those previously mentioned beginning with WC and the code W1. / North: all the zip codes beginning with N. / South: all the zip codes beginning with S.

33 It should be noted that Rudolf Zwirner, a former gallerist long established in Cologne and father of David Zwirner (who is the owner of one of the biggest galleries in the world), gives a stark observation of the state of the current German art market: due in particular to high taxes, German galleries are extremely dependent on fairs that take place abroad, especially Art Basel (Zwirner, 2019).

34 Cf. "Esther Schipper, gallerist: "'Berlin is less accessible to young artists, so it's gentrifying'", *Le Journal des Arts*, issue no. 524, May 24 2019.

35 The gallery scene in other more or less peripheral cities has been analyzed by various researchers, each with a focus on a different city: Anna Uboldi for Milan (Uboldi, 2020), Jérémie Molho for Istanbul (Molho, 2014), Amin Moghadam for Dubai (Moghadam, 2012), Kim Hakhee for Seoul (Kim, 2007), and Amy Y. Zhang for Beijing (Zhang, 2019).

3. Galleries and international art fairs: the success of a relatively deterritorialized system

1 The Venice Biennale was created in 1895 in Italy, and the São Paulo Art Biennial was created in Brazil in 1951. The German biennial, Documenta in Kassel, dates back to 1955. They are the three oldest biennials in the world, as well as the most influential ones.

2 This does not prevent gallerists from conducting business and making transactions during biennial vernissages, as they know that many important collectors will be in attendance.

3 See Marylène Malbert's works for more on the post-war Venice Biennale and its commercial tensions (Malbert, 2006).

4 She was the artistic director of the fair at the time.

5 The source for most of these numbers is the *Artnet News* issue from March 2, 2016.

6 Incidentally, the FIAC emphasized that it would not modulate its costs in a strictly linear fashion, but rather by tiers.

7 Galeries Lafayette is a high-end department store in Paris and a sponsor of the contemporary visual arts.

8 Furthermore, the FIAC assumed the accommodation costs for foreign galleries in the Lafayette Sector by providing each one with a studio apartment.

9 Art Paris is the second most important generalist art fair in Paris (after FIAC until 2021, then after Paris + by Art Basel from 2022 to 2024 and Art Basel Paris since that time).

10 As we will see in the second part of this book, generally speaking, half of the amount of the sale goes to the artist, and the other half is retained by the gallery.

11 This is a classic position in the sociology of work. It has been utilized for several remarkable interviews, notably by Donald Roy and Michael Burawoy (Fournier, 1996).

12 While the owners of large galleries frequently travel in business class (the wealthiest among them may even travel in first class or on a private jet, but this is very rare), such is not the case for the smaller galleries and most gallery directors; they tend to travel in economy class when flying for professional reasons. It is uncommon for these directors to also travel in business class, even when they are going to particularly distant destinations.

13 Another source, the French Comité Professionnel des Galeries d'Art (Professional Committee of Art Galleries, CPGA) estimated that its members made around 40 percent of their revenue at fairs on average in 2018.

14 Obviously, this number is accurate up to the outbreak of the COVID-19 pandemic in early 2020.

15 In 1996, in the middle of the decade during which auction houses began to take a more pronounced interest in the contemporary art domain, the five largest fairs at the time (Art Basel, Cologne Messe, Chicago Art Fair, the FIAC, and ARCO) came together to form the association ICAFA (the International Contemporary Art Fair Association), which intended to regulate access to art fairs and ban auction houses from participating in them in order to avoid any competition that was deemed underhanded.

16 The departure of many of its main artists also largely contributed to the gallery's downfall.

17 Cooper, 80 years old at the time of this interview, celebrated the 50-year anniversary of her gallery in 2018.

18 In doing so, fairs reproduce the phenomenon that also takes place in gallery districts, which was analyzed in the previous chapter.

19 As regards sales in a gallery's space, it is during a vernissage that this characteristic of heightened, fleeting competition is the most intense between potential buyers.

20 Nathalie Obadia, also a gallerist, who runs a competing gallery to that headed by Daniel Templon; a rather unusual situation in the art market.

21 When they have one of the best spaces at a fair, gallerists often downplay the importance of the location, generally preferring to attribute their success to the quality of their presentation but they frequently express their dissatisfaction when they are assigned an undesirable location.

22 After this interview took place, the gallery opened another location in Lyon, the second-largest city in France.

23 Following the outbreak of the COVID-19 pandemic in 2020, nearly all art fairs in the world had to be canceled, sometimes after already having been rescheduled for later in the year.

24 In 2020, due to the COVID-19 pandemic, organizers decided, exceptionally, to reschedule the fair to the month of September, before the fair was ultimately canceled. In 2021, the same postponement was scheduled and in 2022 the fair was able to resume its usual dates in June.

25 In 2020, the COVID-19 pandemic also impacted Art Basel Hong Kong, causing it to be canceled and replaced by a simple online show with virtual booths. It was not, however, particularly successful.

26 The Grand Palais Ephémère was built as a temporary structure that was meant to replace the historical building of the Grand Palais while it was undergoing major renovation works for several years until 2024.

27 Artissima, in Turin, is the leader of these three Italian fairs, as it has the largest international scope (Quemin, 2013a).

28 In 2020, the group's influence was nevertheless particularly disturbed by the COVID-19 pandemic, forcing them to cancel Art Basel Hong Kong—as previously indicated—as well as their flagship event, Baselworld, which was dedicated to watches and jewelry. The Art Basel fair in Switzerland was rescheduled to September of that year, and was ultimately canceled; and Art Basel Miami Beach shared the same fate.

29 In the first few years of the Art Basel fair, each event was named based on the following pattern: Art 1'70, Art 2'71, Art 3'72, etc.

30 The number of visitors to major art fairs is similar between Art Basel and ARCO, at around 90,000 people. As a comparison between Art Basel—the primary fair in the world—and Venice Biennale—one of the largest and most influential biennials—in 2017 the latter drew in 615,000 visitors (with over 23,000 people per day during the preview days) (Trefor Williams, 2018). The number of visitors even reached 800,000 in 2022.

31 A perfect example is the Art Cologne fair; this dropped to 200 exhibitors in 2017 after previously reaching 350 galleries, which severely damaged its reputation.

32 This bench was intended to give a sense of the scale for each work of art that was presented next to it.

33 Hence, when it comes to biennials, Documenta (which is one of the top biennials in the world in terms of influence), is a fairly German-oriented event, with its main focus centered on its German visitors. This is a weak point when compared to its only real competitor, the Venice Biennale. In order to remedy this, and not to be overtaken by its competitors, the 2017 Documenta event took place for the first time in two different cities: Kassel in Germany, and Athens in Greece. This demonstrates that MCH Group's strategy is well suited to an international approach that more broadly characterizes the current structures built around contemporary art.

34 Essentially, unlike several other European contemporary art fairs of its scope, like Vienna Contemporary in Austria and ARCO in Madrid, Art Berlin did not receive any financial support from either the local or national governments.

35 The company had experienced a difficult financial period and overextended its exhibition halls in Basel, forcing it to declare losses; this explains the disengagement from these local fairs. Even worse, its main client Swatch announced that summer that it would no longer participate in the Baselworld watch and jewelry fair, which was the company's flagship event that had launched its development. This withdrawal therefore made other exhibitors doubt whether they would participate in the event. The head of MCH Group was forced to resign in August 2018, while their stocks plummeted in the Zurich stock exchange, forcing the board of directors to react. MCH was already obligated to reduce its expenses, which it therefore did by withdrawing from regional fairs and reworking the Baselworld model. It should be noted that in 2020 the fair, which was supposed to take place at the beginning of May, also had to be canceled due to the COVID-19 pandemic.

36 At the very beginning of the 1980s, when Francine Couture wrote her doctoral thesis on chromos in Quebec (Couture, 1981), or at the beginning of the 1990s, when Raymonde Moulin addressed this topic in France (Moulin, 1992), chromos borrowed stylistically from the impressionist painting style for its pleasing quality in terms of mass appeal. It seems to me that, as the chromos market has in a certain way made contemporary art more accessible, it has been flooded with artworks that take their inspiration from the most iconic and saleable contemporary pieces, adapting them to fulfill a new demand that is further from impressionist art, which almost exclusively prevailed during the 1980s and doubtless into the 1990s as well.

4. Sales: a fundamental undertaking

1 Conversely, in his study on pricing schemes for selling artworks in galleries, Olav Velthuis indicates that a gallerist receiving over 50 percent of the value of a piece is considered unethical (Velthuis, 2002, p. 133).

2 Even large galleries may remunerate some of their artists following this pattern, such as the gallery with locations in Paris and Brussels from which this information was obtained. This is even more common for star artists.

3 This is less true for photography fairs, such as Paris Photo, due to the very fact that they offer multiples. As this gallerist explained in 2020: "Paris Photo is not an easy fair, because the booths aren't that much cheaper than at the FIAC, but people take much longer to buy, they know that the works are multiples, so they say to themselves that they can come back later. We have to work really hard to finalize the sale."

4 A staff member of a famous gallery with abnormal commercial tactics once offered to pay me a 10 percent commission on any sale that I facilitated, and even 20 percent for some artists that are difficult to sell! I never followed up on this offer. It is important to note that such generous practices, and even more so such conditions, are highly exceptional.

5 The more flattering designation of director is also a form of symbolic compensation for the staff who are given this title.

6 This kind of observation clearly shows how, even in the gallery world, there are extremely different segments that follow different norms and codes (Becker, 1982).

7 And yet, not all galleries exist within the same network. There are great similarities between certain galleries, which are particularly reinforced by highly contrasting client overlap rates. As the director of a French gallery puts it: "We clearly share some of our clients with Almine [Rech], with Templon, with Obadia too, but almost none with Lelong, well, at least as far as I'm aware."

8 This kind of information would have been completely impossible to gather if I had not been so thoroughly integrated into the art gallery world.

9 At least in the case of the most successful gallerists.

10 Note that in this configuration, works of art—despite their extreme singularity and their unsubstitutable nature on which economic theory generally insists—are considered here to be fairly substitutable; it is the artist's signature above all else that is sought by the buyer, even more so than the characteristics of the "products" (Moulin, 1995).

11 Contemporary art galleries often operate in the secondary market, at least when they have enough contact with collectors who are sufficiently well off to be able to develop this portion of their business. It is not often highlighted, but is often sought after. When asked how much of their revenue came from the secondary market, large galleries often estimated the amount to be around 10 percent, thus presenting it as a small part of their overall operations. As this Italian gallerist concedes: "The secondary market is very important for galleries today. We can talk about it more easily today, but for a long time, it was practiced in complete discretion, in a somewhat shameful way." A sign of this shift: on several occasions, the gallerists who stated that 10 percent of their revenue came from the secondary market mentioned that it would be a good idea to develop this sector within their own establishments.

12 Olav Velthuis indicates three "scripts" for increasing prices: periodically, according to supply and demand (a model that is widely rejected by galleries, as it can lead to excess); with each new solo exhibition; or else depending on the recognition that the artist has over time (Velthuis, 2002, p. 66).

13 To situate the valuations in terms of price points, in 2018 (at the time of the interview) and to compare them with a more objective level of recognition than

that expressed by his own gallerist, this artist was in fact ranked in the 19,580th position on the Artfacts website.

14 Jean-Bernard Métais came out in the 71,151st position in the Artfacts ranked list in 2018.

15 Recall that price points are not the only factor that structures the various spaces within the art market, or even the sub-spaces within each of them. I have already indicated that the "chromos" market and the contemporary art market are by no means opposed in terms of price points.

16 Here again, gallery managers, with whom I conducted several interviews, had assured me that they would only agree to discounts greater than 10 percent for large pieces or for artists who were difficult to place. Neither of these two conditions were in effect here, but the gallery nevertheless gave a discount of almost 30 percent (at least, according to the buyer).

17 Through a mutual friend, the young woman came to meet me to tell me about her plans and ask for some advice. I vehemently dissuaded her from opening a contemporary art gallery without first having some familiarity with the local scene and its players, especially the collectors who were likely to become clients. Having therefore given up on her plan following our conversation, she thanked me for my advice a few years later.

18 It is therefore very surprising that, in his doctoral thesis on the determinants of prices for contemporary art, Olav Velthuis could believe that between the opening of an exhibition and the possible conclusion of a sale, there is no particular effort made to sell the works (Velthuis, 2002, pp. 87 and 88), when the exact reverse is true. The degree of familiarity with galleries and their modes of operation seems therefore to be a weak point.

19 Despite this qualifier, a great number of participants—which is indisputably the case with the Venice Biennale—are not art professionals at all, but merely collectors, especially important ones.

20 During the 2017 Venice Biennale, the two exhibition spaces for the Pinault Collection in the Serenissima—la Punta della Dogana and the Palazzo Grassi—simultaneously hosted a spectacular presentation of the artist Damien Hirst.

21 While Olav Velthuis was very estimable in wanting to study pricing in the domain of contemporary art, the crux of his approach focuses on the advertised price. As he was so poorly integrated into the world of galleries, it was impossible for him to understand the full importance of a practice such as the discount, which often significantly alters the final transaction price from that which was initially announced.

5. Sociability and friendship: resources for the gallerist occupation

1 Even auctions, although they depend less directly on interpersonal connections, rely largely on these relationships. The main staff of auction houses very frequently bring business to their place of work by playing on their personal friendships with clients who entrust them with objects to sell. Potential buyers

are also involved in relationships that predate the sale, as specific events are set up for them, such as private visits or cocktail receptions in which the auction house staff cultivates close relationships with them.

2 The same is true when galleries suggest delivering and hanging pieces (even little ones) at their clients' residences, like small photos: this gives them access to their collectors' private spaces and provides them with information on what else they collect! It will then be easier to personalize their offerings by appealing more specifically to their tastes.

3 Raymonde Moulin also pointed out another motivation of collectors: financial profit, or even speculation.

4 Here as well, Raymonde Moulin indicated the existence of this form of motivation in the 1960s, but she presented it as being very gendered and frequent in collections by women who were connected to traditional "good works" (Moulin, 1967, p. 240 onwards).

5 This is particularly true for major galleries, but the smaller ones also develop similar activities on their own scale.

6 Even after directly contacting its author, it was not possible to acquire the thesis that Veerle Dobbeleir devoted to these events, studied from an ethnographic approach 30 years ago.

7 In the most influential galleries, actresses, especially the most famous ones and those with an intellectual aura, are particularly desirable as guests.

8 In their work on elite circles and the clubs that host them, Sébastien Chauvin and Bruno Cousin clearly illustrate how private and professional sociability are intertwined and reinforce each other (Chauvin & Cousin, 2010 and 2016).

9 In chapter 1, I showed how much consideration goes into the invitations for openings and the accompanying dinners, at least for those sent by the largest galleries. The invitations are made of heavyweight card stock with carefully chosen typography to best honor the guests (Veblen, 1899). For seated dinners, this is complemented by little place cards indicating the assigned seat, and is generally decorated with the same refined writing.

10 Those two different forms of addressing people in French reflect the degree of familiarity with one's interlocutor.

11 At least until COVID-19 came on the scene, in early 2020, which set back this invitation economy.

12 She also focused on collection agents who have to be highly skilled in managing their emotions.

13 Cousin and Chauvin focus on the professionals: a tennis instructor and a yoga teacher/masseuse, with a socially inferior social status compared to their very wealthy clients. They note that if there is a relationship of subordination, it is combined with a form of authority or legitimacy and a friendship that must be sparked and developed in order to succeed professionally (Cousin & Chauvin, 2019).

14 As Cousin and Chauvin say: "one's friendship with one's tennis or yoga instructor is further proof of the passion that they have for what they teach" (Cousin & Chauvin, 2019, p. 91).

15 It is obvious that the specific form of "professional friendship" analyzed here is not invoked only for happy occasions. Gallerist friends are also there for collectors if they suffer a major blow (not only the death of a loved one), that may affect them. It might be unusual for gallerists to visit their collectors in the hospital when they are sick, but it is commonly accepted that they inquire how they are and show their support over the phone.

16 The same phenomenon can be seen in fashion, in the *haute couture* sector. It is common for the designer who, at least traditionally, most often gives their name to the company and whose personality is absolutely essential in the business, to be supported by faithful clients who are "friends".

17 This initiative, called "Homegrown" consisted of bimonthly online exhibitions. From this, 10 percent of the sales were donated to the World Health Organization to fight COVID-19, and the rest of the profits went to the artists.

18 This anecdote was told during an opening dinner, where the alcohol was flowing, thus releasing inhibitions. It is not at all certain that such an anecdote would have been told so freely during a formal interview.

19 Studying the case of two professionals working with very wealthy clients, Cousin and Chauvin note: "In order to become 'friends' with one's clients and to keep them as such, it is essential to know how to do things for them free of charge, with complete objectivity in the short run, 'giving them gifts', and showing little signs of caring, entering the economy of gifts and counter-gifts that co exists with the commercial and formalized system of priced services purchased elsewhere." The tennis instructor mentioned earlier referred to a gallerist among his relationships, whom he considered to be a hard worker. He added, "he's like me. He's a hustler. He is always looking for clients all year round. He gets really friendly with them and keeps them for life" (Cousin & Chauvin, 2019, p. 90).

20 It is difficult to distinguish between friendship developed by gallerists for their clients and a "pure" friendship insofar as it is possible to believe that a feeling is nurtured and cultivated, in particular for what one can get out of it, whatever the nature of the "return on investment." This comes more generally from well-being, as well as the function of integration associated with the social link (Bidart, 1997). The critique of the utilitarian approach in the social sciences as developed by Alain Caillé opens fascinating lines of inquiry when applied to the area of feelings (Caillé, 2005).

6. Beyond sales: the other activities of contemporary art galleries

1 It should be noted that during my field observations I learned about what amounts to an apprenticeship for the gallery world that takes place well before entering the professional sphere. As previously indicated for traditional French auctioneers ("*commissaires-priseurs*", a profession for which people must pass an entrance exam, which itself is also subject to educational prerequisites) a large portion of the skills utilized by gallerists come from their social

background, their family connections (Quemin, 1997 and 2002b). There is no professional degree or academic track to become a gallerist or work as a gallery director. In France, the proportion of graduates from business schools (of unparalleled prestige) is significant. Another means of accessing this sector is through artistic studies, particularly art history. Even today, though higher education has developed a great deal in recent decades, some very prominent gallerists have not completed higher education degrees, which nonetheless does not prevent them from achieving remarkable success.

2 When discussing the completely distorted or truncated perception of the activities performed by certain occupations within the art market, we may also consider auctioneers. The fact of banging a gavel during auctions is generally thought to be not only the flagship activity, but also the core of the profession, whereas in reality the most visible parts of the profession are only a very small portion of it (Quemin, 1997).

3 In addition to the three main groups ranging from the smallest to the largest entities, the IFSE report distinguished two subgroups at each end of the spectrum. The galleries were distributed as follows: 29 percent had less than €150,000 in revenue, and 29 percent had from €150,000 to €400,000 (i.e., 58 percent were small galleries); 25 percent of galleries were midsize, earning between €400,000 and €1.5 million in revenue; finally, 17 percent of the entities, the "top galleries," exceeded this amount. Of the top galleries, 12 percent were in the range between €1.5 million and €5 million, and only 5 percent were beyond (but the latter accounted for 50 percent of total transactions, compared to only 1.5 percent for the 29 percent that constitute the smallest establishments) (IFSE, 2020). The IFSE statistics covered a set of 700 galleries with a total sales amount of €890 million. It should be noted here that all figures related to private transactions should be taken with the utmost of caution.

4 The previously referenced principle of the interest in selflessness (Bourdieu, 1996) is illustrated here, even though it is somewhat performative in this case.

5 The word that is more used today in the art market is "backers."

6 The intervention of financiers in the art market is fairly widespread; but mainly in the auction sector, where it can lead to considerable profits. Thus, according to the Bloomberg website, the guarantor of Leonardo da Vinci's *Salvator Mundi*—which sold at auction for the record price of $450 million in 2017—would have received between $90 and $150 million on this sale alone (Bloomberg.com, December 20, 2017).

7 The social world of contemporary art galleries is constantly abuzz with rumors and gossip. As Norbert Elias shows very well, these exchanges of information, whether founded or not, help to shape the group and its sense of community (Elias & Scotson, 1994).

8 Before this buyout, the influential gallery had represented such renowned artists as Richard Long, Bill Viola, and Rachel Whiteread.

9 Alan Bowness distinguishes the four successive phases of artist recognition: by their peers, by critics, by the market, and finally by the general public.

10 It is interesting to note that, since this interview took place, the artist is no longer represented by the very influential international gallery in question.

11 A symmetrical case of an artist's vulnerability in regards to gallerists is that they can find themselves caught off guard when the gallery decides to end the collaboration, when it does not pay its artists in full, or when it does not operate in an efficient manner.

12 It is therefore clear that, as indicated in the chapter on sales, which addresses the practice of setting and adopting prices in particular, analyzing this subject without covering the existence of discounts in depth (Velthuis, 2002, 2003, and 2005) makes little sense. Price reductions are so commonplace that they are even built into contract templates.

13 In reality, many of this gallery's clients (with whom I am friendly) have told me about larger discounts, particularly when it involves paying for the services of an art advisor. In this case, it is more often a 20 percent discount that is agreed upon. However, the practice of significantly lowering prices is still less common for the gallery in question than in its competitor.

14 Beginning to formulate this model in 1967, Moulin outlines it thus: "In something of a muddled dialectic, aesthetic judgment becomes the pretext for a commercial operation, and the successful commercial operation serves as aesthetic judgment" (Moulin, 1967 [1987], p. 490).

7. Recent trends: evolution in the gallery sphere and in the gallerist occupation

1 Note that before Brown, his fellow gallerist Andrea Rosen had joined the David Zwirner Gallery in 2017. In both cases, it did not involve unknown galleries; on the contrary, they were very prominent professionals, who operated in the upper-middle sector of the local New York market.

2 In other words, realistically, in the handful of countries in the world that really count on the international art market (Quemin, 2002, 2006, 2013a, and 2013b).

3 In an analysis that I wrote on gallery participation in contemporary art fairs in 2008, I was surprised to discover that at the time, it was the Viennese gallery Krinzinger that was the most active. Through very high investment in international contemporary art fairs, it managed to make up for the weakness of the market in Vienna, and more broadly, Austria (Quemin, 2013a).

4 Salzburg is certainly also a European city, but its position on the continental scene is much more peripheral than that of Paris. In this sense, it can be said that the former is therefore "less European" than the latter.

5 These four galleries are so closely related, both in terms of their extreme capital intensity and internationalization, and absolutely central locations in Chelsea, that they are frequently presented as a homogeneous whole, or even as a single entity. This is evident in the following press extract: "Four of the largest—Gagosian, Hauser & Wirth, Pace, and David Zwirner—account for around 800 staff, 41 spaces, and more than 300 artists and estates among them" ("Top Galleries Have Never Been Bigger or More Influential. But What Will Happen When Their Founders Are Gone?" *Artnet News*, January 9, 2019).

6 I developed the geographical analysis in the first part of this book.

7 Another example of this geographical expansion strategy to stand out from one's competitors: the biennial (or quadrennial, in point of fact) Documenta has historically been a very German-oriented event, aimed above all at German visitors. This was the biennial's Achilles heel. To remedy this, and avoid being overtaken by its competitors, particularly the Venice Biennale (which has a much more international audience), the 2017 Documenta biennial took place in two different countries: Germany (in Kassel) and Greece (in Athens). Clearly, growing and expanding geographically to occupy even more space constitutes a fundamental trend for players in the contemporary art world, even beyond the market alone, because of the more general competition that has been intensifying over the years.

8 Another illustration of the large-scale strategies that are developed by mega-galleries to highlight the work of the star artists whom they represent is how they use the considerable financial means at their disposal. In 2012, Gagosian, which at the time had 11 galleries around the world, devoted all of its spaces to an exhibition of "spot paintings" by Hirst, featuring 331 of the 1,000 works that make up the whole series.

9 The four names mentioned are, respectively, those of the famous French collector and businessman, of two powerful gallerists, and of a collector who has invested extensively in the market.

10 There is, as a matter of fact, a situation that is fairly similar to this evolution by the field of *haute couture*. In the 1970s, Pierre Bourdieu and Yvette Delsaut described and analyzed a very dynamic space, particularly because young avant-garde designers were then creating and developing their own houses and the brands associated with them (Bourdieu & Delsaut, 1975). While this practice lasted until the 1980s, the most powerful luxury groups—which had become owners of the most established brands—later progressively began to integrate talented designers. Whereas previously, creators who founded their own houses and brands tended to cause the most established luxury fashion brands to become outdated, the fact that these brands appointed them as designers of the most prestigious houses prevented them from standing as real competitors, and ultimately harming the most established players (or agents, to use Bourdieu's terminology again). The field of haute couture—considered here from the angle of founding new houses—is therefore much less influenced by industry tensions today than in the period analyzed by Bourdieu and Delsaut. The widespread introduction of massive economic capital has changed the rules of the game, and guarantees a much more tenable permanence of positions.

11 The "gallery crisis" was mentioned a great deal during the Talking Galleries symposium in 2022. This event was created in Barcelona in 2011, and takes place every year in the same city for art market professionals to share insights on the field.

12 That same year, Anne de Villepoix, who had been active in the Paris art market for nearly 30 years with a spacious installation on rue de Montmorency in the Haut Marais neighborhood, withdrew to a less prominent district in the 11th arrondissement, while still continuing her business.

13 Another example of growth via a consolidation of two galleries occurred in Europe, in the merger of the Baronian and Xippas galleries in Brussels in 2019 (however, the two partners quickly went their separate ways).

14 It should be noted that after having opened a second New York space on the upper floor of a Lower East Side building in 2014, Gavin Brown closed it in the summer of 2019.

15 Both partners had created their galleries in Cologne; Monika Sprüth in 1983, and Philomene Magers in 1991.

16 It is in fact possible to draw a parallel between the merger operations affecting galleries (whether they concern the establishment as a whole or they pool their collectors and all or some of their roster of artists) with the recent mergers that took place in the American auction house world at the same time. As such, in 2019, the galleries Leslie Hindmann Auctioneers and Cowan's Auctions on the one hand, and Rago and Wright on the other, merged one after the other. In doing so, these small and midsize American auction houses intended to face off against unprecedented competition in the domain. When stacked against Christie's and Sotheby's, Leslie Hindmann's turnover was negligible. It was only worth $40 million in 2018, whereas the new entity formed by the merger totaled $65 million in revenue. Wright generated $25 million, and Rago $33 million; with these two alone, they verged on $60 million. Additionally, in recent years, a certain number of regional auction houses have opened a growing number of offices and sales rooms across the United States; such as Skinner Auctioneers (four spaces), and Cowan's and Doyle (eight locations respectively). There are therefore clear similarities with the current policy of expansion and reinforcement for contemporary art galleries.

17 The contemporary art world is abuzz with rumors that market heavyweights such as Gagosian and Pace have reached annual gross sales figures for several years that should now exceed $1 billion (note the use of the conditional here).

18 Even before that, in 1995, the PaceWildenstein gallery stunned the art market by securing the sale of television producer Mark Goodson's collection: a treasure trove of around 50 modern masterpieces including works by Picasso, Francis Bacon, and Wassily Kandinsky. The agreement had been negotiated by Arne Glimcher, the father of Marc Glimcher.

19 On a much smaller scale, at the end of 2020, the French gallerist Emmanuel Perrotin in turn joined forces with two art market professionals—Dylan Lessel and Tom-David Bastok—to create an entity that would specialize in the secondary market. It should be noted that the stature of the three associates appears to have no connection to that of the New York triumvirate; however, it also testifies to an attempt to ramp up investments in the secondary market.

20 The same gallery may sell works sold in the same city in one currency or another, based on the artist's nationality.

21 In reality, I was able to learn that, despite this director's statement, his gallery (and even himself directly) sometimes gives 20% discounts, or even 25% on occasion, specifically to art advisors. His misgivings about these professionals are therefore understandable as their intervention in the sales process reduces the price of the work of art or the gallery share at the end of the negotiation.

22 This characteristic is in fact common among gallerists; nevertheless, they avoid displaying it too openly, and while the profession must necessarily include the notion of representing artists who are financially profitable, it can also include a dimension of financial deficit with some of their artists in order to present a more unselfish image.

23 Conversely, the fervor for Chinese artists has fizzled out. The movement in their favor seems to have been more a fad than a real market transformation.

24 This is a clear example of Pierre Bourdieu's famous formulation, "youth is just a word" (Bourdieu, 1993).

25 "Almost one third of solo shows in US museums go to artists represented by five galleries," *The Art Newspaper*, April 2, 2015. A total of 590 personal exhibitions for contemporary artists were taken into account, considering the main exhibitions organized by a total of 68 museums between 2007 and 2013.

26 On the more general notion of "quality" in art, I will again recommend the work of Marian Misdrahi Flores (Misdrahi Flores, 2013). In my own previous work, I also showed that an artist's nationality tends to influence how their work is evaluated and whether it is "quality" (Quemin, 2002, 2006, and 2013).

27 It is not only the works that are sometimes more exceptional. The conditions of their presentation can end up being clearly superior to those offered by reputed museums. Hence, to give another example from the same gallery, the design of the Baselitz exhibition at the Accademia gallery in Venice in 2019 fell very much short compared to the conditions in which the Thaddaeus Ropac gallery in Pantin (in the inner suburbs of Paris) regularly presents this artist.

28 Another landmark event that one could previously have expected from a museum, but that once again came from the same gallery: in November 2018, Thaddaeus Ropac announced that it would now be representing Donald Judd and the Donald Judd Foundation for all of Europe. This announcement was cemented a few months later by the first exhibition of Donald Judd in France in 20 years, as no gallery (or institution) had presented the work of this celebrated artist for two decades.

29 Another example that I can give from the same gallery: in New York in 2017, the Calder exhibition at the Whitney Museum did not make much of a splash in the wake of the Calder/Picasso presentation organized by the Almine Rech Gallery in the same city just before, at the end of 2016.

30 Also in 2017, Philippe de Montebello—the former director of the prestigious Metropolitan Museum in New York, from which he retired in 2008 (at the age of 81 years old)—joined the New York gallery Acquavella as advisor and director. Interestingly, he explained at the time in an interview that he did not yet know what his role would consist of. The announcement of his appointment was made in July 2017, just one month after that of the recruitment of Julia Peyton-Jones by the Thaddaeus Ropac gallery.

31 Note the grandiose title, which has become fairly inevitable, given the inflation of directors' titles that prevails in all major contemporary art galleries; as I mentioned in the chapter of this book dedicated to the analysis of sales relationships. However, it would have been difficult to do any less for such a

renowned and recognized person, who had already been ennobled by the Queen of England for her professional excellence.

32 Gad's reputation was well established; as a member of the selection committee for the "Social Work" section of Frieze London the previous year, she had, in 2015 and 2017, organized monographic exhibitions at the Serpentine Galleries devoted to Arthur Jafa and Jimmie Durham, two artists who were later awarded the Golden Lion at the Venice Biennale in 2019. Her presentation of Jafa's works, which at the time took place at the Moderna Museet in Stockholm, also received the AICA Award for the Best Exhibition of 2018 when it was introduced in Germany; while the show that she dedicated to a rising star on the international scene, Lynette Yiadom-Boakye, was crowned with the Sky Arts Award in 2016.

33 It is important for gallerists to have built up a stock for when a crisis strikes, which results in businesses not turning a profit for months on end. Even if the market is very sluggish, they can then sell a few works from their stock, which can allow them to hold out for several months.

34 This decrease, although very drastic, is much less than that which occurred in 2009, when the auction market fell by 36 percent compared to 2008, even though the global economic crisis was less severe (Artprice, 2021).

35 It should also be noted that figures published about the art market, when they also claim to include private transactions, are not especially reliable. In this particular crisis context, galleries have every interest in overestimating their level of activity, at least *vis-à-vis* the press or in surveys, to maintain confidence in the market. I therefore prefer to consider the much more rigorous data published by Artprice, which restricts itself to the auction (i.e., public sales) segment, and (rightly) ignores private transactions.

36 Beyond fairs alone, the whole calendar of major international events was profoundly affected by the onset of the COVID-19 pandemic, all the way up to the Venice Biennale, which was initially scheduled for spring 2021; and in May 2020, was pushed back to 2022.

37 These galleries that specialize in contemporary art, and represent major players in the primary market, were not the only ones to open spaces in the Hamptons. In doing so, they adopted the same strategy as the three auction houses: Christie's, Sotheby's, and Phillips; as well as the Van de Weghe gallery, which is mainly active in the secondary market.

38 In her short book, *Le marché de l'art. Mondialisation et nouvelles technologies* (*The Art Market: Globalization and New Technologies*), first published in 2000, Raymonde Moulin completely overestimated the impact that the Internet would have on transactions and the digitalization of the art market (Moulin, 2009).

39 In April 2020, the following press release was issued to report on the initiative that, once again, came from Hauser & Wirth, and was quite disconnected from the market:

> "Hauser & Wirth unveils ArtLab, a division devoted to new technologies and research, including a digital residency program for artists.
>
> HWVR, a first in virtual reality exhibition modeling, is launching this month on hauserwirth.com.

> Iwan Wirth, Manuela Wirth, and Marc Payot, co-presidents of Hauser & Wirth, announced today the launch of ArtLab, the gallery's research and innovation division that would explore projects at the intersection of art and technology. ArtLab was formed to create bespoke technology solutions for the most pressing issues in the art world, including greater accessibility and sustainability."

Just a few years later, the hopes that had been hung on this initiative seem to have been largely overestimated.

8. Understanding the gallery hierarchy: how to construct a ranked list of the main contemporary art galleries in the world

1 Countless ranked lists have overtaken websites, newspapers, and magazines: on educational establishments, on hotels and restaurants, on beaches, on tourist sites, on favorite celebrities, on hospitals, on the best cities to live or retire in.

2 In spite of what Larissa Buchholz claims in her recent book on the "globalization" of the visual arts (Buchholz, 2023), her "own" works and mine were definitely not developed simultaneously, and we did not come to "similar" conclusions, as she very surprisingly asserts. Several years after I had published, both in French (Quemin, 2001 and 2002a, b, & c) and in English (Quemin, 2004), on the subject of the internationalization of the contemporary visual arts, she investigated the exact same topic (Buchholz & Wuggenig, 2005). Moreover, she utilized the very same methodology that I had used for my own work. Her main "findings" were absolutely not original and only confirmed conclusions that are clearly mine and that I had published literally years before she presented them as her own. In her early writings, although she cited an extensive bibliography both in English and French, she neglected to mention my conclusions, even though they were readily available in numerous publications.

3 The first edition was published in *Capital* in its 14/08 issue on October 23, 2008.

4 The first edition of the Artfacts classification in *Le Journal des Arts* was published in 2012, in issue no. 371 from June 8–21, 2012. After its success, the newspaper produced an updated list a year later, as had been planned since the first edition. Other publications have since followed.

5 The outline of its general methodology is presented on the following website: http://www.artfacts.net/marketing_new/?Services,Artist_Ranking

6 After doing an online search, I found a 2005 presentation on the (indeed complex) methodology used by Artfacts via the following link: http://www9.georgetown.edu/faculty/irvinem/visualarts/ArtMarket/ArtFacts-ArtistRanking-Forumula-2005.pdf

It is inspired by the following book on economics: Georg Franck, *Ökonomie der Aufmerksamkeit*, Munich/Vienne, Carl Hanser Verlag, 1998.

7 Until 2007, the Power 100 listed architects, as well as companies. In 2007, two star architects still appeared on the Power 100 (Herzog & de Meuron, and

Frank Gehry), as well as two institutions designated as such, and not by the personality of their director (Deutsche Bank and UBS). As of 2008, only individual people have been included on the list.

8 To give an idea of scale, I will provide the figures that I produced for the year 2008 of the 10 largest contemporary art fairs classified by number of exhibitors: Art Basel was far in the lead with 304 galleries, followed Art Basel Miami Beach (248 galleries), Art Cologne (191), Fiera di Bologna (165), ARCO Madrid (164), Art Chicago (158), the Armory Show in New York (158), MiArt Milano (156), the Frieze Art Fair in London (150), and the FIAC in Paris (149) (Quemin, 2013a). It is therefore clear that the figures in terms of the number of galleries in international fairs are often much higher than those of the São Paulo event.

9 In *ArtReview. The Magazine Online*, November 2009.

10 There is, to date, a complete series of 22 successive ranked lists. Again, despite its obvious limitations, the annual edition of the Power 100 since its creation, without exception, testifies to the strong social demand for ranked lists (Blank, 2007; Esposito & Stark, 2009), especially artistic (Quemin, 2013b).

11 The upheavals (and even drastic departures) in the successive editions of the Power 100 strip all credibility from its ranked lists, when we recognize the inertia that automatically characterizes rankings based on a more rigorous methodology. As such, in the Kunstkompass and among the top 100 artists on the Artfacts ranked list, annual turnover is closer to 5 percent, and is sometimes even lower (Quemin, 2013b).

12 Only the Hauser & Wirth gallery is currently split between the United States and Europe (Switzerland and the United Kingdom for the latter) without it being possible to determine which of the three countries stands as the location of its headquarters. This gallery represents an exceptional case of multi-country management.

13 The same issue of *Le Journal des Arts* also offered its readers a "Top 10 independent curators" list, which was introduced as follows: "A subjective selection of professionals from the French scene, some of whom have already marked the landscape of exhibitions with their singular imprint, while others have a bright, promising future." No methodology was mentioned whatsoever, and the list was not ordered; names that should have been self-evident were not mentioned, while other choices completely clashed with their presence in the selection. A "Top 10 of taboos in the art press," a "Top 10 of French champions on an international level," and a "Top 10 of the biggest flops" (again, all unclassified and without any methodology mentioned) were also featured in the same issue of *Le Journal des Arts*.

14 I will later address an unfinished classification initiative by the same company that produces data on art and the art market when I present the methodology that I myself have developed, and is based on ArtFacts data (which I used specifically). I will also mention a very recent initiative that Artfacts adopted two years after the French version of this book was published.

15 Another, rare, quantified assessment of the market found in Moulin's work, in the mid-1980s was that purchases by public authorities represented 8 percent of the French market (in terms of amount), and around 28 percent of the domestic market. By also including all orders, in addition to purchases, these figures rose

to more than 22 percent of the market, and 75 percent of the domestic market (Moulin, 1992).

16 This is why I regularly refer to the data produced by Artprice pertaining to auctions.

17 To better judge the quality of the data produced within the framework of the Art Basel / UBS report, which, in the absence of other sources relating to the market as a whole, is often cited without the slightest critical distance, it is necessary to mention that, for its 2019 edition, McAndrew—the director of Art Economics and author of the report—surveyed 600 wealthy people (through UBS), as well as 500 auction houses (with a 20 percent response rate) and 6,500 galleries (with a 17.5 percent response rate). Such low response rates should already prompt great caution in establishing inevitably unreliable data. The 2019 Art Market Report can be downloaded at: www.ubs.com/global/en/about_ubs/art/2019/art-basel.html.

18 Saying as much is not denunciatory, and solely accounts for the fact that a gallerist's profession falls within the commercial sphere. Even in the pharmacy world—a business that is infinitely more regulated—and whose deliveries of goods are much easier to trace than that of galleries, it is a known fact in a country such as France that pharmacies can (or have been able to) access software that allows them to keep two sets of books so as not to declare the real amount of their profits.

19 Guy Bellavance and his co-authors write about the logic of Artfacts' "circular" qualification (Bellavance et al., 2018).

20 In 2019, the respective Artfacts ranks for these five artists were as follows: 3,485th, 3,379th, 1,257th, 439th, and 102nd.

21 Otherwise, a gallery that makes losses, be they temporary or more lasting, or even structural, can rely on a financial partner, a "backer," who will absorb the gallery's deficit.

22 Here, I have used the names that are mentioned in the Artfacts ranking to designate the various galleries, but I did not include the location that is sometimes associated with them. Quite surprisingly, the Artfacts ranking mentions "Gagosian gallery New York," "Galleria Continua San Gimignano," "Marian Goodman gallery New York," "Sprüth Magers Berlin," "Galerie Max Hetzler Berlin," and "Nathalie Obadia Paris".

23 In October 2023, Artfacts published a newsletter that included a link to its updated list of international galleries, this time ranking the top 100 establishments in the world. Quite surprisingly, there were many changes at the top of the list in the span of just a few months. The most unlikely result was again the position of the Marlborough gallery, which was still ranked in 14th place; a clear illustration of a hysteresis effect (Bourdieu, 1992).

24 In February 2021, once his Artfacts blurb had been rounded out, Nicolas Party was placed in the 1,438th position on the list (before rising to the 972nd position in February 2023).

25 The other sectors of the Art Basel fair are as follows: Unlimited (for monumental or large-scale works), Feature (a curated set of works), Statements (more experimental), Edition, Parcours (works installed in Basel's Old Town), Film, Magazines, and Talks.

26 It should be noted that the Galerie Bruno Bischofberger is mainly active nowadays on the secondary market; whereas, as I have indicated, I have decided here to focus on galleries that are mainly present on the primary market. Moreover, this judgment on the Bischofberger gallery's importance is excessive. This can doubtless be explained (at least in part) by the fact that, in each country, there is a general tendency to overestimate the impact of national players on the international market.

27 One of Larry Gagosian's most spectacular "coups" was to poach Peter Halley from the Sonnabend Gallery in 1992; resulting in a monumental lawsuit filed by the latter. In the same vein, Gagosian quite suddenly appropriated the very prominent artists David Salle and Philip Taaffe from his fellow gallerist Mary Boone.

28 The "estate" designates an individual or a group of individuals who are united around a set of material or immaterial property (or properties) produced by a person and having belonged to them. The artistic estate (which is likened to succession) is the decision-maker of the future of the artist's works. Thus, they often choose to work with one or a few galleries in order to best preserve the interest of the artist in terms of posterity, and their own interests as successors.

29 Based in Saône-et-Loire, in the small town of Chagny (6,000 inhabitants), this gallery deliberately does not have a website, even though it regularly participates in fairs as prominent as the FIAC (and later Paris+ by Art Basel), or Art Basel itself.

30 A few years ago, the gallery announced that it had no fewer than 133 artists.

31 It should, however, be emphasized that this method cannot be used to classify small galleries, along with their less-recognized artists, as there would then be biases that would make this approach much less reliable.

9. The international ranked list of the "best" contemporary art galleries

1 This outcome is a far cry from the aberration produced by the Artfacts algorithm for a long time—that I mentioned in my previous methodological section—which at the end of the first half of 2023 still attributed the third position in the world to the Leo Castelli gallery (and, as previously mentioned, in 2019, it even landed in the number one Artfacts spot!) As I have already indicated, this repudiates any credibility to a ranked list that could be determined by mechanically classifying galleries according to the position that they have been assigned by Artfacts. Even after the company revised its *modus operandi* in the summer of 2023, the newly adopted methodology remains rather obscure and still shows some limitations in the results it provides.

2 It should be noted that, when major galleries recount their history—especially on their website—they almost systematically list their successive relocations and

inaugurations. I have therefore also decided to mention these moves as part of the galleries' development, as they are objective elements that, unlike their financial performances, are fully transparent and clearly illustrate the spatial and economic trajectory of the various establishments.

3 Once again, I must emphasize the impact of the methodology that I have employed: given its top 10 artists, the Thaddaeus Ropac gallery is very clearly the leader of the pack, but if we include the completely exceptional range of star artists (Quemin, 2013) of the Gagosian gallery, the latter could justifiably lay claim to the first place.

4 Unless otherwise stated, all the Artfacts data used dates back to the beginning of 2023.

5 The only notable name missing from this group is Gerhard Richter.

6 However, as I previously mentioned, it could just as easily be asserted that these three galleries rose to a joint third position, or even second position if we acknowledge that the gap between them and Sprüth Magers is negligible.

7 The former's gallery was founded in 1983, and the latter's in 1991; both in Cologne.

8 Hauser & Wirth Somerset was inaugurated in July 2014, and has already welcomed around 1 million visitors, including 100 schools and other educational institutions per year. Entry into this "art centre" (the term used by the gallery) is free, and all donations made by visitors are given to local charity partners. Clearly, the center is very far from following the model of a traditional gallery (Quemin, 2020b).

9 In its first year, Hauser & Wirth Menorca hosted a painting and sculpture exhibition with paintings by star contemporary artist Mark Bradford, as well as an eight-room, 16,500-square-foot tour highlighting the sculptures of Louise Bourgeois, Eduardo Chillida, and Franz West, who were other established artists represented by the gallery.

10 More recently, the gallery opened a second space nearby, next to the iconic Place Vendôme, but it mostly consists of a shop window, with very little space inside.

11 Let us recall once again all of the caution with which a gallery's reported net income must be considered. Moreover, the gallery with the highest sales figure is not necessarily the one with the highest profit margins, if its costs are higher than those of any of its competitors.

12 A significant difference between the two galleries, however, is that the Thaddaeus Ropac gallery is much more involved in developing the progression of artists who are still making their way to acclaim.

13 In 1997, Goodman also opened a bookstore in Paris just down the street from her main exhibition space.

14 The only extension that the gallery can claim of its premises is a smaller space in the courtyard behind its main space.

15 In *Artnet News*, "Art Dealer Chantal Crousel on the Inside Story of Paris's Art Market and Why She's Now Passing the Reins to the Next Generation," February 16, 2021.

16 This is also the case for the Chantal Crousel gallery, even though it landed in the 11th position on my ranking in 2023, as I have previously stated (and was ranked number 10 in 2019).

17 There could have been more similarities between the top rankings of my list and the Power 100, since the latter actually reflects a form of influence, rather than the power that it claims to reveal; however, I have already highlighted the limitations of this indicator due to a very loose methodology (Quemin, 2021).

18 In 2019, Michael Werner, like its fellow gallery Elvira González, represented only nine living or deceased artists. These two establishments are therefore placed at the bottom of the classification.

19 Another sign of the strong connection between Art Basel and the German-speaking world is Maike Cruse, the former director of Berlin's Gallery Weekend, as well as the former director of two Berlin art fairs for almost a decade (Art Berlin Contemporary from 2012 to 2016, and Art Berlin from 2016 to 2019), who was appointed director of the Art Basel fair in May 2023. As the French version of *The Art Newspaper* remarked: "Her ties with Germany and German professionals will be important for this fair, which takes place in German-speaking Switzerland, and has been very popular with collectors from across the Rhine for a long time" (May 4, 2023). Even more than collectors, it was Cruse's proximity to German galleries that Art Basel likely sought; the position was created especially for her.

20 The largest galleries in the world that participate in Art Basel represent very few Chinese artists, as they tend to have a very concentrated focus on Western artists. Even the most sought-after Chinese artists on the market are, for the most part, featured in other circuits, be they galleries or auctions; most of which do not have access to Art Basel (Quemin, 2013c; Yun, 2016 and 2021).

21 Initially based in an apartment when it was founded in 1990, Perrotin moved to Rue Louise Weiss in the 13th arrondissement of Paris in 1997. At the time, this neighborhood was part of an urban planning project to support up-and-coming contemporary art galleries.

22 In 2021, a new joint venture specializing in the secondary market launched on Avenue Matignon when Emmanuel Perrotin teamed up with two other players in the art market, Dylan Lessel and Tom-David Bastok. It is interesting to compare this partnership to the one that Larry Gagosian had announced not long before, on a completely different level, with the major art market players Pace and Acquavella galleries in New York.

23 In 2005, Perrotin moved into a massive 14,000-square-foot space located in a former warehouse in Miami. In 2008, however, the gallerist announced that he would be putting his Florida branch "to rest", and in 2010 the art press reported that he had sold his stakes of this initiative to his partner, Cathy Vedovi, who had previously owned 50 percent of the shares of the building.

24 This Perrotin space was located on Madison Avenue, just below its fellow gallery Dominique Lévy.

25 Perrotin has long been renowned for its various soirees and festivities, all of which contribute to its image.

26 Note, furthermore, that in this top 10 artist list, Sophie Calle is an inexpensive artist in relation to her level of recognition, and Maurizio Cattelan only produces works from time to time. This has a direct impact on the market generated by these artists.

27 Marc Glimcher, the gallery's CEO, is regularly awarded a top spot in the Power 100. Admittedly, this indicator is not intended to reflect a gallery's quality, but the power of those who are in charge. Nevertheless, my ranked list asserts that Pace's leader does not have the power to attract the most prominent and sought-after artists on the market; he is outstripped by his most direct competitors on the New York market (Gagosian, David Zwirner, Hauser & Wirth, and Marian Goodman), most of which are located a stone's throw from the Pace gallery in Chelsea. The White Cube, Lisson, Skarstedt, and Gladstone galleries (all also based in New York), also have better rankings than Pace. It should be noted that this was already true for the Gladstone gallery even before having absorbed a good part of the artist roster of the former gallery Gavin Brown's Enterprise in 2020.

28 In California, Pace first established itself in Los Angeles in the mid-1990s, around the same time it expanded into London; both of these attempts were ultimately unsuccessful, and these branches languished and closed a few years later, due to the absence of the gallery's director, Marc Glimcher. At the time, collectors almost always expected to be able to rub shoulders with the head of the gallery, and only Larry Gagosian managed to bypass this obligation. Pace then opened another California branch in Palo Alto, which it later closed so that it could return to Los Angeles.

29 In London, Pace is located in the heart of the Mayfair neighborhood. For a long time, it was situated at the corner of Burlington Gardens and Cork Street, one block away from Old Bond Street. These two major arteries are home to a very high concentration of eminent galleries that are very active in the art market. Pace has since moved into the immense London spaces left vacant following the closure of the Blain / Southern gallery, remaining in the Mayfair district.

30 Although it was important for Pace to attract a star artist as renowned as Jeff Koons so as to "maintain its symbolic ranking" as a leading gallery, the financial stakes of working with this artist were less significant, since the market for his works had already been very intense thanks to his having been represented by two other mega-galleries. Hence, the perspectives of new sales were more limited than they had previously been.

31 Note that the marginal position is by no means limited to the non-Western space or the southern Hemisphere (Quemin, 2023). In my classification, there are also galleries with low rankings from certain European countries that could be designated as marginal. Such is the case of the Andréhn-Schiptjenko gallery (178th place); a Swedish establishment based in Stockholm (it also has a branch in Paris, where its presence is fairly discreet), as well as Plan B (180th place), based in Cluj, Romania, and Berlin, but originally from the former city. If the more central countries on the contemporary art scene are also represented by galleries with lower rankings on my list, it is because these galleries occupy fairly peripheral positions on their national art markets. Conversely, for a gallery from a marginal country to be present at Art Basel, it must occupy a central place in its national market.

32 Of course, there are very well-known artists whose market success is comparatively much lower, particularly because the medium of their work does not easily lend itself to individual collections, and because institutions (which therefore become the target clients for these artists, especially if they are prestigious) are often quoted lower prices from galleries. Conversely, on the contemporary art market, there are hardly any artists who are extremely expensive (in the long term) who do not benefit from a significant level of artistic recognition. If this is not the case, there must necessarily be a collaboration with wealthy collectors to bolster prices.

33 Although it is common for galleries to maintain privileged relationships with collectors who support them over the long term, most of them maintain a substantial amount of autonomy regarding these financial partners, particularly with regard to their list of represented artists and their lineup.

Conclusion

1 Thus, in a March 2020 press release (resulting from a legal action) issued by the Comité Professionnel des Galeries d'Art (Professional Committee of Art Galleries) in France to challenge the closure of galleries as mandated by the government in order to combat the spread of COVID-19, it was clearly specified that, due to the uniqueness of the artworks, it would be almost impossible to sell works without clients being able to experience them physically (at least on the primary market, which was the focus in this book).

BIBLIOGRAPHY

Adam Georgina, *Big Bucks, The Explosion of the Art Market in the 21st Century*, Lund Humphries, 2014.

Adam Georgina, *Dark Side of the Boom, The Excesses of the Art Market in the 21st Century*, Lund Humphries, 2018.

Adam Georgina, *La face cachée du marché de l'art*, Paris, Beaux-arts éditions, 2018.

Alexander Victoria D. et al. (Ed.), *Art and the Challenge of Markets. National Cultural Politics and the Challenges of Marketization and Globalization*, Cham, Palgrave MacMillan, 2018

Ansaloni Claudia, *The Grand Paris of Contemporary Art*, GIOCA Master thesis, Bologne, Bologna University, 2018.

Appadurai Arjun (Ed.), *Globalization. Public Culture. Society for Transnational Cultural Studies*, Durham, NC/London, Duke University Press, 2000.

Appadurai Arjun, *Modernity at Large: Cultural Dimensions of Globalization*, Minneapolis, MN, University of Minnesota Press, 1996.

Arborio Anne-Marie & Fournier Pierre, *L'observation directe*, Paris, Armand Colin, 2015.

Artprice, *Le marché de l'art 2016*, Saint-Romain-au-Mont d'Or, Artprice, 2017, fr.artprice.com/artprice-reports/le-marche-de-lart-en-2016

Artprice, "Artprice by Artmarket.com : Faut-il redéfinir la notion d'art contemporain en 2020 ?", Saint-Romain-au-Mont d'Or, Artprice, 2020.

Artprice, *Le marché de l'art 2019*, Saint-Romain-au-Mont d'Or, Artprice, 2019 (a).

Artprice, *Le marché de l'art contemporain 2019*, Saint-Romain-au-Mont d'Or, Artprice, 2019 (b).

Artprice, *The Art Market in 2020*, Saint-Romain-au-Mont d'Or, Artprice, 2021.

Artprice, *Le rapport sur le marché de l'art en 2021*, https://fr.artprice.com/artprice-reports/le-marche-de-lart-en-2021

Assouline Pierre, *Grâces lui soient rendues : Paul Durand-Ruel, le marchand des impressionnistes*, Paris, Plon, 2002.

Atencio Demirdjian Tiqui, *For Art's Sake: Inside the Homes of Art Dealers*, New York, Rizzoli, 2020.

Barragán Paco, *The Art Fair Age*, Milan, Edizioni Charta, 2008.

Barragán Paco, *From Roman Feria to Global Art Fair. From Olympia Festival to Neo-Liberal Biennial. On the 'Biennialization' of Art Fairs and the 'Fairization' of Biennials*, Miami, Artpulse Editions, 2020.

Bartelson Jens, 'Three concepts of globalization', *International Sociology*, 15(2), June 2000, pp. 180–196.

Bauman Zigmunt, *Globalization. The Human Consequences*, Cambridge: Polity Press, 1998.

Beaud Stéphane & Weber Florence, *Guide de l'enquête de terrain. Produire et analyser des données ethnographiques*, Paris, La découverte, 1997.
Becker Howard S., *Outsiders. Studies in the Sociology of Deviance*, New York, The Free Press of Glencoe, 1963.
Becker Howard S., *Art Worlds*, Berkeley, University of California Press, 1982.
Beckert Jens & Rössel Jörg, Kunst und Preise. *Kölner Zeitschrift für Soziologie und Sozialpsychologie*, 56-1, 2004, pp. 32–50.
Beckert Jens & Rössel Jörg, "The Price Of Art. Uncertainty and Reputation in the Art Field", *European Societies*, 15-2, 2013, pp. 178–195.
Bell Christopher E., *American Idolatry: Celebrity, Commodity and Reality Television*, Jefferson, NC, McFarland Publishers & Co, 2007.
Bellavance Guy (Ed.), *Monde et réseaux de l'art : diffusion, migration et cosmopolitisme en art contemporain*, Montreal: Liber, 2000.
Bellavance Guy, Casemajor Nathalie, Roberge Jonathan, Sirois Guillaume & Nantel Lyne, "Les données massives en art contemporain : le cas d'*ArtFacts.Net", Communication & organisation*, n°54, 2018, pp. 81–91.
Benhamou Françoise, *L'Économie de la culture*, Paris, La Découverte, collection Repères, 2003 (1996).
Benhamou Françoise, Moureau Nathalie & Sagot-Duvauroux Dominique, *Les Galeries d'art contemporain en France. Portrait et enjeux dans un marché mondi*alisé, Paris, la documentation Française, 2001.
Benhamou Françoise, Moureau Nathalie & Sagot-Duvauroux Dominique, "Opening the Black Box of the White Cube: A survey of French contemporary art galleries at the turn of the millenium", Poetics, August 2002, 30(4), pp. 263–280.
Berggruen Heinz, *J'étais mon meilleur client. Souvenirs d'un marchand d'art*, Paris, L'arche, 1997.
Besnard Philippe & Desplanques Guy, *Un prénom pour toujours. La cote des prénoms hier, aujourd'hui et demain*, Paris, Balland, 1986.
Beyerler Ernst, *La passion de l'art (entretiens avec Christophe Mory)*, Paris, Gallimard, 2003.
Bidart Claire, *L'amitié. Un lien social*, Paris, La Découverte, 1997.
Blanchet Alain & Gotman Anne, *L'enquête et ses méthodes : l'entretien*, Paris, Armand Colin, 2007.
Blank Grant, *Critics, Ratings, and Society: The Sociology of Reviews*, Lanham, Rowman & Littlefield, 2007.
Boorstin Daniel, *The Image: A Guide to Pseudo-Events in America*, New York, Harper and Row, 1961.
Bourdieu Pierre, "Le marché des biens symboliques", *L'année sociologique*, vol. 22, 1971, pp. 49–126.
Bourdieu Pierre & Delsaut Yvette, "Le couturier et sa griffe. Contribution à une théorie de la magie", *Actes de la Recherche en Sciences Sociales*, n°1, 1975.
Bourdieu Pierre, "Le hit-parade des intellectuels français ou qui sera juge de la légitimité des juges ?", *Actes de la Recherche en Sciences Sociales*, n°52-53, 1984, pp. 95–100.
Bourdieu Pierre, *La noblesse d'Etat. Grandes écoles et esprit de corps*, Paris, Minuit, 1989.
Bourdieu Pierre, 'Les conditions sociales de la circulation internationale des idées', *Romanische Zeitschrift für Literaturgeschichte* ,1/2, 1990, pp. 1–10.

Bourdieu Pierre & Darbel Alain, *The Love of Art: European Art Museums and Their Public*, Cambridge, Polity Press, 1997.
Bourdieu Pierre & Wacquant Loïc, 'On the cunning of imperialist reason', *Theory, Culture and Society*, 16(1), 1999, pp. 41–58.
Bowker Geoffrey C. & Star Susan L., *Sorting Things Out: Classification and its Consequences*, Cambridge, MA, MIT Press, 2000.
Bowness Alan, *The Conditions of Success. How the Modern Artist Rises to Fame*, London, Thames & Hudson, 1989.
Brankovic Jelena, Ringel Leopold & Werron Tobias, "How rankings produce competition: The case of global university rankings", *Zeitschrift für Soziologie*, 47(4), 2018, pp. 270–288.
Buchholz Larissa & Wuggenig Ulf, "Cultural Globalization between Myth and Reality. The Case of the Contemporary Visual Arts." *ART-e-FACT*, Strategies of Resistance, (04), 2005.
Buchholz Larissa, *The Global Rules of Art: the Emergence and Divisions of a Cultural World Economy*, Princeton, Princeton University Press, 2022.
Buckermann Paul, "Back from Business: On Commensuration, Construction, and Communication of a Global Art World in the Ranking Kunstkompass", *Kapsula*, 3 (1), 2016, pp. 12–18.
Buckermann Paul, "Ranking Art: Paradigmatic Worldviews in the Quantification and Evaluation of Contemporary Art", *Theory, Culture and Society*, December 2020.
Buscatto Marie, *Femmes du jazz. Musicalités, féminités, marginalisations*, Paris, Editions du CNRS, 2007.
Bystryn Marcia, "Art Galleries as Gatekeepers: The Case of the Abstract Expressionists", *Social Research*, 45, 2, 1978, pp. 390–408.
Caillé Alain, *Don, intérêt et désintéressement. Bourdieu, Mauss, Platon et quelques aut*res, Paris, la Découverte, 2005.
Casanova Pascale, *La République mondiale des lettres*, Paris, Seuil, 2008.
Castells Manuel, *The Informational City. Information Technology, Economic Restructuring and the Urban Regional Process*, Oxford, Blackwell, 1991.
Chiffres clefs 2016. Statistiques de la culture et de la communication, Paris, Ministère de la culture et de la communication, DEPS, la documentation Française, 2016.
Chiffres clefs 2019. Statistiques de la culture et de la communication, Paris, Ministère de la culture, DEPS, la documentation Française, 2019.
Chombart de Lauwe Paul-Henry, *La vie quotidienne des familles ouvrières*, Paris, Editions du CNRS, 1956.
Citerni Francesco, *A New Gallery in Paris suburbs: galerie Thaddaeus Ropac in Pantin,* GIOCA Master thesis, Bologne, Bologna university, 2018.
Clert Iris, *Iris.time. L'artventure*, Paris, Denoël, 1978.
Cohen-Solal Annie, *Leo Castelli et les siens*, Gallimard, 2009.
Coppet Laura de & Jones Alan, *The Art Dealers. The Powers Behind the Scene Tell How the Art World Really Works*, New York, Cooper Square, 2002.
Cousin Bruno & Chauvin Sébastien, "L'entre soi élitaire à Saint-Barthélémy", *Ethnologie française*, 42-2, 2012, pp. 335–345.
Cousin Bruno & Chauvin Sébastien, "Grands cercles et sociabilité des élites mondiales", in Badie Bertrand et Vidal Dominique (dir.), *Qui gouverne le monde? L'état du monde 2017*, Paris, La Découverte, 2016, pp. 186–193.

Cousin Bruno & Chauvin Sébastien, "La dimension symbolique du capital social : les grands cercles et Rotary clubs de Milan", *Sociétés contemporaines*, n°77, 2010, pp. 111–137.
Cousin Bruno &t Chauvin Sébastien, "Entrainer les dominants. Tennis, yoga et service des ultra-riches", *Actes de la Recherche en Sciences Sociales*, n°230, 2019, pp. 76–91.
Couture Francine, *Le marché des chromos à Montréal*, thèse de 3ème cycle, Paris, Ecole des Hautes Etudes en Sciences Sociales, 1981.
Couturier Elisabeth, *Art contemporain : le guide*, Paris, Flammarion, 2015.
Cowen Tyler, *In Praise of Commercial Culture*, Cambridge, MA, Harvard University Press, 1998.
Cowen Tyler, *What Price Fame?*, Cambridge MA, Harvard University Press, 2000.
Crane Diana, *The Transformation of the avant-Garde*, Chicago, University of Chicago Press, 1987.
Crane Diana, "Reflections on the Global Art Market : Implications for the Sociology of Culture, *Sociedade e Estado*, v. 24, n°2, maio/ago 2009, pp. 331–362.
David Géraldine, Huemer Christian & Oosterlinck Kim, "Art dealers' inventory strategy: the case of *Goupil, Boussod & Valadon* from 1860 to 1914", *Business History*, November, 2020.
Davis Fred, "The Cabdriver and his Fare : Facets of a Fleeting Relationship", *American Journal of Sociology*, 65-2, September 1959, pp. 158–165.
Debroux Tatiana, "Une histoire spatiale des membres du CPGA (1947–2017)" in Verlaine Julie (dir.), *Le comité professionnel des galeries d'art, 70 ans d'histoire 1947–2017*, Paris, Hazan, 2017, pp. 150–156.
De Swaan Abraham, 'The sociological study of the transnational society', Amsterdam School for Social Science Research, papers in progress, n° 46, 1995.
DiMaggio Paul, "Classification in art", *American Sociological Review*, 52-4, 1987, 440–455.
Dubar Claude, Tripier Pierre & Boussard Valérie, *Sociologie des professions*, Paris, Armand Colin, collection U, 2011.
Dufrêne Bernadette, *La création de Beaubourg*, Grenoble, Presses Universitaires de Grenoble, 2000.
Durand-Ruel Paul, *Mémoires du marchand des impressionnistes*, Paris, Flammarion, 2014.
Durkheim Emile, *The Division of Labor in Society*, New York, The Free Press, 1997.
Durkheim Emile, *The Rules of Sociological Method*, New York, Simon & Schuster, 2011.
Eichenberger Anita, *The Representation of Women amongst Swiss Art Gallery Owners*, Zurich, University of Zurich, Executive Master in Art Market Studies, 2020.
Eichenberger Anita, *The Representation of Women on the Swiss Contemporary Art Market*, Zurich, Executive Master in Art Market Studies Master thesis, University of Zurich, 2021.
Elias Norbert, "Remarques sur le commérage", *Actes de la Recherche en Sciences Sociales*, n° 60, 1985, pp. 23–29.

Elias Norbert & Scotson John L., *The Established and the Outsiders: A Sociological Enquiry into Community Problems*, London, Sage Publications Limited, 1994.

Erkkilä Tero & Piironen Ossi, *Rankings and Global Knowledge Governance: Higher Education, Innovation and Competitiveness*, London Palgrave Macmillan, 2018.

Espeland Nelson Wendy & Sauder Michael, "Rankings and Reactivity: How Public Measures Recreate Social Worlds", *American Journal of Sociology*, vol. 11, n° 1, July, 2007, p. 1–40.

Espeland Nelson Wendy & Sauder Michael, *Engines of Anxiety: Academic Rankings, Reputation,and Accountability*, New York, Russell Sage Foundation, 2016.

Esposito Elena & Stark David, C., "What's observed in a rating? Rankings as orientation in the face of uncertainty", *Theory, Culture & Society*, 36-4, 2019, pp. 3–26.

Fasche Melanie, *Making Value and Career Building in the Creative Economy. Evidence from the Contemporary Visual Arts*, New York, Springer, 2017.

Faure Sylvia, *Apprendre par corps : socio-anthropologie des techniques de danse*, Paris, La dispute, 2000.

Fialho Ana Leticia, *L'insertion internationale de l'art brésilien. Une analyse de la présence et de la visibilité de l'art brésilien dans les institutions et le marché*, EHESS, thèse de sciences de l'art et du langage, 2006.

Fine, Gary. A. & Rothenberg Julia, "Art Worlds and Their Ethnographers", *Ethnologie Française*, 38 -1, 2008, pp. 31–37.

Florida Richard, *The Rise Of The Creative Class: And How It's Transforming Work, Leisure, Community and Everyday Life*, New York, Basic Books, 2002.

Force Christel H., *Pioneers of the Global Art Market. Paris-Based Dealer Networks, 1850–1950*, Londres, Bloomsbury, 2020.

Fournier Marcel & Roy-Valex Myrtille, "Art contemporain et internationalisation. Les galeries québécoises et les foires", *Sociologie et sociétés*, Volume 34, Numéro 2, "Les territoires de l'art", Automne 2002, pp. 41–62.

Fournier Guillaume, *Quelle place pour les jeunes artistes plasticiens français dans le monde de l'art contemporain ?*, Paris, thèse de doctorat à l'université Sorbonne nouvelle, en cours.

Fournier Pierre, *Deux regards sur le travail ouvrier. À propos de Roy et Burawoy, 1945–1975*, Actes de la Recherche en Sciences Sociales, n°115, 1996, pp. 80–93.

Fraiberger Samuel P., Sinatra Roberta, Resch Magnus, Riedl Christoph & Barabási Albert-László, "Quantifying reputation and success in art", *Science*, 362, n° 6416, 2018, pp. 825–829.

Franck Georg, *Ökonomie der Aufmerksamkeit*, Munich / Vienne, Carl Hanser Verlag, 1998.

Fredet Jean-Gabriel, *Requins, caniches et autres mystificateurs*, Paris, Albin Michel, 2017.

Freidson Eliot, *Profession of Medicine. A Study of the Sociology of Applied Knowledge*, Chicago, the University of Chicago Press, 1970.

Frey Bruno S. & Pommerehne Werner W., *Muses and Markets. Explorations in the Economics of he Arts*, Oxford, Blackwell, 1989.

Fuller Martin, "Less than Friends, More than Acquaintances : Artists Markets and Gallery Openings in New York", *International Review of Social Research*, 5-2, 2015, pp. 120–129.

Fuller Martin & Ren Julie, "The Art Opening. Proximity and Potentiality at Events", *Theory, Culture and Society*, 36, 7-8, 2019, pp. 135–152.

Gabriel Leandro, "Mobilidade espacial de galerías de arte portuguesas e seus artistas na feiras internacionais de arte", *Revista Movimentos Sociais e Dinâmicas Espaciais*, V. 06, n°1, 2017, pp. 121–153.

Gandini Manuela, *Ileana Sonnabend. "The Queen of Arts"*, Rome, Castelvecchi, 2008.

Gautier Michael, *Passion und Kalkül. Zur beruflichen Bewährung in der Galerie*, Frankfurt am Main & New York, Campus Verlag, 2019.

Gautier Michael, "Mapping the Professional Self-Concepts of Gallery Owners : a Typology", in Glauser Andrea & al. (Ed.),*The Sociology of Arts and Markets. New Developments and Persistent Patterns*, Basingstoke, Palgrave Macmillan, 2020, pp. 263–285.

Gee Malcolm, *Dealers, Critics and Collectors of Modern Painting. Aspects of the Parisian Art Market between 1910 and 1930*, New York, Garland publishing, 1981.

Gemelli Valeria, *Female Artists Representation on the Contemporary Art Market: the London Case Study*, GIOCA Master thesis, Bologne, Bologna university, 2020.

Gillmann Fabienne, *Les mutations du métier de galeriste d'art contemporain*, Paris, mémoire de 5ème année de l'ENSBA, 2018.

Gioia Dennis, A. & Corley Kevin G., "Being good versus looking good: Business school rankings and the Circean transformation from substance to image", *Academy of Management Learning & Education*, 1-1, 2002, pp. 107–120.

Glass Ruth, *London: Aspects of Change*, London, MacKibbon and Kee, 1964.

Godart Frédéric, *Unveiling Fashion. Business, Culture and Identity in the most Glamorous Industry*, New York, Palgrave MacMillan, 2012.

Godart Frédéric & Mears Ashley, "Prise de décision créative en situation d'incertitude : le cas de la sélection des mannequins par les maisons de mode", *Sociologie et sociétés*, Vol. 43, n°1, printemps 2011, pp. 175–199.

Goffman Erving, "Symbols of Class Status", *The British Journal of Sociology*, vol. 2, n°4, December 1951, pp. 294–304.

Goffman Erving, *The Presentation of Self in Everyday Life*, New York, Doubleday, 1959.

Goffman Erving, *Stigma: Notes on the Management of Spoiled Identity*, New York, Touchstone, 1986.

Grafmeyer Yves & Authier Jean-Yves, *Sociologie urbaine*, Paris, Armand colin, 2008.

Grampp William D., *Pricing the Priceless. Art, Artists and Economics*, New York, Basic Books, 1989.

Granet Danièle & Lamour Catherine, *Grands et petits secrets du monde de l'art* (Nouvelle édition), Paris, Fayard, Pluriel, 2018.

Graw Isabelle, *High Price. Art between the Market and Celebrity Culture*, Berlin, Sternberg Press, 2009.

Green Nicholas, "Dealing in Temperaments: Economic Transformation of the Artistic Field in France During the Second Half of the Nineteenth Century", *Art History*, 10 (1), pp. 59–78.

Guilbaut Serge, *How New York Stole the Idea of Modern Art. Abstract Expressionism, Freedom and the Cold War*, Chicago, Chicago University Press, 1985.

Halbwachs Maurice, *On Collective Memory*, Chicago, the University of Chicago Press, 1992.

Halle David & Tiso Elisabeth, *New York's New Edge. Contemporary Art, the High Line and Urban Megaprojects on the Far West Side*, Chicago, the University of Chicago Press, 2014.

Hazelkorn Ellen, "Rankings and the global reputation race", *New Directions for Higher Education*, 168, Winter 2014, pp. 13–26.

Heilbron Johan, 'Echanges culturels transnationaux et mondialisation : Quelques réflexions', *Regards sociologiques*, 22, 2001, pp. 141–154.

Heilbron Johan, 'Towards a sociolog'y of translation. Book translations as a cultural world system', *European Journal of Social Theory*, 2(4), 1999, pp. 429–444.

Heinich Nathalie, *Du peintre à l'artiste. Artisans et académiciens à l'âge classique*, Paris, Éditions de Minuit, 1993.

Herstatt Claudia, *Women Gallerists in the 20th and 21st Centuries*, Berlin, Hatje Cantz, 2008.

Hindry Ann, *Claude Berri rencontre / meets Leo Castelli*, Paris, Renn productions, 1990.

Hochschild Arlie R., *Le prix des sentiments. Au cœur du travail émotionnel*, Paris, la Découverte, 2017.

Horowitz Noah, *Art of the Deal. Contemporary Art in a Global Financial Market*, Princeton, Princeton University Press, 2011.

Huber John C., "Cumulative Advantage and Success-Breeds-Success: The Value of Time Pattern Analysis", *Journal of the American Society for Information Science*, 49, 1998, p. 471–476.

Hughes Everett C., *The Sociological Eye: Selected Papers*, London, Routledge, 1984.

Hulst Titia (Ed.), *A History of the Western Art Market. A Sourcebook of Writings on Artists, Dealers and Markets*, Oakland, University of California Press, 2017.

Hutter Michael & Throsby Charles (Ed.), *Beyond Price: Value in Culture, Economics, and the Arts*, Cambridge, Cambridge University Press, 2008.

Institut für Strategieentwicklung, *IFSE Galerienstudie 2020*, Berlin, IFSE, 2020.

Janssen Suzanne, Kuipers Giselinde & Verboord Marc, 'Cultural globalization and arts journalism. The International Orientation of Arts and Culture Coverage in Dutch, French, German, and U.S. Newspapers, 1955 to 2005', *American Sociological Review*, 73(5), 2008, pp. 719–740.

Jeantet Aurélie, *Les émotions au travail*, Paris, Editions du CNRS, 2018.

Joyeux-Prunel Béatrice, *Nul n'est prophète en son pays. L'internationalisation de la peinture des avant-gardes parisiennes 1855–1914*, Paris, Nicolas Chaudun, 2009.

Kaufmann Jean-Claude, *L'entretien compréhensif*, Paris, Armand Colin, 2016.

Kerlau Yann, *Chercheurs d'art. Les marchands d'art hier et aujourd'hui*, Paris, Flammarion, 2014.

Kim Hak-Hee, "The Creative Economy and Urban Art Clusters : Locational Characteristics of Art Galleries in Seoul", *Journal of Korean Geographical Society*, 42, 2, 2007, pp. 258–279.

King Anthony D., *Culture, Globalization and the World System. Contemporary Conditions for the Representation of Identity*, Minneapolis, MN, University of Minnesota Press, 2000, pp. 91–106.

Kostelanetz Richard, *Soho: The Rise and Fall of an Artist's Colony*, New York, Routledge, 2003.

Kurzman Charles, Anderson Chelise, Key Clinton, Lee, Youn Ok, Moloney Mairead, Silver Alexis & Van Ryn Maria W., "Celebrity Status", *Sociological Theory*, 25(4), 2007, p. 347–367.

Lamont Michèle, "Toward a comparative sociology of valuation and evaluation", *Annual Review of Sociology* ,38-1, 2012, pp. 201–221.

Lash Scott and Urry John, *Economies of Signs and Space*, London, Sage, 1994.

Le Wita Béatrix, *Ni vue, ni connue. Approche ethnographique de la culture bourgeoise*, Paris, Editions de la MSH, 1988.

Leibenstein Harvey, "Bandwagon, Snob and Veblen Effects in the Theory of Consumer Demand", *Quarterly Journal of Economics*, Vol. 64, n°2, 1950, pp. 183–207.

Lemarchant Clotilde, *Belles-filles. Avec les beaux-parents, trouver la bonne distance*, Rennes, Presses universitaires de Rennes, 1999.

Lloyd Richard, *Neo-Bohemia: Art and Commerce in the Postindustrial City*, New York / London, Routledge, 2010.

Lorenzen Mark & Frederiksen Lars, "Why do Cultural Industries Cluster? Localization, Urbanization, Products and Projects", in Cooke Philip & Lazzeretti Luciana (Eds.), *Creative Cities, Cultural Clusters and Local Economic Development*, Londres, Edward Elgar, 2007, pp. 155–179.

Malbert Marylène, *Les relations artistiques internationales à la biennale de Venise, 1948–1968*, thèse d'histoire de l'art, Paris, université Paris-IV, 2006.

Markusen Ann & Schrock Greg, "The Artistic Dividend: Urban Artistic Specialisation and Economic Development Implications", *Urban Studies*, 43 (10), 2006, pp. 1661–1686.

Marsan Marie-Claire, *La galerie d'art. Tout savoir*, Paris, Filigranes, 2008.

Maertens Marie, *L'art du marché de l'art*, Bruxelles, Luc Pire, 2008.

Martin-Fugier Anne, *Galeristes : entretiens*, Arles, Actes Sud, 2010.

Martin-Fugier Anne, *Collectionneurs : entretiens*, Arles, Actes Sud, 2012.

Marx Karl, *Capital. A Critique of Political Economy*, Moscow, Progress Publishers, 1887.

Mauss Marcel, *The Gift. Forms and Functions of Exchange in Archaic Societies*, London, Cohen & West Ltd., 1966.

Maximova Marina, "Commercial art galleries as canon-makers: the Moscow art scene in the early 1990s", *Journal of Visual Art Practice*, Volume 19 – Issue 3, 2020, pp. 269–283.

McAndrew Clare, *The Art Market 2019*, Basel & Zurich, Art Basel & UBS, 2019.

Mennerick Lewis A., "Client Typologies", *Sociology of Work and Occupations*, 1-4, 1974, pp. 396–418.

Mennicken Andrea & Nelson Espeland Wendy, "What's new with numbers? Sociological approaches to the study of quantification", *Annual Review of Sociology*, 45-1, 2019, 223–245.

Mercier Cyril, *Les collectionneurs d'art contemporain : analyse sociologique d'un groupe social et de son rôle sur le marché de l'art*, Thèse de sociologie, Paris, Université Paris-III, 2012.

Merton Robert K., "The Matthew Effect", *Science*, Vol. 159, n°3810, 1968, pp. 56–63.

Milo Daniel, "Le phénix culturel : de la résurrection dans l'histoire de l'art. L'exemple des peintres français (1650–1750)", *Revue française de sociologie*, Vol. 27, No. 3, Sociologie de l'Art et de la Littérature, Juillet-Septembre, 1986, pp. 481–503.

Misdrahi Flores Marian, *L'évaluation des pairs et les critères de la qualité au Conseil des arts et des lettres du Québec. Le cas des arts visuels contemporains*, thèse de doctorat en sociologie, Montréal, Université de Montréal, 2013.

Moghadam Amin, "'L'art est mon métier': émergence et professionnalisation du marché de l'art à Dubai", *Transcontinentales,* 12/13, 2012, https://journals.openedition.org/transcontinentales/1339

Molho Jérémie, "Territorialisation d'un marché de l'art émergent : le cas d'Istanbul", *Belgeo*, 3, 2014, pp. 1–16.

Molotch Harvey & Treskon Mark, "Changing Art: SoHo, Chelsea and the Dynamic Geography of Galleries in New York City", *International Journal of Urban and Regional Research*, 33, 2, 2009, pp. 517–541.

Mommaas Hans, "Cultural Clusters and the Post-industrial City: Towards a Remapping of Urban Cultural Policy", *Urban Studies*, 41(3), 2004, pp.507–532.

Morel Jean-Paul, *C'était Ambroise Vollard,* Paris, Fayard, 2007.

Morin Edgar, *Les stars*, Paris, Le Seuil, 1957.

Moulin Raymonde, *The French Art Market: a Sociological View*, New Brunswick (NJ), Rutgers University Press, 1987.

Moulin Raymonde, *L'artiste, l'institution et le marché*, Paris, Flammarion, 1992.

Moulin Raymonde, *De la valeur de l'art*, Paris, Flammarion, 1995.

Moulin Raymonde, *Le marché de l'art. Mondialisation et nouvelles technologies*, Paris, Flammarion, 2009.

Moulin Raymonde & Quemin Alain, "La certification de la valeur de l'art. Experts et expertises", *Annales ESC*, numéro spécial "Mondes de l'art", n°6, novembre-décembre 1993, pp. 1421–1445.

Moureau Nathalie & Sagot-Duvauroux Dominique, *Le marché de l'art contemporain*. Paris : La Découverte, 2016.

Moureau Nathalie, Sagot-Duvauroux Dominique & Vidal Marion, *Collectionneurs d'art contemporain. Des acteurs méconnus de la vie artistique*, Paris, la documentation Française, 2016.

Nahon Pierre, *Pour la galerie. Un marchand et ses artistes, 1973–1993*, Paris, Plon, 1993.

Nahon Pierre, *Les marchands d'art en France : XIXe et XXe siècles*, Paris, Editions de la Différence, 1998.

Negroni Elisabetta, *Via Continua: a Project for galleria Continua*, GIOCA Master thesis, Bologne, Bologna university, 2017.

Nelson Espeland Wendy & Michael Sauder, "Rankings and Reactivity: How Public Measures Recreate Social Worlds", *American Journal of Sociology*, vol. 11, n° 1, July, 2007, p. 1–40.

Oberste-Hetbleck Nadine (Ed.), Zur Geschichte des Düsseldorfer Kunsthandels, Düsseldorf, Düsseldorf University Press, 2014.

O'Doherty Brian, *Inside the White Cube: The Ideology of the Gallery Space* (Expanded Edition), Berkeley, University of California Press, 2000.

Obadia Nathalie, *Géopolitique de l'art contemporain. Une remise en cause de l'hégémonie américaine ?*, Paris, Le cavalier bleu, 2019.

Ohmae Kenichi, *The Borderless World*, London, Collins, 1990.

Paicheler Geneviève, *L'invention de la psychologie moderne*, Paris, L'Harmattan, 1992.

Pardo-Guerra Juan Pablo, *Priceless Calculations. Reappraising the sociotechnical appendages of Art*, European Societies, 2013, Vol. 15, n° 2, 2013, pp. 196–211.

Passeron Jean-Claude, *Le raisonnement sociologique. L'espace non-poppérien du raisonnement naturel,* Paris, Nathan, 1991.

Patry Sylvie (Dir.), *Paul Durand-Ruel. Le pari de l'impressionnisme*, Paris, Réunion des Musées Nationaux, 2014.

Peneff Jean, *Le goût de l'observation. Comprendre et pratiquer l'observation participante en sciences sociales*, Paris, La découverte, 2009.

Peretz Henri, "Le vendeur, la vendeuse et leur cliente. Ethnographie du prêt-à-porter de luxe", *Revue française de sociologie*, XXXIII-1, 1992, pp. 49–72.

Peretz Henri, *Les méthodes en sociologie. L'observation*, Paris, La découverte, 1998.

Perrenoud Marc, *Les musicos. Enquête sur des musiciens ordinaires*, Paris, La découverte, 2007.

Peterson Karin, "The Distribution and Dynamics of Uncertainty in Art Galleries. A Case Study of New Dealerships in the Parisian Art Market 1985–1990", *Poetics,* 25-4, 1997, pp. 241–263.

Piles Roger de, *Cours de Peinture par Principes*, Genève, Slatkine Reprints, 1969 (édition originale : *Cours de Peinture par Principes composé par Mr. de Piles*, Paris, Jacques Estienne, 1708 (Amsterdam and Leipzig: Arkstée & Merkus, 1766)).

Pinçon Michel & Pinçon-Charlot Monique, *Quartiers bourgeois, quartiers d'affaires*, Paris, Payot, 1992.

Pinçon Michel & Pinçon-Charlot Monique, *Grandes fortunes. Dynasties familiales et formes de richesse en France*, Paris, Payot, 1996.

Pinçon Michel & Pinçon-Charlot Monique, *Voyage en grande bourgeoisie. Journal d'enquête*, Paris, PUF, 1997.

Pinçon Michel & Pinçon-Charlot Monique, *Paris Mosaïque*, Paris, Calmann-Lévy, 2001.

Pinçon Michel & Pinçon-Charlot Monique, *Sociologie de la bourgeoisie*, Paris, La découverte, 2016.

Plattner Stuart, *High Art Down Home. An Economic Ethnography of a Local Art Market*, Chicago, Chicago university press, 1996.

Poirrier Philippe (Ed.), *Politiques et pratiques de la culture*, Paris, la documentation Française, 2010.

Pollak Michael, *Une identité blessée. Etudes de sociologie et d'histoire*, Paris, Métailié, 1993.

Quemin Alain, *Les commissaires-priseurs : analyse d'une profession et de son rôle dans les ventes aux enchères*, Thèse de doctorat en sociologie, Paris, Ecole des Hautes Etudes en Sciences Sociales, 1994.

Quemin Alain, *Les commissaires-priseurs. La mutation d'une profession*, Paris, Anthropos-Economica, 1997.

Quemin Alain, *Le rôle des pays prescripteurs sur le marché et dans le monde de l'art contemporain*, Paris, Ministère des Affaires Etrangères, 2001.

Quemin Alain, *L'art contemporain international. Entre les institutions et le marché*, Nîmes / Lyon, co-édition Jacqueline Chambon / Artprice, 2002, 270 p.

Quemin Alain, "De l'espace privé à l'espace professionnel. Les commissaires-priseurs", in Françoise Piotet (dir.), *La révolution des métiers*, Paris, PUF, 2002 (b), pp. 317–344.

Quemin Alain, "L'illusion de l'abolition des frontières dans le monde de l'art contemporain international. La place des pays "périphériques" à l'ère de la globalisation et du métissage", *Sociologie et Sociétés*, volume XXXIV, n°2, automne 2002 (c), pp. 15–40.

Quemin Alain, "The Illusion of the Elimination of Borders in the Contemporary Art World", in Jan Bakos (Ed.), *Artwork through the Market. The Past and the Present*, Bratislava, VEDA, vydavatelstvo Slovenskej Akadémie vied, 2004, pp. 275–302.

Quemin Alain, "Globalization and Mixing in the Visual Arts. An Empirical Survey of "High Culture" and Globalization» ", *International Sociology*, volume 21, number 4, July 2006, pp. 522–550.

Quemin Alain (2010), "Le Marché De L'art : Une Mondialisation En Trompe-L'œil", *Questions Internationales,* Dossier L'Art dans La Mondialisation, n° 42 – Mars-Avril 2010.

Quemin Alain, "International Contemporary Art Fairs in a "Globalized" Art Market", *European Societies*, Vol. 15, n°2, 2013 (a), pp. 162–177.

Quemin Alain, *Les stars de l'art contemporain. Notoriété et consécration artistiques dans les arts visuels,* Paris, éditions du CNRS, 2013 (b).

Quemin Alain, "La Chine et l'art contemporain. L'arrivée de l'Empire du Milieu dans le monde et sur le marché de l'art", in Bret Jean-Noël et Moureau Nathalie (dir.), *L'art, l'argent et la mondialisation*, Paris, L'Harmattan, 2013 (c), pp. 77–98.

Quemin Alain, "The sociology of Art" (chapter 30), in Kathleen Korgen (Ed.), Cambridge Handbook of Sociology, Cambridge University Press, 2017, pp. 293–303.

Quemin Alain, "Ranking Contemporary Art Galleries: a Sociological Attempt from French Case", in *Todas as Artes. Revista luso-brasileira de Artes e Cultura*, Vol. 2, n°2, 2019, pp. 8–22.

Quemin Alain, "What Does Developing a Ranking of Leading Contemporary Art Galleries Unveil about the Importance of the National Factor? An Analysis of Art Basel Art Fair", *Arts*, 9, 105, 2020 a, pp. 1–16.

Quemin Alain, "The Market and Museums: the Increasing Power of Collectors and Private Galleries in the Contemporary Art World", *Journal of Visual Art Practice*, Vol. 19, Issue 3 "Art Markets and Museums", 2020 b, pp. 211–224.

Quemin Alain, *Le monde des galeries. Art contemporain, structure du marché et internationalisation*, Paris, CNRS Editions, 2021 (a).

Quemin Alain, "*Cursus honorum* et vieillissement en art", in Nadeije Laneyrie-Dagen et Caroline Archat (Dir.), *L'art au risque de l'âge,* Editions du CNRS, 2021 (b), pp. 295–318.

Quemin Alain, "Is There Such a Thing as a 'Global South'? Contemporary Visual Arts, the Art Market and Institutions in 'Southern Countries'", in Duarte Adelaide & Pérez-Ibañez Marta (dir.), *The Art Market and the Global South*, Boston, Brill, 2023, pp. 39–56.

Quemin Alain, “Territoires et districts des galeries d’art contemporain à Paris : du 8ème arrondissement et de Saint-Germain-des-Prés à l’avènement du Marais », *Sociologie de l’art*, Au-delà de la valeur. Hommage à Raymonde Moulin, 33-34, 2024, pp. 45–56.

Quemin Alain, “L’amitié comme ressource professionnelle : l’exemple des galeristes d’art contemporain et de leurs ‘amis / clients’ (ou comment effacer la relation marchande pour mieux vendre)”, in Christine Détrez, Kevin Diter et Sylvie Octobre, *Culture & émotions. La dimension affective des goûts*, Paris, Editions du DEPS du Ministère de la Culture et Presses de Sciences Po, 2024, pp. 129–148.

Rannou Simon, *L’attribution des aides publiques aux galeries d’art 2008–2015*, mémoire de Master 2, Strasbourg, université de Strasbourg / Institut d’Etudes Politiques de Strasbourg, 2015.

Ravet Hyacinthe, *L’orchestre au travail. Interactions, négociations, coopérations*, Paris, Vrin, 2015.

Ravet Hyacinthe, *Musiciennes. Enquête sur les femmes et la musique*, Paris, Editions Autrement, 2011.

Ricci Clarissa (Ed.), *Starting from Venice. Studies on the Biennale*, Milan, Et al. Edizioni, 2010.

Rigney Daniel, *The Matthew Effect. How Advantage Begets further Advantage*, New York, Columbia University Press, 1949.

Rindova Violina, P., Williamson Ian O., Petkova Antoaneta, P. & Seyer Joy M., “Being good or being known: An empirical examination of the dimensions, antecedents, and consequences of organizational reputation”, *The Academy of Management Journal*, 48-6, 2005, pp. 1033–1049.

Rius Ulldemolins Joaquim, “Els marxants d’art il’espai urbà. Una anàlisi sociològica del mercat de l’art a Barcelona”, *Revista Catalana de Sociologia*, 17, 2002, pp. 149–184.

Rius-Ulldemolins Joaquim, “Gallery Districts of Barcelona: The Strategic Play of Art Dealers », *The Journal of Arts Management, Law and Society*, 42(2), April 2012, pp. 48–62.

Rius-Ulldemolins Joaquim, “¿Por qué las galerías de arte se concentran en clústeres? Un análisis sociológico de la estructura y dinámica urbana del mercado del arte”, *Revista Española de Sociología*, 2016, Vol. 25 (2), pp. 205–225.

Robson A. Deirdre, *Prestige, Profit and Pleasure. The Market for Modern Art in New York in the 1940’s and 1950’s*, New York, Garland publishing, 1995.

Rodríguez Morató Arturo & Zarlenga Matías I., “Culture-led urban regeneration policies in the Ibero-American space”, *International Journal of Cultural Policy*, 24 (5), 2018, pp. 628–646.

Rodríguez Morató Arturo, Zarlenga Matías I. & Rius Ulldemolins Joaquim, “The cultural clusters of Barcelona. A sociological analysis of types of social interaction dynamics”, *European Urban and Regional Studies*, 23 (3), 2016, pp. 422–440.

Rosen Sherwin, “The Economics of Superstars”, *American Economic Review*, 71 (5), 1981, pp. 845–858.

Roth Alvin E. & Vande Vate John H., 1990. “Random Path to Stability in Two-Sided Matching”, *Econometrica*, 58 (6), pp. 1475–1480.

Rothenberg Julia & Lang Steve, "Repurposing the High Line: Aesthetic experience and contradiction in West Chelsea", *City, Culture and Society*, 9, 2017, pp. 1–12.

Rouet François, *Les entreprises du commerce du marché de l'art,* Paris, DEPS, Ministère de la Culture et de la Communication, coll. "Culture chiffres", 2009–4, avril 2009.

Rouet François, *Les galeries d'art contemporain en France en 2012*, Culture Etudes, Paris, Ministère de la Culture et de la Communication, DEPS, n°2, juin 2013, pp. 1–12.

Rouget Bernard, Sagot-Duvauroux Dominique & Pflieger Sylvie, *Le marché de l'art contemporain en France. Prix et stratégies*, Paris, la documentation Française, 1991.

Russell John, *Matisse. Father & Son*, New York, Harry N. Abrams, 1999.

Saez Guy (Ed.), *Institutions et vie culturelle*, Paris, la documentation Française, 2004.

Saint Martin Monique de, *L'espace de la noblesse*, Paris, Métailié, 1993.

Saint-Raymond Léa, *La Galerie Beaubourg, un électron libre de 1973 à 1993 ?*, mémoire de master 1 d'histoire de l'art, Université Paris-IV, 2011.

Sapiro Gisèle (Ed.), *Translatio. Le marché de la traduction à l'heure de la mondialisation*, Paris, CNRS Editions, 2008.

Sapiro Gisèle, "The Symbolic Economy of the Nobel Prize in Literature: How it Counters or Reproduces Modes of Domination", *Poetics*, 101, 2023.

Sassen Saskia, 'Territory and territoriality in the global economy', *International Sociology*, 15(2), 2000, pp. 372–393.

Sassen Saskia, *Globalization and Its Discontents: Essays on the New Mobility of People and Money*, New York, New Press, 1999.

Sassen Saskia, *Losing Control? Sovereignty in an Age of Globalization*, New York, Columbia University Press, 1996.

Sassen Saskia, *The Global City. New York, London, Tokyo*, Princeton, NJ, Princeton University Press, 1992.

Sauder Michael & Espeland Nelson Wendy, "The discipline of rankings: Tight coupling and organizational change", *American Sociological Review*, 74-1, 2009, pp. 63–82.

Scholte Jan Aart, 'The geography of collective identities in a globalizing world', *Review of International Political Economy*, 3(4), 1996, pp. 565–607.

Schultheis Franz, Single Erwin, Köfeler Raphaela & Mazzurana Thomas, *Art Unlimited? Dynamics and Paradoxes of a Globalizing Art World*, Bielefeld, Transcript Verlag, 2016.

Schumpeter Joseph, *Capitalism, Socialism and Democracy*, New York City, Harper, 2008.

Shchutski Vitali, *Premières galeries privées à Minsk après la chute de l'Union Soviétique : le cas de "Sixième Ligne"*, Mémoire de Master 2 en sociologie générale, Paris, École des Hautes Etudes en Sciences Sociales, 2015.

Shchutski Vitali, *Un 'no man's land' entre l'Allemagne et la Russie ? Les artistes est-européens, la scène internationale et le marché de l'art contemporain*, Saint-Denis, thèse de doctorat de l'université Paris-8, en cours.

Shnayerson Michael, *Boom: Mad Money, Mega Dealers, and the Rise of Contemporary Art*, New York, Public Affairs, 2019.

Single Erwin, "The Art Fair Boom and Its Contradictions", in Andrea Glauser, Patricia Holder, Thomas Mazzurana, Olivier Moeschler, Valérie Rolle & Franz Schultheis (Ed.), *The Sociology of Arts and Markets. New Developments and Persistent Patterns*, Palgrave Macmillan, 2020.

Sinigaglia-Amadio Sabrina & Sinigaglia Jérémy, *Temporalités du travail artistique : le cas des muscien.ne.s et des plasticien.ne.s*, Paris, Ministère de la Culture, collection Questions de culture, 2017.

Sorignet Pierre-Emmanuel, *Danser. Enquête dans les coulisses d'une vocation*, Paris, La découverte, 2010.

Spencer Smith Marc, *Genèse d'un marché d'art. Etats-Unis, 1800–1930*, Rennes, PUR, 2016.

Spoerhase Carlos, "Rankings: A pre-history", *New Left Review*, 114, Nov-Dec., 2018, pp. 99–112.

Stiglitz Joseph E., "The Causes and Consequences of the Dependence of Quality on Price", *Journal of Economic Literature*, 25, March, 1987, pp. 1–48.

Stocco Daniela, *Le marché de l'art à Sao Paulo et à Rio de Janeiro*, thèse de doctorat en sociologie, Paris / Rio de Janeiro, Université Paris-8 / université Fédérale de Rio de Janeiro, 2016.

Stocco Daniela, "The Art Fairs in Rio de Janeiro and São Paulo: Democratization and Access to Art as a Marketing Strategy", *H-ART Revista de historia teoría y crítica de arte*, Issue 4 / January 01, 2019.

Strauss Anselm L., *Mirrors and Masks: The Search for Identity*, New York, The Free Press of Glencoe, 1959.

Stroobants Marcelle, *Sociologie du travail*, Paris, Armand Colin, 2016

Suaud Charles, *La vocation. Conversion et reconversion des prêtres ruraux*, Paris, Minuit, 1978.

Therborn Goran, 'From the universal to the global', *International Sociology*, 15(2), 2000, pp. 149–150 (a).

Therborn Goran, 'Globalizations. Dimensions, historical waves, regional effects, normative governance', *International Sociology*, 15(2), 2000, pp. 151–179 (b).

Thompson Don, *L'affaire du requin qui valait douze millions. L'étrange économie de l'art contemporain*, Paris, Le mot et le reste, 2012.

Thornton Sarah, *Seven Days in the Art World*, London, Norton, 2008.

Throsby David, "The Production and Consumption of the Arts: A View of Cultural Economics", Journal of Economic Literature, XXXII (March), 1994, pp. 1–29.

Tönnies Ferdinand, *Community and Society*, London, Routledge, 1988.

Trefor Williams Glesni, *Exhibiting Works of Art at the Venice Biennale*, GIOCA Master thesis, Bologne, Université de Bologne, 2018.

Uboldi Anna, "Hierarchies and Divisions in the Subfield of Gallery Owners. A Research on Art Galleries in Milan", in Glauser Andrea & al. (Ed.), *The Sociology of Arts and Markets. New Developments and Persistent Patterns*, Basingstoke, Palgrave Macmillan, 2020, pp. 239–262.

Van de Rijt Arnout, Shor Eran, Ward Charles & Skiena Steven, "Only 15 Minutes? The Social Stratification of Fame in Printed Media", *American Sociological Review*, 78-2, 2013, p. 266–289.

van Hest Femke, *Territorial Factors in a Globalized Art World ? The Visibility of Countries in International Art Events*, thèse de doctorat en sociologie,

Rotterdam / Paris, Erasmus Universiteit / Ecole des Hautes Etudes en Sciences Sociales, 2012.

Vasari Giorgio, *Le Vite de' più eccellenti pittori, scultori, e architettori da Cimabue insino a' tempi nostril* (*The Lives of the Most Excellent Italian Painters, Sculptors, and Architects, from Cimabue to Our Times*), Florence, Lorenzo Torrentino, 1550.

Veblen Thorstein, *The Theory of the Leisure Class. An Economic Study of Institutions*, London, Mac Millan, 1899.

Velthuis Olav, *Talking Prices. Contemporary Art, Commercial Galleries and the Construction of Value*, PhD dissertation, Rotterdam, Erasmus Universiteit, 2002.

Velthuis Olav, *Talking Prices. Symbolic Meanings of Prices on the Market for Contemporary Art*, Princeton, Princeton University Press, 2005.

Velthuis Olav, "Symbolic Meanings of Prices: Constructing the Value of Contemporary Art in Amsterdam and New York Galleries", *Theory and Society*, 32-2, 2003, pp. 181–215.

Velthuis Olav & Baia Curioni Stefano (Ed.), *Cosmopolitan Canvases. The Globalization of Markets for Contemporary Art*, Oxford, Oxford University Press, 2015.

Verger Annie, "L'art d'estimer l'art. Comment classer l'incomparable", *Actes de la Recherche en Sciences Sociales*, n° 66-67, 1987, pp. 105–121.

Verlaine Julie, "Soirs de vernissage. Pratiques et publics autour de l'art contemporain à Paris, de la Libération à la fin des années soixante", *Hypothèses*, 2009/1, pp. 285–294.

Verlaine Julie (dir.), *Le comité professionnel des galeries d'art, 70 ans d'histoire 1947–2017*, Paris, Hazan, 2017.

Verlaine Julie, *Daniel Templon. Une histoire d'art contemporain*, Paris, Flammarion, 2016.

Verlaine Julie, *Les Galeries d'art contemporain à Paris de la Libération à la fin des années 1960. Une histoire culturelle du marché de l'art*, Paris, Editions de la Sorbonne, 2012.

Verley Timothée, *Genèse et structure du marché de l'art brut*, Université de Lille, thèse en économie, 14 janvier 2020.

Vidal Oliveras Jaume, *Galerismo en Barcelona 1877–2013. El sistema, el arte, la ciudad*, Madrid, Ministerio de Educación, Cultura y Deporte, 2013.

Vitet Ludovic, *L'académie royale de peinture et de sculpture : étude historique (édition de 1861)*, Paris, Hachette, 2012.

Wacquant Loïc, *Body and Soul. Notebooks of an Apprentice Boxer*, Oxford, Oxford University Press, 2007.

Wallerstein Immanuel, "The national and the universal: Can there be such a thing as world culture?", in A. D. King (ed.), *Culture, Globalization and the World System. Contemporary Conditions for the Representation of Identity*, Minneapolis, MN, University of Minnesota Press, 2000, pp. 91–105.

Wallerstein Immanuel, *Geopolitics and Geoculture. Essays on the Changing World System*, Cambridge/Paris, Cambridge University Press/Editions de la Maison des Sciences de l'Homme, 1991.

Wedlin Linda, "The role of rankings in codifying a business school template: Classifications, diffusion and mediated isomorphism in organizational fields", *European Management Review*, 4-1, 2007, pp. 24–39.

Welsh John, "'Globalizing' academics? Ranking and appropriation in the transformations of the world-system", *Globalizations*, 17-1, January 2020, pp. 126–145.

White Harrison C. & White Cynthia, *Canvases and Careers. Institutional Change in the French Painting World*, Chicago, Chicago University Press, 1965.

Yun Kusuk, *Être exotique en art contemporain. La scène internationale de l'art et trois pays d'Asie – Japon, Corée du Sud et Chine – dans la mondialisation. Création et stratégie de diffusion*, thèse de sociologie, Saint-Denis, université Paris-8, 2016.

Yun Kusuk, *Territoires de l'art contemporain et mondialisation : L'Occident et trois pays d'Asie de l'Est: Japon, Chine, Corée du Sud – 1971–2010*, Paris, L'Harmattan, 2021.

Zarobell John (Ed.), *Art and the Global Economy*, Oakland, University of California Press, 2017.

Zhang Amy Y., "Placing Arts Districts within Markets: A Case Study of 798 Arts District in Beijing", *International Journal of Urban and Regional Research*, January 2019.

Zhang Linzhi, "The Diffusion of Galleries in China", in Glauser Andrea & al. (Ed.), *The Sociology of Arts and Markets. New Developments and Persistent Patterns*, Basingstoke, Palgrave Macmillan, 2020, pp. 287–316.

Zorloni Alessia, *The Economics of Contemporary Art. Markets, Strategies and Stardom*, New York, Springer, 2013.

Zukin Sharon, *Loft Living: Culture and Capital in Urban Change*, New Brunswick, NJ, Rutgers university press, 1982.

Zukin Sharon, Braslow Laura, "The life cycle of New York's creative districts: Reflections on the unanticipated consequences of unplanned cultural zones", *City, Culture and Society*, 2, 2011, pp. 131–140.

Zwirner Rudolf, *Rudolf Zwirner, Ich wollte immer Gegenwart: Autobiografie aufgeschrieben von Nicola Kuhn*, Cologne, Wienand Verlag, 2019.

INDEX